Warren Beatty

Suzanne Finstad received the Frank Wardlaw Prize for literary excellence for her first book, *Heir Not Apparent*. Her most recent work, *Natasha: The Biography of Natalie Wood*, was a *New York Times* bestseller, named the best film book of 2001 by the *San Francisco Chronicle* and chosen as one of the finest books of 2001 by the *Economist*. Several of her books have been adapted into movies, including the bestseller *Sleeping with the Devil*. She lives in California and has a law degree.

Warren Beatty
A Private Man

SUZANNE FINSTAD

Author's note: One of the many rewarding experiences of researching this book was discovering a treasure of rare photographs from Warren Beatty's life, career and family history, a number of which have never been published before. To preserve the richness of detail, most are presented on higher quality stock, in two photo inserts, rather than running throughout the book. The inserts have been designed and positioned with careful attention to chronology to deepen one's appreciation of the surrounding text.

Frontispiece photograph by Curtis Hanson.

Quote on page vii from "Warren Beatty," by Alan Ebert,
Ladies' Home Journal (April 1976).

First published in the United Kingdom 2005
by Aurum Press Ltd, 25 Bedford Avenue, London WC1B 3AT
www.aurumpress.co.uk

This paperback edition published 2006

Copyright © 2005 by Suzanne Finstad, Inc.

This edition published by arrangemenmt with Harmony Books,
a division of Random House, Inc.

A catalogue record for this book is available from the British Library.

DESIGN BY LAUREN DONG

ISBN-10: 1 84513 169 X

ISBN-13: 978 1 84513 169 2

Printed by Bookmarque, Croydon, Surrey

"To some men,
I seem to be what they would secretly like to be
or are afraid of being.
To some women,
I am that fantasy figure,
that object of desire and/or fear.
But none of it is me."

WARREN BEATTY

For my family and forebears,
who formed me in ways seen and unseen

contents

foreword

Early in my career as the *New York Herald Tribune*'s second-string theater critic (actually I thought of myself as a handmaiden to God, in the person of the critic Walter Kerr), an off-Broadway actor approached my desk at the paper and said, "To quote Groucho Marx, if I had a horse, I'd horsewhip you." We settled our differences in the downstairs saloon, agreeing to disagree on the merits of his performance. Early in my career as the *Tribune*'s film critic, Billy Wilder told an interviewer that inviting me to review a movie was akin to asking the Boston Strangler for a neck massage. I was flattered that the great filmmaker had noticed me.

Now, looking back at a forty-plus-year career as critic, I find Warren Beatty stands alone as the one movie star who thanked me for my negative reaction to his performance.

I had first seen Beatty in 1959, on the opening night of William Inge's *A Loss of Roses* on Broadway, in Beatty's first—and last—Broadway appearance. The reviews were generally negative, but Beatty, as the troubled son of a similarly troubled widow, was greeted by a few critics as "definitely a find for the thin ranks of juvenile leads," "earnest and attractive," and having "exceptional skill" as an actor. I certainly agreed enthusiastically with Walter Kerr's assessment of his performance as "mercurial, sensitive, excellent." And I, of course, added "very handsome indeed." I admired him as well on-screen in Elia Kazan's (and Inge's) *Splendor in the Grass*, which won him star status; *The Roman Spring of Mrs. Stone*; and *All Fall Down*.

But the first of his movies that I reviewed after becoming the film critic in 1963 was *Lilith*, Robert Rossen's unintentionally ludicrous 1964 tale of goings-on in a sanatorium for the superrich, with Jean Seberg as a particularly nutty patient, Beatty an occupational therapist-in-training who's involved with her, and some theorizing about connections between love and madness. "Beatty," I wrote, "is noteworthy for his nonacting and his apparent inability to deliver a line without counting to ten. It's either super-Method or understandable reluctance, considering the lines."

John Springer, who had seen Beatty onstage and become his publicist—and was an invaluable professional and personal friend of mine for forty years—extended Beatty's invitation to lunch at a steak house off Times Square. I'd presumed that John was responsible for my first and last "blind" item in a gossip column, with Charlie McHarry, in the New York *Daily News*, asking the next day, "What movie critic had a five-hour lunch with Warren Beatty?" Suffice it to say that I remember a perfectly delightful encounter with a very bright, knowledgeable, and civilized young man with serious interests and ideas about movies. He also told me of a film he was working on with Arthur Penn, whom I knew well for his superb work as a Broadway director.

The last is relevant. Eleven months later, in September 1965, that film, *Mickey One*, opened the New York Film Festival—and I was the only critic who liked it. In fact, I loved it, declaring it "a brilliantly original screen work, visually exciting and intellectually satisfying, a credit to everyone involved." On surface, the story of a nightclub comic on the lam from the syndicate, for me, is basically about fear; about the futility of flight from the unknown, about the self-appraisal that permits modern man to live with the nameless terrors of the unknown. Beatty, I noted, as the man "guilty of not being innocent," revealed himself to be "one of the remarkable young actors of our time." It wound up on my "10 Best" list of that year, its setting, style, and score remarkable. I still think it a film far ahead of its time—and for all time.

Meanwhile—with my noting along the way that *Promise Her Anything* and *Kaleidoscope* did not show Beatty at his potential best—I became the movie critic for *TV Guide* and film-and-theater critic for the *Today Show*.

In 1966, I had served as chairman of the international jury for the Montreal Film Festival. I had had a fine time and kept in touch with its sponsors. The following June, Beatty and Penn invited me to see a rough cut of their second project, *Bonnie and Clyde*. It was passionate love at first sight. The Montrealers phoned me. They had loved *Mickey One* as I had, chairman Rock Demers said—and did I know about *Bonnie and Clyde*? They were looking for a blockbuster opener, since the festival was to be part of Expo 67, the international world's fair, and, boy, did I have an opener for them! It was indeed a night to remember on August 7, 1967. Not officially anyone's critic, I felt free to ride with my husband in a parade of antique cars from hotel to theater and to join a packed audience and its standing ovation at the end of the film. Bosley Crowther, critic for the *New York Times* and my newspaper-days "rival," hated it.

In July, *Vogue* magazine had invited me to review a film, and my rave review of *Bonnie and Clyde* appeared in its September issue. When the movie opened in August, I was able to tell the *Today Show*'s millions of viewers about the film. Among its many triumphs I noted that "Warren Beatty, so often merely a promising performer, fulfills himself as Clyde, revealing every inward weakness and outward ferocity of the man for whom weapons and the driver's wheel provide potency." *Bonnie and Clyde* made my 1967 and all-time best-movie lists.

With only an occasional lapse thereafter, Beatty did, in my view, fulfill the promise of his youth. In *McCabe & Mrs. Miller*, *The Parallax View*, and the superb *Shampoo*, he showed himself a master of character—frontiersman-phony, investigative journalist, Beverly Hills hairdresser-cum-sexpot—as well as a socially conscious filmmaker. He took time out for political activity and returned to do a remake of *Heaven Can Wait* and, after another hiatus, fulfilled many roles in production, innovative structure, and performance in 1981's *Reds*. Another time-out of his, and I found myself enjoying 1990's *Dick Tracy* and 1991's *Bugsy*, though his 1994 third version of 1937's *Love Affair* is a bore. But he triumphed in form, content, and performance in 1998's *Bulworth*, a political fable he wrote, directed, produced, and starred in.

In 1975, Beatty and Arthur Penn had been the guests at the January film weekend at Tarrytown House, weekends I've been running since 1971. Beatty stayed over, and on Saturday we showed *McCabe & Mrs. Miller*, *Mickey One*, *Bonnie and Clyde*, and *The Parallax View*, all of which, with *Shampoo*, *Reds*, and *Bulworth*, are on my list of outstanding American films. Beatty was a splendid guest, funny and discerning in his comments about his own work and that of others. Most of all, however, I remember our private conversations about his future projects and interests.

That was thirty years ago, eleven years after we met. He made an initial and lasting mark on me not only as a filmmaker and a personality, but also as a person. And that person, filmmaker, and personality come clear in Suzanne Finstad's perceptive portrait of the man.

JUDITH CRIST
New York City, September 2005

Rev. Andrew Beaty　*m1.*　Elizabeth　　　　　*m2.*　Sarah Adams
b. circa 1740　　　　　Montgomery　　　*Loudoun*
Swords, Ireland (?)　　　　　　　　　　　*Co., VA*

Rev. John Adams Beaty　*m1.*　Margaret McConihey
b. 1765　　　　　*after 1780*　b. 8-6-1769
VA or PA　　　　　　　　　　Bucks Co., PA
d. 2-16-1849　　　　　　　　d. 1810–1814 (?)
Warren Co., VA　　　　　　　Frederick Co., VA

William Beaty　　　　　　14 other children
b. 1801, Shenandoah Co., VA　with Margaret
d. 8-6-1861, Warren Co., VA

Henry Warren Beaty　*m.*　Mary Lavinia Pomeroy
b. 4-17-1847　　　　　*5-2-1869*　b. 3-24-1847, Warren, Co., VA
d. 8-24-1923, Winchester, VA　　d. 4-29-1931, Front Royal, VA
　　　　　　　　　　　　　　Henry Warren Beaty's double first cousin

William Welton Beaty　*m.*　Ada Virginia Partlow
b. 11-18-1872, Warren Co., VA　*5-15-1901*　b. 5-12-1877, Rappahannock Co., VA
d. 2-28-1946, Staunton, VA　　d. 6-23-1946, Front Royal, VA
　　　　　　　　　　　　　　Daughter of Burrell Taylor Partlow and
　　　　　　　　　　　　　　Ruth Updike Partlow
　　　　　　　　　　　Seven siblings, including: Ira Judson Partlow
　　　　　　　　　　　　　　b. 2-20-1876
　　　　　　　　　　　　m. Andrea Martin, 5-23-1905
　　　　　　　　　　　　　　d. 6-11-1952

Ira Owens Beaty　*m.*　Kathlyn Corinne MacLean
b. 1-18-1903　　　*8-15-1931*　("Tat")
Front Royal, VA　*Wolfville, Nova Scotia*　b. 8-23-1903
d. 1-15-1987　　　　　　　North Sydney, Nova Scotia
Arlington, VA　　　　　　d. 6-26-1993
　　　　　　　　　　　　Malibu, CA

Henry Warren Beaty II　*m.*　Annette Carol Bening　*m1.*　James Steven White
(Warren Beatty)　*3-12-1992*　b. 5-29-1958　*5-26-1984*
b. 3-30-1937　*Los Angeles, CA*　Topeka, KS　*div. 8-1-1990*
Richmond, VA　　　　　　　　　　　*New York, NY*

Kathlyn Bening Beatty　Benjamin MacLean Beatty　Isabel Ira Ashley Beatty　Ella Corinne Beatty
b. 1-8-1992　　　　b. 8-23-1994　　　　b. 1-18-1997　　　　b. 4-8-2000
Los Angeles, CA　　Los Angeles, CA　　Los Angeles, CA　　Los Angeles, CA

Beaty Family Tree

| | *m2.*
12-15-1814
Shenandoah Co., VA | Lavinia Owens
b. 1792, VA
d. 1866, Warren Co., VA
*Daughter of first cousins Ephraim
and Lucinda Owens* | *m1.* | Elias Edmonds
d. War of 1812 |

Lucinda Beaty   m.   William Pomeroy   7 other children
b. 3-7-1822   *1-24-1845*   with Lavinia
d. Unknown

| | *m1.*
5-11-1830
Shenandoah Co., VA | Elmira A. Edmonds
b. circa 1811, Shenandoah Co., VA
d. 12-13-1857, Warren Co., VA
William Beaty's stepsister and first wife | *m2.*
(1858–1860) | Lucina
(surname unknown)
b. 1801
d. Unknown |

William A. Beaty   14 other children
b. 1838   with Elmira

| Elmira Lucy Beaty
b. 3-19-1870
d. Unknown
m. John Bowman | Margaret Ann Beaty
("Maggie")
b. 11-15-1873
d. 5-21-1953 | Roberta B. Beaty
("Bertie")
b. 1875
d. 1957
m. Coleman Ware
d. 1931 | Elizabeth Beaty
("Bessie")
b. 1878
d. 1924 | John I. Beaty
b. 12-1879
d. Unknown |

Ruth Lavinia Beaty   m.   Quincy Damon Gasque
b. 7-4-1906   *6-13-1927*   b. 10-16-1900
d. 2-20-1997   d. 3-8-1982
Alexandria, VA   Front Royal, VA

Jeanne Gasque (Sandidge)   (Ruth) Quincy Gasque (Butler)
b. 11-4-1932   b. 5-31-1935
d. 3-1997, Midlothian, VA   Winchester, VA

| Shirley MacLean Beaty
(Shirley MacLaine)
b. 4-24-1934
Richmond, VA | *m1.*
9-17-1954
New York, NY;
div. 1983 | William F. Parker
("Steve")
b. 2-6-1922
Germany
d. 5-13-2001
Honolulu, Hawaii | *m2.*
1988 | Miki Hasegawa |

Stephanie Parker
("Sachiko")
b. 8-31-1956
Los Angeles, CA

Sources: birth, death, marriage, and census records and/or gravestones

Donald MacLean   *m.*   Mary

Murdoch Donald Thomas MacLean*   *m.*   Annie MacLeod
b. 1833   *3-28-1867*   b. 1846
Little Bras d'Or,   *Boularderie,*   Boularderie, Nova Scotia
Nova Scotia   *Nova Scotia*   *Daughter of John and Christina MacLeod*

Murdoch Thomas MacLean   *m.*   Blanche Henrietta Lehigh
("Murdo")   *10-22-1902*   b. 2-16-1868 (or 1870)
b. 9-19-1873   *Brockville,*   Frankville, Ontario
Little Bras d'Or,   *Ontario*   d. 11-21-1943
Nova Scotia   Brockville, Ontario
d. 6-27-1922   *Daughter of Franklin M. Lehigh*
North Sydney,
Nova Scotia

Franklin M. Lehigh   *m1.*   *Frances Richards*
(1835–1916)   *("Fanny")*
(1832–1872)

Siblings of Blanche:
Eva M. (9-16-1856–9-20-1874)
William Delorma (5-2-1858–9-6-1861)
Elizabeth Henrietta (b. 2-15-1860–d. Unknown)
m1. James A. Lynch (10-12-1879)
m2. Thomas Bertwhistle
Katie (aka Kathleen, Katherine, Catherine)
(10-1-1862–12-8-1939)
William II (1866–1867)
William III (1867–1881?)
All born in Frankville, Ontario

Kathlyn Corinne   *m.*   Ira Owens Beaty   Mansell Lehigh   *m.*   Maisie Johnston
MacLean   *8-15-1931*   b. 1-18-1903   MacLean   *1924*   b. Unknown
("Tat")   *Wolfville,*   Front Royal, VA   ("Sleep")   d. Unknown
b. 8-23-1903   *Nova Scotia* d. 1-15-1987   b. 12-6-1904
North Sydney,   Arlington, VA   North Sydney,
Nova Scotia   Nova Scotia
d. 2-26-1993   d. 7-5-1968
Malibu, CA   Larchmont, NY

Shirley MacLean Beaty   Henry Warren Beaty II   1 daughter:
(Shirley MacLaine)   (Warren Beatty)   Mrs. Arthur Fulmer
b. 4-24-1934   b. 3-30-1937   (deceased)
Richmond, VA   Richmond, VA

* *Murdoch MacLean* is alternately spelled as *Murdock McLean*.

MacLean Family Tree

6 other sons and daughters
born in Little Bras d'Or

m2.
1-28-1875
Frankville,
Ontario

Mary Frances Richard
(Blanche's stepmother)
b. 10-23-1845
d. 3-23-1925
Brockville, Ontario
1 son with
Franklin M. Lehigh:
William IV (Willie)
(b. 1880–d. 1883)

Margaret MacLean ("Wee Wee") b. 4-7-1906 North Sydney, Nova Scotia d. 6-25-1911 North Sydney, Nova Scotia	Alexandra MacLean ("Queenie") b. 4-7-1906 North Sydney, Nova Scotia d. 8-20-2001 Wilmington, NC	*m.* *6-6-1931* *Rydal,* *PA*	Gerald Leslie Eaton b. 10-6-1906 Madras, India d. March 1960	Virginia Kilbourne MacLean ("Ginny") b. 9-27-1908 North Sydney, Nova Scotia d. 9-25-1989 Toronto	*m.* *10-12-1930* *New York,* *NY*	Alexander Albert MacLeod b. 1902 Black Rock, Nova Scotia d. 11-10-1970 Toronto

3 daughters:
Virginia (deceased), Patricia (deceased),
and Judith

3 daughters:
Annabelle (d. 1959),
Jean, and Joan;
1 son: David Lehigh MacLeod
b. 1944
d. 12-6-1998
Montreal, Canada

Sources: birth, death, marriage, and census records and/or gravestones

Origins of Fame

*"Warren and I are not alike
in so many ways,
but we have the strongest bond you can have:
we're blood.*

*"I'm aware all the time
who Warren and I are
in relation to American culture.
That we have this longevity in us is not just about us.
It's about our family
and everything that produced it."* [1]

—SHIRLEY MACLAINE

Siblings Shirley MacLaine and Warren Beatty at the Academy Awards.
Photo by SNAP/ZUMA Press; copyright 1965

1   *The year he turned thirty-eight, the* pathologically private Warren Beatty gave an interview in which he made what may be the most revealing statement he has ever given: "Whatever you have read or heard about me through articles or gossip, forget it. I am nothing like *that* Warren Beatty. I am nothing like what you have read."[2]

Beatty was at the height of his mystique surrounding *Shampoo*, the sexual satire he cowrote and produced—a film in which he played an aimless playboy presumed to be based on him. The true Warren Beatty has been the actor's closely guarded secret.

The first clue is his real name: Henry Warren Beaty, honoring his great-grandfather, a Southern Baptist from a long line of Virginia Baptists dating to the Revolutionary War. Beatty described them once as "a Southern family that went to enormous lengths to maintain privacy," a tradition Beatty has elevated to an art form.[3]

Over the years, when people expressed fascination that the same obscure Arlington couple produced Warren Beatty and Shirley MacLaine, arguably the most successful brother and sister in Hollywood history, two Oscar-winning movie stars with vividly disparate tabloid personas—Beatty as a supposed sexual satyr and recluse, his sister as the champion of psychic channeling—their father, Ira Beaty, would wink and say that he'd always done his best work in bed.[4]

As an old man in the last stages of illness, Warren Beatty's father became fixated on what even he considered the great mystery of his two children's talent and fame, concluding that it "must be their Scotch-Irish genes somewhere way back there."[5]

Ironically, what Ira Beaty failed to see was that he and his wife, Kathlyn MacLean Beaty, known in the family as Tat, were the fount of Warren and Shirley's successes as well as the underlying source of their psychological intricacies.

"The hidden agenda here is my mother and dad," Shirley MacLaine, who was born Shirley MacLean Beaty, said once. "Whatever creative interests Dad had — he taught me to play the violin — were put aside, and Mother was desirous of being an actress all her life, read poetry, and was a great painter. They devoted their lives to us. . . . I think both Warren and I have a need, a deeply felt melancholy respect for the dreams unrealized by our parents, so we fulfill theirs, and ours."[6]

The secretive Beatty expressed his feelings for and about their parents in a coded name he created for his first production company, Tatira, which produced *Bonnie and Clyde*, the film that would establish him as a legend. "Tatira" was a combination of *Tat* and *Ira*, his mother's and father's first names. To Beatty, who measures every word as if it were his last, the name of his company symbolized his parents' importance in his life and to his career.

Ira Beaty's deathbed theory about the origin of his two children's unique fame holds true. The key to Warren Beatty's character and complexity, to the internal conflict that being a movie star created in him, is in the backstory, and the bloodline, of both the Virginia Beatys and the Canadian MacLeans.

How these two families merged through the unlikely marriage of Ira Beaty and Kathlyn MacLean provided the template for Warren Beatty's and Shirley MacLaine's stardom, and offers the first glimpse into the Warren Beatty no one but his family and a very few close friends have ever seen.

To BEGIN TO understand Warren Beatty, one needs to know that he is a Virginian, foremost.

The originator of his line of Virginia Beatys, Andrew Beaty, is a figure of minor intrigue in genealogical circles. The prevailing belief is that he was born in Swords, Ireland, near Dublin, around 1740. According to family lore, young Beaty slapped his stepmother in the face after she whipped his sister for doing a poor job of sweeping the floor. Andrew Beaty's impudent slap in defense of his sister brought Warren Beatty's ancestors to America — an early indication of the rebel and the gentleman in Beatty, and an ironic foreshadowing of his complex connection to his sister, Shirley.[7]

A less colorful version is that Andrew Beaty was part of the second wave of the Ulster-Irish emigration in the 1700s, when crop failures drove nearly two hundred thousand Irish to America. The minority view is that Beaty, a Presbyterian, fled from Scotland to avoid religious persecution.*

The Beaty clan intersect in a belief that Warren Beatty and Shirley MacLaine's first American ancestor departed for colonial America with Richard Montgomery, the British soldier who gained fame in the Revolutionary War by supporting the colonists and who became a general.

Andrew Beaty either enlisted with Montgomery's British army to fight in the French and Indian War, or he left with Montgomery through a family connection. Most Beatys contend that Andrew Beaty married a relative of the general's named Elizabeth Montgomery, though a few claim that he was Montgomery's nephew.

According to Beaty legend, the sex symbol's first ancestor in America served in the French and Indian War as a chaplain attached to a militia commanded by the young George Washington.[8]

Whatever his story, Warren Beatty's precursor, in descendants' accounts, was a religious man. Before permanently settling in Virginia with his second wife, Sarah Adams, Andrew Beaty established a Presbyterian seminary in Bucks County, Pennsylvania.[9] Sarah Adams Beaty, Warren and Shirley's great-great-great-great grandmother, a native of Virginia, is reputed through "family stories" to be a relative of John Quincy Adams, the sixth U.S. president.[10]

Information on the fate of Elizabeth Montgomery, Andrew Beaty's first wife, or their children, is as elusive as the rest of the reverend's personal life — a mystery some in the extended Beaty clan believe that Warren Beatty, famous for his secrecy and his Virginian's desire for privacy, may be perpetuating by guarding access to Bible records.[†]

---

*Andrew Beaty could have been "Scots-Irish," describing residents of the historic province of Ulster in Northern Ireland who were mostly Protestant, with origins that may have been Scottish.

[†]In 1996, the collective Beattys in America (their name is variously spelled as Beatty, Beaty, Baty, Beattie, etc.) organized to document their lineages, known as "Beatty Project 2000." Several decades earlier, Ira Beaty became obsessed with his family tree, perhaps to search for clues to the mystery gene that he believed had spawned his two eccentrically gifted children. In the course of his research, he is rumored to have acquired the original Beaty family Bible, dating back to Andrew Beaty and providing missing names and dates for the Andrew Beaty male line. Participants in Beatty Project 2000 suspect the family Bible is now in the possession of Warren Beatty, who, like his father, developed an interest in his bloodline. True to his reputation, Beatty has not responded to queries from participants in Beatty Project 2000 — either to assist them in documenting the Andrew Beaty genealogical line or even to confirm that he has the family Bible in his possession.

John Beaty, a son of Andrew and Sarah Adams Beaty, was the charismatic precursor to Warren Beatty, matinee idol, and Shirley MacLaine, his actress-proselytizer sister.[11] Beatty and MacLaine's great-great-great grandfather gained fame as a magnetic circuit-riding Baptist preacher in Virginia in the late 1700s. Along the way, he reportedly sired twenty-three children by two wives — which suggests that Warren's father, Ira, was not the only Beaty who did his best work in bed.[12]

The Beaty men were great procreators, beginning by repute with Reverend Andrew Beaty. William, the son of circuit-rider John Beaty, had eleven children. The next in line, Henry Warren Beaty, Warren Beatty's namesake, fathered at least six.[13] "They were all good-lookin' men," observed a female descendant.[14]

John Beaty began studying for the Presbyterian ministry at his father's Pennsylvania seminary, but converted after hearing Elder James ("Little Jamie") Ireland, a famous Primitive Baptist orator born in Scotland who was held in a Culpeper, Virginia, jail for preaching the gospel without a license.[15]

Brother John Beaty began his Old School Baptist ministry in the Shenandoah Valley, "and preached all over that section as long as he was able to ride."[16] Sometime after 1780, he married a Virginian of Irish descent named Margaret McConihey, whose father gave them a farm, as a wedding gift, located near the Blue Ridge Mountains. By the testimony of his kinfolk, John Beaty was devoted to his and Margaret's fifteen children. When three of them died of tuberculosis, he started a graveyard near the house, and then almost gave away the farm in grief.[17]

The great-great-great grandfather of Warren Beatty became an elder, then a deacon, in the Primitive Baptist church, for a time ministering two churches while holding prayer sessions for Methodists on request. He served his final flock at the Old School Baptist church in Browntown, Virginia. In a prelude to Warren, John Beaty's performance in the pulpit and his personal charm so impressed a wealthy female parishioner that she bequeathed him a large mill at Happy Creek, Virginia, where he built a second home.

In December of 1814, when John Beaty was a widower of forty-nine, he married a twenty-two-year-old named Lavinia Owens Edmonds, a widow with a two-year-old daughter, Elmira.* John Beaty became the stepfather of Elmira and went on to father eight more children while in his fifties.[18] Eighty years later, Warren Beatty, at fifty-four, would marry a woman twenty-

---

*Elias Edmonds, Lavinia's first husband, was killed in the War of 1812.

one years his junior, and father four children while in his fifties and sixties.

The phenomenal John Beaty lived to be eighty-three, "an old man and full of days," as his obituary reads. The Old School Baptist left his mark on Virginia's Shenandoah Valley through his twenty-three children and the three churches he built in a region called the Magisterial Fork named Faith, Hope, and Charity. Beaty would be eulogized by his final congregation as "remarkably exemplary in conduct and conversation through life; humility and devotion was [sic] two prominent traits in his Christian character."[19]

Reverend John Beaty's circuit-riding conversion to the Primitive Baptist faith took root in the family for the next one hundred fifty years, continuing its influence on the young Warren Beatty and, later in life, on Shirley MacLaine, a self-described "spiritualist" who would demonstrate a similar intensity to inspire true believers while speaking at New Age seminars.

Until Warren's father, Ira Beaty, moved to Richmond in 1920, the Beaty patriarchs would remain in the Shenandoah Valley, near the river's fork where Reverend John Beaty preached in the 1700s.* Many of them would be buried in Prospect Hill Cemetery, which Warren Beatty still visits.[20] Beatty drew upon aspects of his Virginia forebears to craft the title character in *McCabe & Mrs. Miller*, Robert Altman's elegiac Western about a drifter who ambles into a small town called Presbyterian Church.[21]

The Beatys who descended from Brother John were all faithful Southern Baptists, although John Beaty was the last to preach. The next two generations in Warren Beatty's male line worked as farmers, beginning with his great-great-grandfather William Beaty. William Beaty, who was born in 1801, created permanent confusion in the family tree in 1830 by marrying his stepsister, Elmira Edmonds — the eighteen-year-old daughter of Reverend John Beaty's second wife, war widow Lavinia Owens Edmonds. William's marriage to Elmira gave Lavinia Owens Edmonds Beaty the unusual distinction of being William Beaty's mother-in-law *and* his stepmother.

William and Elmira Beaty named their eighth consecutive son Henry Warren Beaty. Born April 17, 1847, he was the great-grandfather and namesake of actor Warren Beatty. "Warren" was the newly formed county in Virginia where the Beatys resided,† so named in honor of Joseph Warren, the

---

*The word *Shenandoah*, the valley in Virginia that was Beatty and MacLaine's ancestral home, comes from an Algonquin word meaning "Daughter of the Stars."
†Warren County was founded in 1836 as a subdivision of what was originally Shenandoah County.

patriot who reportedly sent Paul Revere on his legendary ride.[22] The Warren County seat became known as Front Royal, Virginia, a town sixty miles west of Washington, D.C., near the border of West Virginia at the northernmost tip of what is now Shenandoah National Park's scenic Skyline Drive. Front Royal was home to the Beatys.

One of the few existing photographs of the first Warren Beaty, taken in his later years, is of a "distinguished-looking gentleman" with gray hair, as described by his great-granddaughter Quincy Butler, a first cousin of Warren Beatty and Shirley MacLaine.[23]

Warren Beatty the actor would show a keen interest in the great-grandfather whose name he inherited. He told a British journalist that the first Henry Warren Beaty was a spy for the Confederacy during the Civil War, a notion scoffed at by other Beaty descendants from Front Royal.[24]

No records of enlistment exist for Beatty's great-grandfather, who was only fourteen when the Civil War began, nor does his name appear on the roster of Warren County Confederate soldiers.[25] He had an older brother, William A. Beaty, who joined the Confederate army as a twenty-five-year-old private in 1863, serving in a regiment of the Virginia Infantry known as the "Warren Blues," organized at Front Royal in June 1861.[26]

The mystery befits the namesake of the secretive actor, as does the clandestine nature of the first Warren Beaty's rumored espionage on behalf of the Confederacy — a subtle foreshadowing of the second Warren Beatty, who would be known for whispering strategies to Democrats' campaign managers in the phantom hours between midnight and three A.M.[27]

Beatty, a champion of liberal causes, maintained that his great-grandfather and the other Beatys did not advocate slavery, despite their support for the Confederacy. During childhood visits to Front Royal, his great aunt Maggie, one of Henry Warren Beaty's daughters, called the Civil War "anything but civil," referring to it as the "War Between the States." "They would never admit the war was about slavery," Beatty recalled. "They said it was about states' rights."[28]

During and following the Civil War, Beatty's great-grandfather worked as a farmhand. When he married at twenty-two, to Mary Lavinia Pomeroy, his choice in brides entangled the Beatys in a web of interrelationships of Faulknerian complexity that was reflective of many playwrights' depictions of the Old South.

The Pomeroys were a prominent Warren County family with no connection to the Beaty family tree. The entanglement arose in Mary Lavinia Pomeroy's *maternal* line: her mother, Lucinda Beaty Pomeroy, was one of the eight children of Reverend John Beaty and his second wife, Lavinia Owens Edmonds.[29] H. Warren Beaty's father (William Beaty) and Mary's mother (Lucinda Beaty Pomeroy) had the same father — the great procreator John Beaty — by different wives, which made Warren Beatty's great-grandparents half siblings. Thus Reverend John Beaty was the grandfather of the bride *and* the groom.

To add to the confusion, H. Warren Beaty and Mary Lavinia Pomeroy also shared the same *grandmother*, through a different branch of the family tree, also extending to the potent John Beaty: Lavinia Owens Edmonds Beaty, the twenty-two-year-old widow John Beaty had wed at age forty-nine.

In short, H. Warren Beaty married his first cousin through not one but two grandparents in common.

The first Warren Beaty and his wife began their married life on a farm in Warren County, Virginia. Mary Lavinia had six children between 1870 and 1880, one of whom died in infancy.[30] The second oldest, William Welton Beaty, was Warren Beatty and Shirley MacLaine's grandfather. Welton, as he was called, grew up as the only male in a house with four sisters, a dominant female presence that would characterize Warren Beatty's childhood.

A confusion of deed records in Virginia showed the Beatys purchasing land throughout the mid- to late 1800s in Warren County, which was plat-ted into streets to form the town of Front Royal. H. Warren Beaty and his family moved onto a lot created at Royal and Second streets around 1885, when Shirley and Warren's grandfather Welton was thirteen. The original Beaty place in Front Royal was a small, two-story frame house their great-grandfather, H. Warren Beaty, may have helped to build, since census records identified him as a carpenter and a "lumber dealer."[31]

H. Warren Beaty started a small factory in Front Royal, on Commerce Street, where he and his son Welton manufactured spokes for wagon wheels and made handles out of hickory. When Welton died in 1946, the county newspaper noted, "Their 'lathes' were always true, the finished articles of the highest class and always up to specifications. There was little or no reason to inspect their offerings."[32]

The observation was revealing of actor-producer Warren Beatty, who showed the same attention to detail crafting his films. And Beatty has recog-nized the tradition of fine craftsmanship he inherited. In 2003, he showed a close friend one of the handles made by his grandfather, with the name "Welton Beaty" cut into the side.[33]

There are other insights into Warren Beatty through the ghosts of his ancestors. His grandfather's obituary included an unusual statement about Welton Beaty and the first Warren Beaty. "These men were inherently honest," reported the *Register*, "it just ran in the family."[34] When Beatty the movie star was asked in 1975 to name the qualities he valued in a woman, he replied, "The quality of honesty is the most important quality to me, in men or women."[35] This distinctive Beaty trait carried through to his sister, Shirley, who said once that she could forgive almost any human frailty except dishonesty.[36]

Their grandfather's obituary tied this truthfulness to the family's Baptist ethics, dating back to John Beaty, the circuit-riding preacher. The newspaper in their Virginia hometown eulogized both Welton Beaty and the first Warren Beaty, "in the words of the Good Book, as 'just men and true.' "

This heritage would hold great meaning for the second Warren Beatty, whose childhood would be spent in perpetuation of these values, before his name became synonymous in Hollywood with sex.

2   *Warren Beatty's father, Ira, devoted* considerable time in his last days to analyzing his parents' tortured relationship, which he felt set the stage for the numerous disappointments in his own life. Ira's damaged soul, Shirley MacLaine believed, was the impetus for her, and Warren's, epic show business careers.

The catalyst for all of it, in Ira's view, was his mother, Ada.[37]

When he was twenty-nine, William Welton Beaty married a teacher who had a one-room schoolhouse in the nearby burg of Little Washington, named after George Washington, who had surveyed the town as a seventeen-year-old.[38] Her name was Ada Virginia Partlow, and she would become a key, albeit enigmatic, figure in the story of her grandchildren's success.

Not much of substance is known about the woman who would cast a shadow over her son Ira's life — and by doing so, trigger what Shirley and Warren call their "marathons of overachievement."[39] She and her seven siblings were born on a farm in Rappahannock County, Virginia, to parents Burrell and Ruth Updike Partlow. Education and achievement must have been stressed on the Partlow farm, because Ada left to become a teacher; one of her brothers went to law school; and her father, Burrell Partlow, eventually was elected mayor of Little Washington.[40]

After Welton and Ada married, in 1901, H. Warren Beaty built a spacious colonial for his wife, Mary, and their four daughters, situated next to the original Beaty place; and the newlyweds, Welton and Ada, moved into Welton's childhood home.[41] Ira Owens Beaty, who would become the father of two Oscar winners, was born in this modest frame house at 9 East Second Street in Front Royal on January 18, 1903.

Ada Beaty hinted at the possible expectations she had for her baby by naming him after her older brother, Ira Partlow, who was finishing his law degree at Cumberland University. Three years later, the Beatys had a daughter called Ruth, after Ada's mother.*

Unlike the prolific Beaty men who preceded him, Warren Beatty's grandfather Welton had only two children, perhaps a metaphor for the emasculated husband his son Ira felt Welton became.

Shirley MacLaine described her father as an unhappy child under the tyranny of a volatile, overbearing mother who bullied and berated him, once locking him in a closet for two days while his father, Welton, stood by impassively. Ira Beaty also recalled being chased by his mother with butcher knives.[42] "One thing my mother taught me well," Ira told his daughter, "and that was how to fear."[43]

Ira's sister, Ruth Beaty, who led a dignified life in Front Royal until her death in 1997, preferred to keep family matters private in the polite Virginia way. More distant kin in Front Royal attested to the accuracy of MacLaine's characterization of hers and Warren's grandparents. Jean Pomeroy, whose grandmother was a Beaty cousin, recalled "a couple of episodes that Ada really worked [Welton] over." Pomeroy remembered: "They had a big argument one day, and Welton was standing on the edge of the back porch, maybe twelve or fourteen inches off the ground, and she didn't like what he said or something or other, and she pushed the washing machine over on him."[44]

Another cousin once observed Ada Beaty "on the front porch whipping Welton with a broom. He was laying down on the porch."[45] Ira Beaty's last thoughts, MacLaine recalled, were of his mother — "trying to figure out how she came to be the way she was."[46]

---

*Ira's middle name, Owens, and Ruth's middle name, Lavinia, both derived from Lavinia Owens Edmonds Beaty, the second wife of Reverend John Beaty.

Ada Partlow Beaty may have felt unfulfilled in her marriage to a "working man" like Welton Beaty,[47] a "jack-of-all-trades" who installed furnaces and fixed electrical wiring.[48]

A snapshot taken of Warren Beatty's grandparents in middle age is a record of their incompatibility. Welton Beaty seems out of place in a suit, and has the rugged, weather-beaten skin of a laborer; his genial features wear an expression of submission. Ada Partlow Beaty, who stands much taller than her husband, commands attention in a stylish coat with an enormous fur collar framing a handsome but stern face. She projects confidence, intelligence, and impatience.[49]

Mason Green, Jr., who worked closely with Ira Beaty in the latter's later years, noticed that Beaty seldom talked about his parents. According to MacLaine, Welton's passive nature "pained" Ira, who yearned for his father to stand up to his domineering, occasionally violent wife.

Ira Beaty, understandably, suffered from low self-esteem, confiding to his daughter that the only encouragement he ever got was from a teacher, who said he wrote well. He told Shirley that his parents rarely showed affection, and he expressed to her and to Warren that he could never envision himself being happy.[50] This specific fallout from their father's past would be at the root of every significant life decision Warren Beatty and Shirley MacLaine would make, consciously or unconsciously.

A sensitive and imaginative boy, Ira Beaty dreamed of running away to join the circus or to become an adventurer, fantasies that involved escape.[51] Instead, he found an outlet for his unexpressed emotions through music, a pattern that was to repeat itself in his son, Warren, who chose the piano. Ira learned to play the drums, but his grand passion was the violin.

He may have gotten the idea from his namesake uncle, Ira J. Partlow, who had established a successful law practice in the tiny town of Welch, West Virginia. Partlow's wife's sister, Martha Martin Burke, was an esteemed violinist who took lessons at the Damrosch School of Music, now known as Juilliard.

Ira Beaty showed promise on the violin, just as his sister, Ruth, did on the piano. Their musical talent came from their father's side. "Like all the Beatys," Welton's obituary states, "Welton had a good voice, sang in the Baptist choir and faithfully attended its public functions." The Beaty talent for singing would surface in Shirley MacLaine, but also—this is less well known—in Warren Beatty.

When Ira took up baseball, his aunt Bertie—one of Welton Beaty's four sisters — persuaded him to quit because "she was afraid he'd break his fingers" and be unable to play the violin.[52] Ira Beaty assimilated the extreme caution of his maiden aunt and acquired a crippling inferiority complex from his severely belittling mother.

Someone had aspirations for Ira Beaty beyond small-town Front Royal, because he spent the year after high school at Randolph-Macon Academy, an army boarding school affiliated with the small, exclusive men's college of the same name.[53] Since Ira Partlow had graduated from Randolph-Macon College, it is logical to assume that Partlow was guiding, and possibly funding, his nephew and namesake.[54]

In the fall of 1920, Ira Beaty enrolled at the University of Richmond, the first Beaty male in his bloodline to leave Warren County, Virginia, in a hundred fifty years. When he left for school, his suspicious mother strapped a money belt under his clothes because "the world was cruel [and] people might steal."[55]

Ira Beaty's photo in the University of Richmond yearbook in 1922 shows a handsome, slightly intense youth with fine dark hair parted in the center — as Warren Beatty would be asked, and would refuse, to wear *his* hair for *Bonnie and Clyde* forty-four years later. Traces of his movie idol son, Warren, can be seen in Ira Beaty's high forehead, scrutinizing eyes, and the guarded yet determined set of his mouth, with its distinctive, sensuously full bottom lip. There is something vaguely sad, and possibly lonely, about the young man in the photograph.

Classmates of Ira Beaty called him "I.O.," for Ira Owens. He was a lackluster student. He played violin in a university string quartet and in the orchestra, where a shared love of music drew him into a friendship with orchestra manager Wilbur "Billy" Southward, a premed student who played saxophone and piano. Southward's son Ronald heard wonderfully amusing stories from his father about parties around Richmond, where Billy Southward and Ira Beaty used to perform with a band while they were in college "but not professionally, or even semi-professionally."[56]

In the middle of Beaty's sophomore year, his life took a mysterious turn. He dropped out of the University of Richmond over Christmas, 1922, and in January he requested that his transcript be sent to Randolph-Macon. His whereabouts for the next twelve months are a matter of conjecture. A director of university relations at the University of Richmond, who saw Ira Beaty's poor grades, thought that perhaps Ira had "found himself" during that period.[57]

Beaty, who had just turned twenty, was seen at dance clubs around Virginia, as recalled by close friend Mason Green, Jr. Green's aunt, who was then in her late teens, spotted Beaty leading the band at dance clubs in Front Royal, Culpepper, and possibly elsewhere. "Young kids in their twenties would travel around the state to different dances . . . so people knew people from all over the state that way."[58] Shirley MacLaine believed that she got her sense of rhythm from her father's talent as a bandleader. "Dad wanted to, I think, express himself in the theater or show business."[59]

Ira Beaty, by Green's aunt's description, cut a striking figure then. "He was quite a dancer. He was apparently quite a popular fellow." The secret behind Beaty's confidence evidently was alcohol. He told his daughter that he started drinking during Prohibition "to seem like a big wheel."[60] His twelve months as a swinging bandleader during the Roaring Twenties at the age of twenty may have been the high point of Ira Beaty's life.

During this interval, by MacLaine's sketchy account, a famous teacher "plucked" her father out of an amateur symphony in Front Royal with an offer to bring him to Europe on scholarship as a violin soloist,[61] a story he would tell Shirley and Warren repeatedly.*

Beaty made the fateful decision not to go to Europe and pursue a career as a violinist. He told his daughter when she was a teenager that the "competition was too rough," and it was an undependable way to make a living.[62] This choice was a defining moment in Ira Beaty's life. "He might have become a concert violinist if he had taken the gamble as a young man," Warren Beatty later mused.[63] Instead, Ira Beaty tormented himself over his decision—the legacy, he believed, of a mother who made him afraid to try. "His mother had been extremely cruel to him," MacLaine later wrote. "She berated him at every juncture . . . so his expectations of success were nonexistent."[64]

In January 1924, the month he turned twenty-one, Ira Beaty enrolled at his lawyer uncle's alma mater, Randolph-Macon College in Ashland, Virginia, transferring his credit hours from the University of Richmond. To Ira, this move signaled the end of a dream. The summer before, his grand-

*Beaty's opportunity may have come through violinist Martha Burke, Ira Partlow's sister-in-law. Partlow's wife, Andrea, died the year before Ira Beaty withdrew from the University of Richmond, and Burke moved into the Partlow house to help Partlow bring up his and Andrea's children. Martha Burke taught violin at Cumberland University and in West Virginia. She, or a colleague, was likely the "famous teacher" who offered Ira Beaty the violin scholarship.

father Henry Warren Beaty—after whom Ira would name his son, and through him achieve vicarious fame—died at age seventy-six. The first Warren Beaty was buried in Prospect Hill Cemetery in Front Royal, next to the ghosts of other Beatys past.

Ira Beaty studied educational psychology at Randolph-Macon, graduating on June 8, 1926. Katharine Hepburn's father, Dr. Thomas Hepburn, received his undergraduate degree from the same small, prestigious men's college in 1900, prior to becoming a prominent surgeon in Hartford, Connecticut, one of several ties to the patrician actress that Warren Beatty would consider significant. Beaty's choice in majors—teaching—certified that he had relinquished any fantasy of being a musician in favor of a more practical vocation.

After two years as a teacher in public schools in Virginia and West Virginia, Beaty transferred his lost hopes of becoming a concert violinist into the pursuit of a prestigious doctorate from Johns Hopkins University, envisioning himself, romantically, as "a philosopher."[65] His sister, Ruth, an accomplished pianist, had been taking graduate courses at the nearby Peabody Conservatory of Music in Baltimore. On June 13, 1927, Ruth Beaty married the principal of Warren High School in Front Royal, Quincy Damon Gasque, whose career as an educator would serve as a benchmark for Ira Beaty. The summer of 1928, Beaty was admitted as a graduate student in education in the Department of Philosophy at Johns Hopkins and assigned to an advisor named Dr. Florence Bamberger, the first woman to be appointed full professor at the school.[66]

To support himself, the cautious Baptist took a job as a part-time professor of education and psychology at a small, tony women's college in Lutherville, Maryland, owned by a Hopkins graduate named William H. Moore III, who had just won the school in a crap game for fifty thousand dollars.[67]

The little town of Lutherville, located ten miles north of Baltimore, was named after theologian Martin Luther by its founding fathers, two Lutheran ministers who felt the need to establish a "school for young ladies" south of the Mason-Dixon Line in 1853.*[68] It still retained its finishing-school quaintness, featuring a riding program as well as the coronation of a May Queen, appealing to upper-crust southern families.[69]

---

*The campus's first incarnation was as a Lutheran female seminary. Its name was changed to the Maryland College for Women in 1895, when it became a four-year university.

William Moore's unlikely other recruit for the fall 1928 faculty of the Maryland College for Women was Kathlyn MacLean, a twenty-four-year-old professor of speech from Wolfville, Nova Scotia.[70]

The small photograph of Kathlyn Corinne MacLean in the faculty section of the *Marylunder* annual bears little or no resemblance to her famous son, Warren Beatty, and only a wistful similarity to Shirley MacLaine, "right through the eyes," as William Moore's daughter Jane observed years later.[71] From her picture, Kathlyn MacLean was more handsome than pretty, with a swan's neck and a slender face fixed in a dreamy expression, communicating a similar kind of longing as Ira Beaty showed in the University of Richmond yearbook photo his freshman year.[72]

The mystery was how Kathlyn MacLean happened to make the journey from the island of Nova Scotia to an obscure ladies' college in Maryland. "I don't think she had a lot of money," observed one of her well-heeled former charges.[73] Students from the first year she taught recalled Kathlyn MacLean speaking nostalgically about Wolfville, and frequently expressing how much she loved it there as if she wished she could go back.[74]

3

One of *Warren Beatty's* earliest infatuations, at the age of three, was his grandmother MacLean, his mother's mother. Shirley, then six, observed from a respectful distance the seventy-year-old's imperious bearing and silver halo of softly waved hair, but Warren, their mother, Kathlyn, noticed, "would snuggle up to her and say, 'Oh Grandmother, you smell so good.'"[75]

Beatty's affinity as a toddler for his maternal grandmother would prove, later in life, to be revealing. Blanche Lehigh MacLean was a formal, and formidable, woman of unusual dignity and refinement, with ethics of steel. She and her husband, Murdoch T. MacLean, a Canadian like Blanche, created an intellectual and quasi-aristocratic home life for Kathlyn MacLean and their four other children that was light years removed from the southern discomfort of Ira Beaty's upbringing.

Blanche Lehigh* had grown up as the youngest girl in a family of reformers blessed with artistic promise and cursed by misfortune. Her grandfather,

---

*The Irish surname Lehigh was originally spelled "Leahy" or "Leehy."

Gideon Lehigh, was a strapping farmer of Irish ancestry who settled in Ontario with British loyalists fleeing the American colonies.[76] He married a plain, sturdy Irish Canadian named Clarissa Kilborn, "hiving" his farmland near Brockville, along the St. Lawrence River, among their sons when they came of age. One of them, Franklin M. Lehigh, would become Warren Beatty's great-grandfather.[77]

Franklin Lehigh, a Wesleyan Methodist, chose an Irish-born Methodist for a bride — Frances Richards, called Fanny, a reverend's daughter.[78] Blanche Lehigh was the last of Franklin and Fanny Lehigh's seven children, born on February 16, in either 1868, 1869, or 1870, depending upon the census taker, or possibly Blanche's vanity. She was christened Blanche Henrietta Lehigh, a name that would suit her magisterial, Puritan character.[79]

Death hovered over Blanche's childhood like a black cloud. She never really knew her mother, Fanny, who died — from causes long forgotten — when Blanche was less than four. Two years later, Blanche's eighteen-year-old sister, Eva, died, or was killed. A brother called William Delorma passed away at three.[80] A second William, named after the toddler who had died, can be found in the church's register of deaths in 1867.[81] That year, Fanny Lehigh named a third infant son William. His name vanished from official records when he was fifteen.[82] There were so many deaths in the family that the township of Kitley created a Lehigh Cemetery to bury them all. The cumulative effect of these tragedies on the young Blanche Lehigh no doubt helped to form the iron-willed character of the woman who would earn the respect of her grandchildren, Warren and Shirley.

With her mother dead, Blanche grew especially close to her older sister Katie (also known as Kathleen and as Katherine).* Franklin Lehigh remarried several years after his wife Fanny's death. His second wife was a thirty-year-old cousin of Fanny's named Mary Frances Richards, described in her obituary as a "remarkable woman in many respects."[83] Perpetuating the family curse, she would lose her only child when he was two years old — the fourth Lehigh son named William to die young.[84]

Mary Lehigh, an early crusader for women's rights, fostered her step-daughters' self-expression. Franklin Lehigh, who had started a prosperous

---

*One other sibling, Elizabeth Henrietta Lehigh, survived the plague of deaths. She married and moved to the prairie province of Saskatchewan before Blanche turned ten. Elizabeth was not mentioned in the obituaries of either Katie Lehigh or Blanche Lehigh MacLean, which indicates that she too may have met an early death.

lumber dealership, "was a staunch liberal in politics," according to the local newspaper.[85] He and his suffragette wife made a decision that helped to set the course for Warren Beatty and Shirley MacLaine's careers: they sent Katie, and later Blanche, to the newly constructed DeMill Ladies College in Oshawa, Ontario, the first college for women in Canada.[86] The college was modeled after Mount Holyoke Seminary, in Massachusetts, by Alfred Byron DeMill, a Methodist clergyman with delusions of grandeur.[87] The wily reverend persuaded men less progressive than Franklin Lehigh to invest in higher education for young women by promising to "turn out the ideal woman . . . learned not only in books but . . . taught that it is no disgrace to make a bed and cook a dinner."[88]

Beatty's grandmother, and his great-aunt, had serious artistic and feminist aspirations. Katie Lehigh, who never married, studied music at DeMill and became a gifted pianoforte instructor in Brockville, the second of Warren Beatty's aunts to teach piano, an instrument that would become one of the actor's greatest passions.[89] And Beatty's grandmother was introduced to the performing arts, a match that would influence the next three generations, not only blazing a trail for Beatty and Shirley MacLaine's stardom, but also establishing Warren Beatty's feminine ideal.

During the week of commencement exercises in June 1892, Blanche Lehigh performed nightly in a scene from *Macbeth*, recited poetry by Longfellow and Kellogg, and sang the part of a fairy in a cantata by Arthur Page.[90] She received her diploma in what was then called elocution.

The "highest Christian" morality was rigorously enforced at DeMill. Students could not leave the school or receive guests on Sundays. Parents were discouraged from visiting their daughters because it might "hinder their studies."[91] Young ladies could visit or correspond with only those people whose names appeared on a list submitted by their parents. Blanche Lehigh conducted herself according to these strict morals the rest of her life, a standard she set for her daughter, and that she expected of her grandchildren. This influence would have a lasting impact on Beatty.

Blanche Lehigh followed the feminist path of her suffragist stepmother, who would be remembered, in a Brockville newspaper, as "a great temperance worker" who "commanded respect."[92] After receiving her diploma in elocution, Blanche continued her higher education at the Toronto Conservatory of Music, enrolling as a voice major. According to a Canadian author, Blanche Lehigh was an "accomplished singer," so Shirley and Warren were endowed with musical talent from their mother's side as well as from their father's.[93] The year she obtained her voice degree from the Toronto Conservatory of Music, in 1896, Blanche set forth, alone and unmarried, for the province of Nova Scotia, a thousand miles away. There she accepted a faculty position at the Halifax Ladies College, in charge of elocution and what she called "calisthenics." She was twenty-eight.

The old-fashioned elocution classes Blanche taught were designed to develop "natural delivery in every form of expression," according to the college catalogue. When Warren Beatty first became famous as a movie actor, he would occasionally mention his grandmother, usually telling reporters that she "taught acting in college."[94] But Blanche Lehigh's classes were more esoteric than that, and demanded intellectual rigor. Her female students recited in front of her, and Blanche individually critiqued them in orthoepy (the study of pronunciation), rhetoric, physiology, sight-reading, English literature, voice culture, and vocal expression.[95]

Blanche Lehigh's quaintly bizarre calisthenics class, a regimen of exercises to strengthen the voice, was equally driven by her perfectionism. She followed a Swedish system of voice and body modulation invented by Baron Nils Posse that promised to "secure perfect normal adjustment of the various parts of the body." Miss Lehigh, it was noted in the course description, taught "perfect health with ease and grace . . . made interesting by fancy marches, and by the use of different apparatus — Indian Clubs, Dumb Bells, etc."[96]

Highly religious in the Baptist faith, not her parents' Methodism, Blanche led morning Bible studies for young women at the college for six years, long past the age when a less emancipated woman in turn-of-the-century Halifax would have felt secure remaining single.[97] When she did marry, it was to a man who was her intellectual and cultural equal. Murdoch Thomas MacLean* was a recent graduate of Dalhousie Medical School, affiliated with Halifax Ladies College, and earned a master's in surgery. "Quite a catch," as a female archivist would later comment admiringly, seeing MacLean's photograph.[98] The cameo portrait of a dashing M. T. MacLean, wearing lacquered wavy black hair and a lavish handlebar moustache, pictured with the ten other physicians in Dalhousie's class of 1899, is a preview of the movie star siblings born two generations later.

---

*Alternately spelled "Murdock McLean," and occasionally identified as Thomas Murdock McLean. Beatty's mother at times went by Kathlyn "McLean," until early adulthood, when she consistently spelled her surname "MacLean."

At the time Blanche Lehigh married her twenty-nine-year-old husband, she was probably thirty-four — identified on the marriage license as a "spinster." Warren Beatty's handsome and eligible grandfather had chosen a strong older woman of creative accomplishment, not a superficial beauty. Beatty would be drawn to a similar type in a number of his serious relationships.

"Murdo" MacLean was born on the picturesque shores of Little Bras d'Or, a saltwater lake covering nearly one-sixth of Cape Breton, a large island settled by Highland Scots off the Atlantic coast of Canada, considered part of Nova Scotia. His Scottish parents, Murdock Donald Thomas MacLean and Annie MacLeod, farmed the land. When he first became a doctor, while courting Blanche Lehigh, Murdo MacLean returned to Little Bras d'Or to practice medicine.

He and Blanche were married in Brockville by a Baptist minister on October 22, 1902, and moved to the town of North Sydney, north of Little Bras d'Or, along the craggy coastline of Cape Breton Island. Blanche quit teaching elocution to start a family, and Murdo MacLean opened a medical office on the first floor of their spacious red-shingled house at 44 Summer Street.*

It was there, on this Scottish island in Nova Scotia, that Warren Beatty's mother, Kathlyn, spent her childhood, and it was there that his sister, Shirley MacLaine, would say that their value system was born, "probably on Summer Street."[99]

4   *Cape Breton Island offered the sort of* mystical tableau of rocky shores, fierce currents, and abandoned lighthouses romanticized in movies, and was poetically described by MacLaine as being on the "windswept shores of the Atlantic."[100] Until 1955, islanders had to ferry across the strait to get to the mainland.

Kathlyn Corinne MacLean, the first child of Murdo and Blanche Lehigh MacLean, was born into this insular world on August 23, 1903. Warren Beatty later would compare his mother to the actress Katharine Hepburn, with good reason: "Hepburn was a progressive with a feminist mother and a

---

*MacLean's first office in North Sydney was briefly at Tutty House.

doctor father. My mother was too. . . . [Hepburn's] name was Katharine. My mother's was Kathlyn."[101] Kathlyn MacLean, who almost certainly was named after her mother's bosom sister, Katie, had an upbringing that was a cross between Hepburn's fabled childhood in Fenwick, Connecticut, and that of Jo March in *Little Women*, a role played by Hepburn on screen and by Kathlyn MacLean onstage.

By the time she was five, the sensible Kathlyn claimed responsibility for a gaggle of closely knit siblings as individualistic as she was. They gave one another nicknames, part of a secret family code. Kathlyn was "Tat." Mansell, her only brother, was known as "Sleep." Twin girls, Margaret ("Wee Wee") and Alexandra ("Queenie"), came along in 1906. The baby of the family was Virginia ("Ginny"), born in September 1908.[102]

Kathlyn, or Tat—the person who would most closely shape the personality of Warren Beatty—was a dreamy child. In girlhood, she wrote romantic poetry about Cape Breton Island and her family's enchanted life there:

Has the sea ever called to you with the irresistible force of command?
The sea, with its great massiveness, its calm dignity,
its merry chatterings, its utter fearlessness, brings with it
all the associations of childhood days.

The nights when troublesome teeth made such a fuss,
this dear old sea, with its ceaseless roar and splash
as the waves dashed against its old friends the rocks,
made fanciful stories run through the imagination,
suggesting fairies, elfs, beautiful white sailed boats
run by wonderful little captains . . .[103]

Tat's first cousin, Jean MacLean, grew up in Cape Breton in the 1900s, around Tat's exceptional family, which provided multiple clues into Warren Beatty's sensitive and complex psyche. Jean MacLean, who knew Kathlyn only as Tat, recalled visits to the rambling two-story on Summer Street that had a storybook quality. "They had a great big house, and Uncle Murdo's doctor's office was attached to the house. They had two live-in maids, one was named Christie, and they had a horse. Marjorie was the name of the horse. They had caretakers that looked after it, and they had all these children, and they just seemed to have lots of fun."[104]

Tat was sleek as a greyhound, a standout athlete like her younger sisters.

All four girls played tennis and swam, and were adoring of their brother, Mansell, who had inherited Dr. MacLean's dark good looks. In middle age, with his hair thinning and his moustache neatly trimmed, Beatty's grandfather MacLean resembled the urbane William Powell as the formal patriarch in the film version of *Life with Father*.

"I don't know that money was something that they thought about or they didn't think about. The father provided for them, and they just had a standard of living," appraised a male cousin who spent time listening to family stories told by Alexandra (Queenie) in her last years. "Queenie brought out photo albums, and she would just laugh out loud and love to reminisce. She had an absolutely infectious laugh."[105]

Like Katharine Hepburn and Jo March, Kathlyn MacLean lost a sibling in childhood, one of the only blights on an otherwise charmed adolescence. Her sister Wee Wee, Queenie's twin, died of diphtheria at the age of five and was buried in Lakeside Cemetery with a headstone inscribed: BELOVED DAUGHTER OF DR. M. T. AND BLANCHE MCLEAN . . . SAFE IN THE ARMS OF JESUS.[106] The loss of a child was especially cruel since Tat's deeply religious physician father, whom she idolized, was on the staff of the first hospital in North Sydney, and performed the first surgery there, on September 22, 1908.

The progressive MacLeans were esteemed on the island, schooled in the same "sensible values" by which Shirley and Warren would be reared.[107] Dr. MacLean helped to initiate the first training school for nurses in North Sydney, and he addressed the original graduating class at the 1914 commencement ceremony. Blanche, described by a local historian as a "noted public speaker," gave the reading. When Tat was thirteen, in the midst of World War I, her mother narrated a concert at North Sydney's first theater, and ended by singing the national anthems of the Allies. Blanche also sang locally, and was featured as a soloist in a repertory company's annual summer tent show. Her performances would inspire all but one of her children, and two famous grandchildren, to pursue the stage.[108]

Blanche MacLean approached her wifely role with the same formality and exacting standards as she had approached her elocution classes. The family took their meals in the dining room on starched white linens, with Blanche ringing a tiny bell to summon the maid. Dr. MacLean began each meal by saying grace,[109] and friends described the MacLeans as possessing "very Canadian," cultivated accents.[110] Blanche had the look and air of a dowager duchess by her early forties. "Ever since I can remember, her hair was white," said a niece.[111]

Shirley MacLaine's impression of her mother's family, which she mentioned in several of her books, was as "controlled, placid, and preeminently polite."[112] Her brother, cut from the same cloth, considered it impolite to discuss the family in public at all.

Blanche MacLean instilled in Kathlyn the same Victorian mores that she herself had followed at DeMill Ladies College. "No dancing or anything like that on a Sunday afternoon," a cousin remembered.[113] The future mother of Warren Beatty — a movie star with a reputation as a Don Juan — was also restricted in her social contact with young men. "There would be a real taboo on certain things," said Cousin Jean MacLean. "Uncle Murdo and Aunt Blanche were very strict [about] boys and dates and things like this."[114]

Blanche MacLean's powerful influence was immediately evident in her daughter Kathlyn's education. The year Tat turned seventeen, in 1920, she was sent to a boarding school on the mainland of Nova Scotia, in Wolfville, the site of Acadia University, a strict, respected Baptist college. It was a choice that would affect the family in profound and unforeseen ways.

The Acadia Ladies Seminary, or ALS, Tat's preparatory school, offered finishing-school courses in the fine arts, with a diploma presented after two years. The MacLeans may have chosen ALS for Tat partly because there she would be under the wing of Mansell, her younger, much admired brother, then a freshman at Acadia University.

If one relative could be said to foretell Warren Beatty's stardom, it was his uncle Mansell, named for Thomas Mansell, the Baptist minister who had performed Murdo and Blanche MacLean's wedding ceremony.[115] Like Murdo, Mansell MacLean was an earlier version of Beatty — tall, dark, and "incredibly handsome," to quote an acquaintance.[116] He excelled at Acadia, in debating and in dramatics, and was described in the college annual as a "deep thinker," one of his nephew Warren Beatty's most defining traits.[117]

While Kathlyn and her brother were away at school that first year, Dr. MacLean was elected mayor of North Sydney, a salaried position he assumed while continuing to practice medicine. According to relatives, Murdo had begun to experiment with plastic surgery, an innovative concept for a small-town physician in Nova Scotia in 1921.[118]

At Acadia Ladies Seminary, Tat expressed her poetic musings in essays mostly about nature and the family she missed in foggy Cape Breton. She showed a predisposition for English literature and a talent for drawing. Another illustration of her mother's imprint: she received private instruction in elocution.[119]

At the end of her final year at ALS, her father died prematurely of a sudden heart attack — a family trait, said a close relative.[120] Murdo MacLean was only forty-eight when he collapsed one morning while preparing to make his medical rounds. Tat had just received her diploma from the Acadia Ladies Seminary when she got word her father was dying. He sent for her in his dying moments.[121]

Mayor MacLean's funeral was reported on the front page of the *Sydney Post-Record*, which described his memorial service on June 26, 1922, as "the largest ever seen on this side of the harbor, the procession being over a mile in length."[122] According to the *Cape Breton Post*, "the whole town went in mourning." Dr. MacLean's family, Kathlyn especially, was bereft. The inscription on the headstone at Lakeside Cemetery in Little Bras d'Or for Murdoch Thomas MacLean reads: THE BELOVED PHYSICIAN/THE LIVES WHICH YOURS HAVE TOUCHED SHALL RICHER BE.[123]

Although Warren Beatty never met his surgeon grandfather, Murdo MacLean's impact on the actor would prove significant.

5   *Dr. Murdoch MacLean's sudden* death opened an unexpected door, one that would lead everyone in his family to Acadia University, the place Shirley MacLaine credits as the instigator of "the dreams and theatrical human expressions" that inspired her and Warren to go into show business.[124]

The catalyst was Beatty's prototype uncle Mansell, who was preparing for his junior year at Acadia when his father collapsed. The stalwart Blanche, who was now fifty-three, moved the family to Wolfville, where they stayed with friends to conserve money.[125] Acadia University, the centerpiece of the MacLeans' new hometown, was set pictorially amid Victorian estates and apple orchards in the Annapolis Valley, west of Halifax.

Tat, who was nineteen, enrolled at the university in the fall of 1922, after a summer of mourning. Warren and Shirley's mother found her calling — and theirs — at Acadia. That Christmas, Kathlyn MacLean appeared in a play called *Mr. Pim Passes By*, presented by the Acadia Players. Tat's picture on the playbill reveals that she wore her reddish brown hair in a slightly longer version of the flapper-style bob popular then. Her face projected the ethereal quality of her poetry.[126]

The high point at Acadia for Tat was a staging of *Little Women* at the Wolfville Opera House, on April 27, 1923.[127] Her handsome brother, Mansell, portrayed John Brooke, and Kathlyn was cast in the starring role, as the feisty Jo March. The actress who played Meg, Maisie Johnston, married Mansell MacLean after graduation—as her character in the play married his.[128]

The following year brought more acclaim to the thespian MacLean siblings, the Shirley and Warren of their generation. Kathlyn appeared in a leading role in *The Feast of the Red Corn* at the Orpheum Theatre in Wolfville, and her younger brother won Acadia's Ralph M. Hunt Oratorical Contest.[129]

Mansell MacLean graduated from Acadia in 1924 with a degree in the arts, but an uncle persuaded him to become an engineer, a choice that would coincide in an unusual way with his nephew Warren's decision to study acting.[130]

That fall, at fifty-six, Beatty's grandmother became a professor of public speaking at Acadia. As a perquisite, she received discounted tuition for Queenie, the only MacLean sibling with no interest in performing.

But Kathlyn yearned to be an actress. She withdrew from Acadia to study drama at the Margaret Eaton School of Literature and Expression, or MES, in Toronto. Innovative for its time, it would become a curiosity from a bygone era. The façade was built to resemble a Greek temple, on which was inscribed the school's motto: WE STRIVE FOR THE GOOD AND THE BEAUTIFUL.[131] The young women at MES were urged to dress simply ("the foundation of true elegance"), and were advised in the school's calendar that "a garment appropriate in a drawing room may be tawdry and vulgar elsewhere."[132]

Warren Beatty's mother and the fourteen other female students of elocution lived in Dundonald House in downtown Toronto, supervised by a housemother.[133] "The difference between the highly proper women I recall at MES and the flamboyant Warren Beatty boggles the mind," observed the son of Dora Mavor Moore, the esteemed theatrical director who taught dramatics to Kathlyn MacLean in 1925.[134] Yet the prim Margaret Eaton image embodied in Beatty's mother and taught by his grandmother—the antithesis of Hollywood glamour—represented, to Warren Beatty, the feminine ideal.

Besides promoting the "ideals of true womanhood," the school taught a voice and movement system created by François Delsarte and later followed by Isadora Duncan.[135] Delsartists subscribed to a semimystical belief similar to what Kathlyn's daughter, Shirley MacLaine, would espouse half a century later: "to each spiritual function responds a function of the body."[136]

The plays Dora Mavor Moore directed at MES were attended by the public and reviewed in the Toronto newspapers. Tat was singled out in the Toronto *Globe* on June 11, 1925, for her "excellent presentation" as Orsino, the Duke of Illyria, in *Twelfth Night*, the last play ever staged at MES.[137]

Kathlyn MacLean received her diploma from MES in June 1925 and was awarded the class prize for interpretation. In what would prove prophetic, the speaker at her commencement closed with the remark, "The greatest of all paths radiating from graduation day [is] the path that leads to the creation of a home."[138]

IF TAT'S DREAM was to become a professional actress after MES, that dream was dashed. Instead, Warren and Shirley's mother took a teaching position. The family's financial straits may have been the reason.[139]

Tat's baby sister Virginia, or Ginny, had started at Acadia in September, increasing the financial pressures. To help pay the bills, Beatty's grandmother accepted a promotion to dean of women that year.

Kathlyn MacLean's teaching post was in a one-building junior college in Alderson, West Virginia, a town so obscure it did not appear on many maps. For the stage-struck, culturally worldly Tat, this turn of events had to be a crushing disappointment.

She quickly became "very best friends" with Estelle Woodall, a demure young debate coach from Alabama. "Mother called her Tat," Woodall's daughter, Jennie Forehand, reminisced. "I can't figure out why in the world my mother went there—this godforsaken, isolated place."[140]

Kathlyn MacLean's trail was easier to follow. Her brother, Mansell, worked as an assistant engineer in Narrows, Virginia, less than fifty miles from Alderson Junior College, on the border of West Virginia.[141] By a curious synchronicity, both towns were within a sixty-mile radius of Welch, West Virginia, where Ira Partlow was a prominent lawyer.

Kathlyn was an exotic flower in Alderson, West Virginia. "My mother just thought that [Tat] was so pretty, and so much fun," stated Jennie Forehand. She cut her hair in a style inspired by the new silent film star Louise Brooks, and looked extremely soignée, if a bit forlorn, in her faculty photo. Tat resembled, vaguely, Charity Hope Valentine, the character her daughter,

Shirley, would play in *Sweet Charity* forty years later. According to MacLaine, her mother's wish was to star in movies.[142]

Tat told her friend Estelle Woodall that she wanted to be an actress. "They were both just killing time there at Alderson," surmised Woodall's daughter. Estelle Woodall's diary noted that the two teachers took day trips by train to places like White Sulphur Springs and the Greenbrier Country Club.[143] "Mother would laugh out loud about that, because she obviously didn't make much money, and she said, 'Well, we could go up there for the day and pretend.'"

Warren Beatty's mother, who was twenty-two, lived in the faculty dorm and never went out on a date, as far as Jennie Forehand knew. "I kind of have an idea that Tat was as prudish and puritanical as my mother." Estelle Woodall loved to tell her daughter, Jennie, about the time she and Tat were strolling down the street in Alderson. "Some boys drove up beside them in a jalopy and said, 'You girls want to go for a nice ride?' And Mother said, 'You have plenty of gas?' He said, 'Yeah.' She said, 'Well step on it then.' My mother was a stitch — like Tat."

Kathlyn MacLean and Estelle Woodall taught only one year at Alderson Junior College. They kept in touch through letters the rest of their lives, as Tat's children, Shirley and Warren, became increasingly famous movie stars, and Estelle's daughter, Jennie, was elected state senator of Maryland — each mother living vicariously through the accomplishments of her talented children.

During Tat's waning days in Alderson, Ira Beaty graduated from Randolph-Macon. Since Beaty spent that year or the next teaching in West Virginia, his path may have crossed with his future wife's that summer, particularly since Tat and her brother lived near Welch, where Beaty's uncle practiced law. If not, Tat and Ira's proximity was a coincidence of the sort their daughter Shirley would consider cosmically ordained and Warren would refer to as a "missed connection," the premise of *Love Affair*, the romantic 1939 film he would remake and costar in with his wife, actress Annette Bening, in 1994.[144]

Mansell MacLean moved to New York that summer to join an engineering firm. For reasons not known, Kathlyn deferred her dream of becoming a professional actress and returned to Wolfville to re-enroll at Acadia. She was twenty-three.

For the next two years, 1926–1928, Kathlyn MacLean and both of her sisters were students at Acadia University at the same time that Blanche

MacLean was dean of women. Beatty's mother would be remembered there as an accomplished stage actress. "Everyone looked up to her," recalled a graduate who knew her then.[145]

Tat's younger sister Ginny, who would become a television actress in Toronto, appeared in plays at Acadia with and without Tat, often produced by their mother, Blanche. Blanche also judged debates for the Acadia debating team, which Tat's sister Queenie joined. The MacLean family, including Kathlyn's brother, Mansell, who had performed with her earlier at Acadia, was regarded in Wolfville as an acting dynasty, a distinguished legacy that would not be lost on Warren or on Shirley, who once referred to her mother's family as the Canadian Redgraves.[146]

Louise Brownell, one of Ginny MacLean's close friends at Acadia, noticed a strain on the sisters as daughters of the strict dean of women. "Mrs. MacLean was very proper, and expected everyone to be on their very best behavior, be little ladies at that age. I think it was hard on Tat and Ginny and Queenie. Ginny, that I knew — because the rules were rules, and if she broke them it was very upsetting to her mother. They had to watch their step more than the rest of us."[147] This, too, would play out for Shirley and Warren in the next generation, when their father was a school principal.

Kathlyn's stringent Baptist upbringing continued at Acadia. Students were required to attend daily chapel. Tat and her classmates had to sign out when they left the dormitory and sign in before a ten-o'clock curfew. Blanche sat on the Acadia judiciary council and "meted out punishment" to anyone who broke a rule, including her own daughters.[148]

Tat, more than Ginny, "took it in her stride," according to Louise Brownell. "Tat was the romantic type. A happy person, and you felt happy around her." Warren and Shirley's mother was tall and willowy, "not pretty pretty" in the opinion of Brownell. "She had a strong face."

During those two years, Tat had a serious "escort," whom Louise Brownell remembered sketchily as an attractive premed student.[149] Nothing more is known about Tat's love affair, or what became of her doctor beau. This was just one of Beatty's mother's secrets.

Kathlyn MacLean graduated with a bachelor of arts degree in 1928, the same year as Queenie, the "quiet" sister.[150] Queenie, or Alexandra, left Wolfville to begin a career as a dietitian at Mount Sinai Hospital in New York, where Mansell was working for a subway builder named Samuel R. Rosoff.[151]

It was then that Kathlyn MacLean made the mysterious decision to move to Lutherville to teach speech at the Maryland College for Women, which is where the seeds were planted for the familial feelings of failure — and, conversely, inspiration — that would compel both Warren Beatty and his sister, Shirley, to achieve stardom.

6   *There were pieces missing from the* stories told to Warren and Shirley MacLean Beaty about their parents' courtship. Their mother never disclosed what drew her to a small town in Maryland, isolated from her family, or why she set aside her goal to become an actress.

To the mystically inclined MacLaine, it was the pull of fate, aligning her mother and father to fulfill their children's destinies as movie stars.

Tat's truths about Lutherville may never be revealed. The observation of her students that she had little money suggested that she had chosen fixed employment over the instability of being an actress, a trait she shared with Ira Beaty, who abandoned the violin for the same reason. The need for security may have been part of what drew the fatherless Tat and the emotionally impoverished Ira together.

Kathlyn MacLean and Ira Beaty made distinctly different first impressions on the campus where they met, an early clue to their deeper discord. "She was extremely popular with all the students, and he wasn't," said Mabelle Symington Moore, a belle who enrolled in 1929 and married the provost, William Moore, the next year. "He was sort of a know-it-all . . . he was full of himself."[152] If he was, it was false bravado — the same insecurity that led to Beaty's occasional use of alcohol.

The *Marylander* photograph of Professor Ira O. "Beatty" (as his name was misspelled) almost seemed to be of a different person than the romantic, pensive youth who had started at the University of Richmond eight years earlier. This Ira Beaty, only twenty-five, appeared prematurely middle-aged, slightly jowly, with barely a trace of the poetically handsome boy he was at seventeen.[153]

By his second year, Warren Beatty's father had won over his students at the ladies' college. "All the girls were in love with him,"[154] said Winifred

Wokal Morrison, who was voted most beautiful, and who took both psychology and education from Beaty. "He was a very good teacher, actually." Her impression of Beaty was as a dyed-in-the-wool man of the South.

Even though it was a small school and the faculty shared a dormitory, no one at the Maryland College for Women seemed to know when, during their three years as unmarried professors, Miss MacLean and Mr. Beaty started their romance. "We all suspicioned it for awhile, as young girls would," said Morrison.

In a letter to her alma mater, Kathlyn MacLean described her future mate pointedly as teaching part-time "while taking his Ph.D. at Johns Hopkins University."[155] As the daughter of a respected physician, Tat clearly placed importance on Ira Beaty's receiving his doctorate. Ira Beaty later told their daughter Shirley that he "wanted to contribute to the betterment of the human race and saw education as the way."[156] Ira Beaty's humanitarianism appealed to the poet in Kathlyn MacLean and would reproduce powerfully in the ideals of their son. Ira and Kathlyn also shared the same conservative Baptist values.

Beaty chose musical appreciation for schoolchildren as the topic of his doctoral thesis, affirming his longing for the concert career he let pass by.[157] When his advisor suggested he take courses at the Peabody Conservatory of Music, Ira Beaty studied violin under the conservatory director, Otto Ortmann, a musical figure of historical repute.[158] Ortmann had become obsessed with determining the physiologically correct way to play the piano and wrote a revolutionary book explaining his theories in 1929, a year before Ira Beaty studied with him.*[159]

Warren Beatty's mother, who was hired to head the Speech Department at the Maryland College for Women, revealed her yearning to perform again. "She would do funny things and all the girls would laugh. Imitate people and stuff like that," said Mabelle Symington Moore. The first year she was there, Tat MacLean persuaded the dean to let her direct a play. "I don't think they'd ever had drama at the school," recalled Winifred Wokal Morrison. "We had a stage that hadn't been used for years."[160]

During the summers, Tat performed with a local repertory company that

---

*While Ira Beaty was taking violin lessons from Otto Ortmann at Peabody, professional pianists visited Ortmann's lab, submitting to precise measurements of their wrists, finger extensions, and arms, part of his rigid regimen to play piano the anatomically correct way. Vladimir Horowitz was a devotee of the Ortmann technique.

came to be called the Barnstormers, using the college gymnasium for their shows—the Beatys' "vaudeville" period, the couple referred to it later.[161] Ira Beaty joined in some capacity.[162]

In their third year teaching at Maryland College, Ira Beaty and Kathlyn MacLean's lives took a series of fateful turns. Toward the end of spring, Ira was recommended as a Ph.D. candidate and prepared to take his final examination in May of the next year, 1932.[163]

The previous October, Tat's thespian baby sister, Ginny, married Alexander Albert MacLeod, an intense Cape Bretoner on the executive staff of the YMCA in New York.[164] In time, MacLeod would become the unrevealed inspiration for one of Warren Beatty's most passionate and profound films.[165] He also would be associated with the family's most shattering secret. Kathlyn's other sister, Queenie (Alexandra), had also gotten married, after working as a dietitian at Mt. Sinai Hospital in New York.*

As the oldest and only unmarried sister, Tat, at twenty-eight, may have felt increased pressure to wed that summer. Or perhaps the timing was related to Ira Beaty's applying for his doctorate, affording him an additional sense of security. Whatever the impetus, Warren Beatty's parents were married on August 31, 1931, under circumstances that, by Kathlyn's later description to her daughter, portended conflict.

Kathlyn MacLean chose to be married in the drawing room of her mother's house in Wolfville, so she could introduce Ira Beaty to her Canadian family. She and Ira drove to Nova Scotia with Ira's difficult mother, Ada Beaty, and possibly accompanied by his sister, Ruth, who played the piano at the wedding ceremony.

Tat must have had misgivings, for she told her daughter, years later, that marrying Ira Beaty was something she felt she *had* to do, "even though so much of it seemed questionable." She loved Ira, and it had "already gone too far."[166] Two years later, Ira Beaty told a classroom of his students that "men married either for money or for looks."[167]

The newspaper in Wolfville, where the MacLeans were a prominent family, described the nuptials as "one of the season's loveliest weddings," further reporting that, "Mr. and Mrs. Beaty left on a motor trip. . . ."[168] Kathlyn Beaty would relive this moment for her daughter, Shirley, many times through the years. MacLaine wrote about it in *Dancing in the Light*:

---

*Queenie's husband, Gerald Eaton, was an Acadia graduate employed as a chemical engineer. They were married in Rydal, Pennsylvania, the state where they would reside.

As Mother was saying goodbye to her mother, setting off on a new life in America, she was horrified at the raucous argument Ira and his tyrannical mother were having while packing up the car. Mother told me that for the first time she felt a flicker of fear: "Am I making a mistake?" she remembered asking herself . . . but she said she couldn't help herself . . . so she stuffed herself in the car with the new family she was marrying into and had a torturously confusing trip back to Virginia. She felt compelled to endure each mile of that journey . . . and then when Warren and I came along, she understood why.[169]

Tat's apprehensions may have arisen as much from her concern about Ira Beaty's alcohol use as from his damaged psyche, since his nickname for her, Scotch, was said to express both her Scottish heritage and her disapproval of his drinking. Ironically, these flaws in Ira *attached* Kathlyn to the relationship. Tat, who lost her father at a young age and took responsibility seriously, had a self-sacrificing nature that fit Ira Beaty's complex weaknesses like a straitjacket binding them both. Ira Beaty had a hold over Tat MacLean that was more powerful than love: he *needed* her.

Ira and Kathlyn MacLean Beaty returned to the Maryland College for Women in the fall of 1931 wearing a newlywed's glow.[170] In January, Ira Beaty's application for his doctorate was accepted, with the expectation he would take his oral examination in the spring and launch his married life with Tat as a doctor of philosophy.[171]

Instead, Beaty's thesis was rejected and he was denied his Ph.D. by Johns Hopkins — shattering the dream he had created to replace his imagined career as a concert violinist. Ira blamed his female advisor, even though a different academic had made the final decision, based on a belief that Ira had insufficiently researched the topic.[172]

Beaty's ego was permanently destroyed. He would still talk about his stolen Ph.D. with a business partner thirty years after the fact. "He really felt like he had been dealt, I guess, kind of a dirty deal not getting his Ph.D."[173]

His failure at Johns Hopkins resurrected Ira Beaty's childhood feelings of worthlessness instilled by his mother, and the Ph.D. that eluded him became a symbol of the impotence that was a dominant part of the atmosphere in the house where Warren Beatty grew up — to powerful effect.

The Good Son

"You're the captain of the football team!
Those other boys look up to you . . .
You've got to run with the ball."

SPLENDOR IN THE GRASS
Bud Stamper, William Inge's character
based on Warren Beaty, 1952–1955

Warren Beaty (#61) on the Washington-Lee High School football team,
Arlington, Virginia, 1954. *Courtesy of Arthur Eberdt*

7   *Instead of starting the summer of 1932*
as Dr. and Mrs. Beaty, Ira and Tat left Lutherville for the small town of Waverly, Virginia, where Ira accepted a job as school principal. It was there that Shirley MacLaine would be born and Warren Beatty conceived.

Kathlyn Beaty later ascribed their move to Waverly as a decision made necessary by the Depression, but in truth, Ira Beaty had lost his confidence, resigning himself to a life of caution.[1] "The little episode at Johns Hopkins probably blunted his opportunities to achieve what he was otherwise capable of," analyzed a friend of thirty years.[2]

Waverly, the Beatys' new home, was an amiable little town about sixty miles south of Richmond that hailed itself as the peanut capital of Virginia. When Shirley MacLaine became a star, magazine profiles either omitted Waverly from accounts of her childhood or erroneously reported that MacLaine spent her early years in Waverly, Virginia, on a peanut farm.[3]

Her parents, in fact, rented an ordinary white-shingle house with dormers and a screened-in porch in the center of town, at 307 Gray Avenue.[4] The only thing distinctive about the snug frame house where both Shirley MacLaine and Warren Beatty were conceived was the interior, which their mother decorated in a style that was avant-garde for Waverly, Virginia, in 1932, showcased by a bold red kitchen accented by a slick black lacquer ceiling. It was "kinda arty" was the polite description of the family who lived there next.[5]

Kathlyn Beaty perhaps was expressing her frustration at being the wife of the local principal in a one-school Virginia town, as well as her "acute disappointment" in her husband, a sentiment shared, sadly, by Ira himself.[6] They kept their disillusionment painfully concealed. The dignified Murdo and Blanche MacLean had taught Tat not to burden others with her feelings; Ira "repressed his emotions in drinking."[7]

The Beatys may have considered their stature diminished by Ira's position as principal of the Waverly School and Kathlyn's role as his muse, but they left an indelible imprint on the community, and on the students they taught, who exalted them. Waverly, which had a population of less than two thousand, was dominated by two genteel Virginia families, the Grays and the Wests. The former Elizabeth West, a student of the Beatys, regarded it as "a rare privilege for us to have the Beatys there . . . it was the depth of the Depression. To have people like that—he was brilliant, and she was talented and brilliant. They did wonders."[8]

Tat and Ira Beaty's interactions with the Waverly students offered a revealing glimpse of the way they would shape the personalities of their two Oscar-winning children, and of their own musical and dramatic talents begging to be expressed. Beaty formed a school orchestra at Waverly and became its conductor, which called to mind his stint as a dance bandleader in the twenties and put into practice his doctoral studies on the effect of music on schoolchildren. He also directed the school's glee club. "He really was interested in encouraging young people to do their best," recalled Mary Grammer Tyler, who was in the glee club. "I remember seeing him play the violin to illustrate to the students what should be done."[9]

Hannah Allen, the teacher most admired at Waverly School, considered Ira Beaty an "excellent educator."[10] Beaty, who taught algebra in addition to his duties as principal, set high standards and used innovative techniques. Mary Tyler recalled:

He did something I had never heard of before nor after. He had us students stand in a line and one by one we would be given a problem which we would "do in our heads." If we couldn't do the problem we had to sit down—very much the same as a spelling bee. It was a real exercise for the mind!

Ira Beaty blossomed in the esteem of the Waverly community. Elizabeth West, who was a popular ingenue in 1932 when Beaty became principal, found him "very dapper," in a shirt and tie every day, with trousers fashionably creased. "He was a handsome dude, and very stately," observed West's younger cousin Elmon Gray, who would become a state senator and was then in second grade.[11]

Gray was "scared to death" of Principal Beaty, as were many of the primary school students, an experience his daughter, Shirley, would have in a few years. "He would roam around the school. You would see him. He was imposing."

Though Beaty was considered "lazy" by a few Waverly parents, he demanded perfection, especially in music.[12] "He required successful results," as Mary Tyler put it.

Elizabeth West's experience foreshadowed Ira Beaty as a father. When West, whom Beaty considered a talented pianist, paid more attention to her teenage boyfriends than to practicing before a concert, "he let me know, in no uncertain terms, that he was very disappointed in me, and thought that I was wasting a gift, a talent—and he *shamed* me." West was shaken by Beaty's harsh response. "But I must admit, I did go on and major in music in college . . . he apparently had more appreciation of what I was about than I did."

Kathlyn Beaty, though more reserved than her husband, was dynamic in her influence in Waverly when Ira was principal from 1932 to 1936. "She made an enormous impression on my young mind," said Elizabeth West, who was a pretty, sociable teen. West gaped as Kathlyn swept into the school auditorium on cold days, her tall, lithe frame elegantly wrapped in a long raccoon coat. "Her enunciation, her whole manner, was grace . . . I—even at that age—could appreciate anybody who could come in and pull talent out of a country high school."

Warren Beatty's mother staged a full-scale musical at Waverly School. Elizabeth West, who costarred in a two-person play, *Nevertheless*, directed by Mrs. Beaty, was moved to tears by Tat's staging of the song "Blue Moon," performed by a young girl alone on the stage, beside a blue velvet curtain, in a dress that was a contrasting, exquisite shade of blue. "Mrs. Beaty just did incredible wonders with the lighting system at that time—it made her skin just look like moonglow . . . and it was just . . . ooh, enchanting . . . she made us feel like—well, there was Hollywood in Waverly, Virginia."

Kathlyn Beaty had inherited her mother Blanche's perfectionism, another trait that would be instilled in her son, Warren, who would show a similar aesthetic creating the color palette for his film *Dick Tracy*. "Mrs. Beaty was so exacting, and such a perfectionist, and we worked so hard. But oh, the way she would drill me in elocution and enunciation!" recalled West.[13] Tat had her students recite phrases like "Around the rough and rugged rock" to improve their pronunciation—an idea Warren Beatty later borrowed for the film *Bugsy*, where his character repeats as an elocution exercise, "Twenty dwarves took turns doing handstands on the carpet."

The Beatys' second autumn in Waverly, Kathlyn became pregnant, soon after her thirtieth birthday. Shirley MacLaine said later that her father had an "eighth sense" about women and knew when Tat had conceived before she did — demonstrating a mystic sensitivity to women's cycles that Warren Beatty reportedly inherited and put to different use.[14]

Kathlyn Beaty passed the early months of her pregnancy with Shirley by taking daily walks while Ira worried about supporting a child. In February of 1934, when Tat was seven months pregnant, Beaty focused on a new, smaller dream. He wrote to the registrar at Johns Hopkins, stating that he hoped to get his name on the approved list of school superintendents in Virginia. The registrar agreed not to reveal that Beaty's dissertation had been rejected, and informed him that he could present himself for his final oral examination for his Ph.D. at any time.[15] Despite this favor, Ira Beaty was bypassed for a superintendent's position, a cringing disappointment that coincided with the birth of his daughter, Shirley, on April 24, 1934.

A friend of Elizabeth West's named Margaret Brittain spotted Ira and Kathlyn Beaty in a cornfield that April. "Mr. Beaty took her out in the field so he could walk her through the rows of corn to induce labor," as Brittain recalled, an appropriately unorthodox prelude to the arrival of Shirley MacLaine.[16] Her birth, at St. Luke's Hospital in Richmond, was more conventional. The pediatrician was Dr. Wilbur "Billy" Southward, Ira's saxophone-playing buddy from the University of Richmond. Southward, according to his embarrassed son, was among the conservative Virginians who would be shocked by MacLaine's New Age beliefs years later. "My dad was sort of a curmudgeon, and he said if he had known how Shirley was going to turn out, he'd have put her back and raised the afterbirth." Kathlyn Beaty, according to MacLaine, determined her daughter's destiny within twenty minutes, naming her Shirley, after Shirley Temple.[17]

Ira Beaty occasionally babysat his daughter while he gave private violin lessons, keeping her in a nearby crib. One of his adult violin students also had a baby, Jack Griffin. Ira Beaty and Jack's father placed their infants side by side in the same crib while the two men practiced the violin, "so Jack loved to say later that he slept with Shirley MacLaine," tattled a chum.[18] Jack Griffin's father and Ira Beaty played violin at the theater in the next town during silent movies. "My dad talked about the Beatys up until his death. He would say, 'They're just the finest people I've ever known.'"[19]

Shirley MacLean Beaty was remembered in Waverly as a robust toddler with "kind of chestnut-colored hair, and a lot of it for a little girl."[20] A snapshot exists of this interlude in the Beatys' lives, before Warren came along. It was taken during a faculty outing in the summer of 1935 and kept by Senator Elmon Gray, the second-grader in 1932 who was terrified of Principal Beaty.

The photograph shows the small Waverly faculty gathered on the lawn in front of Horace Gray's summer home in Gloucester Point, with Ira Beaty front and center, dressed in a shirt and tie, even on a holiday. He wears a smile that appears strained, and is holding little Shirley up for the camera in a way that is at once tender and that seems to announce, prophetically, that she—not he—is the future star. Kathlyn Beaty stands at the rear of the group, her tall frame leaning forward, her head slightly bowed, as she peers up at the camera, her intelligent eyes squinting in the sun with a quizzical expression, exactly like Warren's in countless movie stills to come.

By the end of the next summer, Warren had been conceived, and the Beatys would be gone from Waverly.

8   *From the time he was conceived,* Warren changed the dynamics of the Beaty family. When they learned of his coming, the Beatys left Waverly so that Ira could find a higher-salaried position, and Kathlyn felt she should stop directing school plays to focus on motherhood, becoming a "sort of a housewife," as Beatty later put it.[21]

By the summer of 1936, Ira Beaty's sadly diminished aspirations were to be hired as a principal in the city of Richmond, a goal that eluded him like the ones that preceded it. He came frustratingly close that fall, becoming the principal at a combination high school and elementary school in Westhampton, an enclave of Richmond designated as outside the city limits—a metaphor for all of Ira Beaty's yearnings that were disappointingly just beyond his reach.* (One of the first words Shirley, then two, learned was *binge*, darkly foreshadowing the fallout from her father's escalating feelings of inadequacy.)[22]

Henry Warren Beaty was born the following March 30, 1937, in Richmond,

---

*Beaty reputedly started the year, briefly, as principal in the small town of Hopewell, south of Richmond, and transferred to the Westhampton School when he heard there was an opening.

the city of patriot dreams that would be his home for the first eight years of his life and that would define him forever as a southern gentleman. Dr. Southward, the Richmond college friend of Ira Beaty's who delivered Shirley, attended Warren's birth at St. Luke's Hospital. Tat and Ira's decision to name their son Henry Warren Beaty, after the exacting craftsman eulogized as a "just man and true," announced their high ideals for Warren, the sort of boy who would take those ideals to heart.

Beatty's first great love was his mother, Kathlyn, an all-consuming and mutual adoration that established a pattern for the sweeping romantic affairs that would become part of the Warren Beatty mystique.[23] Tat's complete enchantment with her son may have begun with his physical resemblance to her dashing brother, Mansell MacLean, as well as to the handsome physician-father she had loved and lost in girlhood. As a baby, Warren had the dark curls and the cupid's face of putti painted by European artists of the Renaissance.

Whatever the cause, Warren had "an effect" on his mother, as Beatty later acknowledged. "My mother, ah, *liked* me very much," was his typically understated way of expressing it, though he admitted to writer Norman Mailer once, "Yes, my mother adored me."[24]

Warren's sister, Shirley, who turned three a few weeks after he was born, felt displaced in Kathlyn Beaty's affections. She later told the London *Times* that her mother "made it clear that Warren was the favorite," an attitude MacLaine ascribed to an intrinsic belief on Kathlyn Beaty's part that males were superior, a view of their mother that Warren disputed.[25] Beatty saw his mother as a "feminist" in the same mode as his grandmother Blanche MacLean, the stepdaughter of a suffragist for women's rights. "Warren has a different version of our life," MacLaine has said.[26]

Shirley considered herself a loved but "unrecognized" child, a toddler placed in a crib so her father could teach the violin, an onlooker while her mother directed school plays, second best when her brother Warren was born.[27] Alfred Adler, a disciple of Freud who made a study of birth order, referred to first-born children as "dethroned" by the birth of the next sibling, a concept that seemed to define Shirley's reaction to her adorable younger brother.[28]

After Warren came along, Shirley Beaty literally began to scream for attention, biting her hand until it bled to get a reaction from the undemonstrative and undoubtedly bewildered Kathlyn, who consulted a pediatrician and was advised to "turn a hose" on Shirley.[29] Instead, Tat enrolled her three-year-old in Richmond's respected Julia Mildred Harper School of the Dance.

As an adult, MacLaine offered different versions of why she was in dance class at such a young age, usually saying it was because she had weak ankles and her mother wanted to strengthen them. At other times she said that there was "something wrong with my feet," or that her mother was training her not to "waddle like a duck."[30] Julia Mildred Harper regarded Shirley's lessons as "therapeutic," according to Harper's daughter.[31]

Early in her acting career, MacLaine told *Look* magazine that she took dance lessons because she hated dolls and had "a need to express myself."[32] Elizabeth Jackson, a neighbor from Waverly, recalled Shirley at two and half saying she wanted to be a dancer.[33] When MacLaine was thirty-five, she reflected, "Mother often reminds me that from the age of three I always said, 'I want to be a little dancing gal.' She's told me that, good God, so many times . . . maybe I needed freedom of expression, but how the hell do you know that at three?"[34]

A neighbor of the Beatys from Richmond recalled Kathlyn as the one encouraging little Shirley to study dance and develop her talent, something Tat talked about in later years to her pastor, Dr. Ben Wagener.[35] "I can remember story after story about the dedication she put Shirley through early, and it seemed to click."[36] MacLaine, who described herself as having been a "lonely" child,[37] recalled:

> I was not very assertive in dancing class. But Mother continually encouraged me to step up more — to go to the front of the line . . . it frustrated Mother a great deal. I don't think it bothered Daddy very much. Maybe Mother saw herself in me and didn't want me to make her mistake of being too cautious.[38]

Whichever origin was true, Shirley became obsessed, at three, with becoming a ballerina. Years later, a high school friend would comment on Shirley's twisted feet from being put *en pointe* at such a young age.[39]

At home, three-year-old Shirley "took charge" of her baby brother, alerting her parents to diaper changes in order to get their attention.[40] Beatty was called "Little Henry" then, after the title character in the popular thirties comic strip *Henry*, about a cartoon toddler drawn with a disproportionately big head, a high forehead, and no hair.[41] "The way to upset Warren," MacLaine later tipped, "is to call him Henry."[42]

The Beatys lived on the corner of Park and Granite, a block from the school where Ira was principal, in a middle-class neighborhood of modest frame houses on the west side of Richmond. Tat and Ira's closest friends were the assistant principal and his wife. "They practically lived, as we say, in each other's shadow," a teacher recalled.[43]

The Beatys also socialized with Ira's University of Richmond classmate who delivered Shirley and Warren, Dr. Wilbur Southward, a prominent surgeon on the north side of Richmond. "All the stories [my parents] told about the Beatys were fun stories," said Ronald Southward, then a playmate of Shirley's.[44]

Despite their three-year age difference, Shirley — remembered by her first-grade teacher as a poised, outgoing, intelligent, "darling little girl" with long red curls — was Warren's best, and most imaginative, friend.[45] "I know it seems unbelievable," MacLaine said later, "but we played together all the time. We were close until I went to junior high school."[46] The two siblings would grab onto the back of the milkman's truck as it pulled out of their driveway, or swim in puddles of melted snow on the street at Christmastime, collapsing in front of their house and pretending to have heart attacks.[47] "They were pranksters," chuckled their babysitter. "They'd lay down in the street like they'd been run over. They were little imps."[48]

Beatty would look back with intense nostalgia on his Rockwellesque childhood in Richmond, which he considered one of the happiest times of his life. When he was a guest on a television show in the seventies, the host surprised him by showing a snapshot that MacLaine had sent of Warren when he was about three, standing next to her in their front yard in Richmond. In the photo, Warren smiles radiantly while six-year-old Shirley, her hair in long tendrils with a huge bow, appears deep in thought. Beatty stared at the picture for a long time, clearly moved.[49] "I was happy. I can't explain it to you. 'Fools give you reasons, wise men never try.'"[50]

By contrast, MacLaine considered their "conventional" upbringing in Richmond a "cliché" that bored and provoked her. "They build a fence of protective intimidation around you. And you keep jumping the fence, and they keep bringing you back, and what they succeed in doing, finally, is teaching you how to jump. They made me an investigator, a revolutionary, a person who wants change."[51] Adler, the Freudian-trained expert on birth order, believed that firstborn children who felt they had not regained their parents' favor from a second sibling "sometimes rebel," the pattern Shirley Beaty appeared to be following.[52]

The opposing ways in which Warren and Shirley reacted as children to the strict Baptist religion that Reverend John Beaty had introduced to the family over a century before, and that their mother, Kathlyn, practiced as devoutly as her mother, Blanche, had, revealed the fundamental difference in the siblings' natures.

By the time she was in her teens, the individualistic Shirley considered God and Jesus "mythological," and seriously questioned the Baptist teachings.[53] Warren, a tender and affectionate little boy, embraced his parents' values from earliest childhood. "He can look back at all those Sunday-school picnics we went to and think one thing, and I can look back and think another," said MacLaine.[54] Later in life, Beatty described his father as a "basic Baptist Puritan." Warren was one of the faithful.[55] "We were brought up as Baptists, and attended church and Sunday school regularly," he said once, early in his career — before he stopped revealing anything about his family.[56]

His defeated father, Ira, was the shadow across Warren Beatty's childhood. When Beatty was in his sixties, he acknowledged that he and his father "never really had an emotional connection," a rare personal disclosure.[57] "You have to be very, very careful what you say," he once explained, when he was asked to comment on his sister's candid appraisal of their parents, "so I don't say anything publicly about my family or my close friends unless it's very, very positive."[58]

As a girl, Shirley found it easier to connect with Ira Beaty. "If I wanted something from my father, I would put my little feet together pigeon-toe style, tilt my head, and smile. I got what I wanted every time."[59]

Ira's detachment from his son may have resulted from his personal frustrations, which were obvious even to the teachers at Westhampton, who noticed he had a "short spark."[60] "We all knew his ambition was to become a principal in the city of Richmond," said Virginia Ingram Guest, who taught for five years under Beaty. According to Guest, Beaty compensated for what he considered his loss in prestige by behaving occasionally like a despot. "I learned very early that there were people that got along with him and people who didn't."[61]

During the Beatys' third year in Richmond, Ira had a disastrous falling-out with his assistant principal, for reasons that are unclear. "Something happened," said Guest, who was teaching at Westhampton then. "They had a quarrel, and we understood that Mr. Beaty never spoke to his assistant except through the janitor." The next year, Beaty's assistant principal transferred to a different school.

Ira Beaty's career setbacks made him more withdrawn at home, particularly from Warren. "Dad adored having a daughter, but he didn't know what to do with a son," said MacLaine. "He was much cooler with Warren because he stimulated all the unresolved things about Dad. Warren was Dad's mirror, and he didn't want to look into it."[62]

The young Warren Beaty found affection and support from the females in his family, beginning with his doting mother, Tat. "My mother always said things that made me laugh," he offered in explanation. "Our bond was very strong."[63]

When Warren was very young, the Beatys took a trip to Canada during one of the long summer holidays Ira enjoyed as a school principal. Warren spent time with his aunt Ginny and his grandmother MacLean, solidifying his bond with intelligent, strong-minded females like his mother and sister — and establishing a pattern for his future relationships. "If a boy starts off liking women," he said later, "there's no reason he shouldn't continue to feel that way."[64]

Kathlyn MacLean Beaty prepared Warren and Shirley for their visit by telling them about their physician grandfather MacLean, often reminding them that their grandmother MacLean had been dean of women at Acadia and that two of their aunts, their uncle Mansell, and she had all graduated from Acadia University. MacLaine said later that she had been hearing so much about Acadia University that by the time she and Warren arrived in Wolfville with their parents, they believed that Acadia "was the seat of knowledge in the Western world."[65] Kathlyn Beaty told Warren and Shirley they had "good genes," making it clear that "much was expected of them."[66]

This explicit missive to achieve under the banner of Acadia evoked the progressive spirit of the four MacLean women — especially Blanche MacLean, who retired as dean of women the month Warren was conceived, when she was sixty-seven. "I don't come from a family where the females hovered quietly in the background," Beatty said once. "Both my mother and my grandmother taught drama when it was still called 'elocution' and they were vibrant women. And Shirley — well, she was certainly never dull!"[67]

As a small child, Warren was inexplicably drawn to his regal Canadian grandmother. Blanche MacLean's mastery of voice and movement from the classes she taught created an impression, in Shirley's description, that she "flowed when she walked" — a feminine mystique that cast a spell on the young Warren Beaty, despite his grandmother's rather severe looks and imposing dean-of-women manner.[68]

At seventy, Blanche MacLean took pains with her clouds of soft white hair and came to the dining room in the evenings perfumed and in formal attire. Three-year-old Warren responded to her Victorian propriety and finishing-school manners like a swain, dressing up for dinner expressly for his grandmother and wanting to be as near to her as possible. His mother later told Shirley that she thought there was something "profound" between Warren and his grandmother MacLean.

Shirley's recollections of her first trips to Nova Scotia were of clam hunts at Evangeline Beach, along the rugged coastline near Wolfville. Their mother made sure Shirley and Warren absorbed the high-minded values established on Summer Street by her father, Murdo, North Sydney's surgeon-mayor. As he got older, Warren Beatty developed a scholar's interest in medicine that he told his close friend Peter Feibleman he believed came from his physician grandfather MacLean.[69]

While on summer trips in Canada, young Warren was especially affected by his aunt Ginny, an actress in Toronto. Virginia MacLean MacLeod had become involved in leftist political causes with her husband, Alex, whose sense of social responsibility had been roused early in their marriage when a fellow executive at the YMCA gave him a Marxist pamphlet to read.[70]

To an impressionable young boy with Warren Beaty's ideals and intelligence, Alex MacLeod was an irresistibly romantic figure. Described as a warm-hearted man of "extreme brilliance," MacLeod enlisted in the army by manipulating his age, and was sent overseas at thirteen to fight with the Cape Breton Highlanders 185th Battalion in World War I. The Highlanders' sobriquet, "the Breed of Manly Men," was one MacLeod aspired to early in his youth, when he became disturbed by conditions in the Sydney coal mines.

By the time Warren made the first of his boyhood trips to Canada, his uncle Alex had quit his position at the YMCA to crusade across the country for human rights and denounce Hitler, organizing the League for Peace and Democracy in Toronto.

MacLeod became the editor of a left-wing journal after traveling through Europe between 1935 and 1939 to support and raise capital for the anti-fascist cause. Beatty's uncle was the first North American eyewitness to the Axis' armed intervention against the young Spanish republic, returning to Toronto to help found the Canadian Committee to Aid Spanish Democracy. Ginny MacLeod shared her husband's convictions. During Warren Beaty's early trips to Toronto at the advent of World War II, his actress aunt was promoting the National Labour Forum on the radio in support of her husband's causes.

The parallels between Beatty's glamorously leftist uncle and aunt Alex and Ginny MacLeod and the American journalist John Reed and his wife, Louise Bryant, would become more pronounced as Warren got older. At the time he and his sister made their childhood visits to Toronto, Warren was too young to have heard of John Reed, the author of *Ten Days That Shook the World*. Years later, when he discovered Reed's love affair with Louise Bryant, blending art and left-wing politics, Beatty's boyhood fascination with his radical-chic aunt and uncle would lead, in part, to his making of the film *Reds*.[71]

As a child, especially after his first trip to Canada, Warren thought of himself as a member of an acting family, similar to Shirley's concept of the MacLeans as the Canadian Redgraves. "It's really something that runs in the family," he said when he first became a film star. Beatty described acting as "a form of expression that I was aware of at an early age."[72]

Warren and Shirley playacted together, inventing a game they called Jolly Store, which MacLaine mentioned once in an interview after she and her very private brother became famous. "We would set up orange crates and lots of bottles and cans and dishes. We would make believe we were sales people in a store, and imaginary characters would come in and ask for different concoctions we would mix together. That was the whole game and Warren is going to kill me for telling you that."[73]

Warren's Beaty heritage influenced him as subliminally in boyhood as did his theatrical MacLean genes. Tat and Ira Beaty told their two children they had "excellent bloodlines" and came from "pioneer stock" on their father's side, with the implied understanding that Warren and Shirley would live up to their distinguished Virginia lineage.[74] Warren took a special interest in his ancestry, particularly in the first Henry Warren Beaty.

The family made regular summer visits to Front Royal, home to the Beaty clan for more than one hundred fifty years. Warren and Shirley and their parents stayed with Welton and Ada Beaty in the house where Ira grew up, or next door, in the big colonial built by the late Henry Warren Beaty and occupied by two of Warren's great-aunts, Maggie and Bertie Beaty. The year Warren was nine, both of his Beaty grandparents died. In subsequent summers, the family stayed with Warren's great-aunts or with Ira's sister, Ruth, whose husband, Damon Gasque, was still principal of Warren High School. Ruth Beaty Gasque was a model of Virginia respectability, a hospital volunteer and both the choir director and organist at the First Baptist Church.[75]

Shirley MacLaine would later recount these summer trips to Front Royal with the candor that was said to run in the Beaty family. MacLaine recalled watching her grandmother Ada Beaty chase her grandfather Welton through the house, "armed with a huge metal skillet . . . with every intention of hitting him over the head."[76]

Shirley's impression was that her father's family had a difficult time expressing emotion, a characteristic that Ira Beaty had in common with his reserved wife. In MacLaine's opinion, Ira Beaty had "conflicts" with his sister — a precursor, Shirley believed, to what would become a complicated sibling dynamic between her and Warren.[77]

As an adult, Beatty would focus on pleasant and discreet memories of his father's family — the measure of a polite Virginian, a trait that endeared him to his extremely private Front Royal relations, especially his aunt Ruth, who "didn't care for Shirley," a friend observed. ". . . I think it's because they were the same temperament."[78]

When Beatty paid a nostalgic visit to Front Royal in the summer of 2000, he stopped by the white colonial house built by his namesake, where his great-aunts, and later his aunt Ruth, lived. He took pictures of the outside and walked slowly through the rooms, pausing to reflect to the new owners, "I used to spend a lot of time in this house when I was a child."[79]

Young Warren continued to be surrounded by strong, individualistic, creative women on his visits to his father's relations. His grandmother Ada dominated the Beaty family until her death in 1946. Ruth Beaty Gasque, like Beatty's maternal great-aunt Katie Lehigh, was a respected pianoforte instructor. Ruth's two daughters, Warren's only Beaty cousins, would become accomplished pianists with a graduate degree from the Peabody Conservatory and a Phi Beta Kappa in music from Randolph-Macon, respectively.

Warren had especially fond feelings in boyhood for his great-aunts Bertie and Maggie Beaty. Beatty's dowager great-aunts had opened a millinery shop in Front Royal and were well known as stylish, "snappy" older women.[80] As a young boy, Warren would sit and listen for hours to their stories about the "War Between the States" and his great-grandfather Henry Warren Beaty's alleged exploits as a spy for the Confederacy.

Warren, who was sweet-natured, with southern manners, endeared himself in childhood to his Beaty maiden great-aunts and to his father's sister in Front Royal, just as he attached himself to his grandmother MacLean, his MacLean aunts, his mother, and his sister. "Everything he did was all right," in the opinion of Ruth Beaty Gasque.[81]

Warren was the only son born in his generation of Beatys and MacLeans.* Ira Beaty's sister, Ruth, had two daughters; Tat's brother, Mansell, and his wife, Maisie, had one daughter; Queenie and Gerald Eaton had three daughters; and Ginny, the youngest MacLean, would have three daughters with Alex MacLeod. The impact on Beatty from all this feminine adoration, validation, and affection was enormous. "My childhood was very strongly and very positively affected by women. My mother, my sister, my aunts, my great-aunts, cousins — all of whom were women — and I was fortunately not smothered by them."[82]

From Warren's perspective, he seemed born to please, and to be pleased by, women.

9

*Even as a small child, Warren's inter-*action with his father was largely cerebral. Ira Beaty, a true educator, made it his mission to teach his two children how to read before they started kindergarten. Beatty interpreted this as his parents "encouraging a high level of self-esteem in both kids," as opposed to the less positive notion of pressuring them to achieve. "Shirley and I didn't have parents who were engaged in pointing out limitations."[83]

Warren's first overachievement was learning to read at age four, and thus impressing his mother as being "insatiably curious" — though plainly it was his distant father whose approval he was seeking.[84] The love and longing Warren felt as a child for his father was associated with *Dick Tracy*, the comic strip about the straight-arrow crime buster, which Ira read to him from the newspaper to teach him to read. "It was my favorite comic when I was growing up in Richmond, Virginia. I was thrilled by the color, the characters, the simplicity. Good was good, bad was bad, red was red, blue was blue."[85]

Dick Tracy was Warren's earliest childhood hero. He later explained why, a carryover from his Beaty ancestry: "Tracy is a good man. He is straightforward and he doesn't lie."[86]

In his sister's view, there was a deeper association. To her, Dick Tracy was like their father — a dapper dresser who saw the world in black and white.[87] Whether or not Warren Beatty considered Dick Tracy a version of Ira Beaty,

*Late in life, the MacLeods had a son, David, mentioned later.

his affection for the comic strip pointed to a desire to connect with a father whose career defeats made him difficult to access emotionally.

Ira Beaty's high standards of accomplishment for his two children — the result, perhaps, of his own limitations — extended to Westhampton School. Beaty persuaded Hannah Allen, the most respected teacher at his school in Waverly, to join the faculty at Westhampton so she could teach Shirley and Warren. Shirley started the second grade with Miss Allen as her teacher, the year Warren turned four.

That same year, Ira Beaty decided to try a second time for his Ph.D, still frustrated in his efforts to become a principal in the Richmond school district. Johns Hopkins scheduled his new final examination for May 1941.

As a boy, Warren thought of his father as a scholar, and of himself as a Virginian, with the idealism that the word *Virginian* historically connoted. The state capitol in Richmond is distinguished by its lifelike marble statue of George Washington, a Virginian, sculpted by Houdon, surrounded by busts of the seven other U.S. presidents born in Virginia. Statues of Civil War soldiers and Revolutionary War patriots from Virginia stand in Richmond public squares, decorate esplanades, and form a boulevard called Monument Avenue. Warren Beatty's Virginia role models were sculpted into statues he saw every day in childhood during the patriotic years surrounding World War II.

In Warren's view, his Beaty lineage and his father's academic background connected him to this Virginia legacy. "I grew up around people who had an interest in history, and you can't be interested in history without being interested in government."[88] Beatty's great-grandfather Burrell Partlow, Ada Beaty's father, had been mayor of historic Little Washington, Virginia, and, at the time Warren was born, his father's uncle Ira Partlow (Ada's brother) was the assistant attorney general of West Virginia.

The young Warren was beginning to cast himself in a similar role.

Beatty's mother provided an ethereal counterpoint to his boyhood fascination with government. The romantic Tat read poetry to Warren and Shirley from the time they were small children, reciting verses in "soft, measured" tones, gracefully enunciating, illustrating the beauty of language and the effectiveness of the voice, teaching them to express their emotions through the use of their hands.[89] Kathlyn Beaty believed that feelings were communicated through the hands, and hers were refined and elegantly articulate, as Warren's would be. The year Beatty became a movie star, actress Joan Collins and photographer Irving Penn commented separately on his expressive, "almost feminine" hands.[90]

A Virginia friend of Kathlyn Beaty's believed that she was directing her artistic yearnings into Warren and Shirley. "It was probably a need with her. She gave as much as she could to the children. To help them learn to act, she read poetry and stories to them, and then they'd discuss it all together."[91]

Shirley, who made her stage debut at four in a ballet recital for Julia Mildred Harper at the Mosque Theatre in Richmond, later described Kathlyn as her "stage mother."[92] Anne George, a classmate who took dance with Shirley when they were seven or eight, recalled Mrs. Beaty encouraging her daughter. "Shirley probably took every lesson they had to offer."[93]

Kathlyn fostered Shirley and Warren's talents by doting on them. Ira Beaty demanded perfection and could be harsh, as he had been in Waverly with the piano student he "shamed" when her performance fell below his standards.[94] "He was the principal and he ruled the roost," observed a childhood friend who played with Shirley and Warren at the house on Park. "We were all sort of afraid of him."[95]

Shirley Beaty, who attended the first through third grades at Westhampton when her father was principal, felt more oppressed by Ira's authority than did Warren, then too young to start school. In the same way that Kathlyn was expected to be exemplary at Acadia because her mother was dean of women, Shirley felt constrained at Westhampton.[96]

Shirley felt similarly restricted in their Richmond neighborhood, where the Beatys were considered "almost eccentric" because Kathlyn Beaty had been an actress.[97] "Mrs. Beaty used to work in the yard in her shorts and a big straw hat and *no one* did that then," said a neighbor from the early 1940s. ". . . she wasn't bohemian, just theatrical — she walked to her own drummer, and Mr. Beaty was this stable scholar. They made an odd couple."[98]

Kathlyn Beaty cared deeply about what other people thought, MacLaine said later. When her husband requested that she not go outside in her floppy hat and shorts to garden anymore, Tat seemed to withdraw, in the perception of her children. One of Kathlyn's motherly pieces of advice to Warren and Shirley, a carryover from her own parents' Cape Breton rules of comportment, was not to reveal their feelings because it was impolite.[99] Beatty would follow this family etiquette to the extreme.

MacLaine later analyzed that it was this exaggerated concern about what other people thought that made her an individualist. Young Shirley reacted to the neighbors' conservatism, and to her father's authority at school, with carefully concealed mischief, including emptying neighbors' garbage pails on their front porches.[100] Warren tagged along with his big sister, but his basic nature, unlike Shirley's, was not to rebel. Like his mother, Beatty tended to internalize his emotions and attempt to conform.

This difference between the two siblings may have arisen from Warren's closeness with his mother. Shirley had a desperate need for their parents' attention after her brother was born, even entertaining thoughts that she was adopted. Warren Beaty felt more than love from their mother. He knew he was *adored*.[101]

THE SUMMER IRA BEATY was scheduled to retake his final examination for his Ph.D., in June of 1941, he withdrew his name from the registry at Johns Hopkins. His letters to the registrar earlier that year, asking for scholarship money and referring to "several uncertainties in plans and possibilities," hint at the struggles he was facing.[102]

Ira Beaty's loss of nerve, lack of funds, or a possible second rejected thesis reinforced his image of himself as a defeated man, despite the high regard in which he continued to be held as an educator by such estimable teachers as Hannah Allen.

Whatever "possibilities" he hoped might be forthcoming in 1941, Beaty remained at Westhampton School, outside the Richmond district where he felt he belonged. His eroding confidence as the United States entered World War II manifested itself through personality conflicts at Westhampton, where he would "occasionally let go,"[103] and through his secret weakness, alcohol.[104]

Both Warren and Shirley were aware, at that young age, of their father's failings and his feelings of resignation, which they interpreted differently. "In my case," Beatty said in his fifties, "well, actually, my father, I felt, was philosophic, deeply philosophic, in relation to failure. And I became less driven because of it, and I'm grateful for that."[105] His sister recognized failure's cautioning effect. "Our mother taught us to be inspired, to overachieve; he taught us to be careful because if one dares, one can be hurt."[106] MacLaine would remember their father's light blue eyes as "filled with suspicion."[107]

While Ira Beaty struggled to support the family on a principal's salary, the Scottish-frugal Tat counted their pennies, reminding Warren and Shirley to "save for a rainy day," muttering darkly about the difficulties she and Ira suffered during the Depression early in their marriage.[108] Years later, Ira Beaty told his daughter he "could've been a big-shot Ph.D. in psychology" or a "fine musician at Carnegie Hall" if he hadn't gotten married and had children to support.[109]

Kathlyn Beaty, who had not performed since summer stock at the Maryland College for Women, began to act and direct in a Richmond little-theater group, telling Warren and Shirley her dream had been to be a movie actress, and "she often talked about what she could have been."[110]

The powerful unspoken message from both of their parents to Beatty and MacLaine was that marriage was a form of imprisonment that required sacrificing one's artistic dreams.[111] But it was a mixed message. Kathlyn Beaty also told Warren and Shirley that her primary desire was to have a family and that she was fated to marry Ira so that she could give birth to them. Ira Beaty would say to Shirley, "Sure, I would have seen Europe [as a violin soloist], maybe been wined and dined by royalty, but if I had done it, I probably wouldn't have met and married your mother and we wouldn't have had you and Warren. So I think I did the right thing."

This ambivalent view of marriage from their original role models created a conflict in Beatty and his sister that would persist all their lives.

EVERY SATURDAY of their childhood, and every day in the summertime, Kathlyn gave Shirley a quarter to take Warren to the eleven-cent matinee, a shared thrill that brought brother and sister even closer. "The Ashton Theater!" Beatty later would exclaim. "Wow, the afternoons we spent there as kids, watching Cagney movies!"[112]

From the time Beatty was four and MacLaine turned seven, they had favorite actors or actresses and would give each other "movie star names," though both said later they never fantasized about becoming stars.[113] For Shirley, who was older and more aware of the subtle tension in the house, the movies were an escape.[114] Warren, a kindergartner, simply adored movies, and his sister.

Shirley seemed to intuit, from the age of three, her mother's yearnings, deciding then, "I was the woman who could do what she hadn't done."[115] By eight, she had mastered Tat's first directive to make herself noticed in dance school. Classmates from the Margot Johnston School of Dance, where she was studying at the time, recall how Shirley, the tallest in the class, nonetheless would "step up to the front and in the middle."[116] Every day, Kathlyn

Beaty tied an enormous daffodil-yellow ribbon atop Shirley's long copper-colored curls, creating an enchanting effect with her daughter just as she had created staging the song *Blue Moon* in Waverly.[117]

Beatty, who was five then, later described his sister as his "first crush."[118] Anne George, a friend of Shirley's from dance recitals and the neighborhood, noticed how Warren, "a cute little guy," liked to spy on them.[119] When the Beatys attended Shirley's recitals at the Mosque Theatre, Warren went backstage with her ballet class, and was observed as a shy little boy standing behind his older sister.[120] Through the years, Julia Mildred Harper and Margot Johnston were heard to say that they taught ballet to both Shirley and Warren Beaty, a claim Beatty aggressively denied.[121] According to a Virginia friend of Kathlyn's, Warren "looked in" on Shirley's ballet class, wanting to join, but deciding against it because of peer pressure that "ballet was for sissies."[122]

Warren's tender affection as a child for his older sister was complicated by sibling rivalry, according to MacLaine. Or as she put it, "we both liked to be King of the Mountain."[123] If that was true, for Warren the competition was fierce. Margot Johnston's sister Grace, who played piano for the dance classes, bluntly observed, "Shirley was the one with the talent."[124]

Before Warren started school, Kathlyn Beaty began to recruit him and Shirley for cameo roles in plays staged by her Richmond little-theater group. Warren Beaty made his acting debut there at age five. "My mother gave me a walk-on part in a play she was directing. I walked across the stage, saying nothing, and that was it. She told me I was very good."[125]

In Shirley MacLaine's later, emphatic view, their mother was "programming" them to succeed in show business to fulfill her own fantasies of performing, and their father's, and to discredit Ira as a model of caution because Kathlyn "saw her husband as a disappointing failure."[126]

Beatty, soft-spoken and carefully diplomatic like his mother, took a gentler position. "I don't mean this disrespectfully of Shirley, because . . . I think the world of her . . . but I think that when people write, they say things about themselves . . . and when Shirley writes about my father and my mother, she's writing about herself. And I didn't see it that way."[127]

As adults, Beatty and MacLaine agreed that they saw their parents differently. "My concept of my family as a child is not at all what my sister has written. Everyone's got a right to their own concepts and interpretations. But our memories and the shadings of those memories are just different."[128]

MacLaine would add, "You'll get more straight answers out of me than you can get out of Warren. I think in terms of black and white, the specific and the definite. He's a respecter of gray."[129]

Beatty's explanation has been that acting was simply in his and his sister's genes, as opposed to a dream of his parents they transferred to him and Shirley. "What made me want to try it in the first place? I don't know. I don't know. This probably has some . . . embarrassing root."[130]

At the time of his stage debut at five, Warren and eight-year-old Shirley began to play out scenes from wartime movies they'd seen together at the Ashton Theater, and often parading in top hats.[131] After Cagney, Warren developed a fascination with suave French leading man Charles Boyer, and walked around the Beaty house saying, "Come wiz me to zee Casbah," a line inspired by Boyer's film *Algiers*.[132] "By the time he was five he was a wow imitating Boyer," Kathlyn Beaty would recall, "then he went through a Milton Berle stage."[133]

"I went to the movies all the time, but it never occurred to me to be an actor," Beatty remarked in his fifties.[134] His interest when he was "a kid," he said once, was to direct—a logical choice since his mother was directing plays.[135]

Kathlyn Beaty had other expectations for her son. Forty years after Warren's walk-on debut, she told a writer that she knew that her son would grow up and go on the stage.[136]

10   *In the summer of 1942, at the height of* World War II, Westhampton School was annexed by the city of Richmond, placing it in the school district Warren's father had coveted for six years. By a perverse turn of events that he derisively called "peanut politics," Ira Beaty was transferred just when he had realized his goal. "The superintendent of schools was very elderly, and very cranky, and he and Mr. Beaty didn't get along, so the superintendent put him in the smallest school in the city," recalled a science teacher at Westhampton.[137]

Ira Beaty's formal portrait as principal of Westhampton—showing a well-dressed, balding, dignified middle-aged man—underlined the indignity he must have felt at being transferred to an elementary school with only six students in each class and a faculty of seven.[138]

Asked as an adult whether Ira Beaty was a disappointed man, Warren Beatty answered, "I don't want to simplify how I saw my father or what I think about my father. . . . And maybe I'll talk about it someday . . . but it sure as hell isn't going to come from some sort of superficial kind of thing."[139] Shirley described what it was like at home. "I was told mostly, 'Don't try too hard to dare because you'll end up making a fool of yourself.'"[140] What their father's disappointments and disillusionment symbolized to Warren was that failure was not an acceptable option and that humiliation was worse than death.

One positive consequence of Ira's transfer was the Beatys' move to Ginter Park, a fashionable older section of Richmond, near the Julia Mildred Harper School of Dance and closer to George Thorpe Elementary School, where Ira now worked. "It was a white-glove, little hat, everyone-knew-what-everyone-else-was-doing-and-they-helped-you-try-to-be-the-best-you-could-be neighborhood," as Julia Harper's daughter described Ginter Park.[141]

The house in Richmond where Warren Beaty lived from kindergarten through second grade — a narrow two-story with a front porch — was on Fauquier Avenue, a leafy boulevard with a wide center esplanade, sidewalks, and steps up to each front yard.

For Shirley, who was eight, the move was liberating, since she no longer had to attend a school where her father was the principal. She and Warren could walk to Ginter Park Elementary, the sort of idyllic schoolhouse found in movies of the period.

The Beaty household had certain characteristics of this idealized image of the American dream, and as an adult, Warren Beatty cherished memories of his Ginter Park childhood. One of those memories was his family's cele-bration of Christmas, an event Beatty recalled with special fondness. "Well, Christmas for me is — you know, my father was a teacher, so there was a Christmas vacation going on, so Christmas took on all kinds of resonances in my life. I always think of Christmas as a nostalgic [time]."[142]

But there was a troubling undercurrent to Beatty's Ginter Park boyhood. His father's dissatisfaction with the petty politics of the school district created the valid impression "that it might not have been a good time for the family," as recalled by a George Thorpe Elementary student whose mother was a friend of Kathlyn Beaty's.[143] Seagram's whiskey was the skeleton in the closet. "Out of his frustrations," MacLaine said later, "my father probably turned to drinking."[144]

Shirley first noticed Ira's drinking problem when she was about ten and

Warren was seven. "I remember one time we were going to the seaside. I'm sure my dad was drunk. There was this drawbridge, and it was raised, but he just kept on driving towards it anyway. I remember I was in the back seat, shrieking, and Warren was next to me, doing the same. It was dark, and it was raining. It was like a scene out of Dracula."[145] On another occasion, Shirley saw their father "hit Mother when we were driving in the car. I associate a lot of his drinking with driving."[146]

The polite and respectful Beatys never talked about Ira's alcoholism or his occasional violence.[147] Even as small children, Shirley and Warren considered it a silent cross to bear. "I'm sure I was afraid of my father," Beatty later confessed. "That has to go back pretty early because my father was a gentleman."[148]

To a child, especially his son, Ira Beaty was an intimidating figure. Patricia Stewart, who attended George Thorpe and was Warren's age, described Principal Beaty as a "forceful, big man with just a booming, booming voice, and I was afraid of him." Stewart's mother was a friend of Kathlyn Beaty through the Red Cross, where they both volunteered in the war effort. Though Stewart was not aware that Ira Beaty drank, she said "it would not have been talked about amongst the children in those days."[149]

Ira Beaty's drinking changed not only him, it also changed Warren. As he started school and his father's apparent alcoholism altered the dynamics of the family, Warren began to turn inward. "I was a lonely sort of kid, I don't know why. There are certain changes a kid makes. You don't know why. You begin to cut yourself off from people."[150]

Actress Julie Christie, Warren Beatty's romantic partner through parts of the 1960s and 1970s, once alluded to his extreme sensitivity as a child. After praising his risk-taking as a filmmaker, Christie observed, "He's done it by building up great reservoirs of courage, and I think he's built up those reservoirs himself. I don't think he was born with them."[151]

As a young boy, Warren looked up to his older sister as a role model of assertiveness. "All through our childhood," he told the author of an anthology, "she was bigger and stronger than I was, and it seemed to me that she always knew what she was doing."[152] Shirley, a budding tomboy, acquired the nickname "Powerhouse" as the only girl on the sixth-grade softball team, hitting fifteen homeruns to end the year with a .425 batting average.[153] "She was quite an athlete," Beatty said later.[154]

"I used to protect him when we were in school," MacLaine said once. "If anyone picked on him, I'd deck them. Warren thought that was nice of me, but he wasn't all that appreciative — he was and still is totally capable of taking care of himself."[155] Beatty would later comment on his sister's depiction of herself as his protector in childhood by saying, "I'm not going to run with that ball."[156] On another occasion, he said he didn't need Shirley's help, "she wanted action."[157]

Patricia Stewart thought Warren was in frail health then. When Stewart's brother went to the Beaty house in Ginter Park to retrieve a bicycle he had loaned to Warren, "It was in the garage, and he didn't think Warren had ridden it at all. He got the impression that Warren was sickly, and they were so polite they didn't want to say."[158]

Beatty described himself as having been a "bookworm" in those years — an escape, perhaps, from the reality of his father's drinking. "I had always been chided for being non-athletic," he said of his grammar school years.[159]

Ira Beaty's mercurial personality, provoked by alcohol, intensified Warren's emotional ties to his mother, and to women generally, and made him wary of human nature. "I think I have a tendency to *trust* women more than men," Beatty would later concede. "Although I'm not sure I'm a hugely trusting person."[160]

He found acceptance, and praise, on the stage. The year he started at Ginter Park Elementary, Warren was cast in a class play performed before an audience of parents — his "first real acting part," as he later referred to it:

> It was a Christmas play, and I played the part of one of three toy soldiers under a Christmas tree. All three of us wore soldier suits, and we were required to take a bow to music. I made a big, sweeping bow, the biggest of all, holding my soldier's peaked cap in my hand. I loved it. My mother told me I was very good. I did it right, she said. I didn't waste it.[161]

Beatty's vivid recollection of being onstage as a toy soldier, and eliciting his director mother's approval, suggested that this might be the "embarrassing root" of his eventual desire to become an actor.

In a foreshadowing of his Hollywood image, Warren fell for his first leading lady as a bit player in his mother's little-theater production of *My Sister Eileen*. "I was seven then, and felt I was kind of cute. Everybody in the cast had a crush on the actress who played Eileen. I was the young, young, young one with a crush on Eileen. I got in everybody's way most of the time. Shirley was in that play too. I thought she was good."[162]

As Beatty later analyzed it — rightly — there was logic to his movie-star reputation for falling in love with actresses almost exclusively. As he explained it, "the word [actress], to me, is somewhat equated to womanhood. Because my mother was an actress of sorts — she taught acting. My mother's mother taught acting. My sister is an actress. I understand actresses; I love actresses. My fantasy about womanhood comes from the people I know. It comes from my mother, from my sister, from the women that I've loved."[163]

As a boy, Warren continued to be tugged between his mother's stage productions and his studious inclination toward history and government, the province of his academic father. After learning to read at four, he "took to it like a duck to water."[164] Ira Beaty was similarly taken with words, telling meandering, witty stories at the dinner table and coaxing Warren and Shirley into conversation about religion, philosophy, politics. "I've been fascinated by politics since I was a kid," said Beatty. "My father was in school government, and he used to bring politicians around. I'd listen to them talk, watch them."[165]

When Warren was in the first grade, his father's uncle Ira Partlow was appointed acting attorney general of West Virginia, a position he held for the next seven years, until Warren was in junior high school. Partlow, a Democrat, talked politics with Tat and Ira at the Beaty house. Kathlyn later told Uncle Ira, as she called him, that she liked to "sit and listen to [his] views on the times," and once wrote to him, "I've always admired your sane and unemotional approach to world politics."[166]

Shirley MacLaine, somewhat at odds with her mother's statement, felt that her parents liked politicians who "moved" them, like Franklin Roosevelt, whose presidential fireside chats she and Warren listened to on the radio with their parents.[167] MacLaine remembered once seeing Ira Beaty weep as the "Star-Spangled Banner" was played at the end of the night on television. Her rather poignant childhood image of her father, one that Warren appeared to share, was of a "big man," sparkling with wit, who had a "desire to make the world better."[168]

According to Beatty, "as a kid, I thought I wanted to go into law, into politics."[169] His uncle Mansell MacLean got a law degree after becoming an engineer, his great-uncle Ira Partlow was a lawyer and attorney general, his late grandfather Murdoch MacLean had been mayor of North Sydney, and his great-grandfather Burrell Partlow had died while still mayor of historic Little Washington, Virginia.

Growing up in a house of idealists, in a family of politicians, in the state known as the "Mother of Presidents," six-year-old Warren Beaty entertained fantasies about being elected president.[170] After Beatty became a movie star and expressed an interest in politics, he was repeatedly quoted as having said at six that he wanted to be president, an inaccuracy the hairsplitting Beatty later took pains to correct.[171] "This is a misquote. I didn't say it. I *thought* it. Every young American boy wants to be President, for a minute."[172]

That same year, 1943, Warren's uncle Alex MacLeod, the romantic radical married to Warren's actress aunt Ginny, was elected to the Ontario legislature. MacLeod ran as a Labor-Progressive, but with his leftist leanings was considered a Communist, effectively becoming the last sitting Communist in Canada's Parliament and swiftly earning a reputation as the best speaker in the House.[173]

The dashing MacLeods passed through Virginia for a visit after the election, when Warren was six years old. According to MacLaine, their father "hated Communists" and pointedly took his in-laws to historical sites in the capital to make the point that the United States was a democracy.[174] Beatty, who had fond feelings for his magnetic Uncle Alex, took a more understanding view in adulthood than his sister of Ira Beaty's anti-Communist stance, saying, "I'd call my father someone who wanted to be fair," and describing his mother Kathlyn as "more liberal" politically.[175]

Warren's emotional connection to his MacLeod relations deepened over the next few years, after his aunt Ginny gave birth to a son named David — Warren's only male relation on either side of the family. Beatty seemed to have a protective feeling toward his little cousin David Lehigh MacLeod, whom he saw during occasional family summer trips to Toronto — a tenderness that eventually would turn to anguish and then shame.

Toward the end of World War II, as Ira Beaty's patience at George Thorpe Elementary was fraying, Kathlyn accepted an emotionally demanding role in a three-act play by Martin Flavin called *Children of the Moon*, being staged at a neighborhood little theater. She enlisted Shirley and Warren to play minor parts.

According to MacLaine, Ira became extremely agitated during rehearsals, complaining that Kathlyn was becoming the "bitch" character she was portraying, and was neglecting her duties as a mother and a wife. He insisted that Tat quit the play.[176]

Beaty's extreme reaction to his wife's immersion in her role was especially revealing because of the parallels between the character and Kathlyn, which clearly touched a nerve in both him and her. In the play, Tat's character goes insane after years of resentment over setting aside her dreams in order to rear a son and a daughter with a husband cursed by a tainted gene.

Kathlyn began to speak erratically under the stress of her husband's disapproval, agreeing that she had "become" the character.[177] Finally, she deferred to Ira's wishes and quit the play. The experience had an intense effect on everyone in the Beaty family. Tat seldom performed in little theater afterward, though she would continue to direct plays intermittently. Shirley perceived her mother as a frustrated actress tethered to a husband and family, and she was determined not to allow that to happen to her.[178] Warren, typically, internalized his feelings about the incident, though his future experiences as an actor would suggest the impact of his observing his mother losing herself in her character in *Children of the Moon*. He would have a difficult time losing himself while playing a part.

THE SUMMER AFTER Warren completed first grade, his father began to look for a new job, in Arlington, Virginia, saying he was tired of the "overpowering women" at George Thorpe Elementary.[179]

To cheer him up, Shirley made a Dick Tracy Father's Day card for Ira.[180] She would find it among their late parents' belongings forty-seven years later, when Warren was starring in *Dick Tracy*, a film he conceived as an homage to the happiness he felt as a small child — before their father's drinking introduced a darker dimension to the family.[181]

Warren's father's attempts to extricate himself from Thorpe Elementary, in June 1944, coincided with the events surrounding D-day. Later that summer, as World War II was drawing to an end, the Beatys took a family trip to New York to visit Kathlyn's ever-more-successful brother, Mansell MacLean, and his wife, Maisie. Mansell had become chief engineer for the Samuel Rosoff Company and was supervising the construction of subway systems in New York and Mexico. He lived on property known as Byron Estates in Larchmont, an exclusive enclave of Westchester County, north of New York City.[182]

Mansell took the Beaty family to Manhattan, an experience that awed seven-year-old Warren, who was so emotionally affected by his first glimpse of Times Square he would preserve it in his mind and attempt to recreate it through the eyes of the Kid character in his film *Dick Tracy*.[183] He was similarly overwhelmed by his first Broadway play, which his uncle took the family to see that summer. The new musical *Oklahoma!* had struck a chord with wartime audiences reassured by the play's American storyline and infectious Rodgers and Hammerstein score. "I was thrilled by it," Beatty said later. "I fell in love with musicals."[184] Before the Beatys left New York, they bought the cast recording of *Oklahoma!* for Warren. It came as a set of 78s and would make history as the first complete "original cast album."[185]

When they returned to Richmond, and Warren started the second grade, his father's jittery tolerance for George Thorpe Elementary snapped. The rumor among teachers in the district was that Ira still bore a grudge about being assigned to the smallest school. "He wasn't going to take that," recalled Virginia Guest.

In the middle of the school year, Ira Beaty abruptly resigned.[186] He and Kathlyn withdrew Shirley and Warren from Ginter Park Elementary, and the family left Richmond during the Christmas break.

Throughout that trying autumn of 1944, seven-year-old Warren's greatest pleasure and source of comfort was playing the cast recording from *Oklahoma!* He listened to it constantly, swept away from the tension in the Beaty house as Broadway baritone Alfred Drake, who played the cowboy hero Curly, burst into, "Oh! What a Beautiful Morning!"

Beatty would recall, "I listened to the songs over and over . . . I'll never forget that overture."[187]

11   In January of 1945, the Beatys moved to Arlington, Virginia, the city adjacent to Washington, D.C., which Warren Beatty and Shirley MacLaine both would consider their hometown, and where their parents would reside for the rest of their lives.

Ira Beaty's unfortunate luck followed the family there from Richmond. When the Beatys got to Arlington, the position that Ira expected as principal of Washington-Lee High School "did not work out," by his polite later description.[188] "I think they had a little political war or something on the school board and he kind of got jerked around," recalled his friend Mason Green, Jr.[189] The demoralized Beaty, who had a family to support in an unfamiliar city, took a job as a juvenile probation officer for Judge Hugh Reid of the Arlington Juvenile and Domestic Relations Court at a salary of three thousand dollars.[190]

The family moved into a newly built, tiny, two-story redbrick "center hall colonial" in Dominion Hills, at the top of a winding curve of nearly identical pristine colonials on North Liberty.[191] "It was naked like Levittown," said a friend of Warren's who lived down the street.[192]

Mason Green, Jr., whose family was in real estate, speculates that "seventy percent of the people in Arlington were government workers, from all over. It had the cemetery and Robert E. Lee's home, but very few things with historical significance."

Because of the Beatys' proximity to Washington, D.C., Warren would see more of his great-uncle Ira Partlow, whose duties as West Virginia's attorney general at times brought him to the capital. Within a few months of the family's move to Arlington, Franklin Roosevelt died in office, moving Kathlyn Beaty to tears, and World War II ended. Warren's great-uncle Ira became acquainted with FDR's successor, Harry Truman, and Partlow would stop by the Beaty house on North Liberty to talk politics, giving the young Warren a keyhole view of the machinations of government.[193]

Ira Beaty later told a court archivist that "he soon found he could not afford to raise a family in the Northern Virginia area on his salary,"[194] an anxiety that Warren and Shirley felt keenly. "All I remember is we always only had $300 in the bank," MacLaine observed.[195]

Ira Beaty's disillusion over the position he was promised at Washington-Lee took on a more bitter irony that year when his sister Ruth's husband, Damon Gasque, was promoted from principal of Warren High School in Front Royal to superintendent of the Warren and Rappahannock County school districts, the goal Ira pursued unsuccessfully in Waverly ten years earlier.

The cumulative effect of so many searing disappointments on a man of Ira Beaty's intellect and character found its sad outlet in binge drinking that was anguishing for his children to see and strained his marriage to "Scotch," as Ira often called his Scottish-Canadian wife, Kathlyn.

Beatty once said, revealingly, that he looked to his mother and sister for approval as a child, and he would not comment on his father.[196] He confided somewhat in Deborah Korsmo Ruf, the psychologist mother of the bright young actor who played his Kid counterpart in *Dick Tracy*. Beatty told Ruf he respected his father but there were "problems," and that his father was "not a happy person."[197] Shirley described Ira in those years as an inconsistent drinker who was "tough" on her and Warren.[198] Ruf's impression was that Beatty found this extremely confusing. "I think his experiences with his father affected him quite a bit."

At age eight Warren created a sanctuary for himself out of the windowed walk-in closet situated in the middle of his tiny upstairs bedroom, which was next to Shirley's. He put a desk, a chair, and a light fixture in the closet so he could lock the door and have privacy to write, read, or think.[199]

After he became famous and known for secrecy, MacLaine mentioned her brother's closet in a few interviews as a metaphor, saying, "Even as a kid Warren had a private world no one could penetrate . . . he'd go in there and write or read for hours . . . he could shut everyone out."[200] She also said, "I wished I had such a place, too . . . that's where he planned his battles. He was always determined, but never unkind or overbearing."[201] Beatty once teasingly referred to MacLaine's remarks as his sister's "story" when asked whether he used his childhood closet as a hideout and for reading—but admitted, finally, that it was true.[202]

By the time he completed second grade, Warren had become almost fixated on reading, possibly to impress or feel closer to his father, who had taught him to read and placed such importance on learning. Early in his career, when reporters remarked on his "sexy" half-closed eyes, Beatty attributed it partly to his constant reading as a child, saying, "I have used my eyes more than most fellows do. I've been reading ever since I learned how to."[203]

Both Beatty and MacLaine would comment on their light-sensitive blue eyes, a trait they inherited from their Scottish mother, Kathlyn, who squinted in sunlight. When he first got to Hollywood, Beatty told a writer, "The California sun is so bright that it's hard on the eyes, so I keep them half-closed to protect them."[204] Photos from his boyhood often feature Warren peering through half-scrunched eyes.

Besides enjoying it as a place to read, the young Warren Beaty probably used his walk-in closet as a haven during his parents' arguments, which MacLaine said were provoked by Ira's drinking. Their parents' bouts bewildered Shirley and Warren. MacLaine later wrote that she would observe their mother relaxing in a long bath, lost in thought, and wonder "if she might be thinking about how to get out of her life."[205]

What made the situation so emotionally intricate were Ira Beaty's many admirable qualities. Paul D. Brown, a retired Arlington County Circuit Court judge, used to read Beaty's probation reports on juvenile offenders and considered him an excellent, "extremely relaxed" probation officer and "a hell of a nice guy."[206] There was never any indication, to Brown, that Beaty had a problem with alcohol. It was this dichotomy that confused

Warren, who later told a screenwriting partner that his father "became a different person" when he drank.[207]

As an "emotional release," young Warren sang, the trait of Beaty men before him — though their singing was done in Baptist church choirs.[208] Warren's passion to sing seemingly was inspired by his strong emotional connection to the musical *Oklahoma!* The summer after the Beatys moved to northern Virginia, they returned to New York to visit Warren's uncle Mansell MacLean. "I asked to see *Oklahoma!* again," Beatty recalled. "My father took me, and left me at the theatre."[209]

That fall, unable to make ends meet, Ira Beaty quit his job as a probation officer, accepting a modest eight-hundred-dollar salary increase to become principal of Thomas Jefferson Junior High.[210] An Arlington newspaper noted Beaty's appointment as principal, with an unintentionally sad postscript that he was "preparing for a Ph.D. at Johns Hopkins" — suggesting that Ira had not released that dream, and the magnitude of what a Ph.D. symbolized to him.[211]

In September 1945, Warren started third grade at Stonewall Jackson Elementary, while his sister prepared to enroll at Swanson Junior High, the rival school to Thomas Jefferson, where their father was now principal. Shirley, who was still driven by a need to command their parents' full attention, made straight As and led the teams in basketball, softball, and track, hoping her troubled father would notice her more if she surpassed his high standards.

MacLaine's underlying insecurity, at twelve, was her looks. She was the tallest and skinniest girl in her class, with unruly red hair and a freckled face. "I used to brush my hair at night, wondering if I'd ever be pretty enough to satisfy one man for life."[212] Shirley Beaty's aspiration was to be an astronomer or a physicist, foretelling, in some measure, her future interest in metaphysics,[213] a bent she inherited from Ira, who used to spend Sunday evenings at Johns Hopkins pondering metaphysical concepts with his philosophy classmates while he was courting Tat.[214]

Kathlyn Beaty began to direct plays for the Arlington Little Theatre, casting her daughter in occasional small roles, while Warren helped with props or lighting.[215] Shirley used her nascent acting talent to pretend that she was actress Rita Hayworth, since they both had wavy red hair and danced.[216]

That year, Warren discovered a different sort of actress from the distinguished thespians in his mother's family. The object of his boyish affection was June Rowe Weaver, the leading lady in several of his mother's plays. A glamorous twenty-eight-year-old, June had dark auburn hair that fell in cascades and a face made for close-ups, which she accentuated with crimson lipstick, false eyelashes, and dark penciled brows. Her eight-by-ten glossy showed June in a tight beaded gown with a plunging bodice and a fur stole that bared one shoulder, exposing her décolletage. Nine-year-old Warren was hopelessly love-struck.

Shirley, still a gangly preteen, set out June's costume changes between scenes and developed her own fascination with the actress, who bore a slight resemblance to her titian-haired idol, Rita Hayworth. "[She] used to follow June around in the dressing room," said Weaver's sister, who recalled June giving Shirley one of her bracelets.[217]

Warren mooned over Flaming June backstage while helping with the props. "June was so sweet to children," commented her sister, "and at that point she didn't have any of her own."[218]

When the play closed, Warren, who was finishing third grade, wrote to June Weaver with a proposal of marriage. June saved the letter, which she would show to her daughter after Beatty had become a movie star. "He had written her this letter that he wanted to marry her when he grew up."[219]

The fact that, at nine, Warren Beaty sent a formal, handwritten marriage proposal was an early signal of his deep feelings about marriage — in contrast to his sister, whose solemn vow was not to let herself become trapped in wedlock like her mother.

June Rowe Weaver not only was the first woman Warren Beatty proposed to, she had also offered the devout young Baptist his first glimpse of the Hollywood version of an actress. By coincidence, Warren got his first look at a woman in the nude at around the same time, "an image that was to be forever etched in his consciousness," according to his future wife, actress Annette Bening. The viewing took place when young Warren was escorted into the wrong art class at the Corcoran Gallery in Washington and walked in on a female model standing in the center of the room, completely naked. "Needless to say, he was riveted," said Bening. "Unfortunately, the man who took him in was mortified . . . [and Warren] never went back to the Corcoran again."[220] However, as with June Weaver, he liked what he saw.

That spring and summer, as Warren was preparing to enter fourth grade, his family went through convulsive changes. Both Welton and Ada Beaty died during the first half of 1946, ending what MacLaine perceived as her grandmother Beaty's reign of terror.

Two years earlier, Warren's adored grandmother MacLean fell ill while visiting a cousin in her hometown of Brockville, Ontario, and died shortly afterward in a Brockville hospital. She was laid to rest in the MacLean family's beloved Cape Breton, next to her husband, Murdo, just before Thanksgiving of 1943. The *Cape Breton Post* eulogized Blanche MacLean as "a woman of exceptional ability . . . generous to a fault, kindly in disposition, and a recognized leader of society.[221] Warren, who was only six at the time, lost one of his feminine ideals, and would seek to recreate the bond with his grandmother the rest of his life through deep friendships with accomplished, strong-minded elderly women.

His once handsome scholar-father's long, grim struggle to achieve his career aspirations came to its bittersweet, incongruous end in September 1946, when Ira, now portly and bald, resigned as principal of Thomas Jefferson Junior High to become a real estate agent for the George Mason Green Company. "I think he probably figured he'd make more money for his family," observed Mason Green, Jr., whose father hired Beaty. Green, a contemporary of Warren's, knew Ira Beaty "like an uncle almost." Even as a child, "I was aware of [Ira's] story," said Green. "He hoped to get his doctorate — one of the panel was female, they had to approve his thesis, and one of them objected to it — we were all aware of it."[222]

It must have appeared unimaginable to the ethereal Tat that she had evolved into a real estate salesman's wife in the American suburbs. "Both of my parents came to think of themselves as failures," MacLaine said of this juncture. ". . . it was a house of disappointment and longings, and my brother and I felt all that. I think we pushed ourselves to succeed partly because we were responding to that overwhelming sense of failure in the house."[223]

Kathlyn, who was dignified in any circumstance, wrote a family letter to her husband's uncle Ira Partlow later in this period that shows she was a supportive wife but hints at the disappointment she and her husband felt at his new occupation. In her small, neat handwriting, she stated, "Ira makes an excellent salesman and his educational background helps him every time he turns around." The letter reveals several indications of stress. After describing a sale Ira had made, Tat wrote, "It was all quite a strain on him nervously but he did a beautiful job, and everyone is pleased." Elsewhere, she mentioned that Ira was seeing a diagnostician for an ulcer "and his whole metabolism is out of gear."[224]

This lent support to MacLaine's account that her frustrated father internalized most of his emotions and suppressed them with liquor, which he hid under the bed. "There were some dramas with him, though. Every now and then he'd come home drunk, set something on fire, leave again until the wee hours, then return and sleep till noon."[225] The arguments between Ira and Kathlyn Beaty escalated.

Shirley was so disturbed by her parents' strife she distanced herself from the family that fall, her first year in junior high, by taking dance classes every day. "I was much more interested in being a physicist or an astronomer or an inventor . . . I got into dancing to get out of the house."[226] Once she started, she willed herself to excel in order to overcome what she perceived as the pattern of failure in the house.

MacLaine enrolled at the renowned Washington School of Ballet in Washington, D.C., which required her to take a bus into the city for an hour and a half each way, a grueling schedule that bordered on the masochistic, and which she described as "a lonely and different life."[227] She got up at six and arrived home at one-thirty in the morning. "Why did I drive myself? I had this obsession about being a ballerina, that's all. Nothing else in the world was important to me."[228]

Beatty later described his sister as "extremely ambitious," imputing her feelings of incompletion to a "strained parent-child relation."[229] For MacLaine, the more problematic parent was Kathlyn Beaty, not Ira. "My mother was seemingly the passive one in our family, but as we all know, a really intense mother controls it all. We only saw our father through our mother's eyes."[230]

Shirley, at the impressionable age of thirteen, was affected by their parents' acrimony that fall in a different way than was Warren, who was ten. As a daughter, she was also privy to secrets of her mother's that were better left untold. Kathlyn took Shirley aside and told her that she would leave their father if it weren't for her and Warren.[231]

Warren, by contrast, felt swaddled in his mother's "boundless faith" in him.[232] Fifty years later, when a reporter described MacLaine to him as a "tough character," Beatty would correct this misconception of his sister Shirley with a trace of sadness.[233]

"The broadstroked parent, my father, was the one who drove me to try to figure out what was going on," MacLaine explained. "But the mystery is the passive one who doesn't communicate. That's the source of your trouble. And so it ended up being the mother figure in my life that I was continually trying to understand. Even in drunken states, my dad would get into it. I used to say to Mother, 'Why are you being so emotionally diplomatic about this?' And she said, 'Diplomacy is what keeps the world from going to war.'"[234]

As siblings with the shared and secret trauma of their parents' arguments and their father's drinking, Warren and Shirley formed the primal and indissoluble bond of soldiers who face combat together. MacLaine would come to believe that their parents' discord was the reason her brother waited until he was almost fifty-five to get married, and why she required a marriage that would not "enclose" her.[235]

Warren, the dutiful Baptist son, formed a different perspective from their painful collective experience. "I never had anything against marriage. It's just I had mixed feelings about divorce. A marriage is forever. I was the product of a marriage that lasted for 54 years before my father died . . . I felt that if you didn't have the stamina to stay in it for life then you shouldn't make the promise."[236]

At ten, Warren found a refuge from his parents' conflicts through music, just as his father, Ira, had escaped from Ada and Welton Beaty's arguments in Front Royal by playing the violin. Beatty's instrument was the piano, which he had been introduced to on both sides of the family.

"He used to work everything out on the piano," recalled MacLaine.[237] When he was in his twenties, Beatty conceded that playing the piano "eased tension" for him.[238] He began to take piano lessons from a female teacher in Arlington around 1946, and demonstrated that he had inherited the family gift. "I took lessons from her at one point," recalled a grammar school classmate, "to try to learn to play like Warren."[239]

One of the sadnesses of Ira Beaty's drinking and its psychic damage to Warren and Shirley was that his decision to sell real estate was an expression of his love for them. It was important to Ira, recalled Mason Green, to afford to send his daughter to dance school in the city. "He and Scotch led a kind of dedicated life for those kids; they themselves lived very modestly."

Over the years, Ira Beaty became a "real crackerjack" salesman, and a wonderful storyteller, in Green's estimation. According to his family, Ira's bonhomie was a façade — similar to his hubris as a bandleader, which he confessed to Shirley came from a bottle. "He was a big talker, and quite a man-about-town," as a friend from their Baptist church in Arlington described him. According to Green, Ira "did pretty well" financially as a real estate salesman, but his sterling quality was his character — the Beaty family trait.

WARREN AND HIS SISTER began to diverge the year Shirley started Swanson Junior High. Shirley became interested in boys and increasingly consumed by dance class. Although MacLaine considered herself "different" and not terribly happy, she and her friends at Swanson, recalled a classmate, "were all really, really popular."[240]

Warren continued to retreat to the haven of his walk-in closet, but emerged in the fourth through sixth grades as an outgoing cutup. Susan Morse, who met Warren Beaty in fourth grade and became his first girlfriend, had vivid memories of him as a clown with a gift for mimicry. Both Morse and Mike Durfee, a Dominion Hill neighbor who became a pal of Warren's, considered him an extrovert. "He was doing jokes in elementary school," recalled Durfee.[241]

Warren and his friends in the neighborhood rode sleds down the hills in their backyards during the winter, and went trick-or-treating together on Halloween.[242] Unlike his sister, who felt confined by these conventions, Warren embraced Dominion Hills family values.

Two of the traits for which Beatty would be lampooned in Hollywood were in evidence when he was in fourth grade, according to Susan Morse and Mike Durfee: Warren squinted, even indoors, and he had an odd habit of pausing frequently when he was talking. "Kind of a hesitation," explained Morse, ". . . like he couldn't find the words."

Beatty's pauses were particularly intriguing from a psychological standpoint, since his mother and his grandmother were rigorous instructors of elocution, and his mother spent hours reciting poetry to him from the time he was a small child, demonstrating how to use the voice as an instrument.

Warren may have become self-conscious because he was under the scrutiny of elocution teachers, causing him to take extra pains to find the right words. He might have been rebelling from the regimented diction of his mother and his grandmother. Possibly his hesitation in speech was a side effect of his troubled life at home.

Mike Durfee believed that Warren's "awkward" speech was a "personality" characteristic, like a professional comedian's signature trait — "not a speech defect." Both he and Susan Morse observed that Warren and his sister were adept at dramatic flourishes.

He lived up to his reputation as an entertainer when Susan Morse invited him to dinner. The young Beaty did a few impressions for the Morses, "and yes," recalled Morse, "we think he may have sung Al Jolson's 'Mammy'!"[243]

To Warren at nine, there was nothing offensive about Al Jolson performing "My Mammy" in blackface. "It's something about Virginia," he later mused. "I grew up in an atmosphere where not only were there no black people but a Catholic was exotic."[244]

As an adult, Beatty would deny his sister's characterization of their southern father as a man who said "nigger" and was prejudiced against blacks. "I think my mother and father have always been very fair politically," he told a Richmond paper in 1975. "His [Ira's] fairness means something else today . . . I don't think he's a bigot at all. And my mother is considerably more liberal."[245] More recently, Beatty said, "My parents would have been appalled if anyone had accused them of being racist."[246]

In the forty years Mason Green knew Ira Beaty, Green, a conservative, was never certain what Ira's politics were. "But it wasn't his or Scotch's style to be argumentative about politics." Beatty defined his parents as "implicitly liberal" on most issues, and once told *Time* magazine that they brought him and Shirley up with "a good, healthy, early feminist point of view."[247] This was certainly true on his mother's side, beginning with the early suffragist who brought up his grandmother Blanche, and extending to his aunt Ginny, who spoke on the radio to promote leftist causes.

Warren first noticed his mother's similarities to Katharine Hepburn, who came from a similarly progressive family, the year he was nine, when he saw a rerelease of the 1940 film *The Philadelphia Story*, starring Hepburn and Cary Grant. According to Beatty, he began a "one-way love affair" with Hepburn then. "No doubt it had something to do with her being a slim, rock-ribbed, highly principled northeastern WASP. My mother was too . . . she liked to act. My mother did too." Beatty would associate Katharine Hepburn with Kathlyn Beaty afterward as a "symbol of perpetual integrity."[248]

Another rereleased movie that "knocked him out" was *Love Affair*, a romantic shipboard melodrama that cast his favorite leading man, Charles Boyer, as a playboy and Irene Dunne as a singer who reforms him, a film known for its sentimental, bittersweet ending that turns on a play of fate.[249] Warren found it deeply moving. "This is a movie I always wanted to make," he said later. "I wanted to make this movie when I was a kid."[250]

Forty-seven years later, Warren Beatty would remake *Love Affair*, playing the Charles Boyer role. His costar would be his actress wife, Annette Bening, and the film would feature Katharine Hepburn as his character's cherished aunt.

By the time Warren was in sixth grade, 1948, his regular moviegoing partner, Shirley, was finishing her last year of junior high and was seldom at home, partially to avoid their parents' arguments. The Beatys were among the first in Arlington to get a television set, and Warren tuned in every Tuesday night to watch the first year of the *Texaco Star Theater*, on NBC, transferring his obsession with Charles Boyer to Texaco's rotating emcee, comedian Milton Berle, who came onstage each Tuesday night in a different costume, puffing on a huge cigar.[251]

Warren, a natural mimic, began to "do" Berle — as Kathlyn put it — at home, at school, everywhere. "He had a fascination with Milton Berle," observed his friend Mike Durfee. "He could do just a superb imitation of Milton Berle and his routine."

Warren's blossoming reputation for telling jokes, and his preoccupation with comic Milton Berle, suggests that he was using humor as another release from a home life that was becoming more stressful as Beatty prepared to enter junior high in 1949.

According to MacLaine, Warren and their mother absorbed most of the emotional fallout from Ira's turmoil.[252] "There was a lot of my father staying out, and wondering where he was on Mother's part, but I didn't feel it, because I was on a schedule you wouldn't believe . . . my father's drinking was much harder on Warren."[253]

Her brother's reaction, as MacLaine recalled, was to "close off," the same behavior Kathlyn displayed under stress. Two of Shirley MacLaine's lasting, poignant images of her younger brother as a teenager were of Warren alone in the dining room singing to Al Jolson records, or of "Warren sitting at the kitchen table eating tuna-fish salad and reading Eugene O'Neill."[254]

Warren's withdrawal from the strife set off by his father's drinking, in the opinion of his sister, set the stage for Beatty the auteur filmmaker, the person in control of every aspect of a movie as writer-producer-director-star. "That's why he's more comfortable behind the camera, in the total-control aspect. He has to have control over everything. That was his ticket to survival. Mine was expression."[255]

As a star in his midfifties, Warren Beatty posthumously described Ira Beaty in this way: "My father was a very reasonable man. Cerebral. A teacher. Sentimental. Outwardly jovial much of the time, in a way that concealed a basic Baptist Puritanism. Let's just say that he wasn't overconfident. Or materialistic. He was married once."[256]

Ira Beaty made only one comment about his son to the national press after Beatty became famous. It was just two lines: "I'll tell you this much about Warren. He was always a good boy."[257]

12 *The fall that Warren Beaty started* junior high, 1949, his sister began high school, a three-year period of sweeping transformation for both. Warren cut a swath for himself at Swanson Junior High, impressing his friends as an apparent extrovert. At home, he was in the long shadow of his manically ambitious, gifted older sister.

Shirley Beaty made the cheerleading squad, earned straight As, and was elected president of the Sub-Debs, a popular sorority at Washington-Lee, where there were more than nine hundred students in her class alone, largely made up of the bright and competitive children of diplomats and other government officials. "She was just *going* to be a cheerleader, and there was nothing that was going to stop her," Shirley's friend Mary Lou Munson was to observe. "And she pretty much did that with everything."[258]

Shirley continued her frantic pace at the Washington School of Ballet, and began to perform in ballets for the Children's Theatre of Washington, which were occasionally staged at Constitution Hall and accompanied by the National Symphony Orchestra. Her best friend, Dottie Rector, recalled, "She just danced, and danced, and danced, and if you ever looked at Shirley's feet, you would wonder how she could stand up."[259]

By the middle of the year, Shirley had overextended herself to the point that her sorority voted her out as president. Mary Lou Munson, a Sub-Deb sister, speculated that Shirley had an overactive thyroid, but the truth was that MacLaine pushed herself to succeed because her parents, in her view, had failed, because *much was expected* of her and Warren, and because "it was really a plea for my father's love."[260]

Warren, the twelve-year-old spectator and successor to this orgy of accomplishment, displayed a similar intensity for the piano. After mastering chords, he spent countless hours teaching himself to play by ear, entertaining his friends with his improvisations of popular songs. His musical tastes ran to jazz, Jolson's "Everybody Rag with Me," and the haunting theme from the film *Laura.* Another favorite, revealing Beatty's romantic nature, was "Deep Purple," which had lyrics reminiscent of the poetry his mother wrote as a young woman ("*And as long as my heart will beat, sweet lover we'll always meet, Here in my deep purple dreams*").

When no one else was home, Warren retreated to the basement and memorized lines from the plays of Eugene O'Neill or sang to Al Jolson records, indicating his desire to perform, which he concealed even from himself. Beatty later told a French journalist that he may have "held back" from acting in his youth because his sister's early success discouraged him, and because his mother and grandmother had taught drama. His initial attraction to the piano may have been that it was a form of expression that was uniquely Warren's within his nuclear family. Once he discovered his passion, he pursued it feverishly, to stay in the game with Shirley in "an ambitiously competitive household."[261]

As a teenager in the early fifties, Beatty also had concerns that acting was not a masculine interest, the same anxiety he had felt as a small child when he shrank from participating in Shirley's ballet class. MacLaine's high school boyfriend Bill Mallon, an athlete, recalled how Warren "bust out laughing" when a "flooty tooty" male dancer leaped across the stage when Shirley performed in *Swan Lake* at Constitution Hall. "His father looked at Warren like he was going to kill him. I thought it was kind of funny."[262]

Mallon, who was a football player and a year ahead of Shirley, caught her eye her first semester at Washington-Lee, so she asked him to a Sadie Hawkins dance. Even as a cheerleader dating a football player during the conformist fifties, MacLaine was an original, in her dress and in her energy level.[263] While leading cheers for the basketball team, she got so exuberant, she started to curse, "so I had to calm her down," recalled Dottie Rector, the captain.

"Sometimes she was a little bit oddball, I thought," reflected former beau Bill Mallon. Once, when Mallon drove Shirley home after a date, she sat in the car, staring at a row of radio towers in the distance. "Finally I said, 'Are you okay?' . . . When she came back on earth there and started talking to me, she said she pictured herself over there, jumping from one tower to the other."

Mary Lou Munson described Shirley as possessing a "curious mind," and recalled how she would talk to people of different faiths about their beliefs. "You'd think, 'My goodness, she's going to convert tomorrow,' but the next day she'd be talking to someone else with that same open-eyed, kind of drinking-it-all-in look. She was just trying things on."

Shirley had less enthusiasm as a teenager for Baptist teachings, either the strict version practiced by her mother and late grandmother MacLean, or the Primitive Baptist preaching style of her ancestor Brother John Beaty, whose charisma she inherited and would use to promote her own avant-garde spiritual beliefs decades later.

"She asked me to go to a Baptist Revival meeting with her one night," Bill Mallon, who was Catholic, remembered. "They had one of those week-end things where they were up there preaching the fire and brimstone — you know, 'If you see the light and if you feel this, come up and be saved.'"

Ira and Kathlyn Beaty told Shirley they expected her to remain a virgin until she got married, part of the strict morality in the house where Warren Beatty grew up, which he described as a "middle class atmosphere with all its rigidities."[264] Both Beatty and MacLaine obediently adhered to this code while they were living at home. Shirley bristled at these Baptist precepts; Warren embodied them.

To their demure mother, a graduate of the prudish Margaret Eaton School, sex was a topic exclusively in the realm of the ethereal. When, as a teenager, Shirley tried to discuss with her mother the intense feelings she had for a boy, Kathlyn Beaty told her, "Go stand under a tree and then wonder and think about yourself."[265]

Shirley's father, as Bill Mallon noticed, could be harsh. When Mallon brought Shirley home one night forty-five minutes past her curfew because of car trouble, a furious Ira was waiting for them, "standing in the kitchen, leaning against the sink." MacLaine said later she felt tremendously stifled by the Baptist strictures their parents imposed on her and Warren, mores that she said became embedded — making it difficult to "do things just for the fun of it," even after she became famous. "My trouble is, I'm really a terminal Protestant. I've never taken the time to enjoy all this stardom stuff, be-cause I don't think of myself that way." MacLaine would conclude: "I think fun is really important, as important as obeying the Golden Rule and abol-ishing war and electing the right candidates."[266]

The same Protestant inhibitions created a conflict in Beatty after he be-came a movie star: he was determined to enjoy life yet paradoxically felt that he lacked permission to do so. When he married for the first time, at age fifty-four, he said that the most important thing he could teach his children "is that it's great to be happy. You don't have to worry in order to get through life."[267] The root of Beatty's angst, as he called it, was "basic Baptist Puritanism," combined with the aura of disappointment — of putting duty before one's dreams, of possibilities lost — that clung to his parents, and thus to Warren and Shirley, like southern moss.[268]

Bill Mallon, a husky football star in high school, considered Shirley's kid brother "kind of a little runt," and encouraged Warren to drink milk so he would fill out. Mallon assumed that Warren Beaty would become a serious pianist as an adult "because he was always in there playing the piano, and he was really good."

Shirley's sorority friends held this same view of Warren in junior high, based on their encounters with him at Sub-Deb meetings at the Beaty house. Dottie Rector described thirteen-year-old Warren as "very quiet"; Mary Lou Munson thought of him as a cute, skinny kid.[269] "He'd come running in and stick his head around the door, and we'd all say, '*Warren!*' and tease him. And he would run and hide . . ."

By the time he finished eighth grade, Warren Beaty was a gangly five foot eleven, with a sprinkle of freckles across his nose and dark hair. Though she would later make jokes about how much prettier her brother was, in 1950, Shirley — not Warren — was the Beaty who would be noticed first. At sixteen Shirley Beaty was June Allyson cute, a sprightly redhead with shoulder-length waves. "Shirley was always 'on,'" as her friend Mary Lou Munson expressed. "She was always performing, she was always the center of attention. She would just walk into a room and people would gather around."[270]

That fall, Warren began to extend himself socially when he was elected vice president of a Swanson Junior High eighth-grade class club that primarily planned dances. No one but Warren was aware that this was the first step in a careful strategy to alter his image and redirect his life. As he later revealed to writer Lillian Ross, "In my early teens, I decided that I didn't want to miss any of the advantages of a normal life."[271] He began a physical transformation as well, catalyzed by his sister's husky boyfriend. Mallon remembers that "about three or four months after I was dating Shirley, I went to the house, and her mom said, 'Well, you did it.' And I said, 'What's that?' She said, 'Warren's drinking about a gallon of milk about every three or four days.'"

That Christmas Eve, Shirley invited her athlete boyfriend for a holiday meal with the family, Bill Mallon's first exposure to the family secret. As Mallon recalled, "Warren's mother got to the point where she was really upset because Mr. Beaty was really late, and she was afraid that he was at the office, or whatever, drinking." When Shirley and her beau returned to the house after running an errand, Ira Beaty had arrived home, drunk and abusive. As the tension escalated, Ira directed his rage at Kathlyn. "They were arguing about something and Mrs. Beaty said, 'You should have come home,' and he said, 'Don't tell me! You don't run my life!'" recalled Mallon. "[Mr. Beaty] was very nasty, and . . . threatening to really harm somebody . . . and finally he made a threat on Shirley's mother."

Mallon, a bruising two-hundred-pound tackle, stood up to Ira Beaty, warning him he had better sit down and shut up, calling him a horse's ass. "He sat down like I hit him with a ton of cement."

The incident on Christmas Eve was traumatic for everyone present. Warren, a still-scrawny thirteen-year-old, withdrew, both physically and emotionally — the response he had inherited from Kathlyn. "He went upstairs. He kind of got out of the room from his dad," said Mallon. Shirley, who "was quite upset," apologized, over and over, to Mallon.

As Bill Mallon continued to date Shirley the rest of the school year, he sensed that Ira Beaty was ashamed. "I went to Shirley's house probably a month or two months before Mr. Beaty even had enough nerve to get up and find a newspaper. . . . Couldn't even look me in the eye."

MacLaine later wrote movingly in *Out on a Limb* about a conversation she had with her father toward the end of his life, when she asked him why he drank so much. Ira Beaty began to cry, saying he felt that he had wasted his life, and his talents, because he had been taught not to believe in himself, "and whenever I think about how afraid I am I can't stand it, so I have to drink."[272]

Bill Mallon observed that Shirley never drank anything stronger than a milkshake or an orange freeze because of the disturbing example of her father's alcohol abuse — a policy Warren Beatty was to follow at Washington-Lee and, in large measure, for the rest of his life.

Adhering to the family's code of polite silence, Warren and Shirley never discussed their father's threats, or Ira's drinking, either while they were growing up or in later years. Once famous, Beatty would mention it publicly only by allusion, referring to "certain family problems," adding elliptically: "I've had a lot of struggles . . . I could tell you about struggles."[273]

Virtually no one in Warren's circle of friends in Arlington, and only a few from Shirley's, had any idea that their father was a binge drinker, another illustration of Virginia politesse. The family was able to conceal the situation because Ira restricted his abuse of alcohol to the privacy of their home or in a car. Mason Green, Jr., did not consider Ira an alcoholic, though their daily contact did not begin until Warren had graduated from high school. "Ira was a very social fella — let's put it that way. He liked to take a drink — more than one on occasion — but I never saw him pass out, and I never saw him fall down, and I never saw him behave any way except as a gentleman." It was the Jekyll-and-Hyde quality that confused Warren. His father was a gentleman and a scholar, but his insecurities made him an occasional nasty drunk. According to MacLaine, on one of those occasions, Ira struck his wife.

As a result, Warren Beatty would develop a complicated contempt for rage. In 1992, Beatty said, "My adrenalin begins to tick when I sense that something violent may occur. I don't look forward to it, and my response is not a particularly liberal response — I want to end it as efficiently as possible. I think getting into fistfights is stupid and embarrassing and degrading."[274]

As a slight thirteen-year-old in 1950, Warren found solace and a deeper understanding in two novels, *Tender Is the Night* and *Look Homeward, Angel*.[275] The first, written by the alcoholic F. Scott Fitzgerald, is about an alcoholic, and includes elegant and accurate descriptions of inebriation in polite society — literature the analytical young Warren could use as research about his father's bingeing and as reassurance that he and his family were not the only ones with the problem.

Look Homeward, Angel, "the most important book for me during my teens," Beatty said later, provided a character with whom he could personally identify, a boy coming of age in a dysfunctional southern family who dreams of escape. The young Warren had even more in common with the book's author, Thomas Wolfe, who acted in college and grew up in nearby Asheville, North Carolina, the son of an alcoholic father and a resentful mother whose stormy marriage blighted Wolfe's childhood. *Look Homeward, Angel* was Wolfe's semiautobiographical story.

The obvious parallels of his life to Wolfe's would not have escaped Beatty. "I went on to more Wolfe after that," he recalled. "*Of Time and the River* and *You Can't Go Home Again* — but the first one was the big one." Beatty's enduring fondness for Thomas Wolfe's novels was an early indicator of his attachment to writers with whom he identified, as would be the case, later, with John Reed.

As a young actor, Warren Beatty offered an insight into the lure that books held for him, saying, "Reading — if it is interesting — shuts out everything else."[276] This doubtless explained his private closet sanctuary as well.

13 *Shortly after their father's upsetting* behavior on Christmas Eve, Shirley went through a personal crisis that would have a ripple effect on the rest of her life, and on Warren's.

The trigger was a decision by Mary Day, cofounder of the Washington School of Ballet, to replace Shirley in the starring role of Cinderella in a spring ballet at Constitution Hall. Day believed that a growth spurt had made Shirley too clumsy to dance the lead, and too tall, at five foot seven, to become a prima ballerina. When Shirley heard Day's pronouncement, she wept.

MacLaine later described in four of her books an anguishing scene that she said occurred on the stairwell of the Beaty house after she lost the role. As she went upstairs, MacLaine recounted, her father berated her for trying to exceed her talents and asked her to give up dance — just as he had given up the violin. "I cried so hard I vomited," was MacLaine's wrenching reconstruction of her confrontation with her father. "He stepped over the vomit and went to the kitchen to fix himself a drink."[277]

Beaty wore a pained expression when asked about the incident, forty years later. After a long silence, he said, "I didn't grow up with those things," repeating his refrain that he loved Shirley but this was *her* version of their childhood.[278] MacLaine's rejoinder was that Warren was not at home when it occurred.

Bill Mallon remembers Shirley's disappointment and an earlier occasion when Ira criticized her voice, telling her she was not qualified to be a professional singer. MacLaine recalled, "He said only people who had been classically trained had the background to perform and be accepted."[279]

It was Kathlyn who suggested that Shirley become an actress, a development that would have an enormous impact on Warren. Tat came up with the strategy after Day retracted Shirley's title role in *Cinderella*, while Warren was finishing eighth grade. "Mother called her up and said, 'Fine, Shirley wants to be an actress anyway,'" related MacLaine. "That was news to me . . . Mother wanted me to be a success and neither Miss Day nor anybody else was going to intimidate me."*[280]

---

*MacLaine wrote later in *Dancing in the Light* that her mother manipulated Day into giving her the role of the Fairy Godmother in *Cinderella*, which she danced despite a broken ankle she had cracked in midperformance. The story was accurate in all but one revealing detail: Day cast Shirley as a wicked stepsister.

Mary Day's rejection intensified MacLaine's flaming ambition, which her high school sweetheart had recognized on their first date. "She really wasn't one I'd ever thought would be someone I'd marry," Bill Mallon mused. "Her career was the most important thing to her." As Dottie Rector, their class's homecoming queen, stated, "We all knew that Shirley was going to . . . make it. We just did."

When Shirley completed her junior year, she beseeched her mother to let her spend the summer in New York taking an intensive course at the School of American Ballet. MacLaine's plan was to move to New York permanently, as soon as she graduated from high school, and then join a classical ballet company, thereby proving Mary Day wrong.

Tat overruled the reflexive caution of her husband, and Shirley moved into a hotel for girls in New York to train for the ballet.[281] By midsummer, Warren found out that his seventeen-year-old sister had been cast in the chorus of a revival musical at New York City Center and was invited to tour with the company in Berlin that fall, Shirley's senior year in high school.[282] The musical was *Oklahoma!*, the first Broadway play the Beatys had seen as a family, and whose cast album had become Warren's saving grace.

Kathlyn, whose dream Shirley was now living, wrote exuberantly to a relative that fall. She explained in her letter that Shirley had seen a notice on a bulletin board that two dancers were needed for *Oklahoma!* to represent the west at the Berlin Arts Festival. Shirley decided to audition "for the experience," wrote her mother, and was "amazed" to be chosen ahead of three hundred professional dancers. A contract for $100 a week plus expenses was "plunked down in front of her," Kathlyn recalled proudly. "Not wanting to tell them her age, [Shirley] asked if she might have time to think it over. They gave her until ten o'clock the next morning."[283]

Shirley's invitation to perform in Berlin mirrored Ira's invitation at nineteen to tour Europe as a violinist almost fatalistically. Like her father, she rejected the offer, opting to finish high school, a decision the Beatys claimed Shirley made. MacLaine would assert that she succumbed to pressure from one or both parents.[284] The truth probably was somewhere in between.

In the middle of August, Warren and his parents visited New York for a week. While there, they saw Shirley perfom twice onstage at the City Center in *Oklahoma!*, an experience that must have been emotional for Warren at fourteen, because of both his deep feelings for his sister and the personal meaning the Rodgers and Hammerstein score held for him.

Tat reported on the trip in a letter to Warren's great-uncle Ira Partlow, who had retired as attorney general of West Virginia and was now a circuit judge, and in frail health. Her note reveals the pride and vicarious pleasure Kathlyn took in her daughter's Broadway debut. She described Shirley's thrill at making her own money, at learning more about dancing, audiences, and professionalism, "and most of all about making her own way in a big city under very trying circumstances."[285]

While she was in the chorus of *Oklahoma!*, MacLaine realized that she was happier in musical comedy than she would be in a ballet company, "and I knew I would be good."[286]

Underneath her bravado, Shirley—a vulnerable teenager—bared herself in a letter she wrote on August 21, 1951, to her best friend, Dottie Rector, in Arlington. She began the letter like a typical high school girl, reporting on her latest romance—a Georgetown student named Whitey. Shirley closed by revealing to Dottie what had inspired her to continue through the hardships and loneliness: "hope" and "faith in God."

Shirley's other inspirations that summer in New York were lines from Rudyard Kipling's classic poem "If" ("If you can keep your head when all about you/Are losing theirs and blaming it on you, If you can trust yourself when all men doubt you . . . If you can dream—and not make dreams your master . . . Yours is the Earth and everything that's in it . . .") and a song—"You'll Never Walk Alone," the powerful and moving ballad from *Carousel*. The lyrics were by Oscar Hammerstein II, who wrote the songs in *Oklahoma!* that had comforted her brother, Warren, since he was seven.

14 When Shirley returned from New York for her senior year in high school, in September 1951—the year Warren finished junior high—she had already made arrangements with her mother to return to Manhattan to study acting and singing in the spring, on the condition that she enroll in college.[287]

Her classmates at Washington-Lee considered Shirley a Broadway star already. "She came back singing every single song from *Oklahoma!*," remembered a friend.[288] Other than that, she was the same Shirley, recalled Susan Morse, then a junior high cheerleader: "She was just really nice. She didn't have that stuck-up, stuck-on-herself feeling."[289]

Warren Beatty shared this likable trait with his sister after he became famous; it was inherited from both parents, especially his father. "Ira wasn't high-falutin'," as Realtor Mason Green, Jr., expressed it. "He should have had a Ph.D., but he was very down-to-earth and practical. He kinda punctured pretentiousness a little bit."[290] In MacLaine's view, their father's dislike of "phonies" was a prejudice against success, since he hadn't attained it. Possibly this was true, but it also arose from the Beaty tradition of honesty, which created a natural disdain for pretentiousness in Ira, and in Warren and Shirley.

Shirley Beaty blazed through her senior year at Washington-Lee. Her triumph was starring in, and choreographing, a stage version of the 1947 June Allyson–Peter Lawford movie musical *Good News* — to such amazing effect that it still would be discussed in awed tones forty-five years later.[291]

Warren, the gangly, slightly goofy book lover, had already initiated his metamorphosis when he was elected vice president of the dance committee and began to guzzle milk, emulating Shirley's football-hero boyfriend, Bill Mallon. By summer — when his sister was cast in *Oklahoma!* on Broadway — Warren intensified his physical training, hoping to qualify for the ninth-grade football team at Swanson Junior High, part of his master plan to attain the "advantages" of a so-called "normal life."[292] This kind of detached, analytical thinking, mature for an adolescent, would set a precedent for Beatty's behavior in Hollywood as an intricate strategist, both in his career and in his personal life.

Although he did not express it, part of Warren's motivation was to compete with, if not outdistance, his compulsively overachieving sibling, something his sister freely acknowledged. "We are very fond of one another, but we both have a very healthy, competitive nature. We like to outdo each other."[293]

Beatty later admitted that he was *driven* to make the football team. "I struggled with football for awhile. That was important to me: to prove something."[294] By excelling in sports, Warren also could end the pattern of oppressed males that began with his grandfather Welton and plagued his father, Ira. He could prove himself a man in the mold of Bill Mallon, whose football physique had made Ira cower when he became abusive under the influence of alcohol. As a teenager in the conservative fifties, Warren, moreover, felt the need to dispel any doubts that his interest in the arts made him effeminate.[295] What better way to prove his manhood than to play football?

Beatty accomplished his objectives in ninth grade with startling results.

"He changed dramatically," recalled his sister's friend Mary Lou Munson, who had considered Warren a "skinny kid" when she saw him at Shirley's sorority meetings the year before. "I wasn't paying attention, but I saw that he had changed drastically. He looked like a hunk later on." When Shirley's exboyfriend Bill Mallon saw her once-"rangy" kid brother Warren at a game, "I was surprised by how big he'd gotten and how filled out."

By the end of football tryouts the summer that Shirley performed in *Oklahoma!*, Warren had made the first team for the fall season his last year at Swanson Junior High, reinventing himself as a football player. "I would say if you had to identify a kind of transition I made as a child, it was from being what they call a 'bookworm' into what they call 'an athlete.'"[296]

His mother's powerful aesthetic still tugged at Warren, pulling him toward the family business of acting. That fall, as ninth-grade football practice began, he went to see *A Place in the Sun*, starring Elizabeth Taylor and Montgomery Clift. Beatty would later tell Charles Grodin, his costar in several films, that *A Place in the Sun* was the reason he became an actor.[297] It is easy to understand why the film had an impact on Warren Beatty as a teenager. The movie, considered director George Stevens's masterpiece, is based on Theodore Dreiser's novel *An American Tragedy*. Clift plays a young factory worker reared in strict religion who falls into a doomed and obsessive love triangle with the owner's wealthy daughter, portrayed by Taylor, and another factory worker (a blowsy Shelley Winters). Warren could identify with the dark and handsome Montgomery Clift, as well as the repressed character Clift played. Elizabeth Taylor, at twenty, was in the lush bloom of her youth.

Warren either denied or suppressed this impulse to act at fourteen—or, as he told a Hollywood journalist later, "I got most of my acting ambitions temporarily pounded out of me in high school football."[298] With football, he had achieved the cliché of social success for boys in fifties America, but it was not personally satisfying for him. "I hated every minute of it," Beatty said after he became famous, "worrying all the time that I might get my nose splashed over my face, or my teeth kicked in."[299]

As a movie star, Beatty would be ridiculed for making this seemingly narcissistic remark, but its true meaning was more deeply rooted. While he was on the team, he withstood intense pressure from both of his parents to quit football because they considered it dangerous. His doting mother expressed her anxiety in a letter she wrote that fall: "Warren made the first team in football and is playing an excellent game. We have gone to most of the games, but I don't enjoy it much. It seems as if I am always watching to see if No. 44 comes to his feet all right."[300]

Ira Beaty — whose aunt Bertie deterred him from high school sports because she worried he would break a finger and be unable to play the violin — expressed his paranoia to Bill Mallon. "He was saying, 'Bill, I really got a problem. How can I get Warren to stop playing football?' . . . He said, 'What if he breaks his finger? Gets his teeth knocked out?' . . . I'd always come home a little bruised up, and back in those days you didn't have all these face masks."

Tat was more enthusiastic about her son's piano lessons with a teacher in Washington, D.C., happily reporting his progress to Ira Partlow. Even during the years he was obsessed with football, Warren's heart was in music. When Shirley's friends were at the Beaty house that year, "Warren played songs from *Oklahoma!* endlessly at every gathering," said one.[301]

The fall he started to play football, Beatty's life was changed through an introduction to a person whom he described in later years as "a great man."[302] Warren's idol was a minister at Westover Baptist, a popular church in Arlington with a large congregation. His name was John Raymond, a sandy-haired, boyishly attractive bachelor in his early thirties who wore glasses. "He was the youth leader and he just took such an interest in a group of us," said Judy Evans, a friend of Warren's from Swanson Junior High, which was located across the street from Westover Baptist Church. According to Evans and others, John Raymond "just had charisma, and could communicate, and was genuine."[303]

The Baptist youth minister had a unique gift for connecting with teenage boys. "John sort of took them under his wing," explained his widow, Mary, who married Raymond a few years after Beatty graduated. "He called them 'his boys.' My husband felt his call was to young men; that's who he had a really strong, life-changing effect on. There was an open-door policy for them. He would go to their games. He was, I think, a mentor."[304]

Warren, who was deeply impressed by John Raymond, began to attend Sunday school at Westover Baptist, where Tat later gave recitations and would be a lifelong congregant. Ira Beaty's church attendance dwindled in Arlington in pace with the setbacks in his career as an educator. By the time Warren met Pastor Raymond in 1951, "Mr. Beaty showed no interest in the church," Mary Raymond noted. "Warren's mother was the one in the family that encouraged faith, not the father."

"I taught him how to tie a Windsor knot," John Raymond later reminisced.

"I guess that's the first thing I remember about Warren. He started attending church here when he was in ninth grade. And one Sunday morning shortly after, I saw him staring at me — staring — and I asked him if something was wrong. He said, 'No, I was just wondering how you manage to make a nice knot like that in your tie.' So I showed him." In Raymond's view, Beatty "was the sort of boy adults always liked because he seemed more mature than his years."[305]

Warren attended Westover Baptist Church through the end of junior high and eventually was elected president of its popular Sunday school program, whose attendees numbered in the hundreds.[306] "He was a very good church-goer," John Raymond said in middle age. "Once he joined he was very faithful about attending, all through high school."[307] In later years, Raymond spoke highly and often of Beatty, recalled the minister's widow. "Warren always went one hundred percent in whatever he was involved in — sports, his church — and so that's the picture I have of Warren from John."

During ninth grade and throughout his three years at Washington-Lee, Warren looked to John Raymond as a role model, consulting the Baptist minister for advice and guidance. "Kathlyn told me that she thought he had a lot of influence on Warren," recalled Betty Hawthorne, Tat's friend of long standing.[308] As Raymond's widow confirmed, "There was a very close relationship between John and Warren."

Ira and Warren's strained father-son dynamic created a void that John Raymond filled in Warren's life in 1951, during the critical interlude when he was preparing to enter high school. As Mary Raymond noted, "John never felt that there was a real warm relationship" between Warren and his father, "but that was just a feeling, there was nothing said."

That November, Kathlyn sent a long letter to Ira Partlow with family news in which, ironically, Ira Beaty's devotion to Warren and Shirley was evident on every page, as was Tat's.[309] She wrote of the stress Ira was experiencing having to sell real estate to support the family, and hinted at her own apprehensions. Although Tat reported that Ira had had a successful business year, she noted to his uncle that he was seeing a doctor every week for shots to stabilize his metabolism.

Kathlyn also commented on world events in her letter to Partlow, expressing hope that Churchill's reinstatement would help restore the economy and that he would not compromise with Stalin — further proof that politics were discussed in the Beaty household. She revealed her Canadian roots ("Ira says I have too strong a British outlook so I'm not a fair one to judge") and a more conciliatory nature than her husband, remarking, "It sure is an upset old world isn't it, or maybe it's because we're living in the midst of changes."

She ended the letter expressing regret that she and Ira hadn't been to Front Royal in ages and referring, as she did throughout, to Warren and to Shirley. "Children the age of ours need constant looking after, and they are too busy to go away — so we stay home most of the time."

Six months after he received Tat's letter, Warren's great-uncle Ira Partlow died. He was eulogized in the *Rappahannock News* for his contributions and integrity as a lawyer and a judge, for his tenure as attorney general of West Virginia, and as "a Christian and a gentleman," traits that defined the family legacy passed on to Warren Beatty.[310]

Toward the end of 1951, Warren's respected politician uncle Alex MacLeod lost his reelection to the Ontario Parliament, where he would be remembered as the last sitting Communist in the legislature, and as "a foeman worthy of anyone's steel." His political adversary, the Conservative premier Leslie Frost, was heard to say, "Without him in the legislature, some of the lights went out."[311]

Warren's increasingly prominent look-alike uncle, Mansell, the third theatrical MacLean sibling, surged further ahead in business when Warren was in ninth grade, forming MacLean Grove & Company, a New York engineering firm with lucrative contracts to build tunnels under the Rhine and to construct the New England Thruway, commissions that would lead to one of Beatty's first jobs.

In June of 1952, Shirley graduated from Washington-Lee near the top of her class. Warren celebrated the end of junior high with his first formal date, to the ninth-grade prom. He asked neighbor Susan Morse, a pert brunette on the cheerleading squad. The couple double-dated with Warren's pal Mike Durfee, a high achiever who would become known as the "class politician."[312]

A snapshot of the two couples taken on prom night shows the girls — dressed in white taffeta — arranged side by side, with their dates posed like bookends. Warren stands on the far left, wearing a blue serge suit and the stiff posture of a soldier, his eyes slyly suggesting mischief and merriment. In contrast to Durfee and his prom date, who smile for the photographer with no signs of an emotional connection, Warren and Susan Morse are holding hands, their fingers intimately intertwined — offering at least one clue to the ladies man Beatty would become.

That summer, shortly after he turned fifteen, Warren bid farewell to the older sister who had been his closest companion through childhood and a comrade in the house of their parents' domestic disturbances. As she left for New York at eighteen, Shirley announced to her father, and to her mother, that she was not going to college. "I told my father the world would be my teacher and I would learn well."[313]

In reality, Shirley MacLean Beaty had not strayed from the MacLean ideals, or from the Beaty legacy of honesty. Her goal when she left home was to "contribute something to society . . . and to some art form," she later told a writer in Toronto, where her aunt Ginny MacLeod supported human rights causes. "I couldn't care less about Hollywood, or the money or the people or their way of life . . . you can't find anyone who'll tell you the truth."[314]

While Warren waited for football practice to begin so he could try out for the high school team, he pursued a summer romance with Susan Morse, his first official girlfriend. Morse's memories of Warren Beaty at barely fifteen were of an awkwardly attractive boy with squinty eyes, whose ears kind of stuck out, and who had other teenage deficiencies.

What Warren did possess was a sweetly endearing appreciation for females of all ages, as the only male child on both sides of the family — the adored and adoring son, grandson, cousin, nephew, and brother.* "One could see his tendencies," as Morse coyly suggested. "I mean he *really did* like girls."

Throughout the summer of 1952, Warren comported himself in Susan Morse's company with the Victorian propriety of Tat's house rules at the Margaret Eaton School. Their most risqué date, as recalled by Morse, was an innocent game of spin-the-bottle, chaperoned by Warren's parents.

Warren, it seemed, was his mother's, *and* his father's, puritan son. "I definitely grew up in Virginia thinking in my early teens that I would marry the first woman that I had sex with and would stay married to her for the rest of my life."[315]

15 *That summer, as he prepared to start* high school, Warren developed a bad habit that would follow him to Hollywood and become a Beatty trademark, one that tested the patience of his

---

*Beatty's sole male cousin, David MacLeod, was born when Warren was seven, and Warren considered himself the only male in his generation of Beatys and MacLeans.

friends. "He would keep you waiting," said Susan Morse. "He had a sense of the dramatic, and he would like to make a grand entrance, not really a disregard for someone else's time, but it began to feel a little bit that way."

John Raymond, Beaty's minister mentor, considered it "the only thing I myself didn't appreciate about Warren, for a while . . . I thought it was unnecessary." In Raymond's opinion, Warren's habitual tardiness, even to church, "was part of the picture — so that he could stand out a little more. He'd be the last one to arrive. And, too, he'd be the last one to leave . . . I'd ask Warren about it and he'd say, 'One thing about me, I just can't get out of that bed on weekends.'"[316]

The year that his first film, *Splendor in the Grass*, was released, Beatty confessed to a friend in the press corps named Joe Laitin that he had a compulsion to be late, and that he considered it a disease. "I had to get over it," he told Laitin, "and for that reason I'm upset now if I'm . . . late, if I keep people waiting."[317] But Beatty did not find a cure in 1962, as he informed Laitin at the time. In 1998, his staff was using the acronym WFW: code for "Waiting for Warren."[318]

His friends' impression was that Warren began to arrive late to create his own dramatic flair in order to compete with his older sister's legacy at Washington-Lee. Shirley Beaty, in the estimation of Warren's high school chum Tom Calhoun, was already a "legend" when he and Warren arrived as sophomores in the fall of 1952.[319] Warren rarely talked about his sister to Calhoun or to his other male pals. He opened up more to a female friend at Washington-Lee named Idell Simms, who gleaned that he was close to Shirley and that "she was a very positive influence in his life, [especially] since their parents were older."[320]

Warren's admiration for Shirley, and for her talent, made his sister an even tougher act to follow. "He was certainly not eager to ride her coattails . . . ," Calhoun observed. "He wanted to make it on his own." During that pivotal summer, Beaty assessed how to make his name at Washington-Lee. "He had to make some decisions about football versus politics," according to Mike Durfee, "and I don't think he wanted to do all of the business of student government. He picked athletics."

Warren's choice in the summer of 1952 was also a reflection of his time and place, as Calhoun, a teammate on the Washington-Lee football team, reflected: "Athletic prowess was overvalued at that time . . . that was just what you did." Warren focused on the sport with Zen-like discipline. "Football became a very important part of my life, a very important part," he said later.[321]

As tryouts intensified that summer, "things just sort of cooled off" in his romance with Susan Morse, a pattern he would follow throughout his life: once he committed to a project, or to a person, Beatty immersed himself to the exclusion of everything else. If his consuming interest was a subject he could research, he often achieved a mastery of the topic, as he would with the life of John Reed, or Howard Hughes, or certain medical conditions.

Warren successfully applied this technique at fifteen to football. He not only made the Washington-Lee High School team as a center and a line-backer, but he also redesigned his physical frame. At the start of his first season, Warren Beaty was listed as five foot eleven and one hundred sixty pounds. Within a year, he grew two inches and gained twenty-five pounds.

He followed Bill Mallon's regimen, drinking several quarts of milk at each meal, and he continued to add bulk through high school, often eating three meals at a sitting at a burger joint called Tom's with Arthur Eberdt, the team's quarterback.[322]

Warren and Art became "fast friends," bonded by the parallel experience of having older siblings who had excelled at Washington-Lee before them, coincidentally in the same class. "My brother was an All-American in high school," observed Eberdt. "Then I came to play football after him. Warren and I were both following." Eberdt noted that when they graduated, "Warren and I got as many honors as anybody."

For Warren, his prowess at football was more than a ticket to popularity or parity with Shirley; it validated his masculinity, a process he seemed to view as a ritual. "Some things you want to do," he explained, "like playing a piano. Some things you do to prove something — maybe it has to do with at a certain age in high school you want to prove you're a man."[323] According to Eberdt, Warren was "a big bruiser, and you don't mess around with guys who did well on the football team. He wasn't a sissy."

Tom Calhoun, another of his teammates, evaluated Warren as a football player in this way: "He was a second team, all-county, playing a not-so-glamorous position — center and linebacker, unglamorous position — but he got a lot of recognition for play. He was a good player. A well-prepared player. He was a good size for that day."

Warren's meticulous preparation distinguished him on the football field, just as it would as a filmmaker. While he was at Washington-Lee, he sought the advice of his friend Art Eberdt's father, who had been an All-American at the University of Alabama as a center, the same position Warren played.* "So after every game," recalled Eberdt, "Warren and my dad would sit down and talk. Warren would still be in his uniform and they would talk and chat—very, very serious—about all the mistakes, and the parts that Warren had done in the game."[324]

As a small child, Warren had a natural affinity for older people, especially if they could impart wisdom, commencing with his grandmother MacLean and his great-aunts Bertie and Maggie Beaty. During high school, his friends noticed, "he was always good around adults. Very intelligent, well spoken."[325] This trait had blossomed into a sincere and shrewd tendency to cultivate mentors who would be helpful to Warren, either personally, such as minister John Raymond, or on the football field, as with Eberdt's father. Years later, Beatty told Tom Calhoun, "Everything I found useful in life I learned in football."

Warren played the game the way he approached whatever he undertook: "in depth, all out, with passion," in his quarterback's description. "He hit very hard, he was tough, but he never got angry in football. Our record was usually like seven and three each year . . . and Warren was All-State."

Beatty really wanted to be quarterback—the position Eberdt played—something he kept to himself in high school but later confided to production designer Paul Sylbert when Sylbert was making sketches for *Heaven Can Wait*, a film in which Beatty directed himself playing a quarterback for the Los Angeles Rams. "He always dreamed about being a quarterback," revealed Sylbert, who considered the position a better match for Beatty's personality than center. "He's a director! He's not the guy bent over, shuffling the ball."[326]

The year Warren Beaty was a sophomore at Washington-Lee, 1952, it was considered impressive just to make the team, given that his class alone had 1,100 students. Until shortly after he graduated, schools in Virginia were segregated, something Beatty would marvel at forty-three years later. "I grew up in a high school that didn't have a single black student. This is actually the largest high school south of the Mason-Dixon line in the United States—that is in the old states, the Confederacy."[327] When a federal judge ordered the integration of Warren High School in Front Royal, Virginia, in 1958, Warren's uncle Damon Gasque, who was superintendent of schools, sided

---

*Eberdt's father went on to play center in the early days of the NFL, opposite such legends as Bronco Nagurski, and was introduced to his future wife by Coach Paul "Bear" Bryant.

with ministers who felt that local school boards should have the option to integrate.[328] Even as a youth in Virginia, Warren had liberal leanings. "By the time Brown [*Brown v. Board of Education*] came along, I was just graduating from school and it all seemed like a pretty good idea to me. But I do remember the signs 'Colored' and 'White.'"[329]

Warren's carefully plotted transformation in high school would extend beyond excelling in football. He eventually aimed for class office, made consistently high marks, and participated in extracurricular activities — symbolized by his receiving the senior class superlative of "Best All Around." It was the confidence of a cherished son. "If I told my mother that on Thursday I was going to move the city of Cleveland over to somewhere in the Antilles," Beatty said once, "she would be impressed, then surprised, and hope that I wouldn't work too hard."[330]

The more intuitive of his friends perceived that Warren's hubris concealed a reserved and emotionally complex person. "When I was in high school," Beatty later admitted, "I think I did extend myself more than was really comfortable to myself. I didn't after I left there, and that's the only time that I ever did: to feel accepted, to feel liked."[331] Idell Simms was permitted to see the private Warren. "I think Warren was really a very serious, very internal kind of person — he had his own little well that he dipped out of — but publicly he was the captain of the football team, and the this, and the that, and he could not appear to be vulnerable at all."

Warren quickly fell in with an elite clique, to which he was granted further entrée by joining Phi Lam, one of the "secret societies" that included the Sub-Debs, Shirley's former sorority. Beatty's friends were a mixture of Phi Lams and girls from their sister sorority, the Tau Deltas, along with his closest football buddies — Art Eberdt, Tom Calhoun, and Tommy Bransford — and student government standouts like Mike Durfee.*

The first year Warren was at Washington-Lee, Art Eberdt was elected president of the sophomore class. "Mike [Durfee] and Warren and I were good friends and we were kind of the leaders," said Eberdt. "We three kind of ran the school."

Beaty stood out quickly as a "magnet" to girls, in Tom Calhoun's turn of phrase. After his tentative ninth-grade romance with Susan Morse — who

---

*They were an accomplished group. Mike Durfee would become a pediatrician and Art Eberdt a physician; Tom Calhoun would graduate at the top of his class at Duke and excel in business, as would Tom Bransford.

would later marry Mike Durfee — Warren as a sophomore began to pursue senior sorority girls he met through Phi Lam. One of the seniors he fancied was an extremely feminine cheerleader who had been on the squad with Shirley the year before. Her name was Janet Smith, a Tau Delta. "Warren just started showing up at the sorority meetings," recalled Smith.[332]

Even though Smith was a senior and had a boyfriend, Shirley Beaty's younger brother caught her eye. She described Warren as "very mature for his age," an early blooming that seemed to have occurred overnight. Beaty's five-eleven frame gave him stature beyond a tenth-grader, and Smith swooned over his half-closed blue eyes ("those eyelashes!"). Warren's boyish features, which would be an asset as he got older, were the only clue to his true age. "His baby face used to upset him," said his friend Tom Calhoun. "No one ever asked me for my I.D. and they always asked for his, and it was a curse that he had this baby fat around his baby face. But he outgrew that."

His most dramatic quality was what one male classmate defined as Warren Beaty's "presence." It was an attitude, and a look, that Janet Smith found alluring, even though he was only a sophomore.[333] "Warren just had a style — he didn't horse around and get loud, like boys will. He was low-key." He reminded Smith of "somebody depicted in a movie as a college boy, with the V-neck sweater . . . he just sort of seemed to be so much more sophisticated, like he had made a study of what he was supposed to act like."

Whatever its origin, the look was effective. By the time he pledged Phi Lam in October, Beaty was dating several attractive sophomores, had piqued the interest of cheerleader Janet Smith, and had infatuated another senior Tau Delta named Nancy Dussault, the star of Washington-Lee's theater department. Dussault, a vivacious redheaded singer-dancer, would achieve fame on Broadway by twenty-two, become the first female cohost of *Good Morning, America*, and later costar as the wife of actor Ted Knight in the situation comedy *Too Close for Comfort*.

The popular Dussault, who was dating a senior on the football team, said later that her crush on Warren was "considered shocking . . . me, Nancy, dating a k-i-d."[334]

According to his teammate Tom Calhoun, Warren had an almost mystical power to seduce — adults or teenagers, females or males. "He could mesmerize people if he chose." One of his classmates, Grace Munson, described Warren's technique, which was a combination of physical intimacy and focused intensity. "He just liked to talk . . . he liked to talk at school — he'd talk in the hall, talk after school — and he liked to talk *real close*. Right in your face."[335] Warren's conversations were distinguished by long pauses, as he appeared to struggle for the words to express his thoughts.

His close friend Idell Simms considered Warren's pauses — which some in high school thought he used for effect — to be evidence of his carefully concealed insecurities. "Very often actors — they're not as sure of who they are, and there's a little bit of hesitation."

Another clue was Beatty's preference for one-on-one conversations. "I don't know if he even came to big parties," observed his quarterback chum Eberdt, "or big social gatherings . . . the more drinks, the volume goes up. Warren just never went to those." The concentration he conveyed in a private tête-à-tête was an essential element of Warren Beatty's charm; underneath his extrovert pose, he was basically shy. He also preferred conversations with depth as opposed to the superficial chatter of parties. "He liked to talk more with the teachers," noticed Eberdt. "He liked to talk with older people."

Warren's lifetime of charming females on both sides of his family not only gave him confidence with girls, but also created the ideal boyfriend. "He'd lean up against the wall with his arm," recalled Janet Smith, the senior on the cheerleading squad whom Warren pursued that fall, "and look down at you . . . and boys didn't do that then. He would say things to me that other boys didn't say, and he'd say this in this really low voice. That was so unusual for a boy that age."

Warren's attraction to older girls, and, in particular, to Nancy Dussault, was linked to his strong feelings for the MacLean women. "I've always been in love with actresses," he would later say on more than one occasion. "My mother was an actress. My sister is an actress. The girls I've been involved with have always been actresses. Sometimes I regret this. I like beautiful, intelligent, charming women and it happens that a lot of them are actresses."[336]

The parallel to his sister was obvious with Dussault, a redheaded actress-dancer with animated features that resembled Shirley's. Like Shirley, Dussault had taken Washington-Lee by storm as the star of the school's showcase musical production, in her case, *Brigadoon*. Dussault was also a friend of Shirley's.

By that fall, Shirley Beaty was struggling to pay the rent on a fifth-floor sublet near Columbia University, which she shared with a series of twelve roommates over twelve months.[337] Beatty later said that their parents sent Shirley a twenty-five-dollar weekly allowance, which MacLaine stopped accepting after she got her first job in summer stock, dancing in the chorus of *Kiss Me, Kate* at Music Circus, in Lambertville, New Jersey.[338]

Ira Beaty had severe misgivings about his daughter's show business aspirations, "because he always thought that in some way I would be hurt. Of course that was really him talking about himself."[339] In fact, life was difficult for Shirley that fall in New York as an eighteen-year-old unemployed dancer. She lived on peanut butter and free lemonade from the Automat to pay for voice and dance lessons, hoping for another professional job.[340] In an October 1952 letter to her close friend Dottie, Shirley "spoke of missing Washington-Lee and the kids."[341]

Nancy Dussault was perceptive enough to realize that her boyfriend had similar ambitions. "Warren, of course, was a big wheel in high school. But it's funny, I always had the idea that what he big-wheeled in — football, politics — was not really his cup of tea." She sensed that he wanted to do "kooky, artistic things — call them what you will — character things, goof things."[342]

Warren was still in denial about his thespian leanings, or had pushed those desires aside, either because of Shirley ("he wanted to be his own person," as his friend Idell Simms said), or out of concern that he would be thought of as a "pansy," as he acknowledged later.[343]

What Warren learned from playing football those years that he considered invaluable had to do with truth. "I couldn't con anyone into anything. I was there with the tackle or the block or I wasn't. There was no choice. You just had to do it."[344]

16 *Warren Beaty's sophomore romance*

with Nancy Dussault was not exclusive, at least not on his part, a common practice in their set at Washington-Lee. "We all ran around together . . . we didn't have to 'go with' anybody," noted friend Charlotte Kehart.[345]

By December, Warren had succeeded in dating senior cheerleader Janet Smith, whom he took on a double date to see the Western *Way of a Gaucho*.[346] When they ended the evening snuggled on a sofa in front of a blazing fire with the lights off, Smith was even more impressed with his romantic college-boy behavior. "Warren was a different experience from other boys, who were either so shy they didn't talk or touch, or so cool in a macho way that they'd not let you know if they were interested . . . I appreciated and understood when he came on to me in a romantic way. Made your knees weak."[347]

Warren's moves remained fifties chaste, according to Smith. ("He didn't get fresh other than kissing.") Beatty referred to these years later as his "straight-laced beginnings."[348] Smith, who had an older boyfriend, sensed that Warren was upset she would not commit exclusively to him, an impression that Beatty later confirmed. "After all, I came from Virginia, where it was expected. I once thought monogamy was a goal to be striven for in earnest."[349]

Despite this, his close high school friend Idell Simms intuited, at the time, that Warren "would be hard to marry."[350] She felt that he consciously chose girlfriends who were interested in careers as opposed to marriage or who, like Janet Smith, had serious beaus. "I don't know what gave me that impression. Probably he did. Certainly when he was with Nancy Dussault, I knew that he would never marry her. He dated very 'safe' people."

This paradox in the young Baptist Warren Beaty — desiring yet resisting marriage — was the precursor to a conflict that would stalk him most of his life. The roots of Beatty's ambivalence about marriage were at 930 North Liberty Avenue, the site of his parents' arguments, and their mixed message that getting married dissolved their dreams *and* was their greatest fulfillment.

Beatty's religious regard for his parents' commitment to each other, in spite of their "ups and downs," as he euphemistically described their tumult, was what deterred him from marrying. "That phrase, 'until death do us part,' uh, I always said if you're going to stand up and make this sort of promise, then you really ought to keep it," he said in an interview as a bachelor of fifty-four. "I wasn't exactly prudish about this, but I think I would have been called a strict constructionist . . . my solution was to not get divorced. And one way to not get divorced is to not get married."[351]

Beatty associated most of his parents' conflicts with the arguments that arose when his father was drinking, a trauma he certainly witnessed on other occasions besides the Christmas Eve when Bill Mallon had to intervene. "I'm sure he had bad experiences with it," said his friend Art Eberdt. "Probably why he never drank. He never spoke about it too much."

Much later on, when he lived in Hollywood, Beatty told his friend Paul Sylbert, and others, that he decided early in life that he would never drink or take drugs because of his father's heavy drinking.[352] Tom Calhoun, his Washington-Lee teammate, observed that Warren needed to be in control, of himself and his circumstances — probably due to the powerlessness he felt observing his father's outbursts and the uncertainty he experienced in a house where no one knew when the next binge would occur.

"He always drank tea," observed Eberdt. "As far as I know, Warren never drank alcohol. Never smoked . . . at graduation each year, we'd go to the beach at Ocean City . . . we didn't see Warren too much because he was usually dating some girl. We'd hang out and drink beer and act stupid and all that, but he didn't . . . and so he was kind of on his own. He was pretty private."

Warren Beatty also came of age in an era — the fifties — that was "so innocent," as Eberdt commented on their high school years at Washington-Lee. "I didn't know what drugs were . . . we were a wholesome group. We were weird by today's scale."

Throughout high school, Warren Beaty's primary influence continued to be his Baptist youth minister, John Raymond, who made a practice of cultivating impressive young men as role models to recruit other teenagers into the Baptist church.[353]

Beaty was the perfect acolyte.

As Tom Calhoun recalled, "Warren liked this pastor . . . he got to know him and kind of talked it up with the rest of us, and he got a group of us guys to go with him. We ended up going with Warren to Sunday school for a while." Warren's male friends, Calhoun included, found his mentor "very charismatic," but they stopped short of embracing Raymond's Baptist religion.

"He came over once to the house and tried mightily to get me to join the church, and I turned him down. As I thought about it, it was a bit of a hard sell . . . I found the message a little too literal for my taste." Calhoun took exception to the John Raymond school of oratory. "I guess I stopped going when the pastor gave a sermon about the celestial All-Star baseball team with Jesus batting cleanup, and Paul batting third, and Peter leading off . . . I think we all kind of drifted away." All of them except Warren Beaty, the great-great-great grandson of the circuit-riding Baptist preacher.

Calhoun assumed that like him, Warren was not "particularly religious, he just liked this pastor." But as their mutual friend Idell Simms noted astutely of Warren, "If it made a strong impression on him, Warren probably would not have shared that with us."

For Warren, the experience at Westover Baptist Church was profound. After teaching Sunday school, he served as a royal ambassador, according to Kathlyn Beaty's pastor, Dr. Ben Wagener. "Baptists have what they call an

R.A., which is a mission action group. I can remember Warren was a royal ambassador."[354] Bert Thurber, who was in a Sunday school class taught by Warren Beaty, had a vague recollection of him preaching the sermon one Sunday as guest youth minister.[355]

At a certain point in high school, under the stewardship of Pastor John Raymond, Warren made the life-altering decision to be baptized in the Baptist church, which required total underwater immersion, and which Baptists believed could occur only when a person was old enough to make a conscious choice to be a Christian.[356]

Warren Beaty's baptism as a teenager, a two-step process, began with his formal profession of faith during a Sunday service at Westover Baptist Church, the dramatic event that also occurs at Baptist revivals.

"It was highly ritualistic," explained Bert Thurber, a relation of the Beatys who was baptized at Westover at approximately the same time as Warren. To profess his faith, Warren stood up in front of the congregation to declare himself for Christ, and his baptism by immersion took place during a subsequent Sunday service. "They had a baptismal pool where you might expect to find an altar—right at the center of the church, behind the pulpit," related Thurber. "I was baptized in the same sanctuary as Warren. It was a tub, basically, a big tub, but it had a glass front such that it would hold in the water, so it meant that people in the congregation could actually witness your being baptized, and your being immersed." The ceremony, which took place toward the end of the church service, was a dramatic spectacle, especially for someone as private as Warren Beaty.

"Basically," said Thurber, "you would come in from one side of the tub and the minister would come in from another side. The water would be up to about your waist, maybe a little higher, and then you would take a hold of the minister's arm, and he would take a hold of you, and he'd say whatever he was going to say. And then he would sort of swing you backward, and then lift you up."

After he became an actor, Warren Beatty reflected on his immersion baptism with John Raymond, the pastor's widow would recall. "He told my husband that the only worthwhile thing that happened in his life was his profession of faith."[357]

While Warren formally became a Christian, his sister was undergoing her own transformation at the end of 1952. After weeks of being unemployed, Shirley got a job as a dancing mannequin in the Servel Refrigerators "Show of Stars" that would be touring the South the winter of 1953.[358] On

December 4, 1952, she wrote to a friend in Virginia that she had changed her last name to "MacLaine" after the audition, "because no one could pronounce Beaty," which often came out sounding like "Beety."[359] According to Warren, "Shirley took mother's name and changed the spelling [from MacLean] so as not to be confused with the toothpaste."[360]

One of Shirley MacLean Beaty's Sub-Deb sisters got together with the newly christened "Shirley MacLaine" during the Servel industrial tour, when Shirley arrived in her showgirl costume. "That was probably the last time I saw her in person . . . she seemed suddenly swept into a very sophisticated mode."[361]

When MacLaine returned to Arlington for Christmas shortly before the Servel tour began, "I remember she wore a fur coat and she had long hair, sort of Veronica Lake," said Warren's high school friend Idell Simms. "I remember we were all very impressed with her fur coat."

Her first head shot as Shirley MacLaine shouted GLAMOUR! in the way a worldly adolescent girl might envision it — in a sultry pose, heavy on the dark lipstick and false eyelashes, and with Rita Hayworth hair.[362] It was suspiciously similar to the black-and-white glossy of June Rowe Weaver, the shapely leading lady in Shirley's mother's play, whose costumes Shirley had laid out each night when she was twelve.

"She was only a child — eighteen or something, a kid," remarked Nora Bristow, an experienced dancer, or "gypsy," who shared a Pullman car with MacLaine during the industrial road show in 1953. The Baptist-bred teenager had to grow up fast on the road, according to Bristow. "We were there to entertain these salesmen at industrial shows . . . our big showgirl used to come in and say, 'Okay germs, take a look around, 'cause I can see the men here, and you can't!'" By the end of the tour, MacLaine had been given what Bristow considered a showgirl's education: "Most theater people know how to speak, know which fork to use, and keep their mouths shut."

As his eighteen-year-old sister pirouetted around a Servel refrigerator dressed like a Rockette in towns along the eastern seaboard, Warren Beaty completed his first football season and continued his chaste conquest of the most popular senior girls, often at a fifties hangout called the Hot Shoppe, where they went for milkshakes. Beatty later told talk show host Dick Cavett that when he was dating in high school, he believed that he would lead the sexually conservative life of his daddy. "Oh, yeah. I grew up in a very, almost— I don't like the word *puritanical*, but I grew up in that American atmosphere of a certain amount of constrictions."[363]

At the same time, Warren as a sophomore was demonstrating the qualities that would set him apart with women as a movie star. "We would sit in the car and neck . . . ," recalled Janet Smith. "He probably was dating lots of other girls, but he made *me* feel important to him — because he would 'handle' me sweetly, tenderly, sexy, with soft-spoken words."

In New York, Shirley was experiencing the same strong pull as Warren toward their parents' traditional values. After struggling in vain to be cast in the chorus of a Broadway stage show, MacLaine nearly quit show business in 1953 to marry a graduate student who was attending nearby Columbia University, an Ira Beaty conservative who did not want her to pursue a career.[364]

That April, Warren's older sister decided to give musical theater one last "fling" by auditioning for the chorus line of a new Rodgers and Hammerstein musical called *Me and Juliet*, opening at the Majestic Theater on May 28, 1953. After being rejected twice, MacLaine auditioned for a third time and was hired as a dancer for the show, a turn of events that tested her relationship with her disapproving fiancé.[365]

In June, as Warren finished his sophomore year, his sister received her first publicity, a short article accompanied by a showy headshot in a Washington paper, with the headline, "Shirley Beaty in 'Me and Juliet.'" Hoping to break out of the chorus line, Shirley spent part of her salary that summer on three acting lessons from Joan McCracken, the leading lady in *Me and Juliet* — the only acting classes Shirley MacLaine would ever take.[366] "There was something there that she definitely did have, had, or has," observed Lorraine Havercroft, who danced in the chorus with Shirley that summer in *Me and Juliet* — "a sparkle about her."[367]

Warren spent the summer on a construction job with his quarterback chum Art Eberdt, building up muscle for their junior year of football.[368] After her senior year triumph in *Brigadoon*, Warren's steady girlfriend Nancy Dussault enrolled as a voice major at Northwestern University, in Illinois, a decision Warren would monitor closely.

17 The universal comment about Warren Beatty the movie star made by the friends who knew him at Washington-Lee is that he was essentially the same person at fifteen, sixteen, and seventeen that he seems to be on-screen. "He's sort of himself," observed his quarterback pal. "He's Warren Beaty."

It was more than Beatty's screen persona that his high school friends found familiar; his *personality* remained constant over the years, despite his fame. "Warren has never changed," declared his friend Idell Simms.

High school was the laboratory for Beatty's emerging identity, a blueprint for his adult behavior. For Warren, Washington-Lee was Hollywood in microcosm. After a summer working construction with Art Eberdt, he came back in the fall of 1953, for his junior year, at his adult height of six foot one, with new muscles and extra bulk filling out his frame to a husky 185 pounds — weight that Beatty put on to play football in the same way he later would put on a yellow trench coat and a fedora to play Dick Tracy.

A month after school started, one of the Tau Deltas got a letter from Nancy Dussault. Dussault raved about Northwestern University and the "gorgeous specimens" at fraternity parties there, "but none can take the place of Warren," she wrote. "I really miss him."[369]

While his previous girlfriend carried a torch for him at college, Warren was circling a junior at Washington-Lee named Ann Read, a "gorgeous, husky-voiced" redhead his friend Art Eberdt would call "the love of Warren Beaty's life in high school."[370] According to his quarterback pal, Warren and he were in competition for Ann. "Warren won," Eberdt said simply.

"Everybody was in love with Ann," noted Grace Munson, her close friend from first grade until Read's death in 1995.* As Tom Calhoun confessed, "I guess we were kind of awed by her." Read, a sophisticated beauty who wore her auburn hair in a bouffant, was a cheerleader, a Tau Delta, and a professional jazz singer crowned Miss Arlington "on a lark" the summer after eleventh grade.[371]

Warren gravitated to Ann Read for many of the same reasons he was drawn to Nancy Dussault. As Calhoun observed, "She was sort of in the world of entertainment, and that was the attraction for Warren." Once again, the prototype was his sister, Shirley, and most significantly, Warren's Scots-Irish, titian-haired mother.

---

*Ann Read Colgan died of cancer August 5, 1995. Beaty may have dated Ann a few times in junior high. Her scrapbook includes a program from one of Shirley's high school plays, suggesting that Ann attended with Warren, though Grace Munson does not recall Ann dating Beaty then. Other friends, and Ann's daughter, are unsure.

Warren and Ann were "the dream team," as a classmate from Washington-Lee described their high school romance.[372] "He was captain of the football team, and she was a cheerleader," said their friend Idell Simms. "She and Warren would go to see plays together," added Read's daughter Shannon, who kept Ann's high school scrapbook, which still has the pressed flowers from her dates with Warren. "There were cute little notes of where they would go after dances."[373]

Even though his steady was the most desirable girl in high school, Warren continued to pursue other girls while he was involved with Ann Read, as he had during his relationship with Nancy Dussault, the pattern he would follow when he got to Hollywood.

While he was dating Ann Read, Warren initiated another practice that would become part of his Don Juan mythology: long, amorous conversations on the telephone. Grace Munson, Ann's lifelong friend, recalled Warren's fixation with the phone, a habit that would become his Hollywood trademark. "He would talk on the phone *a lot* — not just to Ann, but almost anybody." After Beatty became a sex symbol, the phone would be referred to in jest as his "second most legendary appendage."[374]

His technique on the telephone was similar to the way he created a sense of intimacy in his face-to-face conversations, when, as Munson recounted, he would talk "real close." Warren held the phone receiver next to his lips and used soft, suggestive tones barely above a whisper, very like the soothing and seductive way his mother read poetry to him when he was a little boy, demonstrating what she had learned in elocution courses about using the voice as a subtle instrument. "The voice means everything to me," Beatty said later, explaining why he spent hours on the telephone. "I enjoy it . . . I respect text, facts and so on but I'm really interested in sub-text — nuance and inflection. That's what you get on the phone."[375]

The telephone also provided the illusion of intimacy without actually having to be in anyone else's company. Idell Simms believed that Warren went out with other girls in addition to Ann for the same reason he chose steady girlfriends who were not interested in getting married: to guard against genuine emotional intimacy. "He had a lot of girlfriends. Warren was a ladies' man. He wasn't, really, but that's the way it came off."

In Simms's opinion, Warren was wary of revealing himself to one person in a committed relationship because it could expose his vulnerabilities. To appear vulnerable was dangerously close to weakness, his father's curse. "Warren would rather die than show a real emotion," Ann Read later told a

Washington writer, reinforcing their friend Idell Simms's theory.[376] Beatty admitted to this neurosis in one of his first interviews, before *Splendor in the Grass* came out. "The hardest thing in the world is to show your real self . . . expose real emotions. It's painful."[377]

This was arguably the reason he needed the "emotional release" he got from playing the piano, or from singing. Despite his popularity, Warren in high school was essentially a loner who valued his privacy. "He doesn't like probing," appraised his Arlington pal Art Eberdt. "He never has liked it. He doesn't respond well to that. In fact, he just shuts up. He can play mental games with you if he wanted to."

Throughout high school, Beaty continued to express himself, and his emotions, through the piano. In later years, he was oddly self-deprecating when he talked about his playing, saying, "I never practiced; I'd just picked up enough facility to get away with a simple rendition of 'Tea for Two.'"[378]

"Warren was a magnificent pianist," a close friend from his junior year, Charlotte Kehart, refuted. "He was a serious young man and a good student." Beatty's habitually harsh assessment of his piano skills goes beyond modesty; it carries the unmistakable echo of his father, Ira.

Art Eberdt characterized Warren as "gifted" on the piano, a belief shared by Eberdt's wife, Carolyn, who was a sophomore at Washington-Lee when Ebert and Beaty were seniors. "He was a natural — he'd hear something and then he'd sit down and he would play it by ear."[379] Carolyn Eberdt was especially impressed by how kind Warren Beaty was. "He was friendly to everyone, even us tenth graders. At lunch, he'd eat with us . . . there was something warm and nice about him."

According to Tom Calhoun, there was something that Warren found interesting in everyone. "He was very genuine," in his quarterback friend's words. "He had a sweetness." This was the same endearing quality that Warren demonstrated from the time he was a small child, and one that would characterize him throughout his life. "He'd never demean anybody," continued Eberdt. "Actually, I never heard him criticize anybody."

Conversely, Warren Beaty had a risqué streak bordering on the inappropriate, what his friend Tom Calhoun called his "outrageous" side. "But I think he was careful about the setting. For example, when we were going around in a group, he would drop by a friend's house and the friend's mother would be there. Warren might seize her in his arms and throw her on the couch and pretend to start making love to her. But he was very careful about which mother he chose, and he never attempted it with my mother, who would've passed out or perhaps died. So I think he did a little calculation be-fore he did some of these stunts. But he was known for these stunts."

Beaty's "stunts" generally seemed to be of a sexual nature, in Calhoun's retelling. "I can remember him in the high school cafeteria, seated at a big table — and he usually had a number of girls around — and just to be outra-geous, if he had a peanut butter and jelly sandwich, Warren might turn it vertically and open it and start licking it in a very sexually suggestive way. And of course I was mortified, and of course the girls were sort of giggling dangerously. Or if someone bit down on a banana in his presence, he might scream out in agony and bend over . . . but at least he would do it in a place where it wouldn't necessarily get him into trouble."

These flashes of inappropriate, aggressive, or unwelcome sexual behavior would surface in a more disturbing way a few times after Warren Beatty be-came a movie star. This paradox in the otherwise sweet-natured Beatty may have been a backlash from the Baptist moral code he followed in his youth. "In the fifties when I was a kid," he said once, "I was walking around in a mode of behavior that related to centuries of Protestant repression. Every cell and fiber around you was influenced by religious upbringings of the past. It was a very puritanical time and I didn't act out in the way that I should have."[380]

In its milder form in high school, Warren's acting out was a continuation of his clownish behavior, humor that was "out of the box," as Eberdt called it, citing as an example the inscription Warren wrote in Eberdt's yearbook, ". . . you are pregnant with potentialities."[381] The quarterback found this as-pect of Warren amusing. "I enjoyed his humor. It wasn't straight humor — he would say different things, weird things, funny things." Mike Durfee, a top student, pronounced Beaty a "supreme wit."

In mid-November of Warren's junior year, Shirley wrote to her closest friend from high school to report the end of her engagement to the graduate student at Columbia University who opposed her career. "He was of Euro-pean background and his morals were not the same as Shirley's — in other words, he thought it perfectly all right to have an affair — Shirley thought not. She called it off."[382]

There was another reason, undisclosed in MacLaine's letter: his name was Steve Parker — or at least that was the name he used; his real name, ac-cording to church records, was William F. Parker, one of the many deceits surrounding the smooth thirty-two-year-old who had swept into nineteen-year-old Shirley's life a few months before and taken control.[383]

They met by happenstance when Shirley and a dancer with a small part in *Me and Juliet*, Lorraine Havercroft, stopped for a hamburger at the Theater Bar, across from the Majestic, where Steve Parker chose to have a drink that night.[384] As Parker, a divorced acquaintance whom Havercroft described as a "go-getter type and opportunist," strolled past her, she introduced him to the teenaged Shirley MacLaine. Parker, a part-time actor with "visions of being a producer, director, and doing big things in the theater," as Havercroft characterized him, was handsome in the slick style of con men and gamblers, with wavy graying hair and a small dark moustache that looked as if it had been drawn with a pencil.[385]

Lorraine invited Parker to sit down, "so he sat across from Shirley and he was absolutely taken by her. She was doing the goofiest stuff you could ever imagine — putting the fork in her nose, and a pencil in her ear, and making faces, and laughing. She had a wonderful laugh. And he thought this was the cutest thing he'd ever seen."

Their introduction electrified both Shirley MacLaine, who felt what she called a "shock of destiny" that she "*had* to marry him," and Steve Parker, "who had a fascination with her," said Havercroft, "and thought, 'Wow — this girl could do something in the theater.'"[386] After Parker escorted Shirley home, he returned to knock on Havercroft's door, a visit he denied to a jealous MacLaine, even though the encounter was innocent, according to Havercroft. "The reason he came back," said Havercroft, "is he wanted to know more about her, he was so enthralled." Parker's lie caused a rift between Shirley and Havercroft, the first deceit in a trail of betrayals.

By December 10, 1953, less than a month after her letter to Dottie Rector to announce the breakup with her student fiancé, Shirley MacLaine the chorus girl was scheduled for a screen test for a United Artists movie, under the influence of her new and ambitious fast-talking thirty-something swain.[387]

"Steve" Parker's qualifications for his role as Svengali to MacLaine — like the stories he told about his past — were an embroidery of lies, half-truths, and fantasy as phony as his first name. Parker claimed to be the son of an American diplomat (or an engineer) and said that he was brought up in Siam (or in Japan, a country that fascinated him); he identified himself as an orphan at fifteen and boasted that he had served as a paratrooper in World War II.[388] Any detail that happened to be true was accidental.

His show business credentials in 1953 were tissue-paper thin. Parker's acting credits were from army information films, a few television programs, and in mostly Shakespearean off-Broadway plays.[389] When he bumped into Havercroft and MacLaine,[390] he was living at the Lambs Club, occasionally staging their shows; at the time, he was directing *The Devil and Daniel Webster.*[391]

What William Frederick Parker did have going for him was a shrewd intellect, and the ability to lie convincingly. As Havercroft described him, "He was probably an entrepreneur type, probably had a mind that was a little bit circuitous. He probably could do well being a trickster or doing fraud stuff." These were qualities that would serve him well launching the show business career of Shirley MacLaine.

Shirley was flattered by Steve Parker's interest, and attracted to his suave good looks and apparent worldliness. More powerfully, she was magnetically drawn to his confidence and to his unwavering belief that her talent and his razzle-dazzle could make her a star — traits that were painfully absent in her father, Ira.

Within a month of their meeting, the thirty-two-year-old Parker proposed to the nineteen-year-old MacLaine, a turn of events that propelled Ira and Kathlyn Beaty to New York City, where Lorraine Havercroft was eyewitness to a backstage drama.[392]

"I do remember, when it all came out quite rapidly that Steve and Shirley were going to get married, that 'Mom and Dad' — and it's very possible that Warren was tagging along with them, I'm not sure — but there they were in the hallway on the second floor of the Majestic Theater in their hat and coat. As soon as they found out, they came roaring up from Virginia to try and save their poor child. You know, she was only eighteen [*sic*]. I remember all this very clearly. I know the mom had a big fur coat on, and the dad with his hat — almost as if they sort of burst through the doors, right past the stage manager, and dragged their kid out of the show — that kind of an attitude."

Someone enlisted the aid of Pastor John Raymond — most likely Kathlyn, possibly Warren — which illustrates the depth of the family's concern about Parker.[393] "My husband actually went to New York," Raymond's widow recalled. "He, at the time, was the assistant pastor with responsibility to youth, and so he took that responsibility seriously and followed up with the youth in the church. But Shirley was not interested."

The Beatys nonetheless succeeded in blocking MacLaine's immediate plans to marry Parker. The showdown was intensely painful for the family —

Warren included, as time would tell. "Steve was the enemy for the parents," declared Havercroft, who had a hazy memory of Shirley's brother in the hall at the Majestic when the battle over Parker occurred. "I kind of see a little figure lurking in the background, kind of going, 'Duh . . . what is all this?'"

By comparison, the complications in Warren's love life the last semester of his junior year seemed as evanescent as bubbles blown through plastic wands at children's birthday parties. Nancy Dussault spent the month of February at Northwestern wondering why he hadn't answered her letters and knitting him a pair of socks for his seventeenth birthday, which the elusive Warren would only tell her was in March.[394]

A few weeks later, when Shirley turned twenty, Steve Parker persuaded her to try out for a new musical choreographed by Bob Fosse called *7½ Cents* — later retitled *The Pajama Game*. Shirley decided to double audition, both for the chorus and for the understudy to lead actress Carol Haney, a smoky-voiced singer and exceptional dancer with a distinctive little boy's haircut.[395] "I had to fight like the devil to become understudy," recalled the competitive MacLaine.[396] To increase her chances, she chopped off her Rita Hayworth waves to look more like Haney. MacLaine's new pixie hairdo, which she later would famously claim to style with an eggbeater, suited her impish humor and would come to be considered Shirley MacLaine's "look."

While his driven older sister made the newspapers in Arlington and Front Royal that April and May — she had been chosen for the chorus *and* as Carol Haney's understudy in a new Broadway musical — Warren campaigned to be elected president of the student council, an office that would be assumed in the fall, his senior year at Washington-Lee.[397] When he lost after an intense competition with his friend Mike Durfee — whose campaign slogan "I Like Mike" was patterned after Eisenhower's "I Like Ike" the year before — Beaty conferred with Pastor John Raymond, a follower of politics.[398]

The defeat was a blow to Warren, the legacy of being Ira Beaty's son.[399] "I have trouble walking away from things if I haven't succeeded," he later confessed.[400]

THE PAJAMA GAME, with Shirley in the chorus, opened on Broadway on Thursday, May 13, 1954, to sensational reviews — for the musical and for Carol Haney, which the canny Parker had predicted. The pleasure was muted for MacLaine. After a lifetime of dance lessons and ferocious ambition, she felt invisible as one of the nameless dancers in a chorus line. With Parker encouraging her, she decided to try out for *Can-Can*, where she thought she had a better chance of being noticed.[401]

Less than a week later, on a Wednesday evening, she arrived at the theater to dance in the chorus of *Pajama Game* depressed and a few minutes late, due to a tie-up on the subway.[402] In a moment that MacLaine described later as happening "only in cornball plots," the frantic stage manager pushed her into wardrobe and told her to get onstage to replace Carol Haney, who had injured her ankle that afternoon when she slipped during the matinee.[403] Haney would be out of the show for a month.

Shirley, who had rehearsed the star role only once, even though she was Haney's understudy, quickly phoned Parker, who sped to the theater to critique her performance.[404] It was an inspired one, from the very first big jazz number, *Steam Heat*, when MacLaine dropped her black derby hat during the complicated choreography and blurted out, "Oh, shit!"[405] The audience, who had hissed and booed when it was announced before the curtain went up that an understudy would be replacing Haney, gave Shirley MacLaine a roaring ovation when the curtain went down.[406] MacLaine felt oddly lonely as she stood on the stage in triumph, saying later, "I had worked for this moment since I was two."[407]

Immediately after the show, Shirley asked everyone in the cast of *The Pajama Game* to sign their autographs on a paper towel. She gave the souvenir to her mother, as a symbol of the dreams Kathlyn MacLean put aside for her family and that Shirley MacLaine had dedicated her life to fulfill.[408]

In the fable of what happened next, a fiction that MacLaine herself has floated, Hollywood producer Hal Wallis, a seeker of talent who would title his autobiography *Starmaker*, "happened" to be in the audience that Wednesday to observe Carol Haney, but instead saw her understudy, Shirley MacLaine, and instantly signed her to a movie contract.[409]

In truth, Shirley MacLaine's legendary "big break" may owe as much to Steve Parker's savvy as to serendipity. Contrary to the MacLaine myth, Hal Wallis was not in the audience on that fateful first night that Shirley stepped in for the disabled Carol Haney.[410] Parker *was* there, making detailed notes on how to improve his girlfriend's high-profile performance for the several weeks she would be replacing Haney.[411] The aggressive Parker coached Shirley on her lines five nights in a row until six A.M., set up appointments for her to meet producers and agents, and gave away tickets to producers so they would see his fiancée in the starring role.[412]

Hal Wallis, a former production head at Warner Brothers and the force behind myriad films, including *Casablanca*, showed up to see *The Pajama Game* on what MacLaine most frequently identifies as the *third* night she substituted for Haney.[413] In all likelihood, Wallis was there by the hustle of Steve Parker. "I've wondered that myself," observed Lorraine Havercroft, Parker and MacLaine's inadvertent matchmaker. "I do know that he was bringing people in, because he was that entrepreneur type person, and he knew something good—Shirley was unique and different. People did ask that question. Nobody really knew what the answer was."*

MacLaine's talent, however, was uncontrived. Wallis found her electrifying, an "instant star."[414] After the last number, the producer went backstage to talk to her. He recalled, "She got very excited, but was shrewd enough to arrange for me to meet her later with her manager, Steve Parker."[415] Wallis, MacLaine, and Parker convened at the Oak Room of the Plaza Hotel at midnight. By the time Wallis paid the check, he had offered Shirley MacLaine a movie contract contingent upon a screen test.[416] As he explained, "She had a nice, pleasant face, a little like the sad, mobile faces of great clowns. She showed a nice figure and a winning offbeat personality."[417]

While Wallis made arrangements for the screen test, Shirley asked her parents to come to New York that June to sign the tentative contract, since she was still a minor.[418] Warren, who was on summer vacation after his junior year, went along to see his sister in *The Pajama Game*.[419] It had been ten years since Mansell MacLean had taken the family to *Oklahoma!* The fact that his sister was now starring in a Broadway musical stirred Warren's deepest emotions. "I just thought she was wonderful."[420]

By their separate descriptions of that summer visit, Warren, his sister, and Steve Parker revealed how painfully insecure Shirley MacLaine was about her talent—the lingering effect of Ira Beaty's disparaging comments, which had been meant to protect her and Warren from his own disappointments.

As Beatty recalled, "The realization seemed to come to her in that show that she was more interesting than her techniques as a dancer, about which she had always had a lot of anxieties."[421] Steve Parker, who quickly deduced

---

*MacLaine told the *Saturday Evening Post* seven years later that Wallis wanted to leave the theater shortly after he sat down, "but a friend of his, Bob Goldstein, who was with him, persuaded him to stay . . . and said to him, 'Maybe this kid is good. Let's watch her for awhile.'" Her revealing postscript suggests that if Parker did not solicit Hal Wallis directly to come to the show, he may have prearranged it with Goldstein.

the family dynamic after meeting Shirley, said later that she sometimes had "terrible illusions of inadequacy."[422]

The underlying source of MacLaine's feeling of inadequacy was dramatized for Parker before the Beatys left New York, when Shirley approached her father to sign the contract with Hal Wallis's production company. Ira balked, concerned that his daughter was even less prepared to succeed in Hollywood as an actress than she had been as a dancer. Parker continued his big push to make Shirley a star. "Steve would tell my father, 'Listen, this kid shouldn't dance, she can act. Let her try it.'"[423]

Seventeen-year-old Warren witnessed with anxiety another battle of wills between his sister and father over the brash Steve Parker. Like her son, Kathlyn Beaty was too reserved to make a scene; internally, she was churning with concern over Shirley's much older, divorced boyfriend, whose tenacity seemed crass and opportunistic to the refined Canadian. Ira was more volatile. As MacLaine recalled, "My father and Steve had a terrible argument one night because dad didn't want Steve to encourage me in something he thought I would fail at. He said, 'She's a dancer only, and that's all. Let her do just that and not make her unhappy by putting ideas into her head.'"[424] Ira Beaty's attitude only fueled his daughter's ambition to act. "I was filled with the success drive," said MacLaine. "But that was because I really felt I didn't have any talent."[425]

Ultimately, Ira signed the contract, but the family left New York that June deeply distressed by thirty-three-year-old Parker's control and influence over Shirley, who was barely twenty.[426] Still, despite the most recent altercation with his sister's hard-sell boyfriend, Warren returned to Arlington in a burst of enthusiasm as he prepared to start his senior year in high school. "He was excited to death about Shirley's hit with *The Pajama Game*," said his friend Charlotte Kehart. "He had to come tell us — those of us who were involved in that kind of stuff — he had to come tell us!"

Things soon would take a very different turn.

18 *After seeing his older sister in the star-*
ring role in a Broadway musical, Warren Beaty accelerated his high school regimen of overachievement. He spent the rest of the summer of 1954 in training for varsity football, basketball, and track, becoming what he later

called "hyperathletic," the path he had chosen for a success distinct from Shirley's, despite feelings about football that could be charitably described as love-hate.[427]

Shirley MacLaine's budding fame was well known at Washington-Lee and in the Beatys' neighborhood in Arlington, where she was now viewed as a star. Warren said nothing to his friends then about wanting to become an actor. He was still in apparent denial, worried he would seem effeminate or as "copying" his sister.

Ira Beaty was excited by his daughter's big break on Broadway, which he reported to his pals at George Mason Green Realty. It was obvious to Mason Green, Jr. that Ira was proud of Shirley's achieving the success that had eluded him, despite their clashes over her ambition and Steve Parker — both of which the cautious Baptist considered brazen and believed would cause Shirley great pain. Kathlyn Beaty, who prized the *Pajama Game* autographed paper towel given to her by her daughter, repeatedly told friends at church the story of how Shirley was pushed onstage to replace Carol Haney. "She was thrilled."[428]

The Beatys' acute anxiety about Steve Parker had diminished somewhat by the end of June, when a mended Carol Haney returned to her starring role in the show and Shirley went back to the chorus line. After seeing her screen test, Hal Wallis placed MacLaine under a five-year contract to make two movies a year, but she was not scheduled to begin until December, if Wallis chose to cast her in something. The crisis, for Tat and Ira, had been averted.

Warren started his senior year at Washington-Lee in September 1954 on top of the world. His girlfriend, Ann Read, was the reigning Miss Arlington and had a following in Washington, D.C., nightclubs as a jazz singer with the Chick Reed Quartet. Beaty made the First Team All-Suburban and Second Team All-Northern Virginia in varsity football that fall and decided to try to conquer student politics by running for president of the senior class. It promised to be a golden year in the life of Warren Beaty.

While Warren was carefully preparing his campaign for class president with Pastor John Raymond, his sister made the *New York Times* on September 12 as a result of another freak mishap involving Carol Haney, setting into motion MacLaine's second break-of-a-lifetime — one that would make her a movie star and eventually coax Warren to Hollywood.

MacLaine embroidered the story in later years, saying that director Alfred Hitchcock was in the audience of *The Pajama Game* to consider Carol Haney for a "kooky" movie role on a night when, by chance, Haney was out with laryngitis.[429] Hitchcock, said MacLaine, saw her instead of Haney and cast her in his movie. "It was like a destiny," MacLaine told PBS. "That little angel on my shoulder or something. Really, I feel that way."[430]

MacLaine's retelling of her legend was an embellishment of a story that had several variations from the start. As she told the tale correctly in earlier years, it was someone who worked with Hitchcock—not Hitchcock himself—who saw her perform for Carol Haney when the latter got laryngitis. Shirley described him as a "talent scout" for Hitchcock; journalists identified her mysterious benefactor as Hitchcock producer Herbert Coleman, who either phoned Hitchcock at dinner to rave about MacLaine or sent him a telegram from the matinee, depending upon who was telling the story.

According to MacLaine's dancer friend Lorraine Havercroft, the gossip on Broadway was that Steve Parker had arranged for Hitchcock's producer to see Shirley in the starring role when Haney had laryngitis in September, just as some believed he had set up Hal Wallis to see MacLaine when Haney injured her ankle in May. "Steve got all kinds of people to come see her. He could have been somewhere, or did something. Who knows? But they were there."*

Alfred Hitchcock at the time was casting *The Trouble with Harry*, an off-beat mystery-comedy about a missing corpse, and was looking for a leading lady with "something unusual," as MacLaine described it—"and if that's what he wanted, he got it."[431]

What persuaded Hitchcock to cast MacLaine, by everyone's account, was the "startling" screen test she had made for Wallis, directed by stage veteran Daniel Mann.[432] *Time* magazine would refer to MacLaine's test a few years later as a "classic."[433] *Cosmopolitan* called it "one of the most interesting bits of film in the backstage history of the movies."[434]

For the test, MacLaine, wearing almost no makeup, sat on a stool, dressed in a short sweater, shorts, and long black stockings. As Mann asked her ques-

---

*In May 1956, MacLaine told a magazine that her performance was "bad" the night Haney got laryngitis, "[so] Steve took me home and helped me rehearse all night. I must have been better in the next day's matinee because Alfred Hitchcock's New York representative sent him a telegram that brought him to New York to see me." This account raised the possibility that Parker had invited Hitchcock's producer, Herbert Coleman, to see MacLaine in the matinee. Another version, in a biography of Hitchcock by Donald Spoto, avers that Coleman went to *The Pajama Game* because his daughter asked to see it. Contradicting Spoto, the April 10, 1955, issue of *American Weekly* reported that Coleman saw the play with his coproducer, Doc Ericson, not his daughter.

tions about herself, the camera moved in close on Shirley's expressive face while she answered with disarming candor. The screen test ended in full view of MacLaine dancing, without music, to a few short bits from *The Pajama Game*.

Daniel Mann called the screen test "animal-like" in its naturalness.[435] One journalist wrote, "Old hands at Paramount could not recall a performer since Audrey Hepburn who displayed such virtuosity and casual charm in a first test."[436]

In Hitchcock's assessment, MacLaine was "unique—which belongs to the making of a star, the rare quality we want."[437] Based solely on her screen test, Hitchcock offered Shirley the female lead opposite the handsome John Forsythe in *The Trouble with Harry*. Hal Wallis agreed to loan his pixie-haired contract player—who had never been in a movie—to the famed director, whose crew was already in Vermont preparing to start filming.

MacLaine had less than a few days to determine her fate. On September 16, she accepted Hitchcock's offer to costar in his new movie, and the next day she eloped with Steve Parker.

Over the years, MacLaine would relate that she and Parker were married at the Marble Collegiate Church in New York City after a Wednesday matinee, with Norman Vincent Peale performing their marriage ceremony. According to Marble Collegiate Church archives, Shirley Beaty married William F. Parker on Friday, September 17, 1954, with Reverend J. Franklin Shindell officiating. There was no family recorded in attendance.

MacLaine kept her marriage to the "enemy" a secret from the Beatys for at least several days, notifying them by cable after the fact. When Warren and his parents learned that Shirley had eloped with Steve Parker, they were in shock. Grace Munson, whose parents were close to Tat and Ira and who was a confidante of Warren's girlfriend Ann Read, wrote about the fissure in the Beaty family that fall to her older sister, Mary Lou, Shirley's good friend in Tau Delta:

> Did you know that Shirley Beaty is married to that actor-producer guy? She got married 3 weeks ago. That girl will never know what she's done to her family. They are very upset because they don't like him and she just sent a telegram or something about 2 or 3 days after she was married. Warren has gotten very bitter about the whole thing and I don't think Shirley will ever mean as much to him again.[438]

For Warren, the fact that the sister he loved dearly — his "first crush" — had secretly married a man he and their parents considered destructive and had warned her not to wed was a betrayal of their close sibling bond. Warren's rupture with Shirley over her hurtful elopement with Steve Parker would be at the root of the tension between brother and sister when Beatty first became a movie star, an undercurrent people would speculate about for decades, usually ascribing it to professional jealousy or sibling rivalry. When he was thirty, Beatty "let it be known that some past childhood 'thing' remained between him and his sister," the closest either of them came to revealing the private, and more painful, truth.[439]

Tat was so distressed about her daughter's secret marriage she wrote a letter to Shirley "warning her about her husband," but decided in the end not to mail it. Warren's mother kept the letter in a drawer in her bedroom for forty years, where Shirley would find it in a moment of symbolic significance.[440]

Shirley's decision to marry Steve Parker, one that would bring her heartbreak in addition to alienating her brother, was something she felt she "had" to do, in the same way her mother had told her she felt "compelled" to marry Ira Beaty twenty-three years earlier. Tat's reaction as she rode away from Nova Scotia as a new bride with Ira and Ada Beaty was a shiver of fear. Her daughter responded just as viscerally on her own wedding day. "I nearly fainted during the ceremony," MacLaine said, "because deep down I knew I was doing something I wasn't ready for."[441]

Shirley had passionately contradictory feelings about Parker. She considered him "overly" charming when she met him, saying later that she didn't love him or even *like* him. Yet in her first book, MacLaine wrote about falling in love with Parker immediately, how the world came alive for her when they met.[442] She considered the debonair promoter "very handsome"; Parker also stimulated her mind, giving her books to expand her worldview and providing the endlessly inquisitive MacLaine a human riddle she would never quite be able to solve.

At fifty-six, with the benefit of hindsight and a divorce, MacLaine concluded, "Steve was the great love of my life . . . however, I married a man who I unconsciously knew would never be home, so I wouldn't have the problem of this intimate, cloistered relationship I saw in my own family."[443]

While that may have been true on an unconscious level, Shirley MacLaine in 1954 was not that worldly. She was the very moral daughter of two old-fashioned Baptists, and she thought she was in love. MacLaine would find it hard to believe, in her fifties, that she was "ever that girl of 20 who married far too young, thinking it was forever."[444]

There were practical considerations as well to Shirley's decision to elope. She was still a minor when Hitchcock offered her the female lead in *The Trouble with Harry*; by marrying Steve Parker, she became an adult for legal purposes and could sign the movie contract herself, emancipating her from the control of her more circumspect father. She was also leery of moving to Hollywood alone, if that was where her movie career would take her, and Parker refused to go there with her unless she married him.

Alfred Hitchcock's overnight "discovery" of Shirley MacLaine, the lucky understudy, would be reported in the fifties press as a "Cinderella story," a label that MacLaine, who had been training rigorously as a dancer and on the stage for seventeen years, resented. In this regard, Ira Beaty showed staunch support, setting aside his personal misgivings about Shirley's elopement and the risks of show business to admonish the *Washington Star* for calling his daughter's success a storybook tale. Ira told the reporter that it was a "*sweat* story book tale," pointing out, "There was a lot of work and sweat on Shirley's part over the years."[445]

The month his sister eloped and became a movie star, Warren Beaty's ambition was directed at winning his election for president of the senior class, a "big deal" at Washington-Lee.[446] The race was especially significant to Warren as a way to blot out his defeat for student council president.

Although his football friends said he won "by acclamation," Warren Beaty meticulously choreographed his race for senior class president, campaigning in his class of one thousand like a dark-horse candidate.[447] "That wasn't an easy victory for him," recalled Reverend John Raymond, who was advising him, "but Warren worked on it from the beginning."[448] As Grace Munson said, "I can remember clearly being backed up against the hall with his leaning on me, convincing me that I should vote for him."

Munson found Beaty's behavior unappealing and egotistical, an opinion shared by a few others, including the senior class sponsor, who considered Warren "cocky."[449]

The young Warren Beaty was aware of the possible distancing effect of his popularity, good looks, and intelligence, and the impact it might have on his winning the election, John Raymond disclosed later. "Warren was worried that there would be a certain amount of resentment that he was too popular, so he decided that the way to counter that was to run a campaign in which he looked a bit inept."[450]

The Baptist minister assisted Warren, although Beaty — exhibiting the behavior that would define him as a movie star and as a filmmaker — had his own unique ideas, and he wanted to be in control.* "What Warren chose to do," said Bert Thurber, who heard the story from Pastor Raymond, "is he created this speech in which he literally planned and practiced being an inept speaker, being awkward, being a little shy. I don't remember John using the word *stammer*, but the notion of stumbling over his words and so forth — he certainly said that Warren planned that, and practiced that, and did that."

"It was interesting to see how he worked it," Raymond said a few years after helping Beaty with the campaign speech. "He not only wrote a serious speech but he was also very shrewd — if that's the right word — to plan certain faux pas and deliberate pauses and the inclusion of phrases such as, 'What I meant to say was —.' In other words, he strove to make this very planned speech a natural-sounding affair."[451]

What was even more fascinating was that the rehearsed pauses and practiced fumbling were the same ways Warren stumbled and hesitated to find the right words in everyday conversation. Art Eberdt, who was class president their sophomore year, felt that Warren "liked the drama" associated with politics and speeches, "but he wasn't as gifted as some of them were to be spontaneous in impromptu speeches. He hesitates, he draws his speech out, measuring his words." Warren's cleverly orchestrated faux pas in his campaign speech may have been an artful way to conceal this weakness as well as evoke sympathy from less popular classmates.

"According to John it worked beautifully," said Bert Thurber. "Warren got up there and he sort of hemmed and hawed, and acted awkward, and the kids felt really sympathetic for him and to him, and they supported him, and he won . . . John said that Warren was particularly effective in winning the sympathy of the girls. The girls just felt sort of sorry for him, and they just soaked it up."

His minister mentor's last public comment on Warren's speech was revealing: "I guess you could say that it was his first true performance as an actor." As Thurber was to observe, "I've often thought when I saw the way Warren played *Bonnie and Clyde* — sort of this inept Clyde Barrow in that

---

*Pastor Raymond was eager to help Beaty because he was fond of him and, "as I understood it," recalled friend Bert Thurber, "John thought it was good for the Church to demonstrate that Christian kids, Baptist kids, could be every bit as successful as any other kid, and so he wanted them to be winning student government elections."

early section, where he's awkward and fumbling and so forth — I often in my mind imagine that that must be somewhat the way he played the role of running for senior class president."

As a young movie star, Beatty would be quoted as saying he won the race for senior class president through "politics, all politics — just go around like a cheerful hypocrite."[452] Although he later denied calling himself a cheerful hypocrite, his high school campaign introduced Warren to an aspect of politics he found distasteful, because of his family predisposition for telling the truth.[453] The notion of "politicians shaking hands and saying, 'Good to see you'" struck him as a form of hypocrisy since no one could feel that way about everybody they met all the time.[454] Beatty believed this entry-level hypocrisy hinted at other promises politicians would not keep, a concern that would emerge as a theme in several of his movies, especially *Shampoo*, and later, *Bulworth*.

BY THANKSGIVING of Warren's senior year, his sister had made an almost complete break from the past. Shirley had finished *The Trouble with Harry*, and she and Steve Parker were living in a tiny beachfront apartment in Malibu waiting for Hal Wallis to cast her in a movie. MacLaine's relations with her family were strained, according to Tat and Ira Beaty's church friend Betty Hawthorne. "They kept that wedding, and that marriage, kind of in the background . . . they didn't have too much to say about it."

Shirley sent a Christmas card from "Mr. and Mrs. Steve Parker" to her loyal Arlington friend Dottie Rector, writing that she was "very happy." But there were tremors in the foundation of her marriage after only a few months. As Parker told *Look* magazine later, "I didn't want to be Mrs. Shirley MacLaine and I began thinking about putting my knowledge of Japan and my knowledge of show business together."[455]

Shirley showed poignant signs of missing her family that betrayed how young she was. "On her birthday, she always wanted her mother to send her a present," recalled Hawthorne. "Her mother told me. She said, 'It doesn't matter what it is, she just wants a present from me.'"

Warren experienced the first flush of vicarious fame from having a sister who was a Hollywood star in January, when *Look* magazine pictured Shirley on a full page with actor James Dean as one of the "bright new stars of 1955."[456] A few weeks later, when actress Betty Grable tore a ligament, MacLaine was asked to replace her in a dance number on a CBS variety show called *Shower of Stars,* airing live on February 17, 1955 — the public's first glimpse of Shirley MacLaine on camera.

A proud Ira Beaty wrote to Julia Mildred Harper, the Richmond ballet teacher Tat chose for three-year-old Shirley after she started to shriek for attention when Warren was born. Ira's handwritten note, in an angular script with flourishes resembling Warren's, shows how much he admired his daughter's talent — though Shirley felt only his criticism and caution.

"You predicted that [Shirley] would be a success as a dancer — and how right you were!" Ira Beaty wrote to Julia Harper. He mentioned that Shirley had taken a stage name and proudly informed her first ballet teacher that his daughter had been offered "several movie deals" when she filled in for Carol Haney on Broadway. "Mrs. Beaty and I felt that you ought to know what you started!"[457]

By the time Warren turned eighteen, on March 30, 1955, his older sister was a full-fledged celebrity. Two weeks earlier, after a dazzling debut on CBS dancing for the injured Betty Grable, *Life* magazine published a pictorial on her called "Shirley On Way Up," winking at her success via "other dancers' misfortunes" and including a photo of MacLaine, with a mink draped over one shoulder, in intense conversation with her "manager" husband, Steve Parker.[458] She had started filming her second movie, *Artists and Models,* starring the popular comedy team of Dean Martin and Jerry Lewis.

His sister's success was a heady brew to a high school senior like Warren, as his friend Idell Simms recalled. "She was just enough older that she was a little bit out of his league, a little bit out of his world — but then I think that influenced him."

One of the last movies Warren and Shirley saw together in their brother-sister tradition was the first Dean Martin and Jerry Lewis comedy, *My Friend Irma,* in 1949, the year Warren started junior high and Shirley enrolled at Washington-Lee. When the second Martin-Lewis picture came out later that year, Shirley and Warren "drove our parents crazy by cupping our hands and screeching around the house, holding huge invisible grapefruits the way we had seen Dean and Jerry do it."[459]

Shirley's skyrocketing career during Warren's senior year in high school demonstrated to him that show business was not just a pipe dream, as their father Ira had forewarned, and may even have whispered to his subconscious that he and his sister were destined for greatness — as his encouraging mother inculcated in him and Shirley from earliest childhood.

After he became a movie star, Beatty would maintain that he was never in a high school play, but he was in two of them his senior year, after Hal Wallis put his sister under contract and Hitchcock cast her in a film.[460] Warren played a trial attorney in the first production, costarring his friend Art Eberdt as a judge. Photos taken of the play show a surprisingly beefy Warren with a mild case of teenage acne as the prosecuting attorney, questioning a peroxide-blond classmate in the witness chair as Eberdt, the judge, observes from the bench.

In later years, Eberdt would forget the name of the play but remember that Warren "always tried, even in these plays, to do really well. And when you try too hard you overdo it—and now and again he would. We had a couple of very gifted actors who sort of stole the show from all of us. Warren and I had the long lines and all of that, but this goofy guy, Roy Kennedy, was just a naturally funny person. Warren wasn't spontaneously funny and neither was I, but this guy was." Eberdt pronounced Warren, as an actor, "about as good as I was, which was fair."

In fact, Warren's heart lay elsewhere. Like his daddy, his true passion was music. The depth of that passion, like all things important to Beatty, he kept private, as his teammate Tom Calhoun discovered when they attended an Arthur Rubenstein concert at Constitution Hall. "I do remember being slightly shocked when after the performance, Warren talked about how Rubenstein 'missed a few notes but that it was a fine performance,' and myself saying, 'Who are you to say?' But then as I read more about Rubenstein, including his autobiography, I realized that he did miss notes and didn't care." As Calhoun recalled, "Warren said Horowitz was the better pianist, Rubenstein was the better musician." Beaty's personal favorite was the great black jazz pianist Erroll Garner, whose style he imitated.

Warren occasionally had a beer or two on his nights on the town in Washington, D.C., with Calhoun, though when he did, he was extremely responsible. He once spent the night sharing Calhoun's double bed rather than drive home. "I don't remember either of us really getting drunk, but he, I guess, thought he did that night. I can never remember Warren drunk." As Eberdt would comment, "His father was an alcoholic. Warren went the other way. His dad was wide open, wild, and all over the place."

One of Beatty's most admirable traits, throughout adolescence and after, was the respectful way he treated his disappointed, occasionally eruptive father, even though they had no relationship. "He was always a dutiful son,"

Tom Calhoun observed of Warren. "I don't think he was ever on the outs with his family at all."

That May, Shirley wrote to Arlington friends that she was learning comedy at Paramount "from the boys," Dean Martin and Jerry Lewis, while Warren assumed center stage during Class Night at Washington-Lee, starring in a spoof written by classmates that mirrored his future as if it could be seen through a crystal ball. He was cast as a producer named J. J. Cinema; his girlfriend Ann Read played Lola Ginabrgeewhiz, a starlet in the curvaceous mold of Gina Lollabrigida; and Warren's close football chum Tom Bransford portrayed an agent. As an actor-producer in Hollywood, Warren Beatty would follow this pattern for forty years, costarring in films with a succession of actress girl-friends, then his actress wife, and casting his friends in supporting roles.

As an eighteen-year-old playing J. J. Cinema on Class Night, Warren was extremely nervous backstage, harshly critical of himself after being upstaged in his first play by a classmate who got more laughs. The competitive Warren, who was emceeing, "almost went over the top a little bit," said his first girlfriend, who recalled a few risqué jokes, "but he had a flair."[461]

Kathlyn Beaty, who attended the spoof, persisted in her unwavering belief in her son's manifest talents, convinced now that Warren would become a performer, as she predicted when he first walked across a stage at age five under her theatrical direction. She told a Washington reporter, later, that when she saw Warren's performance on Class Night, "I knew he had that touch of genius."[462]

A week later, Warren took Ann Read to the senior prom, the last formal appearance of the dream team. After Beatty became famous, Read was quoted in a tabloid saying that they ended their relationship because "he told me the only reason he would marry would be to have a child—and that would be to satisfy his ego," a quote Read told her daughter, later, was a "misstatement."[463]

"Ann would probably have never married him," observed Idell Simms. The consensus among their circle was that Ann, who had a career as a singer, though she eventually married and had two children, was "too much like Warren" for them to remain a couple. "She never got the one break that would have taken her to the top," mused Grace Munson. ". . . Ann was just a wonderful, marvelous person. I'm not sure if Warren was as wonderful as she was. And I don't think it has anything to do with him breaking her heart."

Tom Calhoun asked Warren at the time what qualities attracted him to a woman. "They had to really fascinate him. It had to be someone pretty special—it could be beauty or something else, but it had to be well above the norm." His true aphrodisiac, as Calhoun figured out, was *talent*—in men or in women.

Beatty guarded his more sacred beliefs, including his deep respect for his Baptist mentor, John Raymond. When he first became a movie star and was famous for dating glamorous actresses Joan Collins and Natalie Wood, Beatty would be quoted as saying that the "underpaid, overworked, harassed minister" was the most successful man he ever knew.[464] Raymond thought as highly of Warren Beatty to his last days, according to his widow, Mary. "He always kept up with what was going on in Warren's life."

A few years after Warren left Arlington and began acting, John Raymond married for the first time, later in life, to a woman younger than him. It would be a happy marriage, and he would have four children. Warren Beatty would marry late in life, too, at fifty-four, to a woman substantially younger than him. It would be a happy marriage, and Beatty would have four children.

AS SENIOR CLASS PRESIDENT, Warren Beaty delivered the invocation at his high school commencement on June 10, 1955—arriving late, for effect. His difficulty in deciding what to do after graduation reflected the embarrassment of riches his genes, and his hard work, had bestowed on him, exemplified by his senior yearbook superlative "Best All Around," the goal he had set for himself in junior high.

The second Henry Warren Beaty lived up to his family name, receiving a prize at graduation from the George Mason chapter of the Sons of the American Revolution for excelling in honor, service, courage, leadership, and scholarship.

Beatty said later that he was offered ten college football scholarships that spring. Three were listed in the school newspaper: four years' tuition from the University of Virginia, four years' tuition from George Washington University, one year at Bullis Preparatory School. In the end, Warren turned them all down. "We talked about that," recalled quarterback Art Eberdt, who accepted a football scholarship to Duke. "We debated and debated and debated. And he decided no."

Warren Beaty's reasoning revealed who he had become at eighteen. He rejected football because it was too violent, because failure was not an option

("I developed into a fair player . . . but never would have been as successful in college football as they seem to think I would have been"), and because he did not want to pursue something unless it made him happy ("I just didn't enjoy football that much — the most important thing is a certain joy in doing something just because you enjoy doing it").[465] All derived from his parents' influence.

Warren spent long hours in deep conversation with his friend Charlotte Kehart's father that spring, debating what he should make of himself. "My father was an admiral in the navy, so Warren would come and talk to him about professions and things — what he should do when he grew up." Kehart's father was also a friend of Warren's successful uncle Mansell MacLean, whose photos in stage performances at Acadia Warren strongly resembled. Beaty told Charlotte's father he was torn between music and law. He decided, finally, to follow his uncle Mansell's lead, possibly influenced by Charlotte's father. "Warren went to college with the intention of becoming a lawyer," recalled Kehart.

He chose Northwestern University, in Illinois, where Nancy Dussault was beginning her junior year as a voice major, still enraptured with Warren. "I assumed he was going to Northwestern, which had a theater department, and because Nancy was there," said Warren's friend Tom Calhoun, "but Warren told me that it was not that clear to him at the time."

When he was in his fifties, Warren Beatty told a group of students at Oxford that he went to Northwestern to study law "while trying to conceal the darker reality that I wanted to go into the theater."[466]

19 *At eighteen, Warren Beaty must have* had an inkling that he would never be a lawyer, because the summer before his freshman year at Northwestern, he pleaded for a part-time job from the manager of the National Theatre in Washington, D.C., further evidence to his close friends that he was "enamored with the stage back then."[467]

After he was famous, Beatty liked to describe his summer job at the theater as being a "rat-catcher," a title that began as a joke when the manager of the National teased him that they could use someone to stand in the alley outside the performers' stage door and fend off rats with a broom.[468] Warren accepted the position chasing away rats, a sardonic metaphor for his future career in Hollywood, as he later acknowledged wittily, saying, "I never saw any rats — except, that is, on stage."[469]

His summer as a "rat-catcher" became part of Beatty's show business biography, though it was more hyperbole, and Warren's self-deprecating humor, than an actual job description. Art Eberdt, who had done construction with Warren the previous two summers to build up their muscles for football, recalled him working at the National Theatre as an usher. "Because he invited me down there. He said he would sneak me in."

Actress Helen Hayes, who performed in *The Skin of Our Teeth* at the National in July of 1955, had fond remembrances of young Warren long after that scorching summer, a fact that would delight Beatty, who showed a similar affection at eighteen for the white-haired legend of the stage as he had felt for his theatrical grandmother MacLean when he was a boy of three. "Did she remember me?" he once asked a reporter who mentioned that Hayes had reminisced about Warren's summer as an usher. "Isn't she wonderful? But I wasn't an usher. I was a rat-catcher. I was hired to make sure no rats went on stage during a performance."[470]

His actual title that season, as he defined it later on his résumé, was secretary, a job that included errands and opening theater mail. Besides endearing himself backstage to Helen Hayes, eighteen-year-old Warren struck up an astute friendship with legendary theatrical director George Abbott, then nearing seventy. Among copious credits, Abbott wrote and directed *The Pajama Game* and *Me and Juliet*, the two Broadway musicals in which Shirley was in the chorus, and Abbott had made the arrangements for Hayes's play at the National. Warren was mature enough to appreciate the elderly Abbott's genius, and canny enough to assess his value as a mentor. "Now there's an interview," he said later of Abbott.

In his recurring role as a protégé, Warren sought career counsel from George Abbott that July. Based on Abbott's response, Warren was already considering acting before he enrolled at Northwestern. "I remember talking to [Abbott] at the time. I'd been offered some football scholarships. He said, 'That's right, go back to school. Your sister might make it by not going to school, but you better not try.' That sweet man, offering me words of advice."[471]

Warren's flirtation with his sister's bold choice to bypass college ended, for the moment, with his questioning of Abbott. Like his prudent father, he enrolled as a university freshman, despite yearnings to perform. Though he "vaguely intended to go into law and then politics," Beaty's decision to enter the highly regarded Speech Department at Northwestern in Illinois that fall — in the footsteps of Nancy Dussault, Ann-Margret, Charlton Heston, Patricia Neal, Paul Newman, and others — exposed the "darker reality" that his inclination was to pursue the theater like his maternal grandmother, mother, uncle, two aunts, and sister.[472]

Within a few days, Warren became extremely close to a football player on the freshman team from Ohio named Andy Cvercko, who lived on the same floor in his dormitory, McCullough Hall. Cvercko, a brawny tackle who would make First Team Academic All-American at Northwestern in 1958, First Team All-American in 1959, and turn pro, was an accomplished athlete and student in the mold of Beaty's friends on the Washington-Lee football team. "Warren and I pretty much hung out together all the time most of that year. Then when it came down to rushing the fraternity, we went to most of the rush parties together and we had talked about pledging the same fraternity; however, he liked Sigma Chi better than Delt, but we still remained friends."[473]

Beaty dithered about whether to play football after he met Cvercko and almost joined the team as a walk-on, "but one look at some of the behemoths they had out there and that wasn't what he wanted," as he told Tom Calhoun, his teammate from high school. Beatty said later, "I stopped playing football. I was in the process of consigning myself to a more effete way of life."[474]

If that effete life meant the theater, Warren envisioned himself as a writer, or a stage director like his mother Kathlyn — some profession in the arts with a degree of stature, which was how he viewed his pedigree, according to Cvercko.[475] "His parents [had been] faculty members at a university . . . and Warren was well educated in literature and the arts. He was very literary, and that had an influence on me. We were both serious about academics."

Beaty talked to his pal Cvercko about trying to find a way to combine law with theater, possibly working for the Screen Actors Guild, like actor Ronald Reagan. He discussed his intent to study law with a Sigma Chi friend, Sargent Hoopes, who noted, "Anything [Warren] did at that time, he was serious about."[476]

Though he was drawn to theater and felt a sense of moral responsibility to pursue politics or law, Warren Beaty's first love was still the piano. "He was usually entertaining everybody," said Cvercko. "At all the rush parties, he would sit down and start playing and everybody would gather around and start singing." When Shirley MacLaine was interviewed for *Photoplay* that fall as "Hollywood's Newest Find," she told the reporter that her little brother was "trying to decide between being a jazz musician or a lawyer."[477]

BEFORE HE ARRIVED at Northwestern, Beaty had already acquired a female following. "Nancy Dussault was talking a lot about this great guy who was coming—he was a football star, he was handsome and everything," recalled Eleanor Wood, a petite and pretty cheerleader three years ahead of Beaty in the speech department.[478] "Somehow we connected. I don't remember how, exactly. I was in a sorority, and he would come to the sorority house to play the piano—he was really good, it sort of sounded like Erroll Garner."

In a replica of his first year in high school, Beaty started dating Kappa Kappa Gamma Ellie Wood almost immediately, and the popular senior cheerleader was his girlfriend the rest of the year, "virtually the only freshman heard of to do that," noted a fellow Sigma Chi.[479] "Warren wasn't a kid, in a way," observed Wood. "He was very mature, and he had a lot of—just magnetism . . . he was quite a flirt. He would always hug all the other girls in my sorority, but why not? He was just beautiful. He was everything Nancy said—and more." The mannerisms Warren had been exhibiting since junior high, consciously or unconsciously—mannerisms that would define his movie star persona—he employed to full effect with Ellie Wood, beginning with shy pauses between words "and his eye blinks—yeah, he had all that charm."

Andy Cvercko described Beaty as an occasional "party animal," but his drinking was *de minimis* per Cvercko, and in the observation of Sigma Chi Sargent Hoopes, "Warren was *controlled*. We did a lot of partying. We'd hit the bars in Chicago, where the music was." Even in bars, with his fraternity brothers, Beaty behaved like a courtly Virginian, "very polite, overly polite," said Hoopes. "He was just a gentleman in his mannerisms and everything, and all the women loved him." Warren, his fraternity brother noticed, "liked the older girls."

Beaty seldom mentioned his sister, now a Hollywood and Broadway star, either to Ellie Wood or to his fraternity friends ("He wasn't the type to brag," said one Sigma Chi), but he dropped Shirley's name during rush week with uncharacteristic braggadocio.[480] A Northwestern classmate who was later in a campus variety show with Beaty recalled, "He came through rush week and he said, 'I'm Warren Beaty, Shirley MacLaine's brother,' and I would say, 'I'm Dennis Marlas, Jim Marlas's brother.'" Marlas did not find this offensive. "He was a kid, you know? He might have been proud of his sister or something."[481]

In fact, the ultraprivate Beaty rarely mentioned to anyone else at Northwestern that his sister was actress Shirley MacLaine. The exception was his close friend Andy Cvercko, with whom Warren shared his secret desire to act. "He mentioned he had a sister who was in Hollywood and he told me he was going to be an actor." Beaty also told Cvercko he had this in mind when he turned down football scholarships to attend Northwestern. "He chose Northwestern primarily because of the speech school, the theater school. That was his primary goal and objective the whole time."

Warren's hidden agenda to follow his sister into acting took on a greater, and more glamorous, urgency in October when Shirley's first movie, *The Trouble with Harry*, began playing near campus. A few days before, MacLaine started her third film, *Around the World in 80 Days*. One of her costars was Warren's childhood idol Charles Boyer, the sophisticate he imitated at six with Shirley in the Beaty living room in a top hat and with a French accent.

He was excited by Shirley's career, according to Cvercko. "At that time, he talked about his sister a lot. I knew that they were communicating some, because he knew what was going on, and he knew what movies she was going to be in." Warren made it clear to his friend that he intended to be a *movie* star. "He was a very serious student, but his primary goal was always theater, and specifically movies. That's all he talked about."

Beaty concealed his dream from his girlfriend Ellie and even from Nancy Dussault, who described it as a "strange year" for Warren. "I knew that he wasn't very interested in college, but he would never tell me exactly what he was interested in. He certainly didn't mention acting."[482]

Beaty's covertness went beyond privacy; by his later statements, he kept to himself his plan to become an actor in case he failed. "No one in their right mind sets out to be a movie star," he said twenty years later, sounding like Ira, "because it seems like a capricious gamble to take."[483] In addition, at a virile eighteen, Warren still had misgivings about actors being perceived as "pansies," saying it was a "stupid way for a man to make a living."[484]

Moreover, he was aware of the frustration his sister was facing in Hollywood under contract to Hal Wallis, which MacLaine had come to view as indentured servitude; she wanted to choose her own films and extricate herself from Wallis's "ownership" under financial terms she deemed unfair.[485] Shirley also effectively had been abandoned by Steve Parker, who went to

Japan to start a production company using her celebrity as his entrée, and showed little interest in returning to California or to Shirley—the kind of emotional pain and duplicity that her parents, and Warren, had anticipated from Parker before she eloped. MacLaine chose to stay the course with her absent husband, "because I don't like to make promises that I can't keep," and for the illusion of emotional security.[486]

During this period, Shirley began seeing a psychotherapist, as Warren would after he moved to Hollywood. "I did it for a lot of reasons," said MacLaine. "I wanted to know more about *me*. I was subject to depression, and the adjustment to success wasn't easy."[487]

A week after his sister's first film came out, the movie version of *Oklahoma!* was released, an event with enormous emotional resonance for Warren—the musical was the first Broadway play he had seen, the revival was Shirley's first professional job in a chorus, and the songs had both inspired Warren through adolescence and provided a release from the stress of his parents' arguments. "I went to see it about a dozen times," Beatty recalled.[488]

As the year progressed, Warren inched closer toward the arts. He sat in on a few drama classes taught by Alvina Krause, the doyenne of Northwestern's theater department, and he appeared in the play *Under Milk Wood* with his girlfriend, Ellie Wood.[489] Their relationship was serious enough that Beaty spent Easter break at Wood's parents' house in Maysville, Kentucky.

A photo of Beaty with Ellie Wood posing at a Sigma Chi formal that spring sparkles with the glamour of Montgomery Clift and Elizabeth Taylor in *A Place in the Sun*, the film that had inspired Beatty to become a movie star. Wood's bare shoulders shimmer above a flouncy fifties party dress, and her short dark hair resembles Taylor's as she smiles with the satisfaction of being the prettiest girl in the room. Warren is in a white dinner jacket, his hands nonchalantly in his pockets as he beams at the camera, radiating confidence, charisma, and the optimism of youth.

Decades later, Beatty would tell Ellie Wood that their college romance reminded him of the love story between his character and Natalie Wood's in *Splendor in the Grass*, "because we never really consummated our love." According to Ellie, she and Warren were sexual innocents: "It's unheard of in this day and age!" Beatty later confirmed that he was still a virgin then: the influence of his Baptist morals and his belief that he would marry the first woman with whom he had sex "seemed at the time the only way out of giving in to a completely unmanageable id."[490]

In the final weeks of his spring semester at Northwestern, several things happened to Warren Beaty that would have an immediate and permanent effect on his life. "I remember he talked about the possibility of coming out for football, even though he didn't have a scholarship," said Andy Cvercko. Warren debated whether to try out for the team during spring training, "but I can date when I went from the physically threatening to the theater," he said later.[491] As Beatty told the story, the catalyst was his close friend Cvercko:

> I came back to the freshman dorm and a friend of mine, who went on to become an all-pro tackle, was drunk, and he was throwing up into one of the urinals in the bathroom, and they came and got me and said, "You have to come in here; you're the only person he can talk to." I walked in and saw the urinal he had thrown up into. I remember seeing a couple of Brussels sprouts and what looked like a lamb chop . . . I said to myself, "You know, this is a different stomach. My stomach is not like this. I don't think I have the right one for football," and I never went back.[492]

Beaty remained close to Cvercko afterward and said nothing about what had happened, or that he had decided never to play football again, but to become an actor. "I didn't realize it had such a profound effect on him," Cvercko reflected. "Gee, just think — he could've been a football star."*

Beaty ended his year at Northwestern onstage in the annual Waa-Mu variety show, a student production "considered a Broadway show — it was huge," said a member of the men's chorus from that spring.[493] Nancy Dussault was the featured performer in the Waa-Mu Silver Jubilee Show of 1956. Warren Beaty appeared in two musical numbers, both with intimations of his future, similar to his Washington-Lee Class Night performance as J. J. Cinema.

One of his production numbers was a solo, a rarity for a freshman. Beaty dressed as an Indian chief in full-feathered headdress and war paint to sing "The Wigwam Wooing of Wigawama," backed by a line of college showgirls. The number ended with Warren, arms outstretched, belting his song like his vaudevillian parents and maternal grandmother in summer stock. His other musical number was as one of a male trio of politicians. The still-husky Beaty

---

*Cvercko made All-American the next two years at Northwestern under coach Ara Parseghian and, after graduating with a degree in engineering, went on to play offensive line for the Green Bay Packers, coached by the legendary Vince Lombardi.

suited up like a Texan, bursting out of a black shirt, beige sport coat, and ten-gallon Stetson, clenching a cigar between his teeth, and holding a placard that read, VOTE FOR ME. He and his fellow politicians sang a song, with appropriate foreshadowing for Warren, called "We Kiss All the Girls."

Ira and Kathlyn Beaty came up from Virginia to see the show, and Ellie Wood's parents drove up to Chicago from Kentucky. "We were all sitting in a hotel room together before the show, so I got to meet Warren's mom and dad," recalled Wood, who also performed in the Waa-Mu musical. "I remember his mom as being very shy, extremely shy, soft spoken — and the dad a cigar-smoking, bigger-than-life kind of guy."

Karen Skadberg, a showgirl in Beaty's solo as the Indian chief, remembered seeing Shirley MacLaine backstage after a performance, when Warren "very proudly introduced her . . . I don't think I knew until that point that Warren Beaty was her brother."[494]

MacLaine was four months pregnant, an unplanned event that had occurred while she was filming *Around the World in 80 Days* in Japan at Christmastime. She had barely seen Steve Parker since then — a painful separation for her, alone in Hollywood expecting their first child while Parker set up production, and a separate life, in Tokyo. "Divorce or death are final — clean-cut," she said later, "but I honestly believe that the state of suspension — of waiting — is the hardest of all to live with . . . the complete aloneness was frightening."[495] For Warren and his parents, their prophecy about Parker was being realized.

Shortly before summer, Warren contracted an illness that his fraternity brother Sargent Hoopes and his Arlington friend Tom Calhoun recalled as mononucleosis, and Cvercko thought was "a serious flu." Beaty lost a significant amount of weight and, according to Calhoun, ate raw-egg milkshakes trying "to bulk up" — the beginning of his raised consciousness about the effects of diet on one's health.

When Warren said his farewells for the summer to his roommate, varsity tennis player Vandy Christie,* and to his friend and confidant Andy Cvercko, "he was planning to come back to Northwestern," said Cvercko.

Early that summer, Shirley's closest friend from high school, Dottie Rector, got an unexpected call from Warren, who was playing cocktail piano at a sleek, slate-blue bar in Washington, D.C. Dottie, who had been in frequent touch with Shirley through her rise in show business, had not seen Warren

---

*Carlisle "Vandy" Christie died in 1992.

since he was in junior high. Rector encountered Warren Beaty at nineteen at a pivotal crossroad — possibly *the* pivotal crossroad — of his life.

"He looked me up because he was puzzled about what to do. He didn't know whether to go back to school. He was into music. He really liked playing the piano, and he had of course taken drama at Northwestern . . . he was perplexed about whether to go on into theater, or movies, if he should just go for it then — into show business — or go back to school."[496]

Dottie, who was home from college for the summer, was surprised that Warren had sought her advice. "I mean it was quite a compliment, and I certainly did adore Shirley, there's no doubt about that — we seemed to be on the same wavelength . . . and Warren knew that I wanted very much to go into theater, but he also knew the restrictions I had with my Victorian mother. So he would come by and pick me up, and we would go riding, and just talk . . . he just wanted to talk about the decisions he had to make."

Beatty said later that he found Northwestern "slovenly and lackadaisical," that his classes did not excite him — but he clearly was torn at the idea of dropping out of college.[497] "He was moody and perplexed," described Rector, who went to the club several times to hear Warren play piano. "He couldn't decide; he was really tossing it around."

Warren Beaty's chief concern about going into show business was that he would be perceived as either imitating his sister or capitalizing on her fame. "That was puzzling him," said Rector. "He felt he did not want to follow in her footsteps, and he was afraid of the main thing: that of course they'd be associated as brother and sister. He wanted to make it on his own. That was very important to him."

Beaty's struggle that summer had to do with more than art versus law; he was wrestling with his conscience, knowing that his ultimate decision would involve the acceptance, or rejection, of the life and values his father lived, a life that Warren had dutifully assumed, since childhood, he would replicate.

Dottie Rector was impressed, that June, with the way Shirley's scrawny little brother had grown up. "Oh, he was very handsome, very handsome, and he was sweet, and he was a nice person. We laughed, and of course we talked about Shirley a lot, but he really talked about himself, what he was trying to accomplish, and how he would do it, and whether he should go back to school . . . because he really hadn't made up his mind. He was thoughtful, and asked probing questions. I just told Warren to go for it, if that's what he wanted. And I certainly believed in his talent."

Beaty decided to spend the rest of the summer in New York and explore the possibilities, one of the few decisions he would make in his life partially on impulse. "I let intuition guide me . . . I didn't say to myself, 'I'm going to New York to be an actor.' I just knew I had certain needs—one was to get the hell out of school. I just drifted into New York . . . I could have gone to Phoenix."[498]

In typical understatement, Beatty later would describe his concerned parents as "skeptical" about his pilgrimage to New York. "They knew where Shirley was going," as Rector observed, "but I think that Warren was more of a surprise to them."

It was the decision that would change his life's course, one that defied everything his timorous father represented. "I suddenly got tired of conforming," Beatty said later. "Why do it? I asked myself. Why? I just quit and came to New York."[499]

Ironically, he would credit Tat and Ira with empowering him to seek his bliss in the great unknown, saying, "I think that that decision comes largely from the confidence, the sense of identity that is given to you in your upbringing, in your home, in the people around you, and your own ego strength."[500]

The significant difference in Warren's and Shirley's views of their parents at the time each departed Virginia was one of perception. Shirley had spent her childhood dancing frantically to get Kathlyn and Ira Beaty's attention after her brother was born, while Warren basked in the knowledge that he was absolutely adored by Tat—lending credence to Freud's axiom that a man who has been his mother's darling keeps for life the feeling of a conqueror.

20 *Warren Beaty, the good son, was to* define his wayward arrival in New York in the summer of 1956, at age nineteen, as the moment when he became his own man, "the moment when you have to say, 'Gee, I probably shouldn't do this, but I am going to do it anyway.'" He compared it to "the story of the little lion who grows up in a cage and finally he's strong enough to tear the cage apart but he doesn't know it."[501]

He told the *Washington Star* a year later that his parents were "most willing" to support him, but he wanted to go it on his own, the fierce route through the jungle initiated by his fearless sister.[502] Unlike Shirley, who had flung herself headlong into the fray, the methodical Warren began his summer of experimentation where the Beatys spent their first summer in New York, at Byron Estates, his uncle Mansell MacLean's mansion outside the city, in Larchmont — "until I found my way about."[503] Warren felt the same sense of awe alone in Manhattan at nineteen as he had from his first glimpse of Times Square with his family at seven. "New York enervated me — it seemed to be a lot to cope with at first, but I was excited about it."[504]

Beaty's handsome prototype MacLean uncle helped to launch the next generation of sibling thespians by offering Warren a job to make ends meet while he explored his options.[505] Mansell MacLean's company, MacLean-Grove, had been awarded a contract to build the third tube of the Lincoln Tunnel, in Manhattan, and Mansell hired his nephew as a construction worker. For decades after he became famous, Warren Beatty's stint as a "sandhog" digging tunnels under the Hudson River would show up as a curiosity in his show business résumé. "It was terribly boring work, and that's no pun," he said afterward.[506]

While he worked construction for his uncle, Beaty vacillated about his future. He told friends what he really wanted to do was play piano, like jazz maestro Erroll Garner, a dream he seemed to consider out of reach. "If I had really put myself into playing the piano, I think I would have been a professional," Beatty said five years later, describing himself as "pretty talented, but . . . sloppy."[507]

The fact that Warren degraded his skill as a pianist was understandable, considering the severe standards by which his father judged musicians. Ira Beaty's hypercritical attitude was probably the result in part of being tutored at the Peabody Conservatory of Music by Otto Ortmann, whose rigid approach to playing the piano included measuring the hands for proper placement of the fingers on the keys, a yardstick by which Warren inevitably would consider his playing "sloppy." The more profound reason was his father's voice inside his head, rehashing the fear of failure *he* had had at nineteen debating whether to pursue a career as a violinist.

At the same time, Warren continued to struggle with his conflicting feelings about acting. After he made his first film, Beatty told a columnist, "I never wanted to be anything else but an actor . . . I wanted to act so much that after one year at Northwestern University I went to New York."[508]At other times he said the opposite, usually suggesting he had wanted to be a director. "I never really intended to become an actor," he remarked in a long, insightful interview in 1972. "I don't know how it really began. I wanted to be around the theater, direct or whatever."[509] He has also said, "I don't particularly *like* acting."[510]

Part of Beatty's ambivalence could be traced to his concern at five that joining his sister's ballet class in Richmond would make him a "sissy," the same anxiety he felt about acting once he had reached junior high, when he decided to try out for football. One of the roots of this homophobia may have been Warren's sister, who has said, "There's something missing in a man who's an actor," and who expressed disdain for any man who "has a mirror out all the time . . . that sort of man, ooooh — forget it! . . . I like a man to dominate me anyway. I can't stand a man who doesn't dominate me."[511]

Beaty also was still grappling with his conscience. He felt the sting of disapproval from his cultured parents, who thought acting was an "unstable and not very dignified" profession for a male, an attitude reflected in the names that Tat and Ira chose for their daughter and son: Shirley, for Shirley Temple; Henry Warren, for Warren's Baptist great-grandfather, a name suited to a lawyer, not a movie star.[512] Even though Kathlyn had groomed Warren for the stage, and her brother Mansell had performed at Acadia, the distinction was that although the MacLean family was associated with the *theater*, Mansell MacLean had become a successful engineer and respected attorney.

His parents' and the MacLean influence was evident in Warren, who later told *Time* he originally wanted to write for the theater or be a "stage director — that was legitimate!"[513] He chose to alight in New York, he was to say, "because I thought that was the foundation of the theater."[514]

Warren Beatty's most revealing anxiety about acting was his admission, in his twenties: "I was afraid of it — I still am."[515] This fear was at the core of his cover-ups, denials, and circumlocutions about whether he wanted to be an actor. "I didn't know who I was or what was inside of me. I was always interested in the theater, but I'd shoved it aside for everything else . . . it's hard to explain — but I knew I was good. I had to prove that."[516]

As he so often would, Warren had a secret plan that summer, tucked away from prying eyes, to save face if he did not succeed. His covert mission was to be accepted as an acting student by Stella Adler, the famed New York drama teacher who was the mentor to Marlon Brando, the moody and magnetic star trained in the Method, an acting technique based on the teachings of Russian director Konstantin Stanislavsky. Adler, an imperious, highly theatrical former actress, was a contemporary of Kathlyn's from a family of respected Yiddish stage actors. She studied in Paris with the legendary Stanislavsky, whose technique she believed was based on an actor's ability to create *truth* in his performance by using imagination. After he was a movie star, Beatty confessed his strategy of trying to meet and impress Stella Adler to a French journalist and later revealed that he had put aside part of his wages as a sandhog to pay for Adler's class in case he found an entrée.[517]

His gravitational pull toward acting was the natural evolution of Warren's childhood perception that he, like Stella Adler, belonged to a family of actors — the theory that the MacLeans were the Canadian Redgraves, postulated by his sister Shirley. As Beatty said soon after, "My mother taught acting, and I guess it was just there."[518]

Being introspective, Warren also recognized that "a person can't be encouraged to go into an art form — people become actors because of a need within themselves."[519] Beatty declined to name *his* emotional need to perform, though he later provided a clue that the origins were in his and Shirley's home life, saying, "Two actors in one family — takes a lot of neurosis to produce that!"[520]

As the summer progressed, Warren began to enjoy himself in New York.[521] He wrote letters to Cvercko about his experiences, anticipating their reunion at college in the fall. Then his plans changed abruptly. "I got a letter from him," as Cvercko recalled, "and he said that he was not going to return to Northwestern, that he had been introduced to a well-known theater coach." How Beaty met Stella Adler is unclear, but it was not through his sister. According to MacLaine, Warren never asked for her help or even advice. "I could understand that," she said years later. "It isn't easy, especially if you're ambitious, to live in the shadow of a sister who had made it first."[522] At the time though, Shirley, who was only twenty-two, found her little brother's distancing from her perplexing.

Beatty's later version was that his career was born that summer on impulse. "It just happened, and I knew that it was right. I remember that I just decided that I wasn't going back to Northwestern; that I would stay in New York. Now whether or not that was a good decision, it's certainly been a profitable one . . . all the really best things I've just done instinctively, and I can't tell you why or how."[523]

This interpretation belied Warren's carefully thought-out strategem to meet Stella Adler that summer and persuade her to invite him to study with her in New York. He revealed as much in a letter to his pal Cvercko. "What swung the deal for Warren was that this well-known acting coach decided to coach him, and that made his decision. Apparently she pretty much chose who she wanted to work with, and he said that she agreed to take him on and to teach him, so he decided to stay there and never came back to school."

Nineteen-year-old Warren, who had a special touch with women of a certain age, charmed Stella Adler, a still-flirtatious, honey-blond fifty-five-year-old who was known to show favoritism to attractive, young male students, as she had with Brando.[524] As Beatty later said slyly, "She liked me. A lot."[525] He ascribed Adler's fancying him to a lucky break, saying she "convinced me that I couldn't make a mistake. She seemed to convince Brando of that too. . . . but she was very good for a young male ego and enabled me to start."[526]

In future years, a comparison would be drawn between Marlon Brando's early career path and Warren Beatty's, beginning with Warren becoming Stella Adler's pet, as Brando had been.[527] This gave rise to the possibility that Warren, the master strategist, had used Brando's trajectory to fame as a blueprint for his own. Whether that was true or not, his friendship with Adler would be the first in a series of profound relationships with older women cast in the mold of the special bond he had as a child with his maternal grandmother.

Beaty's decision to quit college that summer created a schism with his mother and father, who were expecting him to return to Northwestern. Decades later, as a successful actor-director-producer-writer, Warren Beatty would say, "I think it was easier for me to drop out of Northwestern than if I had come from a family which had no education. I think my father secretly admired it. He was happy that I would 'do' something. My father spent so much of his life thinking, that he would never have encouraged me to stay in school."[528]

In the moment, however, Tat and Ira Beaty, whose adult lives had been dedicated to education, and to their children, were devastated by Warren's decision to drop out of school. Beatty said in his twenties, "It's been traumatic for my mother and father to have raised two kids who have become successful in a way-out profession."[529] A close friend in Manhattan noted in a letter written in 1957 that Warren went home to Virginia only once during his first two years in New York, evidence of the strain with his parents.[530]

Warren Beaty's struggle to make this choice stemmed from the fact that he was doing more than choosing a profession; he was rejecting a way of life. His decision to study with Stella Adler was the first step on a path leading him far from Virginia — and the Beaty-MacLean Baptist values of his youth — into temptation.

Enfant Terrible

*"No matter what the reason behind your 'troubles,'
you are well on the way to becoming a large mess,
albeit in the eyes of the world you are
an enormous success."*

A PIECE OF THE ACTION
Clifford Odets's unfinished play about Warren Beatty, 1962

Warren Beatty circa 1961, after he filmed *Splendor in the Grass*.

21 *A different Warren Beaty would* emerge after he quit Northwestern to study acting with Stella Adler. He moved out of his uncle Mansell and aunt Maisie MacLean's Larchmont estate and into a rooming house on Ninety-ninth Street in New York City, renting one tiny room from a "classic Jewish mother" and living "day to day" until classes began in the fall.[1] "I had a furnished room," he would recall. "It cost me thirteen dollars a week. The bathroom was in the hall."[2]

At the end of August, Warren became an uncle for the only time, under circumstances that validated his and the Beatys' antipathy for Shirley's husband. Even through the last stages of MacLaine's pregnancy, Steve Parker remained in Japan, and Shirley had to drive herself to St. John's Hospital in Santa Monica when she went into labor, checking out three days after she gave birth in order to return to work.[3]

Warren's niece was called Stephanie Sachiko Parker, a name that would become a symbol of Beaty's brother-in-law's deceit. Shirley had chosen "Stephanie" as a feminine form of "Stephen," which she believed to be Steve Parker's first name; it was actually William.[4] *Sachiko* translates into English from Japanese as "happy child," and was the name, Parker told Shirley, of a waif he tried to adopt in "the Orient" in World War II — a story that MacLaine told the press when she announced their daughter's birth.[5] As she was to find out many years later, there was never a war orphan named Sachiko. This was merely one in a skein of lies Parker wove together from the time MacLaine met and married him.

The only thing authentic about the name chosen for the Parker's baby was her ebullient personality. By a miracle, Stephanie Sachiko was a "happy child." Steffi, or Sachi, as she alternately was called, inherited the MacLean/MacLaine Scottish red hair, was fair skinned with a freckled complexion, and had elfin features that were a virtual reproduction of Shirley's — a resemblance that over the next few years would be promoted in cutely staged mother-daughter photos on the covers of magazines such as *Look* and *Life*.

Warren may have gone to California to visit Shirley and his niece that

September, because he later told a revealing story set in what he described as his first trip to Hollywood at nineteen. "I went to the Crescendo. Remember the Crescendo? And there was a lovely big piano. I sat down and started playing, doing my best Erroll Garner imitation. Pretty soon there was a beautiful black woman standing beside me. At first I thought, 'Hey, that's flattering.' Then I looked at her again, and I saw that she was seething, ready to explode. 'You got a lot of nerve, kid,' she said. And I looked around to where she was looking, and there was Garner with a party of people."[6] Beaty's reaction told volumes about his sensitivity to embarrassment or humiliation, another imprint of his father's failures. "I abandoned the piano," he said simply.

With his life's passion eliminated as a serious career choice, Beaty focused his intensity on Stella Adler's acting class, which was delayed until late October because Adler was directing a play.[7] He moved out of the rooming house into what he called a "garret," a cramped, furnished fifth-floor walkup, at 52 West Sixty-eighth Street.[8] The apartment, two rooms vacated by a drug addict that rented for forty-eight dollars a month, was so depressing that Warren refused to let anyone inside.[9] Besides the cheap rent, its chief attraction, to Beaty, was an abandoned beat-up piano, and possibly its location diagonally across from James Dean's old apartment, number 18 — sacred ground to anyone studying with Adler following the Method actor's fatal crash in his Porsche the prior September 30, a few days before the premiere of *Rebel Without a Cause*.[10]

Beaty, who was making thirty dollars a day as a sandhog, stashed his summer wages to pay for Adler's class, which was two hundred fifty dollars a week, surviving on peanut butter in living conditions that were grim.[11] "The apartment was a junk heap, I mean a real junk heap because a junkie had lived there before and the smell was still there. I never unpacked my bags during the whole year I was there. I knew I would get outta there."[12]

Beaty noodled on the cast-off piano in the apartment to relieve his frustrations, as he had when he was living at home in Arlington. When fall approached, he moonlighted as a piano player at a nightclub on Long Island called the Blue Room, which enabled him to get a union card.[13] With self-effacing charm and his inherited complex to degrade himself, he told people he was a "mediocre" pianist playing "honky-tonk cocktail-hour piano," as opposed to the professional pianist he felt unqualified to become.[14]

Sometime that summer or early fall, Beaty lost his virginity, an event that coincided with his decision to reject the life his father led. His first sexual experience, which he was too much of a gentleman to discuss, transformed him from an innocent flirt to a highly sexual man-child with enormous confidence in his power to attract the opposite sex.[15]

This metamorphosis occurred, significantly, while Stella Adler was grooming Beaty to be her protégé, a role that Warren — the cosseted favorite of his mother, grandmother, aunts, and great-aunts — understood and played well. Adler's belief in him "equipped me with a certain amount of arrogance — arrogant self-confidence, I should say — which enabled me to bluff my way through a few sidescrapers."[16]

By a coincidence, Ellie Wood, Beaty's college girlfriend, lived a block away in New York and was studying at the Actors Studio, where Lee Strasberg taught his interpretation of Stanislavsky's method. When she tried to reconnect with Beaty that fall, "he didn't want to have anything to do with me. He was going in a different direction and didn't want to continue a relationship."[17] For Warren, Ellie represented his Protestant past, and he was living in the prodigal present.

A close friend of Beaty's from Stella Adler's studio, Lenn Harten, observed his new swagger with women. After class, Beaty would be standing on the sidewalk talking to Harten, "and Warren would say, 'You see that girl coming down the street? I'm gonna kiss her when she gets here.' At that distance, you couldn't tell if she was fifteen or eighty-five! And they would just melt. They didn't know who he was. They just kinda melted. Warren had that effect on them. He has that certain smile."

After a "puritan" adolescence spent believing he would marry the first girl with whom he was sexually intimate, Warren's decision to lose his virginity and embrace sex without the obligation of marriage was like releasing a genie from a bottle. A friend later described it as a fortuitous awakening. "He suddenly realized he had this gift: to attract women, and that was it. He could never resist using it."[18]

Beaty began his first term of basic technique at the Stella Adler Acting Studio at Lexington and Seventy-seventh Street the end of October 1956, two weeks after the New York premiere of his sister's new movie, *Around the World in 80 Days.*

Warren, who would make a lifelong habit of aligning himself with the masters, considered Adler "the greatest teacher of them all," impressed by her past associations with Stanislavsky and with the left-wing Group Theatre, where she had starred, to great acclaim, in Clifford Odets's masterpiece *Awake and Sing!*[19] Beatty later told Odets's biographer that as a young man in New York, he "idolized" Clifford Odets — an actor who became a leftist playwright and was known for his affairs with beautiful and gifted actresses — because he "made poetry where there was no poetry" and "gave the theater a form it didn't have."[20]

Later on, Beatty would maintain that he studied acting with Adler "as a sort of 'in'" to directing in the theater.[21] Directing for the stage appealed to Warren, who grew up watching his mother direct in little theaters, and who saw the stage "as a place to control and manipulate," an understandable desire for the son of an alcoholic.[22]

Once his acting class started, Beaty quit his day job in construction, where his flair for theatrical late arrivals was not appreciated. A MacLean cousin noted, "My father went with Mansell and met Warren when he was working as a sandhog. As a matter of fact, the day that my father went to meet him, Warren had arrived late for work, and Mansell tore a strip off of him."[23] Beatty later said dryly, "I was not what you'd call the world's outstanding sandhog."[24]

To support himself, Beaty picked up a second part-time job as a piano player and lounge singer, working between nine P.M. and four A.M. at a bar owned by Frank Clavin on East Fifty-eighth called the First-Nighter. He described himself as "no Carmen Cavallaro,* just a half-baked piano player."[25] Though Beatty later would tell *Time* magazine it was a "bin," the First-Nighter was a rather chic bar that featured a spinet piano in the center of the room in front of a fireplace, where Warren entertained patrons such as journalist Chet Huntley for a hundred twenty-five dollars a week.[26] "Beatty was a hell of a draw for the seven or eight months he was here," the manager recalled. "He played good piano, he sang fine, and he built up quite a following for himself . . . he was a pleasant guy."[27]

Beaty never mentioned that he was Shirley MacLaine's brother, either at Clavin's bar or to anyone at Stella Adler's studio. "As far as I knew, there was no contact there, and he wanted to do it on his own," said Lenn Harten, one of his first friends at the Studio. The closest Beaty came to mentioning MacLaine occurred when he was looking for an apartment to rent with Harten. "We were going up the stairs of this building, and Warren said, 'My sister used to live next door.' And I says, 'Really, was she in the business?' He

---

*Cavallaro, known as the "Poet of the Piano," had a flashy style imitated by Liberace and was the unseen pianist playing for Tyrone Power in *The Eddie Duchin Story*, released that year.

said, 'Oh, she's a dancer, she lives out in California now.' So that's the only thing I knew about her. I didn't know who it was or anything."[28]

Beaty spent much of his free time while he lived in New York looking at apartments with Harten to replace his "dark, gloomy" hovel on West Sixty-eighth, occasionally accompanied by Mike Ryan and James Tolkan, two other pals from Adler's class interested in sharing a large apartment. "The four of us hung together," explained Harten. At times, Warren became so depressed in his ex-junkie's lair that he stayed with Harten, a sensitive war veteran from Rhode Island.

Their quest for an apartment was complicated by Warren's prerequisite that it come furnished with a piano, his stress reliever. Beaty's increasing intensity was similar to that of millionaire Howard Hughes, Jr., with whom he would develop a fascination. As a producer, Hughes would become so engrossed in a film during postproduction that he would forget to eat, sleep, or change his clothes. "Warren had a great power of concentration, but it would take him away from many other things," recalled Harten. "Some things he would just float out of his mind. We'd be driving along looking for apartments and he would drive right by the street. His mind would be God knows where." Harten would carry on a conversation with himself to see if Beaty was paying attention. "I'd say, 'Yeah, that's right.' Long pause. I say, 'I don't think so. Well *maybe.*' Then he'd come out of it and say, 'Huh?'"

As further evidence of his self-absorption, the inside of Warren's car — an old Chrysler given to him by one of his aunts and known among his friends as "the Tank" or "the Mack Truck" — was full of unpaid parking tickets. "I took the tickets one time," said Harten. "They were green, and I cut them into the shape of Christmas trees at Christmastime and hung them around my apartment." The unpaid parking tickets were also a symbol of Beaty's poverty. He ate Special K for every meal, since he had no money and no kitchen, only a hot plate. He lost weight, and his poor nutrition lowered his resistance to illness.

Warren's focus was on getting ahead in show business, and with women. In both cases, he exuded confidence, possibly because, for him, the two were intertwined. "I think Warren already had it in his brain that he'd be a star," observed Harten, to whom Beaty revealed some of his strategies. "He'd say he never had a problem getting into an office — anybody's office — because he could always get by the receptionist. Warren could get around any gal, believe me, he had a technique. He had a way about him." According to his friend, Beaty loved women, "but he was business, business, business, too." MacLaine said once, "Warren wanted success as much as I did, and I think both of us wanted to prove something to our parents."[29]

Although he had visions of directing, and said that playwright Clifford Odets was his idol, Beaty gave all indications that he wanted to act. His influences were James Dean, the ghostly muse of every acting studio then, and Marlon Brando — or so Beaty told actress Rita Gam, who performed a scene in class with him for Stella Adler to critique.[30] Like Brando, Gam observed, Beaty spoke softly and tended to mumble. His elocution, ironically, was Beaty's Achilles heel as an actor. "Sometimes Warren would talk with his teeth a little close, and some people would say that they weren't hearing it," said a classmate.[31]

Charles Carshon, his sight-reading teacher at Adler's studio, felt that Beaty merely "did okay" in class. "You wouldn't have noticed him — he didn't look a thing like he looked later on, he just didn't have that glamour at all."[32] At nineteen Beaty still had his football crew cut and, unlike other young actors, he never wore jeans. He preferred khaki trousers and white dress shirts in the manner of Howard Hughes. But at Stella Adler's, Warren Beaty's appeal registered with female students, who found him warm, charming, and "tremendously shy . . . this was really the All-American boy . . . Warren was so nice back then."[33] To certain older women, Beaty projected a ravishing sensuality. "I remember some little old lady saying that he could sweep her into bed with his eyelashes any time," recalled Harten. ". . . he just kind of blushed."

His estrangement from his parents, and from Shirley, left Warren lonely in New York, despite his sexual magnetism. When Adler asked the class of 1956 who among them had no place to go for Thanksgiving, Beaty raised his hand.[34] Two of his friends from high school, Idell Simms and Tom Bransford, passed through Manhattan over the holiday and looked him up. He was playing piano at the club, and to Simms it seemed "he very much wanted to be his own person and to make it on his own." MacLaine took her brother's attitude personally, saying she was "being punished for having made it to the top before him."[35]

Kathlyn Beaty, who had encouraged her children's talents in lieu of pursuing her own, took a job the end of the year at the Hecht Company, a department store in Washington, D.C., a decision reflecting her suddenly empty nest. MacLaine, who would see her husband a total of only six weeks out of the next year, spent Christmas of 1956 alone in Malibu with Sachi, now three months old. "True, I could always scream for help in the direction of Arlington," she said afterward. "I knew my parents would help me . . . I guess it's a question of self-discipline." She did not call Warren for emotional support, MacLaine said, because she considered him "preoccupied with himself and being a success . . . he had just decided to be an actor himself. So he had his own problems."[36]

Beaty started the second term at Stella Adler's in February 1957 just as he had the first: trolling for apartments with Lenn Harten, hoping to escape his dingy cave on Sixty-eighth. He had formed a close friendship with a wealthy aspiring actor-singer from his sight-reading class named Mitchell May, whose parents kept a permanent suite at the Blackstone Hotel, mostly for their son's use. It was the site of parties until dawn for selected pals of the big-hearted May, including Warren Beaty.

"We were all very good friends," recalled the late Mitchell May's then fiancée Verne O'Hara, a sophisticated English socialite. "They were sort of guys on the town together, and the other kids were all wealthy, but Warren fit right in. We had a lot of fun; he was very sweet." Beaty's entire dress wardrobe, as O'Hara would remember, consisted of "one black tie and — I've never forgotten this — it must have been about an inch wide. It was the fashion then, and he tied it so often that it spiraled."[37]

Because of his close friendship with her eventual husband, Warren saw Verne O'Hara almost daily for the next three years. O'Hara got to know Warren Beaty as well as anyone could know him then, observing, "Warren's a very strange person. He keeps a lot of stuff to himself."

When Beaty did open up, he confided to O'Hara and Mitch May that he was receiving no financial help from his parents. "I don't think it was there to give," observed O'Hara. "Warren told me that his father was an alcoholic, but an intellectual." Both May and O'Hara understood that Warren was "not terribly friendly" with Shirley and that the problem was personal, not career rivalry. "He thought her relationship with her husband was weird." According to O'Hara, "I don't think it would have occurred to Warren to ask her for help."

Shirley MacLaine had serious concerns of her own. The Parkers' marriage had become the subject of Hollywood gossip, much of it warranted. MacLaine, who resented being deserted by her husband, began attending parties on her own and developed a crush on Daniel Mann, who had directed her memorable first screen test for Hal Wallis and was directing a movie she filmed that March called *Hot Spell*.[38] "I had affairs all during my marriage," MacLaine said later. "It wasn't a sexual commitment between Steve and I at all . . . Steve and I had an open relationship."[39]

Privately, MacLaine was torn apart over Parker's abandonment of a marriage that she, at least, had entered in good faith. She wrote to a friend that spring that she was very lonely because Steve had been in Japan for over a year, of how much she adored Sachi, and her yearnings for another child.[40] Steve Parker's feelings about the relationship were manifested in an autobiographical film he produced a few years later, with MacLaine in the title role, called *My Geisha*, about a movie star whose director husband is overshadowed by her success, so he moves to Japan.

That same March, Beaty's friend Mitch May got an audition for the part of a youth in a fifteen-minute Sunday-morning religious serial on CBS called *Lamp Unto My Feet*. The program had been on the air since 1942, dramatizing simple moral stories with resolutions from the Bible. May chose to perform a scene from a Sinatra film, *The Tender Trap*, for his audition, and he asked Warren to help by reading the other part during his tryout.

Beaty took his friend Mitch's request seriously. "It was the other fellow's audition," observed Lenn Harten, "and Warren worked hard on it. We'd go to this Chinese restaurant over on Broadway, and I used to work with Warren on the lines."

When Mitch May auditioned for *Lamp Unto My Feet* in the middle of March, it was Beaty who caught the eye of the CBS casting director, Liam Dunne, a former newspaperman with the vaguely amusing looks of a character actor — which the elfin Dunne later became, specializing in "doddering old coots."[41] Dunne would be the first in a triumvirate of well-connected homosexuals to champion Warren Beatty's early acting career.

Pamela Ilott, a female pioneer in television and the executive in charge of religious soap operas at CBS, recalled, "The genius — really genius — behind getting Warren a start is Liam Dunne. He was remarkable. He discovered Steve McQueen for a *Lamp Unto My Feet*. All these people — George C. Scott — all of them, all thanks to Liam. He was full of fun; a delightful, delightful person."[42]

Beatty characterized his first professional acting job on *Lamp Unto My Feet* as a "fluke," saying later that he was cast in his friend's role on CBS "to my dismay almost, because I began to work then and didn't really *want* to."[43] (May, a true friend, was pleased for him.) After he became famous, Beatty's stock statement was that he never aspired to act, only to direct. "I was running away from acting," he described it in his thirties.[44]

This may have been slightly disingenuous. Lenn Harten, who studied with Beaty at Adler's studio and considered himself Warren's closest friend then, never heard him express a desire to direct, or write — only to act.

As a further indicator of Beaty's impulse to perform, while studying acting with Adler he paid for singing lessons from a vocal coach named Minnie Rutkoff. "I *know* he would have wanted to do a musical," said his friend Harten. This was not surprising, considering his feelings about *Oklahoma!* Like playing the piano and making love, singing was one of Warren Beaty's private passions.

But the Virginian in Beaty found performing undignified, even unmanly — setting up an internal conflict that was to plague him through most of his career. Even after he starred in *Bonnie and Clyde* and *Shampoo*, Warren Beatty would look back on his first role at CBS and say, "I fell into a job acting, and since then I have been working . . . the truth is that it never occurred to me to be an actor, and sometimes I wonder if it has yet."[45] The opportunity for stardom was another of the temptations that beckoned Warren on his new career path in New York.

It was apropos that Beaty, the once earnest young Baptist, would get his break in show business being cast on a Sunday-morning religious show that began as a Sunday-school program."[46] His official debut as an actor was on Sunday, March 24, 1957, playing an essentially moral eighteen-year-old with a scattered attention span. Lenn Harten wrote a letter the next day mentioning it to his mother, who knew of Beaty through her son's close friendship, with the comment, "Warren did a terrific job, but it was easy, because he's exactly like that himself. You talk to him for five minutes and find out he hasn't heard a word you've said and then says, 'Huh?'"

22   *A week after* Warren *appeared on* Lamp Unto My Feet, the day he turned twenty, he picked up the proofs for his first head shots as an aspiring actor — showing him in profile, with his athlete's brush cut, looking wholesome and appealing.[47] He sent one to John Raymond, his minister-mentor.

Over the next several months, Beaty set about to reinvent himself as a movie star, a process similar to the self-transformation he plotted successfully in junior high. After he got the part at CBS, Beatty said later, "I realized this was some kind of train to latch onto and, at the same time, my sister was becoming a movie star, so it didn't seem so unrealistic to me and I saw the possibility for enormous amounts of money, so I went ahead and did it."[48]

This comported with Verne O'Hara's impressions of Warren as extremely ambitious to act and make money, probably because he was living in near poverty. "It all came about at that time because it was forced to come about," observed Beatty. "I needed money and I wasn't that good a piano player."[49] At twenty, he saw stardom as "a perfect way to make a lot of money."[50]

Becoming a movie star would also allow Beaty to keep pace with his overachieving older sister in the adult version of their sibling game of King of the Mountain. He confessed later in life, "As a young actor I had a need to be rich and famous."[51] Acting in movies matched these goals more closely for him than theater.

He also may have been intimidated by the stage. Beaty, in fact, saw acting as a way to overcome his insecurities about performing, his innate shyness, and his occasionally awkward speech — as "a tool for expressing myself, for becoming more comfortable."[52] Unlike his grandmother and mother, who were serious, highly trained thespians, or his sister, an instinctually gifted actress, the young Warren Beaty was both honest and self-critical enough to recognize his limitations as a performer and to tailor his aspirations accordingly. "I don't think I ever had a great need to be a great actor," he said in his thirties.[53] Of course, being Warren, he would demonstrate ambivalence.

The first step in his transition to stardom was to change the spelling of his last name from "Beaty" to "Beatty." He said later that he added the extra *t* for pronunciation, so people would say "Batey" instead of "Beety," a common mistake.[54] However, a MacLean cousin recalled, "Tat told us he added the second *t* so it would balance in lights. She told us that 'Warren' and 'Beatty' would end up balancing in lights. He wanted it to have the same number of letters."[55]

Warren Beatty — the name of the movie star that Henry Warren Beaty II was creating — emerged in New York in the spring of 1957 to the excitement of an important theater agent named Maynard Morris, who worked for MCA, the premier talent agency, which also happened to represent Shirley MacLaine and had branches on both coasts.*

---

*It was outside Morris's office at MCA in New York where Paul Newman and Joanne Woodward, two other aspiring theater actors he represented, met in 1953 (Gary Arnold, "Acts of Love," *Washington Times*, 29 November 1992).

Maynard Morris may have heard about MacLaine's younger brother through the MCA grapevine, spotted him on *Lamp Unto My Feet*, or been alerted to his looks and talent by the infatuated Stella Adler. Agent Stark Hesseltine, then Morris's assistant, took credit later for discovering Warren Beatty.[56] "Maybe I've just been lucky," Beatty said that June, "but . . . people come to acting schools and watch you work. If you're good they say so and if you're bad they say so."[57] It was also conceivable that Liam Dunne, the CBS casting director taken with Warren in March, had tipped Morris.

However the introduction was made, Maynard Morris became the second admiring and influential homosexual to foster Warren Beatty's career, the first being Dunne. Dunne's and Morris's homosexuality, and Hesseltine's, was understood in show business circles, "though in those days," observed Dunne's CBS colleague Pamela Ilott, "one never talked about it." Eleanor Kilgallen, who worked with Morris at MCA, observed that Beatty was one of Morris's "pigeons," a favorite client who got special treatment. "Those were kind of lean days with Warren; he didn't have a great deal, and Maynard, who was wonderful . . . I think he would take him out to dinner and feed him when he looked like he was hungry."[58]

Beatty, the ex-prankster, derived a little-boy's pleasure from embarrassing the refined and at times prudish Maynard Morris by making off-color remarks. "He would regale us with stories," recalled Eleanor Kilgallen, the well-bred daughter of a respected newsman, James Kilgallen, and the sister of society columnist Dorothy Kilgallen. (Eleanor wore gloves to lunch and "little porkpie hats," according to an industry friend.)[59] "One of his tall tales, which of course stuck in my mind, was that when he really needed the dough, there was a house of ill repute on West Fifty-eighth Street where in the evening he used to play the piano. I remember that because Maynard almost had a heart attack. I think Warren just made it up to shock Maynard!" Neither of them was aware that Beatty played piano at the First-Nighter on Fifty-eighth.

Part of Warren Beatty's new movie-star-in-the-making persona involved the selective use of profanity for scandalous impact, the antithesis of his true nature as a polite Virginian with Southern Baptist convictions. "Maynard was so stunned by him because Warren's language could be quite colorful," Kilgallen went on to say. "He would throw comments into the conversation which would throw Maynard — you'd think he was going to have a coronary. He'd say, 'Oh Warren! Oh Warren! Oh! Oh!' He'd say, 'Eleanor's here,' like

I was some nun or something that Warren shouldn't talk that way. And of course this delighted Warren and he did it all the more."

Beatty would take this language with him to California to try to break into movies, acquiring a reputation as a "Hollywood bad boy." Cy Spurlino, his former Sigma Chi brother at Northwestern, recognized Warren's tactics immediately. "I don't remember how long it lasted, but he was known for really having a foul mouth then, and I can remember thinking about the fact that that really wasn't Warren Beaty. He was doing that to get publicity, so to speak. I mean Warren's a smart guy, and he knew — he had the natural type of thinking to do things that would make him a success in movies."

Morris and Kilgallen both plainly adored Warren, charmed by his boyishness and sweetness, which came through despite his blue language. "The thing I admired so much about him," said Kilgallen, "was it never crossed his mouth who his sister was. He was always Warren, very confident of himself. I think it was Jerry Zeitman on the coast in the *Variety* division of the company who finally tipped us off: 'Don't you know who he is?' Shirley MacLaine was to us, at that time, of course, a big star — she was in the flicks, really making a big impact — but Warren never mentioned that he knew anybody in the theater. Never ever." (Though by a curious synchronicity, two of the people from the movie MacLaine was making at the time, *Hot Spell* — director Daniel Mann and actress Shirley Booth — would play significant roles in her brother's career in the near future.)

Eleanor Kilgallen met Warren Beatty for the first time in the spring of 1957, when Morris, who booked actors for the stage, brought his prize discovery into MCA's Manhattan office for Kilgallen's scrutiny, hoping she could find TV work for him to capitalize on his small first part in *Lamp Unto My Feet*. Kilgallen enlisted the aid of Monique James, her West Coast MCA partner, another well-educated journalist's daughter.

Beatty obliged Morris in his efforts to cast him in television shows through the representation of Kilgallen and Monique James, but as he told a French writer a few years later "it was theater I wanted."[60] Warren's reflexive orientation toward the stage reflected his upbringing by an intellectual father among the theatrical MacLeans, a cultural mind-set that would contribute to his recurring ambivalence about being a movie star. "There was a greater part of me that found some solace in the dignity of this process. There was no area of life that the theater was unable to enter. One could carry intelligence as far as one wanted in the theater, as long as the making of money and the acquisition of fame were not the primary goals."[61]

Kilgallen understood astutely that Warren aspired to be a stage actor because of the theater's prestige, "but I think he always wanted to be a movie star." She described this as "sort of a snob point of view . . . they all want to say they have earned their credentials by going through that process." With Beatty, it was reinforced by his internal conflict over rejecting his family's values for what he considered the more superficial pleasures of stardom.

Warren Beatty burst memorably into the MCA offices with Morris that spring to meet the gracious Kilgallen and the other ladies of the television department, acquiring the nickname the Octopus, "because he loved pretty girls, and we had a pretty girl working with us, Nancy Franklin, who had been an actress before she joined our group — and we always thought Warren had, like, ten arms, because he would wrap himself around you, and it was really quite an experience. He came in to charm the office group, you see — it's just that he would zero in because Nancy was a cute-looking gal . . . Warren was very taken with her and would bat his extra-long eyelashes at her and envelop her in one of his octopus-like embraces."[62]

Nancy Franklin found Beatty's approach too aggressive for her taste, though she considered him "luscious" to look at. "He was on the make for everybody, and I didn't want to fraternize. He was *always* asking me out, kind of in a teasing, charming way, like, 'Oh come on, Nancy. Why won't you?' He was very, very persistent."[63] Franklin finally went to lunch with Beatty a few times at Schraft's, just to let him know she was not interested in him romantically. ("He was very nice after he got off of that.") Beatty's conversations with Franklin suggested he maybe had second thoughts about dropping out of Northwestern. "He talked about football a lot, how much he liked it."

Verne O'Hara was both an eyewitness and an earwitness to Warren Beatty's romantic exploits in those years, since he often stayed with her and Mitch May in their two-bedroom suite at the Blackstone Hotel. "Mitch supported him. He had no money." O'Hara, who was considered an unsuitable fiancée by her future mother-in-law because she was divorced, told a "very funny story" involving May and Beatty. When Mitch May's wealthy parents arrived at the Blackstone unannounced one night, O'Hara quickly switched rooms with Beatty so the disapproving Mays would not find her sharing their son's bedroom. "And they came in, and Warren and Mitch were in bed [together] in the other room. I think his mother went to her grave believing Warren was gay. Not her *son*, but Warren."

O'Hara, who observed Beatty in action, appreciated the irony. She described her suite mate as a "very sexual creature. Warren would call all these girls who didn't have a collective brain between them. He'd get on the phone and talk about sex — you know, he was wooing them, and it was so juvenile as far as I was concerned. I'd come from Europe, and we don't behave like that. He was in his twenties, but he was a teenager."

Although O'Hara had great affection for Beatty, she did not find him physically appealing, because "he mumbled all over the place. I never understood why all these girls were so mad about him. It just used to drive me nuts." She also noticed that Beatty had what O'Hara called "one cross eye," possibly a mild form of a medical condition known as strabismus. Nine years later, Paine Knickerbocker, a San Francisco film reviewer, would criticize the same traits in Beatty, writing: "He is an odd young man to have become a star . . . his voice is often inarticulate, and no one has ever figured out what to do with his head of hair. But perhaps his principal problem is that he suffers from a slight strabismus, so that he cannot look directly into the camera, to furnish that unflinching stare which has marked film heroes since William S. Hart."[64]

Warren was exceedingly aware of his looks and his health, according to O'Hara, making it safe to assume that he, the compulsive analyzer, had diagnosed the cast to his eye and devised ways to ameliorate it, an idea borne out by the fact that the condition diminished.

Beatty's strabismus, if that is the correct diagnosis, had no effect on his ability to stare unflinchingly into a woman's eyes, other than his friend Mitch May's unimpressed fiancée, who saw the results in their communal suite at the Blackstone. ("Oh honey, it was one a night.") None was a serious romance, in O'Hara's observation. "I mean, he wanted one *every night*. Warren concentrated on that more than his career, I would say, and my ex-husband Mitch was right there with him."

Beatty's career ambitions were obvious to others, namely Dick Seff, then a young talent agent at MCA, who observed Warren "sitting on the couch outside in the reception area, day after day, hoping somebody might notice him."[65] According to Nancy Franklin, his MCA crush, Beatty seemed to "know" he would make it, the same self-assurance that struck his actor pal Lenn Harten. That April, when Warner Brothers showed an interest in Beatty, he asked Harten to walk past their corporate offices with him, and when they saw the WB logo for Warner Brothers, "Warren made a joke that he had the same initials," a joke he would repeat, famously, while trying to finance *Bonnie and Clyde*.[66]

Actress Rita Gam, one of Grace Kelly's bridesmaids a year before, who spent four months that winter into spring preparing a scene with Warren to perform in class for Stella Adler, felt that "he had a secret that the rest of us didn't know, and that was that he knew he was going to be a star." Beatty also displayed early directorial talent, according to Gam, who was several months pregnant when he asked her to be his acting partner. Warren selected an emotional husband-wife scene for them to perform from A *Hatful of Rain*, in which the character Rita Gam portrayed was pregnant. "He was smart enough to utilize what was there in a real way, and actually he was directing me all the time . . . I think he was trying to get rid of my sort of upper-class Park Avenue accent, which I think I had at the time, I'm not sure, and get me into sort of blue-collar America. So he had me chew gum, which of course, again, was the director coming out in him . . . he was a really terrific director."

Like Dick Seff at MCA, Gam considered the detail-driven Beatty a "very eager beaver," to the occasional irritation of her then-husband, Viking publisher Thomas Gynzburg. "We went through my whole pregnancy working on the scene . . . and my ex-husband would say, 'When are you going to stop feeding chicken sandwiches to that cowboy and forget about acting? Get rid of him!'"

Beatty's money pressures had become so severe there was a question as to whether he could afford to continue taking classes. As the spring term drew to a close, Stella Adler promised to help him look for a scholarship so he could return for his third term, beginning October 1957, a prospect that looked increasingly dim.

His classmates would recall the scene that Warren Beatty performed with a pregnant Rita Gam late that April as extremely affecting.* Gam herself remembered it as a rare instance when Stella Adler was kind in her comments to Gam. "I love Stella . . . but she was tough."

Adler, a teacher with an artist's mercurial personality, chose to visit her actress temperament on Beatty a few weeks later, when students showed off their acting skills on the last day of the second term. Warren played the piano while Lenn Harten and seven other male pals sang "There Is Nothing Like a Dame" as a salute to Adler.

"Most of us were doing scenes," Harten recalled, "and at the end of the

---

*Curiously, several of them thought Gam and Beatty performed a scene from *Our Town*, not A *Hatful of Rain*.

day, Warren comes on, and he gets up onstage, and he kind of hesitated when he spoke. He says, 'Is it okay if I do a song?'" Beatty had chosen something close to his heart: an elegantly melancholy jazz tune called "Little Girl Blue," from a forties musical by Rodgers and Hart. It was the title song in a debut album that year by Nina Simone, who played piano and and sang soulful jazz in Manhattan nightclubs, where her path and Beatty's may have crossed.

Warren brought a young woman to play piano while he sang the wistful ballad for Adler in front of the class. Its lyrics are about a lonely girl counting raindrops, with a bittersweet last verse that may have reflected how Beatty was feeling, alone and struggling in New York:

> No use old girl
> You might as well surrender
> 'Cause your hopes are getting slender and slender
> Why won't somebody send a tender blue boy
> To cheer up little girl blue

"Warren started singing," recalled Lenn Harten, "and then Stella would stop him right in the middle of it and she'd say, 'No! Do this and that.' And then he'd start again, and she'd say, 'No! You shouldn't be thinking of the *words*' . . . And she got up on this little stage to put across what she was trying to say, and Stella did not have a singing voice, she'd kind of *scream* — and the poor girl at the piano didn't know Stella or how Stella could be, and she scared the *hell* out of the girl."

Beatty, who was sensitive to criticism and mortified by failure, continued valiantly with his tender song, trying to please the tempestuous Adler. According to Harten, "At the end of this thing, Warren says to Stella, 'In other words, don't sing again; is that what you're telling me?'" Adler's reply stayed in the memories of Warren's classmates for years after. "She said, 'Oh, stop bothering me. You should be bothering me with your Shakespeare, not your songs. You're gonna be a big star someday and you're going to bother *everyone*.'"[67]

Stella Adler's words were almost instantly prophetic.

A few weeks later, on the first of June, Beatty went to the J. Walter Thompson advertising agency to read for the lead in a *Kraft Television Theatre* live drama on NBC called "The Curly-Headed Kid." The script was about a young hitchhiker who is saved from being hanged on a murder charge by a crusading, alcoholic columnist who realizes the kid was falsely identified based only on his curly hair. The distinguished character actor

Raymond Massey had been cast as the columnist, and popular teen actress Nancy Malone was playing Massey's daughter, who becomes entranced by the young drifter.

Beatty, who was semiestranged from his parents and sister, said at the time that the role of "a rebel, a vagabond, a kid who went from town to town searching for affection and attention" was a part that "came to me easily."[68] He told his father that Maynard Morris had arranged the audition, but it was Marion Dougherty, a female casting director with a resemblance to Shirley, who chose Warren for the role. Dougherty was undaunted by the fact that Warren Beatty's sole acting experience consisted of a fifteen-minute religious program; she was not even aware that Beatty had studied with Stella Adler. "I knew he was into the Method. All the kids were doing that Brando mumbling, and they thought that was the big thing."[69]

Dougherty had a reputation for spotting unknown young actors with talent and casting them in starring roles, and she had a feeling about Beatty. "He was so gorgeous, he was just darling. I always go by the reading, but it did call for a lovely-looking young man, and he was that."[70] The director, Peter Turgeon, had final approval.

According to Ira Beaty, Shirley overheard a few people at CBS in Hollywood talking about a "hot property in New York named Warren Beatty," said to be close to getting the lead in a Kraft special. She phoned her brother to ask him about it. A few days later, as Ira Beaty told the story, Warren's agent, Maynard Morris — who had no idea who Warren's sister was — warned Beatty that he had almost been replaced in the Kraft drama by "some jerk kid brother of Shirley MacLaine's." Shirley, as their father observed, "must have been trying to pull a few strings" for Warren, "but they've done everything themselves that they had to do."[71]

Within a week, Warren Beatty was cast in "The Curly-Headed Kid" and signed with MCA, news that made its way into the small print of one of the West Coast trade publications, which mentioned that he was Shirley MacLaine's brother.[72] (In another parallel to Marlon Brando, it was Maynard Morris who sent Brando to the audition for *his* first major acting job, as Nels in *I Remember Mama*.[73] Brando was twenty, the same age as Beatty.)

Two of his pals from his eight months at Stella Adler's, Lenn Harten and Mike Ryan, happened to see the piece in the trades mentioning Beatty and were stunned to find out he was related to movie star Shirley MacLaine. That Saturday night, recalled Harten, "We had to meet Warren in front of his apartment to go to a party, and so on the way over to the party — we had planned this—my buddy says to Warren, 'Gee, have you seen that movie *Around the World in 80 Days* yet?' Warren said yes, and Mike said, 'Did you see that dame, the MacLaine broad? Wasn't she something?' And Warren kind of turned red, kind of embarrassed, and he said, 'You guys know, don't you?'"

After being cast as the curly-headed kid, the brush-cut Beatty was instructed to get a permanent wave and to use a curling iron on his hair, a minor indignity for the starring role in a prestigious live *Kraft Television Theatre* production.

Stella Adler's sardonic prophecy that Beatty would "bother everyone" once he was famous began to unfold during rehearsals, when imposing stage veteran Raymond Massey, who was sixty-one, complained that he couldn't hear Warren speak his lines. Nancy Malone, the ingenue who was playing Massey's daughter and Beatty's girlfriend, kept Warren from getting fired:

> I was the hot kid in television, like the Sarah Jessica Parker of that era, only younger, sixteen, and Warren was the cutest thing I'd ever seen in my whole life. I went mad for him.
>
> Long story short, Warren was mumbling and fumbling, and Raymond Massey was hard of hearing, and he had a problem hearing Warren and understanding him . . . well Warren didn't know anything about technique, and I would go and say something to him, kind of sotto voce—"Lean back because the camera really can't get Mr. Massey," and blah, blah, blah. And Massey was getting angrier, and angrier, and angrier at Warren: one, because he couldn't hear him, and he didn't hear his cues, and two, because Warren kept blocking the shot.
>
> . . . Massey, if memory serves correct, went to the J. Walter Thompson people, who were the advertising agency who put the show on, and complained about him. So I—being fearless—went and said, to the effect, "He stays."[74]

Neither Beatty nor the casting director, Marion Dougherty, knew at the time that Nancy Malone had intervened to prevent Warren from being replaced the week of rehearsals, though as Dougherty recalled of an earlier discovery, "Once, the director on another show called me and said, 'I want to get rid of this kid' after the first day of rehearsal, and I had him come in to talk to me — and that was Jimmy Dean."

According to Harten, who helped Beatty prepare for the role and audio-taped the final broadcast for him, Massey was as much at fault. [Warren] said Raymond Massey couldn't remember his lines so they were feeding them to him through the earpiece, and it was live, so it messed up the timing. Warren was a wreck, because it was his first real big show and he was the star, but he was the unknown."

Years later, Beatty took the blame in good humor. "It was my first big job, and I was the kid, and I didn't know what I was doing, and they couldn't understand a word I was saying, because I was running around mumbling, and stumbling, and I thought that was acting."[75]

The Thursday morning of the live NBC broadcast, June 26, 1957, the *Washington Star* ran an article called "Arlington Lad Starring in TV Title Role Tonight," with a short sidebar headline that was Warren's worst nightmare: "Kraft Discovery Is Kid Brother of Shirley MacLaine." Four unnamed class-mates from Washington-Lee High School tipped off the newspaper that Beatty was MacLaine's brother, a fact that was confirmed by their "proud father, Ira O. Beaty." Ira told the *Star*, "Warren asked me not to reveal this. He wanted to make it on his own, and not trade on his sister's reputation." It would be one of Ira Beaty's last published remarks about either of his children.

The Sunday before, Pastor John Raymond had announced the time and date of Warren's first starring role to the congregation of Westover Baptist Church, urging them to watch what would possibly be Beatty's most humiliating performance.[76] His television agent, Eleanor Kilgallen, winced while she sat through the live one-hour broadcast as Warren "talked through clenched teeth, in total terror, his jaw locked," as a furious Raymond Massey struggled to hear what he was saying. Because of his muffled speech, the sensitivity Beatty brought to his characterization of the falsely accused kid — not unlike that of James Dean, casting director Marion Dougherty's earlier find — was overlooked.

"I was very, very bad," Beatty said later. "I knew it, and so did everybody else."[77] The next morning, Kilgallen tried to smooth things over with the casting director. "Marion said, 'Why doesn't he speak and open up his mouth?'" Dougherty "joshed" Beatty about it years later. "I said, 'You know, Warren, you nearly got me fired after that show.' We were screaming with laughter."

Beatty would repay the favor several times over after he became a star. He hired Marion Dougherty to cast his film *Love Affair* in 1994, and when Dougherty's elderly mother was diagnosed with shingles, "he got me a whole list of people to call who were experts, and was very concerned about it, it was very sweet. I've always felt he acted like a very sweet brother to me."

23 *Maynard Morris, Beatty's devoted*

theater agent at MCA, had long talks with Warren about his acting after "The Curly-Headed Kid," which should have made him an immediate star.[78] "We probably all had at him," said his television agent, Eleanor Kilgallen. "But actors being the children that they are, there's a way to do it and a way not to — I'm not of the Strasberg school to lacerate somebody . . . it was live television, there were no retakes; it was a very scary thing."

Kilgallen recognized that Beatty's clenched-teeth delivery was partially Brando inspired, and to some degree a strategy, "an idiosyncrasy that would label him a little different from the rest of the kids on the block, 'cause he always knew how to play that." Her worry, and Morris's, was that Beatty's *Kraft Television Theatre* debacle would deter television producers from casting him in a starring role again, a concern that was well founded. "I think it stayed with some people, it really did."

With his family sensitivity to failure, Beatty considered himself a "disaster" in "The Curly-Headed Kid," "and after that, doing TV became a struggle for me."[79] His lockjaw portrayal was the symptom of a deeper concern than stage fright, inexperience, intimidation, or a desire to emulate Brando: Beatty found it "painful" to reveal himself, or his emotions, an essential element of transcendent acting.[80]

This fear of letting himself go, of losing control, had its roots in Warren's childhood, watching his father lose his temper while drunk, and the unsettling experience of observing his mother confuse her identity with the insane character she played in *Children of the Moon.*

Despite his occasionally clownish behavior, Beatty was naturally reserved and he was a loner — traits more closely associated with the writer he would become than with a movie star. He confessed that he was emotionally inhibited, and still sought relief by singing. "That's the way I release some of what's going on inside of me. Everybody's got to be able to release himself, everyone has to talk to someone."[81]

Playing the piano was Beatty's other outlet from his loneliness and pent-up tension, along with his newly discovered passion: sex.

ALTHOUGH "THE CURLY-HEADED KID" set him back with television exec-utives, Beatty's prestigious credit as the star of a live *Kraft Television Theatre* production gave him cachet with stage directors, who were encouraged by Maynard Morris, Warren's doting and well-connected theater agent. Before the *Kraft* special had even aired, Beatty was approached for the lead in a Broadway play called *Counsel for the Defense*, based on the sensational Leopold-Loeb murder trial in 1924.[82] He had also gotten a surprisingly good, and prescient, review in *Variety* for his almost inaudible performance oppo-site Massey, described as "a little too grunt and groan," but "amiable, per-sonable and [he] can act . . . he'll be around for some time to come."[83]

The day after he starred on *Kraft Television Theatre*, Beatty went home to Virginia to see his parents, proving how eager he was to redeem, and prove, himself in their eyes — especially those of his mother, whom he put on a pedestal. "I think they had some amount of parental caution and skepticism about the theater," was Beatty's wry explanation, later, of their brief estrange-ment, "and I'm sure that would have increased had a few years gone by and nothing happened."[84] The visit fully restored Warren to Tat and Ira Beaty's good graces, where the good son would remain, later disclosing that he tele-phoned his parents every Sunday of his adult life.[85]

Shirley, who had finished *Hot Spell* and was perpetually lonely with her husband living in Japan, happened to visit at the same time, as she wrote to the friend who had counseled Warren the summer before about whether to become an actor. "She was alone, and longed to see her family, so she upped and went to Arlington," recalled Dottie Rector. MacLaine recently had moved out of her tiny Malibu apartment and into a house on Berry Drive in the Valley, "the first time she had her own things around her." A thrifty Scot like her mother, Tat, Shirley the movie star told her old friend from Virginia that "she was enjoying buying secondhand or on-sale furniture — never full price."[86]

Their July visit to Arlington to see their parents in 1957 was Shirley's first encounter with Warren since he had followed her into show business the previous July, as MacLaine commented archly in a letter to Rector afterward, writing, "My actor brother was also home and we had a wonderful time fighting and arguing about the pros and cons of Actors Studio. He being a devoted follower and I think it's a pile of crap."[87]

Beatty, who was still enthralled by Stella Adler and her past association with the Group Theatre, returned to New York on July 10. He immediately contacted Lenn Harten to critique his performance in "The Curly-Headed Kid" on Harten's audio recording. Warren arrived "four hours late as usual," Harten noted at the time.[88]

Within a few weeks, Beatty told his friend he had a couple of movie offers, and he was reading a script for the lead in a Broadway play called *Compulsion*, based on the same infamous murder trial as *Counsel for the Defense*.[89] The two productions had squared off in what the *New York Times* called a "smoldering rivalry" to get to Broadway first, a victory that went to *Compulsion*.[90] After offering Beatty the starring role in *Counsel for the Defense*, the producers canceled the play, concerned they could not compete with *Compulsion*, which was adapted from a celebrated novel by Meyer Levin.

"All the young actors in New York were ecstatic about *Compulsion*," remembered Eleanor Kilgallen. The plum role was a character named Artie Straus, based on Richard Loeb, the charismatic, disturbed mastermind of two rich college boys' scheme to commit the perfect murder. Beatty was possessed to play Straus; he was intrigued by the character and anxious to overcome his mumbling debut to prove his mettle in the theater, his family legacy.

Beatty prepared for the audition by carefully studying Meyer Levin's novel, unwinding at Rockaway Beach on Long Island, his favorite because it was private and quiet. In a Kodak picture Harten snapped of the future movie star that summer, Warren is sitting on an army blanket on the sand, gazing at the Atlantic Ocean "like he was looking into the future."

On August 5, the *New York Herald Tribune* reported that Roddy McDowall, Dean Stockwell, and Warren Beatty were the actors in contention for the coveted lead role in *Compulsion*. All three got callbacks for a second audition, although Warren told Lenn Harten that it had been his understanding that Meyer Levin, the author and playwright, had selected him to play Artie Straus.

When Beatty appeared for his second reading in front of the producer and director, something went awry, he told Harten afterward. "Evidently Warren just got the feeling from them that they already had somebody else in mind. He said, 'You don't *want* me in this role, do you?' And he got up and walked out. That's before he was known by anyone really, so I mean Warren had the talent, he had the guts. He just got up and walked out."

Beatty was also bothered by script changes made by the producer, Michael Myerberg, which he felt destroyed the integrity of Levin's play. The playwright agreed with Beatty. "Meyer was very outraged about what had been changed," said his widow, Tereska Levin, "and he didn't want the play to be called '*Compulsion* by Meyer Levin.'" Levin forced the producer to open on Broadway with the theater marquis stating, "*Compulsion* — producer version."[91]

The part promised to Beatty went to Roddy McDowall. Beatty's only public comment about the experience, later, was to say, "I had a lot to learn."[92]

After coming within a hairbreadth of starring in two Broadway versions of the Leopold-Loeb case, Warren Beatty's only acting job that summer was a small part in an Alfred Hitchcock series on NBC called *Suspicion*.* Demonstrating how far into obscurity he had fallen in the television world since his starring role on *Kraft Television Theatre*, Beatty's screen credit on *Suspicion* was as "Henry Warren Beatty."[93] One of the stars of the episode, noted stage actor Pat Hingle — who would play Warren's father memorably three years later in *Splendor in the Grass* — would have no recollection of Beatty playing a boy hiding under the boardwalk at Coney Island, "the best I'd ever seen him do," appraised Harten.[94]

Beatty's living conditions in a junkie's former apartment were almost as squalid as his character's in the Hitchcock anthology. He was down to a threadbare few dollars by September, when Joe Scully, the casting director on CBS's *Studio One*, got a call from Shirley MacLaine's agent at MCA, recommending Beatty for the respected series — a favor Warren knew nothing about.[95] The story was a docudrama re-creating Orson Welles's 1938 "War of the Worlds" radio broadcast through a series of vignettes. Beatty's segment was of three college buddies in a card game, listening to the radio during Welles's broadcast of the hoax alien invasion.[†]

---

*The episode, filmed August 19, was called "Heartbeat" and starred David Wayne as a coronary patient mistakenly advised that his heart is healthy, only to drop dead celebrating the false diagnosis — the signature Hitchcock twist.

†Character actor Vincent Gardenia starred in a separate vignette. Twenty years later, Beatty loyally cast Gardenia in his film *Heaven Can Wait*. As a producer, Beatty would find creative ways to remember people from his past, sometimes naming characters after them, a private game similar to artist Al Hirschfeld's practice of hiding the name of his daughter, Nina, in his caricatures of Broadway stars.

"The Night America Trembled" aired live on September 9, the first *Studio One* of the 1957/58 television season. It was praised as an "interesting premise," but slow paced, featuring an "able" cast.[96] Warren Beatty's part was too small to be mentioned by name, but he made a little money and a new close friend, Clinton Kimbrough, who was in the cast, along with character actor Warren Oates, who played one of the other boys at the card table.

Kimbrough, a talented stage actor from Oklahoma who had been offered a creative writing scholarship to Princeton, was the sort of glib, razor-sharp eccentric Beatty would gravitate to in his male friendships — in the vein of future pals Jack Nicholson and comedian Garry Shandling. "Clint was a very, very brilliant, articulate person, and had an unbelievable vocabulary at his command, something that really aroused Warren's interest," said a mutual friend.[97] The at times clownish Beatty enjoyed witty repartee, and people who made him laugh were an antidote to his and Shirley's fear that they would lead unhappy lives in the pattern of their parents.

Before the fall term at Stella Adler's, Warren Beatty created a new, more sophisticated image for himself, growing out his football crew cut and parting his hair to one side. When he arrived late the first two days, Adler teased him about his "big ego" since he had been on television, joking, "You'll have that knocked out of you this term!"[98] Beatty later would credit Adler for instilling that arrogance: "She convinced me that I couldn't make a mistake . . . before I started making films, some of the confidence had to be knocked out of me."[99]

In truth, Beatty was struggling to make ends meet, unable to pay for Adler's classes and barely surviving on cereal. When a severe strain of the Asian flu swept through New York at the end of September, he was felled by it, too weak even to move his car at night. Warren was too proud to ask his parents or anyone else for help, just as Shirley had been when she gave birth to Sachi alone in Los Angeles.

Lenn Harten was Beatty's lifeline, bringing him a quart of milk, soup for his hot plate, orange juice, a bottle of aspirin, cough drops, tissues, and a newspaper. "Warren couldn't thank me enough and wanted to give me a buck, but I wouldn't take it," Harten wrote at the time, noting that his friend was "in bad shape" with a very high fever.[100]

According to Beatty, his illness escalated into hepatitis that October, caused by "bad food" and near starvation — his eating habits of the previous fifteen months. He lost 35 pounds in two weeks, dropping to 155, and he could barely dress or get out of bed. Beatty described this time later as the "bleakest period of my life," and as "a story of a young man in trouble."[101] The hepatitis left him physically depleted, and he worried that he would never work again.

Beatty went to a hospital to get medication and tried to cure himself with a diet of yogurt and health foods, drinking the special raw-egg shakes he had devised when he had mononucleosis the spring he left Northwestern. "He didn't eat all the bad things we ate," observed Verne O'Hara. "He was very, very health conscious, and it was at the time when none of us even knew what it was all about. And he *never* drank." His concern about his health would be a lifelong obsession for Beatty thereafter and would lead him to study medicine with the dedication of a physician, an interest and aptitude he believed he inherited from his surgeon grandfather, Dr. Murdoch MacLean.

When Stella Adler's secretary informed Beatty that there were complications finding him scholarship money, he dropped out of class, making a forced choice to learn by doing. "I was weak as a sick cat . . . some mornings I barely had energy enough to kick myself out of bed. Funny thing though, about then was when I got kind of cocky."[102] Warren Beatty's eight months at Stella Adler's studio would be the extent of his professional training as an actor. "From these sessions I developed my own method," he said once, explaining that he "backed into" a scene by starting several lines before the ones to be filmed. "This gets me into the mood. It's like taking a running leap."[103]

His lack of formal education in drama was a delicate issue for Beatty, growing up with elocution professors and a father who considered a Ph.D. the holy grail of his career. Through the years, when asked about his acting style or technique, Beatty would associate himself with the prestigious lineage of Stella Adler. "I guess my training comes out of that kind of strain that goes back to the Group Theatre and that kind of thing. I wasn't with the Group Theatre, but I studied in New York as an actor. I don't know if I think of 'style' so much."[104] Beatty's respect for the Stanislavsky method was evident the month he withdrew from Adler's studio, when he asked Harten for audiotapes of James Dean — a student of Lee Strasberg's and a protégé of Elia Kazan's — so he could study them.[105]

Warren Beatty survived the autumn of 1957 through the grace of Liam Dunne, the CBS casting director who had given him his first job on television in *Lamp Unto My Feet*. Dunne chose Beatty that October for another Sunday-morning religious program, the aptly titled *Look Up and Live*, originally hosted by a young Merv Griffin. Dunne suggested Warren for the teenage son in a five-part morality series narrated by Hiram Sherman called "The Family," with each episode featuring a different family member in crisis.[106] Character actors Edward Andrews and Louise Platt played the parents.

Pamela Ilott, the series' executive producer, would recall, "Liam was not only talented, but he had a big heart. He would call me sometimes and say, 'So-and-So's phone is being cut off, could you write him a five-part or something in next week's show so he can get another credit and get employment?'"

Beatty's first segment in "The Family" aired live on CBS's *Look Up and Live* from ten-thirty to eleven Sunday morning, October 14, while Warren was experiencing a raging fever and "sounding terrible," according to a friend.[107]

Julius (Jack) Kuney, who produced the series and hired Beatty, became a trusted friend once Warren found out that Kuney's family was from Arlington and that his nephew played football at Washington-Lee. "My goodness," recalled Kuney, "he could talk about anything and everything, and I discovered . . . I learned about his sister."[108] Kuney's impression was that Warren "wasn't getting along with Shirley at that time, that he was living on his own, not depending on riding her coattails." Beatty did not bring up his parents, which Kuney took as another indication he wanted to make it on his own. "He was terribly ambitious, terribly ambitious . . . somebody who was on the road to success."

Beatty confided in the producer that he had a speech problem that caused him to hesitate between words. "I was a stutterer," said Kuney. ". . . And we did discuss it, because I was a speech therapist." In Kuney's view, Warren's speech tics were a way of "rebelling" against his mother and grandmother's rigid rules of elocution. Their discussions evidently helped Beatty. After the fourth episode of "The Family," Lenn Harten's mother wrote to Harten, "Tell Warren we all noticed a big improvement in his speech compared to the show he was on a few months ago."[109]

Although he said he had no desire to be a great actor, Beatty approached his role as the teenage son in "The Family" with an artist's dedication. The director, Roger Englander, remembered, "He would call me in the middle of the night to ask me something about characterization, and line reading, and he was so intense about doing it just right, as if he had been studying all the time about it. And it wasn't a very important show. It was a charming series, but still it was a daytime sort of pseudoreligious program. So I was very impressed by that—a little annoyed at first, but then I thought, 'this is terrific.'"[110]

Englander had one other encounter with Beatty, after he had been a movie star for many years. "I was walking down Fifty-seventh Street, and he was walking the other direction, toward me, and he stopped and said, 'Do you remember me? I'm Warren Beatty.' . . . How could you forget! It was kind of sweet and unimpressed."

During the five-week series, Beatty formed a tender connection with Bennye Gatteys, the pretty, musically inclined sixteen-year-old who played his kid sister. "He would walk me home from rehearsals and buy me an apple on the way home and we'd just talk."[111] At the end of that October, Gatteys wrote in her diary, "Guess what? I found my big brother. My friend, my companion, my big brother."[112]

Gatteys's impression was that Beatty wanted to succeed in the theater. He asked her to help him read for a starring role in the Broadway play *Winesburg, Ohio*, and rehearsed it six times with her before their audition. Beatty told Gatteys he admired actor Spencer Tracy's naturalism.

Warren's endearing sweetness came through in his portrayal of the generic teenaged son—and in his treatment of his television kid sister, whom he discouraged from studying with Stella Adler, warning Gatteys, "she doesn't like young actresses, just young actors." When the series ended in November 1957, Warren Beatty remained Bennye's "friend for life," Gatteys said, though their paths would seldom cross. "If you're his friend, he is a true friend. . . . that's the thing I think about him the most, is that he is truly there for you."

IN EARLY DECEMBER, Beatty lost the starring role in *Winesburg, Ohio*, to George Grizzard after a second audition, a turn that left him him not only "very disappointed," as Gatteys recalled, but also unemployed.

Liam Dunne, his guardian angel, immediately put Beatty in a CBS daytime series called *The Verdict Is Yours*, a reality-based courtroom show with actual attorneys and a real judge, and scripts that called for the actors to improvise. Since Dunne cast Beatty as the defendant, he was in five consecutive episodes.

That winter, Beatty began pursuing Diane Ladd, a shapely twenty-five-year-old blonde who had appeared in *The Verdict Is Yours*. A former Copacabana dancer and aspiring actress from Mississippi, Ladd shared an apartment with model Judy Loomis, future gossip columnist Rona Barrett, and, at times, Suzanne Pleshette, an up-and-coming, husky-voiced stage actress with a small role in *Compulsion*.[113] Beatty dated Ladd for a short time, and as she recalled, "He'd take me home and kiss me goodnight — then say hello to my roommates and kiss them, too. I thought I was special when he kissed me goodnight. But the boy was out to kiss 'em all."[114]

In her memoir, Rona Barrett wrote less than flatteringly about Beatty then, recounting a time he pounded on their apartment door at four A.M., saying he was hungry and identifying himself as "Di's guy." When Barrett opened the door, "this huge creature lunged forward, grabbing and screaming like some wild maniac, 'I'm gonna rape you! This is it, baby!' . . . then I heard Diane say, 'Oh, my God. It's only Warren.'" Barrett's critical assessment of her roommate's suitor was that Warren liked being mothered, avoided commitment, and "was a little boy who will probably never grow up . . . afraid to find out who and what he is."[115]

Beatty's behavior with Barrett was reminiscent of the sexually aggressive clowning that Tom Calhoun noticed in high school, when Warren would pretend to make love to his friends' mothers or suggestively lick a sandwich in front of girls, a peculiar contrast to his normally sensitive and respectful treatment of women.

Rona Barrett's negative feelings about Beatty at twenty were a minority view, but she was not the only woman to question his dating habits. A female Stella Adler student took pride in being "the one girl from class he didn't get."[116]

According to Bennye Gatteys, "all the older ladies had crushes on him, and kind of like in a motherly, but definitely attracted way." Nancy Malone, his smitten sixteen-year-old costar on "The Curly-Headed Kid," tried to explain Warren Beatty's appeal in 1957. "He just had the best smile in the whole world, and you just kind of melted when you saw that face. I'm not terribly tall — five four — and he would look down, and his smile was a light from heaven."

Another girlfriend of Beatty's was Jan Norris, a sixteen-year-old actress from Pittsburgh he met on Broadway when she replaced the ingenue playing Ethel Merman's daughter in the musical *Happy Hunting*, while Warren was auditioning for *Compulsion*.[117] Norris, who would be cast several years later as Juanita, the high school temptress who seduces Beatty's character in *Splendor in the Grass*, was a light-complexioned redhead, similar in coloring to Beatty's sister, Shirley, and in temperament to his mother, Tat.

"Jan was so delicate — porcelain almost — soulful, sweet, refined," said a director who met her while she was dating Beatty.[118] Like his first girlfriend in junior high, Jan Norris considered Warren "kind of goofy," a friend rather than a boyfriend — though she would keep his handwritten love notes to her up to her death. "She had many nice things to say about him," recalled Norris's son, who also remembered hearing her say, "Warren dated anything that walked."[119]

Beatty's sister attributed his multiple girlfriends to a fear of intimacy created by the volatile example of their parents' relationship, just as she would come to view her own unconscious motivation in choosing to continue to remain married to a man who lived on a different continent. "I can honestly say I've never really been married," MacLaine said at seventy. "I can admit it now. I stayed married so that I wouldn't *get* married."[120]

In 1957, at age twenty-three, Shirley was still hoping for a traditional family life with Steve Parker, expressing a longing for two more children and a poignant desire to move to Vermont with Parker and Sachi to run a country store.[121] Instead, she sent her year-old daughter alone on an airplane to spend Christmas in Japan with Parker while she spent the holiday lonely and unfulfilled in California, waiting for her next three movies — *Hot Spell*, *The Sheepman*, and *The Matchmaker* — to be released.[122]

Beatty, a conservative Virginian in his heart, asked Verne O'Hara to help him choose Christmas presents for Shirley and his niece. He was bewildered by his sister's lifestyle with Parker, the man who had come between them. "She was married to this guy that lived in Japan, and it was a very weird relationship," commented O'Hara, "because they'd be sticking this kid on a plane back and forth to Japan, and Warren thought it was very strange."

24 *Both Warren Beatty and Shirley*

MacLaine started the year 1958 with television offers. In February, Shirley signed a $500,000 contract with NBC for two specials; the same month, Liam Dunne cast Warren in five episodes of a soap opera on CBS called *Hotel Cosmopolitan*, a rotating serial about a hotel detective. "Very often," Beatty recalled, "I had little more to do than walk across the stage, but I earned about three hundred dollars a week."[123]

By mid-March, Warren told friends he expected to do a war movie soon, an offer that never materialized or that the ever-strategic Beatty rejected.[124] "I had a number of offers to come out [to Hollywood], but I just didn't want to come out yet . . . they didn't offer me anything really good. I would have taken it."[125]

In the back of his mind, Beatty wanted to prove himself on stage, the family business. On March 29, he kept body and soul together by doing an episode of a live NBC anthology series on Saturdays at noon called *True Story*, playing a student who put his scholarship at risk by cheating on a test.[126] Though he was unaware of it at the time, this obscure show would change the direction of Warren Beatty's career.

Beatty supplemented his meager acting income by playing piano at the First-Nighter, and spent the spring trying to get hired to perform in summer stock at the Clinton Playhouse, in Clinton, Connecticut, where he once ferried agents Maynard Morris and Eleanor Kilgallen so they could watch Rita Gam, another of Morris's clients.[127]

Charlotte Harmon, who produced the plays for the Clinton Playhouse with her husband Louis, and had an apartment in Manhattan at the Osborne, recalled, "Warren lived down the street, and he kept coming every day, asking the doorman if he could come up."[128] Though he was desperate to be hired, and his sister's movie *The Sheepman*, costarring Glenn Ford, was playing in theaters at the time, Beatty never mentioned that he was related to Shirley MacLaine.

Still weak from hepatitis, Beatty went six weeks without an acting job, trying all the while to get Harmon's attention. In May, the loyal Liam Dunne cast him in fifteen episodes of *Lamp Unto My Feet*, the same Sunday-morning religious series in which Dunne had cast him, instead of Mitch May, the year before.[129] "I played a son who couldn't communicate with his father, and a sailor who came home from the service and couldn't adjust to his family again, and things like that."[130]

That month, Stark Hesseltine, the assistant to Beatty's theater agent, persuaded Ned Manderino, who was directing two musicals and a drama at the Clinton Playhouse that summer, to interview Warren. "I knew from the beginning I was going to hire him," recalled Manderino, who was taken with Beatty. "You know that first impression? He could sing and play the piano, and gave a very dynamic reading, and he had an *aura* . . ." Beatty's "aura qualities," according to Manderino, were an amiable eagerness, good humor, and a sexually electric presence that Manderino would compare to the "lethal grace of a tiger."[131] Warren Beatty's only deficit, in the director's observation, was that "he had pimples."

Beatty kept up his barrage, prodding Hesseltine to make daily phone calls to Ned Manderino. By the end of spring, Charlotte Harmon agreed to hire Warren Beatty for her summer stock company. "He was so persistent. Just to get rid of him I took him. And he was rather nice looking."

The gentlemanly Manderino offered a few words of advice to his greenhorn leading man. "I told him that he had to start using Clearasil, and he began to use Clearasil. And I told him he ought to start using dental floss. So he began to use dental floss."

When rehearsals began in the middle of June for the opening musical, *The Happiest Millionaire*, Beatty quickly alienated the company, all seasoned stage actors. As Manderino recalled:

> First rehearsal was called for eleven A.M., and the other actors were there at ten, ten fifteen, saying hello — knowing one another from previous engagements in New York and elsewhere — and there's no Warren. One minute before eleven, Warren arrives. . . . There were people in the company who felt that he was doing a Jimmy — James Dean. He just kind of slouched in, didn't say anything — didn't make any contact with anyone.
>
> And so the rehearsal began, and he was lost. And mumbling. Didn't know his way around the stage, in a haze. At the end of the day, some of the veteran actors voiced negative feelings that they just could not work with him.

For a second time in his short career, Beatty was saved from being fired by an admiring colleague — in this case his director. Manderino spent the ten-day rehearsal period, including dinners, privately coaching Beatty to prepare him for opening night on June 28. "One of the things that happened at the restaurant the first night — it was sort of amusing — was that whenever the waitress came to the table, Warren would always jab his finger into her stomach." Manderino had suggested that Beatty create a unique physical gesture for his character, Angier Duke, and use it onstage. At the director's prompting, Beatty wagged his pointer finger at the waitress instead of jabbing her in the stomach with it. "So I said, 'Well, Warren, maybe you should use this, wagging your finger, for the characteristic gesture,' and he did it."[132]

When *The Happiest Millionaire* opened at the Clinton Playhouse on

June 28, 1958, Warren Beatty was the only member of the cast to get applause after his first scene. "I still remember his entrance on opening night," said Manderino, Beatty's Henry Higgins. "Warren entered from one side of the stage and moved quickly to the other side of the stage, and suddenly sparks flew, and the scene just really came alive, and on his exit, the audience applauded . . . all of the seasoned summer stock actors, they were just left with their mouths hanging. . . . Warren was so happy that he grabbed me and kissed me on the cheek."

Manderino bought a box of gold stars afterward, "and each day I would put a gold star on Warren's T-shirt, because I thought that he was a star." The director later wondered what might have happened to Warren Beatty if he had been sent back to New York after Charlotte Harmon wanted to fire him. "Might he have said, 'Well, I'm not an actor'?"

Forty years later, a journalist for the London *Times* would refer to the "finger-point" — the "characteristic gesture" that Manderino suggested at the restaurant — as Beatty's "staple acting gesture . . . it is as regular as Clint Eastwood's squint or Jack Nicholson's lip-smacking smile. You can easily tell when Beatty is squaring up for a big speech by the unfurling of one or both forefingers . . . he waves his finger so much he might as well be conducting at the Metropolitan Opera House."[133]

In Manderino's appraisal, Beatty's gesturing with his right index finger pointed up — which had phallic implications — became a source of security in his acting. It was also, interestingly, a screen gesture characteristic of Cary Grant's, one of Warren Beatty's Hollywood role models.

During his summer at the Clinton Playhouse, Beatty would continue his lone-wolf lifestyle, requesting a room in an old-fashioned boarding house run by an elderly landlady, while the rest of the troupe stayed in cottages adjacent to one another. "He was simply gorgeous, very polite to everyone, and very much a recluse," in the description of Jean Voland, the wife of Herb Voland, the star of *The Happiest Millionaire*. Beatty drove a "funny old car," which Ned Manderino observed was cluttered with empty cigarette packs. He claimed not to smoke, a combination of denial and wishful thinking, since smoking was at odds with Warren's health-conscious diet and his increasing medical concerns.

When *The Happiest Millionaire* ended its run, on July 5, Beatty started rehearsals for his role as the younger romantic lead in the musical *The Boyfriend*. After rehearsing all day, he would stand in back of a full house to watch theater veteran Herb Voland play the complex character Big Daddy in

Tennessee Williams's *Cat on a Hot Tin Roof*, the second play of the Clinton summer season.

As Voland's wife recalled of Beatty, "He went to every performance and went backstage and talked to Herb, and wanted to know 'why did you do this,' and 'why didn't you do it this way,' . . . he was the most incredible student I've ever seen in my life."

Beatty's internal conflict between the dignity of the stage and the lure of the screen recurred that summer when he confessed to Manderino that Shirley MacLaine was his sister, and indicated that he wanted to be a movie star. "At the beginning of rehearsals, we would get a lunch break or something, and somebody from the box office would come out onto the theater lawn and tell him, 'Warren, Hollywood calling.' And this happened three or four times. Finally he told me that it was his sister. She never told the person at the box office who she was, it was always 'Hollywood' calling."

In early July, Beatty began to be seen with Elizabeth Hubbard, the young actress cast as his girlfriend in *The Boyfriend.* Hubbard, a regal blonde, would go on to fame playing the aristocratic Lucinda Walsh on *As the World Turns* and garner several Daytime Emmys. "Once she arrived, he stopped having dinner with me," commented Manderino, who observed Beatty and Hubbard "squeezed close to one another whenever I saw them together." Warren, the health faddist, was intrigued by the fact that Hubbard's mother was a homeopathic doctor.

"Oh, I was never his girlfriend," demurred Hubbard, whose memory of Warren Beatty at twenty-one was "this fantastic joie de vivre, his sense of humor, and also how ambitious we all were. We were all young; we just wanted to be the best we could be." Beatty helped the actress get an agent, which she found "quite sweet."[134]

By the last half of the month, when Elizabeth Hubbard and Beatty costarred in *The Boyfriend,* Beatty had resumed "stalking girls," as he playfully described his bachelorhood then.[135] "He was, what do you call it — a womanizer . . . and he talked about it to me," recounted Ned Wertimer, one of the experienced actors in the repertory company that summer. "He used to discuss with me some intimate details, which — I just looked at him and said, 'Okay.'"[136]

Word drifted back to Charlotte Harmon, the producer at the Clinton Playhouse. "Warren was a very nice guy," she would say of him, "[but] I think he made love to everybody in the cast." Harmon eventually phoned Ned Manderino, complaining that Beatty was bothering the girls backstage and warning the director that it had to stop. "Warren came over to my room, across the street from the theater, and I told him what Charlotte said, and he didn't say anything. He just said okay, and he walked out. No argument or anything of that kind." Earlier that summer, Manderino was to recall, "Warren told me in so many words that, 'Oh, that's Charlotte, she'll want to snip your balls off.'" Beatty ultimately got the last laugh, according to actor Ned Wertimer. "I know that he finally went after her daughter later on, who was just beaming."

Paul Tripp, creator of the children's television show *Mr. I. Magination*, and a guest star that summer at the Playhouse, was fond of Beatty, who babysat in Clinton for Tripp's ten-year-old son. As an actor, Warren Beatty impressed Tripp less. While he and Beatty were performing together in Gore Vidal's satire, A *Visit to a Small Planet*, Tripp made a wager with Charlotte Harmon that Warren Beatty "would never make it" in show business. "Three years later," chuckled Harmon, "I said, 'Paul, give me the ten bucks right now.' I couldn't believe it!"[137]

Ned Wertimer, the actor in the company to whom Warren revealed the details of his sex life that summer, was also in the Vidal play and offered Warren pointers. Wertimer evaluated Beatty, paradoxically, as "very intense, assured, and *un*sure."

By the end of summer stock, Beatty was at his best, and his worst. While he was in rehearsals for the final play, A *Hatful of Rain*, he asked actor Allan Miller, his costar, if they could switch roles so that Beatty could play the lead, a war hero struggling with a narcotics addiction. The director, Jerry Solars, clashed with his young lead, who had strong opinions about how he wanted to play the addict. "He took Warren outside to bawl him out, because he was undermining the director's position," observed Wertimer, who played a drug pusher. This battle of wills continued throughout rehearsals as Beatty "maybe gave in a little bit, but it always came back to his own approach to the work." As one castmate observed, "the director was not particularly that brilliant."[138]

Wertimer had his own rankling experience with Beatty onstage. The two were performing a scene in which Wertimer's character tries to lure the addict with a pad of heroin. Beatty was supposed to recoil at the sight of the heroin. "Here I'm a threat to his life, and he's got to have the drug—it's the whole downer, 'hatful of rain'—and [Warren] went all the way across the stage and he adjusted a *clock* next to me, and went back again! And it threw the whole scene. The importance of my position was thrown. I've never forgotten it."

When Wertimer asked him about it afterward, Beatty just shrugged. His close friend at Stella Adler's, Lenn Harten, felt that Warren was trying a James Dean trick. "Jimmy used to do things like that."

Thirty-odd years later, Beatty tried to explain what he was attempting to accomplish as a young stage actor then. "My first and primary need unquestionably was in getting the moment right. That made me transcendently happy . . . I didn't give a shit if there was an audience or not."[139]

In a preview of what would happen a few years later, under more notorious circumstances, Beatty came through the fractious experience winning praise from critics. The review in the *Clinton Recorder* extolled, "Warren Beatty as Johnny has either seen a junkie — or director Jerry Solars has a profound knowledge of drug addiction."[140] As Ned Wertimer noted philosophically of the turmoil between director and star, "Out of those conflicts come good drama, as they say."

By an unusual coincidence, Warren Beatty was not the only future Hollywood legend babysitting part-time for the troupe at the Clinton Playhouse that July and August. Allan Miller, the actor who switched roles with Beatty, hired a teenage babysitter who was still spelling her name as "Barbara" Streisand to watch his children while he and his wife, actress Anita Cooper, performed in *A Hatful of Rain*. "She was so hungry and eager," Miller would observe of Streisand, "but she had absolutely no acting ability at that time. She followed us all around. We didn't know she could sing." According to the vigilant Charlotte Harmon, who would close the playhouse after the end of that summer, "She was the only one that turned Warren down."

When Beatty left Clinton, Connecticut, that August for his dismal closet-sized apartment on Sixty-eighth Street, an infatuated stranger was making arrangements for a professional introduction. This secret admirer was a man, and he would turn Warren Beatty into both a Hollywood movie star and a respected New York stage actor, the two ambitions that rivaled for his attention.

25   *When he returned to New York after* doing summer stock in 1958, Beatty began to move in different social circles. His verbally gifted pal Clint Kimbrough introduced him to a coterie of theater friends who studied with Lee Strasberg at the respected Actors Studio, including Kimbrough's roommate, Tomas Milian, a colorful Cuban.

The ambitious trio of Beatty, Kimbrough, and Milian personified flaming youth within a certain strata of New York actors toward the end of the Eisenhower era: passionate about life, about love, about art, about music. As Milian sketched it, "My friendship with Warren was — you know when you are walking down Central Park West with someone, and through the smiles, and the giggling, or the reactions of the person, you can tell if the person likes you, that you are simpatico to them? And that was Warren's reaction toward me. All of a sudden he would start singing an opera aria or something, and I was very surprised. I said, 'My God, do you sing opera?' and we would talk about that."[141]

Milian occasionally invited Anna Maria Barraque, a comely Cuban friend related to department store magnate Bergdorf Goodman, to the Actors Studio soirees with her Cuban roommate, Margarita. Beatty often was there. "They were all starving," Barraque reminisced, "but they knew other people who already had made it, and they would have parties all the time. Whoever could, brought a bottle of very bad wine. They treated Margarita and me as though we were sort of separate, like little ladies . . . I had the fondest time with all of them."[142]

Anna Maria Barraque dated Warren Beatty throughout fall of 1958. Her description of him during their romance was of a Virginian: polite and charming, but reserved. Beatty was still frail from health problems, driving the same "beat-up old car" littered with parking tickets and empty cigarette packs. He had begun to wear glasses, scholarly horn-rims, for nearsightedness, and continued to squint in light of any kind, his heritage from Tat. "I remember him good-looking, but not to faint," as Barraque put it.

As often as not, Beatty's dates with his Cuban girlfriend were walks through Greenwich Village, since he had no money. "I don't remember even having dinner with Warren, but we went out all the time. I remember once asking how long are you all going to continue living on cornflakes?"

Although Beatty never mentioned Shirley to Anna Maria Barraque, "he spoke about his mother and father, and I think he had gone to see them at one point." Beatty told Barraque how religious his mother was, and though he kept his feelings about his faith to himself, and was not known to attend church, Tomas Milian would observe: "One of the qualities that I appreciate and remember from Warren was his decency."[143]

Beatty occasionally took Anna Maria to see plays at the Actors Studio, where she got the impression he wished he could study with Strasberg, like

Beatty's handsome Canadian maternal grandfather, Murdoch MacLean, a physician and mayor.
Dalhousie Medical Alumni Association

Blanche Lehigh MacLean as Dean of Women at Acadia University in Nova Scotia—the grandmother Warren adored as his feminine ideal.
Courtesy of Acadia and Karen McKay

Little Women staged at Acadia in 1923. Warren's mother, Kathlyn MacLean *(third from left)*, as Jo, his lookalike uncle Mansell *(standing at rear, in center)* as John Brooke, and his aunt-by-marriage Maisie Johnston *(fifth from left)* as Meg. . . ."the Canadian Barrymores." *Acadia University Archives*

Ira Beaty's romantic photo in the 1920/1921 University of Richmond yearbook, before abandoning his dream to be a concert violinist; later, his son, Warren, would forgo the piano. *University of Richmond, courtesy of Mary M. Maxwell*

Tat, the aspiring actress *(third from top)* in her Louise Brooks bob, pictured with her friend Estelle Woodall *(second from top)* with the faculty in the Alderson Junior College yearbook. *Courtesy of Senator Jennie Forehand*

Kathlyn MacLean's and Ira Beaty's 1930 faculty photos at the Maryland College for Women, where they courted and where Warren's and Shirley's fates were determined. The Marylander, *courtesy of Jane Banks*

Ira Beaty *(seated on the grass)*, proudly holds up Shirley at a faculty outing near Waverly, Virginia, while Kathlyn stands at rear *(second from right)*. *Courtesy of Senator Elmon M. Gray*

Richmond circa 1942. As her expression attests, Shirley Beaty felt dethroned by her winning little brother. Warren adored his fiercely talented older sister and their mother, Kathlyn *(second from left)*, whose light-sensitive blue eyes and Scottish complexion they both inherited. *Photofest*

Shirley and Warren in Richmond, best pals; the photo Beatty later viewed with great nostalgia.
Photo by SNAP/ZUMA Press; copyright 1942 by Movie Studio

Ira Beaty's formal portrait as principal of Westhampton, where his disappointments began to take their toll through alcohol.
Dementi Studio

June Rowe Weaver, the actress Warren Beaty proposed to at nine, when she starred in a play directed by his mother in Arlington, Virginia. *Courtesy of Heather Harris*

Shirley Beaty *(fifth from left)*, the tallest ballerina in the Washington School of the Ballet, performing *Hansel and Gretel* in 1948. *Courtesy of Sandy Burditt*

Warren at the ninth grade prom in Arlington with his first girlfriend, Susan Morse, and his rival for student council president, Mike Durfee, who later married Morse. *Courtesy of Dr. Michael and Susan Morse Durfee*

Mike Durfee *(far left)*, Art Eberdt *(second from left)*, and Warren *(third from left)* "kind of ran the school." *Courtesy of Dr. Arthur Eberdt*

Shirley Beaty at seventeen *(second from left)*, with high school beau Bill Mallon *(at left)* and best friend Dottie Rector in Arlington, 1951.
Courtesy of Dorothy Rector Turmail

Warren's first "older" girlfriend, Janet Smith *(first row, second from left)*, a Washington-Lee cheerleader. Shirley is second from right. *Courtesy of Janet Smith Filia*

Nineteen-year-old Shirley (*center*) in the Broadway chorus of *Me and Juliet* in 1953, a few months after changing her name to Shirley MacLaine. *Photo by Will Rapport, courtesy of Lorraine Havercroft*

Though he said he never took drama, a newly husky Warren Beaty played a lawyer in a high school production. *Courtesy of Dr. Arthur Eberdt (seated behind bench)*

Shirley's sultry first headshot as Shirley MacLaine, which she signed for her friend Lorraine, "Love always, Shirl." *Courtesy of Lorraine Havercroft*

Shirley MacLaine, in her signature pixie haircut, with husband Steve Parker, who would betray her, as her parents and brother protectively forewarned. *Photofest*

The "dream team," Washington-Lee football star Warren Beaty and cheerleader Ann Read, at their senior prom in 1955. *Courtesy of Shannon Gabor*

The 1956 Sweetheart of Sigma Chi formal at Northwestern, with Ellie Wood. *Courtesy of Eleanor Wood Walker*

First headshot, taken in 1957, as Warren "Beaty." Rev. John Raymond kept this framed on a wall until his death.
Courtesy of Mary Raymond

Beatty in his embarrassing first starring role on television as "The Curly-Headed Kid," pictured with Raymond Massey and Connie Van Ess.
Copyright ZUMA Movie Stills Library, ZUMA Press

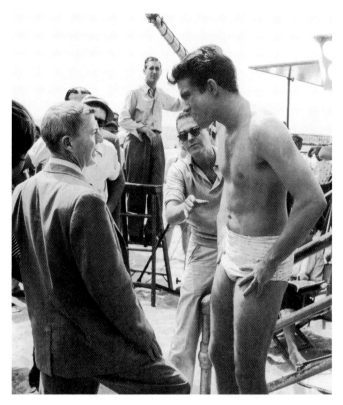

As a struggling young actor, Beatty refused to trade on his sister's fame and barely survived an attack of hepatitis. Here, in a bit part billed as "Henry Warren Beatty," in "Heartbeat," a November 1957 episode of the Hitchcock series *Suspicion*. *Photofest*

Beatty's more sophisticated new look in his second term at Stella Adler's. *Courtesy of Ned Manderino*

The cast to Beatty's eye is visible in this photograph with director Elia Kazan, taken in 1960.
Courtesy of Verne O'Hara

Beatty *(in white shirt)* onstage in *A Hatful of Rain* at the Clinton Playhouse, with his perplexed costar, Ned Wertimer *(far right)*, the summer of 1958.
Courtesy of Ned Wertimer

Jeanne Rejaunier, the former model Beatty arranged to meet in 1959 after spotting her headshot at MCA.
Courtesy of Jeanne Rejaunier

As Milton Armitage *(left)* in *Dobie Gillis*, with star Dwayne Hickman and guest actress Anita Sands, who turned down Beatty's odd request for a date.
Photofest

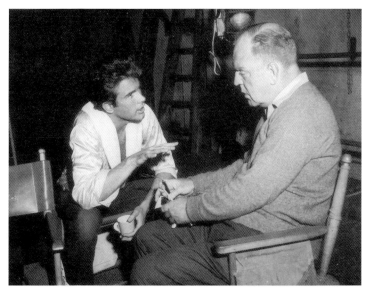

With William Inge, who wrote *A Loss of Roses*, *Splendor in the Grass*, and *All Fall Down* for Beatty, for whom Inge seemed to have an unrequited love.
Courtesy of JoAnn Kirchmaier

Joan Collins signed this to their English friend Verne O'Hara, "Up the British— Love, Joan." Beatty signed, "Down the British—Love, Warren."
Courtesy of Verne O'Hara

The disastrous premiere of *A Loss of Roses* at the National Theatre on October 29, 1959, the night Shirley Booth *(far left)* quit the play. Carol Haney, whose sprained ankle launched Shirley MacLaine's career, is at right. *Copyright* Washington Post, *reprinted by permission of the D.C. Public Library*

Beatty and fiancée Joan Collins with his publicist and confidant John Springer's children—the closest he and Collins would get to family life after her traumatic abortion. *Courtesy of June Springer and Gary Springer* his friends.* Most of their crowd were up-and-coming members of the Studio interested in theater, such as Kimbrough and Milian, Ben Piazza, a young Dennis Hopper, and a few famous names such as Gore Vidal. "At one point Montgomery Clift and Roddy McDowall became part of the group," said Barraque. ". . . I wasn't crazy about Dennis Hopper. He played up to both of them, Clift and MacDowall, a lot, and we all knew Dennis Hopper was not gay . . . he wanted them to think that maybe he was, too." As far as Barraque could discern, Beatty was not close to anyone in their clique other than Clint Kimbrough, who was remembered by Milian, his roommate, as "one of the purest and nicest persons I've ever met."†

Beatty maintained his affectionate friendship with his well-to-do classmate at Stella Adler's, Mitchell May, known in his social set as "Buzzy." Beatty fell in with Buzzy May's rich crowd, which included Ted Otis of the Otis elevator family, an extra in the movies, and "Georgie" Hamilton, a nineteen-year-old aspiring actor whose mother was a Memphis belle. "I remember meeting George Hamilton at the Blackstone," said one of the gang, "and he had just bought himself a Chesterfield coat, and I think it was summertime, and he was wearing this Chesterfield coat, he was so proud of it. George, when he went out to Hollywood, had to have the Rolls-Royce and the whole trappings of the 1940s stars. He was the biggest narcissist I had ever known. He couldn't pass a mirror without standing in front of it, gazing upon himself for the longest time."[144]

By this point, May had married Verne O'Hara, his English society girlfriend. None of Buzzy May's clique knew exactly where Warren Beatty lived. "It was so grungy that he never wanted any of us to go there," explained O'Hara, "I mean, he was poor . . . he had nothing. So here he's going to the Stork Club, and anywhere he wants to go, he came with us. We were spoiled brats."

In August 1958, soon after Warren Beatty returned from the Clinton Playhouse, he was summoned to meet the gentleman admirer who would change his life, the last of the trio of influential homosexuals responsible for his early career.

---

*Lee Strasberg, who headed the Actors Studio, taught the Method based on Stanislavsky's original emphasis on "emotional memory," or recalling an incident from one's conscious past to convey the emotion in a scene. Adler instructed her students to use their imagination.

†Clinton Kimbrough died of pneumonia on April 9, 1996, in Ada, Oklahoma.

William Inge, a respected and successful playwright from America's heartland, had won the Pulitzer Prize for *Picnic* in 1953, and wrote the classics *Come Back, Little Sheba* and *Bus Stop*. That fall, he was preparing to go into production on a movie he was writing in collaboration with the respected director Elia Kazan.[145] Inge was looking for a young man to play the costarring role of a high school youth from the Midwest, with everything going for him, whose first love takes a tragic, and finally bittersweet, turn. The script, still in progress, was then called *Splendour in the Grass.**

Inge, who grew up in Independence, Kansas, a lonely and repressed homosexual, heard a true story of similarly star-crossed young lovers when he was a boy, and he told it to Elia Kazan at the end of 1957, when Kazan was directing Inge's play *The Dark at the Top of the Stairs*.[146] Inge felt that the simple story of lost love would not translate well as a play or a novel, so Kazan told Inge, "If you write it, I'll do it [as a film]."[147] By early spring in 1958, Inge, who had never written a screenplay, submitted an early draft of *Splendor in the Grass* to Kazan, who later described it as a "dramatic narrative with dialogue." The director began to "rearrange" the script, "cut[ting] out hunks."[148]

The last Saturday in March, as Kazan was scheduling a second read-through of what he referred to in his journal as the "Bill Inge movie," Inge happened to watch *True Story*, the short-lived noon serial on NBC. By chance, it was the episode where Beatty plays a high school boy who cheats on an exam. Inge found Beatty captivating.[149] After seeing *True Story*, the playwright believed that Warren Beatty was the young man he must have to play Bert, as the character of Bud was then called, in *Splendor in the Grass* — as Inge would inform Beatty when they met.[150]

Elia Kazan was more focused on casting the actress who would play Deanie, the virginal high school girl tragically in love with Bud. The star he had in mind from the beginning was Natalie Wood, whose poignant performance as a schoolgirl three years earlier in *Rebel Without a Cause* with James Dean lingered in Kazan's subconscious.[151] When he heard gossip that Wood, who was on suspension at Warner Brothers, was "washed up," he thought of

---

*Both William Inge and Elia Kazan used the British spelling, "splendour," taken from William Wordsworth's poem, *Ode to Intimations of Immortality*, which inspired Inge's title. The studio changed the spelling to "Splendor." For consistency, the studio title, *Splendor in the Grass*, is used hereafter.

Lee Remick, but she had become pregnant in May and would be unavailable the rest of 1958, so the director returned to his original choice of Wood.[152]

In September, soon after Warren Beatty returned to New York from Clinton, Kazan received approval from the Motion Picture Production Code for the basic story of *Splendor in the Grass* and began to consider locations for filming, while Inge worked on the script.[153] Sometime in the interval of August to September, William Inge sent for Beatty to come to his apartment at 45 Sutton Place South so he could meet the struggling soap opera actor he had been imagining since March as the ideal high school boy for his film. The go-between, according to both Beatty and Inge, was Maynard Morris, Beatty's effete theater agent at MCA.[154]

William Inge's reaction to Warren Beatty in the flesh was a *coup de foudre*. John Connolly, the playwright's live-in secretary, was a witness. "I think it was a foregone conclusion in his mind as to who was going to play the part. Once Bill saw Warren and got the feel of him, he was exactly what Bill wanted to write about. I may go even so far as to say that he may have tailored scenes with Warren's personality in mind."[155]

"He was the kind of boy everyone looked at," was Inge's rapt description of Warren Beatty, based on their first meeting. "He seemed . . . just perfect."[156]

According to Connolly, Beatty was unsure of himself when he arrived at Inge's apartment. "You can imagine, here he was coming up against the big guns, and nervous as hell, anxious as hell. People keep saying that he was a suave, smooth — he wasn't. He was feeling his way, and he learned very fast." When the secretary escorted Beatty to meet Inge, "he introduced himself as, 'I'm Warren Beatty, Shirley MacLaine's brother?'"[157] To Connolly, a sophisticated literati who later became an acclaimed lighting director, Beatty was a naïve and eager twenty-one. "I don't want to use the term puppy-like, but you got that impression . . . he looked like to me a college jock, and gives that impression of, 'Where's my football? I'm going out and toss them around today.'"

John Connolly's quick read of Beatty, reinforced by future encounters in the company of Inge, was that he had "unending ambition, all starting from being, quote, 'the brother of Shirley MacLaine.'"[158] Beatty, whom Connolly considered "very calculating," was patently aware that a starring role in an Elia Kazan film written by William Inge would establish him as a movie star, and he wanted it as badly as Inge wanted him.

After that first meeting, as Inge and Kazan continued with pre-production on *Splendor in the Grass* — including a visit to Kansas in October scouting for locations — "Warren came over on a number of occasions to the apartment at Sutton Place," recalled Inge's secretary. The sensitive playwright was completely smitten with Beatty, determining in his mind that he was going to star "a would-be actor and cocktail lounge piano player" in his first original screenplay, directed by the illustrious Elia Kazan.[159]

"They would hang out," observed Connolly, who found it difficult to discern whether Inge and Beatty were devoting more time to "the movie, the script, or just buddy-buddy friendship. Bill felt comfortable in his presence, he liked the kid; he wanted to show him his appreciation of his talent, and really to discover the talent . . . Bill felt that he could *mold* him, and mold his writing to the talents of Warren Beatty."

Connolly believed that Inge "may have had fantasies" about becoming Beatty's lover, but the playwright's puritanical upbringing constrained him. "I doubt if Bill ever expressed them in any form, shape, or matter. Warren was an overwhelming presence, even at that age and in that position. He just came on like the boy next door that I want to know."

Inge told his niece, JoAnn Kirchmaier, one of his few confidantes, that he had intense feelings for Warren Beatty, to a point that Kirchmaier believed her uncle was in love with him. "I think he was, probably."[160]

Beatty was aware of Inge's infatuation and "vamped" him, according to the ever-present Connolly. "Oh yes. Well, listen, you take one look at that incredibly beautiful face, and that sort of, 'Gee gosh, wow, I'm just a little kid from Podunk, Iowa.'" Or as Beatty's agent, Eleanor Kilgallen, observed, "Inge thought [Warren] was the cat's pajamas and Warren had a way of ingratiating himself to anybody that he turned the charm on, and of course he wanted that [movie] so very, very badly."

Whether Beatty went further than vamping with Inge, hoping it would secure the part in *Splendor in the Grass*, remains between him and Inge. Beatty certainly had the ambition. As Inge's secretary observed, "There are a lot out there who are pushing, but Warren tops it all." Considering Beatty's anxiety since childhood about being perceived as a "pansy," and his behavior in a similar circumstance that same fall, it was unlikely that he had an affair with Inge. Anna Maria Barraque was with Beatty during the parallel incident when a Greek male director tried to seduce him at a small gathering at Clint Kimbrough's apartment. The group had just attended the married director's off-Broadway play:

I was sitting on a chair, this director was on the sofa in front of me, and I guess Warren must have been on the floor — and I was fascinated, because for a long time this director was trying to convince Warren to have an affair with him. And he kept saying, "You don't have to feel badly about it. Most people are bisexual." And Warren kept saying no. But it was the argument back and forth, "why you should," and "why I don't want to." And I never said a word.

William Inge's niece, JoAnn Kirchmaier, stated it simply. "My uncle was gay, and Warren Beatty wasn't." Moreover, as his live-in secretary observed, Inge was too ashamed of his homosexuality, and too Kansas-polite, to put himself, or someone else, in a compromising position. "Bill never wanted to be around beautiful young men without someone else being there . . . so there would be no question, I assume — Bill, I'm sorry to say, was more of a closet type than you could imagine." In Connolly's estimation, Inge was 99% percent asexual; "his social life was boring as whale shit."[161]

Whatever the sexual undercurrent to their relationship, Beatty must have felt an affinity for William Inge, who was similar to his father in many ways, and had even studied elocution. Like Ira Beaty, Inge had a repressed childhood, little confidence in his talent, was once a frustrated teacher, and became an alcoholic. "He really was a very scholarly person," said Connolly, "he was quiet, afraid of his own shadow, but extremely nice to people." Kazan described his frequent collaborator as "sensitive, modest, helpful . . . he was just a dear, decent man."[162] Many years later, Beatty told Dick Cavett, "I liked the [*Splendor*] story and I liked Inge."[163]

Inge, who was in Alcoholics Anonymous and in intense psychoanalysis, supplanted Reverend John Raymond as a mentor to twenty-one-year-old Warren Beatty that fall, the second father figure to stand in for the emotionally inaccessible Ira Beaty.

In their increasingly parallel lives, both Warren Beatty and his sister had established friendships in 1958 that would thrust their careers into the upper echelon of stardom and, just as important, offer them serious roles — the artistic standard they demanded of themselves as scions of Beatys and MacLeans.

While Beatty was fastening himself to William Inge that year, Shirley MacLaine, through Dean Martin, was becoming the self-styled mascot of the Rat Pack. This contributed to Frank Sinatra's choosing her that fall as their costar in the film version of James Jones's novel *Some Came Running*. In the film, she played Ginny, a heartbreaking floozy as fragile as Ira Beaty's confidence, a part Sinatra shrewdly predicted would win her an Academy Award nomination. "When I started in movies, no role seemed right for me," observed MacLaine. "After Ginny, there seemed to be no role I couldn't do."[164]

Beatty envisioned Bud Stamper, the high school athlete Inge was tailoring for him in his screenplay for Kazan, as his breakout part. "He wants to prove to himself that he can act," the playwright insightfully observed of Beatty, "and he's devoted his entire self to it."[165] Beatty fidgeted through the fall and into winter, waiting for *Splendor in the Grass*. On December 11, 1958, the Hollywood trade papers reported that Warner Brothers had purchased the film for Natalie Wood, but "as it turned out," Inge later noted, "we didn't start the picture right away."[166]

To pay the rent, Beatty took a few-weeks recurring role that month on the CBS soap opera *Love of Life*, as a son who disapproved of his father's romance with Vanessa Dale, the serial's lead character. With the private knowledge that William Inge was crafting the starring role in a Kazan picture for him, Beatty had acquired a swaggering self-confidence, a bravado that Bonnie Bartlett, who played Vanessa Dale, viewed as "cockiness."[167]

"He was always 'on' with everybody, and I didn't like him," declared Bartlett, a respected actress married to actor William Daniels, both graduates of Northwestern prior to Beatty's year there. "I didn't think he was sincere. I really thought he was very full of himself . . . mostly he talked about girls."

Beatty came on even stronger backstage with the females on the soap opera than he had at first in Clinton, possibly to offset the homoerotic attention he was getting from William Inge. To Bartlett, Beatty was an annoying presence in the dressing room. She considered him "young and very gauche," an opinion she felt was shared by her female castmates. "At one time I said to him, 'Somebody must have told you somewhere that you were gorgeous or something . . .' — oh, he came on so bad!"

Beatty even enlisted the aid of one of MCA's cub agents who used to work for the Ford Modeling Agency, Neil Cooper, to put him in touch with starlets. When he was at MCA to confer with Morris or Kilgallen, Beatty would stop by Cooper's office to look through headshots of actresses represented by the agency and instruct Cooper which ones he wanted to date. "My father was notorious with the ladies in his own right," conceded Cooper's son, Lucas.[168]

Jeanne Rejaunier, a striking former model under contract to MCA, got a phone call from Neil Cooper early in 1959. "He wanted me to meet a guy named Warren Beatty, 'a young guy that's newly in New York, just came here, wants to meet you, he saw your picture . . .' Neil told me that he was Shirley MacLaine's brother. In fact, he said Warren had been looking over all the photos up there and he picked me."[169] Rejaunier found it "interesting that MCA would let [Warren] do that," discovering, soon after they met, that Beatty was "very enterprising for a young man."

Rejaunier, a Vassar graduate who would quit acting to become a novelist, went out with Beatty intermittently through 1967, describing him as a "very fast operator" with "sexual savoir faire." Within a short time, Beatty introduced her to William Inge, hoping to get her a part in an Inge play. Rejaunier knew that Inge was homosexual, "[and] I teased Warren about it. I used to tease him about all these guys that were after him, the gay guys. He would sometimes play along with the joke — he never would say that he ever was involved with them, but he would joke about it sometimes, although I never believed that he would. I'm sure he wouldn't."

Unlike Bonnie Bartlett, Rejaunier got to know Beatty the Virginian, who was tactful, close to his parents, a voracious reader. Their dates were to piano bars, where Beatty played Broadway show tunes for her. "He was just a really sweet guy."

The December he was on *Love of Life* with Bartlett, Warren Beatty's creative integrity was rewarded when he finally got to play the lethally charming fraternity-boy murderer based on Richard Loeb, the part he had lost twice on Broadway the year before. The two-week staging of *Compulsion* was at a playhouse in Fort Lee, New Jersey,* but it had the cachet of being the first production of Meyer Levin's play performed as Levin had written it, rather than the "producer's version" that Levin and Beatty objected to on Broadway.[170] Levin supported the Fort Lee production, announcing that he would attend opening night.

Beatty, who was on hold for *Splendor in the Grass,* considered this staging of *Compulsion* a possible "big break," remembered Verne O'Hara. He told a reporter later that the first two rows were filled with agents. "I really thought I was hot shit . . . I thought, I don't want to do something until I do something that's good."[171]

---

*The North Jersey Playhouse where Beatty performed was owned by future best-selling novelist Robert Ludlum, then an actor.

The actor had matured considerably since his disastrous first rehearsal at the Clinton Playhouse the previous summer. Wayne Tippet, who had a supporting role in *Compulsion* with Beatty at the North Jersey Playhouse, found him "very pleasant. He was young and technically he was kind of raw . . . but pleasant."[172]

Beatty invited Ned Manderino, the director who had coached him in Clinton, to the opening, on December 9, 1958. Manderino attended with Jan Norris, Beatty's occasional girlfriend, and the three celebrated that night with a dollar spaghetti dinner. "Jan told me that Warren wanted me to see it because he wanted my comments," said Manderino. In his assessment, the play was badly directed, and Beatty did not demonstrate "the definitive kind of stage presence I had seen him do." The critic for the *Bergen Evening Record* praised David Rounds, who played Leopold, as the "standout" performer, but said that Beatty "was equally able in portraying the more manly and attractive Loeb character."[173]

Tippet, who shared the stage in Fort Lee, did not get the sense that anyone in the audience was electrified by Warren Beatty, but he was "compelling," in Tippet's professional view. "I think probably people thought he was a comer, because he had a certain amount of charisma about him."

In the future, virtually all extant biographical information about Warren Beatty, including his own publicity material, would claim he was "discovered" when William Inge and director Joshua Logan happened to see him in *Compulsion*. In truth, neither Inge nor Logan saw him in the play. Inge, who was already shaping *Splendor in the Grass* for Beatty, stated later, "Just for the record, neither Josh Logan nor I even knew that Warren had played in *Compulsion*."[174]

Two other men with show business connections apparently did notice Beatty on stage in Fort Lee that month. One of them, according to director Rodney Amateau, was Herbert Bayard Swope, Jr., a Palm Beach aristocrat who was an executive at Twentieth Century Fox Television. Swope would recommend Beatty to Amateau for a part in the television series *Dobie Gillis*.[175] The other was a talent scout for Josh Logan on the lookout for a young unknown to star in Logan's next picture, most likely tipped off to attend *Compulsion* by Beatty's dogged and admiring theater agent, Maynard Morris.

Warren Beatty's two and a half years of semiobscurity as an actor, and his anonymity as a ladies man, soon would come to a sensational end.

26 *By the mystical intersection of talent,* luck, and timing that the gods of fame conspire for the chosen few, Beatty's two weeks performing in Fort Lee, coincided with a sweeping ten-day talent search in small theaters for an unknown actor to star in a movie called *Parrish*, a melodrama set on a tobacco plantation, based on a popular novel that year by Mildred Savage.

Director Josh Logan launched the talent quest on December 13, 1958, through columnists and via conference call with radio hosts across the country. He described the boy he was looking for to play Parrish McLean as if he had seen Warren Beatty through a crystal ball.[176] Logan's ideal was a "sturdy, stalwart" newcomer with some stage experience, who looked eighteen; a "man-boy" who appealed to girls, and whom Logan could turn into a star, beginning with speech lessons.[177]

When the New York director's talent scout spotted Beatty onstage in Fort Lee that December, Beatty "made an impression."[178] Logan subsequently arranged to meet him in January, with the possibility of screen-testing him for the starring role in *Parrish*.

While waiting for his appointment with Josh Logan, Beatty was barely keeping himself in cornflakes through another favor from Liam Dunne, who put him in an episode of a new religious series on *Look Up and Live* produced by Jack Kuney, the Virginian who had befriended him on "The Family" in 1957. Beatty and costars Warren Berlinger and Broadway actress Sandra Church appeared in the final segment of a morality trilogy called "The Hipster, the Delinquent, and the Square." The show aired live on January 25, 1959. Berlinger described Warren then as attentive, pleasant, "and very, very aware of what was going on."[179] Sandra Church's impression of Beatty was as "another actor on the make."[180]

Toward the end of the month, as his sister's film *Some Came Running* was officially released amid expectations that she would be nominated for an Academy Award, Beatty got a bit part as "somebody's boyfriend" on the soap opera *The Brighter Day*, starring Hal Holbrook.[181] Kirk Lang, a classmate of Shirley's from the same fraternity as Warren's at Washington-Lee, went to a few parties with Beatty in Greenwich Village that winter. "And I said, 'Well, why in the hell don't you go out to Hollywood?'" Lang recalled, "because Shirley had made it. I said, 'I'm sure she could be of some help.' And [Warren] said 'Oh no, if I'm going to get there, I'll get there on my own.' He had a great deal of social confidence. . . . I knew he'd make it, you could just tell — and just a very nice person, a very generous person. Good guy."[182]

Director Josh Logan's diary for 1959 shows that on January 30, a few days after his forgettable role on a Sunday-morning religious show, Warren Beatty arrived at Logan's penthouse on West Fifty-fifth, hoping to enthrall the director into choosing him to star in *Parrish*.[183] Two weeks earlier, Logan had signed the attractive but inexperienced twenty-one-year-old daughter of stage and film actor Henry Fonda, one of his dearest friends, to a five-year option contract. Jane Fonda, a former Vassar student who had studied art in Paris, became interested in acting the previous summer after meeting Lee Strasberg's daughter, Susan, who encouraged her to join the Actors Studio.[184] Logan decided to make a screen test of Jane, who had her father's lean intensity and the edgy energy of a thoroughbred colt, to see if her "physical appearance, acts, and poses" were "suitable" for movies, "specifically *Parrish*."[185]

Logan's plan to ensure the film's commercial success was to hire established stars Vivien Leigh and Clark Gable as the mother and stepfather of tobacco heir Parrish McLean. That way, he could cast the unproven Fonda as one of Parrish's love interests and introduce a new male "discovery" to play Parrish. Logan later wrote that when he met Warren Beatty at his penthouse that January to consider him for the part, "he was all a director could hope for: tall, humorous, extremely male. He even sat down at the piano and played and sang."[186] Beatty found the manic-depressive Logan's enthusiasm "exciting to be around," candidly disclosing that he related to the fifty-year-old director because "he hates to reveal himself too."[187]

Beatty's chief competition for the role of Parrish the "stalwart man-boy" included puckish Michael Callan, who was playing Riff in *West Side Story* on Broadway using the name Mickey Calin; Anthony Perkins, who had costarred in several movies, including *The Matchmaker*, a nonmusical precursor to *Hello, Dolly!* in which Perkins played Shirley MacLaine's boyfriend; and Tom Laughlin, a former football player from Wisconsin with a few movie credits, including a small part in Logan's film adaptation of *South Pacific*.

Laughlin, who lived in Los Angeles and had a wife and children to support, was as poor if not as malnourished as Beatty, and just as motivated to win the starring role in the film — demonstrating the brash confidence that would compel him to write, direct, and star in the counterculture classic *Billy Jack* twelve years later. "I wanted to test for *Parrish*," recalled Laughlin, "and Josh thought I was too husky, and too much of a football player, all-American hero. So I lost forty-six pounds in six weeks, and I paid my own way to New York."[188]

After eliminating Anthony Perkins as too well known, Logan introduced rivals Warren Beatty, Tom Laughlin, and Michael Callan separately to Jane Fonda, suggesting that each of them rehearse with her.[189] The director set February 4 for the first of two days to film tests of the three competitors for *Parrish*, beginning with a love scene opposite either Fonda or actress Suzanne Pleshette, whom he had cast as another of Parrish's girlfriends. Logan slyly planned to choose whichever actor generated the most potent sexual chemistry on film with the two actresses.[190]

By the director's arrangement, Fonda first rehearsed with the more experienced and driven Laughlin, "because Josh felt she was really frightened and insecure," as Laughlin would recall. ". . . I'm staying in a two-dollar-a-night, flea-bitten hotel off Times Square with rats all over the place, and Jane is living up on Fifty-ninth overlooking the park in this four-story place that for me was just beyond opulent. I had never seen anything like that. But I would go up there and work with Jane and rehearse . . . we argued all the time about God, and all the philosophical principles—great theological discussions." Laughlin's impressions of the young Jane Fonda were poignant. "I sensed in Jane an enormous purity of heart, a little naïve, a tremendous intellect that was just going crazy for something to latch onto."

Susan Stein, Fonda's equally high-born roommate, was the daughter of Jules Stein, the head of MCA, the talent agency that represented both Beatty and Shirley MacLaine. "I don't remember if the first time I met Warren was at Josh's office or when we were rehearsing," mused Fonda, "or whether he came over to the apartment I shared with Susan, but we rehearsed together before the screen test."[191] Fonda's initial impression of Warren Beatty, the starving soap opera bit player who would become as famous as she would, was "that he was totally charming, and gorgeous . . . he always seemed confident. Yeah, it was interesting."

Beatty's account was slightly different, for reasons that are unclear. "We didn't know each other," he said. "The first time either Jane or I appeared in front of a [movie] camera was doing that screen test."[192] Over the years, Beatty would tell an amusing anecdote about what happened during his movie test with Fonda, part of Logan's three-way competition to see which young and hungry actor displayed the most sex appeal with her.

"They had [Jane and me] sitting next to each other, talking," Beatty recounted a few years after the screen test. "Then Logan called out, 'Kiss her,' and I leaned over and kissed her on the cheek. Logan demanded to know if that was the best I could do, so I threw myself on Jane and kissed her and held that kiss, and they called cut and we held it, and they called cut and we held it, and somebody finally pried us apart. 'Well,' I said to myself, 'that felt pretty good.' Logan signed me for the role, didn't even wait to see the test itself."[193] When he was fifty-four, Beatty repeated the story, adding, "We were thrown together like lions in a cage and told to kiss. Oh my God! We kissed until we had practically eaten each other's heads off. We thought this was all very effective."[194]

Curiously, no one other than Beatty would remember this passionate screen kiss with Jane Fonda, including Fonda. "My memory is different from Warren's," stated Tom Laughlin, "and frankly it's quite accurate." By his recollection, Laughlin tested with Suzanne Pleshette before Beatty's test with Jane Fonda, and it was *his* kiss that was memorable:

The first scene that was to be done was the one where the girl seduces Parrish. Parrish is lying on a table, and he's been filled with bee stings, and she rubs calamine lotion on his chest, and that gets to be hot, and she sexes him up, and they have the big kiss. Now remember, I'm there, Warren Beatty, and Callan—they were surrounded by agents. Warren hadn't done anything yet, but he had Shirley MacLaine, and there were like five MCA suits there, and I got nobody. I didn't even have an agent.

And so we do this scene, and Suzanne Pleshette—it's her scene—and when she goes to kiss me, the big kiss at the end, I'm a creative actor, and I wanted to make an impression. That was more important to me than anything. So as she's coming down, I grab her by the hair at the back of her head, and I hold her there for a minute. She's a little startled, because what the hell am I doing? And I suck her down on me, and that's where we had this incredible kiss. And she took over from there, and was incredible. Then you heard everybody start to giggle, and then Logan cut. No one would *say* "Cut, cut." So that's my clear memory.

After the kiss, I ran out of the place . . . and Suzanne Pleshette said, "Who is that? Who is this guy? Where does he come from?" I had them buzzing. Now whether it happened with Warren, too, I don't know. But that was the first day.

Director Daniel Petrie, then an apprentice, was in the studio observing on the historic day Warren Beatty and Jane Fonda filmed their first screen test. Like Fonda, Petrie had no memory of the dramatic second kiss Beatty described giving Fonda, or of Logan's yelling, *"Cut! Stop! That's enough!"* as it was reported later.[195] "All I remember is sitting in the room, with no portfolio really, just allowed to be a fly on the wall, seeing the tests, and being so impressed with both these young people. There was pretty much no problem of whether or not they were going to be stars. She was devastating, and I got a kick out of the fact that she looked so much like her father."[196]

What Petrie did notice about Warren Beatty from his screen test, interestingly, was what Verne O'Hara had detected as a crossed eye. "It was not that he was cross-eyed but that he has a *cast* in his eye," explained Petrie. "One eye operated a little bit differently than the other one . . . however—by the tilt of his head—he disguised it extremely well. But it certainly didn't prevent you from coming to the conclusion that this guy was major, just major. And in later years, I thought, you know, it was just Warren Beatty, it wasn't a guy with a cast in his eye."

Tom Laughlin, who had not had a real conversation with Beatty during their competition, misjudged him at a glance as "just a good-looking rich kid, brother-of-a-star." On the second day of their screen tests, with a new scene to play, Laughlin, who was as determined as Beatty to win the part of Parrish McLean, continued to grandstand:

I went to Josh and said my ticket was up for my air flight, and I didn't have money, and it was desperately important for me that I go first. Now I was planning this, because I knew there might be some interest with "what's this crazy guy gonna do?" So I went first, and everyone was there—Beatty was there, Callan was there, and the girls were there.

The scene is where Parrish comes in and says, "I don't care. Here, take the keys to the car, I'm walking out." And so we go to do the scene, and Logan's standing next to the camera, and I turn with my back to him, but I come around with this unbelievable rage, and I say, "As far as I'm concerned, you can take your car and take a fast flying fuck at the moon," and I throw the keys in Josh's chest. And I hurt him.

I bolt off, and I go up the stairs—it was this little studio in New York—and then finally the applause started, and Logan comes running upstairs, [saying], "Oh my God, you're a genius, that was incredible, but I can't use it. You know what Jack Warner would say if he ever heard fuck you?" So he said, "Tom, if you want this part you have to do it again." So I went down, and I did it, but I didn't say "fuck you." I said, "leap at the moon" or something. But I knew, as an actor, that if somebody dares to go do something really outrageous and it works, you can't come on afterwards except to look bad. How do you top it? So I just left and went to the airplane. So I didn't watch Mickey, and I didn't watch Warren, but I left them with that.

Josh Logan made an ecstatic note in his diary to put Tom Laughlin in the next film he directed after *Parrish*. A week later, the *Hollywood Reporter* announced that Logan "stuck to his guns and nabbed 'unknown' Warren Beatty for *Parrish*."[197] The following day, Shirley MacLaine was nominated for an Oscar for her moving portrayal of the mistreated Ginny in *Some Came Running*, just as Frank Sinatra had predicted. Shirley had achieved Hollywood's highest honor at twenty-four, within a day of Warren's first starring role in a movie at the age of twenty-one, accomplishments their talented but passive parents had only fantasized for themselves.

"This boy is the sexiest thing around," Logan would later and famously say to *Time* magazine when asked about the young Warren Beatty.[198] The compliment was sincere, since the director swiftly signed Beatty to the same five-year option agreement to star in five pictures that he offered Jane Fonda, the only actors Logan had ever placed under personal contract to his production company.[199] "Warren," Tom Laughlin explained, "had a masculinity none of the other beautiful guys had."

The year 1959 clearly was meant to be Warren Beatty's moment in time. On the same February day as Beatty's first screen test with Jane Fonda, the head of production at Warner Brothers in Los Angeles sent a letter to Elia Kazan, who was rehearsing *Sweet Bird of Youth* on Broadway, promising to "alert the boys here" to look for a boy of nineteen to twenty-one to star in *Splendor in the Grass*.[200] Kazan wanted to start filming in August, unless he was contractually obligated to Twentieth Century Fox to direct the film *Wild River* first.[201]

The timing coincided with actress Natalie Wood's return to Warner Brothers that February after a seven-month suspension. The studio had resolved its dispute with the former child star using the lure that she could play Deanie Loomis, the fragile teenager in *Splendor in the Grass* whose first love ends in tragedy, a role with painful parallels to Natalie Wood's own life. Natalie Wood was drawn to Deanie as a moth to the light, just as she was to "Gadge" Kazan,* whose psychologically nuanced work she revered.

William Inge, who already had cast Warren Beatty mentally as Deanie's athlete boyfriend, Bud, was at first "dubious about Natalie," whose promise in *Rebel Without a Cause* seemed to flicker after Warner Brothers put her in a pair of shallow movies with Tab Hunter that featured only her beauty. "But Gadge wanted her," Inge said later, "and he was right."[202] After meeting privately with Wood, the director discovered she was "disgusted with her image" and had a "desire for excellence" in her work.[203] Kazan preferred to cast actors whose personalities matched the characters they were playing, and he quickly assessed the vulnerable and intelligent Natalie Wood as "true blue with a wanton side held down by social pressure," similar to the sweet-natured Deanie.[204]

Inge was still rewriting the screenplay, further refining the part of the high school football hero to fit Warren Beatty, who continued to visit the playwright frequently at his apartment on Sutton Place.[205] Jane Fonda, who had become pals with Beatty while they were preparing to costar in *Parrish*, thought at first that he was Bill Inge's boyfriend.[206]

After both Beatty and Fonda were famous, she often would be included on the long list of his girlfriends, but their relationship was more like brother and sister. "Warren and I became friends — not lovers, but friends," said Fonda. Beatty's intimate circle recognized the distinction. "He did only hang out with Jane," affirmed Verne O'Hara, who still sometimes shared her husband's hotel suite with Beatty, and was thus able to observe his bedroom partners firsthand. In O'Hara's evaluation, "Warren was of the good girl/bad girl school in those days." Jane Fonda, who had graduated from Emma Willard — similar to the seminaries for young ladies both Tat and Blanche MacLean had attended — was the former. As Tom Laughlin noted, "Jane was not a sex machine. She was a sensitive, beautiful, caring person . . . what would you look to, Eva Marie Saint? That kind of sensitive, beautiful quality."

When he went out with Jane Fonda in 1959, Beatty entertained her with tales of his carnal adventures, which seemed to surprise and amaze the essentially Baptist son of Ira and Kathlyn Beaty as much as they did the sheltered Fonda. "We mostly talked about sex," Fonda recalled, laughing. "I mean, we talked about lots of things — I'm not saying that we didn't talk

---

*"Gadge," short for Gadget, was Elia Kazan's nickname.

about professional things, but . . . maybe it was because I was just his friend that Warren would talk to me about his lovers, which I found fascinating."

Beatty described himself then as a "kid in a candy store," slightly overwhelmed but enormously pleased by his unexpected good fortune.[207] Harry Crossfield, a writer-producer of *Captain Kangaroo* who became acquainted with Beatty when their mutual friends Mitch May and his wife offered him their Blackstone suite, observed that he had "an insatiable thirst for sex. It was twenty-four hours a day . . . I mean Warren would stop women in the street. He had a great gift of picking up ladies. He would just put on the charm, and women thought he was just the cutest little thing that ever came around. Not sophisticated, but just a cute boy, with a sweetness."[208]

It was Beatty who introduced Crossfield to the woman he would marry, Anna Maria Barraque. "I was doing the backer's audition for Mitch's musical on Broadway," explained Crossfield, "and Warren had asked whether he could bring these two Cuban girls. And I said, 'Do they have any money?' '*I don't know.*' I said, 'Are they going to invest in this show?' '*I don't know.*' So they came, and that's how I met my wife."

According to Crossfield and to Mitch May's first and second wives, the Blackstone Hotel belonging to May's Bronxville-based parents was the site of innumerable sexual romps during Beatty's temporary residency there. "It was an orgy room," in the description of Crossfield, who stayed there from time to time as a bachelor. "Warren enjoyed orgies . . . he was game for anything."

Gita Hall, a Swedish actress who married Mitchell May after he and Verne O'Hara divorced, recalled a second embarrassing incident at the Blackstone involving Beatty, Mitch May, and the inopportune arrival of May's mother. "Warren had some girl there — I guess they both had a girl, definitely Warren did — and Mitch's mother walked in and opened the door, and there they were. She was not expected. So she walked in on a sort of compromising situation, and of course Warren and Mitch both blamed each other, and tried to hide. And I guess they were caught with their pants down. I think Mitch's mother quickly closed the door as I remember — he never did tell me what punishment she inflicted, but it had to be something severe."[209]

"It happened all the time," revealed Crossfield. "One time we even put a tape recorder under the bed when Warren was there and taped him." Crossfield, similar to Jane Fonda, would recall, "When Warren wasn't talking sex, or women, I don't remember what he *was* talking about . . . we were all very screwed up in that way. Immature." In his sixties, Beatty offered a similar rationale for his hypersexual behavior then, analyzing that his Protestant upbringing had constrained him from "acting out" the way he should have in his teenage years, implying he had a delayed adolescence.[210]

Harry Crossfield, who produced a short-lived musical with Mitch May on Broadway in 1959, had an exquisite tenor voice, and, for a lark, performed in piano bars with Beatty—similar to the lounge act Dustin Hoffman and Beatty would parody thirty years later in *Ishtar*. Beatty and Crossfield even used foreign accents as part of their cocktail-lounge shtick. "Warren really wanted to learn how to sing well," remembered Crossfield, who toured as an opera singer, "and I took him to one of my voice teachers at the time, a guy named Carmen Galliardi. I don't know how long that lasted, because Warren didn't have two nickels to rub together."

Beatty even entertained the idea of composing music.[211] In addition to studying with Galliardi and the voice coach he employed at Stella Adler's, Beatty collaborated with composer Rick Besoyan, and sang with an accompanist he referred to girlfriend Jeanne Rejaunier.[212] Ira's influence still shadowed him. "I have a pretty good voice," Beatty said at the time. "I never recorded professionally, but I made a demonstration record that my agents thought was pretty good. Might do something about it some time. But it's like my piano playing. I studied for a year or so, was pretty talented, but I'm sloppy."[213]

Beatty nonetheless exuded confidence that he would be a movie star, buoyed by his five-picture contract with Josh Logan commencing with *Parrish*, and by the devoted patronage of William Inge, who had positioned him for *Splendor in the Grass*. When Tom Calhoun, Beatty's high school football buddy, was flown to New York that spring by accounting firms recruiting him from Duke, "Warren kept trying to get me to stay in New York [and act] with him. I remember he said, 'All you need to succeed in this business is brains,' and he knew that I had brains. But what he didn't know was I'm not a risk-taker—it would have seemed so outlandish to me. And, too, I didn't think I had any talent, and I'm sure that's true, and I was pretty skeptical that all you needed was brains. I was pretty sure you needed talent. At least some talent."

Warren Beatty's strategy, then as always, was to cultivate exceptional mentors; or as Jane Fonda expressed it, "He had a way of collecting talent. You know, he hadn't even kind of been discovered yet, but he was already looking for talent in [writer] Mead Roberts, William Inge. He was already creating . . . making friends with people who had talent. It seemed like he knew a lot of really talented people."

Beatty's alliance with Inge bore fresh fruit just before spring, when the Pulitzer Prize–winning playwright summoned the actor from his hovel on West Sixty-eighth to Inge's Sutton Place apartment. As Beatty told the story, "Inge called me one day and asked me to come over right away to read a play he had finished, even before he had it typed up . . . he said that he had a part in a play for me. I was recovering from an attack of food poisoning. I had been sick for three or four days, hadn't shaved or anything, but I left the house immediately. On the way I stopped in at a cafeteria and ate some food and came out thinking to myself that tasted pretty good, that's all right. Suddenly three husky fellows closed in on me. For a moment I thought they were going to hold me up right there in the middle of the day; then one of them flashed a badge in front of my face and another stuck a gun in my back. They turned out to be the FBI, but they had the wrong man. It frightened me so much that I ran back into the cafeteria and was sick all over again."[214]

The play Inge had in mind for Beatty, A Loss of Roses, was a tense triangle with oedipal overtones about a young gas station attendant living with his widowed mother in Depression-era Kansas. Their lives are thrown into turmoil by a middle-aged tent-show actress whom the son seduces. "I had deliberately set out to write a play about . . . how it is between a mother and a son, how it really is when there is too much love."[215] Inge, who was afraid to fly, wrote a first draft on a train ride in 1957 but set it aside after becoming discouraged.[216] The play "suddenly looked good" to him at the end of 1958, when he envisioned Warren Beatty as the son, whom Inge described in a letter as possessing such sexual confidence "he feels a wreath has been hung on his penis."[217]

The Festival of Two Worlds in Spoleto, Italy, announced that A Loss of Roses would have its world premiere there in June, then canceled it on February 26 for lack of funds, foreshadowing a long, tortuous saga that lay ahead for Inge.[218] A few weeks later, the theater press reported A Loss of Roses as William Inge's next Broadway play. Inge asked Elia Kazan to direct, and sent a letter to Kazan in March wondering if he should change the title and suggesting actress Shelley Winters to play the possessive mother.[219]

Beatty told his publicist later that year that both Inge and Kazan had offered him the lead in A Loss of Roses on Broadway, with Kazan directing, a dream scenario that evaporated in March.[220] "It's a fine play and it's going to be a sure as hell hit . . . but I'm caught," Kazan wrote to Inge on March 24, referring to his obligation to direct the film Wild River. "I've ducked and dodged the 20th Century Fox business for three years . . . if their script doesn't turn out soon, I'll do *Splendor*. If it does, I'll do our picture next."[221] A few days later, Inge issued a press release saying he had shelved *A Loss of Roses*.[222]

To Beatty's further frustration, *Parrish* collapsed like an undercooked soufflé at the end of March, his twenty-second birthday. Josh Logan had been unable to persuade Vivien Leigh and Clark Gable to play Parrish's mother and stepfather, and he himself had severe misgivings about the final script.[223] Logan withdrew as the director of *Parrish*, taking his two new contract players, Jane Fonda and Warren Beatty, with him.

In less than a month, Beatty went from three starring roles in a Broadway play and two movies — *A Loss of Roses*, *Splendor in the Grass*, and *Parrish* — to none, leaving him with only a bit role as "somebody's boyfriend" on the soap opera *A Brighter Day*, and a dormant contract with Joshua Logan.

He decided it was time to go to Hollywood.

27 *As he was leaving for the West Coast,* Warren Beatty saw his name in a gossip column for the first time. It was written by Dorothy Kilgallen, the influential sister of his MCA television agent, "and a Warren fan in those early days."[224] Kilgallen's widely read column in the *New York Journal-American* reported on March 31, 1959, "Jane Fonda's been seen about town with Warren Beatty, a young actor who may become the hottest of all cinema properties."

Eleanor Kilgallen, who was equally fond of Beatty as her sister, appreciated the irony that Warren, her "hot" young MCA client, could barely afford breakfast and was desperate for an acting job. Beatty also was in fragile health, recovering from food poisoning and still weak due to his bout of hepatitis. Kilgallen finessed a television audition for him on *Playhouse 90* via her partner in Beverly Hills, Monique James, and then arranged to take a business trip to Los Angeles with her assistant, Kelly Lachman, so she could personally shepherd Beatty to his reading at CBS. Kilgallen further displayed her "deep affection" for her unemployed actor by paying for Beatty's first airplane ticket to Hollywood. "I don't talk about that part," she recalled modestly.

"So we get a hold of Warren," continued Kilgallen, "and I said, 'Get your good suit. You have to have one suit to show up.'" Beatty, as she would remember, "had sort of a navy blue job, and a white nylon shirt . . . so out we go to the coast, Kelly and I in the front of the plane, and I guess Warren was sitting in the rear somewhere."

As his agent and her assistant checked into the Beverly Hills Hotel, Beatty tagged along, until it became clear "he had no place to stay." The tactful Kilgallen refrained from suggesting he call Shirley MacLaine, who was in town to attend the Academy Awards the following week, since she had been nominated for *Some Came Running*.* "Though Warren said nothing specific to me, I had a feeling that staying with his sister was not an option . . . he was not out there looking for her."

Kilgallen and her secretary's mothering of Beatty extended to hand washing his one white shirt in the bathroom of Lachman's hotel suite so it would be clean for his *Playhouse 90* audition, then finding a spare sofa for him in the apartment of Monique James's assistant, Ina Bernstein. "Poor Ina was not thrilled at the thought of Warren Beatty. Her father also lived in the same complex, so she was scandalized that suddenly she had a male roommate. It wasn't in the days where that was the thing to do. But anyway, long boring end to the story, he did not get the part."

Beatty's spate of bad luck continued during his first few weeks in Hollywood, after Eleanor Kilgallen returned to Manhattan, where he had given up his dismal walk-up. "I hung around . . . thinking something would surely happen. I was still a hermit. At that point I was very run down physically. My liver was acting up again. Things were a drag. I didn't have much money. I didn't have many friends, and I didn't have any work."[225]

Warren Beatty's spirits flagged further that April after he learned that Josh Logan had agreed to direct a campus romance for Warner Brothers called *Tall Story*. Logan had planned to cast Beatty in the starring role as a college basketball hero pursued by a coed, played by Jane Fonda, on the hunt for a husband. The studio, and Logan's agent, insisted he cast the fey Anthony Perkins as the star athlete Fonda hoped to snare, a choice the director strenuously opposed, as he wrote to Fonda later:

When I had to switch to *Tall Story* because the *Parrish* screenplay was so poor, I tried to get Warner Brothers to use Warren for the male lead. They said, "No, you have to have somebody with some kind of a name in *Tall Story*, especially if you are going to use Jane Fonda, who has not appeared on the screen so far." So, with great reluctance, I agreed on

---

*Susan Hayward received the Oscar that year for *I Want to Live*.

Tony Perkins. I have always liked him personally, but I did not think he was the right man for this job and I thought Warren was. By not using Warren in a picture, I lost his contract.[226]

After juggling three star-making roles and a five-picture deal with Logan two months earlier, "I didn't have a job," Beatty said simply.[227]

Monique James, his MCA agent in Los Angeles — who would acquire the nickname "Starmaker" — cast her net in the shallower waters of television, securing another audition for Beatty on the CBS showcase *Playhouse 90*, where one of her other young clients, Robert Redford, would first get noticed. Beatty was cast in a small role in a World War II drama called "Dark December," directed by the respected Franklin Schaffner and starring Barry Sullivan, James Whitmore, Richard Beymer, and Lili Darvas. When the program aired on April 30, Beatty was singled out for praise in the review in *Variety*, which noted that he "briefly contributed a memorable character."[228]

Ironically, Warren Beatty would be better remembered that spring for playing Milton Armitage, the rich and insufferably vain rival of the title character in *The Many Loves of Dobie Gillis*, a situation comedy starring Dwayne Hickman and Bob Denver as a girl-crazy teenager and his beatnik pal. According to the producer, Rodney Amateau, Beatty came recommended by Herbert Bayard Swope, Jr., the Fox executive who had seen him onstage as the arrogant college-boy sociopath in *Compulsion*.[229] Swope, who grew up on Lands End, an estate in the Hamptons described in *The Great Gatsby* by F. Scott Fitzgerald, who occasionally summered there, had an intimate understanding of the stuffy, egotistical Milton Armitage persona. "And he came back to me and said, 'I got just the guy to play him,'" recalled Amateau.[230] When Amateau's wife, Sandra, the daughter of George Burns and Gracie Allen, met Beatty, she made the wisecrack to her husband, "Not your type, he's a class act!"

Beatty, who urgently needed the paycheck, signed with Fox for a recurring role on *Dobie Gillis*, and returned to New York in early May to spend a few weeks before filming began, staying in Mitch May's suite at the Blackstone. His great supporter, William Inge, was still not ready to set up *A Loss of Roses* for Beatty to star in on Broadway, though he had been in touch with George Cukor about directing it. In May, Inge wrote to Josh Logan, who was desperate to direct the play, saying he had "only tentative plans" to open it around Christmas.[231] Beatty was reluctant, probably due to his mixed experiences at the Clinton Playhouse. "Because it's not fun, it's work doing a play," he said later. Beatty's criteria—having *fun*—governed both his and his sister's life choices, their conscious means of avoiding becoming trapped as MacLaine perceived their parents had been.[232]

The ambitious Beatty pressed his agency, MCA, to devote more energy to getting him movie roles. "Nobody in the picture department was doing anything, to our knowledge, trying to get him a job in pictures," remembered Kilgallen, his television agent. "We were trying to work with Maynard with the theater stuff." As ever, Beatty refused to trade on his sister's fame, which was at a high point after her Oscar nomination.

"He never made any attempt to utilize any opening of doors that some people would do normally because of who he was," recounted Kilgallen. "I have a great admiration for the way, from the beginning, Warren seemed to know that he had a big career ahead of him and how determined he was to make it all happen by using, in addition to his talent, his considerable charm, good looks, smarts, and political savvy to get him there. Would that the current crop of vapid, up-and-coming stars had that kind of know-how going for them. He is a wonderful success story."[233]

Beatty's pressure on MCA led to Metro-Goldwyn-Mayer expressing interest in offering him a movie contract based on his *Parrish* screen test—if studio executives liked how he looked on film when he started *Dobie Gillis* in mid-May. Earlier that month, movie and gossip columnist Louella Parsons interviewed Shirley MacLaine for a profile syndicated through the *Los Angeles Herald-Examiner*. After mentioning MacLaine's new film, *Career*, Parsons added, "Her brother, Warren Beasley [sic], is a New York actor and she's hoping he'll come to Hollywood."[234]

Before he left New York, Beatty saw Jane Fonda, who was rehearsing for a two-week appearance in *The Moon Is Blue* at the North Jersey Playhouse, to acquire stage experience before making her film debut in *Tall Story*. Dorothy Kilgallen faithfully publicized their date at Johnny's Keyboard, a popular piano bar, in her May 15 column, promoting her sister Eleanor's client as "promising young actor Warren Beatty." In private, Beatty affectionately referred to the columnist as "Dolly May," the code name for Dorothy used by her family and close friends.[235]

A few days after Beatty entertained "good girl" Jane Fonda, the *New York News Sunday Magazine* featured a front-page color portrait of English starlet Joan Collins wrapped in a hot-pink sweater and pursing fuchsia-painted lips at the camera. Collins, a glamorous brunette, hazily resembled Elizabeth

Taylor, who had starred in A *Place in the Sun,* the George Stevens film that had inspired the teenage Warren Beatty to become an actor. Collins's provocative pose in the Sunday magazine inspired other thoughts in Beatty. After studying her photograph, as he later told Collins, Beatty made a point to observe her onscreen, "to decide whether he would like to meet me in person."[236] Warren Beatty left for the West Coast in May 1959 with this as one of his objectives.

Beatty flew into Hollywood the second time under somewhat more auspicious circumstances. Jay Kanter, one of MCA's top talent agents, met him at the airport, by the prior arrangement of Edd Henry, the New York agent who had elicited interest from MGM to test Warren Beatty for a movie contract. "We took care of him as a corporation," explained Henry's assistant at the time, Marvin Birdt.[237]

Kanter and his wife, the former Judith Balaban, a friend of Rita Gam's and another of Grace Kelly's bridesmaids, took over for Ina Bernstein, Beatty's skittish roommate of the month before. "Warren had no special place to stay, so he hung out at our house," recalled Balaban — a polite way of saying that Beatty was broke. The Kanters, who lived in the heart of Beverly Hills near the Kirk Douglases and the Robert Wagners, and who were extremely social, had previously offered the room over their garage to an up-and-coming publicist named John Foreman, who became a successful film producer. Balaban later wrote, "John Foreman and I, deciding Warren had a unique charm, bet someone else that we could make a star of him in the industry within a month, just by talking him up at parties. Nobody had seen him act, and though he appeared only in one *Dobie Gillis* episode after his arrival, our plan worked even better than we'd dreamed."[238]

Intent on becoming a movie star ("and making a lot of money," according to a New York pal), Beatty impressed MGM executives sufficiently for them to offer him a five-year term contract at a salary of four hundred dollars a week, which the starving Virginian viewed as a mixed blessing.[239] His increasingly successful sister, who was preparing to film the musical *Can-Can* with Frank Sinatra, had been offered two hundred thousand dollars a picture, but was still bound by her original contract with Hal Wallis at what she derided as "the equivalent of 50 cents a week."[240] MacLaine told the *New York Times* that May that she would never sign anything again but a laundry bill, a piece of wisdom listened to closely by her cautious brother, whose shared experience observing their parents' restricted lives caused him to further embrace freedom of choice.[241] "I didn't want to be told what to do," Beatty said of MGM's offer, "and I had the feeling they were going to tell me what to do, or at least try to!"[242]

Beatty's poverty, however, was compelling, as was his desire to be a success in films. He signed the five-year contract with Metro,* which had him, suddenly, "rolling in money," and gave him a shot at becoming an MGM movie star, though from Beatty's point of view, his signature was in erasable ink.[243] He shrewdly negotiated a provision that "barring no conflicting dates," MGM would release him to make *Splendor in the Grass* for Warner Brothers "if Inge wants him."[244] MGM had Beatty in mind to star in a youth film called *Strike Heaven on the Face*, about a high school rumored to have a sex club, based on a first novel by a high school English teacher that critics dismissed as "flimsy" and "salacious."[245]

With his first regular paychecks as an actor, Beatty took a room at the Chateau Marmont Hotel — an ersatz seventeenth-century French castle on Sunset Boulevard known to be an artists' retreat — and attended to his fragile health. "I went to a doctor. He put me on a special diet, no drinking and all that, got me back in shape."[246] Maintaining his health, and abstaining from alcohol and drugs, would remain Beatty's lifelong preoccupation, even as he began his paradoxical pursuit of la dolce vita in Hollywood. "Four hundred dollars a week. I was not used to this kind of money. It coincided with a certain liberalization of my life style. I was having a very good time."[247]

On May 21, he filmed his first appearance on the sly situation comedy *The Many Loves of Dobie Gillis*. The episode was called "The Best Dressed Man," and pitted Beatty's rich-boy narcissist, Milton Armitage, against the everyman Dobie Gillis in a wardrobe contest to impress the prettiest girl in their high school, played by the talented and precocious Tuesday Weld. Herbert Swope's aristocrat's intuition that Warren Beatty would be right for the role proved accurate. Beatty told Deborah Sherwood, one of the regulars in background scenes, that he knew the character inside and out, "he *was* Milton. Tops in everything, handsome . . . all Milton had that Warren didn't have was money."[248]

Beatty's effective impersonation of Dobie's handsome and spoiled rival carried through to the set at Fox Western, where he was viewed by much of the cast, including the amiable Dwayne Hickman, the star of the series, as aloof, egotistical, and superior. "I mean I was Dobie Gillis, and yet you never

---

*Metro-Goldwyn-Mayer, or MGM.

would have known. Denver and I—Bob Denver and I—used to stand and look at each other, you know, because Warren had this personality, that he projected, that was like a *star*."[249]

Rod Amateau, who often directed *Dobie Gillis*, recalled, "Max Shulman, who created the series, used to say, 'Warren's a star. The only thing is, nobody knows it except him!' And I didn't laugh at that. It was Max's line, but I didn't laugh at it, because it was true." In Amateau's opinion, everyone on the series was playing himself, "and don't think that was easy. There's no Milton, there's no such fella. It's Warren. And there's no Dobie Gillis; there's Dwayne. Tuesday was always the girl everybody in the world wanted to sleep with. People on the street wanted to sleep with her."

Amateau found Beatty "pleasant to work with, his behavior on the set was professional, he knew his lines, he knew his marks, you told him once, that was it. He put a lock on that character. Good manners, very good manners." There were also indications, on *Dobie Gillis*, that Warren Beatty took a great interest in the way he looked on camera. Amateau was amused by Beatty's habit of combing his hair in the reflection of the lens before he said his lines, or asking the camera operator to reblock scenes to show his best angle.

According to Hickman and Denver, the crew resented Beatty as conceited. "I remember once they locked him in the dressing room," said Hickman. "He couldn't get out the door. It was one of those cheap, knock-down dressing rooms with material on the sides that you just put up like four walls, but they made it so the door wouldn't open." When Beatty discovered he was trapped, he cleverly disrupted the scene that was being filmed by singing loudly, knowing the crew would have to let him out. "*Opera*," recalled Hickman. "Which I thought was a strange choice. In fact, I always thought Warren was strange, frankly. Very private, very hard to get to know, and kind of in another world—you could look at him and you'd think that he was thinking of something else. He was gone, he wasn't there."

It was the same absentmindedness, self-absorption, or intense distraction that Warren's friend Lenn Harten had noticed in their Stella Adler days. Dwayne Hickman and Bob Denver interpreted Beatty's detachment as an indication that he thought the TV series beneath him. "I had the feeling that he didn't want to be there very long, you know what I mean?" mused Hickman. "And I also felt that his handlers, maybe Monique, or other people, wanted to move him into movies." Denver, who played the offbeat Maynard G. Krebs, considered Beatty "great in the part, but we all thought he was not long for episodic TV."[250]

Warren Beatty's sights were set high, even with respect to films. "What I do remember," remarked Jane Fonda, "and I'm not good about the timing, is realizing that Warren was much more self-conscious about wanting a career, and sort of seeing a vision for himself. Very early on he made a list of the directors that he would work with, whereas it never would have occurred to me, and I think part of it has to do with gender. I don't remember the list— Kazan was on it— it was just the existence of the list that fascinated me more than the names on it."

Beatty later told film editor Dede Allen he wanted to work with only certain directors, "and the best," because he could learn from them, a concept that came naturally to the son of former college professors and the grandson of a respected director of Canadian stage productions.[251] As he said later of his first weeks under contract to MGM, "I wasn't doing anything that meant anything."[252]

When the dubious *Strike Heaven on the Face* was shelved in June, a wary Beatty had "some disagreements" over what picture Metro would put him in next.[253] He balked at most of the studio's suggestions, complaining that the only wardrobe at MGM that fit him was Clark Gable's.[254]

His discriminating nature was reinforced by the example of his sister, an Oscar nominee with equally vocal opinions about doing quality work. When Beatty started *Dobie Gillis*, Shirley MacLaine was interviewed by the *New York Times*, expressing her contempt for "pictures where the white girl never ends up with the Negro guy even though it was inevitable in the context . . . I dig a dollar as much as the next person, but I want to be part of something that's real. I want to make pictures that are an expression of the people, that are authentic . . . if everyone told the truth, then no one would be offended."[255]

Shirley's and Warren's at times disdainful attitude toward movie stardom was a by-product of their cultivated, socially progressive MacLean genes and the Beatys' Baptist reverence for the truth, or as MacLaine told the *Times*, "I'm not what you call part of Hollywood. Not because I don't like them, but because I like what I am better . . . in any case, I won't be doing this all my life."[256] Less than a month later, Shirley MacLaine was on the cover of *Time* magazine, closely followed by the cover of *Look*, with the caption "Hollywood's Free Spirit," another example of Ira and Kathlyn Beaty's influence, in this case inspiring their children *not* to conform.

That summer, Warren tangled with Hollywood's established powers over the next movie MGM suggested for him, *Studs Lonigan*, a 1920s Chicago gangster drama adapted from a novel by James T. Ferrell and directed by Irving Lerner, who went on to direct television's *Ben Casey*. Beatty would say later that he turned down the starring role, a recollection disputed by the film's producer-screenwriter, Philip Yordan.[257] "I offered Warren the lead," acknowledged Yordan, "but he couldn't get along with the director, Irving Lerner, and Lerner fired him."[258]

Gerald Medearis, a Harvard theology student who replaced Beatty as Lonigan,* later heard a third account from actor Jack Nicholson, who had a bit part in the film, one of Nicholson's first movie roles. "Warren *wanted* to play the lead. He told Jack Nicholson they turned him down because he wanted too much money." According to Medearis, "Jack wanted to play the lead, too. He was very disappointed he didn't get the part, but Jack was a really nice person."[259]

Whichever version of why Beatty was replaced as the star of *Studs Lonigan* was accurate, each pointed to the fact that he was an actor, and a person, with strong convictions, just as he had shown when he walked away from *Compulsion* on Broadway, a position supported by Meyer Levin, the disenchanted novelist. The same was true with the author of *Studs Lonigan*, who publicly repudiated the film version of his novel as "stupid and foolish."[260]

Beatty, who felt "oppressed" under contract to MGM ("I was turning into citrus fruit after three weeks"), telephoned Eleanor Kilgallen in New York, divulging a private plan to extricate himself.[261] "He used to call me on Mondays and play the piano. And he was very antiestablishment—he wasn't in control of his life, they were going to assign him to some crazy lousy picture, et cetera et cetera—and he said, 'You know what I'm doing? I'm saving every one of these [MGM] checks and I'm not cashing them.'"

Beatty's righteous position with MGM resulted in his being tossed out of the Chateau Marmont that summer when he could no longer pay his bills.[262] "I was extremely naïve about movies when I came to Hollywood," he later told a documentary filmmaker. "I wanted to make a movie with Greta Garbo, but I couldn't do that. I had a serious problem, and there was just nothing that could be done about it."[263]

Beatty relocated to the faux-medieval Montecito Apartments on Franklin Avenue in the Hollywood foothills, using his meager *Dobie Gillis* wages to pay the rent. One day in the elevator, he bumped into the impishly amusing Michael J. Pollard, a diminutive stage actor who was in California

---

*Medearis used the screen name Christopher Knight.

to break into television. "All the New York actors used to stay there, or at the Chateau Marmont," recalled Pollard, who had shared an elevator with horror star Boris Karloff the morning before he saw Beatty. "It was all different then, it's like real quiet and spooky."[264]

Beatty and the childlike Pollard, polar opposites physically and by nature, seemed fated to become friends. They had first met in an elevator in New York in 1957, as Beatty was leaving the studio after the disastrous "Curly-Headed Kid." "I told Warren he was good on the *Kraft* show, and he said, 'Really?' I said, 'Yeah, really.' He said, 'Could you hear me?' I said, 'Yeah.' So we've been friends ever since." After their second chance encounter on an elevator, at the Montecito, Pollard spotted Beatty the next morning on the set of *Dobie Gillis*, where, by coincidence, Pollard had been cast to play Maynard G. Krebs's loopy-cool cousin Jerome. "It was like those movies where two people meet, and then they meet again at a dinner party, and go, *Gasp!*"

Warren Beatty and Michael J. Pollard became unlikely pals, with Pollard as another in Beatty's gallery of talented eccentrics who made him laugh. "He was just a guy Warren thought was funny," observed the director of *Dobie Gillis*. Pollard's take was very direct. "Warren was always such a — really a neat guy, from the beginning. We just hit it off, you know?" He considered Beatty one of his "alter egos," the other being Bob Dylan.

Except for rare instances of insecurity — such as when he met Inge and blurted out that he was Shirley MacLaine's brother — Beatty told only a few people about his famous sister. Michael J. Pollard was one of them. Pollard recalled, "Warren used to drive me home. I don't drive a car, so he used to drive Shirley's. She had, like, one of those MGs she lent to him . . . one time at Roma's, Frank [Sinatra] was sitting with Shirley MacLaine, and I walked by, and she'd go, 'Oh, you know my brother, Warren.'"

The fact that Shirley loaned Warren her MG convertible, a gift from producer Hal Wallis when she moved to Hollywood, proved that she wanted to help her fiercely independent younger brother, contrary to some of his friends' beliefs. "I kept saying, 'Isn't she going to help you?'" recalled New Yorker Harry Crossfield, "and Warren said no. I thought that very strange. I got the idea that she wouldn't help him. They'd never gotten along very well, that was my impression. They were not talking to each other. Warren didn't want to discuss it."

Alluding to his hurt feelings over Shirley's elopement and to the tension her unusual marriage to Steve Parker had caused, Beatty characterized the relationship as, "There was a period when it was not all honeysuckle. But that was just brother and sister problems. It happens in any family and had nothing to do with our work."[265] His refusal to capitalize on his sister's fame was part of his gentleman's code of the South; or as he put it, "I think that there are certain things you have to do on your own."[266]

At the beginning of his uneasy alliance with MGM, and while he was first appearing on *Dobie Gillis* at Fox Western, Beatty held out hope that *Splendor in the Grass* would begin production at Warner Brothers. Sometime that summer, apparently, he met Elia Kazan, an introduction that came about through the kindly Inge, according to Beatty, Kazan, and Inge.[267] The director, unaware of Inge's tailoring the role of Bud for Beatty, was considering other actors to play Natalie Wood's tender first love in *Splendor* while evaluating whether the script for *Wild River* was sufficiently ready to start filming.

"Bill [Inge] said he'd seen this fellow and he liked him and would I meet him," Kazan said of his first encounter with Warren Beatty. "So I met him and took a walk with him."[268] Kazan, who believed that directing was 80 percent casting, and was then a great admirer of Freud, analyzed the characters in his scripts and chose actors whose personalities mirrored them, based on his psychoanalysis of the actors.[269] "I take walks with them. I go to dinner with them . . . I'm looking for someone who can *experience* the experiences of the role . . . and gradually you say, 'He's got the part in him somewhere.'"[270] Kazan liked Beatty "right off," and saw in him the earnest but flawed football hero Bud in *Splendor in the Grass*. "Warren had been a high school football player, uncertain and charming," Kazan recalled when Beatty was sixty-two. "He still is."[271]

After his walk with Beatty, Kazan reported his impressions to Inge. "And I said to Bill, 'He's awful *raw*. He's awful new. He's rather clumsy, but I'm ready to try it with him and do it with him if you are.' And Bill said yes. He thought he was perfect for the part. Now that was Bill's suggestion. I didn't know Warren Beatty."[272]

Warren Beatty's initial, and everlasting, impressions of Elia Kazan were those of a devoted acolyte, an eager student recognizing his teacher. After Kazan had directed him, Beatty said, "I always have the feeling that the first ten or fifteen seconds of meeting someone are terribly valuable because all the subconscious knowledge that you have about a subject or a person is immediately brought to bear, and you make a snap judgment whether you like to or not, and automatically you make an assessment of them. I remember that my first impression of Kazan was one of a person with great vitality and sensitivity . . . now since I've worked with him, he has to me assumed a thousand colors."[273]

On June 9, 1959, as the trades reported that Beatty was "set as a semiregular on *Dobie*," his patron saint William Inge sent a telegram to the chief of production at Warner Brothers: "I THINK WARREN BEATY THE MOST PROMISING YOUNG ACTOR I KNOW AND I WOULD LIKE TO READ HIM FOR SPLENDOR IF YOU SIGN HIM COULD YOU LET HIM DO A PLAY SOMETIME BEST WISHES BILL INGE."[274]

A week later, the New York press announced "definite" plans to open on the first of the year *A Loss of Roses* on Broadway, the Inge play with the too-close mother-son relationship the playwright intended for Beatty, with Arthur Penn as the director.[275] Penn, whose first play on Broadway, *Two for the Seesaw*, had opened the year before, was Inge's third candidate, following the departures of Kazan and then George Cukor, who had "changed his mind," another harbinger of doom.[276] The playwright must have sensed that Kazan would postpone *Splendor*, for as Beatty said, "Inge asked me if I'd do his play . . . first, and I agreed."[277]

With an MGM contract, plus the covert knowledge that he was Inge's personal choice to star in a Broadway play and both Inge's and Kazan's preference for the lead in *Splendor in the Grass*, Beatty, not surprisingly, "drifted above them all" on the set of *Dobie Gillis* that July, in the director's turn of phrase. "But [his manner] was always sweet," Amateau said slyly, "the way you speak to your pets."

After Warren Beatty became a movie star and was nominated for multiple Academy Awards, Dwayne Hickman and his costars perceived that he wanted to deny that he was ever on *Dobie Gillis*. Amateau, who saw him in later years, said Beatty found it "hysterical" that he had once played Milton Armitage. "He thought the whole thing was very, very funny . . . a mistake of youth. No ill will about it, just something funny that happened to him."

In 1990, Beatty told *TV Guide* that he was grateful for the series. "It kept me eating. And I got to work with great people like Tuesday Weld and Michael J. Pollard, and it kept me from doing a bad movie [for MGM]."[278]

Beatty's only friend on the show, besides Pollard, was Deborah Sherwood, a pretty blond extra aspiring to write fiction and the girlfriend of producer Ben Kadish, Josh Logan's partner. Sherwood was a listening ear to Beatty, who had not been seriously involved with anyone since Ellie Wood at Northwestern, four years before. He seemed lonely to the already-attached Sherwood. Beatty often phoned her late at night at the Studio Club, a residence for young women—a Hollywood version of the dormitory in Toronto where his mother stayed when she studied drama at the Margaret Eaton School of Literature and Expression. "I could never figure out why Warren was calling me. He wasn't calling me to ask me for a date or anything, he was calling to talk. And the phone at the Studio Club was out in the hall. It was not an easy thing for me to do, to settle into a conversation like that."[279]

Sherwood could tell that Beatty had a romantic interest in her ("he kept inviting me into his dressing room"), but neither one pursued it out of respect to Kadish. One day, Warren asked her in exasperation why the girls he found most attractive "are always already involved with other men."[280] Unlike his sister, Beatty had not analyzed the possibility that he was drawn to unavailable women to avoid getting married, a subconscious way to protect himself from reliving the painful arguments he and Shirley had witnessed between their parents.

Beatty compensated for a lack of emotional intimacy through sheer volume. "God knows, he was not at a loss for female companionship," observed Sherwood, who found Beatty "aggressive in chasing girls; he'd call and call a girl even after turndowns." Michael J. Pollard recalled watching his friend "pick up girls" in Shirley's MG at the Chateau Marmont, and once witnessed actor Tim Everett, who had dated Jane Fonda, accost Beatty while Everett was in a drunken stupor. "I remember Timmy was, like, at this party at the Montecito, and he was yelling, and poor Warren was sitting in a chair, and [Timmy] was yelling at Warren, and I know Warren. I'm sure he didn't want to get into a fight because he didn't want to mess up his face, right?"

Beatty also haunted the Studio Club, where Deborah Sherwood lived and where starlet Kim Novak had recently rented a room. The Studio Club, as Sherwood explained, "was sort of like a sorority house for aspiring actresses, models, writers, young women at that time who usually didn't take apartments. They locked you in at night. There was a housemother, and you could have men over on the ground floor, certainly not up to the room. And Warren came over and had dinner with me there, but I think he may have gone over there to check things out."

Underneath, Beatty was still the sweetly polite, mischievous boy who had amused Susan Morse in the fourth grade singing "My Mammy" and impressed her by playing the piano. Sherwood, who saw this private Warren Beatty, considered him a "clown," as Morse had, with tactful manners. "He was fun. I recall him breaking into little songs and dances. The memories that stand out are Warren doing a little soft-shoe, or moving to the piano between takes to play my favorite songs. He played just like a cocktail pianist." Beatty's standard was "Wait Till You See Her," another song of romantic longing by Rodgers and Hart, who wrote "Little Girl Blue." The lyrics were equally idealized ("I'll never be willing to free her / When you see her you won't believe your eyes"). His taste—musicals, like *Oklahoma!*, that ended with the hero marrying the girl—revealed the sentimental Virginia boy looking for true love in the tradition of his Baptist youth.

Late in June, the "other" Beatty made a play for Anita Sands, an eighteen-year-old guest star in an episode called "Dobie Gillis, Boy Actor." Sands was cast as a high school girl with the lead in the school play, a spoof of *Gone With the Wind* about a southern belle romanced by a Confederate officer, played by Beatty, as Milton Armitage. In the episode, Beatty used a southern accent and wore a Confederate uniform, similar, he averred, to the first Henry Warren Beaty, his great-grandfather, a Virginia Confederate in the Civil War. A few months later, Beatty would give a photograph of himself as the Confederate soldier to Joan Collins, the sultry brunette whose magazine cover sexually excited him. As a joke, Collins wrote on the back, "*What a ham!*"[281]

Teen actress Anita Sands, *Dobie*'s version of Scarlett O'Hara, found Dwayne Hickman "a charming kid," and described Beatty then as diffident and callow, "elegant at not being there."[282] When he asked her for a date, she was stunned. "We had no relationship whatsoever, except for talking about 'stand here, stand there,' and I was a very repressed kid, I'd never been on a date. I was thinking, 'What? Where is this coming from?' It was like he wanted to go from zero to eighty miles an hour, if the girl were ready for that. I said, 'Oh, no!' I don't think he understood the reason why."

Sands's impressions of Beatty comformed with that of the majority of the cast and crew. "He was invisible. He literally didn't talk to anyone, or hang with anyone, or make noise. No talking, no friendship."

According to Rod Amateau, "One person that could stand up to Warren like nobody else was a woman called Doris Packer." Packer was the heavyset, older character actress who played Milton Armitage's formidable and extremely proper mother, and she bore a resemblance to Beatty's grandmother Blanche MacLean. "She'd give him a look. She'd say, 'You filthy little boy.' And . . . 'You've done the unpardonable.' She made Warren . . . not squirm, but he was uncomfortable." Twenty years later, Beatty would give Doris Packer a small part in his sexual satire *Shampoo*.

As the summer of 1959 progressed, Beatty's high hopes for stardom ebbed again. Kazan decided to film *Wild River* in August, postponing *Splendor* until 1960. Beatty confessed to Deborah Sherwood that he purposely sang off-key during an audition for a minor role in *The Pink Jungle*, a Ginger Rogers musical about the cosmetics industry that never made it to Broadway, so he would be available to star in *A Loss of Roses*, even though his agent believed that MGM would not permit him to do the play.[283] Arthur Penn favored Dennis Hopper to play Kenny, the part Inge had written with Beatty in mind, and as rehearsals drew near, Penn began testing other actors as well, including Robert Vaughn.[284]

The studio's contractual noose was tightening around Beatty. MGM executives told him he "wasn't ripe enough" for the movie roles that interested him, and he had a growing disdain for the parts the studio was offering him, and for their advice that he "could be the next Troy Donahue."[285] Beatty rejected the embarrassing *All the Fine Young Cannibals* — MGM's attempt to exploit the fan-magazine popularity of newlyweds Natalie Wood and Robert Wagner — with his part going to his New York chum George Hamilton.[286] Soon after, Beatty turned down the studio's offer to play one in a "phalanx of beatniks" in *The Subterraneans*, starring French actress Leslie Caron, who would become his girlfriend amid worldwide scandal four years later.[287] His rejection of *The Subterraneans* appeared in Sidney Skolsky's Hollywood column with a description that made Beatty cringe: "Shirley MacLaine's kid brother Warren turned down his first [*sic*] offer at MGM."[288]

Beatty later described this period as "trying times, waiting for a movie part to materialize."[289] He released his tension by playing the piano and singing around the house, as he had since childhood, financing his holdout for quality pictures through his modest Milton Armitage money. "From the beginning, I definitely had some feeling that if I was to go out and just take the gigs and do the press and be in the public eye, I wouldn't live much of a life. I would live a pretend life of story after story on celluloid, and I didn't want to do that."[290]

His *Dobie Gillis* director recognized something unusual in twenty-two-year-old Warren Beatty that he admired. "He had a *life plan*. It wasn't a life plan about 'I want to get ahead,' it was a life plan that 'I wouldn't do a thing like that, that's not me.' You could *see*. You could see that everything Warren did was a car on that train. You knew that he'd never knock up a girl. You knew it. You knew that he'd never drive drunk. You knew it. You knew that he'd never . . . tell an executive to go fuck himself. He might *think* it, and he might imply it, but he would never do it. And he wasn't somebody like

Sammy Glick*; it wasn't that at all. Everything was kind of easy, and charming, and nice. I was impressed with Warren because he had a life plan and he stuck to it."

28

On July 21, Jane Fonda flew to Los Angeles with Tony Perkins to start *Tall Story*, the Warner Brothers romantic comedy that Josh Logan had hoped would make movie stars of both her and Warren Beatty. After months of near misses in high-profile films and on Broadway, Beatty's sole acting job continued to be his "semiregular" role on *Dobie Gillis*. "I got the impression that he was pretty much a nobody," said his friend from the television series Deborah Sherwood.

Even Beatty's natural charm was being severely tested. At the Studio Club, where he dined with Sherwood partly to meet young actresses, "*they* were all looking for producers," Sherwood observed. "I remember there was one girl that was dating [playwright] Gene Ionesco — she was going to be the new Kim Novak, redhaired. So I don't think they were particularly interested in Warren. The girls there were in the big leagues — a lot of them probably had better credentials than Warren at the time."

Beatty later confessed to his actress girlfriend Joan Collins how anxious and alone he was feeling that spring to summer, referring in an interview once to "three bad months" in Los Angeles before he became involved with her.[291] His obsession to meet the English starlet when he got to Hollywood temporarily dimmed after a friend took him to see her in *The Big Country*, a Western starring Gregory Peck released a few months earlier. "Well, he was very disillusioned by what he saw," related Collins. "And he came away saying I was not so hot after all. Fortunately, he was mixing me up with Jean Simmons."[292] By chance, Collins was also in a Western with Peck that year, called *The Bravados*.

Once Beatty realized that the genteel British brunette in *The Big Country* was not the English starlet whose seductive photograph on a magazine cover had caught his eye, he tried the same modus operandi he had used in New York when he asked Neil Cooper to introduce him to MCA actresses

---

*The Budd Schulberg character who climbs to the top through ruthless means in the novel *What Makes Sammy Run?*

after looking over their headshots. "I'd always thought Joan Collins was the end, the dream of the world. So I told my agent, 'Listen, I've just got to meet this girl.'"[293]

While he was waiting for an introduction to Collins, Beatty's sympathetic pal Deborah Sherwood set him up with an actress named Greta Chi, who lived at the Studio Club. "I introduced him here and there. But I don't think it lasted very long. She was just drop-dead gorgeous, Eurasian, and I think as soon as men met her they dropped whoever they'd come to pick up that night." Beatty's brief romance with Chi was mentioned a few times in gossip columns in the Hollywood trades in July, along with reported dalliances with young actresses Diane Baker and Stella Stevens.

Beatty also saw Jane Fonda that summer, while she was in town filming *Tall Story*, but "it was no romance with Jane," confirmed her then beau, agent Alexander Whitelaw.[294] "Sandy" Whitelaw, a self-described "relatively glamorous" European with social credentials and little money, became friendly with Beatty after an unusual introduction at Fonda's apartment one evening, as Whitelaw arrived unannounced when Jane was expecting Warren. As Whitelaw explained, "I was not having a good time with Jane; we were breaking up then." When he knocked on Fonda's door, "She said, 'Warren?' and I said 'No, it's me.' And then we started having a huge fight. I stuck my fist in a mirror, and right then Warren showed up. Instead of saying, 'Jane, is this man bothering you?' he sort of said, 'Listen, I know what you guys are going through. I once had a problem like that [when] I threw a bed out of the window in Philadelphia.' He was extremely nice in that situation. I'm very fond of Warren."

In Whitelaw's peer appraisal of Beatty, "I don't think Jane was big enough fish for him. I think he was after Joan Collins . . . Warren's always had this quality of being a star fucker. No question about that."

Whitelaw's theory that Beatty preferred actresses with a degree of fame had psychological implications that related to the females he had loved as a child—his mother, grandmother, aunts, and sister. During Beatty's first month in Hollywood, his sister was nominated for an Academy Award and was on the cover of three national magazines, *Life*, *Look*, and *Time*. Within a few weeks of his friend Fonda's arrival to make *Tall Story*, Fonda was on the cover of six: *Vogue*, *Glamour*, *Harper's Bazaar*, *Ladies' Home Journal*, *McCall's*, and *Esquire*. This was a standard with which Warren not only was familiar, but also had been brought up to expect.

In addition to respecting thespian talent, Beatty was drawn to actresses in the curvaceous mold of June Rowe Weaver, the leading lady from his mother's little-theater group whom he proposed to at nine, setting up a potential conflict in his psyche between the two types. Joan Collins fit into the glamour category, as well as reminding him of Elizabeth Taylor in A *Place in the Sun.* "I remember a conversation on the phone with Warren about Joan Collins," said Sherwood. "How beautiful she was, and how she looked like Elizabeth Taylor." Beatty was quoted later as saying, "I'd really been out of my mind trying to meet this girl."[295]

Early in August, he got his first glimpse of his dream girl—though at a worldly twenty-six to Beatty's twenty-two, Joan Collins was more woman than girl. The sighting took place at a restaurant in Beverly Hills, and was almost certainly staged for Beatty by Mort Viner, an MCA agent who represented him on occasion and was Shirley's agent and close friend. Viner and his wife, Barbara, invited Collins to La Scala, where Beatty just happened to be dining with Jane Fonda. When Collins arrived, she got the distinct feeling she was being observed "a bit too boldly" by what she appraised as the "rather appealing and vulnerable" young man at the next table. When Barbara Viner told Collins that her intense admirer was Shirley MacLaine's brother, "Warren something-or-other," Beatty lifted his glass at Collins and continued to stare. "That went on a lot," Jane Fonda commented dryly. "You know, when you'd be with Warren, and he'd be looking at somebody."

Beatty's attention was diverted from Joan Collins on August 4, when Arthur Penn suddenly withdrew from A *Loss of Roses.** Inge seemed "stunned" at losing a third director and "was beside himself," observed actress Barbara Baxley, a close friend whom the playwright wanted to cast as Lila, the stag show actress who tempts young Kenny.[296] Baxley suggested Daniel Mann, who had directed Shirley MacLaine in her unique first screen test and had worked with Inge before, directing *Come Back, Little Sheba.*

Arnold Saint-Subber, the Broadway veteran who was producing the play, intuited trouble, but William Inge's reputation as a Pulitzer Prize winner who "only wrote hits" assuaged him.[297] Fox executives, who credited Inge with the same Midas touch, had already purchased the movie rights to A *Loss of Roses* for four hundred thousand dollars and were thinking of Marilyn Monroe to play the unstable small-time actress in the film version.

---

*Penn's publicized reason was to devote more time to directing *The Miracle Worker*, which was opening on Broadway that October. According to Inge's close friend, actress Barbara Baxley, Penn's wife fell ill.

Beatty, who was frustrated "sitting out in California doing nothing," ignored his agent's warnings that MGM would not release him to star on Broadway in *A Loss of Roses*.[298] He contacted the studio, "and I said I didn't want to stay out here any more under contract . . . I said, 'I'll go back to New York and do a play,' and they said, 'You can't do a play,' and I said, 'I can, too.'"[299]

Beatty plotted his exit strategy from MGM while carrying out the next phase of his plan to meet Joan Collins. The facilitator, this time, was Jay Kanter, the MCA agent whose wife, Judith, and pal John Foreman had conspired to make Beatty a star by taking him to Hollywood parties, and who were both close friends of Joan Collins. As Collins recalled the setup, Foreman invited her to a party one Saturday night given by Tyrone Power's widow, and when the actress resisted, "John was insistent we go."

The evening proceeded like a highly choreographed Virginia reel. According to Judith, the Kanters arrived at the party first, bringing Beatty.[300] By the time Collins walked in with Foreman, Beatty was seated at the piano, dazzling a circle of listeners gathered around him with a clever impersonation of Erroll Garner. When Collins mentioned how good the attractive young piano player was, Foreman said, on cue, "I think it's Shirley MacLaine's brother, Warren something-or-other." The rest of the evening, Collins hovered near the piano, "watching and listening," while Beatty appeared to be "totally absorbed in his music," smiling up at her once or twice.

The next day, when Collins came home from a day at the beach, there were six messages on her answering service to call Warren Beatty, and the phone was ringing with Beatty on the line. "We had not even exchanged a word and yet he had managed to get my number," Collins noted admiringly, unaware of Beatty's well-directed set-up.

Beatty made a date to meet his goddess that night at eight, suggesting a Mexican restaurant in Beverly Hills. The sophisticated Collins, excited by her young swain's self-confidence, ardor, and "physical packaging," overlooked his adolescent "spots," her English expression for acne. When she scrutinized him that evening, Collins, who had a quick wit, was especially impressed by Warren Beatty's mind, his clear blue-green eyes, and his "beautiful hands," the instruments of creativity his poetic mother had trained him to use expressively. The actress also found the wildly interested Beatty a refreshing change from her older married lover, George Englund, who dangled her with empty promises to leave his wife, actress Cloris Leachman.

For Beatty, Joan Collins represented the seduction of Hollywood as opposed to the dignity of the stage embodied by his grandmother, mother, and aunt. Beatty was over the moon about Joan Collins, and expressed it as floridly as the Rodgers and Hart love songs that moved him. "She's got eyes that are big pools and she looks like a rain goddess in the rain," he told one magazine writer.[301]

Beatty's nervousness at twenty-two in the company of the significantly older, infinitely more cosmopolitan object of his desire — "a real woman" — was evident by the fact that, contrary to his nature, he chose the restaurant where they spent their first date for its margaritas, and drank "countless" of them, Collins recalled. Like his father, the intense Beatty felt more relaxed and less insecure under the influence of alcohol; unlike Ira, Warren exercised enormous self-discipline to avoid drinking and drugs, painfully aware of what he called the "awful" consequences. "The next morning when you think back and say I was great last night, witty, relaxed, really 'on,' it's a terrible temptation to have a few drinks so you can do it again."[302]

Fortunately for Beatty, he found another way to release tension while spending the night at Joan Collins's apartment north of Sunset. "Before I began going around with Joan, I used to sing around the house," he said a few months later. "But when she's in town and I'm seeing her, I find I don't sing at all. I think that singing is a form of emotional release. If you're able to express that emotion in some other way, then you don't sing."[303] Collins said forthrightly of her first time making love with Beatty, "The die was cast. We became inseparable . . . I would stagger to the studio to work on *The Seven Thieves* and he would call me eighteen times a day. We couldn't bear to be apart." Beatty also empathized with Collins because her first husband, English actor Maxwell Reed, was abusive to her when he drank. "Joan had been married to an awful man," said her friend Verne O'Hara. "A drunk. And she had to pay money to him."

The essentially unemployed Beatty, who had nothing but time, demonstrated the same consuming devotion to his beloved as he still felt for his mother, spending hours on the Fox lot during the middle of August watching Collins rehearse *The Seven Thieves*, a caper film displaying her both in and out of an extensive wardrobe.

To prepare for her role, Collins took stripping lessons at Fox from exotic dancer Candy Barr, whose equally infamous boyfriend, mobster Mickey Cohen, observed — alongside Beatty, who observed Cohen. "Cohen," he would recall, "was very quiet, soft-spoken, kind of heavyset. It was only afterward that I realized who I had met. You would see these people and there would be that *atmosphere*."[304] Beatty stored the memory, along with Hollywood stories he heard about Ben Siegel, intrigued by the way a gangster could use show business to conceal his darker side — which would become the theme of his film *Bugsy*.[305] "I have some sort of déjà vu fascination with the Hollywood of that period."[306]

Around that week, Beatty met Daniel Mann, Inge's last-minute replacement to direct *A Loss of Roses*. Rehearsals had been moved up to the first of October, and Mann was casting the play. At Inge's request, he read Beatty for the male lead. Mann, who had twice directed Shirley — who had a crush on the married, rumpled-looking director during the filming of *Hot Spell* — liked her brother right away, according to Inge.[307] "He seemed so right for the role," Mann said later, with irony.[308]

Nevertheless, Beatty spent an anxious five weeks "hoping he would get the lead," according to Joan Collins, who was aware that her handsome young boyfriend would rather be in movies. Relying on Inge's support to get him cast, Beatty made the bold decision to return the money MGM had paid him, gambling on the belief that a starring role on Broadway, as opposed to the roles being offered to him as a contract player, would get him noticed for important films. "I felt that a good part in a William Inge play was worth the chance."[309] Beatty collected the checks he had not cashed, borrowed the remaining $2,600 from MCA, and settled with MGM, agreeing to do a picture for them in the future.[310] As Kilgallen recalled, "Metro-Goldwyn-Mayer thought he was probably a troublemaker, and he got out of the deal."

The other stress in Beatty's life that September was his torrid relationship with Collins, who had agreed to meet for a drink with her wealthy married lover, who was trying to persuade her not to end their affair for an "out of work child actor." The "insanely jealous" Beatty stalked her while she was with Englund at the Cock and Bull, on Sunset, circling around the restaurant in his car for two hours and "steaming" as he watched his "Butterfly" give the expensively dressed Englund a passionate kiss in the parking lot. The next day, with the help of her analyst, Collins chose Beatty, whom she called "Bee," rejecting the father substitute her married boyfriend had represented, in her therapist's view.

Beatty celebrated his triumph over Englund by taking Collins to La Scala, where he had first gazed at her while having dinner with Jane Fonda. He asked his sister to join them, a gesture that indicated his strong feelings for Collins and the newfound security he no doubt felt dating someone whose fame was on a par with Shirley's—and, in all likelihood, to impress the fickle Collins.

MacLaine invited the two lovers to a luncheon on the set of *Can-Can*, where she demonstrated the racy French dance for a political delegation that included Soviet premier Nikita Krushchev and his wife, a story that made both *Time* and *Newsweek*. A roving photographer snapped a candid moment documenting the undiscovered Warren Beatty sitting on the set with his movie star sister, still in her dancer costume, and sex symbol Joan Collins, dressed against type in school-boy short pants, her legs crossed mannishly in a pose of sexual confidence. Beatty, wearing a worn jacket, black horn-rimmed glasses, and a serious expression, looked like a graduate student who had wandered into the wrong building. "Without his glasses he was practically blind," noted Collins.

A few weeks later, Warren Beatty signed a two-year contract to play Kenny Baird, the conflicted son in *A Loss of Roses*, the part Inge had intended for him since the play's second draft. This casting news created a frisson among theater veterans who were shocked that the male lead in William Inge's new Broadway play had gone to a "complete unknown" who had once worked as a sandhog.[311]

Beatty filmed his last episode of *Dobie Gillis* ("The Smoke-Filled Room") at the end of September, and suddenly "he was gone," noticed Dwayne Hickman. "One day, like after the first few episodes, I said, 'Where's Warren? Isn't he in a play?'" Beatty's wordless departure for Broadway, after distancing himself from the television series, left his costars somewhat embittered. Director Amateau was philosophical. "How can you be resentful or angry about someone who tells you the absolute truth and then goes and does it?"

Beatty, who had gambled his movie deal at MGM for a chance to star on-stage in an Inge role, departed for New York at the end of September "nervous and excited" about his break, recalled Joan Collins, who remained in Hollywood to finish *The Seven Thieves*, adding to her new boyfriend's anxiety.

Verne O'Hara was among the first in Manhattan to greet Beatty, who was staying with her and her husband, Mitch, at the Blackstone. The chic O'Hara, who had known Collins in London, was startled at Warren's transformation in the few months since she had seen him. "He met Joan Collins; he absolutely flipped. That was like his first movie star that he ever met. And he came back to New York and he said he had to find an apartment for her, and it had to be very glamorous because she was, you know, a movie actress, and she had tons of clothes, et cetera, et cetera, and he asked me if I'd go with him to look for apartments."

Beatty arrived in New York a few days before rehearsals for A *Loss of Roses*, where a series of backstage crises had preceded him. The most acute involved Inge and director Danny Mann, who was refusing to cast the playwright's friend Barbara Baxley as Lila, the small-time carny actress whom Kenny seduces and then abandons. Mann's position on the issue was an early catalyst in turning the already unstable stage production into "a nightmare," in the description of Burry Fredrik, the show's production stage manager.[312]

Mann's choice to play Lila, ironically, was Carol Haney, the dancer whose sprained ankle in *The Pajama Game* had turned her understudy, Shirley MacLaine, into a star. Haney, a superb dancer and choreographer, had never acted in a drama before and "wanted the part desperately," recalled Fredrik. While Inge was auditioning Haney for the role, Baxley telephoned him from California. "Barbara was standing on the cliffs of Malibu saying, 'If you hire Carol Haney, I'm jumping off the cliffs.' . . . It was very, very difficult for Bill, and of course it was ultimately Danny's decision."

Many years later, after Inge and Baxley were deceased, Danny Mann revealed the "very, very personal" explanation he offered Bill Inge as to why he would not cast Barbara Baxley as the carny actress reduced to stag films. "She happened to have been a woman who was not a woman, whatever her sexual preferences were . . . and there's no reason why a lesbian could not have soft and tender love, but in my mind's eye it was what I sensed was a wrong quality for the play."[313]

In his struggle with being homosexual, Inge had considered marrying Baxley the year before.* Mann's refusal to cast her as Lila for the reason he gave Inge "threw Bill back fifteen years in his analysis," the director later confessed, "which was a terrible thing for me to do, but, not realizing it, completely innocent."[314]

Years later, both Burry Fredrik and John Connolly, Inge's live-in secretary, would take issue with Mann's characterization of Baxley as a lesbian. "I think Danny Mann just had it in for Barbara for some reason," observed

---

*Barbara Baxley said later in an interview archived in the William Inge Collection that she had a "deep love" for Inge, "and any homosexual experience [of his] was acceptable to me, as long as I didn't have to deal with the people."

Connolly. "He may have gotten the wrong impression of her, or just wanted to hurt Bill in order to cut him off from putting her into that play."

Mann's interference created "a war" between Baxley and Inge, as Baxley would recall. Shortly after, the actress chose to marry "somebody Bill didn't like," said Baxley. "I was furious and I wouldn't even see Bill for a year. He was hurt and I was hurt."[315]

The role of the mother in the play's oedipal triangle was cast a month before Carol Haney replaced Baxley as Lila, under circumstances that portended a different kind of instability. For the part of Helen Baird, a controlling personality unnaturally close to her son, Inge chose sensitive character actress Shirley Booth, who had starred in his play *Come Back, Little Sheba*, winning a Tony, and later an Oscar for the film version. Booth had "reservations" about her unsympathetic character and the play, but was "talked into" accepting the role by her agent, and out of "nostalgia" for Inge, who promised he would rewrite and enlarge her part during rehearsals at the New Amsterdam Theater.[316]

The arrival on October 5, the first day of rehearsals, of a young and nervous Warren Beatty was akin to lighting a match to the already combustible mix of egos, power struggles, and conflicts in personality. That same morning, adding to Beatty's insecurities, Louella Parsons reported from Hollywood, "The George Englunds' reconciliation didn't take and he's been seeing Joan Collins."[317] Beatty called Collins "constantly" from New York, remembered Collins, whose presence in his life had created new pressures. "I remember the kind of change in our Warren in a way," noticed the motherly Eleanor Kilgallen. "Joan was the one who took the rather rough-edged Southern boy and taught him the ways of sophistication, which he readily learned, and employed."

Mann scheduled rehearsals for the first three weeks in October, with the world premiere of *A Loss of Roses* to be held in Washington, D.C., during tryouts, the play's preview period, followed by another week of tryouts in New Haven, before opening on Broadway.

As soon as Beatty got to New York, he went to see Stella Adler, and told his old pal Lenn Harten "of course his mother and father would be there" on opening night to watch him perform.[318] Beatty's conferring with Adler was the first clue that he felt out of his element starring on Broadway with masters of the stage such as Shirley Booth. Audrey Wood, the powerful agent who represented Booth, Inge, *and* Mann, heard comments from all three about Beatty. She was told that he was "dreadfully uncertain," repeatedly interrupting rehearsals to ask Mann questions, constantly wondering about his character's "motivation," a habit that at times led to "acrimonious discussions."[319] Beatty clearly was groping for the techniques used by Method actors, training he missed when he had to withdraw from Adler's studio.

A few of his veteran costars resented Beatty's exacting efforts to improve his performance on their time. Mann recalled, "Shirley Booth came to me at one point and said, 'Danny, are you directing the play or are you teaching an acting class?'"[320] Robert Webber, a handsome character actor cast as the villain who coaxes Lila into stag films, reacted personally. "I couldn't stand Warren Beatty," he later said emphatically.[321]

Decades later, Beatty referred to the experience obliquely, saying, "I was a joke among people I knew, because I would rehearse forever . . . that always struck me as my greatest weakness, if I wanted to make a profession out of the theater, make money, be hired, be rich, be famous. I thought, 'I don't want to do that. I just want to keep doing it until this crazy thing happens.'" He was possessed with *getting the moment right*, with the transcendent feeling that something extraordinary, and unexpected, might occur the further one got into character. For Beatty, rehearsing over and over helped him to shed his Virginia reserve and draw him out; or as he described, "the scene always gained more life" with each repetition.[322] This tendency eventually would lead to his famous compulsion to request innumerable takes on film sets.

Booth eventually complained to Daniel Mann that the director was devoting too much time to Beatty, as the stage manager recollected. "Danny said, 'Shirley, you don't need me, you're a marvelous actress, you can do it. The kid needs me.'" Booth became "upset by this," according to her agent, and to Burry Fredrik. "She said, 'This is a very complicated play, and I too need help.'"[323]

Carol Haney, whose showier part as the smalltown temptress overshadowed Shirley Booth's, said later that she found *Booth* "very difficult."[324] As costar Robert Webber noted war-wearily, "It's just not a good play. It was very badly cast. Shirley . . . God, Shirley was so wonderful, but Shirley wanted to rewrite the play and make her a nicer lady . . . Carol Haney was a dancer, she wasn't an actress."[325]

Warren Beatty became the fall guy for the simmering tensions offstage — some of it deserved. Fredrik, who as production manager witnessed the behind-the-scenes dramas, and who, as a nonactor, could be objective, conceded, "It was very difficult, and it's all about Warren. He was difficult, but I loved him. He was just his own man, like he was all of his life, and it didn't matter to him that this was his debut in the theater." Mann, a director from the old school, considered Warren "a juvenile delinquent," saying later, "There were great problems with Beatty."[326]

Burry Fredrik was Beatty's sounding board. "I remember spending many, many a time with him in the dressing room because he did have certain problems. What they were I don't remember." In her analysis, Warren was trying to emulate his sister, Shirley, "to be as successful *as*. She was somebody he looked up to at that moment. She had made it, and he thought, 'Well, that's what you do in this business, you make it.'" Fredrik also recalled Beatty brooding over personal matters, which meant Joan Collins. "Everything about this man exuded sexuality, pleasantness."

Another source of resentment toward Beatty during *A Loss of Roses* was his special relationship with Inge. "It was very obvious," observed Fredrik, "that not only had Bill fallen in love with him, but this was a very charismatic young man starting his career. It was clear that Bill was smitten, and that the 'smitting' — or whatever word there is for it — I don't think was necessarily reciprocal with Warren, other than how you advance your career."

Beatty's favor, and influence, with Inge was proved earlier that summer, when his buddy Michael J. Pollard spotted him at the airport in Los Angeles with Marlon Brando and Inge. "We said hi . . . ," recalled Pollard, "the next thing I knew I was in that play." Beatty and his easygoing pal, who played a wily neighborhood boy called Jelly, clung to each other throughout the production like the last two survivors on a life raft. "Everybody in the cast hated each other except Warren and me!"[327] Pollard assumed the role of Beatty's comic foil. "Me and Warren were clowning around a lot, and Danny Mann would get so mad. He'd come running down into the aisle, and they had to bring the curtain down during rehearsals because he used to get so angry. Warren thought it was hysterical."

When Mann and his renegade cast arrived in Washington, D.C., for three final days of rehearsal prior to the play's world premiere, Audrey Wood demanded script changes and insisted that the director pay less attention to Warren Beatty, or else her client, Shirley Booth, would quit the show.[328] In truth, Booth had already tipped the stage manager that she would hand in her notice on opening night. "I had a mutiny on my hands," recalled the stage manager. "Robert Webber actually yelled, *'Mutiny!'* Robert was leading, and talking about, having a rebellion in the company."[329]

After several days of frantic rewrites by a traumatized Inge,* Warren Beatty made his debut on the legitimate stage on October 29, 1959, at his hometown theater, the National, where he had chased rats for Helen Hayes four years before, trivia reported in the local press. Ira and Kathlyn Beaty, but not Shirley, were in the audience on opening night, recalled Pollard, who met his friend's parents after the show. Seventeen years after she had praised the five-year-old Warren for walking across the stage in her little-theater production in Richmond, Tat MacLean Beaty's prediction for her only son had come true. In what would set a precedent, Beatty garnered good reviews under the duress of a doomed production.

Although the *Washington Post* stated that Beatty's inexperience failed to make his character fully dramatic, the paper's theater critic admired the actor's "shy, humorously boyish quality," praising his effectiveness in conveying Kenny's "inner distress."[330] According to *Variety*, Beatty showed "opening night jitters, made worse by stage accidents. For instance, his zipper jammed while he was putting on his pants, so he donned Miss Booth's apron."[331]

Inge's work fared less well than that of his protégé, referred to in reviews as an "unfinished play."[332] Shirley Booth, whom critics called "skillful but passive in an undeveloped role," quit on opening night, true to her word,[333] plummeting the production from a nightmare into "a disaster," in the stage manager's words.[334] Booth, who had never left a play before, agreed to perform until New Haven, so Mann could work with her emergency replacement, veteran actress Betty Field, who had accepted as a favor to Inge.

Joan Collins, who had finished *The Seven Thieves* and committed herself, body and soul, to Beatty, took a midnight flight from Hollywood to Washington, D.C. She moved into the Willard Hotel with Warren, who received her like a man seriously in love, which his friends Pollard and the Mays believed him to be. Pollard, who would remain close to Beatty, considered Joan Collins "the only girl he ever loved until, I think, he met Julie [Christie]." Beatty took Collins to Arlington to meet his parents, with whom he remained in constant touch, keeping him connected to his Virginia roots and values. "They were kind, humorous people whom I liked instantly," Collins

---

*According to stage manager Burry Fredrik, Mann cut an entire scene and set, eliminating a character played by Joey Heatherton, who was fired.

observed of Tat and Ira Beaty, "and I could see from where Warren and Shirley inherited their intelligence and good manners."

Beatty discouraged his actress inamorata from accepting a movie she had been offered by Fox, *Sons and Lovers*, because "he did not want me to go to England and leave *him* . . . he said he needed me with him." Collins recalled that November as a "tricky time in Warren's life," a rare understatement from the actress. The press on both coasts were reporting *A Loss of Roses* as "in trouble" during its previews in Washington, an alarming turn of events for a play by William Inge, who had never written anything but a success, either commercially or with critics.[335] Beatty, who had risked his MGM movie contract, was now under severe financial and career pressure.

Burry Fredrik, whose job was to keep the production together while Mann rehearsed Betty Field during the day and directed Shirley Booth at night — while Inge cut and replaced scenes — recalled, "The actors were furious. They were playing the original script at night and trying to deal with rewrites all the time at rehearsals."

As they foresaw the play's epitaph, the company turned cannibalistic, preying on one another and assigning blame.* The only two who remained aloof were Pollard and Beatty, "who was sitting in his dressing room the whole time playing his guitar, or some musical instrument."[336]

In most future accounts, Beatty would be singled out as the satanic element in the play's demise. Later magazine profiles, including a notorious piece in *Esquire* by Rex Reed, cited him as the reason Shirley Booth quit the play, but that was not how Booth felt, according to her sister, Jean Coe.[337] "Shirley just didn't like it. She didn't much care for the morals of the play, and she got out as soon as she could and didn't go to Broadway with it." Shortly after, Booth went on to star as the lovable maid Hazel in the eponymous popular television series. "It was nothing to do with Warren Beatty," declared Coe, Booth's closest confidante. "I want to make it perfectly clear that is not true."[338]

Beatty *was* a demonic presence to Daniel Mann, who later sighed, "We don't have enough time," when asked to discuss directing Warren Beatty. "I

---

*In addition to Beatty and Booth, Mann held Inge accountable, saying in the *Kansas Quarterly* in 1986 that Inge was "unavailable" to discuss rewrites. Inge's secretary, John Connolly, who delivered script changes to Mann, believed it was *Mann* who was distracted — by *Butterfield 8*, the Elizabeth Taylor film he had just been hired to direct. Inge told the *Toledo Blade* in 1960 that he had "differences" with Mann, and also laid the blame on miscasting.

don't know what his troubles were in those days, but I inherited them."[339] After Booth quit the play, Mann threatened to fire Beatty, the third time in his short career that Beatty faced this threat.*[340] Dennis Cooney, Beatty's understudy, recalled that "at one point there was a remote possibility I'd replace Warren in Washington, but the differences were solved."[341]

According to Pollard, "[Warren and I] were like the scapegoats . . . that Danny Mann — he was like a murderer or something, you know? He almost killed us during rehearsals." In Pollard's view, Beatty did nothing to provoke the director. "[Warren] was getting exasperated with this Danny Mann. He'd tell Warren — because Carol Haney was the leading woman — he'd go, 'Warren, teeth and hair, just think teeth and hair.' Warren said, 'Teeth and hair? Teeth and hair is like the worst thing you can think about on a girl.'"

A few years earlier, Mann had almost fired actor James Dean while directing *him* in a play. "Of course he thought Jimmy was very sick," Mann's widow, Sheri Mann, recalled, "but Jimmy and Warren were arrogant to a point that they were destroying the play. They were going off and doing these weird things that really took them out of the scene. They would look around, or change something, or be very self-indulgent . . . Danny had a temper, and it never came out unless he was totally frustrated with someone. With Jimmy Dean he jumped across the footlights, ran down Walnut Avenue, and said, 'If I get you I'm going to kill you, you son of a bitch.' I don't know if he did that with Warren."[342]

Pollard believed Mann was envious that Beatty was dating Joan Collins, who watched them rehearse a few times in Washington, D.C. "I'm sure, because she was glamorous . . . she just did that *Girl in the Red Swing*.† And he was [the] worst to Warren in front of his girlfriend . . . it was like really personal. He'd *get* to you."

Despite being the company's whipping boy, or the troublemaker of the production, Beatty managed to impress reviewers as a future star. Richard Coe, the drama critic for the *Washington Post*, evaluated, with some prescience, the hometown boy's future as an actor when Beatty left for New Haven that November, writing, "Warren Beatty has a clean, ingratiating quality . . . but he is unable to project more than himself, and passive

---

*The first was on "The Curly-Headed Kid," followed by the Clinton Playhouse.
†Collins played showgirl Evelyn Nesbit in *The Girl in the Red Velvet Swing*, based on Nesbit's scandalous under-age affair with Gilded Age architect Stanford White, who was murdered by Evelyn's jealous and deranged husband, Harry Thaw.

understanding. He is theatrically uninteresting because he does not yet have at his command the voice or technique to color the role and thereby move us . . . I don't doubt that Beatty will score emphatically with those who further performing careers and that for some years he will be playing just this type of part on stage, screen and TV."[343]

A despondent William Inge spent the week of preview tryouts in New Haven agonizing whether to close the play, which the *New Haven Register* called "fragile and generally abortive."*[344] Inge, "a real poetic kind of guy," as Pollard described him, was not up for the battle. Beatty defended his friend Inge the next year, saying, "I felt it might have been a much better play if we'd had more try-out time with it out of town . . . the play deserved more."[345]

On November 22, less than a week before its Broadway opening, the *New York Times* referred to A Loss of Roses as "in crisis."[346] Robert Webber recalled that it was the producers who made the final call to take the play to New York that week. According to Fredrik, they had to stage twenty-one performances on Broadway to fulfill their contract with Fox for the movie rights.[347] The cast received the news like an invitation to sail on the *Titanic*. "When we left New Haven, Betty Field started to get onto the train and said, 'Oh, my back went out.' Just a lovely lie so that her understudy would have to play most of her performances in New York."[348]

Inge's married niece, who lived in the Midwest, said, "I bought a beautiful dress to go see *Loss of Roses*, and it had roses on it — I never spent quite so much money on a dress — and they called me and said, 'JoAnn, don't come, it's gonna fail.'"[349]

When A *Loss of Roses* opened at the Eugene O'Neill Theater on November 28, Webber would recall, "Everyone in the cast realized the play was a bomb. You could feel waves of apathy and disinterest from the audience. It's not a pleasant sensation."[350]

Years later, an unnamed cast member was reported as saying that Beatty changed his lines and blocking on opening night, confusing Carol Haney so badly she ran to her dressing room in tears.[351] The tale may have been apocryphal, since Haney never mentioned it and neither the stage manager nor Pollard saw it occur.[352] If true, it was reminiscent of Warren's odd, James Dean–like behavior onstage in A *Hatful of Rain*. Beatty may have been at-

---

*Beatty again got good notices — this time for his "physical gusto" and clear expression of the character's "emotional quandary."

tempting to improve the script, since he said later, "I'd get laughs at times when I shouldn't be getting laughs. The play was about a boy in trouble, and I didn't think it was funny, but the audience reacted as if I were doing boffo scenes."[353]

Warren Beatty celebrated his first, and last, opening night on Broadway in the company of loyal friends from his years of struggle in New York, along with his costar Pollard and Pollard's date, Jane Fonda. He wore an Italian suit selected by Joan Collins, showing off the suit, and the starlet, after the play. Eleanor Kilgallen was not the only person struck that night by the contrast between the older, sophisticated Collins and "their Warren," whom Kilgallen remembered as having only one nylon dress shirt.

Lenn Harten, who had kept his buddy alive with cream of mushroom soup cooked on a hot plate, found Joan Collins "very snobbish. I felt like saying to Warren, 'Hey! Do you know what you're doing? Please get another gal!'"[354] Director Ned Manderino, whose coaching kept Beatty from being fired in Clinton, encountered his former protégé's new girlfriend backstage as they left for Sardi's. "We walked down the street and I didn't know who she was, so at one point I asked her, 'Are you an actress, Joan?' Warren took me aside and got really mad. Then later on, I found out she had done those biblical films, *The Sun Goddess?** I didn't see Warren too much after that."

When the reviews came in at dawn, delivered to Sardi's, Inge's play was savaged, while everything came up roses for Warren Beatty. The all-important *New York Times* review by Brooks Atkinson called him "earnest and attractive." The *New York Mirror* reported that he "dominates the proceedings." The *Daily News* stated that Beatty was "definitely a find for the thin ranks of juvenile leads." The *New York World-Telegram* praised his "exceptional skill." The *Wall Street Journal* and *New York Post* showed more restraint, pronouncing him, respectively, "good" and "able." The line most often repeated, in future years, was from Kenneth Tynan of *The New Yorker*, who described Warren Beatty as "sensual around the lips and pensive around the brow."

Beatty's most glowing print review came from the influential Walter Kerr, who used such adjectives as "admirable, mercurial, sensitive, excellent" to describe the neophyte actor's performance.[355] Judith Crist, who was then a young critic at the *Herald Tribune* and later reviewed theater and movies for the *Today Show*, had a similar reaction when she saw Beatty on

*The correct title is *Esther and the King*.

opening night in *A Loss of Roses*. "I was just bowled over. Walter Kerr was, at that time, the [senior] *Herald Tribune* theater critic. And the two of us were absolutely knocked out by (a) the appearance of this beautiful young actor, and (b) by the quality of his performance; and we used to kid each other about being a Warren Beatty fan club."[356]

The sensitive Beatty told *Theater World* a few months later, "I read the reviews with mixed emotions. I was happy for myself but I had a sick feeling for the show. I really thought it would run."[357] His friend and patron, the gentle William Inge, was shattered by the viciousness of the critics, who seemed to take pleasure in shredding not just his play but him personally. "William Inge, I regret to report, has finally written a very bad play," Richard Watts, Jr., wrote cattily in the *New York Post*.[358] Another reviewer wrote, "Shirley Booth withdrew from the part of the mother a few weeks ago . . . there is no doubt that Miss Booth knew what she was doing."[359] Inge's niece JoAnn Kirchmaier recalled, "It just broke his heart. He said, 'I'm just . . . I'm no good.'"

The cast of *A Loss of Roses*, minus director Danny Mann — who had left to start *Butterfield 8* — played out its contractually mandated three-week danse macabre. "After opening night the theater was never more than half-full," Webber would recall.[360] "For the last matinee, the Saturday matinee, Warren came to the stage door and said, 'I can't go on. I'm sick, I'm throwing up. I've had it,'" revealed the beleaguered stage manager. "I said, 'I don't care how sick you think you are, I'm not putting one other understudy on in this play. . . .' Warren knew I meant it, and he also knew he wasn't sick."[361]

Robert Webber's antipathy for Beatty blossomed into overt contempt in New York, according to Pollard, and Mitch May's wife, Verne. Webber "absolutely *loathed* Warren," said O'Hara. "I mean really hated him. And I must say one thing about Warren; he didn't care one way or the other. He didn't hate him back. But he knew that this guy hated him."

To amuse each other, Pollard later would admit, "We'd do things onstage that had nothing to do with the script." One night, when actress Betty Field, as the hovering mother, could be heard in the background washing dishes, Pollard blurted, "What's with your mother?" — which wasn't his line — sending Beatty into convulsive laughter. During other scenes, "we'd kiss each other. We were like Laurel and Hardy. The play was supposed to be about Warren and his mother. Actually, it was about Warren and me, sitting on the stoop laughing."[362] No one seemed to notice. "By this time," admitted Fredrik, "with everything else in mutiny, I just thought when is this going to be over? We couldn't wait."

The final performance of *A Loss of* Roses was on December 19, 1959. As Webber said later, "It was a relief to get the closing notice."[363] Beatty and Michael J. Pollard, who had bonded like brothers, would greet each other as Kenny and Jelly from then on, symbols of their tour of duty. At the closing, "Me and Warren made a pact never to work with Danny Mann again."

To Warren Beatty, the play, despite its star-crossed history, represented the starting point of his career.[364] As Dick Seff, an MCA agent out of New York, said, "He had a kind of royal entrance into the theater in that he had the advantage of [his sister Shirley's] entrée, which separated him from a lot of other handsome young people; and then he had the talent and the charisma. The play was a flop but he was effective in it. There was a buzz about him, there's no question. The same way there was for Jimmy Dean in *The Immoralist*, or Brando in *The Truckline Café*. Those also ran a week or two, but everybody in town seemed to know they were in them. You just sort of heard around town there was something going on. And Warren had that kind of impact."[365]

One of the people Beatty had electrified was already beginning to strategize how he was going to turn the young actor into a movie star.

29

Warren Beatty's canny admirer in December 1959 was John Springer, a respected and well-liked publicist who headed the East Coast branch of the successful public relations firm of Arthur P. Jacobs, representing, among others, actress Elizabeth Taylor.

After seeing Inge's failed play at the Eugene O'Neill Theater, Springer was so certain Beatty had star quality that he went backstage to introduce himself, offering to promote him without pay until Beatty began to earn more money as an actor.[366] "From the first time I saw you in *Loss of Roses*," he later wrote to Beatty, "felt you had to be a big star, came back and discussed the idea of our working with you and you signed with us, we have known exactly what we wanted to do."[367]

John Springer's initial assessment of Warren Beatty in an in-house memo for the Arthur P. Jacobs Company read: "In addition to being a good actor, Beatty's youthful, handsome and seems to have elements that made Paul Newman, James Dean, Montgomery Clift."[368] While the publicist was backstage, he outlined for Beatty the star-making strategy he had in mind, saying that he would build him up as a "teen-age idol" first, "taking advantage of everything possible to get your name known."[369]

The press agent could not have appealed to the innately private Virginian at a more receptive time. Beatty's high-minded ideals to follow in the family tradition on the stage had begun to wobble even before his Broadway debut; after the fiasco of A Loss of Roses, Beatty told Springer he "wasn't particularly anxious to do another play."[370] His focus was on becoming a movie star.

Typically, Beatty kept to himself how he felt when A Loss of Roses collapsed, even from his comrade Michael J. Pollard, who recalled, "He didn't talk about that stuff." Lenn Harten, who had helped identify Beatty's mistakes on "The Curly-Headed Kid" by listening to an audiotape of the show with him, could detect when Warren was feeling vulnerable. "I think being in that play sort of scared him."

It was clear, from his later comments, that Beatty was profoundly scarred by his involvement in such a colossal failure, one over which he had had no personal control — a core issue that emanated from his childhood experiences. "If you are in a flop, you are very disappointed and your ego and bank balance are both deflated," he once remarked of performing onstage.[371] A few years later, Beatty said he refused to put his fate in the hands of "four critics who decide whether you're going to be allowed to keep doing the play."[372] After the personality wars on A Loss of Roses, he also became leery of the behavior of costars onstage. "I'm very dependent upon the attitude of other actors to keep the ball in the air . . . I really was not in control of who those other players were and whether we were all playing volleyball in the same way."[373] The seeds had been sown for his future as an auteur filmmaker.

The depressing nature of William Inge's characters — smalltown Midwesterners with foiled dreams — also deterred Beatty from performing in the theater, for reasons that had to do with his parents. "I found it masochistic to have to be in a negative frame of mind night after night, this kind of enforced and repeated unhappiness."[374]

There was another facet to Warren Beatty's rejection of the stage for movies at twenty-two, a corollary to the formerly devout Baptist's overwhelming attraction to sex symbol Joan Collins. "Fame and fortune are seductive," Beatty confessed many years later. "The medium of movies is very exciting and very seductive."[375]

John Springer's proposition to make all that possible was so tempting to Beatty that it eclipsed the invasion of his privacy the plan required, which included, as Springer would recapitulate in a letter, "having you meet editors and writers who would be responsible for breaks at the right time, getting you in columns . . . hounding [them] to meet you until they gave in out of sheer desperation . . . following it up every minute, using every advantage we could to keep the fact that you were coming and you were the one to watch — the hot new star."[376]

Beatty and the ethical, family-oriented Springer liked, and understood, each other from their first meeting, forming an affectionate relationship that was as much familial as professional. Springer called Beatty "Kid," and Beatty called Springer in the middle of the night to sing tunes like "The Best Is Yet to Come."[377] Springer, Beatty said later, was one of the few people in the business he respected.[378] "John was a father figure to him, I know that," remarked Peter Levinson, a former Springer associate.[379]

During their initial encounter, Beatty laid out his career ground rules, telling Springer that he was wary of television unless it was "prestige," making it clear he would not sign a term contract with a movie studio because he wanted to choose his own films, and pointing out that he could sing, as he claimed to Springer, "well enough to be able to do a musical and to record."[380]

After the meeting, the press agent sent a missive to his West Coast partner, Arthur Jacobs, writing that Warren Beatty was a "hot property" and advising Jacobs that the actor was "cooperative about publicity . . . although is inclined to be a little too outspoken about what he thinks of other actors, of movie producers, etc. He has agreed that he will hold his opinions on such subjects down until he has acquired more standing himself . . . he could alienate a large segment of Hollywood if allowed to talk unchecked."[381]

Beatty signed with the Arthur P. Jacobs Company on December 15, and Springer went to bat for him immediately: blanketing the press with the actor's reviews in *A Loss of Roses*; setting up interviews for him with columnist Earl Wilson, *Glamour*, *Theater*, and a syndicated radio show; arranging a layout for him with Joan Collins in a fan magazine. At the end of the month, Daniel Blum announced that Beatty would be receiving the Daniel Blum Theater World Award as a "promising newcomer."

Beatty's most cherished aspiration was still to play Bud in *Splendor in the Grass*, which Inge was refining for him during the three weeks *A Loss of Roses* was on Broadway. "He was absolutely writing it with Warren in mind. We all knew that," said the stage manager, Burry Fredrik, who heard Beatty's and Inge's discussions at the O'Neill. "Bill Inge was enormously taken with him, enormously taken." She also noticed Kazan stop by the theater occa-sionally to work with Inge on the *Splendor* script.[382]

Beatty's first wave of real success that winter served to deepen the ten-sions with his famous sister. "Warren is resigned to being asked about her in interviews although he hopes that that will eventually die down," John Springer apprised his Los Angeles–based associates after Christmas. "Confi-dentially, he and Shirley do not get along very well and haven't seen each other for some time."[383]

In his romantic life, Beatty was deliriously happy. He and Joan Collins remained in New York for a few weeks after A *Loss of Roses* closed on De-cember 19, going to nightclubs and Broadway shows, partying with the Mays, and posing for their fan-magazine layout. Verne O'Hara, whose hus-band had semisupported Beatty, shared their Blackstone Hotel suite with Warren and Joan, and the two couples went out regularly together. In O'Hara's observation, Beatty and her close English pal Collins were ideally matched. "He was mad about her—it was the first person that Warren was mad about. She was really right for him." As O'Hara explained, "Sex *drives* Joan. She was besotted with him. And he was besotted with her." Beatty's close friend Michael J. Pollard, who spent considerable time with him and Collins at the Blackstone, had the same view. "I'd be dancing with Joan Collins and from the bedroom I'd hear, '*Get your hands off my girl's ass!*' . . . 'Okay, Warren.'"

Dorothy Kilgallen wrote a headline item in her column that December about an incident involving Collins and Beatty at a party that illustrates the depth of his passion: "Guests would give a good deal to know what Christo-pher Plummer said—or did—to insult beautiful Joan Collins. At any rate she was so incensed she threw a drink in his face, and her adoring escort, Warren Beatty, was all set to fight the English actor when cooler heads per-suaded him it would be smarter to exit."[384] Beatty referred to the episode later, saying, "I felt like calling him up and telling him that he'd better watch it or I'd kick his tail in the next time I saw him—he was drunk."[385] For Beatty, the incident was not only an act of gallantry triggered by his fury at Maxwell Reed, Collins's alcoholic first husband, but also a painful reminder of similar instances from his childhood.

Beatty continued to be defensive about Collins's reputation as a sex sym-bol, telling one magazine that "she could be one of the great light comedi-ennes if she ever had a chance."[386] His attitude revealed his competing desire, or need, to be involved with an actress who was the caliber of his mother, grandmother, aunt, or sister. He encouraged Collins to "stretch" in her work, even directing her to walk out on *Sons and Lovers* as the cast was leaving for England, because he thought the story was not "appealing" — an act that caused Fox to put Collins on temporary suspension. "Of course Warren's motives were not entirely selfless," Collins reflected. "He needed me with him and he was getting publicity over our liaison." Ironically, her replacement in the film, Mary Ure, won the Academy Award. Years later, Collins would name the role in *Sons and Lovers* as the one part she wished she had taken, though she would not call it a regret. "'Moi, je ne regrette rien,' as Edith Piaf said."[387]

On December 21, Dorothy Kilgallen reported Joan Collins's nuptials as near, writing, "Chums predict she'll become the future bride of Walter [*sic*] Beatty, the handsome young actor, early in 1960."[388] Kilgallen was correct about Beatty's intentions, according to Verne O'Hara. "He did want to marry her," revealed O'Hara, who went shopping with Beatty for the engagement ring at David Webb's. "It was like a huge gold dome with emeralds and diamonds in it. . . . [Joan and Warren] were fabulous together! And when Joan's in love she's one hundred percent giving." Collins's devotion was proven by her sitting through eight of Warren's twenty-one performances in *A Loss of Roses* in the half-empty Eugene O'Neill Theater.[389]

Like so much in his life, Beatty kept the engagement ring a secret, either biding his time or waiting for the perfect moment to propose. His new mentor, John Springer, a veteran of show business romances, described Beatty's relationship with Collins in a note to Arthur Jacobs, "He is, shall I say, very romantically involved with Joan Collins and it is conceivable, but not definite, that they will be married. Collins is very possessive of him and he seems to be totally gone on her. It could wind up as a sort of Franciosa-Winters deal,* but at the moment, it's going strong."[390]

The couple returned to Los Angeles in mid-January, renting a small studio apartment at the Chateau Marmont. Beatty's impressive debut in a three-week Broadway catastrophe had not ignited the kind of excitement in Hollywood he had hoped, and to add to his anxiety, Kazan was having second thoughts about casting him in *Splendor* after seeing his *Parrish* screen

---

*Springer was referring to Tony Franciosa, the handsome, dark-haired actor who electrified Broadway audiences as Polo in *A Hatful of Rain* in 1956 and began a highly publicized romance with eight-years-older Shelley Winters. Franciosa and Winters had just filed for divorce following a brief, tempestuous marriage.

test. "It looked like I had that job, but Kazan saw this other screen test, and he said, 'I've got to be very honest with you. I don't know if I want you.'"391

Beatty set up a command post from their apartment at the Chateau, Collins recalled, "making three hundred fifty calls a day—two hundred fifty to his agent, twenty-five to Bill Inge, who was doing all he could to get Kazan to test Warren . . . he was never happier than when he was on the phone." Beatty had an instant and photographic memory for phone numbers—in his sixties, he would still be able to recall the numbers of people he had met only once forty years earlier—and an unusual gift for dialing faster than a machine, a trick he would demonstrate in future years, after it had become part of his mythos.

Although Joan Collins had begun to feel like a "sex object" living with the ever-amorous Beatty in his twenty-two-year-old prime, "we were good for each other," she conceded. Beatty introduced her to carrot juice and health food, and tried to persuade her to stop drinking and smoking, even though he still smoked, albeit without inhaling. Their wealthy friends the Mays took a house in Palm Springs that winter, and the two couples socialized on weekends. "They were *fun*," extolled Verne O'Hara. "One time we went to Disneyland. I had the best time in the world—ever, ever!"

The only gray cloud over the couple's romance was Beatty's uncertainty about his career, undoubtedly the reason he had not given Joan Collins the engagement ring yet. "I couldn't get a job in film," he stated bluntly.392 When his friend from *Dobie Gillis*, Deborah Sherwood, ran into Beatty with Collins at a party, she found him "uncharacteristically a bit depressed."

By the middle of January, Natalie Wood had signed her contract for *Splendor in the Grass*, creating a sense of urgency in Beatty, according to Eleanor Kilgallen. "Maynard was knocking his brains out, you know, that Warren would get a good crack at that." In what was likely Maynard Morris's doing, producer Walter Mirisch requested that Beatty audition for the doomed hero, Tony, in the movie version of *West Side Story*, the sort of romantic Broadway musical Beatty had fantasized himself in since he'd seen *Oklahoma!* at age seven.393 Director Robert Wise liked Beatty well enough to bring him back for a second audition that winter, making a note that he had an "excellent quality," but Wise questioned whether Beatty's singing voice was right for the part.394 Beatty's desperation became apparent when he agreed to test for the lead in *Where the Boys Are*, at MGM.395

That same week, he filmed the pilot episode of an ABC anthology series with stories about the supernatural called *One Step Beyond*, a showcase for movie star Joan Fontaine, whose husband was the producer. Beatty turned down a recurring role on the series, saying, "I want to be free to make my own choices, I don't want to be tied up," a metaphor for the next thirty years of his life.[396] In the episode, called "The Visitor," he played Fontaine's husband, seen first as an older man whose car goes off a cliff to his death. After the accident, Beatty's character appears to Fontaine as the ghost of his youth. "I remember him as a good, no trouble, and pleasant actor," reflected Fontaine.[397] The script supervisor offered an amusing image of Beatty as a "nut" and a "smart-ass" who flirted outrageously with Fontaine, then forty-two, knowing her husband was the producer.[398]

Joan Collins would recall being introduced with Beatty as a couple to the Robert Wagners that February, "double-dating" at nightclubs and Beverly Hills parties or playing poker and charades together. Collins shared confidences and went shopping with Natalie Wood, whom she described with affection as a "girl's girl." The suave Wagner, called "R.J." by intimates, told Hollywood columnist Sidney Skolsky that he kept his eye on promising young actors, and named Warren Beatty as one he was "enthusiastic" about, describing a fight they staged as a joke at a recent party.[399]

The same month, Beatty enrolled as an airman third class in the California Air National Guard, in Van Nuys, to fulfill his military service. While waiting for his assignment, he continued his incessant phone calls to William Inge and Maynard Morris, begging them to persuade Kazan to reconsider him for *Splendor in the Grass*. For the second time, Inge presented Warren Beatty with a golden opportunity.

On March 2, 1960, Kazan, encouraged by Inge, flew to Los Angeles to direct Beatty in a screen test with Natalie Wood. The test began the following morning, on Stage Four at Warner Brothers, in Culver City. As Beatty described that fateful day:

> I complained about a couple of things, and [Kazan] said, "Really?" And I said, "Why don't I go over here, and I'll play the piano a little bit?" He said, "Really?" About thirty minutes later, Karl Malden wandered in. Kazan said, "Well, Karl, you take over." I thought I had disappointed him.
>
> That night, we meet at Natalie's house, and he's [Kazan's] being fairly distant with me, so I thought, "Well, I guess I didn't get this movie." Suddenly he grabs me by the lapels and shoves me up against the wall. He says, "Look, kid, you got the part, okay?" He says, "You

know that thing where you said to me that was not a good idea that I had?" He says, "Keep doing that. That was good. I need that." And I felt a chill start at my heels and go up my back to the top of my head. Because I thought, unless I'm stupid, I'm not going to be poor, because I've got a shot, and I can do something with it.[400]

Beatty would also offer a slightly different version of the conversation with Kazan that was to change his life, saying it occurred in a car, after the screen test, on the way to Chasen's, with Kazan telling him, "Kid, you got the picture. I don't even have to see the test. I need you to help me direct this movie."[401] By either account, Kazan's invitation to Beatty to participate and challenge him set a precedent for Beatty's relationships with future directors, at times to catastrophic effect.

Though he said he felt in that instant he would never have to worry about money again, the fifteen-thousand-dollar salary Beatty got for *Splendor* was not his most important cause for elation. "I don't think I've ever been mainly motivated by money," he said when he was forty. "I'm paid so much more money than I'd ever expected. I've been very lucky in that area. But it's only interesting as a symbol."[402] The greater glory for Beatty, the son of two professors and the grandson of another, was the opportunity to learn from a master of his craft like Elia Kazan. "I knew from the moment I began working with him that he was a wonderful teacher. *Splendor in the Grass* was my very first film, and therefore I was at my most susceptible."[403] Beatty's experience with Kazan called to mind the ancient expression: When a student is ready, the teacher will appear.

Kazan's rationale for choosing Beatty to play Bud Stamper was simple and direct: he liked to cast unknowns essentially playing themselves, "not actors portraying something."[404] The director could not have found more authentic casting, since William Inge had crafted Bud, the sensitive high school football hero, *for* Warren Beatty. "There's something so very right about the casting of Warren, too," Inge said at the time, "as an active, physical boy, cautiously raised, almost cursed with a conscience."[405] In effect, he was describing Beatty.

Kazan's notes on the character of Bud, Beatty's alter ego, offer further insight into a deepening conflict in Beatty's psyche, which Inge must have observed and incorporated into the character: "He is being pulled by three different teams of wild horses in opposite directions . . . he is full of desire, yet he's a good, dutiful boy." Kazan wrote further of the internal schism in

Bud/Beatty: "There is a wild streak in Bud . . . he has sadism, wildness, danger in him. The opposite face of Puritanism."[406]

Kazan, twice psychoanalyzed and a student of Freud, had even submitted the script to a psychiatrist for an analysis of each character, and the director had prototypes among people he knew, according to his script notes. He identified Bud with his own sons, Chris and Nick; Bud's father, the domineering Ace Stamper, he associated with Hemingway, among others; Bud's submissive mother reminded Kazan of the wife of Spyros Skouras, the president of Twentieth Century Fox.[407]

Bud's relationship with his father had undertones of Beatty's with Ira; like Ira Beaty, Ace Stamper suffers humiliating failure, and like Warren, Bud drops out of college to pursue an occupation his father considers tenuous. Intriguingly, Inge created an older sister for Bud named Ginny, a free spirit rebelling against their parents and of whose choice in men the family disapproves. Inge kept to himself whether his reshaping of Bud in the image of Beatty extended to Beatty's sister and parents; however, when the mother of Beatty's high school girlfriend Ann Read saw *Splendor in the Grass* in Arlington, her comment was, "That's his family; that's Warren's life!"[408]

Inge, who was in a position to know, made an insightful observation about his protégé. "Warren plays love scenes best when they are on a more idealized level," the playwright advised a Warner Brothers producer, citing *Splendor in the Grass* as an example. "I feel it's hard for him to be bluntly sexual or earthy."[409] Inge's observation about Beatty as an actor reveal Beatty's Protestant inhibitions, and his essentially romantic nature, carryovers from his Virginia youth.

Shortly after he was cast in *Splendor* — two long years after Inge first began to tailor the part of Bud for him — Beatty celebrated his twenty-third birthday at a surprise party in Los Angeles. The next day, his high school football buddy Tom Calhoun, who had graduated from Duke and was now in the air force reserve, looked him up on his way to basic training. Calhoun found his old friend "much the same" as in Arlington. "He liked to wear crisp white dress shirts without a tie, unbuttoned, sleeves rolled up. Warren's idea — I don't think he ever realized it, maybe he did — but he liked the thought of cruising up and down the boulevards in a Thunderbird in, I guess, his white shirt. He seemed excited to be there. He was always enthusiastic and upbeat, and that's the way he was. He was just enjoying the life, and extolling the brains of the people he met out there — not all the gorgeous chicks, but the smart people. I thought that was interesting."

Beatty recited to Calhoun the poem by Wordsworth from which Inge had taken the title of *Splendor in the Grass*, and told his friend how many talented writers and directors he had met or wanted to meet. "That was not the prevailing view of Hollywood — at least not to people like me, just from what I read, of semiliterate studio heads and bubble-headed blondes — but Warren found the really bright people." Beatty later told an interviewer he was attracted to people who "work hard and are intelligent."[410]

During that visit, Tom Calhoun also noticed that the same cautious nature that had led Beatty to bunk at the Calhouns' after a few drinks while in high school was still in evidence when Beatty was on the cusp of stardom in Hollywood. "Warren was concerned about things that he shouldn't have been concerned about. For example, Joan Collins was hot for him. And he for her — he said, 'She's the most beautiful woman I've ever met, and she had this very hard life. She was married at fifteen and abused, and she wants to marry me.' And he said, 'But I haven't been in the army yet.' He was like a normal person, like a normal kid of his age, and had the same concerns. He had thought about them."

Beatty's hesitance to marry Collins was not, as it would be misinterpreted, a disinclination to get married; rather, it was out of respect for marriage, "which I took very seriously . . . a marriage is forever."[411] According to Calhoun, Beatty told him, "I'm too young and I haven't even been in the army yet."

A few days after Calhoun's visit, as Beatty was preparing to go to New York to start shooting *Splendor in the Grass*, Joan Collins discovered she was pregnant — "just like a bad novel," in her arch recollection. Beatty, whose life was defined by meticulous planning, was puzzled about how this could have occurred. According to Collins, he soberly discussed their options, which did not include marriage. "We were too young and immature to make it work. Besides which, he was practically penniless and exceedingly ambitious." Collins, who was twenty-seven to Beatty's twenty-three, reluctantly agreed to have an illegal abortion in New Jersey, arranged by their mutual friend Judith Kanter,* the same person, ironically, who had arranged for them to meet.[412]

According to Kanter, the three flew to New York together, sharing a room at the Hotel Beverly. Beatty notified his publicist, John Springer, beforehand that he was flying east with Collins to start the Kazan film and he wanted to

*Judith Balaban Kanter Quine.

be "incognito." Springer noted in an April memo to his partners, "Warren doesn't wish anybody, for the moment, to know when he is arriving or where he is staying . . . why this is, I don't know."[413]

The morning of the abortion, Collins, hidden behind a head scarf and dark glasses, had hysterical second thoughts. Beatty, who was distraught, panicked that a child out of wedlock would damage their careers—as had happened with Ingrid Bergman—just as he was about to star in his first movie. "Frightened to death that Joanie would be maimed and we would not know how to find her, Warren and I parked our car on a side street in the New Jersey town," recalled Kanter. She and Beatty sat in a coffee shop, listening to a jukebox play "Love Is a Many-Splendored Thing," while Collins had her backstreet abortion.

Joan Collins was still pained at the thought forty years later.[414] Beatty, the once devout Baptist, kept his religious, moral, and ethical feelings about Collins's abortion private, though he said, when he was fifty-four, "I always wanted to have children."[415]

30 *Beatty started "Splendor in the Grass"* the day after he took Joan Collins to get her abortion, adding an emotional element to the tension he was experiencing starring in an Elia Kazan movie as an unknown immediately after the nightmare of *A Loss of Roses*. "I'm a bit scared and worried," he admitted to a reporter from the *New York Times*, "but I'd try anything involving Bill and Gadge."*[416]

Kazan inspired this feeling of devotion in his lead actors by forming an intimate bond with them before filming began. "He spent a lot of time with Warren," said the assistant director on *Splendor*. "Individually. A lot of talking, and more talking—that's what he did with actors. Kazan can get under your skin and really make you feel that you're the only one he's ever thought about and you're ready to do anything. It's like, 'Here I am—take me.' I mean he was brilliant."[417]

The director, whom actress Natalie Wood likened to a psychologist, had already psychoanalyzed Bud's/Beatty's "problem" to be his father, so Kazan treated Warren like a son, knowing he craved that relationship.[418] Beatty

*"Gadge" Kazan.

later told a psychologist, "While you're in the show, Gadge makes you feel loved. He's a great father."[419] For Kazan, the reward was on screen, in the actor's performance. He said once, "You have to treat [movie] stars in a certain way that bores me. When you get these young guys . . . they'd do anything. They were great, full of eagerness. They say that fighters come to fight. These guys — Dean, Brando, Beatty — they came to act. You couldn't stop them."[420]

To get Beatty into the spirit of the 1920s, the setting for Bud and Deanie's high school romance in *Splendor*, the director invited him into his dressing room and played "music of the period on a Victrola," recalled a member of the crew. "He'd bring Warren into the room and talk to him for long periods of time."[421] From their discussions, Beatty believed that the key to Bud was that he "failed to rise to the occasion with Deanie," a weakness Beatty was trying to communicate in his performance.[422] As a "kid actor," he said later, he was so impressed by Kazan's organizational capacity, flexibility, and openness that, "I would have done anything he wanted."[423]

After he had secured Beatty's unwavering loyalty and respect, Kazan shrewdly sent him to Pat Hingle, the veteran actor, formerly in the navy, who was playing Bud's father, hard-driving narcissist Ace Stamper, the one responsible for destroying Bud's happiness with Deanie. "Kazan and I," observed Hingle, "that was the third movie that we had done, and we'd done three plays on Broadway. I was in *On the Waterfront* with him, *Cat on a Hot Tin Roof* onstage, *Wild River* I narrated. And he knew there was no actor that he could hire would play Ace better than me . . . Warren, hell, hadn't done anything. Warren had been in a Bill Inge play that didn't succeed."[424]

Kazan's strategy was to establish a relationship between Beatty and Hingle prior to filming so they would behave like father and son in their scenes together. "At the time that Warren was cast, I had a near-fatal accident," revealed Hingle. "I fell fifty-four feet down an elevator shaft and was almost dead. I broke everything. I landed upright, so I broke hips and knees and ankles and ribs, and that sort of thing. That lurching walk that Ace Stamper has — that was as good as I could walk. And so I used to, this was before we started the film, Kazan would have Warren come up and take me to the park in the afternoon, because I was still in a wheelchair. I was living on West End Avenue, and we'd roll down to Riverside Park, and sit there and talk and everything, and I got to know Warren pretty well."

After his days at the park with Hingle, Beatty came up with the idea that

Bud and Ace Stamper should roughhouse with each other in a few scenes to show their father-son competitiveness. "You know the way people punch each other in the shoulder in a friendly way, hitting harder each time until somebody calls it quits?" explained Beatty. "I suggested doing that and we used it."[425]

The neophyte Beatty was the ideal student for Kazan's school of naturalism, particularly since Bud, in effect, *was* Warren. Beatty used the same number — fifty-one — on Bud's football uniform as he himself had worn when he played center at Washington-Lee, something his parents noticed when they saw the film the next year. "We have a hunch he asked the director if he could use the number," Ira Beaty said, "maybe to show all of us back home he hasn't forgotten."[426] For the detail-driven, perfectionist Beatty, Kazan's request for input from his actors was deeply satisfying. "It's wonderful to work with Kazan," Beatty commented then. "He'll accept anything that makes good sense."[427]

Beatty's feeling of security with the serious artist Kazan was threatened by the presence of Natalie Wood, who arrived in New York by luxury train in a $6,500 mink, a gift from Robert Wagner, who accompanied her, along with their pals Elizabeth Taylor and Eddie Fisher.[428] As Bob Jiras, Kazan's makeup artist, observed, "This was the first picture Kazan did where he used a real movie star. And Natalie *was* a movie star at the time. She came with R.J. on the *Twentieth Century*, and it was like a movie star *should* arrive — you know, with tons and tons and tons of luggage."[429]

Barbara Loden, the talented actress who played Beatty's/Bud's sister, and who later married Kazan, noticed "Warren's contempt for anything strictly Hollywood, and what can be more Hollywood than a Hollywood-raised star like Natalie? And he went to extremes to show it, his contempt."[430]

By Natalie Wood's later account, "After he got the role, a few misunderstandings crept in. Warren had heard rumors that I didn't want him in the film, that he was too much of an unknown, that we needed an established male star to carry the picture at the box office. None of this was true. But Warren believed it. And being a new face in films, he was anxious to do his best. Instead of talking to me about the gossip, Warren acted quite aloof."[431]

At the same time, Beatty felt privileged to be in a movie with Natalie Wood because she had been in *Rebel Without a Cause* with James Dean, and therefore possessed what he called a "sacred flame."[432] Both Kazan and Nicholas Ray, who directed *Rebel*, were perceptive enough to recognize

Wood's sensitive intelligence and willingness "to do anything to be good," and each director initiated the process by stripping off her makeup until she was "naked and gasping," in Kazan's famous phrase.[433]

Unknown to Warren Beatty, but well known to the analytic Kazan, was Natalie Wood's identification with the fragile Deanie. As Wood described her, "Deanie's a girl who tried always to do the right thing despite many conflicts."[434] Wood's cross to bear was her controlling mother, who had instilled in her daughter a superstitious fear of dark water and had forbidden Wood to marry her high school boyfriend, who shot himself in despair. Wood was forced to relive these painful themes while filming *Splendor*, in which her character tries to drown herself after breaking up with Bud.

Beatty, who had to confront harsh emotional truths about his father while playing the conflicted Bud, was also despondent that Joan Collins was leaving for Italy in mid-June to star in *Esther and the King*. "I was dismal about going to Rome," recalled Collins. "Warren was very jealous at the thought of me being around other men, especially Italian men." One Saturday, Beatty sent Collins to the refrigerator for chopped liver in a deli carton from Reuben's, in which he had hidden her engagement ring. According to Collins, Beatty was "grinning like a schoolboy." The actress, who intuited that the timing was due to Beatty's "strong guilt" over her abortion and insecurity that they would soon be apart, nonetheless was thrilled by his marriage proposal. Beatty set a tentative wedding date for the end of the year, and from then on, Collins refused to remove her engagement ring, even in her biblical costumes for *Esther and the King*. To Beatty, marriage was a serious proposition, and monogamy "a goal to be striven for in earnest." As he put it, "After all, I came from Virginia, where it was expected."[435]

Before Collins left for Rome, she and Beatty set up housekeeping in a tiny apartment furnished with English antiques. They were glowing like newlyweds, according to Verne O'Hara, who saw them daily. "He finally found an apartment on Fifth Avenue, and it was a lovely apartment. I don't know if Warren could really afford it, but [it was] a fabulous apartment, and I must say they were very, very happy together."

On May 9, 1960, the first day of filming on *Splendor in the Grass*, Joan Collins and Robert Wagner were at Filmways Studios to watch Kazan direct their significant others in what the director hoped would be "a poem in praise of young love."[436] Observing the master of cinema had to be bittersweet for the two, since, as actors, Wagner and Collins were "utility infielders," in Joan Collins's phrase. While Collins had a cheeky sense of humor about her B movies, Wagner was trying futilely to break out of his "pretty boy" roles as his wife's movie career began to soar.[437]

Beatty, who described *Splendor* as a "turning point in my life," felt the pressure, particularly with Collins leaving for Italy.[438] Castmate Barbara Loden found him "insecure . . . he was always taking [vitamin] pills — especially the first few days. He did tell me once that he'd had something wrong with him physically — hepatitis or something. He tired easily. He was always asleep in his dressing room when he didn't have to work . . . Joan Collins was around quite a bit. He had pictures of her in his dressing room. They seemed very close."

Beatty also lacked formal training and was in the intimidating company of consummate actors such as Pat Hingle, who considered Warren "green as grass." Both Beatty and William Inge, who was on the set frequently, conceded that he did not really know what technique he used as an actor, or whether he followed the Method. Beatty called his acting "intuitive," and Inge said, "He's hard-working and instinctive. He's got a healthy ego. And a good ego, a really sound ego, has its negative side, too."[439]

Beatty quickly annoyed the crew by asserting his opinions to Kazan, and to Inge, who continued to court Beatty, observed Inge's secretary. "Bill wanted his words to be read, or said, as he had written them. But with Warren, he sort of tailored the thing to Warren. 'Well, would it be better if I said such and such?' would say Warren, and Bill would say, 'Well,' and on it would go."[440]

To some degree, Kazan was responsible for Beatty's attitude, since, as he once said, "I don't particularly like obedience or servility in an actor . . . I try early in the procedure to encourage them to say what they think and come forward with their own ideas. I tell them frankly: 'I probably won't use one idea in twenty.'"[441] As Beatty remarked, "Kazan would get mad if you *didn't* tell him what you felt about a scene . . . he would eventually do it the way he felt, which is correct."[442]

In Beatty's case, the director appeared to have created a monster. "The enemy — who none of us liked — was Warren," said Bob Jiras, "B.J.," the makeup artist who toned down Natalie Wood's exotic look. Jiras, who instantly adored Wood and eventually became Beatty's close friend, observed, "It was as if Warren Beatty had *already* been a movie star, had already made twenty movies. That was his attitude. I rather got a kick out of that — I don't want to say *respect*, but I *did*. The arrogance! And the crew didn't like him, either. The crew gave him a name. It was 'Mental Anguish.' When he'd come on the set, it was, 'Here comes Mental Anguish.' Then it was short-ened to M.A. Natalie did it, too."

Even Kazan found Beatty problematic at the outset. Inge later wrote to Kazan, "I know you told me, during the first few weeks of shooting on *Splendor*, what a pain in the ass Warren was but I never really saw it for myself."[443] Beatty said later he thought he was "hot stuff" at the time.[444] Robert Aiken, an actor and astrologer who helped prepare Beatty's astrological chart for Collins that spring, recalled that he would often say, "I'm a narcissistic son-of-a-bitch."[445]

In the same way his father had concealed his insecurities through false bonhomie, Beatty cloaked his fears of failure in arrogance. "This was my analysis of Warren," actress Barbara Loden said after *Splendor*. "That he was scared. So I'd laugh at him, and he'd laugh back with me. He seemed to enjoy the fact that I was seeing through his act."

Loden observed the dichotomy that was emerging in Beatty, which was similar to the split in Bud between dutiful son and wild rebel noted by Kazan. "I think Warren is afraid of being a movie star," Loden appraised while they were filming *Splendor*. "I think he's got this conflict inside him. He's an intelligent boy with rather high standards . . . and I think he's going to have a hard time with it from now on. On one hand, he's intelligent and seems to have a contempt for the Hollywood way. On the other hand, he wants to be a part of it. Why not? His sister is. It's not easy, a conflict like this . . . I fear he'll end up being a big star without respecting himself." Inge had a similar intuition about Beatty during *Splendor*, predicting that he might give up acting at some point.[446]

Beatty, who had intricately ambivalent feelings about being an actor, viewed Kazan's set as a "think tank," in the assessment of one of his few friends on the production. "Warren was — is — a great observer and student of anything. What he was always doing was soaking up what people knew, and what they do, so *he* could do it."[447] Beatty's strength as the producer he was to become, his eye for talent, was already in evidence. He made mental notes on a few of Kazan's crew for future reference and was to say of charac-ter actress Zohra Lampert, who had a small but pivotal role as the waitress Bud marries instead of Deanie, "She's one of the best actresses I've ever worked with."[448]

Throughout filming, Natalie Wood provoked Beatty simply because she was a Hollywood star in a Kazan picture; Beatty provoked Wood with his at-titude. "They didn't seem to like each other," noticed Loden. "It was like a professional jealousy — as if each was afraid the other was going to get more attention. There was this coldness."

Wood described Beatty later as "difficult to work with," pointing out that he was "insecure at the time."[449] She, Kazan, and Loden recalled the director worrying that their dislike for each other was affecting their love scenes.[450] "Warren wasn't coming through," observed Loden. "Kazan said, 'Pretend it's Joan, Warren.'"

Shortly before Collins left for Rome, Beatty's supporter Dorothy Kilgallen reported in her June 10 column that a newspaperman had visited the set of *Splendor* requesting information on Warren Beatty. When the unit press agent said he was Shirley MacLaine's brother, "that set off a hydrogen bomb," wrote Kilgallen. "Warren flipped. 'From now on,' was his order, 'I want it stated that she's my sister.' Most flicker experts believe he'll wind up a bigger star than Shirley."[451]

This item, by MacLaine's later comments, initiated what Hollywood gossips would refer to for decades afterward as the "feud" between Shirley and her brother, Warren. "It got started without me," MacLaine said a few years later. "I didn't even know we were having a feud until I started reading 'I'm not Shirley MacLaine's brother; from now on she's my sister.' And everyone kept bugging me about this holy war we were supposed to be having."[452]

The item seemed to create further distance between Beatty and his sister immediately. A few days after Kilgallen's column, Beatty and Collins were photographed at a benefit with MacLaine and Steve Parker. Beatty's friend Lenn Harten observed, "I don't think Warren and Shirley were really on speaking terms. They sat apart from one another." The prior evening, Harten had been with MacLaine, Parker, and actor Jack Lemmon, who had recently completed filming *The Apartment* with MacLaine in New York. During the evening, Harten would recall, "Jack Lemmon mentioned to me, 'I never knew that Warren was Shirley's brother. She never brought it up.'"

The private tension between Beatty and his sister over his brotherly concerns about Steve Parker had somehow become confused, or entangled, with his almost courtly insistence not to trade on her fame — and that had been misconstrued in the press, and possibly by MacLaine, as hostility. The item in Kilgallen's column, which was widely repeated, seemed to trigger whatever residual sibling rivalry remained from their childhood competition to be King of the Mountain. "Little things build up," was Beatty's description of what he and MacLaine were going through. "You build up a little head of steam."[453]

The last half of June, Beatty suffered in Joan Collins's absence, calling her constantly in Rome from Riverdale, the section of the Bronx where most of the location scenes in *Splendor* were being filmed to create the illusion of small-town Kansas. Beatty's costar Barbara Loden noticed he "didn't mix much" with anyone in the cast or crew.

Beatty and Collins were so miserable without each other that twelve days after she left, the actress flew to New York from Rome for a weekend. When Collins returned to Italy, she hired a London dressmaker to design her wedding gown, and Beatty sent cables stating, "CAN'T WAIT TO SEE YOU IN DRESS!" Verne O'Hara, the unwitting voyeur to Beatty's love life at the Blackstone before he met Collins, was astounded at his total fidelity. "I'd stop by the apartment and he'd be there on his own, and that was *never* Warren."

Beatty's sensitive portrayal of Bud Stamper in *Splendor* reflected his complete dedication to the role, and Kazan's intensely personal style of directing. "Gadge knew how to get the best out of any actor he'd ever worked with — those piercing eyes of his — he was like the father figure of all times," observed John Connolly. Six years later, Kazan would say of Beatty's performance, "I think that he has never been better since."[454]

Kazan was equally effective with Natalie Wood, using a different strategy. He manipulated Wood into performing the scene where Deanie tries to drown herself in a reservoir after the breakup with Bud, knowing that Wood's terror of dark water would add to the pathos. Since Wood could barely swim, Kazan placed his right-hand man, Charles Maguire, underwater. "She was petrified," recalled Maguire's widow. "Charlie had to hold her before she could even be put in the water. Someone took a picture of Charlie holding her, and he came home with a still photo. The poor thing."[455]

By early July, when the conflict-ridden *Splendor* company was shooting at the Riverdale Country School for Girls, "I think I was the only one Warren was talking to," recalled Larry Shaw, son of the still photographer Sam Shaw.[456] During Joan Collins's visits, she and Beatty lightly socialized with Wood and Robert Wagner, as they had in Hollywood. In Collins's absence, Kazan's two stars remained aloof. "Warren told me Natalie was stuck-up," said Shaw, who was apprenticing as an on-set photographer. "I avoided her because I was kind of on Warren's team." Wood and Robert Wagner, who was present throughout filming, spent most of their weekends at a house in the Hamptons they shared with Elizabeth Taylor and Eddie Fisher, as Taylor would recall.[457]

Beatty spent his free time with Larry Shaw, who was a few years younger and shared "a lot of common interests." Shaw noticed that Beatty was extremely focused on his health. "He was a very good athlete, too, and I'm a good athlete, but he was better than me. I freely tell you he was better than me. And we would throw a football. I was health conscious myself and I wasn't lifting weights, and he told me it was very important."

Beatty understood that how he looked on camera was part of his currency as a movie star, and he approached the maintenance of his face and form with his characteristic intense curiosity and perfectionism. "When Warren was in *Loss of Roses*, the makeup made him break out horrendously, horrendously, so he was very concerned about what he was going to do," said Verne O'Hara, who recalled Beatty seeking treatment from a dermatologist. He had evidently noticed his father's receding hairline, or was worried because his maternal grandfather and uncle, Murdoch and Mansell MacLean, had gone bald by middle age. According to O'Hara, Beatty, who had naturally thick hair, "went and got hair plugs, too, not too much after the dermatologist. That was the first time I'd ever heard of that." At twenty-two, he was already shrewdly focused on how to prolong his career as a leading man.

Shaw said later, "I should have listened to him. Not many people were doing weight training at all, and Warren was doing it. He wasn't just doing it to pump up his muscles like an Arnold Schwarzenegger. My coaches didn't believe in it, and we were discouraged from weight training. I'm telling you, he's a smart guy."

Others viewed Beatty's attention to detail with respect to his looks as sheer vanity. Donald Kranze, one of the crew who disliked him during *Splendor*, considered Beatty "six feet of pure ego." Kranze once observed Beatty "in front of a mirror, a set stage . . . he's got a straight pin, right? He's putting that pin into each eyelash and separating them, and moving them forward." Beatty, who was six foot one, also occasionally wore lifts. O'Hara noticed them at the Blackstone, and Wayne Tippet, a costar in *Compulsion*, loaned Beatty his "elevator shoes" to wear onstage. By the end of the production, "he wore them down. I guess he thought he needed to look taller."

According to John Connolly, who accompanied his boss, Bill Inge, to Riverdale that July, Beatty wanted to be noticed. "I remember being in a small, quote, cocktail lounge with Kazan, Bill, Warren Beatty, Natalie Wood, Robert Wagner, and Joan Collins . . . there were a dozen or so girls from the college outside giggling, and talking, and teasing each other, daring each other to come in . . . and totally ignoring Warren. Joan Collins they fell over; Natalie Wood they knew because she was a child star. Warren's nose was out of joint. *Splendor* hadn't obviously been finished, and he was a no-body—just a friend of Joan Collins. Warren *determined* to make up for that."[458] Before the cast left Riverdale, according to assistant director Donald Kranze, Beatty had a gaggle of teenage groupies, "waiting for him to shoot his scenes, drooling."

But his romantic energy was directed solely at Joan Collins, whom Beatty claimed to have sent "at least 10,000 cables" during the eight weeks she was in Rome shooting *Esther and the King*.[459] Collins was equally addicted to Beatty. At the end of July, with only a few weeks of filming remaining, she left Rome without notifying her agent so she could spend forty-eight hours with Beatty, telling reporters at LaGuardia Airport that she had a dentist's appoint-ment in New York. Kranze, who had dinner with Beatty and Collins in Riverdale that weekend, described them as "very lovey-dovey in the restau-rant, kissing and holding, and I was a little bit uncomfortable, to tell you the truth."

As Collins was leaving to finish *Esther and the King*, Beatty became con-vinced she had been unfaithful to him in Italy. "Warren seemed to be both-ered, and lonely, much of the time," observed Barbara Loden. He may have unconsciously baited Collins when she left for Rome because he had doubts about their passionate relationship. As Loden commented, "Warren said to people that they were going to get married. But this I didn't believe."

That week, when the *Splendor* cast returned to Filmways, the Wagners had dinner with actor Robert Evans, their Manhattan neighbor, to celebrate the fact that Wood had been cast in *West Side Story*. Evans, the future head of Paramount, recalled Wood saying she was "having a difficult time" with her costar, Warren Beatty.[460] As Wood later wrote, "Between takes, Warren and I went our separate ways." She was also exhausted from playing Deanie, and had been scheduled to begin grueling dance rehearsals in Hollywood the day after she completed *Splendor*.

Early in August, with his two stars both under stress, Kazan shot the poignant last scene of *Splendor in the Grass*, in which Bud shyly introduces his lost love Deanie to the comparatively plain woman he has married, and the star-crossed former sweethearts wish each other well. Beatty, as Bud, stands in the doorway of his modest farmhouse watching Deanie's car drive off, as Natalie Wood's voice is heard reciting the lines from Wordsworth's poem, "Though nothing can bring back the hour of splendour in the grass . . . we will find strength in what remains behind." Kazan considered it "one of the best things, certainly, that I've ever done on the screen—the last fifteen minutes of that picture are just heartbreaking, I think."[461] Their earnest and touching performances as Bud and Deanie validated Kazan's instinct in casting Warren Beatty and Natalie Wood as what he believed them to be, "two awful good kids."[462]

At the wrap party for the cast and crew in the middle of August, Kazan gave Beatty a hand mirror that said, "GOOD GOD, WARREN!"—a gag gift that was self-explanatory.[463] In his memoir, the director would write, "Warren wanted it all and wanted it his way. Why not? He had the energy, a very keen intelligence, and more chutzpah than any Jew I'd ever known. Even more than me."[464] Kazan said at the time that Beatty's inquiring mind was stimulating, adding prophetically, "but he needs a strong director and a challenge."[465]

Beatty said simply of Kazan, "I love the guy."[466] In the future, he would credit the director for teaching him 50 percent of everything he knew about filmmaking.[467]

Elia Kazan's interpretation of the ending of *Splendor in the Grass*—a movie in essence written for, and about, Warren Beatty by William Inge— provided a lesson that Beatty and his sister were still learning, the implicit lesson of their parents' lives: "you have to accept limited happiness, because all happiness is limited, and that to expect perfection is the most neurotic thing of all."[468]

31   *While Beatty was filming the emo-* tional last sequences of *Splendor in the Grass*, in August, he sent a cable to Joan Collins in Rome on the first anniversary of their meeting, stating, MY LIFE BEGAN ONE YEAR AGO.[469] Collins, who was still angry over his suspicions that she was having an affair, engaged in a highly publicized "flirt" with her Italian costar, Walter Chiari, as she completed *Esther and the King*, further provoking Beatty and signaling deeper problems in their relationship.

Careerwise, Beatty fretted about what film he should do after his impressive debut in *Splendor*. At this critical juncture, he was summoned for two weeks of reserve duty at George Air Force Base, in Victorville, California. Beatty, whom John Springer described with a wink as "constitutionally unable to write letters," deluged Joan Collins with cables from the military base, pleading to see her in her wedding dress.[470] When she spent a weekend with him at a nearby inn the middle of September, Beatty was not a happy soldier, in the actress's observation. She found him edgy, depressed, and insecure about his career, sidelined in an air force base.

Kazan, who had signed Beatty to three more pictures, was still in postproduction on *Splendor* and had given no indication when, or whether, he might direct Beatty in another film, causing the actor to feel displaced professionally and personally, since the director had treated him like a son.

William Inge continued his ardent promotion of Beatty, agreeing in September to adapt James Herlihy's newly released novel, *All Fall Down*, for producer John Houseman with the understanding that Beatty would play a pivotal character.[471] "I think he made *All Fall Down* for Warren," expressed Inge's niece and confidante.[472]

While Inge wrote the screenplay at MGM, Beatty tried to reconcile his diminishing bank balance and lofty ideals. "He had been spoiled by his first film being of high artistic caliber," observed Joan Collins, "and now he wouldn't settle for anything less." At the time, Beatty said he only wanted to make films that were "really worthwhile" or he would diminish Kazan's respect for him, an inchoate expression of the longing he felt for a satisfying relationship with Ira Beaty, who had high standards and an interest in psychology, like Kazan.[473] It was apparent from such statements, and from his actions, that Beatty was seeking a mentor similar to Pastor John Raymond, a moral compass to guide him through the temptations and hazards of Hollywood. When filming on *Splendor* ended, Kazan ceased to play that role.

Charles Feldman, the Famous Artists agent who stepped in to become twenty-three-year-old Warren Beatty's role model that fall, if not his moral compass, was a shrewd Hollywood insider in his late fifties with the elegance and politesse of Cary Grant and the continental looks of Charles Boyer — two of Beatty's childhood heroes. They met on a flight to New York, as Beatty was preparing to start *Splendor in the Grass*, and "hit it off," said Beatty. "He was more fun than almost anybody I had met in Hollywood of the older guys. I liked his sense of humor about the movie business and the people in it, his objectivity, his lack of drive."[474] In effect, Feldman was the anti–Ira Beaty, a Hollywood pleasure-seeker who exuded a joie de vivre, the life force that Beatty and his sister, Shirley MacLaine, had been seeking since childhood and had dedicated their adult lives to embracing.

Mitch May's wife, Verne O'Hara, who knew Beatty extremely well by 1960, said bluntly, "Charlie Feldman was the father he never had, the father he always *wished* he'd had. Warren's father was a drunk. He had a *terrible* relationship with him. Charlie was suave and worldly and successful in every area—all the things Warren wanted to become."

Feldman saw in Beatty a future star and a kindred spirit. Both of them knew their futures were in producing, not as an agent or an actor, and neither one believed in signing contracts, making it easy to extricate themselves whenever a deal, or a relationship, took a negative turn.[475] Jane Fonda marveled at Beatty's ability as a young actor to negotiate "special commissions" with agents, or to represent himself. In 1961, Fonda starred in *A Walk on the Wild Side* for Feldman, a legendary ladies' man with a preference for beautiful actresses or models, "and I can tell you that in my perception, one of Warren's most important mentors was Charlie Feldman. Charlie was very important to him, not just in a career way. As a role model: the way he lived, the way he handled women, the whole thing."

That fall, as Beatty floundered waiting for his next movie role, Feldman offered to loan him money, and advised him not to star in a film he was close to accepting.* "I want to thank you for that and tell you that I won't forget it and that you were damned right, I think," Beatty wrote to Feldman afterward in a short typed note, adding puckishly, "By the way—what do you think of my typing?"[476]

Photographer Larry Shaw, whose father was Feldman's creative producer, was around Feldman and Beatty then. "Charlie treated him like a son. If Warren liked a cashmere sweater that Charlie had, 'Take it.' 'You want some free advice on the contract?' He'd take a phone call from Warren any time of the day or night . . . Charlie thought Warren was brilliant and talented, and he liked that. Warren *is* brilliant. I'm surprised he's an actor."

In fact, Beatty had begun to express a serious interest in writing scripts, and he had a visionary's gift to foresee the future of filmmaking. A year after he met Feldman, in 1961, Beatty told a film magazine he thought the studio system in Hollywood would "undergo a big change" by 1968. Not only was the prediction accurate, but Beatty would be instrumental in effecting it through a film he produced, *Bonnie and Clyde*.[477]

In the fall of 1960, as Feldman loaned Beatty money to keep him afloat, Beatty's more traditional father figure, John Springer, continued with the brash plan he had devised to make "the Kid" a teen idol before his first movie, *Splendor in the Grass*, had even been released. The Arthur Jacobs

---

*The film was apparently *By Love Possessed*, the third role rejected by Beatty that went to George Hamilton. The character's name, ironically, was Warren Winner.

Company's next step was to "create an image" of Warren Beatty as a sex symbol. "And he wasn't," Springer said bluntly.[478] To attract girls and elicit interest from the press, the agency decided that Beatty should behave as an enfant terrible, similar to the way he used to playfully shock Maynard Morris and Eleanor Kilgallen—the opposite of his exceedingly courteous Virginia manners, as his fraternity brother at Northwestern was to observe.

Beatty, who had made a deal with the devil when he decided to become a movie star, went along with the ruse. As he later explained, in mixed metaphors, "The entire meat-grinding snowball of the economics of the movie business requires a new young commodity to be interesting in some way, and I think probably it's not so easy to make someone so interesting. To make them famous, and to develop grist for that mill, certain choices have to be made. And usually with a young man, it's that he's very rebellious and an enfant terrible, et cetera—and just to get it out of the way, sometimes you comply. You just say, 'Well, I'll give you what you want.'"[479]

Ira Beaty had a favorite joke illustrating his son's circumstance, which Beatty repeated in his early years as a movie star. "My father tells a story about a man who is captured by cannibals in the jungle and is about to be boiled. He says to himself, 'There is nothing I can do about it, so I may as well enjoy it.'"[480] This would become Warren Beatty's guiding philosophy as a star.

Shortly after his transition into Hollywood's "bad boy," when Beatty first met Hedda Hopper, the prim gossip columnist, "all he talked about was sex, and I couldn't print it," she later wrote.[481] Gerald Medearis, who had replaced Beatty in *Studs Lonigan*, met him with Joan Collins that fall at a party. "It was a little 'A' party, and people came to the door and just sort of sat around, and Jack Lemmon was there, and we had cocktails and made witty remarks. I started to shake Warren's hand, and he wouldn't shake my hand. He was inarticulate, and vain, and stuck on himself. He played that image up, and he liked the fact that people criticized him for it. He used it as kind of PR."

The "other Warren," as Springer referred in house to the real Beatty, was the person described by Pamela Mason, actor James Mason's wife, who gave frequent parties at their showcase house in Beverly Hills: "Warren would often sit at the piano and play quietly for hours. He was very intelligent and intellectual."[482]

It was at one of the Masons' parties the fall after filming *Splendor* that

Beatty met his "demigod," playwright Clifford Odets.*[483] Beatty was absolutely stunned, he said later, to see Odets — "who embodied the radical spirit of the Group Theatre of the 1930s" — dancing with Rita Hayworth at a "silly party" in Hollywood where the other guests included starlet Mamie Van Doren.[484] Beatty told Odets's biographer, Dr. Margaret Brenman, that he saw the playwright sitting in a corner that night, "sought him out, and tried to cultivate a relationship with him."[485] Beatty later confessed, "I was really a fool. I said, 'Can I talk to you later? I can't believe you're Clifford Odets!' I went over to Clifford's house . . . he rented a house on Beverly Drive in the flats of Beverly Hills."[486] By Beatty's accounts, he "fell at Odets's feet," and eventually discussed collaborating on a film.[487]

Sheri Mann, the widow of Daniel Mann, recalled the end of the evening differently. "Danny was at Clifford Odets's house, and Warren said — Danny never got over this — Warren said very arrogantly, 'Listen, Clifford. Why don't you write with me, and I'll share fifty percent with you?' They were both sitting there, their jaws dropped, and when he left, Clifford said, 'Who the fuck is that?' And Danny said, 'Well, it's this kid, Warren Beatty.' Clifford said, 'Well, I've never seen anyone so pushy and arrogant in my life.'"

There was no doubt that Beatty worshipped Clifford Odets, a romantic figure to him. In a number of ways, Odets's life and career were the blueprints for Warren Beatty's. Like Beatty, Odets had begun as an actor. His plays, occasionally adapted into films, a few of which Odets directed, were artistic with political themes, which Beatty admired. In his personal life, Odets was involved with gifted and striking actresses like Frances Farmer, and he married an Oscar winner, Luise Rainer. "Warren wanted to *be* Clifford," analyzed Dr. Margaret Brenman, Odets's close friend and a Harvard psychologist.[488]

Despite Odets's initial reaction to him, Beatty was invited into Odets's inner sanctum that fall. "Clifford," conceded Brenman, "was a hero-worshipper himself, and maybe he was flattered by Warren's attention." Beatty used to bring Joan Collins, who'd fall asleep on the sofa while he listened raptly as Odets told stories over red wine and charcoal pills until five A.M. Beatty told Brenman later he wondered why the playwright spent time

---

*In his fifties, Beatty was quoted as saying he met Odets at Romanoff's when he was twenty or twenty-one, which is inaccurate, as documented in Odets's journals, Beatty's contemporaneous interviews, and other sources.

with him, a kid actor. The truth was that Odets's career had declined by 1960, and he was flattered that Beatty hung on his every word.

In certain respects, Odets replaced Elia Kazan as Beatty's surrogate father. Beatty discussed this with Brenman after Odets's death, expressing that he had loved Kazan, saying Kazan provided "great insights" for him, "and then he walks away." Beatty believed that Odets "might have *maintained* that kind of love."[489] In his journal the October after he met Beatty, Odets noted that they spent the evening talking about their parents, sharing negative impressions of their fathers.[490] Odets was more bitter than Beatty, who recalled, "[Clifford] would scream about his father at two o'clock in the morning."[491]

Beatty and Collins spent election night 1960 at Odets's house, watching the Kennedy-Nixon returns on television with Cary Grant, the Danny Kayes, and a few other guests. Astrologer Robert Aiken, who was there, recalled, "Warren's liberal sentiments were clear," and he showed "political savvy." Cary Grant, who supported Nixon, was extremely upset when Kennedy won, Aiken remembered, and predicted a war.[492] Beatty's memories of the evening were of Cary Grant arriving with two girls ("always"), how the level of conversation improved in the presence of an attractive female, and of Odets's technique to "get" a girl. According to Beatty, the playwright presented himself "as her savior, and he would analyze her and analyze her." Beatty declined to mention if he copied this tactic, but he made the point that Odets loved women, and that the playwright was never destructive to them because he was "too humane."[493]

In his later years, Beatty would say that the best part of being a movie star was the access he had at a young age to such dazzlingly accomplished people.[494] The crowning experience, for him, occurred that same intense autumn at Odets's house. "There was a fat guy in the room, and I was talking to Clifford and I said, 'Who is that over there?' and he said, 'Oh that's Renoir.' And I said, 'Is he related to the painter?' He said yes. I said oh. And he said, 'Did you ever hear of *Grand Illusion?*' and I said, 'Ah. I think I have.' He says, '*Rules of the Game?*' I said no. He said, 'You should talk to him.' So I talked to him."[495]

Jean Renoir, the son of Auguste Renoir and a lauded writer–film director, moved to Los Angeles from France toward the end of his career. He was the "highest human," in the expression of Beatty's friend Michael Laughlin, an opinion shared by a dedicated following that included Kazan.[496] Beatty's introduction in the fall of 1960 to *Rules of the Game*, a farce with political undertones considered Renoir's masterpiece, impressed him possibly more than any film he would ever see, and would be the inspiration for *Shampoo*.

"Warren wanted to have a friendship with Jean like he had with Cliff, but I don't think that came about," mused Brenman, who was close to both writers.[497] "I got to know Renoir very, very well," Beatty said in 1990. "And loved him, loved him. If I had to pick someone who I think embodies it all, it probably would be Jean Renoir."[498]

To Beatty, the concept of "access" to these glorious talents was not dissimilar to his fascination in childhood for older people of distinction, beginning with his grandmother. In addition to Stella Adler, Odets, Feldman, Renoir, and Inge, Beatty became a pet of aging movie mogul Samuel Goldwyn, who called him regularly to offer advice. That fall, Beatty acquired his second matronly champion in Minna Wallis, Hal Wallis's imperious sister. "She was a very ugly, social woman — social in this Hollywood sense," commented Sandy Whitelaw, an agent in Feldman's office then, as was Minna Wallis. "And she really helped him, and she really adored him. Warren has this very specific thing that he gets along incredibly well with old people. When he was young, most of the people I saw him with were always older people."

In essence, they were *teachers* to Beatty, like his schoolteacher father, mother, and both grandmothers.

BY MID-NOVEMBER OF 1960, when he and Joan Collins were photographed snuggling in a booth at El Morocco amid rumors they would marry at Thanksgiving, Beatty still had not signed for his second movie and he "needed money."[499] He decided he wanted to play a character completely different from Bud, whom Beatty described as a "muffled Puritan boy."[500] He had agreed to a salary of twenty-five thousand dollars to star with Jane Fonda in A *Walk on the Wild Side* because he was intrigued at being cast as an "obnoxious pimp," but the deal fell through.[501]

Late in his career, Beatty would reflect on his resistance to playing heroes, a pattern that began after he starred in *Splendor* and which he was unable to explain.[502] At the time, he said he had "used up all that stuff," and needed to play someone different, "like changing crops"; in addition, he did not want his looks to typecast him, or he would be "stuck in romantic parts."[503] The extremely private Beatty may also have felt exposed as Bud, preferring to hide behind a character who was nothing like him.

His choice that November was "the opposite of Bud": an unsympathetic Italian gigolo in a film starring Vivien Leigh as an aging and lonely American actress in post–World War II Rome entangled with a young escort-for-hire.[504]

The high-minded Beatty, no doubt influenced by his new friend Odets, saw the story as a "political metaphor" for the colonization of Italy. He was attracted to working with acclaimed stage director José Quintero, but the real draw for him was Tennessee Williams, who had written *The Roman Spring of Mrs. Stone*, the novella on which the script was based. Beatty, who wanted to work with the greats, and whose cash flow was at a trickle, "read the Williams story," said producer Louis de Rochemont, "and he started a campaign for the role of Paolo."[505]

Beatty's timing, and choice in roles, was brash even for him. The cast was in London preparing to start filming, "and after searching a year for the boy, they finally settled on a young Italian," recounted actress Jill St. John, who was cast as a starlet visiting Rome.[506] According to de Rochemont, Beatty, still an unknown, was rejected as the gigolo.[507]

When he learned that Tennessee Williams had casting approval and was represented by Audrey Wood, an MCA agent, Beatty began hounding the faithful Kilgallen and Morris to intercede. "Oh, I remember he wanted that badly, so badly, he was out of his mind," said Kilgallen. "And Audrey Wood, who was very protective of her clients — Tennessee being number one on the hit parade — did everything to protect him that she could. And our pathetic little attempts to con her into arranging something with Tennessee, a great star himself, fell upon rather deaf ears. And Warren was determined. He was extraordinary. So we tried to figure out ways, how do we do this?"

A week before filming, Beatty turned to William Inge, a friend of Williams's and an Audrey Wood client. Inge's live-in secretary recalled, "Warren came to Bill and . . . wanted to know where Tennessee *was*. Bill told him that he was on an island out in the middle of the Caribbean somewhere. Warren said, 'Thank you very much,' and disappeared."[508]

Using money he borrowed from Mitch May, Beatty bought a book on how to speak Italian and a round-trip ticket to Puerto Rico to persuade Tennessee Williams, an avowed homosexual, to cast him as the Italian gigolo, Paolo.[509] "He got himself, as I recall in my dim memory, a very loud suit, a suit with a wide white stripe down it," laughed Kilgallen. "At the time we had a thing known as 'Man Tan.' Well, he swooshed that all over his face. Off he went, and several days later I got a wire — it was totally unsigned — from one of the islands. Warren sent it to me. It consisted of two words — which I can't tell you, because it is private, but it was a great two words — intimating that he had made the connection. And then the next thing we knew he got the picture."

As Beatty told the story of his arrival at the Caribe Hilton in San Juan, "I walked into a casino just off the main lobby of the hotel, and sure enough, hunched over a blackjack table, I saw Tennessee Williams, whom I had never met."[510] Beatty knew that Williams believed he had gotten an ulcer from the reviews of his last play. "So I asked the waiter to give me a glass of milk. I sent a note — the character's name was Paolo — and I said on the note, 'Dear Mr. Williams, Anything you want. Paolo.'"[511]

What happened after that is in the realm of Warren Beatty myth and legend. Beatty's anecdote in later years was that when Tennessee Williams saw the "Man Tan," he fell on the floor laughing and told Beatty he had the part, and then Beatty "turned around, got on the plane, and I came back to New York."[512]

At the time, Beatty gave an account that was more consistent with the fact that he spent two days in San Juan.[513] In this earlier version, he said he read Paolo's lines for Tennessee Williams, trying to impress him with the Italian accent he had practiced on the plane. "I never worked so hard in my life. And after awhile, the great playwright came around to seeing things my way, and I got the part. We got along pretty good after we talked awhile. He is sort of set in his ways like older men often are, you know."[514]

In the memoir *Cry of the Heart*, Tennessee Williams confirmed how Beatty had appeared unannounced at the Caribe Hilton casino and sent a glass of milk to him on a tray. According to Williams, Beatty approached him about playing Paolo and later read "fabulously" for him and a friend, with and without an Italian accent. "And I said, 'You have the part, Warren.'" Williams, who was known to embellish such stories, added a postscript. "I went up to bed. There was a knock on my door. When I opened it, there stood Warren in his bathrobe. I said, 'Go home to bed, Warren. I said you had the part.' Warren has no embarrassment about anything. Whenever he sees me he always embraces me. What an affectionate, warm, lovely man."[515]

Verne O'Hara, who went to the airport with Joan Collins to see Beatty off to Puerto Rico and whose husband helped pay for his ticket, considered the ending of Tennessee Williams's tale as poetic license. "I adored Tennessee, who was a big pal of mine, but I wouldn't believe that. I would, but, you know, I wouldn't . . . I wouldn't say that it's authentic if it came from Tennessee."

There is an ironic coda. By coincidence, the Latin actor whom Tennessee Williams had chosen to play Paolo was Tomas Milian, Beatty's Cuban friend and fellow ladies' man from the Actors Studio. "And then

'Snow White' arrived," as Milian would chuckle, referring to Beatty. "So in a sense, Warren and I were both for the same part, but I think he never knew." To Milian's amusement, he *did* sleep with the playwright, only to lose the part to Beatty. "You know how actors are, how you're young, and — so I went out with Tennessee Williams, and I started trying to, in a certain sense, sell myself like the character in the movie, but instead of to Vivien Leigh, to Tennessee Williams. So Warren ended up in the movie dating Mrs. Stone, and in real life, Tomas ended up dating Tennessee Williams!"[516]

Director Peter Yates, then an assistant director on *The Roman Spring of Mrs. Stone*, recalled José Quintero announcing on the London set, where they were waiting for the final word on the casting of Paolo, "We have a hero! Tennessee has asked me to see and talk to Warren Beatty." Yates added, "And of course I didn't really know who Warren Beatty was at the time."[517]

John Springer, Beatty's publicist-mentor, drove Beatty to the airport as he left for his first trip to Europe in early December, instructing the Kid "to be as hard to get as Brando" with fan magazines during filming — an essential element of the new Warren Beatty image.[518] Springer had already set up interviews with film magazines and *Seventeen* as part of the Beatty buildup, and had sent a memo to his London partner to "generate excitement in Europe for Warren Beatty as the hottest new male star." He had also made arrangements for Beatty to be introduced to socialite Fleur Cowles Myer in London, so he could meet "important theater and society people."[519]

Joan Collins, whose parents and younger sister, Jackie, lived in London, accompanied her fiancé, but "the bloom was coming off the rose," as she described her increasingly volatile romance with Beatty. The wedding he had vaguely set for the end of the year did not occur, despite its advance publicity, and he and Collins seemed to share a tacit understanding that it never would, though they remained nominally engaged. For Beatty, who had inherited the family trait of honesty eulogized in the first Henry Warren Beaty — "a just man and true" — it was the *promise* that preyed on him. "It's a lie to vow you'll be faithful 'til death do us part' when you know you'll be faithful only as long as it's still good," he explained, signaling that he was not ready to marry Collins and paving the way for his wandering eye.[520]

Beatty also had an unusual theory that made him wary of emotional intimacy: "If I have a fault in relation to women, it's that I'm too dependent on love. When I'm deeply involved and all is not going well, my creative impulses become somewhat sublimated. I used to think the answer was not to get involved."[521] The underlying source of Beatty's fear — that he had to choose between art and a relationship—may have been Ira and Kathlyn Beaty, whose continuing lament was that marriage had caused them to give up their dreams.

Beatty's wavering commitment to Collins concerned her when she visited him on the set of *The Roman Spring of Mrs. Stone* and instantly discerned that his costar, Vivien Leigh, who was forty-seven, disliked her and "fancied Warren." Leigh had not appeared in a film for six years, suffered from manic depression, and was "a worry," Peter Yates recalled. In future years, Beatty had only tender things to say about the actress he had admired as Scarlett O'Hara. "Vivien Leigh! Well that was a childhood crush and it never became any other way . . . she was a lovely person, a terrific lady, made me feel immensely important, and she was beautiful to look at."[522]

Kazan's warning that Warren Beatty needed a strong director was borne out that winter with José Quintero, whom Beatty found "terrifically responsive to actors," but who had only directed plays, and by Quintero's own admission, was too timid to yell "Action!"[523] "It was a mess," Beatty recalled of the film. "The poor man couldn't find the time to make a movie. Nobody could tell him how."[524]

True to Kazan's prediction, Quintero's weakness brought out Beatty's petulance. The producer, Louis de Rochemont, said afterward, "Warren was a problem for him as well as for everybody else. He tried to upstage everyone and that caused more problems for the director than for me."[525] Quintero, who pronounced de Rochemont "my only distress," nonetheless characterized Beatty, in a memoir, as "never popular with the crew. Out of what I can only imagine to be insecurity, he was arrogant and huffy to Vivien. He kept people waiting."[526]

Beatty took exception, later, to these depictions, telling a journalist friend that he was late only once "because I wasn't called to the set."[527] Vivien Leigh's then companion, Jack Merivale, described Beatty revealingly to a writer as "keeping people waiting to get attention," the same trait his classmates began to notice in junior high as his way of competing with Shirley.[528] A complaint that especially bothered Beatty was from the director, repeated by Jill St. John, who said he took "a lot" longer to put on his makeup than Vivien Leigh.[529] Beatty defended himself privately, explaining that he wore special dark makeup to look Italian that was time-consuming to apply.[530]

Beatty's attitude was due partly to his press agents' makeover of him into a Hollywood rebel to get him noticed. As Collins was to note, "The Warren Beatty sex symbol image was finally emerging for the world to see, and the women to adore, and he was loving every minute of it . . . women were going gaga at the sight of this vision."

Privately, the "enfant terrible" was insecure, as Quintero had perceptively observed. Beatty confessed to a writer from *Film Review* who visited him on the set that *Splendor in the Grass* had been easier for him because "the character I played was nearer to my own." He also felt out of place, since no one had seen him in a movie yet.[531] Assistant director Peter Yates noticed that Beatty appeared "anxious" about his Italian accent, conferring before every scene with an Italian voice coach.

In Yates's assessment, Joan Collins's frequent presence during filming contributed to making it "very difficult" for Beatty, whom Yates regarded fondly. "Vivien probably was jealous of Joan. That was one of the few times Warren perhaps didn't use tact or judgment in bringing her around. Vivien was definitely attracted to Warren, and he was such a strong personality. He was just her type, and she was very vulnerable at that time, since [her ex-husband Laurence] Olivier was getting remarried. I'm sure Vivien would have been open to an affair with Warren if that door had been open, which I don't think it was."

Eleanor Kilgallen, who had gone to great lengths to help her favorite "pigeon" get the part of Paolo, heard nothing from Beatty after his cryptic two-word telegram from Puerto Rico. "And one day I get this lovely letter, all about what's going on with the movie, and all of this lovely stuff. It's all in longhand." As she read further, Kilgallen noticed, to her amusement, that Vivien Leigh had written the letter, from Beatty's dictation, as if she were his secretary. It was on Leigh's personal stationery, part of the joke:

Vivien Leigh

Feb 17th

Dear Eleanor -
    Since I am unable to write letters I am now writing a letter to you. It is being written by my new secretary — Vicky Leigh. She's got an ugly nose & sends you her regards because she too loves you.
    Love to Wilbur & Susan & Kay Brown from my new secretary.

                                                    Love,
                                                    Warren Beatty

WB/
sec/VL

Kilgallen kept the letter written to her by Leigh for Beatty with her other Beatty mementoes. "He obviously conned her one day. Well, I'm sure she was in love with him." At the least, the letter, written toward the end of filming, suggested that Beatty and Vivien Leigh had a playful relationship, and that she was sympathetic to her costar's youthful insecurity.

Three days after he dictated the letter, Beatty was presented to Queen Elizabeth and Princess Margaret at a royal premiere in London, wearing black tie and tails and a look of intense concentration, accompanied by a beaming Joan Collins — his publicists' latest strategy to introduce Warren Beatty as Hollywood's fastest-rising star. Beatty sent an affectionate note to John Springer in New York a few days later, casually mentioning that he had met the queen. It was signed, "Kid," and written on a scrap of toilet paper.

Beatty's whimsical choice in stationery was a comment on his increasing distaste for publicity, a process that crystallized in a single moment during a two-week break in filming that winter, when he and Collins visited France with married actors Paul Newman and Joanne Woodward. "I was in Paris and I opened the door of my hotel room one morning to see this copy of the *Herald Tribune* lying on the mat. And there was this large picture of me. I looked down and my stomach just turned over. I realized that things were getting out of hand, and in the future I would have to try and insulate myself." He was "startled" by it, Beatty said later, "because I wasn't doing any publicity. That instant it hit me. Whether the article said something good or bad about me, it was the same. The same! So I rarely read anything written about me."[532]

His new renegade attitude was unveiled at the wrap party for *The Roman Spring of Mrs. Stone,* in March. Quintero's assistant, Charles Castle, told a Vivien Leigh biographer that Beatty stood up at the party and said, "I want you all to know how much I've enjoyed being in England, even if the film turns out to be a bomb."[533]

Whether or not this anecdote was true — as Peter Yates believed it to be and Joan Collins affirmed — it accurately reflected Beatty's feelings. "So much happened on that film," he sighed four years later to the *New York Times,* indicating his disappointment in the screen adaptation of Williams's admired novella. "The broken-down Roman society of the book certainly wasn't the updated one they fabricated."[534]

Playing the character of Paolo had also been difficult for personal reasons. Beatty, a boy "almost cursed with a conscience," as Kazan once described Bud, was uncomfortable in a gigolo's skin. Like all things meaningful to him, Beatty kept his religious past private, but he hinted at its importance in a conversation with author Lillian Ross when he returned from London, which Ross included in her book *The Player*. "What I'm doing now is still a little bit of a mystery to me," he told Ross. "We were brought up as Baptists, and attended church and Sunday school regularly. To this day, I don't smoke much, or drink. When I had to smoke cigarettes as the dissolute and amoral young Italian in *The Roman Spring of Mrs. Stone*, I could do it, but I didn't like it."[535]

Underneath the enfant terrible, Beatty was still that "muffled Puritan boy," an internal conflict that would intensify now that he was becoming a movie star.

32

On March 12, 1961, Beatty wrote to Eleanor Kilgallen from London, as he was winding down *The Roman Spring of Mrs. Stone*. The typewritten letter made clear his fondness for the television agent who had sponsored him in his cornflakes days, and it captured his mood at a moment of transition in his life, and his career, on the cusp of turning twenty-four:

> *Dear Eleanor,*
>
> *Don't ask me why all of a sudden I'm able to write letters. I don't know. Anyway—I'm through with the picture now. I have just a little dubbing and stuff to do and that will be it. Next I want to go to Paris and then on to Rome and anywhere else that is interesting and everything is interesting.*
>
> *As you know—this is the first time I haven't had to worry about where my next dollar is coming from and it is making a lot of things more enjoyable for me. I have been offered several scripts—but I don't know what I am going to do . . . some people over here have offered me a thing called Bird of Passage (which I am) . . .*
>
> *I think I will be a few more weeks over here in the old world before New York—But who knows, they may call me back to accept an academy award for last year . . .*
>
> *Love,*
> *Warren*

Beatty stayed on to explore Europe for six weeks, while Joan Collins returned to Los Angeles, a drastic change from their lovesick behavior during *Splendor*. Collins said later that they let the relationship "drift," but in her mind "Warren didn't want to get married so I was finished."[536] Technically, they remained engaged; although in the future, Beatty would refer to the engagement as "an exaggeration," suggesting that he no longer viewed Collins as his fiancée in the true sense.[537]

His behavior in Italy that spring was certainly that of a bachelor with no attachments. Actress Julie Newmar, whose film *The Marriage-Go-Round* had just come out, in which she played a brainy Swedish bombshell, recalled Beatty chasing her unsuccessfully all over Rome. "I tell you, though, he is a great charmer, and I can see why women fall for him. He puts his eyes on you as if you are everything in the world at the moment."[538]

Jane Fonda's friend Susan Strasberg ran into Beatty at a café in Rome soon after with Inger Stevens, the beautiful Swedish blonde who would star in *The Farmer's Daughter* on television two years later. Strasberg, the daughter of Actors Studio founder Lee Strasberg, had dinner with Beatty, and the next morning he moved into her Rome apartment, staying two weeks. Beatty borrowed Clifford Odets's "savior" technique to woo Strasberg, comparing family backgrounds, probing her complicated relationship with her parents, and advising the actress to go into analysis. "I found him charming and intelligent," assessed Strasberg, "with a tremendous need to please women as well as conquer them."[539]

Beatty's business in Rome was with Luchino Visconti, an aristocratic Italian director interested in casting him in an art film called *The Leopard*. Strasberg would write about a "strange evening" at Visconti's opulent villa. "He was a salon Communist and sat in his living room surrounded by priceless antiques and a handful of beautiful young men, while advocating Communism for the masses. He seemed enchanted by Warren and ignored his young men to seductively focus on him." Sensing that Strasberg was feeling left out, Beatty whispered to her to meet him in the bathroom. "When we returned to the living room twenty minutes later, we were greeted by six pairs of hostile eyes. To my embarrassment, I realized my blouse was still unbuttoned. I wasn't quite sure how to act, but Warren beamed at one and all an enchanting, ingenuous smile."

Jeanne Rejaunier, the model-actress Beatty began dating in New York in 1958 after seeing her MCA headshot, was living on the Via Nera, across the street from Visconti, and went out with Beatty in Rome that same April. She teased him about Visconti, another older gay man with designs on him who could further his career. Beatty laughed with Rejaunier about his gay admirers, but "he didn't really dwell on it. He was very kind of mysterious about what he was doing professionally. He made it sound like whenever he got a part, he just *got* it — and I'm sure that he probably did anything he could. When I say anything he could, I don't mean anything shady, or sexual, or anything like that with a gay. I mean that he just would turn on the charm . . . Warren had a knack for allowing them to be in love with him *without* coming across. He makes it known that he's straight, and I think that the gays will accept that." Beatty told his publicist, John Springer, that Visconti was "begging" him to star in *The Leopard.*[540]

After falling ill in Rome for several days, an intermittent pattern since he contracted hepatitis, Beatty flew back to Los Angeles, via Paris, without committing to Visconti, or to anyone else. His passion was to portray Broadway director-playwright Moss Hart in the film version of Hart's recent memoir, *Act One*, a jewel of a book that Josh Logan had optioned. The previous November, after Kazan directed *Splendor*, Logan had written to him, "Please tell me something about Warren Beatty, he's dying to play *Act One* . . . do you think he could?"[541]

When Beatty reunited with Joan Collins the first week in May, at a house they were renting on Sunset Plaza Drive, "we argued so much and over such mundane and petty things that the last few months of our relationship are a hazy blur," she said.

Beatty's attention was on his career. After several weeks of fruitless phone calls to Logan and to his MCA agents trying to arrange his casting in *Act One*, he signed a contract with MGM to make *All Fall Down*, the film adaptation of Herlihy's novel that Inge had begun the prior September as a showcase for Beatty. It was now in preproduction, with John Frankenheimer set to direct.[542] Beatty's salary was sixty thousand dollars, double what he received for *Roman Spring.*[543]

Although Beatty said later that he made *All Fall Down* because he owed MGM a picture as part of his 1959 contract settlement, John Houseman, the film's distinguished producer, had assembled an exceptional cast and set it up as an art film, the kind of prestige project with which Beatty wished to be associated. Houseman noted afterward that he acquired Beatty, who still had not been seen by the public in a movie, "almost against my will . . . Inge had suggested him, and Warren Beatty himself had done the rest."[544] Referring to Springer's publicity blitz to make Beatty a sex symbol, Houseman wrote, "In an astonishing campaign of self-promotion, this young man . . . had managed to get pictures of himself, together with feature articles, into every major magazine in the country. Using charm, sex, and unmitigated gall he kept the country's female columnists in a tizzy. Within a few months, before we shot a single frame of film, he had turned a tall, nice-looking, but rather awkward and completely unknown young man into one of the hottest names in the business."

Still Beatty's "number one fan," William Inge had inflated the character Warren was playing in *All Fall Down*, a prodigal son named Berry-Berry, beyond its importance in Herlihy's novel, which had emphasized Berry-Berry's impressionable younger brother (portrayed by the talented Brandon de Wilde).[545] Beatty, still seeking roles with variety, took pleasure in the fact that his character in *All Fall Down* was "neurotic," a change from the gigolo Paolo, though he was aware of what he called the "Freudian similarities" between Berry-Berry, a misogynist ladies' man, and Kenny, the troubled son he had played in *A Loss of Roses*.[546] Both Berry-Berry and Kenny, tailored to fit him by Inge, were unnaturally attached to their mothers, suggesting that Inge may have drawn upon Beatty's close relationship with his mother, Kathlyn, in shaping the characters.

In support of this theory, Inge once noted that Berry-Berry's mother, portrayed in the film by English actress Angela Lansbury, "might once have been considered 'very talented' by the audiences of some brave little-theater group. She comes to satisfy her need for drama by investing her family's life with it," — a nearly exact restating of Shirley MacLaine's observations about Kathlyn Beaty.[547] In another parallel, Berry-Berry's parents frequently argue in Inge's script, and his father, played by Karl Malden, was "the kind of man who had retreated from the world but at the same time held court in the basement by himself and a bottle of bourbon," observed director John Frankenheimer.[548]

IN THE LAST HALF OF JUNE, as Beatty was confirmed to star in *All Fall Down* and his first film, *Splendor in the Grass*, was being previewed for the press, the publicist for Natalie Wood and Robert Wagner released a statement announcing the couple's trial separation — "a shocker," recalled actress Debbie Reynolds. Reynolds typified the reaction in Hollywood, where the Wagners had attended a Warner Brothers gala only a few nights earlier holding hands.[549] Wood had just accepted a Warner Brothers picture called

Lovers Must Learn,* with Troy Donahue as her leading man, scheduled to start filming in Rome in a few weeks, and she had expressed excitement about seeing Europe for the first time with Wagner.

Beatty's former costar had been in seclusion since the night of the breakup, when she arrived at her parents' house "a basket case," her hand bleeding, telling her mother and trusted friends that she had crushed a glass into her palm during a row with Wagner, after stumbling upon him in flagrante delicto at their house in Beverly Hills.[550] In a memoir she began for editor Peter Wyden several years after she divorced Wagner,† Wood wrote, "It is too painful for me to recall in print the incident that led to the final breakup. It was more than a final straw, it was reality crushing the fragile web of romantic fantasies with sledgehammer force."[551]

When Natalie Wood was able to return calls from studio executives who had been trying to locate her for several days, she was too distraught to work, requesting a leave of absence without pay for an unspecified time, for "reasons personal to her," as documented in a letter to the actress from Warner Brothers' legal department on July 3 and countersigned by Wood.[552]

Warren Beatty was in New York and Washington, D.C., while this occurred, doing a week of advance promotion for *Splendor in the Grass,* set up by his press agents and Warner Brothers publicity, which had scheduled photographer Richard Avedon to take publicity stills of him.[553] Beatty's distaste for the PR campaign exposing him to the public was dramatically apparent at a Warner Brothers press conference to publicize *Splendor.* Journalist Lyn Tornabene, who interviewed Beatty afterward, observed him become nauseous on his way to the podium and throw up before he faced the lineup of reporters.[554]

Screenwriter James Toback, a perceptive collaborator and friend later in Beatty's career, was cognizant of the inhibited Virginian that was the inner Beatty. "Being fundamentally very shy and self-conscious, he is not capable of relaxing when he thinks several million are listening to what he's saying. When it's Warren Beatty as Warren Beatty, all of a sudden all these people are listening to what he's going to say. He recoils from it."[555] Beatty's shyness was another facet of his fear of failure, associated, no doubt, with the string of disappointments he observed in childhood as the pattern of his father's life.

---

*The title was later changed to *Rome Adventure.*
†In July of 1966, Wood submitted her "life story" to Peter Wyden, then the executive editor of *Ladies' Home Journal,* and a book publisher. It was written by hand, and in typescript with Wood's handwritten corrections. The excerpts that follow are from this memoir.

He told a reporter that fall, "It's like they expect you to turn on a plug and then you light up like a Christmas tree and you throw off witticisms and things. It's not very realistic."[556]

His contempt at being paraded before the press reached an unintentionally comic nadir during the press conference, when, according to Tornabene, studio head Jack Warner, who had not seen *Splendor in the Grass* yet, introduced Warren Beatty to reporters as "our next big star, Warner Beaker." [557] Despite this gaffe, Beatty answered the inane questions with southern courtesy and his customary honesty, telling reporters, "I can't say enough about Kazan," admitting he would "like like hell to win an Academy Award," and that he considered *Splendor* "terribly, terribly true and important." When he was asked about Shirley MacLaine, Beatty responded sincerely, "I feel very strongly about my sister. I think she's one of the great talents."[558]

His rebellious streak surfaced later in the weeklong press junket, inspired by seeing his anti-Hollywood role model Kazan while in New York. The already skittish Beatty gave a disastrous interview to a reporter with the *New York World-Telegram and Sun*, resulting in a profile called "Mystery Surrounds Mr. Beatty." The writer described in detail how Beatty spent the interview shuffling through cards and notes in his wallet, wandering in and out of the room, making phone calls, and transferring objects from table to table.[559] One of the calls Beatty made was to Kazan. "Kazan doesn't approve of publicity," Beatty told the reporter when he hung up. "He thinks an artist should let his work speak for itself. He's a genius." The comments went into the piece, which became an embarrassing satire.

His pal and image maker John Springer warned Beatty that there should be "no more articles like this," but the die was already cast. Beatty defended himself to Springer by grading the reporter, similar to his teacher-father Ira, pointing out critically that his interviewer arrived late and was "improperly prepared."[560]

Beatty's other phone conversation during the ill-fated interview was with Joan Collins, still in Los Angeles. He took the call from Collins in a separate room, returning with a piece of paper on which he had written her dress and waist sizes, evidently to surprise her with a gift. Collins, who was weary of arguing and had realized that Beatty "wasn't husband material," had decided to do a movie in England "to get away from him," and for the money. Her friend Natalie Wood helped her secure the lead in the Hope-Crosby comedy *The Road to Hong Kong*, filming in London in July. Beatty became upset that Collins had accepted another role he considered "crap," unaware she was doing it to make her final exit. "It was obvious that I had to be the one to end it with Warren. He seemed content to let it drift sloppily along."

A day or so later, on June 29, while Beatty was still in New York doing publicity for *Splendor in the Grass*, Dorothy Kilgallen spotlighted her favorite young actor in her column with an anonymous gossip tidbit: "If the [Wagner] rift ends in divorce, there's nothing Natalie Wood would like better than to become Mrs. Warren Beatty. If that's true, Natalie is auditioning for a punch in the nose from Joan Collins . . ."[561]

The next morning, Kilgallen received a letter from Woodrow Irwin, a lawyer representing Natalie Wood and Robert Wagner, threatening to sue over the item romantically linking Wood and Beatty, who were barely cordial.[562] Beatty's publicist and confidant, John Springer, asked "the Kid" about the Kilgallen column while he was in New York that week. Springer wrote in a memo to Arthur Jacobs, his West Coast partner, afterward: "Warren told me himself that he has never even taken Natalie Wood out."[563] A few weeks later, Springer sent a letter to a colleague stating, "I imagine this story must have started when Natalie and Wagner broke up at the same time that Joan Collins left for Europe to make a picture."[564] The canny Beatty, whose career Kilgallen was always trying to promote, came up with the most plausible theory for the false gossip item that was planted in her column. "Warren figures it must be started by someone who'd be glad to see 'romantic' publicity about him and Natalie with a picture co-starring them coming out," wrote Springer.[565] The likely suspects were at Warner Brothers, where studio press agents were staging advance publicity for *Splendor in the Grass* and its stars, Wood and Beatty, that very week.

Beatty extended his East Coast press trip for *Splendor* into early July so he could spend a day at Josh Logan's country house in Connecticut, continuing his campaign to play Moss Hart in *Act One*, according to Logan's diary.[566] Jane Fonda, remembering the raw first screen test she and Beatty made for Logan two years earlier for *Parrish*, wrote to Logan that same week, congratulating him on his new film, *Fanny*, and adding, "Isn't it exciting about Warren's career? . . . What an instinct you have!"[567]

When Beatty returned to Hollywood soon after, Joan Collins was packing for the film shoot in London she had sought as closure for their disintegrating engagement, a reality Beatty was being forced to accept, as was she. "We looked at each other and I started to cry," Collins recalled. "It was the end, and we knew it. We held each other tightly. Nearly two years of loving and fighting had passed."

A close friend of forty years, production designer Richard Sylbert, said late in life, "Warren told me *he* was dumped in all of his relationships," partings that were extremely difficult for Beatty, who had always had a tender heart and who confessed his dependency on love.[568] "It was always with a whimper instead of a bang, and accompanied by a tremendous amount of separation anxiety and sadness," Beatty said in his fifties. "Well, I hope it wasn't as bad on the other side, but it was always bad with me."[569]

On July 12, at this vulnerable point, Beatty reported to MGM to start *All Fall Down*. On the same day, Delmer Daves, the director of the picture Natalie Wood was to begin that month in Rome, sent a letter to his Italian production manager indicating how traumatized Wood still was by the breakup of her marriage. "Natalie Wood has separated from her husband and is going through an emotional turmoil, has lost eight pounds which she cannot spare, and our studio doctor believes we should not plan on using her," wrote Daves; he replaced Wood with Suzanne Pleshette a few weeks later.[570] Wood, who plummeted to eighty-eight pounds, revealed later she "almost cracked up" that July. This was confirmed by her closest friend, Mary Ann Marinkovich, who described Robert Wagner's infidelity as "shattering Natalie's dreams" that they were a storybook couple.[571]

Beatty, feeling bereft without Collins, began attending a few parties by himself the first week of rehearsals on *All Fall Down*, including, on July 14, a surprise party for Milton Berle, the comic he used to impersonate. Wood arrived late to the same event, escorted by an old friend, millionaire Arthur Loew, Jr., the white knight to actresses in romantic peril.[572] Later that week, Beatty and Wood each attended a soiree for producer Jimmy Woolf. Wood was in the company of another supportive male pal, theatrical producer Peter Glenville, who had rented his London house to Beatty during *Roman Spring* and would lease it to Robert Wagner the next month, when Wagner fled Hollywood to live in Europe, depressed about his career and the demise of his marriage.[573]

The former costars of *Splendor in the Grass* exchanged pleasantries at the parties, which led *Los Angeles Mirror* columnist Mel Heimer, who had seen Kilgallen's bogus gossip item about them, to report that they were "seeing each other."[574] John Springer wrote a letter to Heimer, bringing it to his attention that the item about Beatty and Natalie Wood was not accurate, information that came directly from Beatty.[575]

Beatty's separation anxiety over Joan Collins, and his mixed feelings of nausea, egotism, and insecurity as an overpublicized "movie star" who still had not been seen in a movie, surfaced as soon as he sat down for a table reading of *All Fall Down*. Present were his venerated costars Angela Lansbury, Karl Malden, Eva Marie Saint, and Brandon de Wilde, joined by their intimidating thespian producer, John Houseman and writer William Inge.

Typically, Beatty concealed his nervousness in what was perceived as aggressive behavior. Houseman would recall, "From the start, our most serious problem was young Mr. Beatty. With his angelic arrogance, his determination to emulate Marlon Brando and Jimmy Dean, and his half-baked, overzealous notions of 'Method' acting, he succeeded in perplexing and antagonizing not only his fellow actors but our entire crew."[576]

Beatty's provocative tactics harkened back to the James Dean antics he had tried in desperation, as much as inspiration, at the Clinton Playhouse, when he had also felt intimidated and lacking in formal training. "Everyone came to the first day of rehearsal knowing his lines and ready to rehearse, with the exception of one actor," remarked de Wilde, referring to Beatty, "who kept the script in his hands up until the last day and annoyed everyone else."[577]

There was one significant exception. Karl Malden, the powerful character actor who was playing Beatty's father and often worked with Kazan, was impressed by Beatty's insights during the script readings. "I felt that he was a talented young man. I didn't know [then] that Warren was so brilliant in everything else, but I thought as an actor he was very, very talented, and in discussing the part with Frankenheimer, I remember he was very . . . I was going to say literate, I don't mean that. I mean very sure. He was able to express himself beautifully, in what he felt was right, what was wrong. And right then I knew. I said, 'This boy's very talented.'"[578]

The petulance the rest of the cast observed in Beatty was partially the actor's reaction to sudden fame, which he felt he did not merit since his work had not been seen yet. So no one could find his dressing room, Beatty removed his name from the building directory at MGM, substituting the nonsensical pseudonym "Geyger Krocp," allowing him to rest and maintain privacy — an adult version of the closet hideaway he had created in his parents' volatile household.[579]

During filming, Beatty confided to father figure John Springer that he no longer could do publicity. Since his stomach-churning reaction to seeing his face on a newspaper in Paris — with no control over the photograph or what was written about him — Beatty, at his press agents' direction, had squirmed and stammered through interviews with *Cosmopolitan*, *Horizon*, *Newsday*, *Show*, *Woman's Day*, the *New York Times*, and *McCall's*. In addition to feeling uncomfortably exposed, the Virginia-born son of scholars felt like a fraud being interviewed without something meaningful to discuss. "I was offended by the economics of it. I didn't feel that people really wanted to know about me, and I didn't feel that it was important for them to do an interview with me. The writers who talked with me were usually intelligent people, and I thought they were a little embarrassed at being assigned to do a story on somebody who didn't really stimulate them."[580]

Springer sent Beatty a long letter from New York, advising him in a fatherly way about his career, starting with a private joke about two women they once spotted at their favorite hangout, P. J. Clarke's. The letter provides an intimate glimpse at their relationship and at Beatty's state of mind as fame crashed in on him at twenty-four:

July 27, 1961

Dear Warren:

I've been meaning to write for a long time but you know how it is. I get sidetracked—looking for those two dikes and things like that. I wasn't making much sense when you called me at 6:00 A.M.—or was it 5:00—to say you were going. Morning after—or just morning! . . .

We never had a chance to finish our conversation about you and publicity . . . I think you are in one of the greatest spots, publicity wise, that any young actor has ever been in. And for you to think you don't need or don't want publicity is ridiculous. One of the things which makes you so in demand is that everyone wants the person who is wanted by everyone else. Mamie Van Doren isn't a bad actress but who would hire her if they could get Marilyn Monroe. Marilyn is in demand and publicity has a lot to do with it . . .

Don't forget that not one of the [editors] had ever seen you on the screen at the time they set the story in question . . . these publications have accepted you because we sold you. And they have confidence and trust in whom we sell . . . I think your attitude toward Louella, Hedda and Sheilah Graham is childish . . . you don't have to kiss their behinds—I've forgotten the exact delightful way you put it—but you should be reasonable . . .

If your personal reviews on your first couple of pictures are as great as I think they will be, they, plus the importance you have already gained publicity wise, will establish you as a big star. Then we should re-evaluate our approach and subtly make you more inaccessible . . .

> *I know why Kazan would want to soft-pedal too much press activity*
> *for you. He wants you treated as a serious actor and would hate a*
> *batch of playboy publicity . . . None of us are ever going to let you*
> *stoop to the swimming-pool-with-starlet type of thing. . . . And I'm sure*
> *he must think we're responsible for all the Joan Collins–Natalie Wood*
> *gossip column items . . .*
>
> *And now that all this serious business talk is by the boards, how*
> *about a letter — even on toilet paper if you have to — about what's*
> *happening. How is* All Fall Down? *How are you? What's happening*
> *that I don't read in the columns? What's not happening that I do read*
> *in the columns? When are you coming back to New York? Take care of*
> *yourself.*[581]

Beatty's literary mentor, William Inge, who was present throughout most of the filming of *All Fall Down*, proved how well he understood the young actor to whom he had tailored three starring roles, correctly foreshadowing to a magazine writer, "I think Warren may start closing the doors on the press pretty soon. I doubt if he will give interviews at all much longer."[582]

Toward the end of rehearsals, Beatty and Natalie Wood, who had a joint press tour coming up for *Splendor*, found they were consoling each other when they crossed paths at social events, and were able to put aside their earlier professional jealousies. "Warren and I got to know each other gradually, as people," Wood wrote later in her memoir for Wyden. "He was depressed because his sweetheart had gone to England for a film, and I was devastated over the end of my marriage." At the end of July, Beatty escorted Wood to an industry screening of her other new film, *West Side Story*, their first public appearance together, though they were still just friends, according to Wood.[583] After he was in his fifties, Beatty validated that their relationship developed gradually, saying, "I've never gone from being in love with one woman to being in love with another woman immediately."[584]

As filming on *All Fall Down* began on July 27, Beatty continued to be plagued by his perfectionism and the stress of constant media attention. He refused to work when there were visitors on the set at MGM, complaining that the whispering and shuffling made him nervous.[585] He later defended his right to demand silence as necessary to an actor's concentration, behavior those in the cast and crew who already disliked him interpreted as egocentric. John Frankenheimer, a relatively young director with insight into Beatty, could see that the person Beatty was hard on, actually, was himself.

"Warren was very, very demanding of himself, wanting as many takes as he could get."[586]

Beatty's self-doubts and high standards increased when he saw an early print of his performance in *Splendor in the Grass*, the first time he had seen himself on a movie screen. "I felt terribly frustrated . . . I realized that if I had done the same parts on the stage I would have had the opportunity to come back and do them again, in a better way, trying to find new meanings in them. On the other hand, I knew I was learning how to combat out-of-sequence shooting, how to sustain a performance, and how to come to the set prepared, in my own mind, to play it."[587]

The consummately professional Angela Lansbury, who was cast as Beatty's clinging, borderline hysteric mother in *All Fall Down*, had little tolerance for his learning curve, a trait she had in common with Shirley Booth, briefly his mother in Inge's play. When Beatty ran laps around the set to appear out of breath before one of his scenes as Berry-Berry, "We all stood around and waited and tried not to look embarrassed for him," Lansbury told her biographer.[588] She further recalled how Beatty took an inordinate amount of time "thinking and preparing" before he was ready to go on camera. Frankenheimer concurred that Beatty was not a "team player" in his approach to acting.[589]

The insightful Inge once again saw clearly what others misread in Beatty, pointing out that he was "nervous about making pictures so he's self-protective." Inge believed that Beatty was "reluctant to trust people in charge, so he takes over," a carryover, perhaps, from having an alcoholic father. After he became a producer, Beatty would confirm Inge's observation about him, saying, "I came in very young. Younger than when people become what they call 'movie stars.' I'm also kind of lazy and selfish, and there was a time I probably shouldn't have done movies for other people. I should have been doing them for myself. But I didn't want to work that hard so, rather than do what they said, I would do their movies and, well, nudge people."[590]

Beatty's sole ally among the cast was Karl Malden, whom he likely associated with Kazan, making him feel secure. "Not with me he wasn't introverted," declared Malden. "I liked him very much."

As Beatty's friendship with the emotionally fragile Natalie Wood turned romantic during the troubled filming of *All Fall Down*, "we each brought problems to the relationship," Wood observed.[591] The actress, who was in daily psychotherapy over her trauma with Wagner, and over other painful issues from her past, said after the fact, "Warren and I spent hours ruminating and analyzing each other's problems."[592] In addition to their analytical natures, they had a number of other things in common. One fundamental parallel was that they had both grown up with alcoholic fathers whose drinking created marital conflict. Like Beatty, Wood had an intuitive intelligence, was driven to succeed, possessed a kind heart, struggled with inhibitions, and wanted to be taken seriously as an actor, not merely a beautiful face.

The public, entranced by the combined, almost blinding, beauty of Natalie Wood and Warren Beatty as a couple, became captivated by their romance, especially with *Splendor in the Grass* soon to be released.

The fact that Beatty and Wood began dating that August lent false credence to Dorothy Kilgallen's bogus gossip item from the previous June, which in turn spawned a worldwide scandal, as summer ended, that Warren Beatty had been the cause of the Wagners' earlier separation—a lie made more titillating when old pals Robert Wagner and Joan Collins, each in London making a movie, spent a few evenings together in public. Wood was falsely portrayed in the press as an adulterer and Beatty as a home wrecker, with Robert Wagner and Joan Collins depicted sympathetically as crying on each other's shoulders—when in fact Wagner and Collins each were already involved with his and her respective future spouses.*

The scandal was especially painful for Natalie Wood, who had been the innocent victim in the breakup with Wagner, a truth she concealed to protect him. As she later wrote, by hand, for her memoir, "I have suffered in silence from gossip about my walking away from my marriage to go with Warren. There was gossip and speculation that Warren was in some way responsible for the end of the marriage. It is totally untrue. Warren had nothing to do with it. We began our relationship <u>after</u>, not before, my marriage collapsed."[593]

In time, the myth of Beatty's affair with Natalie Wood would become even more preposterous, with the claim that it began while they were making *Splendor in the Grass*, when, in reality, they had barely tolerated each other then. When he was in his fifties, Beatty debunked this lore to novelist Norman Mailer, saying, "You've got it wrong if you think I've often met women on movies and started some sort of frivolous affairs with them."[594] To support the false legend of Beatty's "affair" with Wood during *Splendor*, writers would later cite Dorothy Kilgallen's bogus gossip item as proof, and then inaccurately report that it appeared in her column during filming, instead of the correct date, one year later, *after* the Wagners' separation.[595]

---

*Actress Marion Marshall and performer Anthony Newley.

The irony of the false mythology was that, in truth, Beatty was a chivalrous figure in Natalie Wood's breakup, a friend to her during her distress over Wagner, one whose developing romantic interest validated her eroding self-worth. For Beatty, who was also on the rebound, Wood fit the actress prototype to which he was drawn, and like him she was a sensitive, intelligent person. Although Joan Collins, the girlfriend she succeeded, would say with amusement, and perhaps some jealousy, that Beatty was "helped enormously" by dating a star of Natalie Wood's magnitude, their mutual close friend Verne O'Hara demurred. "I cannot see Warren using a woman. Warren's quite honorable."

In fact, Beatty was already getting more attention from the press on his own than his privacy-seeking Virginia psyche could process. John Springer's backstage pledge during *A Loss of Roses* to make him a movie star had already been achieved before the public had seen Beatty on-screen, due to the mass exposure from Springer and Jacobs's campaign to sell him as a petulant sex symbol. "I don't know how to assimilate the idea of being thrust out like a product," Beatty told one of his press interrogators.[596] The Faustian pact he had entered into with the Arthur Jacobs Company had exacted its price — his anonymity — which Beatty compared to a girl losing her virginity, "and when you do, you can't get it back."[597]

While Beatty was filming *All Fall Down* that August, Springer and Jacobs were jockeying to get him on the cover of *Life* magazine, and a journalist from *Time* followed the actor around the set for a piece on Hollywood's "new face," irritating Beatty by describing him in the article as having "a comb in his hand." Beatty's high public profile was creating deeper misunderstandings with his famous sister, who received her second Oscar nomination that March for her poignant performance in *The Apartment*. Reporters interviewing Beatty began to describe the two siblings as estranged, writing that Beatty never brought up Shirley MacLaine's name, or that he did not attend industry events with her.

Beatty said at the time that he rarely saw MacLaine because he did not want to "capitalize" on her fame, praising her as a great talent.[598] "I refuse to take advantage of our relationship," he told a British magazine. "Shirley's put a terrific lot of hard work into getting where she is, and that's how I'd expect to get to the top myself. Whether I'm as successful or less successful, I want the results to be on the strength of my own abilities. But it's only careerwise I want to be dissociated from Shirley; I wouldn't want to give anyone the impression I'm not very fond and proud of my sister."[599] For that reason, and because, as MacLaine observed, "he resented being called Shirley MacLaine's kid brother," they were seldom seen together in public, "mostly at his insistence."[600]

At the time, MacLaine was still confused and hurt by her younger brother's distancing himself. When the reporter from *Time* contacted her for a comment to include in their profile, she said of her brother, "I'm crazy about him, but he doesn't seem to want to communicate," a quote that would be repeated ad infinitum as "proof" of their rivalry.[601] Piqued by his sister's criticism in print, Beatty retreated further. His friend Sandy Whitelaw recalled, "There were moments when they didn't speak, and then they made up again, and then they were feuding. I mean he was — for a long time — she was a very big star, and he was just her brother."

In future years, when MacLaine had a more mature understanding of her brother's need to succeed on his own merit, she would see things differently. "The newspapers thought they smelled conflict. They tried to create a sibling rivalry, à la Fontaine-DeHavilland or something like that. They would call Warren and tell him something I supposedly had said about him. If he said nothing they would call it a 'pregnant pause with meaning.' If he said anything at all, usually out of embarrassment at the personal invasion, wham, the comment would appear in a newspaper story."[602]

On a personal level, as MacLaine later revealed, "All the time we were supposedly fighting like cat and dog and not speaking, we were getting together with friends and having dinners and long talks and were as close as ever . . . we only feuded in spurts. I'd lose my temper or he would, and then we wouldn't see each other for weeks."[603] Beatty described their lives then as "separate," largely because of MacLaine's marriage to the absent and opportunistic Parker, a union that Beatty considered not only strange but also damaging to his sister — concerns that would be proven justified.[604] "We're not that close right now," Beatty said honestly at the time. "If I ever get to where she is I might feel more like talking about her and how we both got the way we are."[605]

The bond that formed between Warren and Shirley in childhood was always intact, despite their different lifestyles or the challenge of their working in the same profession. It was reinforced by their strong feelings for their parents, with whom they spent Christmases, a nostalgic time for the sentimental Beatty. It was further strengthened through their family legacy as MacLeans and Beatys, which meant that "much was expected of them," as Tat had instilled in homage to her own formidable parents. When Beatty spent time with the dynamic older sister he had looked up to as a boy in Virginia, "we would reminisce about Washington-Lee High School, the neighborhood pranks, and of course about what had happened to some of our old boyfriends and girlfriends," MacLaine later wrote.[606] What the public, and reporters, did not know was that when Beatty sought life advice, it was either MacLaine, or their parents, whom he asked and trusted.[607]

Beatty's refusal to talk about his sister in the press was a measure of his deep feelings for her, since he guarded all things he considered sacred. He was also increasingly aware of how his words could be twisted in print, and as a southern gentleman, he refused to risk wounding or offending someone he cared about. As he later explained, "I don't talk about other people, particularly who I'm close to. I don't talk about my family. I don't talk about my close friends. I don't talk about things like that because I don't like to have my friends or family think that they're out of control of that. And also when I say things about someone that I know very well, my opinion takes on too much credibility or too much weight. It's too important and I may be reductive, particularly in some sort of interview, or I might be misquoted or something, and there would be a terrific misunderstanding and then people are hurt. So I just don't do it."[608]

He adopted the same protective stance toward Tat and Ira Beaty, blocking access to his parents, and by extension to his past, like a sentinel. An interoffice memo of the Arthur Jacobs Company that fall read, "WARREN BEATTY'S ANSWER TO GOOD HOUSEKEEPING REQUEST FOR INTERVIEW WITH HIS PARENTS IS UNPRINTABLE. NO OTHER CLIENTS I KNOW OF ARE BUILDING BOMB SHELTERS."[609] The Beatys, in turn, respected their children's right to privacy, promising not to comment on them for publication — a promise they honored, as honorable people. According to Kathlyn Beaty, "We made an agreement with the children that we would stay out of public life entirely."[610]

The irrevocable loss of his anonymity, combined with the pressures and perquisites of stardom, created a personal crisis for Beatty, who had craved solitude and had respected the religious teachings of his parents since childhood. With Kazan withdrawing, Beatty now patterned himself after producer–ladies' man Charlie Feldman, as he once emulated Pastor John Raymond, even copying Feldman's signature look, a cashmere cardigan worn over a knit shirt. The inner Beatty, who considered his full-immersion baptism as a teenager sanctified by Raymond as the most meaningful event of his life, was at odds with this movie star persona.

Beatty's contempt for the cheaper aspects of Hollywood fame, yet desiring it, made him surly company on *All Fall Down*, where Frankenheimer, as a "joke," took to calling him Warner Beaker.[611] On August 31, Inge wrote to Kazan from the set at MGM, informing him of Frankenheimer's "fine job" on the film.[612] "Warren, however, is being impossible and I can't figure the kid out. I never before was aware of this mad streak in him . . . the entire company loathes the boy, and I don't think he knows it. He seems totally unaware of anything except himself."

Beatty's problems at times were evident in his performance. Angela Lansbury would recall Frankenheimer suggesting that she berate Beatty before one of their scenes, just to elicit a reaction. "There was nothing in his face," she later told her biographer. "It was completely empty."

One stumbling block for Beatty may have been his antipathy for Berry-Berry, a misogynist and "professional stud," in Frankenheimer's description, the sort of amoral character Beatty had found it uncomfortable to play in *The Roman Spring of Mrs. Stone*. He complained to the *New York Times* later, "Well, there's *no* guy who makes out with *all* women, no matter *how* good he is. And that one did, didn't he?"[613] Beatty also may have been troubled by Berry-Berry's violent treatment of women, particularly the schoolteacher played by Barbara Baxley (the actress Mann had replaced in *A Loss of Roses*, and whom the loyal Inge made sure was cast in *All Fall Down*). The scene with Baxley possibly was a painful reminder for Beatty of his father's sudden rages.

Inge had his own perceptive analysis, which he shared with Kazan in his letter. "[Warren's] so afraid of emotion," he wrote to Kazan, "that he tends to back away from scenes, sometimes, that he could make something great of. And he constructs such barriers when John starts to direct him that eventually John understandably wants to . . . not use him except when he absolutely has to." Inge was concerned that Beatty's part would be diminished, even though his rushes looked good, and that Brandon de Wilde would walk away with the film.

Beatty's self-containment had many origins, beginning with a childhood where there was "little expressed emotion," according to his sister and reflected in photographs of the stately MacLeans and stoic Beatys. This was contrasted with his parents' domestic strife, which reinforced Beatty's natural reserve. His inhibitions as an actor also may have stemmed from the disturbing experience when his mother lost herself in the tormented character she was playing in *Children of the Moon*. Beatty, who was extremely self-critical, was aware of the problem. He said at the time, "The hardest thing in the world is to show your real self to strangers, expose real emotions. It's painful."[614]

Inge, whom Beatty "revered," worried about the actor's edgy behavior and his fear of revealing emotion during the filming of *All Fall Down*.[615] "I finally brought myself to tell Warren (without getting sore and losing my temper, which would have wasted my words)," the playwright wrote to Kazan, "and I think I made some impression. But my guess is it's going to take several years of successful analysis to make him a human being." Once again, Inge would prove prescient.

Beatty's new romance with Natalie Wood—who was still on a leave of absence from Warner Brothers, seeing her analyst daily—manifested the strains each was going through. "Neither Warren nor I was ready for a permanent relationship," Wood wrote in 1966. ". . . at bottom, we both knew it was only an interim relationship. Both of us were not only immature but moody . . . we were both so confused that we thought fighting and hostility meant real emotional honesty."[616]

Beatty's tempestuous behavior on *All Fall Down*, and with Wood, clashed like cymbals the last week of filming, when the company relocated to Key West, Florida. "He asked me to join him," recalled Wood, who packed and unpacked her suitcase during a series of arguments with Beatty. On September 14, columnist Louella Parsons reported that the actress had decided not to go with Beatty at the last minute due to storm warnings. In her memoir, Wood revealed what really had occurred. "When we got to the plane, I started to cry. We decided all over again that I would go with him. But where was my luggage? I had unpacked it. That provoked another argument . . . Warren telephoned me on every stop the plane made en route to Florida. Finally I called a friend and we carted our suitcases on the next plane to Florida . . . it was like a highly-charged movie script."

The drama in his personal life carried over to the location shooting in Key West, where Beatty so exasperated the camera operator that "he flew a camera-bearing helicopter within a few inches of [Warren's] head," according to Houseman. A few months later, Beatty told writer Florabel Muir about an incident involving him and the crew at a restaurant in Key West. "A fellow cut me with a beer glass. They took four stitches in the cut, but I took the stitches out myself the other day and put this butterfly patch on." The actor, whose frequent illnesses led him to study medicine as well as nutrition, explained, "It draws the flesh together, you know, and you don't need the stitches."[617] Typically, Beatty refused to say who cut him or how he had reacted, calling it "horseplay."

The coup de grace occurred on September 18, when Frankenheimer shot the last footage of *All Fall Down*, a scene with the prodigal son, Berry-Berry, in a Key West jail. "Just as a joke," Frankenheimer said years later, "I locked Warren in the cell on the last shot and wouldn't let him out. We all left and he languished there for about two hours. It wasn't an act of retribution; it was honest to God fun, and we're still good friends."[618] Producer John Houseman offered a different account in his memoir, writing, "in a secret agreement with the local police, Warren Beatty was left to languish overnight in a bare cell of the Key West jail while the company flew back to California."

Representatives for MGM told Joe Laitin, a journalist scheduled to interview Beatty when he returned to Hollywood, that the actor had "disappeared," and his press agents' records noted that he did not return from Florida with the rest of the cast and crew.[619] Laitin, who was preparing a major profile of Beatty for the *Saturday Evening Post*, sent a letter to John Springer complaining that the actor had been less than cooperative, one in a flurry of similar letters the publicist had been receiving from other reporters over what Laitin called *"l'affaire Beatty."*[620]

On September 25, a few days after Beatty re-emerged in Los Angeles with Natalie Wood, Springer wrote another of his gentle letters of reproach to the Kid:

Dear Warren:

Forgive me for going into the lecture but I thought you should see this copy of a letter I got today from the Saturday Evening Post.

This isn't the first time I've had this reaction . . . you antagonized Joe Hyams to the point where he told his New York editors that he just wouldn't interview you . . . Jon Whitcomb was delighted with you as a person but said you were impossible to talk to in any normal kind of way . . . Lyn Tornabene, Jon's editor, passed it because she's still under your spell . . .

Bob Ginna of Horizon *was so upset by you that he wanted to cancel the story. Fortunately, Warren Miller stayed with you, got to know you better and convinced him that you weren't as impossible as Bob decided . . . and remember how outraged Mark Nichols of* Coronet *was by his interview — he swore Beatty would never get into* Coronet.

Of course, you retaliated by killing Coronet — *it was you, wasn't it? . . .*

When it comes to the point — and that ought to be just about the minute your pictures are released — that magazines are beating down the doors to get to you, then when you give an interview you can be as wild as you want.

I've been with you on interviews where you were funny, in the Warren Beatty personality style, but also very intelligent and articulate . . . there's no sense of getting a reputation for being impossible when you don't have to and with the people who count to your career. Clift, for example, did that and, in the long run, it has hurt him considerably. He told me that himself. Brando didn't until after he was already important.

End of lecture . . . I miss you.

> *Love,*
> *John*

When Beatty met with Joe Laitin a few days later to complete the interview for the *Saturday Evening Post*, the writer, a former war correspondent and later deputy press secretary to President Lyndon Johnson, found the actor reasonable, pleasant, and good-natured about Laitin's earlier complaints. The avuncular Laitin developed a fondness for Beatty, who liked and respected the writer. Laitin's son Peter recalled, "Warren Beatty actually used to babysit my sister. He's totally a nice guy. My father used to say, 'If you ever get out to Hollywood and there's any way that you can meet Warren Beatty, do it.'"[621]

Over time, Beatty began to confide in Laitin his grievances with the press, especially a misquote in *Time*, "and it's a very important one," Beatty told Laitin, "it has to do with my sister."[622] He explained why he was annoyed at being portrayed holding a comb in his hand. "The guy from *Time* magazine who said I had a comb was a fink because *he* told me to *get* it . . . I think they try to make you more of a nut than you really are." Beatty told the writer he considered fan magazines "pornographic. I think they're trash. I don't think they do anybody any good. Most of them are scandal magazines."

Beatty refuted, point by point, the reporters' criticisms of him in Springer's letter, telling Laitin he was not uncooperative with Hyams, "and I certainly was not rude. Joe Hyams acts like a goddamn jerk sometimes. We sat at lunch and he came up with a lot of wry comments and I gave 'em right back to him. When somebody wants me to be serious, I'm serious. But if some guy wants to come along and sit there and be bored and chop through a salad and smoke a cigarette and have a drink, and he's cracking jokes and he expects me to be serious, then he has his head up his ass."

What he resented most, Beatty told Laitin, was when a reporter would ask him to find "an angle" for their interview. "What kind of shit is that? Let him find his own angle. It's like sitting across from a girl and saying, 'Gee, I wish that I wanted to fuck you.' I mean, what can she say, 'Well, I'm sorry you don't?' If somebody's got something to talk about, then I'm a talkative person."

His camaraderie with Joe Laitin, even babysitting Laitin's daughter, resurrected the inner Beatty, the good son, what Springer called the "other Warren." When Laitin happened to mention that his elderly father, Harry, a retired stage manager, was extremely ill, Beatty visited him in the hospital, or phoned to see how he was feeling, until he died. Springer, who found out about this through the writer, wrote afterward to the Kid, "Incidentally, Laitin will never get over what you did about his father. That's a very nice thing about you, Warren — something like calling the old man every day."[623]

The enfant terrible, who was already in partial retreat from the press, was about to experience *real* fame.

33 *One of the future myths about Warren*

Beatty would be that he was an overnight success. This negated the three and a half years of struggle, near poverty, and tenacity beginning the summer he dropped out of Northwestern at nineteen, and overlooked his baptism by fire in *A Loss of Roses* as well as the intense publicity buildup staged by Springer and company to make him a "theoretical" star, an "unknown" star, a "movie" star for eighteen months before his first movie came out.

All of these elements came together in October of 1961, when *Splendor in the Grass* was finally released, and the public got its first glimpse of Warren Beatty on a movie screen. Warner Brothers sent its dazzling costars, whose romance off-screen was "on fire," in the description of columnists, on a sixteen-day publicity tour. The tour ended in New York, where *Splendor* opened on October 10, eight days before the world premiere of the highly anticipated *West Side Story*, which Beatty attended on the arm of Natalie Wood.

"*Splendor* should establish you as a dreamboat and potentially the hottest young star in the business," Springer had written to Beatty the week before, in a rare instance of what would prove to be understatement by a press agent.[624] An intern at Beatty's talent agency in New York, Jane Alderman, now a teacher, experienced Warren Beatty's impact on female moviegoers that fall as Bud Stamper. "One weekend," as Alderman told the story, "a phone call comes in at MCA, the operator sends it to me, and it's this girl, hysterical, she's going to jump out the window if she can't talk to Warren Beatty. So I said, 'Oh my God! Hold on.' And I had access to all of the clients' home phone numbers, so I put her on hold, and I called him at home. And I said, 'I'm the weekend secretary, I hate to bother you, but I've got this girl on the other phone, and her name is Mary Smith, and she's going to jump if she doesn't talk to you.' And he goes, 'Okay, this woman does this all the time, so you say whatever you want.' '*But Warren, she's gonna jump! Could you call her?*' He goes, 'No, no, no, this goes on all the time.' I thought I was saving a life. He was already used to this, and it was just starting."[625]

Eleanor Kilgallen and Maynard Morris took the once-struggling, sweet young actor — whom Kilgallen and the other females at MCA had affectionately nicknamed the Octopus for his all-embracing hugs — to a fancy lunch with his new girlfriend, then the most famous actress in the world. Beatty, as of old, took a little boy's delight in shocking the fussy Morris at the restaurant with Natalie Wood, as Kilgallen was to recall. "We took them to lunch at a place [where] we all ate on East Fifty-eighth Street, Le Valois, and my dear, we shouldn't have been there because they were entwined, lots of hugs and kisses, and here again, Maynard was saying, 'Oh Warren! Oh Warren!' because the restaurant was rather crowded. But that didn't deter the lovers. They went right at it all through lunch . . . poor Maynard almost passed out; I loved it."

Kilgallen found "her Warren" to be the same person he was when he had only one white nylon shirt. "Warren never gave you a lot of malarkey. Oh, he did with the girls that he would be entwined with, but you accepted him for what he was, and that was it. He wasn't going to kind of *schmickle* you. So I've never felt that . . . he has *ever* really changed very much from where he started."

Beatty spent time with his longtime friends, the Mitch Mays, borrowing May's idea to keep a hotel suite in New York as a pied-à-terre. He replaced his former haunt, the Blackstone, with the Delmonico Hotel, on Fifty-ninth

Street and Park Avenue. Beatty's ironic take on his "overnight" fame, which would be his constant companion, was formed at the Delmonico's front door that October. "The moment I remember the most was after that first picture opened. I was walking out of the Delmonico Hotel in New York and two young girls looked up at me with a look that I could only interpret as adoring, absolutely adoring me. One of them said, 'Oh, my God, you're Warren Beatty!' I said, 'Yes, I am.' And she said, 'Gee whiz, you're nothing!' And that is kind of what fame is."[626]

His ambivalence about celebrity, in certain ways, paralleled his stormy relationship with Natalie Wood, whose glamorous image, cultivated by her controlling mother, was the personification of "Hollywood," which Beatty both loved and loathed. (He later told Dr. Margaret Brenman, "the people are goddamned attractive and goddamned magnetic.") "Natalie always kept everybody waiting an hour while she primped," said Mitch May's then-wife, Verne O'Hara, who spent time with the couple that fall. In private, without the minks and her signature cigarette holders, Wood's aspiration, like Beatty's, was to be in serious films, and she shared his devotion to Kazan.

O'Hara observed the emotional damage from Wood's disillusionment with Robert Wagner that her fans, and even Eleanor Kilgallen, would never see in the sparkling "public" Natalie Wood. "There was something about her, but she was like *dead*. That's the only way I could describe her. And she was with Warren, they were sharing a suite, and it was like you were pulling teeth to have her along." Both Beatty and Wood, for different, equally complex reasons, were seeking happiness — or in Beatty's case, due to his parents' example, *permission* to be happy. Instead of one balancing the other, they matched each other's intensity. As O'Hara observed, "It was not the warm, happy-go-lucky relationship that it was with Joan. I mean Joan's a lot of fun."

Careerwise, Warren Beatty and Natalie Wood were soaring. *Newsweek* named *Splendor in the Grass* the best American picture of the year, calling it "funny, moving, and finally beautiful"; the *New York Times* included it on its list of the ten best films of 1961; Kazan would later cite it as one of his most profitable films. There were dissenters, including the critic for *The New Yorker*, who lambasted *Splendor* as "phony in a particularly disgusting way," but such criticism, plus a minor controversy over Wood's "risqué" bathtub scene, added to the box office appeal and drew more attention to its rising stars.

Beatty's reviews were mostly the stuff of young actors' dreams. One critic wrote that he and Natalie Wood "play the anguished youngsters with exqui-site sympathy and persuasion."[627] *Newsweek* called Beatty "excellent," and the *Hollywood Reporter* praised him as "immensely likable, a not inconsider-able value."

As a perfectionist, Beatty would be aware of the few negative notices he received. The harshest was from the critic for *Films in Review*, who belittled him as "too inexperienced to be able to project *anything*. I'm told Holly-wood hopes to make him a star, but his face, at least in this picture, is on the weak side, and doesn't always photograph well."[628] Beatty's mention in the *Los Angeles Times* hit a sensitive nerve. "For Beatty, it is an auspicious debut—a clean-cut sincerity that more than compensates for his occasion-ally stumbling delivery of it. He is the brother of Shirley MacLaine."[629]

Overall, as Karl Malden was to say, "My personal opinion—this is me speaking—I think Kazan made Natalie a big star. She wasn't. He made Beatty a big star." While they were still in New York promoting *Splendor*, Natalie Wood was given the starring role in the musical *Gypsy*, a part she coveted, and Warren Beatty was featured in an eight-page pictorial in *Life* magazine with the bold headline "It's Warren Beatty . . . The Biggest New Name in American Entertainment," exactly as Springer had forecast. With his family's trademark candor, Beatty told *Life*, "The actor who tells you he dislikes fame is a liar. But there are elements that are distasteful. The actor wants everybody to know him and yet he wants to keep something to him-self."[630] This was the central paradox of Beatty the movie star.

On Springer's advice, Beatty met with a French reporter at Sardi's for a cover piece in *Cinemonde*, sat for a portrait with photographer Irving Penn for *Vogue*, and on November 19, 1961, could be seen on the cover of the *New York News Sunday Magazine*, where he had ogled Joan Collins two years before. The discreet Virginian recoiled at the media exposure, telling one New York writer that the loss of his "wonderful anonymity" made him nostalgic for his old garret. "There's something enjoyable about living in one furnished room with no money and a sense of freedom."[631]

By November, when he and Natalie Wood were back in Hollywood, Beatty still had no plans to star in a movie, though every studio was courting him. *Act One*, his passion project, was canceled, and Beatty had discovered a central truth about himself, one that would contribute to his legendary rep-utation for procrastination: "I've learned that you have to believe in what you're doing body and soul," he told the French writer for *Cinemonde*, "so it takes a long time for me to make choices."[632] The corollary to this self-realization was Beatty's complete devotion once he did make a commitment, another reason he thought things through so carefully.

His caution turned to fear a few days after Christmas, when *The Roman Spring of Mrs. Stone* opened in the United States as the "bomb" Beatty had predicted at the wrap party in London. This was made worse by reviewers competing to express their distaste for the film — a contempt Beatty shared. "I hated *The Roman Spring of Mrs. Stone*," he said a year later.[633] The critic for the respected *New Yorker* called the movie a "painful assault on love," directed "with a sort of finicky languor," adding, "Gavin Lambert, who wrote the screenplay, has provided dialogue of suffocating archness."[634] *Cue* described it as "an elaborately repulsive little picture."[635]

Despite the film's reception, Beatty received several positive reviews, with one critic lauding his gigolo as "phenomenally well played," and another calling him "certainly a young man who bears watching."[636] *Newsweek* singled him out for making his "mercenary gigolo a sympathetic character."

Other criticisms of Beatty had an edge, partly because of reviewers' patent dislike for the picture. "Warren Beatty is the male whore," wrote the critic for *Films in Review.* "Because I am unfamiliar with such low-life, I suppose, he seemed well cast to me, though it's true his Italian accent kept slipping. At least his dead-pan face was appropriate in this degraded role."[637] *Variety* similarly lampooned Beatty's acting, noting that "every once in awhile a little Guido Panzini creeps into his Italo dialect and Marlon Brando into his posture and expression."[638]

The most personal and painful review was from Bosley Crowther, the influential film critic for the *New York Times,* who described Beatty as "a sleek, surly, wet-lipped, sly-eyed youngster who looks as though he has just slipped off an American drug-store stool. Mr. Beatty, who does very nicely as a middle-western youth in *Splendor in the Grass,* is hopelessly out of his element as a patent-leather ladies man in Rome. His manners remind one of a freshman trying to put on airs at a college prom, his accent recalls Don Ameche's all-purpose Italian-Spanish one." Crowther closed his scathing review noting that great expense had been put into the film, "Heaven only knows why."[639]

The experience unnerved the failure-phobic Beatty. "I couldn't go on anymore. I couldn't face making another. Why? It's a question you'd need a treatise to answer. I was insecure. I'd lost the spark."[640] Beatty told writer Dena Reed a few years later that *The Roman Spring of Mrs. Stone* made him so afraid of starring in another picture that might not please him that, "I turned down a million dollars worth of work."[641]

Beatty later estimated that he rejected seventy-five scripts during the next two years, one of the first, and most infamous, *PT 109*, a Warner Brothers film based on President John F. Kennedy's youthful wartime experiences. Kennedy had seen Beatty in *Splendor in the Grass*, "and he wanted me to play him."[642] "I remember," confirmed Senator Edward M. Kennedy, "my brother thought he would be terrific in the part."[643]

Beatty's rejection of a personal request from the president of the United States caused a minor scandal. According to Beatty and to Kennedy's press secretary, Pierre Salinger, Beatty told Salinger that the script was badly written, a concern reinforced by a negative meeting he had with Jack Warner and the producer, Bryan Foy.[644] "Jack Warner kicked me off the lot," recalled Beatty, "because I told Kennedy I didn't think he should allow the movie to be made. I said I didn't think it was very good."[645]

Before Warner threw Beatty out, he asked him to fly to Washington to meet the president and reconsider. "I couldn't say no to the part *after* I'd already met the President and discussed it with him," reasoned Beatty, "so I said I wouldn't fly to Washington. Someone in the office said, 'Why not fly the President to Hollywood?' He meant it as a joke."[646] Producer Bryan Foy, annoyed with Beatty for rejecting the part, planted a gossip item saying that Beatty had told him, "If the President wants me to play him, tell him to come here and soak up some of *my* atmosphere," a remark that would be repeated for years as an illustration of Warren Beatty's narcissistic behavior.[647]

Beatty was so disturbed by the item that he drafted a statement and sent it to John Springer, with the idea of releasing it to the press. He noted that he tried to be articulate, admitting that he was flattered by reporters' attention, but he resented their "putting untrue statements into my mouth to make it look as if I was some sort of egomaniacal idiot." Then he corrected the record on *PT 109*:

> It has been reported in the press that when Jack Warner submitted the script to me and asked me to go to Washington to get atmosphere, I allegedly said "Let President Kennedy come here to soak up some of my atmosphere." Even as a joke I never said it, never thought it. I suppose it makes a good story for the press but I am damned upset at them (the press) making up this lie and attributing it as a direct quote. I particularly resent distortions that reflect on someone else for whom I have

great admiration — actually I don't believe there is any actor who wouldn't be pleased at being considered for the role of President Kennedy as a young man.

I turned down the script for the simple reason, I did not feel I was right for the part. It would be nice if the press printed the truth once.[648]

Ultimately, Beatty chose to keep silent "and not add to the hullabaloo," which would become his standard policy with respect to anything written about him.[649] For him, the incident was offensive, since Kennedy not only impressed him but also rekindled his boyhood interest in politics. "I was terribly upset. Later, when I did meet President Kennedy on another occasion, he was very funny about that."[650] According to Beatty's friend Michael J. Pollard, the first time Beatty met Robert Kennedy, in an elevator, "Bobby Kennedy went, 'You're the guy that turned down my brother in *PT 109.*' Warren was turning down everything!"

Beatty's stressful experiences filming *The Roman Spring of Mrs. Stone* and *All Fall Down* had taught, or reminded, him that he did not want to replicate the pattern of unhappiness in his father's career. He confided to his friend Joe Laitin, "I'm beginning to realize that if you don't enjoy what you do when you get paid, you're missing the whole point. If you don't get a sense of fulfillment out of your work, forget it."[651]

What was perceived as Beatty's bad behavior sprang, in part, from this realization. "I am finding more and more that it's really very hard to please a lot of people. I would say it's impossible. And so I've been allowing that need to please *a lot* of people to slip away from me in the past couple of years, so that I realize now that there will be a lot of people that will dislike me just on principle. There will be a lot of people that resent me. There'll be a lot of people that will *like* me. And there'll be an awful lot of people that just don't care one way or the other. If I allowed myself to be upset by that, then I'd be a pretty upset person . . . all I know is when I'm enjoying my work as an actor and when I'm not, when I think I'm doing well and when I don't . . . there can be an awful lot of those obstacles, and those obstacles can just eat you up. And you find, what am I? An actor or a corporation? Or what am I?"[652]

His second two films had also revived Beatty's insecurities and ambivalence about being an actor, prompted, in part, by a remark of Kazan's to *Newsweek* wondering whether "Warren Beatty will be that good in five years . . . it isn't the bloom that comes off, it's the humanity. The bloom comes on — that wax-fruit look."[653] Beatty was "depressed" by his idol's comment, which he considered "a legitimate warning from Kazan."[654] A year later, when he explained why he rejected the leads in such respected films as *The L-Shaped Room* and *The Victors*, Beatty said candidly, "It's a little complicated to explain. I just didn't feel like acting. I'm not really so sure how good an actor I am, how much I enjoy it, what I want to do, or where I want to live."[655]

Warren Beatty's existential crisis coincided with his trauma over the loss of his anonymity. As he said later, "I felt as if I were being sold like a can of tomatoes. I'm not a can of tomatoes."[656] His hesitation in choosing his next film stretched from days to weeks to months. When he produced *Bonnie and Clyde*, Beatty told writer (and later director) Curtis Hanson why. "I had come to a timid point . . . my instincts then were to go and find stories that had great meaning for me. But I made the mistake of being passive and waiting for the ideas of other filmmakers to become appealing to me . . . it was a very upsetting period, the first year or two years of being famous. Very, very upsetting. I am surprised I handled it as well as I did."[657]

Beatty would show signs of these severe strains the first three months of 1962, while his girlfriend, Natalie Wood, was filming the musical *Gypsy*, a role that was physically and emotionally demanding for the waiflike actress, with its song-and-dance numbers, strip sequences, and the painful parallels to her relationship with her overbearing stage mother. Actress Morgan Brittany, who played the young June, used to watch, fascinated, when Warren Beatty, in the thick horn-rimmed glasses he wore off-screen, came to the set to visit Natalie Wood. Brittany's girlish impression of Beatty was of how reassuring he was to Wood, who sat on his lap and whispered into his ear, while he listened adoringly.[658] Wood, in turn, was sympathetic to Beatty's brooding indecision about his career. But their romance was doomed from the start. "We were both having difficulties. Warren wasn't getting good scripts and I was trying to punish myself for my divorce by sticking to a relationship that was going nowhere."[659]

Under the influence of agent-producer Charles Feldman, Beatty began to explore the deal-making and production end of the business, while agonizing over which movie he should do next. When MCA disbanded its talent agency for antitrust reasons at the end of 1961, Beatty chose to act as his own agent, using the cunning Feldman as a model.

He spent frequent evenings that winter with his other father figure, Clifford Odets, "sitting on the floor at Clifford's feet while he talked," in Beatty's description. He was often accompanied by Natalie Wood, who would fall asleep on the playwright's sofa, like Joan Collins before her.[660] Odets, who had been reduced to writing for television or anonymously "patching" screenplays and was, in Beatty's description, "abused by Hollywood," saw in his young movie star acolyte a way to revive his earlier work. The ambitious Beatty sensed an opportunity to collaborate on a film with one of the greats. They chose a script by Odets called *Fifteen Doves in Flight*, a remake of *Camille*.

Like his sister, Warren Beatty wanted to break a taboo on-screen by showing an interracial romance, and expressed a desire to cast a "Negro girl" in the Garbo role, with him as the star. He and Odets hoped to get the playwright's close friend and Beatty's film god Jean Renoir to direct, and either Jerry Wald or English filmmaker J. Lee Thompson to produce. Beatty and Odets signed a contract, and Odets's journal reflects a meeting between them and Thompson on March 8, 1962. "Lee Thompson and I were turning things down to work on it," recalled Beatty, who was using his new power of celebrity to set up the remake at a studio, since Odets's luster was fading. "If Mozart were alive," the playwright told Beatty, "he'd be writing jingles for commercials."

The collaboration began to sour by mid-March, when Odets's journal records that he and Beatty returned from dinner for an "earnest heart to heart talk," and the playwright formed the impression Beatty was masterminding a secret deal to make him less than a full partner.[661] Three days later, the *Camille* remake, and the Odets/Beatty partnership, collapsed when Fox would not meet the playwright's financial terms.

According to his notes, Odets was "insulted" by what he viewed as Beatty's "neurotic power plays disguised as creativity," describing Beatty as concerned with only his own wants, "riding roughshod" over Odets. He noted that he had "watched Warren closely for five weeks," that Beatty had "many good qualities" and "some talent," but he was "so far gone." Like William Inge, Odets felt that Beatty needed psychoanalysis, writing that he was "on his way to becoming a large mess despite his success." In closing, however, Odets wrote of his "regard for Warren."

Beatty's account of their parting to Dr. Margaret Brenman, Odets's friend and biographer, depicted Odets as having unreasonable expectations, requesting seventy-five thousand dollars from Fox for his idea, and two hundred thousand dollars to begin working on the script, before they even started, which Beatty said he "had trouble getting for him." Beatty contended that he had set up the film at Fox before he knew Odets's terms, and when Odets demanded more money from Fox than the studio was willing to pay, the deal fell apart and Beatty did not speak to Odets for a year. "The relationship blew and I was embarrassed to see him," Beatty told Brenman, characterizing Odets's demands as "cagey and reasonable." Forty years later, when Beatty was honored at a film festival, he would refer to his early associations with legends like Odets, saying, "It's hard for a kid to collaborate with someone of a much older generation, because if you have the humility that is necessary, there's a danger of being arrogant."[662]

Odets was deeply embittered by their falling-out, and was considering writing a play about it, called *A Piece of the Action*, Beatty's "favorite phrase." He began to make notes for the intended play that March, around Beatty's twenty-fifth birthday. Odets started his draft with a description of his final meeting with Beatty. According to the playwright's notes, Beatty called him at two A.M. the night before, dangling six offers, only to "trump" Odets at the meeting, "saying, 'Don't hate me.'" Odets sketched the characters for his thinly veiled play about Beatty: a boy and his sister, neither of whom drink; their dad, a "bad drunk"; and the boy's girlfriend, Natalie Wood, who, wrote Odets, "is working hard, exhausted, is beginning to resent the boy and a break-up is inevitable."

The same March, tension surfaced between Beatty and his long-time patron William Inge over a photograph of Beatty in that month's *Show* magazine — Beatty is in glasses, mugging on the set of *All Fall Down*. Inge had written a caption for the photo that read, "I don't know why Warren Beatty should have gone ape in this picture, unless someone told him he was a second Jimmy Dean."[663] The caption offended Beatty, according to Inge, who later wrote, "I once refused to grant an interview about him because I had found him too unpredictable in his emotional reactions to what is said about him in print . . . I thought the caption humorous and unoffensive. Warren didn't."[664]

Beatty was sensitive about being compared to Dean and Brando (he told one reporter, "I'm myself — honest!"), but clearly there was more to his growing estrangement from Inge.[665] A few weeks after *Show* came out, during Beatty's blowout with Odets, columnist Sheilah Graham, widely read in Hollywood, wrote an item describing Inge as Warren Beatty's "fairy godfather." Graham stated that Inge had "discovered" Beatty, mentioning the play and two films he wrote "expressly for Warren," and reporting that Inge "is currently writing another original movie for the young brother of Shirley MacLaine . . . if it were not for Inge, Warren might still be working as a sandhog on the third tube of the Lincoln Tunnel."[666]

The caption in *Show,* and the subsequent gossip referring to Inge as Beatty's "fairy godfather," with its sexual innuendo, coincided with Beatty's disassociation from the kindly gay playwright who had made him a star, and seemingly was in love with him. Beatty would seldom mention Inge in future years, crediting only Kazan, or sometimes Stella Adler, as the ones responsible for his career. "I think Warren probably distanced himself from my uncle," mused Inge's niece and confidante JoAnn Kirchmaier, "because he didn't want to get — well, because maybe my uncle was after him, I don't know . . . maybe he's embarrassed. Maybe he has the right to be. I don't know."

Inge's live-in secretary, John Connolly, would observe, "Warren just simply went on to bigger and better things, that's all. Warren very calculatedly knew which buttons to push and when. I think he had been aware of that all of his life, overshadowed by his sister. He had to overcome a lot of stuff to say, 'Hey, look at me, I'm here, I'm me.' And now he was established, recognized on both coasts for himself, not because he was, quote, the brother of Shirley MacLaine."

According to his niece, Inge felt betrayed by Beatty's withdrawal from his life, whatever the reason. "Bill was a little, a little — thought that Warren Beatty dumped him and kind of treated him shabbily. I wonder if Warren didn't use him. I think that maybe my uncle might have thought that, but he never said so. My uncle was a gentleman . . . I know my uncle felt he was responsible for Warren's success, and he was hurt by it."

According to Inge's then-secretary, the insecure playwright concealed his wounded feelings. "I suppose he was grateful that Warren even considered him enough of a friend for him to drop by," reflected Connolly, a turn of events that Connolly found tremendously sad. "It would hurt Bill, but he would internalize that."

Clifford Odets's notes for *A Piece of the Action* — the play he was starting to construct that spring dramatizing his aborted friendship with the young star — contained the famed playwright's thoughtful analysis of Warren Beatty. In Odets's appraisal, Beatty needed validation from his father, Ira, which was the reason he "taught himself to be a football hero, so he would be popular." At the same time, observed Odets, "Warren hated that his father was a drunkard." In the playwright's assessment, Beatty began their friendship respecting Odets as a father figure he sought "for assurance he's loved or respected," but after the connection was made, "Warren needed to feel contempt for me, as he had for his own fallen father."

Odets's psychoanalysis — that Beatty gravitated to father figures he revered, put them on a pedestal, and then dethroned them as a way of reenacting his loss of respect for his alcoholic father — fit the pattern of his relationships with Odets and Inge. To some extent, it also was true with respect to Kazan, though it was Beatty who felt abandoned by the director after finishing *Splendor*. As Beatty said to Dr. Brenman a few years later, "People say I must be a shit because Kazan rejected me."

Odets's perceptive study of Beatty for his intended play went on to describe the actor as a boy who "wants to be decent, but has demons," almost identical to Kazan's description of the conflicted Bud/Beatty as a "good, dutiful boy" who has "sadism, wildness, danger in him." At the end of *A Piece of the Action*, the boy — Odets's prototype for Beatty — *becomes* "a piece of the action," and loses his humanity. Yet the playwright ended his notes writing, "I like the boy despite the stories I hear," an indication that Odets's injured feelings, like Inge's, signified how much they missed Warren Beatty's friendship.

Beatty was struggling to maintain his Virginia decency, but he was a twenty-five-year-old sexually charged movie star with his face on magazine covers, women threatening to jump out of windows over him, studio heads begging him to be in their pictures, and no moral compass in Hollywood to guide him. "I made three films in one year — just like that — bang bang bang . . . the sudden success went to my head. But I loved every minute of it; just being able to turn around and get anything I wanted. It wears off, of course . . . but at that time, it had me very mixed up emotionally."[667]

An example of Beatty's "mixed up" star behavior occurred soon after he met another of his show business mentors, talent agent Elliott Kastner. Susan Umbs, a former neighbor of Kastner and his then-wife's, recalled a disturbing blind date she had with Beatty the spring Odets began his play *A Piece of the Action*.[668] It began when Umbs, who worked at the Beverly Hills Hotel, spotted Kastner inside the hotel travel agency on the phone, "and I just popped in the door to say hi." Kastner, who was on the line with Beatty, "said, 'Oh, you should see who I'm standing next to, this wonderful tall blonde Sue' . . . and he handed me the phone." After a few minutes of pleasant conversation, Umbs accepted a lunch date with movie star Warren Beatty at a restaurant a few blocks south of a house he was renting on St. Ives, in Sunset Plaza.

When Umbs met Beatty for lunch the following Monday, "the restaurant was closed, which I guess he knew. Maybe he didn't, but I assume he did." Beatty invited Umbs into his car, presumably to find another restaurant. A few minutes later, they pulled up in front of the actor's house, "which I remember had a circular drive, double doors." Umbs went to the door with Beatty, assuming he needed to get something or wanted to offer her a drink. She found him "terrifically strange . . . because he didn't say much."

As soon as they walked into the foyer, "he literally closed the front door and his pants dropped . . . his hand was on the doorknob, and then it was on his belt." Umbs, startled, told Beatty, "No way this is going to happen," and ran back to the car. "I never touched him . . . I don't even think he kissed me. And that was it, he didn't get what he wanted and the pants were up, zipped himself up. It was so fast it was unbelievable . . . he thought he was so wonderful, that if this isn't going to fly, he wasn't going to waste a minute." Beatty opened the car door for Umbs and drove her back to the restaurant in his sister's MG without saying a word. "This was just the pickup, like I was a call girl or something."

To a degree, Beatty's behavior was an extreme, decadent version of the times he would lick a sandwich suggestively in the school cafeteria or pretend to make love to a friend's mother, aggressive sexual behavior that did not fit with his gentlemanly manners or otherwise respectful treatment of women. More to the point, the "muffled Puritan boy" had succumbed to Hollywood temptation, which had created an internal conflict in Beatty and a deep sense of guilt. "Nobody knows how hard it is to be a movie star," he told *Seventeen* two years later. "I wasn't prepared for it. The egos, the coarseness, the vulgarity."[669]

Beatty was unfaithful to Natalie Wood with these brief encounters, a symptom of their shaky interim relationship, but also evidence of what he considered "an ethical failure," he said later in life. "Anyone who does that has failed . . . that is, if they're lying about it."[670] The singer Cher confessed in *Playboy* later that she was one of Warren Beatty's one-night stands while he was involved with Natalie Wood and she was an unknown sixteen-year-old. "I did it because my girlfriends were just so crazy about him, and so was my mother. I saw Warren, he picked me up and I did it. And what a disappointment! Not that he wasn't technically good, or couldn't be good, but I didn't feel anything. So, for me, I felt there's no reason for you to do that again."[671]

During this period, William Inge told Clifford Odets's biographer that Beatty was a "compulsive satyr."[672] Inge, who felt betrayed by Beatty, may have said this out of spite, but it was apparent that the once devout Baptist was in crisis, struggling with fame, conflicts of conscience, and confusion over his identity. Beatty had begun to see a psychoanalyst, according to Odets's March 1962 journal, a doctor the playwright described as "a strong and wily old campaigner." The "wily" analyst presumably was Dr. Martin Grotjahn, Beatty's therapist in 1964 and for a number of years afterward. Grotjahn occupied what had been the Beverly Hills office of Dr. Peter Lindstrom, actress Ingrid Bergman's first husband.

The internal schism Warren Beatty was experiencing over his Hollywood lifestyle versus the Baptist mores of his Virginia youth was delineated during an interview that spring, at the height of his newly minted fame, while he was rejecting hundreds of thousands of dollars to star in movies that were being offered to him. "There are many different kinds of success," Beatty told the writer. "The most successful man I ever knew was an underpaid, overworked, harassed minister." He was referring to John Raymond. "He didn't live in any big house. I doubt if he ever saw a private swimming pool. Yet, his whole life seemed to be one continuous success. Why? Because nothing was pulling at him, tearing him into parts. He did just what he wanted to. He wanted to help people. Making money never got in his way. It wasn't what he wanted. He was a great man." Beatty went on to say that his fame as a movie star "isn't success . . . to be successful is more important than to have success."[673]

Warren Beaty, the good son, and Warren *Beatty*, the enfant terrible, had become locked in a struggle for the actor's soul. According to John Raymond's widow, Mary, the Baptist minister never lost faith in the good son. He kept the 8-by-10 black-and-white glossy Beatty sent to him while at Stella Adler's, in a frame, next to photographs of other people meaningful in his life and ministry. "That's to say how much my husband thought of Warren — the picture was one that was always on the wall wherever we lived."

Beatty's career indecision and self-doubts about his acting were reinforced in April, when *All Fall Down* was released "too quickly," in his description, or as director John Frankenheimer said bluntly, "MGM dumped the picture."[674] *New York Times* critic Bosley Crowther, who had ridiculed Beatty's "Don Ameche accent" as a gigolo, characterized him as "virtually a cretin" in *All Fall Down*, a description some would associate with Beatty instead of with the unpleasant character he played. This was especially true of Crowther's follow-up line about Berry-Berry: "Surly, sloppy, slow-witted, given to scratching himself, picking his nose, being rude beyond reason to women and muttering about how much he hates the world, this creature that Mr. Beatty gives us is a sad approximation of modern youth."[675] Crowther — who had so infuriated Shirley MacLaine over a biting review of one of her performances that she told *Time* magazine "he made me vomit" — would remain a thorn in Beatty's side, although the actor would eventually, and famously, have the last laugh.[676]

The enormity of the fame Warren Beatty had such difficulty adjusting to after *Splendor in the Grass* could be perceived in a glance in one surreal photograph, taken from behind, as he and Natalie Wood arrived at the Academy Awards that month. Beatty's arm is around Wood, a beacon of glamour in a white mink stole and beaded white halter gown, as they approach what seems like an army of paparazzi blocking their entrance to the auditorium and snapping their pictures in blinding flashes illuminating the sky like lightning.

The press's fascination with Beatty and Wood as the movie star couple of the moment pursued them to Europe in May, when *All Fall Down* was shown at the Cannes Film Festival as the art film it was intended to be. As Natalie Wood was to recall, "Photographers almost fell into our lap as we tried to eat dinner in a restaurant . . . a few cameramen slept outside our hotel rooms in the hall, hoping to catch us in an impromptu moment. We were mobbed wherever we went. After four days, we left [for Paris]. Even if Warren and I were basically more compatible — and we weren't — we couldn't have survived that craziness."[677]

To Beatty, fame was both repellent and seductive. "The external aspects of being a movie star fascinated me, and I found more pleasure in dashing off to Paris . . . and to carrying on with the dolls than in working."[678] The "other" Warren, the sweet Arlington kid John Springer would always consider him, showed tender devotion to Natalie Wood, making sure there was someone in Springer's Paris office "to help Natalie" or take her shopping. "Warren gives bad interviews," as Springer's Paris colleague, Nadia Marculescu, cabled the press agent in New York, "and though I told him, it didn't seem to help. He doesn't answer questions, he mumbles . . . I don't know what he is afraid of, though he says so often he has been misquoted. I don't know if really his mind just wanders off, or if he doesn't care. Otherwise, I think he is absolutely charming."[679]

The Kid wrote to Springer a few days later from the Grand Hotel in Rome to say he was having a ball, and bouncing off ideas for his next film, which he hoped would be either the romantic comedy *Sunday in New York*; an English picture for expatriate director Joe Losey; a Quintero film about Eugene O'Neill; or *Cocoa Beach*, for director Robert Rossen. Beatty signed the letter, impishly, as "Guess."[680]

Natalie Wood, whose divorce from Robert Wagner had just been finalized, was given a painful reminder of what might have been when she and

Beatty ran into her ex-husband and his new fiancée, actress Marion Marshall, at a nightclub in Rome. Wagner, who had been undergoing therapy in Europe and regretted the end of his marriage, tried to reach Wood later that night at the Grand Hotel, where Beatty had the phone tied up for hours with calls to the States plotting his next career move. The actress spent the rest of her first trip to Europe, which was supposed to have taken place a year earlier with Wagner, crying over what she deemed the end of a dream.[681] "Reality had crashed in, and collided with, and destroyed my childhood fantasies," as she later described what she was feeling.[682]

When reportedly the world's most famous celebrity couple flew back to New York in June, Warren Beatty's long-standing ambivalence about whether his profession was a dignified one for a man resurfaced while he was going through customs. As he later told *Time,* "It was embarrassing for me to put 'actor' on my landing card."[683]

In early July, Beatty finally accepted a movie, following his game plan to align himself with respected directors. In this case, it was Robert Rossen, whose gritty drama *The Hustler* had just won the New York Film Critics' Circle Award, and which Beatty had seen three times, admiring its "honest, grainy texture."[684] The picture was called *Cocoa Beach,* set against the backdrop of the Florida missile base. Even though there was no script yet, Beatty committed himself to Rossen, declaring, "I have put myself entirely in Robert Rossen's hands," a statement that shortly would make them both wince.[685]

34

Beatty stayed off and on in Natalie Wood's rental house at the top of San Ysidro, in Bel Air, when they returned to Los Angeles that summer. He waited for Rossen to finish writing *Cocoa Beach,* while Wood considered her options after *Gypsy.* The two movie stars, equally driven, argued incessantly through six months of mutual unemployment, heightening their incompatibilities. "We had constant fights, break-ups and reconciliations," recalled Wood. "Sometimes we were so emotionally spent after a big fight that we laughed at ourselves . . . I felt bogged down in a half-destructive relationship, but I could not bring myself to end the affair and face loneliness."[686]

Wood's troubled sixteen-year-old sister, Lana, who had eloped to Mexico to flee their domineering mother, had her marriage annulled and moved into the San Ysidro house for "awhile." "That's when I saw the problems they were having," she recalled. "Natalie would be ready to go [out] and sitting, waiting for Warren, waiting for Warren, and Warren doesn't show up, and Warren comes in very late, and Warren doesn't have really good excuses. 'Cause he was with other women. It drove her crazy . . . they were probably okay for about a month or so, and then they started really fighting a great deal."[687]

At the end of the year, as Wood signed to make what would be her favorite film, *Love with the Proper Stranger*, Beatty, who was still on hold for *Cocoa Beach*, feverishly pursued a script to produce called *Honeybear, I Think I Love You*, which he described as "one strange day in the life of an indecisive young man."[688] The writer was a talented unknown named Charles Eastman. Eastman and his younger sister, Carole—who would acquire a cult following and an Oscar nomination for her eventual screenplay *Five Easy Pieces*—studied acting in a class taught by Jeff Corey. Two of the other unknowns in Corey's class were Jack Nicholson and Robert Towne, future close friends of Beatty's who would also become Hollywood legends.

Beatty showed vision in his early choice of material with *Honeybear*, a quirky story similar to but predating *The Graduate*. The script was inspired by Charles Eastman's fascination with *Hiroshima Mon Amour* and the "new wave" of avant-garde French filmmakers. According to Eastman, "It wasn't only Warren who was romancing me. Robert Redford was, too . . . a bunch of new directors like Irvin Kershner and Sydney Pollack got very excited about the script . . . and Warren wanted it very badly."[689]

Agent-producer Elliott Kastner, Beatty's newest mentor, arranged a luncheon for him with the writer, whose artistic standards and skittishness to commit were more than a rival to his own. As Eastman recalled, "Warren said, 'You're confusing me because everyone in town wants me and you don't.' . . . We had meetings, and Warren would speak of people like Sandra Dee that should play Honeybear, and that was not right. And he was rather sexually oriented about the character, [that] he wants to fuck her, and this was not right. I was not happy with his interpretation. I was very flattered at his interest."

Eastman also felt that Beatty was not the correct choice for the male lead. "I wasn't just trying to get into Hollywood or get a movie made . . . I wanted something unique. I never felt Warren was right for it because he's a charming, polished guy, and this is about a loser, an inconspicuous person at a wedding that we watch and realize that he's in love with the bride, and he's just getting drunker and saying inane things to everybody . . . so I felt it had a tenderness, and a smallness, that was real and important."

Eastman also disapproved of the enfant terrible in Beatty then. "He would sexualize it — we would screen somebody's film to look at an actor, or for the director, or something he was interested in, and he in those days had a mouth that would start saying all kinds of unquotable things about whoever was on the screen. And it wasn't objectionable, it wasn't charming, one just wondered why." Eastman later understood that Beatty was "unsettled" by all the attention he was getting in Hollywood. "I think Warren had developed protective verbal games, or any number of things to protect himself, because he has remained a very nice guy."

By a coincidence, Charles and Carole Eastman's mother was from Cape Breton Island, where Tat had spent her straitlaced childhood, a common background that, ironically, made Beatty's sex symbol behavior less appealing to Charles, who was unaware that Beatty and Natalie Wood were having problems in their relationship. "Everybody knew that he was with Natalie, and so if you're having lunch with him or having dinner with him, and you see him stop someone on the street, a young lady — to me it annoyed me. . . . He'd come on very strong, very charming, and you had the feeling that he was [saying], 'Where will you be later?' or 'What's your name?' and 'Why don't you join us,' that kind of thing, that he was acting like a single man." Eastman had also heard stories around town about Beatty calling women late at night to proposition them. "I remember feeling wronged in the Natalie Wood phase, but then I'm known as the talented square."

Beatty had been stopping girls, women, even dowagers, on the street to flirt with them since his Stella Adler days, and his phone calls in the middle of the night, already part of the Warren Beatty mystique, were as likely to be to his male friends or to discuss business. When he did call to woo, his signature greeting was, "What's new, pussycat?" Lana Wood, who was around him during and after his volatile romance with her sister, found it impossible to dislike Warren, and so, she said, did Natalie. "He's just wonderful to women, just wonderful. He just genuinely likes them, *all* of them. It isn't even that he compliments you, although he will; it's like he hangs onto every word you have to say, everything that comes out of your mouth is of the utmost interest to him."

Lana Wood recalled having dinner once with Beatty at the Aware Inn, a popular health food restaurant on Sunset, "and this little waitress who I don't think I looked at twice . . . he thought she looked like — it was an artist, like

Rubenesque — he was going on and on and on, and I said 'Okay, fine, whatever, Warren.' . . . But he would do that. Every woman he saw, he would see something wonderful about her, even if it was only one quality."

While Natalie Wood was preparing for *Love with the Proper Stranger*, Beatty began to set up his own company to produce the groundbreaking *Honeybear* script, with Elliott Kastner as his partner. Eastman, its discriminating screenwriter, had underestimated both the screen star's business acumen and his sixth sense about movies. "I had no money," recalled Beatty, "but I was very selective about what I did . . . as soon as I came out to Hollywood I started thinking about how to replace the studio system which was then on its last legs. Although I didn't produce a film until *Bonnie and Clyde* in 1965, I'd intended to produce from the very beginning. I realized that's where the future lay."[690]

In January 1963, the young actor asked John Springer to purchase a trade announcement for his new production company, tellingly requesting "the kind of ad that 7 Arts took welcoming Kazan."[691] Beatty's production company folded when Charles Eastman dithered over signing the contract to release the rights to *Honeybear, I Think I Love You* — the same tactic Beatty had perfected under the apprenticeship of the master Charles Feldman. Eastman kept the star at arm's length, conferring with his close friend from acting class, Jack Nicholson, who had not yet met Beatty. "I didn't sign. I didn't cooperate. I just knew I couldn't. This was not what I wrote it for. Jack was kind of my confidant. He's a smart man, and he saw all the mistakes I was making as far as Hollywood is concerned, and he's realistic, and said, 'Why don't you make the deal?' And so I would run from my meetings with Redford, and Warren, and talk to either my sister, or Jack, or both, and nobody would quite understand why I was so uncooperative."

Once again, Eastman may have misjudged his suitor. Beatty's artistic and commercial instincts would prove golden two years later with the New Wave–inspired *Bonnie and Clyde*, and the poignant loner-loser in *Honeybear* was closer to Warren Beatty's self-image than anyone might have imagined; later in his career, Beatty told a pair of college reporters that he related to playing "schmucks, cocky schmucks, guys who think they know it all but don't," perhaps because they reminded him of the other Warren, the skinny, clownish kid who had impersonated Milton Berle to entertain classmates in junior high and who had played the soundtrack from *Oklahoma!*, over and over, alone in the dining room.[692]

With *Honeybear* up in the air, Beatty, who had not worked for sixteen months, was forced to take an acting job; by a strange chain of circumstances, it would be the ethereal *Lilith*. "I waited and waited for [Rossen] to write [*Cocoa Beach*]. He never did. And by the time he asked me to do *Lilith* instead, I was so broke that I was happy to do whatever picture he wanted. I had sort of committed to do my next picture with him."[693]

The pathological discord that would come between Warren Beatty and Robert Rossen, the director he so admired because of *The Hustler*, had its inception when Beatty expressed concern about the script for *Lilith*, a film he had chosen for no reason other than to work with Rossen.[694] After requesting script changes, Beatty was forced to accept another movie for financial reasons. "Rossen is unhappy with you again," Springer wrote to the Kid on February 1. "He feels you kept stringing him along, making him think you liked *Lilith*."[695] At the time, Beatty was ten thousand dollars in debt.[696] Charles Feldman, his Hollywood surrogate father, had loaned him the money to keep him afloat during his long holdout for artistic material. "People thought I had a lot of money," Beatty explained later, "but I didn't. My business manager said, 'Work or else.'"[697] Ironically, the press accused Beatty of greed, claiming he had turned down scripts because he was demanding too much money.

The film Beatty accepted to make ends meet was *Youngblood Hawke*, a slick adaptation of a Herman Wouk novel for Warner Brothers, directed by Delmer Daves. Beatty's reluctance to make the mediocre *Youngblood* could be read between the lines of John Springer's advice to him that February. "You have plenty of time for 'artistic integrity,'" his press agent wrote to the Kid, "but just about any star who can afford that has to have pretty well established himself as a box-office magnet first." Springer closed with greetings to Natalie Wood, writing, "Love to the Pretty One (or should I say 'the other Pretty One')."[698]

During the next three weeks, Beatty was assigned a dressing room; filmed hair and makeup tests with his costar, Suzanne Pleshette; and phoned or met the director, Delmer Daves, on a daily basis to discuss the script. Five days before filming was to begin in Kentucky, Beatty still had not signed the contract. According to Daves's phone logs, journal, and studio transcripts, Jack Warner set a deadline of noon on Friday, February 22, for Beatty to sign the papers. Daves had waited all day Friday, and most of the following Monday, when a Warners representative finally called Beatty's attorney, who said he "couldn't put a pen in the boy's hand and push his arm." The director phoned Beatty at home that Monday night, warning him "to get off the dime or else we'd be behind the eight-ball." The next day, Jack Warner, the head of the studio, sent the actor a wire notifying him he had been terminated.[699]

Beatty's advisor throughout was Charles Feldman, who had invented the tactic of contract avoidance.[700] Beatty and Feldman had become so close the actor was living in a guest room at the agent's Coldwater Canyon mansion, which Feldman shared with his stylish ex-wife, actress turned photographer Jean Howard, with whom Feldman had remained close, despite his sequence of glamorous girlfriends.[701]

In the process of emancipating himself, Warren Beatty had acquired a formidable adversary in Jack Warner. The actor said later that the studio chief resented him because of *PT 109*, but according to Robert Solo, an executive who worked with Warner, the mogul's bitterness stemmed from Beatty's contract ploy on *Youngblood Hawke*. "They ended up using James Franciscus because they were too far along, so he was furious at Warren. He had a hate-on for him."[702]

Beatty later conceded it was "hard to turn down the money" for *Youngblood Hawke*, claiming that he and the director "agreed to disagree" on the script, which Beatty had hoped would be reminiscent of Thomas Wolfe, his boyhood idol. "I thought they'd intended it along the lines of *Of Time and the River*."[703] For the grandson of Blanche MacLean, it was a question of artistic standards. "At the last minute I couldn't do the picture," he later told his hometown paper in Richmond. "I couldn't bring myself to make the decision."[704]

The experience was as unnerving for Beatty as it was for Jack Warner. Throughout his enfant terrible period, the health-conscious actor chain-smoked sporadically, staying at Feldman's partly so he could play the agent's baby grand piano, his tension-reliever since childhood. That night, Beatty went to a party, where he saw Clifford Odets for the first time since their difficult break a year earlier. "I had just walked out of a picture," as he told Odets's friend Margaret Brenman, "and I was in a tremendous state of anxiety." In what would prove to be a recurring, and admirable, trait of Beatty's, he made the first move to reconcile. "I walked over and said hello to Clifford and we made up." The playwright died six months later. Five years after that, Beatty expressed regret over their lost project. "I had the chance earlier to do something with Clifford Odets. But I was scared of what people would say. You know, who does he think he is at his age? Odets is gone now and that chance went forever."[705]

After deserting Delmer Daves and antagonizing Jack Warner, Beatty decided he needed to start work immediately or he would be "banished," so he accepted *Lilith*.[706] His first gesture was to repay the ten-thousand-dollar note to Feldman, who hosted a farewell party for Natalie Wood in March as she left for New York to start *Love with the Proper Stranger*. Her date was Beatty, but their romance had become "a charade of closeness," Wood wrote later, "a ritual of acting out counterfeit feelings."[707]

Beatty behaved as he had in the last stages with Joan Collins, by pursuing the year's most desirable actresses throughout Europe. The trip was disguised as a favor to Robert Rossen, who had flown to London to test actresses for the title role of Lilith, a seductive patient in a mental institute with whom Beatty's character falls in love. Beatty, who offered to screen-test with the actress candidates for Rossen, had suggested Jean Seberg, who lived in Paris with her fiancé, novelist Romain Gary. His choice provided further proof of Beatty's fascination with New Wave filmmakers, who had anointed the Iowa-born Seberg as their muse in *Breathless*.[708]

For personal reasons, Beatty was also promoting sultry German starlet Romy Schneider, who was filming *The Cardinal* in Vienna, and English actress Samantha Eggar, a freckled redhead in the tradition of his mother, sister, and early girlfriends. Jeanne Rejaunier, Beatty's friend and occasional date of four years, noticed that he was "fascinated" by Eggar. "Romy [has] the edge," reported the like-minded Feldman in a memo to his partners. "Frankly, Beatty likes her, and so do I."[709]

Beatty kept in touch with his role model while in Europe, sending Feldman whimsical telegrams with "love and greetings from the London Pimpernel" after a late evening "working" with Eggar, as John Springer coyly emphasized it in an interoffice communiqué. On his way to Vienna to see Romy Schneider, the actor cabled Feldman, who liked to call himself the Jewish Clark Gable, "regards from young Jewish actresses from the Phantom of Frankfurt."[710] Sam Shaw, the still photographer on *The Cardinal*, sent a letter to Feldman from Vienna. "Everybody's laughing about Warren Beatty coming here to case Romy Schneider for Lilith — she thought he was ridiculous. He gawked and followed her around. She turned him and Rossen down flat — and refused to screen test or play opposite Warren."[711]

His last stop, in Paris, proved that Beatty, the wandering "Pimpernel," was as serious as ever about his work, despite his underlying motives to screen-test with Romy Schneider and Samantha Eggar. Actress Jean Seberg, Beatty's original suggestion solely for professional reasons, was Rossen's clear choice to play Lilith after they met with her in Paris. Beatty was "very enthusiastic" about it, according to Darryl Zanuck, who had dinner with him afterward. The actor showed an "intense interest in French films," re-called Zanuck, and impressed his publicist's European representative as "much calmer and more mature" than he was the year before, at Cannes. The representative wrote to Springer, "I was very pleased to renew my friendship with 'the other Warren.'"[712] Jean Seberg, his new costar, shared this positive feeling about Beatty in Europe, observing, "At the start, Rossen and he had a relationship that was strangely fraternal, very intimate, very like accomplices even."[713]

On Beatty's return flight to New York to start *Lilith*, a red-eye from Lon-don on March 29, 1963, the plane was hit by lightning shortly after takeoff. A hole was torn in the nose of the Boeing 707, which dropped ten thousand gallons of fuel as the pilot managed to make an emergency landing. The near-fatal plane mishap made the evening news on WVNJ radio in New York, which reported, "Aboard were twenty-two American ministers, return-ing from the Holy Land . . . and actor Warren Beatty." In the light of subse-quent events on *Lilith*, perhaps it was an omen.

JEAN SEBERG'S RECOLLECTION of the early bond between Beatty, who turned twenty-six during his star-crossed flight back to New York, and fifty-five-year-old Rossen was another instance of the actor's cleaving to an older, respected authority figure he viewed as a teacher. "Rossen very generously, particularly in the first month, taught me as much as anybody else ever did about making movies," Beatty said later, "in how he handled the studio, how he handled the shooting, how he avoided decision, how he left his op-tions open."[714] The director took Beatty to Maryland to watch him scout lo-cations, and to walk through the mental hospital that had inspired *Lilith*'s story—"a pretty shocking and sobering experience," the actor told a friend.[715]

On his way back to New York, Beatty spent time with his parents in Vir-ginia, as he often did when he was on the East Coast. He mentioned to Springer that Kathlyn Beaty had been "extremely ill some time ago" and said he was "thrilled to see his mother in such good health."[716] When Beatty re-turned to New York, Rossen invited him to a family Passover dinner at his home, another indication of how close they had become. Beatty brought Natalie Wood, in what amounted to their farewell appearance.[717] The ac-tress left for Hollywood shortly after, to complete *Love with the Proper*

Stranger. A few weeks later, Beatty flew back to California for a brief visit before shooting began on *Lilith*.

When he arrived, Natalie Wood had come to the same conclusion about ending their romance as Joan Collins had two years earlier, for essentially the same reasons. Beatty's infidelities were a symptom of their deteriorating relationship, and a signal that he was not ready for marriage. As he tacitly acknowledged, "I've had relationships where I felt that it could be a real nasty trail if I stayed on. But I can't remember not thinking that they were right to some degree, and that a large part of it was my fault when the problem made itself apparent."[718]

In the bravely honest memoir she began a few years later, Wood described her emotions at the time. "I could join Warren or stay in California, alone, without work, without a lover and face my troubles. It would have been easier to go East. I chose the path of most resistance . . . finally I felt I had the strength to say farewell to Warren."

Actor Tom Bosley, Natalie Wood's costar in *Love with the Proper Stranger*, who knew about her earlier attempts to release Beatty, was with her the night of what Bosley called the "final kiss-off."[719] The actress had invited Bosley and his wife, along with their director, Alan Pakula, to dinner at Chasen's. As Bosley was to recall, Wood arrived late because "she was at the airport breaking off with Beatty . . . he wanted her to come and say good-bye to him at the airport, and she decided to say good-bye to *him*." When she got to Chasen's, Wood was "obviously shaken," noticed Bosley, but "she was strong about it." According to her sister Lana, Wood would have liked her romance with Beatty to progress "if he'd been able to stay on the straight and narrow."

In the years after the breakup, a second myth would emerge that Beatty had left Natalie Wood sitting at the table at Chasen's while he disappeared with the hatcheck girl for two weeks, upsetting the actress to the point of a breakdown. In keeping with his no-comment policy, Beatty never bothered to refute the rumor. Both he and Wood had tried to avert gossip at the time, as shown in a June memo Beatty's New York press agent/confidant, John Springer, sent to the Los Angeles office, which stated: "Warren Beatty is very concerned that a lot might be made of the fact that he and Natalie have broken up . . . Warren wants to make sure there isn't a big thing—he says Natalie does, too."[720]

Wood, who first turned to Beatty for friendship, would resume the relationship in that vein after her disappointment subsided, according to her younger sister, mutual pals, and the actress herself, who wrote: "Ironically, we became better friends after we separated."[721]

THE SET, and subject matter, of *Lilith* was a disturbing place for Beatty to land in the wake of his broken romance with Natalie Wood and the pressures in his career. J. R. Salamanca, who wrote the admired novel, modeled the charismatic title character on a schizophrenic who had been his patient when he was an occupational therapist at Chestnut Lodge, an exclusive mental institute in Rockville, Maryland. "She was a brilliant girl, and after she was 'cured' as they called it . . . she wrote a rather celebrated novel called *I Never Promised You a Rose Garden.* She wasn't particularly beautiful physically, but she was just fascinating."[722] Salamanca called his heroine "Lilith," an allusion to Jewish biblical lore that Adam had a wife before Eve named Lilith who was banished because she would not make herself sexually subservient.

Beatty's character, a sensitive but troubled aide in an elite sanitarium who becomes fixated on his sexually beguiling patient, was "a bit of me," admitted Salamanca. "Warren obviously identified with the part to a great extent . . . I think he felt a great deal of sympathy for that character. He just liked the idea that this boy was war weary, and rather cynical about the world and life, and that the lodge was, for him, a kind of refuge."

Beatty's original suggestion of Jean Seberg to play the erotic but mentally ill Lilith showed delicate insight on his part, and on Rossen's in casting her. The beautiful but fragile Seberg—who would take her life at forty-one— would consider Lilith her "favorite part" and once said, "In many ways her world is so much more beautiful and preferable to ours."[723] Seberg's emotional illness and eventual suicide would be brought on by an FBI smear campaign falsely alleging that she had miscarried a child with a leader of the Black Panther organization. Salamanca, who was often on the set, observed, "There was something about Jean that was rather tragic anyway. There was something sad about her. She was a smalltown girl, and she felt that her career might not be going quite the way she'd like it to have. The fact that she committed suicide practically seemed not so much ironic as a part of her destiny." At the time he cast her, Rossen described the blond Iowa native prophetically as having "that flawed American girl quality, sort of like a cheerleader who's cracked up."[724]

To prepare for their roles, the director sent his stars to Chestnut Lodge to perform "psychodramas" with the patients. Beatty would comment afterward that the sanitarium had "a greater sense of reality than Madison Avenue."[725] According to Salamanca, "There was a patient at Chestnut Lodge who Warren liked very much, a very brilliant girl . . . she was a fourth-floor patient and was often isolated in a padded room. But then she would have flashes when she would be very articulate, brilliant."

Jane Fonda's younger brother, Peter, who was cast as a mental patient in a rivalry with Beatty's character over Lilith, declined the director's invitation to visit the "local loony bin place," as Fonda called it. "I think Warren asked me why I didn't go, and I said, 'Well, if they take one look at me they're going to slam me in there.' I really was worried about it. By this time in my life I'd realized my mother had committed suicide when I was ten, and was in an insane asylum, so I said 'Uh-oh. I don't want to go near that place.' I was goofy enough."[726]

Both Beatty and Fonda, in the opinion of the director's daughter, Carol Eve Rossen, an accomplished stage actress, were young, inexperienced actors in competition, "so that it was problematic."[727] Robert Rossen, whom his daughter described as "a bull of a being, very strong," was diabetic and suffered from a rare skin disease.* His doctors had begun treating it with cortisone, unaware that the drug interaction with insulin would lead to his death. "He was very ill," recalled Salamanca, "and he frequently passed out on the set."

Just as with *A Loss of Roses*, and its similarly volatile combination of elements, the *Lilith* production began to self-destruct on the first day, detonated by Beatty, who once again emerged with a reputation as the company's holy terror.

According to Seberg, the "intimacy" she noticed between Beatty and Rossen in Paris "stopped at the first day of filming, and from then on, it did nothing but deteriorate more and more."[728] Beatty, who had not been in front of a camera for almost two years and realized that this film was crucial, turned to the strained, ailing Rossen for the kind of director-actor discussions Kazan had provided on *Splendor* before every scene. According to Salamanca, "Rossen said, 'I hired you because I thought you knew how to act, for Christ's sake. Don't ask me how to play the part. You're supposed to know how to play the part.'" From Beatty's perspective, Rossen had "turned on him."[729]

*Pemphigus foliaceus.

To add to his insecurity, Beatty clearly was aware of, and bothered by, the critics who had mocked his "dead-pan" expressions as Paolo in *Roman Spring* and Berry-Berry in *All Fall Down*. Socialite Afdera Fonda, an ex-wife of Henry Fonda's, who went out with Beatty a few times that spring, recalled that he would study himself in the mirror, concerned that his looks were "a bore. He also had a complex over his sister Shirley MacLaine. 'Shirley's got character in her face,' he would say." Beatty told Afdera Fonda he looked forward to getting wrinkles so his face would look more "interesting."[730] In effect, the critics were pointing out what Inge had expressed concern about on the set of *All Fall Down* — Beatty's fear of revealing emotion, a crippling handicap for an actor and part of the reserved Virginian's deeper-seated fear of revealing himself.

Beatty continued to ask for his character's "motivation," as he had on *A Loss of Roses*. The film crew, which included Tibor Sands, an assistant camera operator, took Rossen's side in their dim view of Beatty's Method techniques. Besides "mumbling," recounted Sands, "Warren would, after 'Action,' spend a horrible long time . . . getting into his part. Stand and look up into the sun, and get inspiration — by this time half of the film was gone from the camera."[731]

Warren Rothenberger, who was preparing a short film on the making of *Lilith*, recalled, "Every time they'd get ready to shoot, Warren Beatty would say, 'Just a minute' when they were ready to do a close-up of him. He'd say, 'I have to get my energy,' and he'd look up to the sky, and he'd start taking deep breaths, and it would drive Rossen crazy. He said, 'I had to hire this son of a bitch. He's driving me crazy.'"[732]

Jean Seberg's skittishness further aggravated the situation. She confessed, later, that she was nervous the first three weeks of filming because she had not worked in America for three years. "I was intimidated by the whole business. I was intimidated by Warren Beatty . . . not intimidated really, but he talked a different language than I did in his work."[733]

Beatty, who was hungering for direction, complained to an aide of Springer's that he felt slighted by Rossen's extra attention to Seberg, who had inspired protective feelings in Peter Fonda. The young actor gallantly leaped to defend her from Beatty, much as his character would in the movie. "I had got upset one day when she had to slap Warren," admitted Fonda. "Warren would stop her hand, but he did it with the side of his hand that was bruising her arm. And I said, 'Rossen, you can't let that happen.'"

The "life imitating art" triangle created tension between Beatty and Peter

Fonda, which was ironic, since it was Beatty who first encouraged Jane Fonda's younger brother to become an actor, perhaps seeing himself in Peter and Shirley in Jane.* "Warren was the first person I ran into who said, 'You should be in movies' . . . I went to look in the mirror right away. I thought I was a skinny little kid that wasn't taken seriously anywhere because I was so skinny."

Jean Seberg, Fonda's damsel in distress, was an eccentric personality, according to J. R. Salamanca. The author of *Lilith* had dinner several times with Seberg and her novelist fiancé, who stayed at a country inn "estranged" from the rest of the company. "Romain didn't get along with anybody else at all. They had a little world of their own . . . but I liked them. Jean was a bit outrageous, and she tried to be. She smoked cigars and things of that kind."

Beatty, who continued to hold Rossen to the standards of his idol Kazan, considered the film, as it progressed, "completely disorganized," which he blamed in part on the director's drinking.[734] Carol Eve Rossen later would concede that her father was a "hard-drinking" man, but she disputed that his alcohol use affected *Lilith*. Beatty voiced his creative complaints to Rossen, as he had been encouraged to do on his first film by Kazan. "I saw he wasn't making a good picture and told him so, which did not endear me to him."[735]

The star also began to make suggestions — another policy of Kazan's that struck Rossen and his crew as impudent. "An awful lot of people were saying to me, 'What the hell do you think you are? A producer?'"[736] commented Beatty.

"He did dispute the director a few times," observed camera operator Tibor Sands, "which in my experience rarely happens . . . he would say his line differently than the director wanted him to do it." At first, observed Sands, Rossen "tolerated Warren's eccentricities . . . I think he was already in a weakened mind." The ailing director's patience with Beatty finally snapped, according to the camera operator, who recalled the specific incident. "I was witness — Warren said to Rossen, 'What's my motivation?' and Rossen says, 'Your goddamn paycheck!'"

In future years, the director would tell journalists that Warren Beatty was "miscast."[737] Beatty offered his own version, privately, to film critic Judith Crist. "Warren had realized that he had made a serious mistake in taking the part . . . Warren gave me the impression — I don't remember a phrase or

---

*Beatty made the suggestion to Peter Fonda at a party in Hollywood when Peter was visiting Jane around the time of *Tall Story*.

anything — that he just felt *stuck*. He had asked for his release and could not get it."[738]

Beatty assumed the posture of a cornered man. "The making of the movie was as crazy as the things that took place in the plot," Beatty told a film journal years later, after Rossen was long deceased. "And I think we were all absolutely up to the level of the characters in the movie. It was hilarious . . . I would say the picture that the making of the movie most resembled was *Gaslight*; I was playing the Ingrid Bergman part."[739]

At the time, it was gallows humor. According to Peter Fonda, the crew so disliked Beatty and his mumbling, they nicknamed him "Whispering Jack Smith." Fonda, who had trouble hearing Beatty himself, blurted, in the middle of one of their scenes, "Excuse me, what did you say?" "Rossen was really pissed off," Fonda remembered. "I thought it was kinda cool." Dorothy Avakian, who was married to Aram Avakian, the film's much-lauded editor, would recall Beatty's dialogue as barely audible. "He mumbled and held his head down, and Aram had trouble cutting the film."[740]

Years later, Beatty revealed to Judith Crist that he purposely sabotaged some of the scenes after his request to be released from the film was denied, deciding, "Okay, I'm just not going to act." Jean Seberg's makeup artist, who admired Beatty's early efforts to make creatively interesting choices, noticed with amusement how he began to "one-up" Rossen by "spoiling takes that Warren didn't think were gonna be good for Warren."[741] Tibor Sands, the director's assistant cameraman, remarked after Rossen died, "We used to say that Warren helped him to his death."

Both Beatty and Rossen later admitted on the record that they had "fights" throughout the filming of *Lilith*, which the director attributed to Beatty's "psychotic" behavior. "There was nothing I could do about it," Rossen told a film journal, "because he's so sick, that he brings his sickness into anything he does."[742]

At the end of May, columnists began to report "clashes" on the set between Rossen and his star, quoting the director as saying, "I was making Oscars when Warren was a baby pissing in a pot."[743] Soon after, Beatty received a letter of concern from Kazan. "The letter upset him a lot," Springer revealed. ". . . it wound up with Rossen volunteering to call Kazan and tell him that it wasn't true at all."[744]

That weekend, a colleague of Springer's visited Beatty on location to counsel him about the "Rossen thing." She reported that the Kid was happy to have someone "'on his side' there," and that he was "really terribly anxious to cooperate."[745]

Beatty had a few allies, including novelist J. R. Salamanca, who found him "very pleasant to talk to" and effective in portraying the world-weariness of Salamanca's alter ego. It was during *Lilith* that Beatty became close with Bob Jiras, Kazan's makeup man on *Splendor*, who had teasingly referred to him then as "Mental Anguish." "B.J. had a wonderful sense of humor," observed Irving Buchman, Jean Seberg's makeup artist, "and Warren needed that because he was playing such a downbeat kind of character."

Beatty also had a sympathizer in Buchman. "Warren always has been a sensitive actor, and Hollywood wasn't into it . . . and Rossen was not in good health and also drank a little bit too much sometimes. Warren really was a loner pretty much on this movie. He was one of those people, earlier than Robert De Niro, who would keep away from the sociology of the set."

The laid-back Peter Fonda, who had thought he and Beatty might bond as the younger brothers of two famous movie stars, instead encountered the Virginian's reserve. "I was curious, you know, and I'd look at him and wonder about him and his sister, and why they didn't talk, because here I was with my sister, also in show biz." Fonda refrained from asking Beatty about Shirley MacLaine. "I felt it was inappropriate to do that. If Warren wanted to tell me, that would be fine, you know, because we shared the fact that we both had siblings in the business. I mean I had a double-header with the fact of my dad."

Beatty spent one of his weekends on location in Maryland as the houseguest of President Kennedy's sister Eunice Shriver. Despite his brushes with the Kennedys, Beatty had not become what he called politically "activated" yet. He would express guilt, later, for not objecting to the war in 1963. "I was busy trying to be a movie star, and this and that."[746]

The tension with Rossen worsened in July when the cast left for Oyster Bay, Long Island, to film on the estate that was doubling for the sanitarium. According to Jean Seberg, the director was so exhausted, so frustrated with Beatty, "he even wanted to bring a lawsuit against him, and other childish things."[747] Rossen omitted Beatty's name in preliminary advertisements for the movie, creating more ill will between the star and director who had started out like father and son.

In John Springer's belief, Rossen was also responsible for an unflattering item in Mike Connolly's gossip column in the trades reporting "Beatty's daily two-hour makeup-and-wardrobe sessions on *Lilith* stemmed from the 45 minutes required to separate and curl his eyelashes, plus an intricate costuming gimmick: seven T-shirts under his suit, each scalloped . . . all to give him that V-look."[748]

Peter Fonda confirmed the accuracy of the T-shirt story. "Warren was very clever . . . it made his pecs look a little bit bigger because he's cut them in a certain way. . . . He had a whole workout set up in his dressing room, pushing weights, pumping weights. I was so embarrassed about my own lack of weight—because I felt I was so skinny and all that—that I was very curious about what Warren was up to, and how he was doing it."

Beatty's thin frame was an indication he had not fully recovered from the hepatitis he had contracted five years earlier. Several in the cast of *Lilith* recalled a nurse visiting the set to give Beatty vitamin shots, including Peter Fonda, who considered him "very health conscious." Fonda also noticed Beatty smoking cigarettes, tangible evidence of the strain he was under. "He was talking about wanting to give it up. He said *I* should not do it. I don't remember when Warren quit, but I know he did 'cause he made a purpose of telling me."

Beatty's fraught experience on *Lilith* would be made worthwhile by a single scene he filmed toward the end of the shoot. Actress Jessica Walter played his old flame, and for the tiny part of her husband, Rossen had cast an unknown stage actor named Gene Hackman, whom he and his daughter had seen at an out-of-town tryout.[749] "Gene of course was 'to die' brilliant," recalled Walter, "and every time he did it, it was fresh, and he just slayed everybody. And Warren, no fool he, I think he really sparked to Gene immediately."[750] Beatty said later it was "fun" to act with Hackman, whom he would remember, and make famous, two years later. Recalling Beatty's mumbling, Jessica Walter would say with amusement, "That's when I learned to read lips."

The crew, the director, and Fonda would show scant sense of humor for Whispering Jack Smith. At the wrap party for *Lilith*, "Peter rounded up some of the crew, including myself, to throw Warren into the pool," admitted Tibor Sands. "It never happened, but he really, really wanted to do it." Paul Sylbert, whose twin, Richard, was the production designer on *Lilith* and would become one of Beatty's closest friends, recalled, "People were lining up to kill him. They were. The crew on the Rossen picture was taking bets, getting him at the end of the movie."[751]

Beatty faced a more serious issue with Rossen. "Warren hears indirectly and believes that Rossen is going to sue him or bring him up on charges or try to blacken his name," John Springer wrote in an in-house memo that month, evaluating the press agency's "Warren Beatty situation." Beatty told his publicist-confidant he felt Rossen was using him as a "scapegoat" to conceal the director's alcoholism and "unpredictable" behavior on the set. "It winds up," wrote Springer, "with Rossen calling Warren all kinds of a 'monster . . . he's driving me into the hospital, etc. etc.,' but having nothing concrete with which to back it up." Rossen had indicated to Springer he would not sue Beatty, but he threatened to edit *Lilith* "so that Warren came out looking bad." At the end of the memo, his publicist wrote ominously of Beatty, "I think we may be in big trouble with him."[752]

Springer and company devoted the coming weeks to meeting with their star client to devise a PR campaign that would, in effect, counteract the plan they had set in motion in 1960 to turn Warren Beatty into a sex symbol by making him an enfant terrible, an image that was now suddenly destructive. "I had a whole part to play up, and I played it," Beatty said later. "I guess because I was too dull to see any other roles. I was supposed to be an *enfant terrible* . . . that was the role that they wanted me to play; certainly I must have wanted to play it, or it wouldn't have been so easy."[753]

The publicist's new campaign was to introduce the "other Warren," the "right Warren," the "Warren Beatty we love," a tactic that Springer suggested include an attack in the press on Rossen, whom he had been told was "planting nasty untrue items" about Beatty. "I begged him to let me retaliate," Springer later wrote to a friend. "But Warren never fought back in the press and never allowed me to. He said the director was sick and scared and alcoholic and he didn't want to hurt him. He said people who knew him would know the stories were not true and he didn't give a damn about the people who believed them. (But he did — he's no less sensitive than anybody else when it comes to attacks on him.)"[754]

Many years after Rossen died, in 1982, Beatty, who had just won an Academy Award for Best Director for *Reds*, would spot Carol Eve Rossen at a Christmas party at actress Brenda Vaccaro's house. As Carol Rossen recalled, "Warren made a beeline for me in the middle of a very, very crowded room filled with men and women who wanted to get something from Warren, whatever that was. And for over an hour we stood talking. It was essentially a monologue on his part with my asking only a few questions. It was almost like an unburdening of his feelings."

In his confessional, Beatty revealed to Rossen's daughter the root of his conflict with Rossen during *Lilith*. "I do not remember the specifics of the conversation," said Carol Rossen, "except I remember one thing. One of the many things that [Warren] talked about was his relationship with his father, the details of which I do not know — or do not remember . . . my impression is that he was acting out on *my* father, and that he had a lot of stuff that he still needed to resolve, like we all have, with authority, with his father. Whatever that was about I don't begin to know. And my dad was the guy that got it."

Beatty's experience with Robert Rossen took a step further in the pattern Clifford Odets had psychoanalyzed two years earlier: Warren Beatty's need to bond with, and then lose respect for, an idealized father figure–teacher, the same way he had lost respect for his own "fallen father." Since Beatty, ever the "good son," withheld his contempt for his own father, he rebelled against his *surrogate* fathers, expressing his disillusionment with Ira Beaty through painful estrangements with Odets, Inge, and Rossen.

According to Shirley MacLaine, their father was aware, toward the end of his life, of the negative impact his drinking and career failures had had on her and Warren. He told MacLaine, "I know you two didn't want to be like me. That's why you turned out like you did. You didn't want to be nothing. Like me."[755]

When he was in his fifties, Beatty reflected on this period in his life, validating Odets's theory. "Rossen, who was a gifted man, was not in good health. And I in retrospect think I didn't help a lot, because I was at that kind of patricidal stage that young actors go through, expecting these older men to be perfect, if they want to be in charge."[756] Having "felled" the alcoholic Rossen, a stand-in for his alcoholic father, Ira, Warren Beatty seemed to have released some inner demon.

He told Springer he was eager to go along with the press agency's revised campaign, bidding farewell to the "enfant terrible." As Springer documented, "Warren feels that this 'image' that has been created — that of the rebel, the wild kid, the type who doesn't give a damn what anyone thinks — is the image he wants to retain. <u>This is to the public.</u> To the industry and to the producers and directors with whom he hopes sometime to work, he wants to be known as a craftsman who cares about his work."[757]

A Legend
in the Making

Photograph by Curtis Hanson

"You've heard the story of Jesse James
Of how he lived and died
If you're still in the need of something to read
Here's the story of Bonnie and Clyde."

BONNIE AND CLYDE
quoting Bonnie Parker

Arthur Penn directs Faye Dunaway and Warren Beatty in a scene from
Bonnie and Clyde on location in Texas, late autumn of 1966.
The photo is by a young Curtis Hanson.

35 *Consistent with the campaign to bury*
the enfant terrible and present the "other Warren"—the Kid who called
Springer in the middle of the night to sing to him and who privately visited
Joe Laitin's dying father—Beatty set his sights on becoming a producer as he
rose from the wreckage of *Lilith* in the fall of 1963.

At the same time, he advised Springer that he wanted the press agency to
project him to the public as a "hotshot bachelor" with "a string of girls," because he believed it would enhance his mystique as a movie star.[1] Springer
had arranged for Beatty to get a special rate on a permanent suite at the Delmonico Hotel, like Mitch May's rooms at the Blackstone, and the actor told
his publicist he thought that it would "add to his 'image' if he were thrown
out of his hotel for wild parties."[2]

Beatty helped Springer write the "blurbs" to plant in Army Archerd's and
Mike Connolly's trade gossip columns. Such as, "Warren Beatty showed up
at his apartment with several cans of film under his arm to find he was having a party. Nobody tells Warren about his parties—they just happen. His
Delmonico bachelor terrace apartment seems to be a Mecca for the swinging set." Or, "Three girls who met each other at one of Warren Beatty's
swinging bachelor parties in New York last week discovered that, in various
years, they had all been Miss Sweden." Springer sent Beatty's gossip bits to
the Hollywood office, adding, "I can promise you that Warren will be reading Connolly and Archerd with a magnifying glass, expecting to see most of
these items . . ."[3]

The stories were mostly hyperbole, with some basis in fact. Beatty, his
press agent noted in the memo to Los Angeles, did give a "wild party" at the
Delmonico for Italian sex symbol Claudia Cardinale, whom he was dating
that September in New York; and Springer made a note in the margins of
the Miss Sweden blurb: "Believe it or not, this is true." Afdera Fonda, the socialite with whom Beatty had what she called a "fling" earlier that spring, described him as naughty, charming, and playful, saying he smelled of honey,
and that he came and went "like a shadow in the night."

Beatty's longtime close friend Mitch "Buzzy" May considered this to be Beatty's movie star persona, not the real Warren, according to May's second wife, Gita Hall. "They always called him a playboy, but Mitch insisted that he was a one-woman man."[4] The private Beatty spoke of wanting children someday, how he needed a woman in his life as a "jumping-off place," but saying he was not ready for marriage.[5] This "other Warren" got permission from the Delmonico to move the piano from the hotel dining room into his suite, so he could play, alone, for hours.

Gita Hall May, a former Swedish actress with a young daughter by her first husband, actor Barry Sullivan, spent considerable time with Beatty after becoming engaged to Mitch May in 1962. "Warren was very polite — you could see he was very well brought up. He had very good manners, unlike some other Hollywood types I met, so he always gave me a very favorable impression. . . . he was a very nice man."

While May's first wife, Verne O'Hara, did not think of Beatty as a one-woman man, she had a similarly high opinion of him, saying, "If it wasn't for his womanizing, Warren would be the perfect man."

To the public, Beatty played up his image as a Casanova, an aspect of his personality that seemed to intrigue, and confound, him. When Charlie Feldman approached him earlier that spring to star as a playboy in a farcical film that Feldman had originally bought for Cary Grant, the agent wrote enthusiastically to a friend, "Warren is crazy to do it" — the beginning of a long journey that would lead Beatty to make the film *Shampoo*.[6]

The script Feldman owned was called *Lot's Wife* and was based on a Czech play adapted by director Billy Wilder's writing partner I. A. L. Diamond. Warren Beatty was eager to do the movie for several reasons. After four dark films in a row, he was anxious to appear in a comedy; the script reminded him of Renoir's classic farce *Rules of the Game*; and Feldman had offered him the opportunity to coproduce it. Most revealingly, Beatty said he was drawn to "the plight of the compulsive Don Juan. It always struck me as a pathetic and funny character, a victim of himself or society or his conquests or whatever — but a victim."[7]

While Beatty was filming *Lilith* on Long Island, he and Feldman looked for a gag writer to punch up Diamond's dated Don Juan script, which they renamed *What's New, Pussycat* after Feldman heard Beatty whisper his trademark greeting to a girlfriend on the phone. The movie star showed a producer's instinct for talent, gravitating to Elaine May, Mike Nichols's eccentric comedy partner, who turned down Beatty's offer to write the script but became a close friend.[8] His second choice was a young Jewish comic named Woody Allen, whom Beatty considered "brilliant" when he and Feldman saw Allen perform at a New York nightclub, the Blue Angel, that summer. Feldman and Beatty offered Woody Allen his first screenwriting job in July 1963 for thirty thousand dollars, which the stand-up comic shrewdly negotiated to include a part in the movie.

While Woody Allen rewrote the script for *What's New, Pussycat* that fall, John Springer sent a letter to Columbia Records trying to elicit interest in Warren Beatty as a singer, "in the light of record successes of unexpected people like [Richard] Chamberlain, [George] Maharis and Vince Edwards." He touted Beatty's experience as a cocktail lounge singer and pianist, describing his style as a cross between cabaret artists Bobby Short and Mabel Mercer, the actor's favorite vocalist. As evidence of how many years it had been since Warren Beatty starred in a movie, his press agent reminded the record company that Beatty was "exceptionally handsome," adding, "I'm enclosing a couple of pictures to refresh you on how he looks."[9] Columbia was interested enough to request a demo record, but nothing came of the queries—which were proof of Beatty's serious interest in becoming a singer, and of his career confusion, exacerbated by the disastrous *Lilith*.

Beatty's other iron in the fire in the fall of 1963 was *Honeybear, I Think I Love You*, the New Wave comedy he still hoped to option from Charles Eastman, its protective writer, with whom he had developed an odd mutual respect. According to Eastman, Beatty felt proprietary about *Honeybear*, and viewed the young Robert Redford, who was getting attention for his matinee idol looks and his intellect, as a rival. "Redford was trying to make a deal in which he would produce *Honeybear*, and I remember Warren's words were, 'Oh, he's trying to—he's imitating me, is he?' I never hear Hollywood *women* openly competitive, it's the men who are very aware of who's coming along, and who's getting the part."

That October, during a trip East, Beatty made a cold call to Arthur Penn at his home, trying to interest him in *Honeybear*.[10] Penn, the respected stage director of *The Miracle Worker* who had dropped out of *A Loss of Roses*, was on the select list of names of people with whom Beatty told Jane Fonda in 1959 he hoped to work someday.

The director met Beatty at the Delmonico Hotel within an hour, carrying a script that was his own passion project, *Mickey One*. The sensitive Beatty felt an instant affinity for the cerebral Penn, who had a deep respect and infinite patience for Method actors—the antithesis of Rossen. Beatty praised

Penn for having the "soul of an artist," while Penn said later that he found Beatty "deeply confused but attractive," with "a reputation for being uncooperative and difficult."[11]

In spite of these red flags, Penn offered Beatty the starring role in *Mickey One*, a low-budget, abstract drama — originally a play — about a comic pursued by the Chicago mob. The director envisioned it in a nouvelle vague style, "meant as the ultimate McCarthy paranoia picture."[12]

Arthur Penn's similarly avant-garde production manager, Harrison Starr, who had worked with Godard and Truffaut, and had helped to attract Belgian artist Ghislain Cloquet to shoot the film, took a dubious view of Warren Beatty.[13] "Not to reflect badly on Warren, I thought we were going for star power, and I thought that was a mistake," said Starr. "I thought we should have looked hard and found an extraordinarily eccentric guy who had still a sufficient charisma to hold the center of the film. Warren was almost too big for the film. And I voiced that to Arthur, and at the same time I could see that Arthur was hooked. Warren is a very bright man, and consequently he can engage someone in real terms, with real substance, and it's hard for a director to turn that down." Beatty, in a way, seduced Penn, the gift he had possessed since childhood. "Arthur is interior," observed Starr. "Almost sometimes neurasthenic ways of working. And I could see how Warren appealed to Arthur."

Starr, a sometime collaborator of Rossen's, had "already heard Warren's reputation. Stubborn, wanted to take control. Forced takes, forced takes . . . if you get in a discussion about a script, you're going to get something from him. At the same time, ultimately Warren wants to run the show." To Starr, a fiercely intelligent production manager, Warren Beatty represented "a challenge."

Beatty, who was waiting for Woody Allen to finish his rewrite of *What's New, Pussycat,* and who did not own the rights to *Honeybear,* instantly committed to *Mickey One,* neither the light comedy he wanted nor the commercial movie he needed. As always, Beatty chose the film for its director, someone he respected who could impart knowledge, following the pattern from his childhood, when his mother had directed him in her Richmond little-theater productions.

Beatty announced plans to star in *Mickey One* in November 1963, as Woody Allen was completing the first draft of the Don Juan comedy *What's New, Pussycat.* On November 22, the afternoon John F. Kennedy was shot, "I was at Stanley Kubrick's apartment on Central Park West, trying to get him to direct the movie *What's New, Pussycat,*" recalled Beatty. As he was leaving Kubrick's building, he heard, on the radio, that the president he had been asked to play in a movie had been assassinated. "I was on my way to a meeting with Woody Allen and Charlie Feldman. We were going to read the latest version of that picture . . . we were all stunned."[14] The impact of that tragedy on Warren Beatty would come out in future films.

Beatty had spent the previous few days with two of President Kennedy's sisters, Jean Kennedy Smith and Peter Lawford's wife, Pat Kennedy Lawford, taking them to lunch and to a private screening of *Dr. Strangelove.*[15] Beatty had also had a Lawford connection on the eve of Marilyn Monroe's death the year before. Natalie Wood said later that she and Beatty had seen Monroe at Lawford's house in Malibu hours before her death, and Beatty would tell journalist Bill Zehme in 1990 that he played cards with Marilyn Monroe the night before she died, although he never elaborated on it.[16]

Beatty spent the Thanksgiving after JFK's assassination with Shirley MacLaine at their parents' house in Arlington, close to the funeral procession in Washington, D.C. The holiday seemed to mark a rapprochement between brother and sister, whose political consciousness had been stirred during the Kennedy years.[17]

After his visit to Virginia to see his parents and sister, Beatty officially formed his first company to produce movies, which he named "Tatira," for Tat and Ira, the truest indication of how deeply he felt about his mother and father. That January, he opened a Tatira office in New York, after attending the funeral of Maynard Morris, the MCA agent who had discovered, and championed, him when he had started at Stella Adler's seven years before.

In early February, Beatty flew back to Los Angeles to discuss Woody Allen's latest draft of *What's New, Pussycat* with Charles Feldman before starting rehearsals for *Mickey One.* While he was there, he attended a party at The Bistro hosted by agent Freddie Fields to promote a few movie star clients Fields hoped would be nominated for Academy Awards. One was French actress Leslie Caron, who was in Hollywood to tape a Robert Goulet television special and to publicize her current film, *The L-Shaped Room.*

According to his friend Richard Sylbert, Beatty had become infatuated with Caron's gamine, doll-like beauty after seeing her in *Gigi* and *An American in Paris*—similar to his fascination with Joan Collins after spotting her on a magazine cover in the late fifties.[18] Caron reportedly reminded him of the winsome young girl in Auguste Renoir's *A Girl with a Watering Can,* said to be Beatty's favorite painting.[19]

Freddie Fields would recall Beatty as flirting with everyone at the party, concealing what Caron was to describe as an "electric attraction" between them, one that would alter both their lives.[20] "Was he flirting with Leslie or was he flirting with someone next to Leslie, or was he flirting with someone behind Leslie?" pondered Fields. "I don't know."[21] At the end of the evening, Beatty left unnoticed with Leslie Caron, whom he had just met.[22]

Caron, who was married to respected English stage director Peter Hall, with whom she had two young children, was not the sort of woman to fall into an affair. She described herself later as "discreet, well-mannered, not at all wild and never wanted to be. I don't like misbehavior of any kind."[23] Caron said she found Beatty "irresistible."[24] Writer Michael Laughlin, the actress's third husband and a friend of Beatty's, understood why. "Warren's success with women is partly because he drops everything to devote himself."

Leslie Caron, who conceded later that her marriage was weak because her husband had become, in his words, "a man possessed" with his work at the Royal Shakespeare Company, and disdainful of her Hollywood career, was vulnerable to Beatty's "strong wooing," as she described it.[25] The affair, however, made her feel conflicted. As she said afterward, "I have been help-lessly in love and known it was wrong."[26]

For Beatty, Leslie Caron not only appealed to his sense of aesthetics, she also was another in a series of actresses with parallels to his sister and mother — a link to his past, to the women he loved. Caron was six years older, thirty-two to Beatty's twenty-six. Like Shirley MacLaine, she had stud-ied ballet as a child, and her mother, a former dancer, lived through Caron's career. Within a few days after Beatty began the romance, Leslie Caron was nominated for an Academy Award for Best Actress. Two of the other nomi-nees were Shirley MacLaine and Natalie Wood.

Beatty and Caron kept their passionate affair a secret as he flew to New York to rehearse *Mickey One* in the middle of February, and she left shortly afterward for London, to see her family prior to starting the movie *Father Goose*. "After a couple of days," recounted Peter Hall, "Leslie told me she was in love with Warren Beatty and had decided to leave me and go back to Hollywood." In future years, Hall was to say he "didn't blame Leslie, I didn't even blame Warren Beatty. He was just the catalyst for a split that had long been inevitable." At the time, the director was "devastated."[27]

Beatty's guilt over breaking up Caron's marriage, and the depth of his feeling for her, were apparent in his communications with Charlie Feldman, who had let him use his house after the breakup with Natalie Wood, and had been his advisor in the forlorn months before and during *Lilith*. Beatty phoned Feldman from New York, telling his mentor that he had a "personal secret," one that he would entrust to Feldman. He revealed the affair with Leslie Caron, saying she was "the one girl in the world" for him, and that Feldman was the only person he had told.[28]

The stress of his illicit affair with Caron, and of rehearsing the complicated *Mickey One*, erupted a few days later over *What's New, Pussycat*. Beatty was concerned that Feldman wanted to cast Capucine, his girlfriend and a French actress of limited range, in the film, and he noticed that Woody Allen's part had become increasingly prominent, while his own was shrinking with each rewrite. On March 1, Beatty wrote a letter to his mentor expressing regret that they had released their "constipated" feelings in a "torrent of hostility," and closing, "So — if you'll accept a moment of honest sentiment — allow me to say that you've been a good and loving friend especially in a period of loneliness for me and that it has been something that has moved me more than a few times. Love, Warren."[29] The next day, Beatty left for Chicago to start *Mickey One*. In a perverse omen, the first day of filming was Friday the thirteenth.

Beatty found a suite with a piano on the twenty-seventh floor of the Astor Tower and largely kept to himself as the struggle for creative control between the equally opinionated star and director, anticipated by the production manager, began to unfold. "We had a lot of trouble on that film," Beatty said candidly, "because I didn't know what the hell Arthur was trying to do and I tried to find out . . . I'm not sure that he knew himself."[30]

Their contention started with a contretemps over Beatty's character, a nightclub comic. "To me the stand-up gags that the guy had to do in *Mickey One* were not funny," observed Beatty, "and that was always my complaint with Arthur, that the jokes were some attempt to attain some sort of universality, some appeal to intellect that I didn't find funny at all. I felt that they were pretentious jokes . . . that was the greatest source of the problem. I felt if I was playing a comedian I ought to be funny."[31] Penn's rejoinder was that "Warren did not want to play the role the way I wanted him to play it."[32]

Harrison Starr, the producer in the middle, recalled, "He and Arthur had go-arounds . . . the role was basically a role of an eccentric, a person whose inner demons were reflected in the world he inhabited . . . and I think that was difficult for Warren to play. He wanted to play it more as a Broadway showbiz guy."

Beatty made a pal of his good-natured leading lady, actress Alexandra

Stewart, a patrician blonde from Canada who moved to France at seventeen to go to art school and was put into French films by Cloquet. "I did a movie in 1963 with Louis Malle called *Le Feu Follet*, a beautiful movie," recalled Stewart, who had a child with Malle. "And one day Arthur Penn is looking for a young girl, Midwestern girl, to play this sort of fiancée of Warren Beatty, who's a pure sort of girl who doesn't know what's going on. And because Louis Malle was already quite a director, Arthur saw his movie *Le Feu Follet* and said, 'That's her — we can give it kind of a European look.'"[33] Stewart, who spoke fluent French and was by then the girlfriend of director François Truffaut, had additional cachet for Penn "because he very much admired Truffaut." Similar to Beatty, Alexandra Stewart found Penn's obtuse New Wave–inspired film "kind of irritating."

While they were making *Mickey One*, Stewart noticed that Beatty seemed to be going through a difficult time. By chance, Woody Allen was performing at a club in Chicago called Mister Kelly, and Beatty took his costar to see Allen perform, mentioning the script for *What's New, Pussycat*, which Stewart hoped might include a role for her. "And I kept saying, 'Warren, do you think you're going to do this movie?' And he said, 'Well, you know . . .' I think he was waiting. He was like Paul Newman, whose sister I played in *Exodus* — these gorgeous creatures, and they're not sure of themselves. And Warren, because he'd just come out of this terrible Robert Rossen thing, he was . . . he sometimes couldn't remember his lines."

Penn's patient direction was the opposite of the combative Rossen. "There was one particular scene, which was difficult, where Warren was alone on the stage," said Stewart, referring to the film's intense climax. "They did that over and over and over. I had such a headache on this, psychosomatic headaches, they had to bring in a sort of old Japanese masseuse during lunch." Roberta Hodes, the crisply intelligent script supervisor, who often worked with Kazan, compared Penn's direction of Warren Beatty to "the feeling of breaking in a young horse," recalling one infamous day "where he did sixty-nine takes to get Warren to behave . . . to sort of settle down and do the performance."[34]

Harrison Starr explained. "That's the way Warren thought he could take control, but he couldn't . . . I think Arthur always took William Wyler as his exemplar. Wyler would go for as many takes as it took to get what he wanted . . . Warren was trying to get what he wanted, Arthur was trying to get what he wanted, and they were just goin' around, and then one or the other was going to get something. But of course, what I'm sure Warren ultimately knew, is that you get him in the cutting room." In Hodes's view, Penn's sixty-nine takes were "probably symbolic of the relationship in some way. Maybe Warren appreciated that he wouldn't take shit from him."

Unlike *Lilith*, Beatty and his director would emerge from their discord with mutual respect. "*Mickey One*, truthfully, I did not enjoy making it," Beatty said later. "I liked it on a personal level, the people involved . . . I do respect the picture."[35] Arthur Penn later would concede that the film suffered from his "youthful excess" as a director, and said of Beatty, "On *Mickey One* we'd had deep disagreements. Warren thought the script was too mannered and intellectual, and I have to admit he was right."[36]

As on *Lilith*, the "artistic differences" between Beatty and his director resulted in what Hodes called "general antagonism towards Warren" on the set, prompted by "arrogance, arrogance, and smart-ass-ness." The lesson, for Beatty, from these recurring conflicts had announced itself. "It was clear to me I should get my act together and make my own pictures or it wouldn't be an enjoyable proposition for me."[37]

Beatty was also under pressure in his personal life. When Leslie Caron returned to the States in mid-March to prepare for *Father Goose*, she stopped in Chicago to see Beatty, showing up on the set of *Mickey One* incognito. "He kept appearing with a woman in sunglasses and a babushka," recalled the script supervisor, "and she came on the set every day. She was passing as — Bob Jiras was the beard, apparently." Beatty introduced Caron as "Mrs. Smith" to Alexandra Stewart, who found their attempt at disguise "adorable." Stewart immediately recognized the star of *Lili*, her favorite film from boarding school, recalling, "I saw eight times *Hi-Lili, Hi-Lo!*'" Stewart was amused that Beatty thought anyone would be fooled by his hiding Leslie Caron under a hat, "with her French accent and blue, blue, blue, blue eyes." Roberta Hodes recalled, "One day I went up to her and I said, 'You know, you look like Leslie Caron.' And of course that blew her cover, and she came the next day without all that." According to the producer, the crew "muted" the fact that the married Caron was staying with Warren Beatty in Chicago.

During her visits, Caron took care of Beatty. "She sat right up front in one of those director's chairs," said Hodes, "and she brought him oxygen. Some of these stars have little bits of oxygen tanks, and she was watching over him, and taking care. It was very long hours, a difficult shoot. And she would take care of him. Very motherly." Hodes also noticed that Beatty "would put something like eye drops in his eyes before the take."

Harrison Starr, who interacted with the cast regularly as production manager, knew about Beatty's oxygen tank and that "he was very conscious of himself physically, though it never was obtrusive." In his observation, Beatty was "very, very deeply involved with Leslie Caron." Despite his overwhelming feelings for the French actress, and hers for him, Beatty flirted with Alexandra Stewart before and after Caron's secret trip to Chicago, often pinching his playful costar. "I pinched him back," she chuckled. "I'm always teasing." Stewart, who was expecting a visit from her beau, Truffaut, succumbed to Beatty's charm, which intensified "the more he knew my boyfriend was coming from Paris. And I don't find American actors, or most actors, particularly charming, frankly. But Warren is so — I mean nobody can deny, or nobody can resist."

The dalliance with Alexandra Stewart was a continuation of Beatty's sexual behavior throughout his romance with Natalie Wood, and at the end of his engagement to Joan Collins, to whom he previously had been faithful. The fact that he referred to such infidelities later as "ethical failures," suggested that Beatty had lingering Baptist guilt about his emerging lifestyle, one reason he was drawn to play the Don Juan character in *What's New, Pussycat*, whom he described as "a man struggling with the sexual revolution."[38]

In certain respects, Beatty's dating pattern replicated his high school years, when he and his clique paired off but also dated outside their relationships. His need as an adult for a loving partnership with one woman, while still seeking affection from others, may also have sprung from his role in childhood as the cherished only son of Kathlyn Beaty, who was also adored by a variety of female cousins, aunts, great-aunts, grandmothers, and his sister.

Alexandra Stewart was not Beatty's only flirtation during *Mickey One*. "When we were shooting in the Playboy mansion," Stewart recollected, "nobody could find Warren at two in the morning." Even the no-nonsense script supervisor, who disliked Beatty, got the impression that he had thoughts of seducing her when they discussed a screenplay she wanted to get produced. "Warren came over to speak to me, and he looked at me — I was older than him of course — and I knew he was considering me as a bed opportunity, and looked me over. It was just going through his mind, 'Is she a lay or not?' If he was looking at me, he must have looked elsewhere, too. There are men like that that can't pass up an opportunity."

In Alexandra Stewart's opinion, Leslie Caron had to be aware of Beatty's indiscretions. "I don't know how anyone *couldn't*." At the same time, Stewart, a self-described "playgirl" then, recognized that Beatty was under strain from concealing his romance with the married French actress, feeling guilty, "and I think he liked me because it's nice to have somebody light, in the middle of that."

Beatty's pressures escalated when Caron left Chicago a few weeks before the Oscars. She told columnists in Hollywood that she was "happily in love" with her husband, Peter Hall, and that Hall and their two children would be joining her in California after he directed his new play.[39] A few days later, on April 5, Peter Hall issued a terse statement from London announcing their "joint" separation, citing unspecified career demands, exposing Caron to gossip on the eve of the Academy Awards ceremony.[40]

Throughout this tense several-week period, Beatty "bombarded" Charles Feldman with cables from Chicago, imploring him to reply about the status of *What's New, Pussycat* "so I can concentrate on the picture I'm doing."[41] Upset by their previous discussions about Capucine, Feldman ignored the wires. When Beatty sneaked into Los Angeles on Sunday, April 12, to spend the day before the Oscars with Caron, he left more messages for Feldman. On Monday, the thirteenth, he returned to Chicago, and Leslie Caron attended the Academy Awards ceremony with her parents, looking "wistful and sad."[42] To add to Caron's regret, Patricia Neal won Best Actress, besting Caron, MacLaine, and Wood.

Three days later, Beatty's delicate and tangled situations with both Leslie Caron and Charles Feldman began to unravel because of this item in a Harrison Carroll column in the *Los Angeles Herald-Examiner:*

> Nobody will admit it, but I hear that Warren Beatty flew here last Saturday night, spent Sunday with Leslie Caron and was back on the "Mickey One" set in Chicago on Monday morning. As I get it, Leslie made several trips to Chicago. The word there was that she was talking to Warren about a part in his next picture, "What's New, Pussycat" . . .

Carroll's gossip item was reinforced by a headline in Sheilah Graham's column the same day proclaiming, in bold letters, "BEATTY WANTS LESLIE FOR HIS 'PUSSYCAT.'"

Feldman reacted to what he perceived as Beatty's underhanded tactics by dictating a blistering five-page letter later that day, which he never sent. In it, he accused Beatty of planting the Leslie Caron items to pressure Feldman into dropping his French girlfriend, Capucine, from the film, putting his protégé on notice that he would "cast the picture and do the film my way."

The rest of Feldman's unsent letter revealed how deeply Beatty felt about Leslie Caron and how upset the actor was by the circumstances of their affair. "If you are not concentrating on the picture it is certainly due to your emotional life," scolded Feldman, adding, "your emotional problems are one thing, the picture is something else again." He went on to state frankly to Beatty, "There are many things I would like to level with you about, and though I am deeply concerned about your emotional life, I am not going to put myself in a position where I am going to crack up because of your personal problems."

Later in the letter, Feldman warned Beatty that the romance with Caron that Beatty found such a "help" to him personally "could very possibly prove otherwise insofar as your career-life is concerned . . . as far as I know the young lady is everything you think she is, and possibly more . . . I hope so for your sake. I hope so for her sake . . . and from what I gather you have pretty well made up your mind."

After deciding not to mail the letter to Beatty, the actor's Hollywood advisor sent a cable to him in Chicago, beseeching Warren to stop planting items in the press, informing him that the script and cast for *Pussycat* had not been approved, and stating simply that he hoped they would see each other soon. Beatty cabled Feldman back immediately to say he understood there were problems with the *Pussycat* deal and he would look for another script in the interim, and to express hope that "we can find a solution."

That same March–April, at the height of his distress, Beatty had dinner one evening in Chicago with Arthur Penn and Alexandra Stewart, leading to a conversation that would plant a seed for the movie that would change not only his career but Hollywood.

Anticipating the arrival of François Truffaut, Stewart happened to remark that an American producer named Lewis Allen had approached Truffaut "suggesting that there was this sort of couple, Clyde Barrow and Bonnie Parker — this young Texas couple who had become sort of famous there because they were handsome, and young, and such and such. I had never heard of them. And so I remember saying to Arthur and Warren at dinner, 'Have you ever heard of this couple, this young couple, Barrow and Parker?' and this and that. And then Arthur said, 'Oh yes, yes, yes . . . yes, absolutely,' and I said, 'Well, because my friend François Truffaut is interested in doing it eventually, and with me playing the role of Bonnie.'" Penn and Beatty, who had discussed making a Western together after *Mickey One*, seemed intrigued, according to Stewart, but it was Beatty whose "little ears perked up."

Years later, Leslie Caron would state confidently, "Neither Warren nor Alexandra Stewart knew anything about *Bonnie and Clyde* while filming *Mickey One*," the first in what would be a skein of conflicting stories, hidden truths, and false gossip misreported as fact about the history of the groundbreaking film.[43] Stewart's tip about Truffaut to her costar during *Mickey One* was one of the truths kept a secret, in this case by the sly Beatty, who did not even tell Caron.

In fact, the treatment for *Bonnie and Clyde* had been written expressly for Truffaut, who was in New York to meet the writers at roughly the same time his girlfriend mentioned it to Beatty and to Penn. By synchronicity, the idea to write a script about Clyde Barrow and Bonnie Parker came to Robert Benton and David Newman, two film buffs who worked at *Esquire* magazine, shortly after Benton chanced to meet Warren Beatty. Benton later would recall this meeting as taking place once the script was completed, but it occurred just before he thought of the idea, in spring 1963, as Beatty was starting *Lilith*.[44] Benton was at writer Herb Sargent's apartment in New York, "adrift" after a painful breakup with feminist journalist Gloria Steinem, then twenty-nine, when Beatty stopped by with Natalie Wood, a close friend of Sargent's wife.* Wood, an accomplished pianist herself, tinkled on a toy piano the melody from the title song to *Oliver!*, which had just opened on Broadway. "And it was so great," remarked Benton, "I mean I fell in love instantly." The writer, who had interviewed Wood during her marriage to Wagner, took little notice of Beatty other than to observe astutely "the difference in Natalie before Warren and after Warren — he really educated her in a way." Three years later, Beatty would become his Clyde Barrow, and Wood would reject the role of Bonnie.

Benton's despondency that spring over his broken romance with Gloria Steinem, on the cusp of fame, kindled his love affair with François Truffaut's films. "I had had in my life, until I got married, a series of the most unfortunate affairs." As a balm, the sensitive Benton went to see "an enormous number of times," *Jules and Jim*, Truffaut's poignant Valentine to the nouvelle vague, about two friends in a love triangle. "It was like a life raft, because it was about somebody surviving." In another instance of synchronicity, Benton and his pal at *Esquire*, David Newman, "were both by chance — or not by chance, well we talked about stuff all the time — reading a book by John Toland on John Dillinger. In that book there is a footnote about Bonnie

*Actress Norma Crane.

Parker and Clyde Barrow. And I had grown up in Texas, and my father had gone to their funeral, and I had grown up with all those stories about Bonnie and Clyde — the people they gave money to, and what romantic heroes they were, and that the kids would go to Halloween parties dressed up as Bonnie or Clyde." Toland's footnote, and Benton's family lore, inspired Benton and Newman to write a script about the fabled outlaw couple in the spirit of the New Wave of European cinema, with the fantasy that François Truffaut might direct.

In an odd way, Gloria Steinem was the muse behind *Bonnie and Clyde*, setting the pattern for a sequence of unheralded women who would help to launch Beatty's cult film. The fairy godmother of *Bonnie and Clyde*, in its early stages, was Elinor Wright Jones, a bright young producer married to a former classmate of Benton's at the University of Texas, Tom Jones, the lyricist for *The Fantasticks*. Elinor Jones and Benton, an art director at *Esquire*, had coproduced a prize-winning short film that told its story through paintings. It was Jones whom Benton contacted first with the idea for *Bonnie and Clyde*. As a bonus, Jones worked for New York–based producer Lewis Allen, who was setting up *Fahrenheit 451* for Truffaut, giving her an entrée to Benton's dream director.

The last week of August 1963, Benton and Newman began outlining *Bonnie and Clyde*, "heavily influenced" by *Jules and Jim* and "some old sort of detective magazines with stories about Bonnie and Clyde," Benton would recall. By the end of November they had seventy-five pages setting forth in detail the story, and the way they envisioned the film, which included a ménage à trois between the couple and the character eventually played by Michael J. Pollard — their homage to *Jules and Jim*. "We didn't know how to write a screenplay, but we wrote a treatment."

Benton staged a reading in his small apartment, inviting Elinor Jones, who brought her boss, producer Lew Allen, and Helen Scott, who had just left her post as director of the French Film Office to work with Allen and Truffaut on *Fahrenheit 451*. Scott had also coauthored a book on Hitchcock with Truffaut, who spoke little English and had great respect for her translations and her opinion.

After the reading, "I was ready to sacrifice my life to do this film," expressed Elinor Jones. "I just thought it was the most exciting thing I had ever come across in my life."[45] At Jones's urging, Helen Scott championed *Bonnie and Clyde*, sending a copy of the treatment to her friend and collaborator Truffaut in Paris that December, with a letter personally recommending it.

As a courtesy, Lew Allen cabled the French director asking him to read the treatment, a gesture that would result in Truffaut biographers' misstating that Allen owned the original rights to *Bonnie and Clyde*.[46]

Elinor Wright Jones was the person who first secured the film rights to *Bonnie and Clyde*, in partnership with her brother, Norton Wright, a former line producer married to an actress in *The Fantasticks*. "We were all François Truffaut–philes," said Jones's brother. "I got involved because I had been a unit production manager. I was very good at the business of taking a script, breaking it down, making the strip board, knowing how many days it was going to take to shoot, and then doing a budget, and I knew some crew guys. So I knew how to make the movie."[47]

Their lawyer, the well-connected Robert Montgomery, negotiated an eighteen-month option on *Bonnie and Clyde* for Jones and Wright in December, scheduled to begin in May 1964, when Benton and Newman hoped to finish the script, and ending on November 27, 1965, a date Warren Beatty eventually would track like a hawk.

In the mythology that would form around Beatty's classic gangster film, Elinor Wright Jones and her brother would be misidentified as husband and wife, portrayed as inept, and reported to have purchased *Bonnie and Clyde* from Benton and Newman for ten thousand dollars. The sum was one thousand seven hundred dollars, Elinor Jones would clarify, "and to us it seemed enormous." For Robert Benton and David Newman, who, as Benton said, "just sort of eked out a living," the money was crucial, and Elinor Jones remains "one of the great unsung heroes of *Bonnie and Clyde*." As he observed, "Ellie and Norton gave us kind of seed money for the script. We used some of that money to go down to Texas, and drive around in Texas, and go to the gravesites, so that David could get a feeling for it."

As the coproducer of *Bonnie and Clyde*, the well-bred Jones, who spoke French, followed up conscientiously with Truffaut, who wrote to her in February of 1964 expressing "interest" in the treatment.[48] Privately, the French director fretted about the language barrier to Alexandra Stewart, who was soon to leave Paris to start *Mickey One* with Warren Beatty. "François had great difficulties in speaking English, this is his enormous problem, obsession. That's why he wanted me as Bonnie . . . and so he kept saying, 'Well, I don't know . . .'"

When Truffaut arrived in New York at the end of March to meet an ecstatic Benton and Newman — around the time Stewart revealed to Beatty and Penn in Chicago that she might play Bonnie — a third party became interested in *Bonnie and Clyde*. As Benton was to recall, "Truffaut thought we should see a movie that we had never seen called *Gun Crazy*, which is a brilliant film. There was a small private screening, and sitting in the audience with us was Jean-Luc Godard. He was there with a girl, not his wife. Anna Karina . . . we were so shy we could barely say hello."

Benton and Newman, who idolized Godard, were unaware that the skittish Truffaut was considering him as a backup director because he could speak better English, or that Godard had an interest in their script, the first of several secrets concealed during this visit to the United States, one of which would involve the equally mysterious Beatty.

In addition to his inspired idea to have them study *Gun Crazy*, an admired low-budget film noir with parallels to *Bonnie and Clyde*, Truffaut spent two days with Benton and Newman at the Regency Hotel meticulously analyzing their seventy-five-page treatment to assist them in writing the screenplay, using Helen Scott as a translator.

Truffaut suggested several changes that would be in the movie Warren Beatty eventually produced. "It was his idea to have Bonnie write her poem, then cut to a Texas Ranger reading it in a newspaper, and then cut to Clyde reading the poem from the newspaper to Bonnie," revealed Benton.[49] Jones, who kept a diary, noted that Truffaut also advised them to break down the treatment into twenty-eight scenes. As he was leaving for Chicago to see Alexandra Stewart, the director mentioned that he had her in mind to play Bonnie, with Harrison Starr as the production manager on location in Texas.[50]

Curiously, Truffaut never mentioned *Bonnie and Clyde* to Starr on the set of *Mickey One*. "He wanted to talk about the picture he intended to make next, which was *Fahrenheit*," noted Starr, who seemed to recall that Beatty "made a point" of meeting Truffaut then, an encounter the actor would keep to himself. "Warren is very, very capable that way." Beatty, who had been put on hold for *What's New, Pussycat* and was looking for a script to produce, or act in, hoped to talk to Truffaut about *Bonnie and Clyde*. As Stewart recalled, "Warren, from time to time, kept sort of asking me about it." The handicap, for Beatty, was that Truffaut spoke only French.

The saga took its next intriguing turn when Jean-Luc Godard visited the *Mickey One* set after Truffaut left, and told Harrison Starr that *he* would be directing *Bonnie and Clyde*. According to Starr, Godard gave him a copy of Benton and Newman's treatment to evaluate, "and wanted to know about shooting it in Texas," with Starr as the producer. Starr discussed financing with the head of Columbia, Mike Frankovich, "and Frankovich wanted to do it for under four hundred thousand, four hundred four."

What was bizarre about this meeting was that Elinor Jones and Norton Wright, who owned the rights to *Bonnie and Clyde,* had no idea that Godard had a copy of the treatment, or that he had asked Starr to produce the movie for him to direct. "I never heard of a Chicago meeting," Jones remarked forty years later. "I just find it amazing." Since Truffaut was unsure he could direct *Bonnie and Clyde* in English, and considered suggesting Godard as a substitute, it was possible that Truffaut had asked Godard to approach Starr in Chicago. The other possibility was that Godard went behind Truffaut's back to try to direct *Bonnie and Clyde.* Either way, as Norton Wright observed, "Ellie and I were absolutely unaware of the Godard–Harrison Starr 'B' story."

The ending to this "B" story involved Warren Beatty. As Starr told it, "Back in Chicago, I have the *Bonnie and Clyde* script on my desk. And Warren comes into my office, as he was wont to do, because he hadn't seen the kind of production that we were doing — he came basically from a Hollywood production setup — and he said, 'So . . . can I read that?' And I said, 'Sure, go ahead.' A couple of days later, he returned it to me. That's the last I heard."

The cagey Beatty would conceal the fact that he read Starr's copy of the *Bonnie and Clyde* treatment, provided by Godard, in 1964. In future interviews about the film, Beatty would consistently maintain that he heard about the script for the first time in the summer of 1965, in Paris. "He took it *off my desk* in Chicago," insisted Starr. "I know he took it off my desk, that I know as well as I know that I was born at a certain time and who my parents were. I remember him saying, 'Can I look at that?'"

Ironically, Beatty provided indirect validation for Starr's account. When he was honored at a film festival in 2002, Beatty disclosed that he had met Godard in Chicago during *Mickey One* in 1964, and that Godard "was interested in *Bonnie and Clyde* at that point" — the "B" story only he, Harrison Starr, and Goddard knew about.[51]

At the end of April, Truffaut confirmed to Elinor Jones and Norton Wright that he was still interested in directing *Bonnie and Clyde,* saying nothing to them about Godard. He told Jones that he would give her a final answer once he had read the new screenplay.

After Beatty completed *Mickey One* at the end of May, he joined Leslie Caron in Jamaica, where she was shooting location scenes for *Father Goose.*

They kept their relationship discreet, renting a walled estate, where Beatty remained in hiding.[52]

The swinging bachelor image he had told Springer he wanted to project to the public was now a concern to Beatty, according to Caron, evidence of the conflict between the Hollywood Beatty and his Virginia past. "He was considered just a playboy. He had spent too much time wooing women in the public eye. Of course it bothered him that he wasn't taken seriously. We used to talk about it. He was in despair about it."[53]

Cary Grant, Caron's leading man in *Father Goose*, was one of the few who saw her with Beatty on location in Jamaica, and he later remarked "how deeply in love Warren Beatty was with Leslie Caron." Grant told Maureen Donaldson, his companion in the seventies, "It's Leslie who was the love of Warren's life. I saw them together on the set and they were bonkers for each other."[54]

It was Grant, ironically, who unwittingly instigated the painful scandal that would doom Beatty and Caron's relationship. It began when Grant invited long-time journalist pal Roderick Mann to visit him in Jamaica toward the end of filming. Mann, who knew Warren Beatty was there, "lurking about," interviewed Leslie Caron for the *London Express*, and mentioned in the piece that Beatty "flew down here amid secrecy." The article, which quoted Caron saying she would decide whether to settle in Hollywood after her children spent the summer with her, inflamed her estranged husband, who had recently filed for divorce.[55]

The day that Mann's interview with Leslie Caron appeared in the London paper, Peter Hall's solicitor amended his divorce suit to charge Caron with four acts of adultery, and naming Warren Beatty as a corespondent, with photographic evidence from a private investigator.[56] Hall also sought a restraining order to enjoin the actress from taking their seven-year-old son and five-year-old daughter out of England.[57] The divorce case made headlines around the world, permanently branding Beatty and Caron as adulterers, though Hall would later confess that he, too, had had an affair during the marriage.

Caron, who was in "shock," flew to France the following night for a costume fitting en route to picking up her children.[58] As she got off the plane in Paris, Hall's lawyer served her with an injunction. The actress hired counsel in London, providing written assurance to the court that she would not take her children out of England without Peter Hall's written consent or a court order. Hall responded by seeking custody of their son, Chris, and daughter,

Jenny, a lawsuit that would cast a shadow over Beatty's romance with Caron and alter both their lives and their careers.

Peter Hall later expressed regret for his actions, which Caron considered an "attack." Hall rationalized his decisions as having been in the best interests of their children, saying, "Quite apart from the dubious stability of Leslie's relationship with Warren Beatty, I did not believe she would make a permanent new life in Hollywood, a place she both admired and loathed . . . the children would be caught up in these hectic changes."[59]

In a memoir, Hall blamed his "ruthless and cynical" solicitor. "He told me that if Leslie took Jenny and Christopher to America, no court there was ever likely to allow them out of their mother's control . . . [saying] unless he served a notice on Leslie as she stepped off the plane, making the children wards of court, I had no chance . . . I had until the next day to make up my mind, and spent a sleepless night. I despise revenge. Was I taking this stand to pay Leslie back for loving Beatty? By the morning, I believed I knew what was best, and told the solicitor to go ahead. I hate the law. Victory depends on who can play the game in the quickest and most cool-headed way."[60]

Beatty, who flew to London to be with Caron, was also in the throes of delicate renegotiations with Feldman to coproduce and star in *What's New, Pussycat*, at a salary of two hundred thousand dollars. His guilt over Caron's custody battle was apparent in a handwritten note he got from Feldman, who had warned him, months before, that the affair might damage his career. "We know of your personal problem," Feldman wrote to him, "and will do anything to cooperate, but you too must be mindful of your money problems . . . Let's make a good film. Love, C."[61]

On July 23, Beatty took a letter he typed himself, confirming his acceptance of *What's New, Pussycat*, to Feldman, who had flown to London. The contract terms were included in the body of the letter, with Beatty's handwritten suggested changes. Typically, he did not sign the letter.[62]

That day, or soon after, Beatty attended a meeting at the Dorchester with Feldman and production designer Richard Sylbert, in which his frustrations of the previous months exploded. He argued with Feldman about his shrinking starring role in *What's New, Pussycat*, and other changes to the script, accusing his mentor of flouting an agreement not to cast Capucine.[63] In the heat of the moment, Beatty walked out in what he later called a "bluffing huff."[64] Feldman retaliated by cutting Beatty out of the movie named after the actor's signature phrase.

"Charlie screwed him really badly," said Sylbert's brother, Paul, a friend of Beatty and of Feldman. "That's a real Hollywood shafting story. And Warren must have wised up from that point on. It was a real lesson in how these boys play."

Beatty, who said later that the script he and Woody Allen wanted to shoot "would have been six times funnier" than Feldman's version ("we would've gotten rich"), viewed *What's New, Pussycat* as the turning point in his career.[65] "I've often thought that one experience made Woody a producer, and me a producer, because never again did we want to lose control over something that we'd created. So when I decided to do *Bonnie and Clyde*, I wanted to do it right."[66]

36   *The one-two punch from Feldman and*

Peter Hall temporarily set Warren Beatty's life on a different course. He and Leslie Caron had been staying in a bungalow at the Beverly Hills Hotel, where Beatty became fascinated with one of the other residents, the reclusive Howard Hughes. Hughes had once produced movies, dated Katharine Hepburn, and was notorious for keeping starlets in apartments around town. "[Warren] wanted to make a movie about him," Caron later told writer Aaron Latham, recalling how she and Beatty used to spy on Hughes and tried to interview his bodyguards. "He was very intrigued because Howard Hughes was so rich and powerful, because he wielded so much power, because of the paranoia and secrecy."[67]

That summer, as Caron sought permission from the court to have her children, Chris and Jenny, visit her, she and Beatty rented what he called "a big Hollywood house with two pools and a tennis court." He later acknowledged, "I only had it so when Leslie's kids were in town they'd have room to play."[68] Beatty stayed in a separate wing during their visits to avoid damaging Caron's custody case.

Jenny Hall, who was five then, recalled, "We were all together in a house on Sunset nicknamed the White Elephant, because it wasn't selling, but we didn't actually know [Warren] was there — it's quite a large house as I remember it, and Warren was in one part of it, and we were in the other. That was a sort of legal thing to do with my parents. I didn't know the legal things, but I know that by law we weren't allowed to see him, so he used to send us wonderful presents. I remember that he sent us, in particular, walkie-talkies — it was great — and bicycles, and stuff like that."[69]

Despite their best efforts, Hall's divorce and custody case was disturbing for Beatty, and traumatic for the well-brought-up Caron, who told Roderick Mann earlier that summer that she now considered marriage "a bit of a farce," and in future years would compare love to a painful disease.[70]

At Beatty's urging, Caron started therapy. "Once he was interested in a woman," she was later to say, "he would never let go. He enveloped her with his every thought. He wanted total control of her, her clothes, her make-up, her work. He took notice of everything. He sent every one of us to a psycho-analyst. He believed the experience was beneficial. He was right . . . Warren went as well, of course, to his own. He was so fond of his analyst — a brilliant and witty man — that he never stopped going."[71]

Beatty's psychiatrist, Dr. Martin Grotjahn, was a penetrating German with a thick accent and a borscht belt sense of humor who had trained at the Menninger Clinic and founded the Los Angeles Psychoanalytic Institute. Grotjahn attracted a coterie of patients from the arts, including actor Danny Kaye, journalist Gail Parent, playwright William Saroyan, and entertainer Merv Griffin, who signed a copy of his autobiography for Grotjahn, "To Martin, the great force in my life who made everything better."[72] Grotjahn's son Michael, who also became a psychiatrist, observed, "My father was a mix of charming and appropriately seductive, but not in a sexual way; he just knew how to draw people out." As an additional attraction for the Baptist-reared Beatty, Grotjahn, who had been named after Martin Luther, was an expert on the Bible. "He never went to church," said his son, "but every two years he would reread the Bible."

According to Shirley MacLaine, her brother was in analysis, like her, to grapple with the after-effects of growing up in a house of repressed emotions, frustrated ambitions, and their parents' discord, which she believed had made Warren wary of monogamy, just as it had lured her into choosing a husband who lived on another continent. Beatty's catch-22 — yearning for an ideal marriage but afraid to commit — may have been part of what attracted him to Natalie Wood, who was jaded about marriage after her anguish over Wagner. Leslie Caron, who had a husband when Beatty met her and became cynical about marriage during her divorce, fell into this "safe" category, as a friend from high school classified Warren's girlfriends even then.

Clifford Odets's journal identified Warren Beatty's primary issue in psychoanalysis as a desire for a relationship with his "fallen" father. This emotional void was punctuated by his rupture with Feldman over *What's New, Pussycat* in the summer of 1964. "Warren wanted that role, and he wanted it badly, and Charlie didn't give it to him," said Larry Shaw, who took still photos for Feldman on the film. In Shaw's observation, Feldman was as shaken as Beatty over the collapse of their father-son relationship. "I can't imagine that being a pleasant time for him. They were too close. It was a real friendship, and it's a shame those things happen."

Beatty's regret over losing *Pussycat* was intensified by the critics' reaction to *Lilith*, Rossen's poetical evocation of mental illness. The film had its first screening at the New York Film Festival on September 19, to what Bosley Crowther of the *New York Times* noted as "a few boos notably mingled with the applause." Crowther found the picture "gauzy and opaque," continuing to delight in skewering Beatty, in this case writing, "Mr. Beatty has a sodden way of moving and a monotonous expression that suggests his character should be getting treatment all the way through the film."[73] "Bosley Crowther has never liked me," Beatty remarked some months later, "but I don't like him either, and I told him so once in Sardi's."[74]

The same "gray Saturday" that *Lilith* was jeered at the New York film festival, *Bonnie and Clyde*, the script that would ensure Warren Beatty's place in cinema history, suffered a setback that put it within his eventual reach. Benton and Newman had completed the screenplay in August and found their ideal director, François Truffaut, preoccupied with *Fahrenheit 451* and a possible film for actress Jeanne Moreau. Alexandra Stewart, Truffaut's choice for Bonnie, was to recall, "Francois said, 'I don't know if I dare, if I have the health' — which of course he didn't — 'to take on a whole Texas shoot like this' . . . and then he said, 'Well, Jean-Luc Godard,' who I had done a movie with, 'he's interested in it, so we can put you on to that.'"

On September 7, Truffaut had written to Elinor Jones and Helen Scott to turn down *Bonnie and Clyde*, mentioning that he had "permitted himself" to give the screenplay to his friend Godard, who "adores it."[75] Whether Truffaut similarly permitted himself to give a copy of the seventy-five-page treatment to Godard in April, or if the wily Godard took it on his own to trump Truffaut, remains a secret.

Eleven days later, Godard attended a screening of his film *Bande à Part* at the New York Film Festival. By the next afternoon, shortly before the screening of *Lilith*, he was at Tom and Elinor Jones's penthouse apartment on West Ninety-sixth to discuss directing *Bonnie and Clyde*. Also there, for what would become a fabled meeting, were Jones's brother Norton Wright, Helen Scott, the two writers, and, it would seem, Harrison Starr.

Godard, who was known to shoot his films quickly, announced over drinks that his schedule was tight and he wanted to start *Bonnie and Clyde* in a few months, raising a red flag for Norton Wright, the cautious and only marginally experienced logistics and money man for his sister. At the time, Wright was a television producer on *Captain Kangaroo*.

"I'm this twenty-four-year-old hot rock, right?" Wright recalled. "And we were sitting there, and we were in the presence of Godard, and I like his *Breathless* but I haven't seen much else that I like about him. I just sensed he was a different kind of person than Truffaut. Truffaut was a humanist, and caring, and he gives all to the cinema screen, and Godard I think is a more egocentric person . . . and he said, in typical show business talk, 'I love the script, I love you guys, I've got a movie to do called *Alphaville*, so what we can do is we can prep this in December, and shoot it in New Jersey in January.' That scared me because it required unusual prep, and a million three budget to weather the locations, so I said, 'You know, it's been written for Texas, in a colorful location, with the summer heat . . .'" As he continued, the nervous Wright at some point mentioned the word "meteorological."

Robert Benton, who was elated at the prospect of the great Godard directing *Bonnie and Clyde*, recalled what happened next. "This is a story that's been repeated, and I think over the years, caricatured . . . had Ellie and Norton had a little bit more experience, because they were both very smart, they would have simply said, 'Absolutely' to Godard, and let the dust fall, and you shouldn't be so afraid that he's going to hold you to a check for a million dollars." Instead, as Benton would recall his nightmare moment: "Godard stood up and very politely said, 'Excuse me, but I'm talking cinema, and you're talking meteorology,' and he excused himself very politely and he was out the door before anybody had a chance to say anything."

Harrison Starr, who has said that he was there at Godard's request, continued the story. "Godard excused himself and didn't come back. And they said, 'Well, where's he going, to the toilet?' I said, 'No. He's gone.' They said, 'What do you mean?' I said, 'That's it. He shoots it his way and you stay out of it, or it won't be shot at all.'"

In one of the mysteries of *Bonnie and Clyde*, forty years later, Elinor

Jones, her brother, and Benton would not recall Starr being at the meeting.* This was also the inference in notes made by Elinor Jones from a conversation she had with Helen Scott shortly after Godard dropped out. In the notes, Jones had written, "Helen felt really strongly that Harrison Starr should have been there, [because] he can handle Godard." Starr found this baffling. "I was certainly at the meeting, 'cause I remember Godard walking out, and I knew that that was the end of this little venture."

"Memories are strange things," Elinor Jones would observe.

Helen Scott, who talked to Godard after he changed his mind about directing *Bonnie and Clyde*, confirmed Benton's and Starr's analyses. "Helen told me Godard's 'a strange, mad guy,'" Elinor Jones wrote in her 1964 notes. "She said Godard's mercurial, that we shouldn't have taken it so rigidly." Scott described the evening to Jones as "a comedy — Godard saying, 'Weather doesn't matter, casting doesn't matter' — and our reactions were hilarious. She said she and Godard knew we were trying to recover our sangfroid, that's why Godard said later he went to the men's room." Helen Scott's last words to Elinor Jones that September were, "Don't feel so desolate. You've had an experience with Godard."

Robert Benton, who had conceived the film with Newman for one of their heroes of the New Wave to direct, was "stricken" by Godard's abrupt departure. "All I know is when I walked out of that apartment, I thought, 'Well, that's it for *Bonnie and Clyde*.'"

WARREN BEATTY had his own reasons to feel gloomy about his future that Saturday night, as *Lilith* drew boos at the New York Film Festival. In October, when it was released in the rest of the United States, the film received mixed reviews. It was praised for its exquisite black-and-white photography by Eugen Schüfftan, but judged essentially as an honorable failure. In the future, Rossen's last work would achieve new respect as a film noir romantic tragedy, and would develop a cult following in Europe, "especially in Scandinavia," noted J. R. Salamanca. "They loved it up there, but in this country it was way ahead of its time, and I think that all of that business about lesbianism and everything put a lot of people off."

Beatty's reviews for *Lilith* were the worst of his career, as critics outdid

*Helen Scott and David Newman, who were also present, died respectively in November 1987 and June 2003.

themselves to capture with wit his self-sabotaging performance under the guise of Whispering Jack Smith. *Variety* described Beatty's speech hesitations as "jarring to the watcher . . . often the audience waits uncomfortably for words which never come while Beatty merely hangs his head or stares into space."[76] *Time* called him "studiously guttural."[77] Judith Crist, his secret admirer during *A Loss of Roses*, "hated the movie," as she recalled her review for the *Herald Tribune*. "When I got to Warren, I said, 'Beatty is noteworthy for his non-acting, and his apparent inability to deliver a line without counting to ten. It's either Super Method, or understandable reluctance, considering the lines.' It's not the kind of thing I said when I got older and kinder."

Beatty was stung by the criticisms, especially Crist's. "She had ridiculed me for slow line readings, and the ring of truth threw me into such a pique that I demanded, 'Who is this woman?' and called her up.* Well, we actually got along." Beatty also phoned Arthur Penn. "I needed some confirmation, so I asked, 'Do you think I need to talk faster?' He said, 'Are you kidding? Everyone does. What have I been trying to tell you for years?'"[78]

As Crist recalled, it was Beatty's trusted publicist John Springer, one of her "true loves," who phoned first. "He said, 'Warren Beatty is coming to New York, and he wants to meet you because he said you were the only critic who knew that he wasn't acting.'" Crist found the approach refreshing. "Usually when I gave somebody a bad review, that person would want to come up to the office and horsewhip me. But I was so taken by his asking John, and John, who knew that I was rather choosy about meeting actors and directors." Crist agreed to meet Beatty, "and leave it to John to arrange a lunch at a steakhouse in Times Square, and I know we made a gossip column the next day. It was the first and last time I ever appeared in a gossip column. It said something about 'What glamorous movie star and movie critic had a five-hour lunch at So and So's steak house yesterday?'"

Beatty hit it off with Crist, confiding how he had botched his scenes to taunt Rossen. Like most women, Judith Crist fell under Beatty's spell. "This conversation was simply marvelous . . . we talked about *Mickey One* and a lot of other things, bitching about other people, and agreeing that we didn't like Robert Rossen's work, and that sort of stuff . . . but the thing that struck me about Warren was that he was so interested, and interesting, as a person. That he had a passion about filmmaking, and it wasn't all centered around

---

*In the interview for the *Washington Times* from which this was taken, Beatty either misidentified Judith Crist as Pauline Kael, or he was misquoted.

his own ego of exploiting his beauty—God knows, he was one of the most beautiful young men! Having known many beautiful actors who couldn't put three thoughts together, he made a remarkable impression on me. And I think that was why we were in almost constant touch. He or Arthur would call me about *Mickey One*."

Beatty's luncheon with Judith Crist would have fortuitous consequences for him and Arthur Penn, in due time, with *Bonnie and Clyde*.

WITH LESLIE CARON'S custody case creating "turmoil" in his private life, Beatty wanted to make a "happy story" that fall.[79] His passion was still to star in and coproduce the strikingly original *Honeybear, I Think I Love You*, with Sandra Dee as a possible costar. When Charles Eastman refused to sell his script, Beatty's producer friend Elliott Kastner set him up in the Sandra Dee sex comedy *That Funny Feeling*. However, the deal fell apart when Beatty requested top billing, and Bobby Darin, Dee's husband, replaced him.[80]

The previous summer, while Caron was filming *Father Goose* with Cary Grant, Beatty had begun to look for a romantic comedy in the Cary Grant tradition for the two of them, the beginning of what would become the actor's pattern of starring in films with the women in his life. In years to come, the press would reverse this to say that Beatty initiated the affairs during filming, but as he later clarified, "I think friendships with people *lead* you to do stories together—not the other way around."[81]

Beatty's string of ambitious artistic failures drew him that October to a genial romantic comedy for himself and Caron called *The Babysitter*, later renamed *Promise Her Anything*. Caron was cast as a single mother with a precocious toddler whom Beatty's character agrees to babysit in order to woo her. "I had the luck to appear in three pictures, one after another, that were shown at festivals and were full of prestige but people didn't go to see them . . . I thought I had better do something popular."[82]

Fortunately for Beatty, his stunning debut in *Splendor in the Grass*, along with his high-profile love affairs, kept him a bankable enough movie star for him to command a salary of three hundred thousand dollars for *Promise Her Anything*. As the film critic for Beatty's hometown newspaper, the *Washington Star*, wrote in a review of the disastrous *Lilith*, "What he does on the screen can hardly be called acting at all . . . yet Beatty unmistakably has that elusive something called star quality; he radiates it."[83]

Using his star power, Beatty persuaded Ray Stark at 7 Arts Films to shoot

Promise Her Anything — which was set in Greenwich Village — in London, so Caron could be near her children, who were at school in England. Beatty, who had been named a corespondent, took his responsibility to Caron seriously. "There was a custody battle going on," he said later, "so it was necessary that I was in the country."[84]

Stanley Rubin, who produced the picture at Stark's request, with Arthur Hiller directing, had no idea that Beatty had pulled those strings. "Ray Stark came to Arthur and to me and said that there was a threat of a Screen Actors Guild strike that might catch us in the middle of preproduction preparation, or even after starting the film — and he said, 'You better go off to London and make this.' And my first reply, I remember this fairly vividly, was, 'But Ray, it all takes place in Greenwich Village, New York.' And Ray's answer was, 'So build it in London.' And so off we went to London, and started building sets at Shepperton Studios."[85]

Before leaving for England, the likable and "hands-on" Rubin, whom Beatty would name, when in his sixties, as one of his favorite producers, "heard stories around town about Warren that made things look as if they might turn out to be difficult." Rubin, who came to respect Beatty as a filmmaker, and for his political activism, felt "he had not matured to that point yet" when they met in February 1965 to read through the script with Hiller, who had just directed *The Americanization of Emily*, which Beatty admired.[86]

Rubin and the equally genial Arthur Hiller brought their wives and young children to London, occasionally inviting them to the set. Beatty impressed both men as professional, with one vestige of his *Lilith* and *Mickey One* behavior. "On every scene," recalled Rubin, "as a scene would come up, Warren, and/or Warren and Leslie, would say in the morning to Arthur and me, 'Well, about this scene . . . what's our motivation?' As if the script were totally foreign to them, as if they had never seen it before . . . after a week or so, 'What's our motivation?' was beginning to drive me crazy, and Arthur."

When Hiller asked if he could use Rubin's two young sons in bit parts for an upcoming scene, Rubin and his wife, actress Kathleen Hughes, spent the night before coaching their seven-year-old and nine-year-old to play a practical joke on Beatty and Caron.

"Well," remembered Rubin, "next day came, and the two boys were brought on the set. They listened to Arthur tell them where they were to move, et cetera, and they did just as he had said. They went into the middle of the set, stopped cold, then they looked around at Arthur and said, 'What's our motivation?' And the whole crew burst out laughing. The electricians up in the rafters were laughing. Everybody on the set was howling. Warren and Leslie took it very graciously. They were very, very amused." Thereafter, noticed Rubin, the requests for motivation "lessened. It might come up, but not with the frequency it had before. I think the joke paid off."

Beatty, who had not been in a comedy since *Dobie Gillis*, seemed slightly insecure at first to Rubin. According to Caron, he was extremely conscientious about his acting. "I think the actor who influenced him most was Spencer Tracy . . . he invented something which was also an important part of Stanislavsky's training: he knew how to listen. Warren had noticed that and incorporated it in his own work."[87]

Beatty's boyish sweetness, which he had tried to conceal in the unsympathetic characters he chose after Bud, shone through in his appealing comedic performance in *Promise Her Anything*, a forerunner to the innocent quality he would project in *Heaven Can Wait*, especially in scenes with his toddler costar.

Beatty's affection for children was demonstrated further with Caron's son and daughter. Jenny Hall would have warm memories of Sunday dinners when she and her brother, mother, and Warren would dine at the London Trader Vic's, an exotic themed restaurant. "I guess the cook was away for the weekend, and Sunday evenings it was just us, and it was like a treat for us kids to go to Trader Vic's because it was fun." Hall thought of Beatty as a "very nice quasi-stepfather . . . and also very glamorous. I was aware at the time how glamorous he was, so that was fun." At the same time, "when you're a child," she said once, "you long for a family life like everyone else."[88]

For Caron, and for Beatty, that winter and spring in London were acutely stressful. While they were preparing to costar in *Promise Her Anything*, Peter Hall's divorce case, which Caron had not contested, went to trial, with signed "confessions," along with testimony from Hall's private investigator, introduced as evidence. On February 5, Hall was awarded a divorce from Leslie Caron on grounds of adultery, with Beatty, as the corespondent, ordered to pay court costs — standard procedure under British law. At a closed hearing, the judge granted custody of Caron's children to Peter Hall.[89]

Thirty years later, a contrite Hall said, "The fact that I had taken legal actions to keep the children, whom Leslie adored, and had succeeded, was something she found very hard to forgive. Only many years later did we become friends again."[90]

Caron, Hall, and Beatty shielded Jenny and Chris Hall from the enormous scandal surrounding the divorce and custody case that winter. "I had no idea," said Jenny Hall, "and I doubt my brother had any idea. We'd been quite used to traveling about, and sort of changing and stuff—not cataclysmically in terms of family, but I mean from my point of view—you don't even question it when you're a kid. So I was not aware of it at the time at all. That means people were protecting us."

His children's emotional pain, Peter Hall conceded in a 1993 memoir, came later. "What happened certainly affected their lives adversely. But how far they have been damaged is difficult to say. They were surrounded with love and care from both of us . . ."[91] As an adult, Jenny Hall would say, with unflinching honesty, "The fact is that I have never really recovered from it."[92]

The extremely private Beatty and the discreet Caron said nothing about her custody case, or the duress they were under, while filming *Promise Her Anything*, although as Rubin would say, "I had the feeling Warren was protective of her." Beatty confided in his sister, who was in London at the time. MacLaine had been the subject of similar gossip, on a smaller scale, months earlier over her love affair with married actor Robert Mitchum, one of several serious relationships she would have after the realization that Steve Parker, her opportunistic husband, was leading a separate life in Japan.

MacLaine's fondness for Leslie Caron, and Beatty's anguish over the custody case, brought the two siblings closer together. A journalist who interviewed MacLaine in London that March wrote afterward, "Warren came to see her at her hotel and they spent the whole night talking . . . she had hardly slept a wink that night. Warren was deeply in love, felt responsible for the turn of events, had just about made up his mind to ask Leslie Caron to marry him." MacLaine, who had complicated feelings about marriage and respected Beatty's judgment, did not advise her brother.[93]

Shirley MacLaine's mostly absent husband and her daughter Sachi's frequent stays in Japan with Parker, or at boarding school, launched MacLaine on a quest for knowledge, and self-knowledge, that took her on pilgrimages between films. At the time she saw Beatty in London, she had been on a spiritual trek through the Himalayas and was writing a memoir about her travels called *It's Better with Your Shoes Off*.[94] The manuscript would evolve into *Don't Fall off the Mountain*, MacLaine's first book, six years later.

Beatty's comments about his sister early in 1965 attested to their reconnection. He told the *New York Times* they had "become close," and that she

was "great fun," telling another journalist, "My sister and I have a very tender, very good relationship . . . I think she's a very, very fine actress. And a
very, very special person."[95]

Beatty's guilt and confusion about his romance with Leslie Caron was
obvious in a candid interview he gave that May on the set of *Promise Her
Anything* to a writer from Toronto, where his aunt Ginny was a respected
television actress and her leftist politician husband, Alex MacLeod, now
wrote speeches for the government.

Asked about his and Caron's plans for marriage, Beatty said somberly,
"There have been many complications and problems. All I will say is that I
want to. But I will wait till it's all over, if it happens, before discussing it . . . it
happens that I love a beautiful girl who's intelligent and charming and has
the talent to be a movie actress. Who wouldn't love Leslie? It just happens
that it attracts a lot of publicity . . . I've not had a quiet romantic life and I
feel embarrassed about it."[96] Beatty's embarrassment, as well as his compulsion to atone by marrying Caron, signified the powerful influence of his
Protestant upbringing, and his conservative Virginia and Nova Scotia roots.

Caron later revealed that Beatty "asked me to marry him — but he was a
difficult customer. I couldn't have survived."[97] His absorption in his career
was one of the difficulties for Caron; the other was Beatty's promiscuousness,
an indication that he was not ready for marriage as defined by his strict Baptist construction of the vows.

Peter Levinson, a colleague of John Springer's, observed Caron's conflict
the previous December at a gala for singer Jack Jones at the Plaza in New
York. "I had a date with a Polish model whose nickname was 'Sweater,' why
I don't know. It wasn't because she was big-busted or anything, but 'Sweater'
was her nickname. At any rate, Beatty was after her that night. He was really
after her. And Leslie Caron, she was his date that evening, and I remember
her just looking so forlorn, like, 'You can't trust this guy.' It was written all
over her face."

Levinson, who assisted Springer as Beatty's publicist during his romance
with Caron, was an occasional accomplice to the star's infidelities. "He used
to cheat on Leslie like crazy. I've probably never seen anybody like him."
Himself a young man-about-town, Levinson occasionally secured phone
numbers for Beatty of the women he wanted to meet, the same service Neil
Cooper provided for him at MCA in the 1950s.

"I remember one time he called me about Bernadette Peters. He knew
she was in this play, this was about 1965, and of course she had this Kewpie

Doll face, and that had an appeal to him. He said, 'See if you can find out where she lives and get the phone number.'" Levinson left the information with Beatty's answering service in a code the actor had devised. "It was a Thursday, and then he called me at home on a Saturday and I said, 'How are things?' 'Things turned out wonderful . . .' or something like that."

Levinson enjoyed Beatty. "He's very likeable because he's so smart, and he was funny, and I was after girls — not like he was, but I was kind of always amused by him. He loved to have these long phone conversations. He'd always ask a lot of questions. Always. 'Okay, when you talked to her, what did she say? What did she seem like? Do you think she wanted to talk to you? You really think? What's your feeling?' It was like a police detective. Every angle. And with these girls, I don't know whether it was phone sex or whatever, but I know he's had a lot of these long conversations."

While Peter Levinson worked with Springer, he also observed the "other" Warren, Tat and Ira Beaty's good son. Whenever the Kid was in New York, Levinson noticed, usually every few weeks, "He'd always go home to Arlington. Every time. He'd go New York to Washington." Levinson was of the opinion that Beatty was on a quest for a particular quality in a mate. "He had all of these babes . . . but he always wanted *smart* women."

BEATTY'S TRUE MISTRESS was his career. "He used to call Springer a hundred times a day," said Levinson. "'Listen, I got an idea. What do you think of so and so?'"

When Beatty and Leslie Caron completed *Promise Her Anything* at the end of May, he began an intensified campaign to find a worthy project and produce his first film. It would commence with an encounter in Paris with François Truffaut that Beatty, in future interviews, claimed was his introduction to *Bonnie and Clyde*.

In the eight months since Godard's exit from the film, Elinor Jones had remained in hopeful contact with Truffaut, while trying to interest other directors in *Bonnie and Clyde*. One of the first directors she contacted, ironically, was Beatty's eventual choice, Arthur Penn, who received a copy of the script in January 1965. Penn declined, via a letter from his assistant, Jill Jakes, who wrote, "Arthur thinks that the material is rich and engaging and that the writers are cinematically hip — what a rare pleasure. But. Though it's not really like *The Chase*, it's nevertheless just enough like it to be unfeasible as a project for Arthur . . ."[98] In the web of peculiar *Bonnie and Clyde* coincidences, Jill Jakes had been Harrison Starr's girlfriend during *Mickey One*, when Starr gave the treatment to Beatty and when both Truffaut and Godard wanted Starr to set up the film in Texas.

After the encouraging praise for *Bonnie and Clyde* from masters of the French New Wave, Elinor Jones and Norton Wright hit a wall with American studio executives, who were accustomed to the frothy Doris Day "sex comedies" of the early sixties. A ménage à trois in the style of *Jules and Jim* shocked them even more than the graphic violence in the script, "and we swore we would not give that up," said Benton of the ménage.

Wright recalled a typical meeting at United Artists, trying to sell *Bonnie and Clyde* to Arthur Krim, the then fifty-five-year-old head of the studio, and his equally conservative partner, Robert Benjamin. The only glimmer of interest Wright observed in the room was from David Picker, who arranged the pitch. "He was the junior member of that trio, but old Mr. Krimm and Benjamin were the guys who were going to say yea or nay. I can remember some conversation with these older gentlemen as to, 'Was there indeed intended in this script a sexual ménage?' 'Was it really that Clyde and W.D.* were, how should I say it, sexually servicing the same woman?' And I said, 'Yeah, yeah, and there's also the suggestion that Clyde and W.D. are getting it on.' And I think I remember Mr. Krim — evidenced either in body language or facial expression — that that was not something that he would want to endorse. And I think he said to me at that time, 'What is it that you do, Mr. Wright?' And I said, 'Well, I'm the production assistant on *Captain Kangaroo*.' And it was like I had torn the American flag up in front of him."

By the end of May 1965, when Warren Beatty and Leslie Caron finished filming *Promise Her Anything* and went to Paris to look for film projects, *Bonnie and Clyde* was at a discouraging impasse. According to Alexandra Stewart, Beatty had continued to keep the project in mind since *Mickey One*. "I'd see Warren in London from time to time, and he'd say, 'What is happening with it?'" That spring, he became more persistent. "And so in the end I said, 'Listen, here's François Truffaut's number, and it's what's his name in New York, he's the one that has the rights.'"† At the time, Truffaut was in Paris preparing *Fahrenheit 451*.

---

*W.D. were the original initials of the character eventually called C. W. Moss, played by Michael J. Pollard.

†Stewart, mistakenly, was referring to Lewis Allen, Elinor Jones's boss, who was producing *Fahrenheit 451*.

Toward the end of May, when Beatty and Caron arrived in Paris, Caron contacted Truffaut, whom she described as "a friend through the Renoirs," to set up a luncheon. Beatty said nothing to her about *Bonnie and Clyde*. "Warren was interested in working with Truffaut and play the part of Montag in *Fahrenheit*," as Caron would recall. "He wished to let Truffaut know this."

Beatty carefully arranged for Caron to meet Truffaut at the restaurant alone. "Warren came at coffee time; he felt a whole lunch would be too laborious as François didn't speak English and he didn't speak French." In Caron's retelling, "During the conversation, Truffaut told Warren that the part [of Montag] was meant for Oscar Werner, with whom he was very close, as he had done, with great success, *Jules et Jim*, but that if Warren wanted to do a film with *me*, he knew of a remarkable script that he, François, had no time to do — *Bonnie and Clyde*."

Several weeks later, Truffaut informed Elinor Jones about his luncheon conversation with Leslie Caron. As he recollected it, "She told me she was looking for a film for her and Warren Beatty. I immediately thought of *Bonnie and Clyde* because it's the story of a couple." Truffaut explained that he was trying to help Jones by suggesting her gangster script to Caron and Beatty, since he had to abandon it for *Fahrenheit 451*.[99]

The mysterious Beatty, who had kept secret, even from Leslie Caron, his prior conversations with Godard, Stewart, and Starr about *Bonnie and Clyde*, gave varying explanations, in later years, for his trip to Paris to see Truffaut. On one occasion, he claimed it was Caron who wanted to meet with Truffaut, to see whether he would direct her in a film on Edith Piaf.[100] Caron would refute this story. "I had no project in relation with Edith Piaf, and did not even mention her name, as far as I recall." More recently, Beatty has said it was he who was interested in an Edith Piaf movie, "and I went to France to talk to François Truffaut about doing it — and he told me about this script, *Bonnie and Clyde*."[101]

In his accounts of the lunch, Beatty never disclosed his desire to play Montag, or his previous knowledge of *Bonnie and Clyde*, although he was extremely honest about Truffaut's reaction to him. "Truffaut was *utterly* bored by me. I think he did not really like me for some reason of principle. I don't know what it was — I could speculate — but he was really nice to me. And he said, 'You know what you oughta do? There's a script that's been kicking around that everybody's turned down called *Bonnie and Clyde*."[102]

Beatty's feeling about Truffaut was correct, from a story heard by Robert Benton, who later got to know the French director quite well. "Warren, who never does anything without a purpose, was trying to talk François into doing — I forget, it was a picture that he wanted François to do — and in order to get Warren, who can be very persuasive and very insistent, off his back, he told him about *Bonnie and Clyde*."

Over the years, the legend of Beatty's Paris lunch with Truffaut was to get almost comically twisted. David Newman, Benton's screenwriting partner, gave his version in a documentary, saying, "Warren Beatty was in Paris making a movie and having, I think, a romance with Leslie Caron. And one night they went to dinner at somebody's apartment, and he found himself sitting next to Truffaut, and Truffaut said, 'There's a movie you should read. Because it's a great part for you.'"[103] Caron's third husband , Michael Laughlin, was certain that Beatty dropped in on Caron and Truffaut at the White Elephant, a gambling club in London, "and I think that Warren probably was thinking, 'Well, isn't there a movie that we could all do together?' And François Truffaut said, 'You know what you should do? There are a couple of young writers who sent me a script, a very good script of *Bonnie and Clyde* and you should do it.'" *The New Yorker* would report that Truffaut told Beatty about *Bonnie and Clyde* in Monte Carlo while the actor was starring in *Kaleidoscope*.[104] Even Truffaut misstated the facts in 1970, saying his lunch with Beatty was in London.[105]

The consistent element, even in the apocryphal versions, was Beatty's response. Caron, who was with them in Paris, recalled, "Truffaut gave the name and address of Robert Benton, and Warren left for New York to see Benton the next day."

Beatty phoned Robert Benton on a Saturday morning in June 1965 from his suite at Delmonico's in New York, saying he had just had lunch with Truffaut in Paris, "and there's this great script I ought to do." The folksy Benton, who was now happily married to illustrator Sally Rendigs since meeting Beatty while in mourning over Gloria Steinem two years earlier, was startled to see the movie star standing in his doorway fifteen minutes later. "The doorbell rang, Sally opened the door, and there was Warren. That was when Warren was *really* Warren. That was when — I've seen women's knees buckle — I mean, I've just seen his power, and it was, and is amazing."

Fifteen minutes after Beatty returned to Delmonico's with the script, he phoned Benton to say he wanted to make *Bonnie and Clyde*. Concerned that Beatty would change his mind after reading that Clyde was in a ménage à trois with his studly getaway driver and Bonnie, Benton told him to call back after he got to page forty-five. "An hour or so later he said, 'Okay, I finished it, I know what you're talking about, I still want to do it.' I said, 'Warren, that's not negotiable.' He said, 'I understand it, and that's fine.'"

Beatty cunningly declined to mention to Benton or Newman that he had read their treatment the year before, in Chicago, or that he had met Godard then. "He said, 'Who do you think should direct it?' And we said, 'Well, Truffaut or Godard.' . . . I had no idea that they knew one another, but that's Warren. Warren keeps cards very close to his vest."

Benton and Newman, who had the right to approve the director as part of their contract with Elinor Jones, found that Beatty had a different perspective. "Warren said, 'You've written a French picture. You don't need a French director, you need a very American director,'" Benton recalled. Beatty suggested George Stevens, but as he later slyly revealed, "I thought *I* might want to direct it."[106] He was similarly secretive about the actress he had in mind to play Bonnie: Shirley MacLaine. "I thought I could get her to do it," Beatty confessed to a reporter at the premiere in Texas a few years later, "then maybe she'd let me direct it."[107]

Warren Beatty's other secret was that he had no intent to play Clyde, which would make it feasible to cast his sister as Bonnie. "I didn't want to be in it at all," he said later.[108] Beatty felt he "wasn't right for the part," an admission that proved that his true calling was as a producer-director, not an actor. "This happens with me often," he revealed to a film audience in 1990. "I don't see myself in a movie very often. I see the *movie*, but I don't see me, because I see who would be right for the part."[109] Beatty's choice was singer Bob Dylan — "because he did look like Clyde" — with MacLaine as Bonnie.[110]

Leslie Caron, who believed that Beatty was in New York with the idea that *she* would play Bonnie to his Clyde, got the screenplay in Europe. "Warren sent me a copy to read. He wasn't sure whether it was a good idea to buy it. He feared it might be too much like a western, and westerns were not fashionable at that time. My only contribution was to disagree with him, say that it was a remarkable script, and push him to buy it." While he was in New York the first of June, Beatty told the writers he would wait for their option contract with Jones and Wright to expire in November. "He said, 'It's yours until the option runs out, and if they make it, then I'll take that chance,'" remembered Benton.[111]

Beatty almost lost *Bonnie and Clyde* a few days later when David Picker, the young production chief at United Artists who had expressed interest earlier that spring, told Elinor Jones "if you can pull it in for eight hundred thousand dollars, let's do this movie," reviving François Truffaut's interest.[112]

Truffaut wrote to Jones on June 18 saying he could direct *Bonnie and Clyde* that summer, with Alexandra Stewart as Bonnie and possibly English actor Terence Stamp as Clyde. Jones agreed to his financial terms a week later. "And I got a telegram saying, 'Tu es Bonnie!'—you are Bonnie—'and we're going to start,'" recalled Stewart.

On June 29, after he and Leslie Caron were back in Hollywood, Beatty phoned Benton. The conversation, according to Elinor Jones's journal, was as follows: "Liked script—sensational. Wants to do. Benton told about Truffaut. Beatty surprised. Benton told him to call us directly. Gave our number."[113] Beatty subsequently left a phone message for Jones with her husband but never called back. According to Benton, Beatty intended to discuss the rights with Jones, and then changed his mind. "He said, 'No, I'm gonna wait for the option to run out, and then I will make an offer that they can't meet.'"

On or near the same day, Leslie Caron phoned Truffaut in France, expressing her enthusiasm, and Beatty's, for the *Bonnie and Clyde* script he had recommended for them a few weeks earlier in Paris. "I felt obligated to be very frank with her and to explain that the project had come back to me," Truffaut wrote to Jones. The director advised Caron to wait until the end of August to see what happened with the script.[114]

Jones, who knew that Picker had run into difficulties at United Artists trying to convince the chairman, Arthur Krim, to finance the film because of the ménage à trois, asked Truffaut if he would consider casting Beatty as Clyde, in the hope that a movie star might attract a studio. Truffaut, possibly aware of Beatty's brief affair with his girlfriend, Alexandra Stewart, wrote back, "I have much admiration for Leslie Caron, but none for Warren Beatty, who seems to me to be an extremely unpleasant person. He is on a short list in my head, with Marlon Brando and a few others, under the title, 'Better not to make a movie at all than with these people.'" Truffaut advised Jones that he would cede *Bonnie and Clyde* to Caron and Beatty if she was unable to fund the film in the next few weeks with Stewart as Bonnie and a young unknown as Clyde.[115]

On August 25, Truffaut informed Elinor Jones that he was no longer interested in *Bonnie and Clyde*.[116] Jones's well-placed lawyer, Robert Montgomery, who had sent the script to every studio, advised her dejectedly "the majors are all frightened of it."[117]

Warren Beatty, who would become the "guiding spirit" of *Bonnie and Clyde*, in Benton's words, had his own dilemmas that August, when Columbia screened an early print of *Mickey One* for studio executives in Hollywood. "People walked out," recalled Arthur Penn's assistant. "It was the gossip at the studio. Arthur, who had put his heart into it, was devastated."[118] As Penn elaborated, "I was able to persuade Columbia to back it on the basis of them not reading the screenplay . . . [and] we made it quite cheaply for an American film, but that did not in any way mitigate their consternation when they eventually saw it. They were very upset." Pauline Kael, then a rising young film critic, would call *Mickey One* a "poor, pretentious mess."[119] The director conceded, "I'd like to go back and remake that film, putting in a nice engaging palpable story."[120]

Beatty, who had predicted its commercial demise, said diplomatically, "It was a very good picture, but nobody understood it."[121] *Mickey One*'s great champion was Judith Crist, Beatty's admirer since *Lilith*, who reviewed it as "a brilliant original screen work" and called Beatty "one of the remarkable young actors of our day."[122] The more common viewpoint, expressed in the *New Republic*, was that Beatty "is never for a moment credible" and that Penn's film consisted of "a bunch of images . . . adding up to nothing."[123] As Crist conceded, "I was apparently the only critic on the face of the earth who liked it."

Harrison Starr, the film's experimental production manager, concluded, "*Mickey One*, I guess you could say, was a failure, if you see it as an individual event. But failure is part of success. If you see it in a bigger context, it's part of *Bonnie and Clyde*. *Mickey One* led to *Bonnie and Clyde* . . . that the old studio system allowed that kind of picture to go through." Beatty, who had met Penn, Truffaut, and Godard as part of the *Mickey One* experience, and read Benton and Newman's treatment during filming, would call the movie the "incubator" for *Bonnie and Clyde*.[124]

As the summer of 1965 ended with the high-minded debacle of *Mickey One*, Beatty was driven, "trying to line up eighty things at once," Charles Feldman chided.[125] He was drawn, still, to artists of substance, meeting with Jean Renoir to discuss starring in a remake of Renoir's *Les Bas Fonds*, which the French director wanted to set in a Los Angeles slum, with Beatty "discreetly burgling houses."[126] Later in life, Beatty would mention his failure to follow through with Renoir, his cinema idol, as one of the regrets of his career.[127] He had also struck up a friendship with playwright Lillian Hellman, with whom he hoped to collaborate, one in the succession of strong-minded grande dames he doted on as he had his grandmother MacLean. Beatty also continued to pursue *Honeybear, I Think I Love You*, telling Charles Eastman, "This has to happen right away."

In the end, he chose to star in *Kaleidoscope*, a caper film set in "swinging sixties" London and in Monte Carlo, with Beatty playing a sophisticated card-sharp in a romance with the "mod" daughter of a Scotland Yard detective—a scenario he may have compared to Cary Grant in *To Catch a Thief*. The producer was his friend, Elliott Kastner, in what was Kastner's third attempt to costar Beatty with the bubbly Sandra Dee. Beatty later called the film "terrible," saying he chose *Kaleidoscope* hoping for a commercial hit, and so that Leslie Caron could remain near her children; but the director, Jack Smight, revealed Beatty's hidden motive: "Warren wanted nothing more than to meet Sandra Dee, and as we used to say in the army, 'score' with her. This was the main reason Kastner agreed to let Warren have Sandra Dee. So much for the producers wanting to protect the integrity of a fine screenplay."[128]

Smight, who had just directed the respected *Harper*, starring Paul Newman, recalled his first meeting with Beatty that October in London. "He came to my house at five o'clock in the morning and knelt down in front of my ottoman. Literally knelt down in front of it, and pounded on it, and *begged* me to do the movie." Smight agreed to make *Kaleidoscope*. He had directed Dee before, in *I'd Rather Be Rich*, "but I couldn't conceive of Sandra Dee playing the role of a strong-willed British girl." Like Rossen, Penn, and Stanley Rubin, "I was warned that Warren would be difficult to deal with, both as an actor and as a human being," Smight admitted. "Jack Warner could not stand him. He said, 'You talk to him, kid, he won't listen to me.' Which is exactly what he said to me about Paul Newman."

As Beatty prepared to start *Kaleidoscope*, the expiration date for Elinor Jones's and Norton Wright's option on *Bonnie and Clyde* drew near. "Warren had further hesitations," revealed Caron, "because he feared the story resembled *In Cold Blood*, which had just come out.* I told him that the film would be forgotten by the time *Bonnie and Clyde* was released." Others discouraged him. "A lot of my friends thought it wouldn't work very well," said Beatty, "because of its mixture of comedy and violence."[129]

Beatty sought advice on whether to buy *Bonnie and Clyde* from "everybody," according to Robert Towne, a talented and soft-spoken young screenwriter he had met some months earlier "in an odd, kind of funny way, by accident" in the outer office of their mutual psychiatrist, Dr. Grotjahn.[130] "I knew who Warren was and I just was quite shocked to see him. He was shocked to see somebody there. We walked out and chatted briefly." The two

---

*The film rights to the book *In Cold Blood* were sold in late 1965.

eventually discussed a script of Towne's for producer Roger Corman, called *The Long Ride Home,* and discovered that they had "roughly the same taste," leading Beatty to place great stock in Towne's evaluation of *Bonnie and Clyde.*

"Warren," conceded Towne, "was a little shaky. He had done a couple of movies that were not as good, that were cultural or commercial failures — and then there was *Mickey One.* And he always had this reputation for being difficult, always arguing, at that time, with his directors." Towne, who was impressed with Beatty's ability to "take apart a script the way no actor or any producer I know could at that time," quickly assessed the problem with Beatty's directors, which Towne found amusing. "He was arguing with them because he was generally right, and nobody likes a smart-ass, particularly a pretty one, telling you that you're fucking stupid and that you're wrong."

Beatty, of course, expressed it more politely. "I knew at that point that if I didn't control a film, and do it exactly the way that I wanted to, that I would lose interest in movies completely. And *Bonnie and Clyde* did re-interest me in movies."[131]

Like Beatty and Caron, Towne recognized the potential in Benton and Newman's New Wave gangster script, "and I probably was someone, as much as anyone, who urged him to do the film. I saw the possibility of what subsequently happened. Certainly I was more vocal about it than anybody else around. I remember saying, 'Just do it. Do it.'"

On November 27, 1965, the date Elinor Jones's option expired, Beatty paid Benton and Newman seventy-five thousand dollars for the rights to *Bonnie and Clyde,* becoming a producer. "I wanted to do it," he said later, "because it was a truly American subject, partly because it had a genuine social-economic background, but mainly in the end because it showed interesting people."[132] All the agonizing Beatty went through to reach his decision had been replaced by an almost religious fervor, a trait that would recur in Beatty's career, and his personal life. "Once Warren is committed," observed Towne, "he's passionate."

37 *As soon as he took the producer's reins* on *Bonnie and Clyde,* Beatty shed his frustrations as an actor-for-hire like a snake discarding its skin, and reemerged as the sweet-natured boy from Arlington, charming everyone in his path.

"That's what makes him be able to do all of these things that he's done," observed Robert Benton, who "truly loved" Beatty from the instant he took over the script, for his heart as well as his skills as a producer. "When you see him in all of these films, what shines through is a kind of innocence. He really is a very innocent, and I think really extraordinary, good person. If you sort of cut the boundaries a little bit wider."

Beatty began by respecting the writers. "Warren had hands off the script," praised Benton. "He would talk about things, but there was never any kind of ownership." By Christmas, Beatty began to question his secret yen to direct *Bonnie and Clyde*. "I was afraid to do it myself," he said frankly.[133] The master of long-range planning since junior high thought he needed more preparation to direct, "[and] I felt that as long as I was the producer and therefore responsible for the end result, and as long as I knew that nothing that I didn't like was going to be in the film . . . it seemed a great waste, really, not to have the best possible director."[134] For Beatty, it was a question of control. "If you produce a film as *I* do, and you're the person who the buck stops with, well let's say you have more control over it than anyone else."[135]

Before starting *Kaleidoscope*, he also began collaborating on a film with screenwriter Robert Towne. The two had become friends during the summer of 1965, and as Towne was to reflect in 2003, "over the years, I guess we've been about as close to each other as anybody in my life, or in his." After Beatty suggested they work on something together, the two came up with an idea through an almost cosmic meeting of the minds. "Warren mentioned that he wanted to do a movie about a ladies' man, and I said, 'Really? Well, I've been thinking along similar lines.'"

Beatty had remained intrigued with the Don Juan character he and Woody Allen envisioned in *What's New, Pussycat*, and he wanted vindication after being cut by Feldman from the movie named after his seductive telephone greeting. As Towne recalled, "He outlined briefly his frustration, disappointment, and the feeling that he got somewhat fucked over on *What's New, Pussycat*."

Towne, who had seen a revival in San Francisco of William Wycherly's bawdy seventeenth-century Restoration comedy *The Country Wife* — the story of a rogue who pretends to be a eunuch — dangled the idea of doing a modern version "about a guy everybody thinks is gay, so he would be able to bang everybody." Beatty liked the concept, suggesting that they make the Casanova character an actor. Towne replied with one word: hairdresser. "And Warren looked at me and he said, 'You're right.' And that was it."

Towne's inspiration for what became Beatty's oversexed hairdresser character in *Shampoo* was his own experience with a girlfriend who, he discovered, was still seeing her hairdresser ex-husband, who told her that Towne would never amount to anything. "I said, 'Where *is* this fucking guy?' I went down to pick her up at the beauty shop, and I saw this guy with his blow dryer, running around the most beautiful women I'd ever seen. And I thought, 'Wow. This guy has got it made. The only rooster in the hen house.'" Towne's then girlfriend was Barrie Chase, Fred Astaire's statuesque dance partner in the late 1950s; her ex-husband was Gene Shacove, a charismatic hairdresser with a harem of girlfriends who owned a shop called the Razor's Edge and drove a motorcycle, as Beatty's character would in *Shampoo.*

Warren Beatty's personal interest in the storyline, at first, was to challenge the "Freudian Victorian assumption" that all Don Juans are latent homosexuals or misogynists.[136] "Some of them just like fucking," he would tell a reporter with a smile, ten years later, while promoting *Shampoo.*[137] When he and Towne jointly came up with the idea, they both envisioned the movie as a classic farce in the style of *Rules of the Game.* "Again, it was one of those peculiar things," said Towne. "I think we both independently came to the table having been great admirers of Renoir." As Beatty left for Europe to film *Kaleidoscope,* Towne started the script, then called *Keith's My Name, Hair's My Game,* shortened to *Hair.*[138]

A few weeks before filming was to begin, Beatty's third effort to "score" with Sandra Dee was foiled when Warners paid her full salary, $150,000, to remove her from the picture, announcing that Dee had a "conflicting commitment."[139] "I had a considerable amount to do with it," confessed Smight. "Because I thought it was a classier movie than to have Sandra Dee in it. It took a great deal of *shmushing,* as we say in the Yiddish language. I had to push very hard to get Sandra Dee out of Warren's mind, because he really was determined to have a go at her." To offset the payoff to Dee, Beatty reduced his salary from $100,000 to $50,000 in exchange for a percentage of the net profits.[140]

At Smight's suggestion, the studio replaced Dee with English stage actress Susannah York, who had attracted attention a few years earlier in the film version of Henry Fielding's masterpiece, *Tom Jones.* "I chose her because of her talent. She's a wonderful actress, and great-looking, and she brought class to the film." The British screenwriters sent a telegram of gratitude to Smight on January 18, 1966, cabling: "NOW IS THE WINTER OF OUR DISCONTENT MADE GLORIOUS SUMMER BY THIS SUN OF YORK."[141]

Beatty's behavior when he got to London sent an even clearer signal that the end was near with Leslie Caron. When he went out to dinner with producers Lewis Allen and Dana Hodgson, who were in London for the filming of *Fahrenheit 451*, he arrived with three British "birds," as Hodgson described Beatty's female companions.[142] Victor Lownes, the manager of the London Playboy Club and a legendary Lothario himself, recalled the actor stopping by to meet the "talent," as Lownes referred to the Playboy Bunnies.[143] "All Warren had to do is come over to my house, or hang out at one of my parties. He knew that if he dropped over, there would be a lot of talent around." Beatty, Lownes would recall, generally was surrounded by "a bunch of girls."

In other respects, the actor displayed his MacLean refinement. Lownes would recount what he considered an important story about Beatty after they met at the London Playboy Club. "Warren discovered that I was a big fan of Mabel Mercer.* And when he discovered that, he told me, 'You know, I never liked you until I heard that you were a fan of Mabel Mercer. And then I started to be more receptive, and I got to like you.' It was revealing about his own taste and character, because Mabel was not exactly top of the Hit Parade."

Beatty also impressed Dana Hodgson with his southern manners. "I was surprised by how extremely nice, and polite, and thoughtful, and sensitive Warren was." Beatty's Virginia core values, the part of him that made him consider his Baptist youth minister the most successful man he knew, were still in evidence. He told a London paper that February, "If Leslie wanted to marry me — absolutely I wouldn't hesitate. But she's the one who is nervous. You've got to remember she's had two marriages give way under her." In the same interview, he commented revealingly, "It just seems to me that people aren't made for each other anymore. Yet I still believe that a fulfilled monogamous relationship can be great — but it takes genius to do it. The investment over the years to a common vocabulary is very exciting. I don't have children of my own and I'm kind of looking for responsibility in a way."[144]

This traditional and sentimental side of Warren Beatty was expressed that same month when he sent a postcard to Eleanor Kilgallen, the motherly MCA agent who had supported his career ten years earlier when he had only one blue suit. He wrote a single line, "When are you coming to London? Love Warren." Smight observed the same tenderness in Beatty when they talked about his sister, Shirley. "He seemed protective of her."

---

*A black cabaret singer with a repertoire of jazz, show tunes, and Cole Porter standards.

Both the director, and Beatty, would say later they had fun making *Kalei-doscope*. "We got along pretty well," remarked Smight. "The one thing he did have was a sense of humor, and I used that considerably in my dealings with him." Beatty's intense Stanislavsky approach did not last long with Smight, a "just-get-on-with-it sort of professional chap," in the phrase of Shakespearean-trained Clive Revill, who played York's father in the film, the inspector from Scotland Yard.[145]

"Warren sort of gave the impression that he was immersed in the Method," said Revill, "whatever that is . . . they're all frightfully serious, and actors in England were different. I just got a feeling Warren needed this picture to get back in the swing somehow. His sister was incredibly successful, and he was the younger, rather unknown, brother . . . he needed something to keep in the race."

Smight, a former television director, kept the pace brisk, with no time for discussions about a character's internal motivation. "Warren tried to put on that New York attitude," he said. "In fact, I cut so many scenes halfway through, because he was trying to put on that 'Methody' act, and we didn't do it that way. We'd get to a certain scene, and he would ad lib something in the middle of the scene, and I'd cut. And he'd say, 'Well, I thought that was kind of funny, didn't you?' I said, 'Sort of.' But he was a good performer. And that's about what I got out of him."

Elliott Kastner's English production assistant, Marion Rosenberg, who found Beatty "always very charming," could see he was restless. "He used to come into the office a lot, and spend a lot of time on the phone, and it was always about *Bonnie and Clyde*. I got the sense that he couldn't wait to get *Kaleidoscope* over with, because it was clearly something that was a big deal to him, and very exciting."[146]

Beatty's original instinct, to cast his sister as Bonnie with Bob Dylan as Clyde, shifted after he decided not to direct the film. According to MacLaine, her brother called her twice "saying he had this great script," acting mysterious.[147] When he mentioned Bonnie Parker to her, "to tell the truth, I didn't know who he was talking about."[148] Beatty, in MacLaine's telling, never actually offered her the part. "I hesitated, and, to Warren, hesitating means turning it down."[149] Beatty's vagueness was a way of keeping his options open, a corollary to his refusal to sign contracts. As he later told a Dallas writer, "The more I got interested in the film, the more interested I got in the role of Clyde Barrow for myself."[150] Once he decided to play Clyde, his sister was out as Bonnie.[151]

The last half of February, Smight took the *Kaleidoscope* cast to Monte Carlo to film card scenes in the casino, where Beatty's cautious nature and need for control, the dual legacy of Ira Beaty, manifested itself in an aversion to gambling. "I got hot flashes once when I lost a Monopoly game," Beatty quipped in his fifties.[152]

Whereas his father's addiction had been alcohol, Warren Beatty's addiction was sex, or sexual flirtation. Tom Carlile, the publicist for *Kaleidoscope*, sent a memo to the studio from Monte Carlo on February 10, stating, "Warren, bless his good fortune, spent almost all of his free time kipped up with a series of six different young ladies before Leslie Caron arrived, including the female feature writer of the *London Sun*, who has been so stunned about it that she has yet to write her piece about him." Carlile closed the publicity report saying he hoped "the little broad from the *Sun* . . . can forget her tingling crotch long enough to write her story."[153]

Susannah York, who had a "bantering relationship" with Beatty, described him as a flirt. "Wouldn't stop ever, actually. So you kind of had to get past that. I mean either you were up for it, or after a bit you'd need to say, 'Come on, cool it, Warren.' I think he was probably always 'on,' never unpleasantly so, but sometimes a little tiresomely so."

Marion Rosenberg, whose female cousin was an object of Beatty's desire when she taught him how a gambler holds his cards, formed an impression about Beatty's flirtatious behavior. "I think he did it just for the sport, but I think if anybody had responded he probably would have run a mile, because he's of a type who just enjoys the chase, but doesn't follow through on the conquest."

York fit into the category of women Beatty could woo without consequence. "I wasn't sort of particularly up for flirting or anything like that," as she said. "I was newly married, and very happily so, and I wasn't really that much a part of the London swinging scene in that way. But I got on pretty well with Warren, and we laughed. Even when I got a bit pissed off with him, at times, he always had a really nice sense of humor, and he was fun, and he would laugh at himself. He was so obviously incredibly good-looking, women were falling all over the place . . . I think Warren would pursue anything in skirts at that time, or anything that was kind of halfway up his street."

When Leslie Caron visited the set to see Beatty, York "felt it was a bit strained. I remember sort of feeling a certain solidarity with Leslie actually, and thinking, 'Ooh, well, I'm totally glad I'm not in her place.'" Beatty expressed his viewpoint about his lifestyle to a London reporter that February, saying, "Look, you're in your twenties once, in your thirties once — you don't get another chance at life. I figure I should be spending my money and my energies now. You can't help but settle down as you get older. So I grab all the fun I can at this moment."[154]

On March 9, 1966, a few weeks shy of his twenty-ninth birthday, while he was in Europe, Beatty registered *Bonnie and Clyde* with the Motion Picture Association. The technicality caught the eye of David Picker, the young United Artists executive who had tried to persuade the squeamish Arthur Krim to buy the script from Elinor Jones. "I used to keep track of what was going on at the other companies as much as possible," Picker was to recount, "and I used to read every day the title registrations when they came in. So one day I pick up the title report, and I see *Bonnie and Clyde*, and I see it's registered by a company called Tatira, so I called and found out that Tatira is Warren's company. And I went into my boss, Arthur Krim, who ran the company, and I go, 'Arthur, Warren Beatty's acquired *Bonnie and Clyde*, so we *have* to make a deal.'"[155]

That same week, Beatty and Caron, who were in London for the last few weeks of filming on *Kaleidoscope*, attended the royal premiere of *Born Free*. Standing to the right of Caron in the receiving line was English actress Julie Christie, the striking blond star of *Dr. Zhivago* who would be called the "Face of the Sixties" and become Beatty's next and longtime love. By chance a photographer at the premiere took a photo of the precise moment when Beatty met Julie Christie, a snapshot that, in retrospect, seems voyeuristic. In it, Beatty's head is turned as he stares with interest at Christie, who is curtsying for the queen, while Caron stands between them, oblivious to her lover's wandering gaze.

Somehow, amid the crush, Beatty managed to have a conversation with Christie, saying later, "Julie was the most beautiful, and at the same time, the most nervous person I had ever met. She was deeply and authentically left-wing, and making this fuss over royalty did not amuse her."[156]

Christie's leftist leanings had a romantic association for Beatty because of his actress aunt Ginny MacLeod, and he was enthralled with the Russian epic, *Dr. Zhivago*, which had come out at Christmas. The writer Buck Henry, who would co-direct Beatty and Christie in *Heaven Can Wait*, observed, "I think Warren thinks every movie is flawed, and he's so compulsive about his own stuff that he's looking for the flaws in other people's work to make it more understandable . . . the only thing he has never said is flawed is his beloved *Dr. Zhivago*."[157] Beatty became infatuated with Julie Christie as the luminous Lara in *Zhivago* just as he had developed a crush on Joan Collins and Leslie Caron from seeing their movies — although his romance with Christie would not ensue for another year.

Three days after meeting Christie, the secretive Beatty sent a letter to John Springer hinting that he said more than hello to her at the premiere. "I finalized the purchase of BONNIE AND CLYDE," Beatty wrote on March 17, "and suddenly everybody seems to want to do it. Jean-Luc Godard wants to do it very much, I hear, and Natalie [Wood], and I had a mysterious feeler the other day about Julie Christie being interested in it . . . Several studios want to make it as it is, and I really don't know what to do next about it."[158]

Beatty promised the writers he would meet their idol, the tempestuous Godard, to discuss directing *Bonnie and Clyde*, "and the thing about Warren is that if he promised he would do something, he did it," said Benton. Beatty told Benton he met with Godard in London during *Kaleidoscope*. "And I always wanted to be a fly on the wall! He said it did not go well." Beatty was pleased to discard Godard. "I don't think Godard could have done it," he said later. "I don't think Truffaut could have handled the language."[159]

Despite early interest in *Bonnie and Clyde* from studios because of his involvement, Beatty encountered the same resistance from American directors as had Jones and Wright. One of the first naysayers was Brian Hutton, a young director friend of Elliott Kastner's. Hutton, who would go on to direct *Kelly's Heroes* and eventually leave the business, ran into Beatty in London "carrying the script under his arm," asking for an opinion.[160] "He didn't even tell me that he was going to produce it. I didn't know really quite frankly whether he was considering it just as an actor, or what. It was all very, very, very tentative . . . that's how his opinion would come about. Warren loves to wind people up, and put people on, and pick people's brains, and that's his game. I think he would just bounce it off people, and they would give him negative reports and positive reports." Hutton's was negative. "What's the message? Kill four or five people and you'll find love and happiness? I told him that I really wasn't interested in it. But you know, I must be one of probably fifty people that he handed the script to."

Any doubts Beatty had were vanquished when he finished *Kaleidoscope* and saw *Promise Her Anything* with Robert Towne at a movie theater in Hollywood. "I remember sitting and watching it with him," said Towne, "thinking something he well knew — that it wasn't very good. And we started to sort of talk about it candidly, and laughed about it." When the conversation got around to *Bonnie and Clyde*, "I said, 'This is a very important film for you to do in many ways.'" The moment was an epiphany for Beatty. "It got to the point where I would have to make a good picture or get myself into trouble. That was when we made *Bonnie and Clyde*."[161]

The headquarters for *Bonnie and Clyde* for the next six months was Beatty's new residence, a small penthouse with a patio at the Beverly Wilshire Hotel, a continuation of the hotel lifestyle Mitch May had introduced to him in 1956.

Beatty focused his initial efforts on hiring a director, typically leaning toward one of the old masters, George Stevens, whose 1951 film *A Place in the Sun* had helped inspire him to act. When Stevens responded with "long silences" over meetings in Chinese restaurants, Beatty phoned Arthur Penn, a suggestion of Benton and Newman's.[162] The writers were unaware Penn had heard about *Bonnie and Clyde* through Alexandra Stewart two years earlier, or that he had turned down the script the year before. When Penn rejected *Bonnie and Clyde* again, saying he was not interested in a gangster picture, Beatty was partially relieved. "Warren," Towne observed, "thought Arthur was a wonderful, interesting director, but he didn't want to repeat *Mickey One* . . . it wouldn't be enough to have a *success d'estime*."

Leslie Caron, who had been filming *Is Paris Burning?*, rejoined Beatty that spring during his quest for a director, and learned the truth about the movie she thought they would be starring in together. "Warren told me he did not think I was right for *Bonnie and Clyde* when I returned to Los Angeles. He felt an American girl should play the part. I agreed with him . . . I returned to England soon after to be with my children and did not follow the developments of 'B and C' anymore except to congratulate him warmly when the film came out."

Caron's account discreetly omitted her breakup with Beatty, a parting that was painful for both of them. Although Beatty never considered the chic Caron, who had a strong French accent, as a realistic choice to play a bank robber from the rural American South, close friends of the actress, such as François Truffaut's wife, Madeleine, described her as wounded when he decided to find someone else to play Bonnie.[163] Caron felt "discarded," particularly since Truffaut had recommended the script to her and Beatty together.[164]

The underlying causes of the breakup were more complex. Like Joan Collins and Natalie Wood before her, Leslie Caron was the one who left Beatty, worn down by his infidelities.[165] "Warren was wonderful, but the difficulties of living with him were too great for my constitution," she said at sixty-four. "He lived a professional life twenty-four hours a day, and everything had to fit in with his public image. It was extremely tiring, and after two years was full of anxieties."[166]

Caron and Beatty also harbored tremendous guilt about her divorce and the custody case, which had placed an extra burden, and scrutiny, on their relationship. When journalist Robert Musel saw Beatty shortly after Caron returned to London, "he was just as vulnerable as you and I, carrying a torch for Leslie Caron, who had ended a long relationship by deciding it would be wrong for them to marry."[167]

From Beatty's own statements, it was clear that he, the Virginia traditionalist, felt a strong desire to be in a fulfilling marriage. He said the next year, 1967, "We move in a time when tranquilizers, polygamy, so many alternatives are offered to working out the difficulties of a marriage. This business of you go with a person, you live with a person, you marry a person, you divorce a person, you marry *another* person—there is no substitute for the particular depth that is provided by time."[168] Yet it was Beatty's affairs that drove Caron to end their relationship, indicating a resistance to marriage that his sister, Shirley, believed came from witnessing their parents' arguments.

Privately, Beatty was anguished when Caron ended the romance, a confession he made to his writer friend Michael Laughlin, who married Caron several years later. "Warren told me how he cried for days when he and Leslie broke up," said Laughlin.

Beatty's deep sense of loss extended to Caron's son and daughter, then ten and eight, who were equally sad he was gone. "All I know is I felt very comfortable with him being around," recalled Jenny Hall, "and he must have been really nice, otherwise I wouldn't have." Beatty tried to stay in contact, "[but] I think it probably became a little bit difficult quite soon after that," said Hall. "My family has gone through so many changes and things . . . he's somebody who doesn't let people drop." As they got older, Beatty would make a point of keeping up his familial relationship with Caron's children. "It wasn't a formal thing," observed Hall. "He wasn't my stepfather, but I feel I can call him and ask for advice about family and stuff. It's a nice feeling of things continuing." To Jenny Hall, that was the real Warren Beatty. "It doesn't sound like a movie star kind of thing, but that is how he is."

As time would pass, Leslie Caron assigned part of the blame for her split with Beatty to *Bonnie and Clyde*, which became his obsession.[169] When Godard, Stevens, and Penn all passed on the script, "I must have sat in meetings where thirty directors turned it down," said Robert Towne, who became Beatty's sounding board that spring. One of them was Brian Hutton. "I was advocating this," recalled Towne, "and Brian said, 'What do you see in it? *You* may see that, but it's not there on the page.' Like so many things, when you're doing it, it takes a certain amount of vision."

Beatty, whose vision never wavered, approached his former girlfriend, Natalie Wood, that spring, hoping she would play Bonnie. In contrast to the optimism he expressed about her in his March letter to John Springer, Wood was not interested.[170] "I guess I wasn't too persuasive," Beatty was to recall. "At that point I wasn't getting a lot of offers and Natalie was riding the crest of her career."[171] Beatty felt more secure having Natalie Wood's movie star power to bolster his own, and when Towne expressed concern that people might dismiss the picture as a "family" project because Natalie was an ex-girlfriend, "Warren's response was, 'You know, she's a *very* good actress.'"

While Wood was demurring, Beatty recalled, "I asked *eleven guys* to direct *Bonnie and Clyde*."[172] With his options shrinking, he decided to go back to Arthur Penn, aware that Penn's earlier film *The Left-Handed Gun*, a sympathetic portrait of Billy the Kid, had a similar sensibility, but unaware that the sensitive and aesthetic Penn was contemplating giving up film directing after several bad experiences with studios.[173] "We talked to Warren about Arthur Penn," said Benton, "and he knew Arthur Penn was the perfect director. And God bless — he said, 'You know, you're right. I'm going to lock myself in a room with Arthur, and I won't let him out until he reads through the picture.' And the next call we got was from Arthur. I don't know how long Arthur stayed in that room."

"I didn't stand a chance," Penn would recall. "Warren can be the most relentlessly persuasive person I know." The deal was struck over lunch at Dinty Moore, in New York, brokered by their common powerful agent, Abe Lastfogel. Lastfogel promised Penn and Beatty, who were both disenchanted with Hollywood and their previous movies, that they, not the studio, would have final cut. "I had capitulated by the time Warren finished his complicated order for a salad," said Penn.[174]

There was one other stipulation, prompted by Penn's experience with Beatty on *Mickey One*. "We made an agreement to be frank with each other about what we were thinking, to say it very forcefully if necessary, and in the case of a complete disagreement, Warren would yield to what I wanted to do."[175] Beatty, who had a long memory of Penn's sixty-nine takes on *Mickey One*, felt that he and the director had "established a vocabulary" together, or as their producer, Harrison Starr, expressed it, "Warren felt he'd worked out the kinks with Arthur and could get what he wanted." As Beatty said later, in a favorite metaphor explaining why he chose to work with people he already knew and respected, "Making a movie is like being on a small plane. You can't get off mid-flight. There are ways, but they're not attractive."[176]

Penn was troubled about how to film the Barrow gang's massacre by sheriff's officers—which he had "worked out how to do" at his home in Stockbridge—and by the ménage à trois with C. W. Moss, the *Jules and Jim* element in the script the writers informed Beatty they would never relinquish.[177] David Newman said later, "Our very first meeting with Warren, he came right out and said, 'I'm not playing a homosexual' . . . [because] he thought it would make him terribly unsympathetic to his audience." According to Beatty, "it was Arthur Penn who suggested it should be removed."[178]

"In those days," recounted Benton, "Warren had a suite at Delmonico's. And we were in this room, and Arthur said, 'Listen, I want to take out the bisexuality.' And we stiffened, and he said, 'Listen to me, okay? Two things. You have not really written a bisexual relationship, you've written a complicated heterosexual relationship. You never feel the equal chemistry from C.W., and it really rings false. And secondly, this is not a movie about bisexuality. This is a movie about people who are outsiders, who are outcast as well as outlawed. Everybody's going to think, oh, they're weirdos, they kill people, and they're going to dismiss them the moment they find out about this. You're doing your characters a deep disservice.' And I think by the time Arthur finished speaking, and speaking so eloquently, David and I were completely convinced. Having spent x number of years hanging on fiercely to one concept, I think he was so right in arguing us out of it, and his logic was irrefutable."

Ironically, Robert Towne, who had long discussions with Beatty about the script in private, conceded that Beatty was reluctant to play Clyde as a bisexual, "but not for the reasons that you may think. Warren was somewhat attracted to the idea of playing somebody to some extent sexually dysfunctional, or not as attractive as he was. He was always trying to get away from the 'pretty boy' image. His main reservations were that it's gonna make this commercially dicey."

Roberta Hodes, Penn's script supervisor on *Mickey* One, recognized then that Beatty "was a very shrewd movie guy," when he read a screenplay that Hodes hoped to get produced. "He said, 'Why do you think anybody would want to come to see this picture? If you want to write about a subject like this, forget about anybody backing it.' He was very astute about what was commercial. I remember the look on his face was totally different from his 'seductive' look."

After the turning point of Penn's persuading the writers to lose Bonnie and Clyde's sexual ménage with C.W., "Arthur thought Clyde should have some sexual dysfunction," Newman remembered, "so we came up with him being impotent."[179] Beatty had a strong opinion about this decision, according to Penn. "He felt that Bonnie and Clyde should finally make love . . . Warren was right. It proved a vital ingredient."[180] What Clyde's impotency added, noted Towne, was an element of suspense, the hope that Clyde would resolve the problem before the movie was over and consummate his love for Bonnie.

While the writers spent the first part of the summer revising the script with Penn, Beatty met with studio heads, while still trying to persuade Natalie Wood to play Bonnie. On June 20, Wood hosted a party for the touring Bolshoi Ballet troupe.[181] A few days prior, Beatty had become infatuated with the prima ballerina, Maya Plisetskaya, then forty-four, whom he met at a private reception at the Beverly Hills Hotel, hosted by Sol Hurok. According to a PBS producer who was there, "She wore no makeup and spoke no English. Nonetheless, she had an intelligence and charm that was captivating, and from the way Beatty behaved that afternoon, it was clear that he had sighted his next conquest."[182]

Natalie Wood, whose parents were Russian immigrants, translated for Beatty and Plisetskaya on their first date, after a performance of *Swan Lake*.[183] "Maya was an amazing woman," Towne extolled. "Her arms truly were like a swan's wings, the most graceful thing I've ever seen in my life . . . in the moonlight, she looked like she was sixteen, if that . . . and very, very homely, and luminous, utterly compelling, but by no stretch of the imagination would you call her pretty. She had the most beautiful eyes you've ever seen; the eyes were very, very sad—somebody who'd seen a lot." Beatty told a female friend that Plisetskaya was "the most beautiful woman he had ever seen."[184]

The Russian ballerina fit his pattern of girlfriends in the mold of Shirley MacLaine: she was a dancer, she was older than Beatty, and she was gifted. The fact that Plisetskaya was married to composer Rodion Shchedrin made her even more appealing to that part of Beatty that feared an intimate relationship.

Though Beatty spoke no Russian when he met Plisetskaya, "I can only say that language was not a barrier," Towne would remark. As the romance intensified that summer, Beatty studied Russian "like a maniac." His tutor was Michel Thomas, a renowned linguist who would teach Beatty several languages for what Thomas discreetly referred to as "personal reasons" — usually related to the native tongue of the woman he was pursuing at the time. "He took French, he took Spanish, he took German, he took Russian, he took Italian," recalled Thomas. "He wanted to click — just practical and functional use of the language in a very short period of time, each time."[185]

Beatty's agent friend Sandy Whitelaw, who had been dating Natalie Wood, helped to interpret with Plisetskaya on a few occasions. "At the time, the cold war was on, and I think Warren thought it was very funny, the idea of him seeing a Russian ballerina and maybe getting her to defect."

That summer, Beatty's discerning eye, inherited from his artist mother, found its perfect occupation as a producer. One of his early ideas was to cast the still unknown Jack Nicholson as C. W. Moss, originally written as a football player who provided sexual services to both Clyde and Bonnie.[186] "My first instinct was to cast Dennis Hopper," recalled Beatty.[187] When the writers eliminated the ménage à trois, he changed his mind and called his old pal, the sweetly eccentric Michael J. Pollard, to play the getaway driver — even though Pollard did not know how to drive.[188] "Michael was really the one," reflected the loyal Beatty.

The search for an actress to play Bonnie would become the centerpiece of the legend of Beatty's landmark film. According to myth, Arthur Penn rejected Natalie Wood, Beatty's choice, though in fact, as Penn clarified, "I never even knew about it until after the fact." Penn's objection was to casting a star as Bonnie. "I said no to the category, not to Natalie."[189]

Beatty's alternate choice was another old friend, by now a movie star, Jane Fonda, the writers' preference. He would say that Fonda turned him down to play Bonnie, but as she explained, "Warren has an incredible way of making you *think* that he's offering you a part — that he's working on this movie, he wants you to be in this part, and then not using you — and you never feel you've been rejected. That's a gift. So I don't really know whether he offered it to me or not. He certainly had me come over and talked to me a lot about it. What Warren did intrigued me, there's no question about it. I thought he had real talent. But I don't know where my head was at that time, and I didn't fight for the part, and I don't think he really said, 'Jane, we have to have you for this part.' He *teases*."

A formal offer was made to Tuesday Weld, Beatty's costar on *Dobie Gillis* and a unanimous choice for Bonnie, whom she vaguely resembled.[190] Weld, who gave birth to a daughter that summer, rejected the role "because I was breast feeding and I thought [the film] was too strenuous. It was really violent . . . I just thought it was a bit much."[191]

While Penn "held out for no star," Beatty pursued actresses with name recognition. "I think that was more characteristic of a movie star not really wanting to be the only horse pulling the wagon," explained Penn. "It's terrifying to think that you're up there, and that's it." Beatty later would name Ann-Margret and Sharon Tate as two of the actresses he offered the part. Others, such as Anjanette Comer, Lesley Ann Warren, and Sue Lyon, informed reporters they had been asked to play Bonnie.[192] "I was turned down by every living actress," Beatty said later.[193]

By the time Penn and the writers arrived to further revise the script and meet with studio executives, the casting of Bonnie had become a male's fantasy. "Warren met us when we got to the hotel," as Benton set the scene. "And we're staying at the same hotel, the Beverly Wilshire, where he had the penthouse. And then we went over to La Scala for dinner, and there was Bob Towne, in a booth with [actress] Sue Lyon."

Beatty's casting sessions for the part of Bonnie mostly took place in various rooms of the Beverly Wilshire, where his penthouse had acquired the nickname "La Escondida," Spanish for "The Hideaway." Penn joined Beatty to interview a seemingly unending parade of young and beautiful actresses soon after he and the two screenwriters checked into the hotel, as Benton would observe with some merriment. "Every time we would go downstairs to the old MFK drugstore, Arthur would be in one booth and Warren would be in another booth. Each was talking to an actress."

The experience established a precedent, according to scriptwriter James Toback, who would later reveal Beatty's insider tip as a producer to "include a small part for a pretty young actress in every motion picture and to schedule auditions for that part late in the day."[194]

At the end of July, Beatty made a last-ditch effort to recruit Natalie Wood, still worried he would be playing the lead in a risky film with no other star to help shoulder the burden. "We met at her house, and she kept taking phone calls . . . it didn't take long to see she wasn't interested in doing a picture with me. Besides, she figured the idea didn't have a chance."[195] Wood said later she was wary because of her stressful experience costarring with Beatty on *Splendor in the Grass*, and her psychiatrist thought she was too unstable to interrupt her therapy to go to Texas. It was a choice she would regret.[196]

According to Sandy Whitelaw, Wood called him that night feeling suicidal. "I was sort of like a semi-boyfriend, semi-confidant. I was one step up from her two gay secretaries. She said, 'I saw Warren again,' and it depressed her, and blah, blah, blah. I had always been told if somebody calls you and says they're going to commit suicide, you should be very rude to them, that you should say, 'Oh come on, for Chrissake, get off it, who gives a shit whether you live or die,' which is roughly what I did to Natalie, and I'm not sure if she took it very well." Wood's live-in assistant, Tony Costello, whose mother found her after an overdose that summer, said the actress blamed her analyst for her suicide attempt by advising her not to go to Texas.[197]

Soon after, Beatty and Penn flew to Dallas to scout locations with their production manager, Harrison Starr, Godard's and Truffaut's original choice in 1964. Starr, who had not spoken to Beatty about *Bonnie and Clyde* since the actor took the treatment off his desk in Chicago, said, "I got a call from Warren. 'Hey, you want to do a picture?' I said, 'What is it?' He said, '*Bonnie and Clyde.*' I thought, 'Goddamn, Warren! Good for you.'"

While they were in Texas, David Picker was closing a deal with Beatty's agent to buy the gangster script he had been chasing for United Artists since 1964. As Picker told the story, "I had to fly from California to Spain on some other problem, and I called Abe Lastfogel. Abe was representing Warren, and Abe said, 'Have Arthur [Krim] call me.' I knew Abe felt he probably had something special, so I went into Arthur and I said, 'Arthur, you have to call Abe, and you have to make this deal. Don't let it go away.' By the time I landed in Spain, *Bonnie and Clyde* was at Warner Brothers. Abe said, 'This is what we gotta have,' and Arthur just wouldn't agree, and I lost it . . . it was heartbreaking that *Bonnie and Clyde* wasn't a UA picture."

Over the years, colorful and conflicting tales of Warren Beatty's *Bonnie and Clyde* sales pitch to Warner Brothers would circulate from people who claimed to be in the room. In all but one version, Beatty groveled before his old nemesis Jack Warner, who still bore a grudge against him for dropping out of *Youngblood Hawke* and rejecting *PT 109.*[198] One executive, Joe Hyams, swore he saw Beatty kiss Warner's feet and beg him to buy *Bonnie and Clyde.* Dick Lederer, Warner Brothers' head of advertising, said he was present when Beatty "got down on hands and knees" in studio chief Ben Kalmenson's executive suite "and crawled across the office, saying, 'You've got to let me make this picture' . . . Benny thought he was nuts and he yelled at him, 'Get off the floor, you crazy bastard!'"[199]

Beatty, who had knelt in front of an ottoman the year before, begging

Jack Smight to direct *Kaleidoscope*, told a reporter for *Time*, shortly after *Bonnie and Clyde* was released, that he lay down on Jack Warner's rug, pleading with Warner to let him do the movie.[200] Five years later, Beatty conceded to film critic Roger Ebert that he "probably possibly" got on his knees in Warner's office, admitting, "I used to do all sorts of crazy things with Jack. He thought I was a little crazy. Well, I am a little crazy. Sometimes I used to think he was physically afraid of me."[201]

When he was sixty, Beatty would deny all the stories, including his own, saying teasingly, "It never happened. It was then—Warners production chief Walter MacEwen who approved the movie. That stuff about me being on my hands and knees is all apocrypha* . . . the real stories, they're even better."[202] As Robert Benton was to observe, "Whatever Warren said—whether he's right or wrong—doesn't matter. In some ways, it *symbolizes* the truth, and symbolizes, to me, Warren's passion for this, his total commitment, that he was willing to drive everybody crazy in order to make it work." Robert Solo, who was a junior executive at Warners with MacEwen, recalled, "it took an awful lot of effort by Walter and myself to con Jack Warner into doing it. Really there was a lot of conning, and pleading, and begging. He didn't like Warren, he was mad at Warren."

By the end of August 1966, Beatty, by whatever histrionics, had a deal memo in place to make *Bonnie and Clyde* at Warner Brothers for $1.8 million, at a salary of $200,000 plus 40 percent of the profits, which Jack Warner assumed would be nonexistent. "They kept cutting down the price of the budget," Towne later chuckled, "and giving Warren more and more, Arthur more and more and more, on the back end. I remember subsequently there was some concern that they owned so much of it, because they got paid so little to do it." After Warner Brothers signed on, Harrison Starr told Beatty and Penn, "Fellas, good-bye," convinced that *Bonnie and Clyde* would become "a studio operation," controlled by the hands-on, less-than-inspired Jack Warner.

With a major Hollywood studio financing him, Beatty the producer began to put together the movie *he* wanted to make, with the precise craftsmanship of the first Henry Warren Beaty, whose "lathes were always true," adhering to the artistic standards of the MacLeans. "I think that, in a way, it

---

*Theodora Van Runkle, who designed the costumes for *Bonnie and Clyde*, recalls Beatty getting on his knees in a studio commissary in 1977 to beg her to do the costumes for *Heaven Can Wait* (which she did).

must have been an enormous relief," commented his friend Towne, "after all the problems that he perceived on these other movies. He was finally in control and could be responsible for one."

As a producer, Beatty's primary directive was to hire talent. "He was a great respecter of talent, and appreciated talent," observed Towne. "Somebody whose taste in everything, from production designers to actors, was without equal, as witnessed by the cast and crew that he assembled."

One of his first recruits was Theadora Van Runkle, a struggling illustrator recommended by designer Dorothea Jeakins to sketch the thirties wardrobe for what Jeakins told her was "a little cowboy movie that won't be much good."[203] "I did not know how to do a movie or anything," said Van Runkle, "but I knew exactly what I'd do after I read the first page. I knew that it would be a huge hit, and I knew that I'd be nominated for an Oscar." Van Runkle, a strikingly tall young widow with two small children, took her costume sketches to Beatty's penthouse, "and there were all these beautiful golden girls walking around in little pleated skirts and bare golden legs, and they were all almost identical and all just irresistible. And Arthur Penn looked at my work and danced me around, and said, 'If our movie can be as great as these drawings, we'll have a hit.'"

A few days later, when Van Runkle met Beatty at the studio and discovered that the Costume Guild had demanded he hire someone older, "I leaped across the room, and I grabbed him by his shirt collar, and I said, 'You've got to give me this job.'" In his emerging modus operandi as a producer, "Warren got on the phone right away to talk to the head of the Costume Designers Guild, a southern woman who swore a lot, and they swore at each other for about five minutes, and when he hung up, he said, 'You got the job.'"

Beatty, as Van Runkle would observe, "has the best manners of any man in Hollywood. Whenever I run into him, he always comes over, embraces me, and kisses me on the mouth, and his kisses, I swear, are the great kisses of all time. His lips are very full, and they're very clean, and his whole presence is scrubbed, and scented . . . he's just—he's got it. It's wonderful, because you feel like he's a member of your family."

What made Beatty effective as a producer were the tactics he had gleaned from his years of cultivating and observing mentors, especially Charles Feldman. "Charlie taught him the use and abuse of power in terms of making deals," said Towne. "How it *can* be abused, and how it can be used. Charlie was abusive with power. From time to time everybody is. But I think he taught Warren where it worked, where it didn't work, how to exploit — and it was usually in the best sense, but occasionally the not best sense — people's weaknesses and their strengths."

Beatty also pulled strings to work with film editor Dede Allen, another artisan he and Penn brought in from outside the studio, advising Warner Brothers that he "refused to hire anyone but Dede Allen to edit *Bonnie and Clyde*."[204] He took a similar position with two obscure actors the studio opposed.[205] The first was his pal Michael J. Pollard, and the other was the little-known character actor he had kept in mind since 1963: Gene Hackman, who he insisted play Clyde's brother, Buck. "Buck Barrow could be played as a buffoon, but he also had to have dignity," said Beatty. "I had only one scene with Hackman in *Lilith*, and I had to work like a demon to keep him from stealing that scene from me. It's wonderful playing opposite an actor like that."[206] Hackman, who was in the hospital and out of work when Beatty tracked him down, was startled by the offer.[207] "I owe Warren my career," he said in 1985. "He's a very generous actor. What if he hadn't remembered me from *Lilith*? Where would I be?"[208]

In the last few weeks before filming, according to Beatty, Arthur Penn nearly quit, worried he had "cut the guts" from the script.[209] Beatty recommended Lillian Hellman to polish it; instead, he and Penn chose Robert Towne, who would make two key contributions: moving up the scene where Clyde and Bonnie pick up a mortician, so that it becomes "a glimpse of their future," and adding the powerful line from Bonnie's mother, "You try and live three miles from me and you won't live long."

The other major development was the casting of the barely known Faye Dunaway, who had appeared in two films that had not been released yet. Peter Levinson later would say he "knew for a fact" that the idea to have Faye Dunaway play Bonnie had come from his boss, John Springer, after Springer saw an early press screening of *The Happening*, Dunaway's second film. Mike Selsman, an agent then married to actress Carol Lynley, claimed he spotted Dunaway starring Off-Broadway in *Hogan's Goat* and that he suggested her to Beatty before anyone else thought of her.[210]

According to Theadora Van Runkle, it was she who first brought up Dunaway, while making the costumes for *Bonnie and Clyde* that would set fashion trends a year later. "I was hanging around at the production office, maybe after a production meeting, and I said, 'Listen, I can't do any more on this until I know who my leading lady is.' And Warren threw the New York actors book at me, down on the table, and he said, 'Well *you* pick someone.'

And I looked through it until I found this picture of Faye Dunaway, and I said, 'Here's your Bonnie.' She had a gardenia in the picture, and it was reproduced so darkly, she almost looked like Billie Holliday."

Dunaway herself was under the impression that Arthur Penn had made the suggestion to cast her, after seeing a sneak of *The Happening*; while Penn would say she came to his attention on the stage in *After the Fall*, adding, "All of us knew Faye slightly."[211]

Without a doubt it was Penn, and not Beatty, who expressed interest in casting Dunaway. After a meeting at the Plaza, the director asked her to fly to Los Angeles, so she could pass the scrutiny of Beatty and meet the writers. "When we met Faye Dunaway for the first time," related Benton, "we all went out to dinner at Café Escobar, a Mexican restaurant on Santa Monica. And Warren was not as enchanted with her as Arthur or David or me. We all loved her, and Warren was uneasy about her."

Beatty claimed later that he "tricked" Penn into thinking he did not want to cast Dunaway, but according to Towne, "I remember Warren, like me, being a little more on the fence."[212] Besides her relative anonymity, Beatty's concern was Dunaway's "extraordinary bone structure," which he and Towne thought might be inappropriate for Bonnie Parker, a local girl trying to look innocent while she held up smalltown Texas banks. "I remember thinking, 'Fuck, man. She looks like something you put on the prow of a ship.' Faye—that face—looks like she could kill you by looking at you."

To convince Beatty, and himself, that Dunaway could play Bonnie, Towne sent her to Gene Shacove, the Beverly Hills hairdresser Beatty would immortalize in *Shampoo*, "to soften the lines of her face." Meanwhile, John Springer called in a favor from the young editor-photographer of *Cinema* magazine and asked him to take photographs of Dunaway, who had just hired Springer as her press agent. The cub editor was Curtis Hanson, the future Oscar-winning writer-director of *L.A. Confidential*.

Shortly thereafter, Hanson got a call from Warren Beatty, asking to see what he had shot. When Beatty saw the way Faye Dunaway looked through Curtis Hanson's lens, he not only approved the actress to play Bonnie, but "Warren offered to have the studio buy my pictures," recalled Hanson. "But I said I'd rather get a ticket to Texas when they made the movie. Good to his word, he called me up a few months later and I went down there, hung out, and took pictures on the set . . . that was a pivotal learning experience for me."[213]

When Dunaway, who only had a few weeks to prepare for the role, was asked to lose weight to give her a Depression-era look, she stopped eating and dropped thirty pounds in days.[214] "She was insanely perfectionistic," said Van Runkle, then a close friend. "She lived on Blackbird diet pills. Warren couldn't have cast anybody who was more perfect for the clothing." The berets that Van Runkle chose for Dunaway to wear in the film were authentic to Bonnie, "and when I was a kid I loved a photographer that worked in Europe named Leslie Gill, who worked for *Glamour* magazine and always put his models in berets with arrow cuffs, and that was my inspiration for that."

Van Runkle's only obstacle, in terms of period authenticity, was her two stars' vanity concerning their hair. "What I wanted was for Faye to wear a marcel wave, and I wanted Warren's hair to be parted in the middle, and then shaved. I thought he was going to faint, and he certainly wasn't going to wear his hair like that! He was going to be *beautiful*. A lot of designers have criticized the hair in the movie, but the fact of the matter is it really does go with the clothes, and makes him look divine." Van Runkle's clothes for Clyde — tweed jackets, vests, and tank-top undershirts — were meant to be "puritanical *and* pure sex," a contradiction that was also true of Beatty.

By mid-September, Beatty and Penn had chosen another Hollywood outsider, stage actress Estelle Parsons, to play Buck's hysterical wife, Blanche. "Everybody in the movie was down on their luck," observed Parsons. "Arthur and Warren were coming off of a bit of a financial disaster with *Mickey One*. Gene [Wilder] and I were newcomers. He wanted to have a movie career; I couldn't have cared less, I just wanted to work with Arthur. Nobody thought of this as any kind of important movie at all."[215]

On September 19, 1966, as Penn's Hollywood outcasts prepared to leave for Texas, Jack Warner sent a memo to Walter MacEwen, the executive who had encouraged him to buy Beatty's script. "Dear Walter," he wrote, "I finished reading *Bonnie and Clyde* and I can't understand where the entertainment value is in this story. Who wants to see the rise and fall of a couple of rats. Am sorry I did not read the script before I said yes. I don't understand the whole thinking of Warren Beatty and Penn. We will lose back whatever we happen to make on *Kaleidoscope* . . . this era went out with Cagney."[216]

To stay in the studio's good graces, Beatty agreed to a press trip to New York to promote the September 22 premiere of *Kaleidoscope* at Radio City Music Hall. He was the mystery guest for the first episode of the new season of *What's My Line*, and the next morning, he appeared on *Today*, his first television interview. Springer, Beatty's loyal publicist, would refer to the

Today segment, privately, as an "unqualified disaster."[217] Barbara Walters, then the cohost, described her interview with Warren Beatty a few years later, writing, "He answered me monosyllabically with an expression of extreme boredom bordering on distaste. Finally, I resorted to the hackneyed but spoil-proof, 'Tell me, Mr. Beatty, what is your new picture about?' . . . after an end-less pause he said, 'Now that's really a very difficult question.' I'd had it. Right on the air, in front of ten million, I am certain, very sympathetic viewers, I said, 'Mr. Beatty, you are the most impossible interview I have ever had. Let's forget the whole thing and I'll do a commercial.'"[218]

A week after the *Today* show, Beatty tried to defend himself in the *New York Daily News*, admitting, "I'm a bad plugger." He acknowledged his "magnificent indifference" during Walters's interview, adding sheepishly, "I didn't even mention the name of the picture."[219] The experience with Bar-bara Walters paralyzed Beatty, who could not tolerate humiliation after a childhood observing his father's setbacks. It would be five years before he agreed to do another television talk show.

When he arrived in Dallas in October to start *Bonnie and Clyde*, "I re-member seeing a bunch of the crew standing around, joking about Warren," Gene Hackman would recall: ". . . he was such a tremendously good-looking guy that they just figured he was a Hollywood dilettante. But he overcame that. As it turned out, he was a lot better at his job than they ever were at theirs."[220] Hackman, an observer to Beatty's creative wars with Rossen, said, "This was as far from the fellow who had been so unhappy on the *Lilith* set as you could imagine. He was the soul of tact and kindness, quite unlike the image of Warren too many people had come to believe."[221]

Beatty instantly won over Bill Stokes, the Texan whose company built the soundstage, who had confused Warren with Clyde Beatty, a wild animal trainer. "Some people here tried to explain to him who he was," recalled Stokes's son, "and the thing that finally sank home was that he was Shirley MacLaine's brother. And his first impression of Warren was this guy with longish hair, his shirt half-untucked, really unkempt looking, he couldn't imagine he had all of this clout, but when he came by to visit, they got along really well."[222] Stokes, whose Texas accent Hackman used as a model for Buck Barrow, found Beatty took his job "very seriously, and was very dedi-cated to make the project work, a very hard worker, very focused . . . there was a lot of weight on his shoulders, especially from the studio, about the budget."[223]

Beatty's tutelage under the master, Kazan, had taught him that "making a really good film is a matter of meticulous planning."[224] Over the years he would recruit several of Kazan's regulars, including production designer Dick Sylbert, producer Charles Maguire, and makeup artist Bob Jiras, who evolved from nicknaming him "Mental Anguish" on *Splendor* to being his emotional support on *Bonnie and Clyde*.

Beatty approached producing like an athlete in training, demonstrating the same focus and drive he used to make the football team. "If you let your energy level fall," he said during filming, "if you get drunk or stay up all night and come in the next morning and have no energy, you are letting down the people with the money . . ."[225] According to Towne, Beatty even abstained from sex. "What I remember most of all about *Bonnie and Clyde*," said Towne, who went to Texas to assist with the script and to write *Hair*, "is Warren never fucking around with *anybody* . . . I mean, not with a soul." Dean Tavoularis, the production designer, commented, "He was like a priest, a saint."[226]

Maya Plisetskaya, Beatty's married love interest, was touring with the Bolshoi while he was filming *Bonnie and Clyde*. "Like so many Russians," Towne would say of Plisetskaya, "she was just full of fun and life — and sadness. I just know Warren was crazy about her, and I could certainly see why." Before he left Hollywood, Beatty had also become involved with Juliet Prowse, another long-legged, red-haired dancer cut in the pattern of Shirley MacLaine, a testament to Beatty's admiration for his sister and possibly his nostalgia for their closeness as children. His fantasies in Texas that fall were about Julie Christie, who had won the Academy Award for *Darling* a month after their encounter at the London royal premiere in March. "I remember him asking me if I liked Julie Christie," said Towne. "And he said, 'I *talked* to her. I think I'm going to try and see her.'"

Faye Dunaway would say later that she and Beatty had a "tacit understanding" during filming to remain platonic friends, because "both of us felt that any kind of romance would be distracting."[227] According to Beatty's close friend Pollard, "Warren didn't do it with Faye because Clyde was supposed to be impotent."

Beatty made a lasting impression on Dunaway's porcelain blond double, a Dallas high school student named Patsy Ann McLenny, who would later move to Hollywood and use the stage name Morgan Fairchild. "I started doing some local commercials, and one night the fella who owned one of the commercial houses called up out of the blue and said, 'Hey, you want to be in a movie? Well, show up at the parking lot of the North Park Inn at four A.M.,'" recalled Fairchild. "As I'm getting off the phone, he said, 'Oh, do you have a driver's license?' And I said, 'Yeah, why?' And he says, 'Can you drive stick shift?' I couldn't, but I lied. So I arrived in the dark, milling around with all these movie people. I didn't know anything about the movies, I didn't know who anybody was, I didn't know what the movie was about. And they put us all on this bus, and we drove for hours out to the middle of nowhere Texas, which is pretty nowhere."[228]

When the bus came to its final stop near Maypearl, Texas, Fairchild wandered off to look for the set. "I was walking down this dirt road, and this kid was kind of shuffling toward me, coming back from that direction. So I said to him, 'Is this the way to the set?' And he looked up, and his face just lit up, and he said, 'Well, uh, yeah, yeah, the uh, it's down that way, it's going on at that farmhouse down there, you should take a look.' And I thought, 'My God, that's the most beautiful man I've ever seen in my life.' And of course it was Warren. He just glowed. He had that real pretty olive skin with pink underneath it, and he just glowed. Even in the dawn."

Fairchild enlisted friends to teach her to drive a stick shift so she could double for Faye Dunaway in the chase scenes. "I looked like I was twenty-two, so nobody believed I was sixteen . . . I would go back to high school and my teachers would follow me around saying, 'What's Warren Beatty really like?' And I'd say, 'He's very smart.' And they'd say, 'Oh yeah, right.' Everybody knows he's very smart *now*, but back then he was known more as a glamour boy."

The fiercely driven Dunaway, while brilliant in the role of Bonnie, was extremely upset about the way she looked in the rushes — "very edgy," noticed Fairchild. Dunaway's friend Van Runkle attributed it to the actress's diet pills.[229] "She kept taking stuff to make — she was just going to, like, disappear for a while," concurred Pollard, who in the spirit of the sixties, spent his evenings doing acid. "She was yelling at everybody."

"They had a lot of problems with Faye," observed Texan Johnny Beasley, who recalled that Dunaway had to be hospitalized briefly, and Beatty, as the producer, took care of the situation. "He was always a gentleman with most people that he dealt with, and he handled it with kid gloves." Don Stokes, whose father's company built the sets and who worked with Beasley, affirmed that Dunaway was "very, very difficult to get along with on the set, and was kind of hell on the crew, and Warren came across the total opposite. He was very warm and engaging."

Traumatized by her appearance in the rushes, Dunaway later wrote how she would sit alone in the cornfields of Midlothian, Texas, "silent, sullen, morose."[230] At one point, recalled Pollard, "I was the only one talking to her, and then one morning I jumped into Warren's car. He said, 'What are you doing?' I said, 'I can't stand her anymore.' Then she got real nice again. It all worked somehow, you know? Like the Yankees work somehow." When it was over, Dunaway would praise Beatty as "a gentleman, a cunning business-man, a great film star, and a very worthwhile person."[231] As Pollard noted, "Warren was, like, really protective of all of us. Like 'don't mess with these people, they're doing a movie here, and they can't be bothered by outside things.'" The same courtesy Beatty had been criticized for requesting, as an actor, on *All Fall Down*.

His creative disagreements were reserved for Penn, a process Beatty and the director seemed to relish, though at times they communicated only through Towne.[232] "We had an argument for an hour, every day, on *Bonnie and Clyde*," Beatty later admitted in an interview for the British Film Insti-tute.[233] Estelle Parsons and Gene Wilder would look at their watches every morning and wait for the hour to pass so they could start filming. "We'd be sitting in the car," described Pollard, "like me, and Faye, and Gene. And Warren and Arthur Penn would be going on and on. I'm sure Warren was asking 'what's my motivation?' And we'd go on waiting, like, 'When's the scene going to start?'" A year later, Beatty would confess, "I like knowledge-able people to argue with me," possibly as a result of observing his parents' charged relationship.[234]

Tat and Ira Beaty flew to Texas in December, the first time they had "seen Warren in action," proof of how proud Beatty was to be a producer, and his continuing gratitude to his parents, whose combined first names, Tatira, would appear onscreen as the company that produced *Bonnie and Clyde*.[235]

During a break in shooting, Beatty and his mother, a heavy smoker, had a conversation that revealed the depth of their feelings for each other, as well as the formality and character of the MacLeans. "Here was this dignified, lovely woman coughing up a storm, with a cigarette dangling from the side of her mouth," recalled Beatty. "And I asked her, 'Do you love me?' . . . my father looked bewildered. My mother looked embarrassed. She said, 'Well of course I do. Why do you ask such a thing?' I said, 'Then do me a favor. Put out that cigarette and never smoke again.' She paused. Then she said okay. She put out the cigarette and never took another, in front of me or anyone else. And we never mentioned it again."[236]

Beatty invited someone else dear to him to visit the set of *Bonnie and Clyde*, Andy Cvercko, his pal who made All-American at Northwestern, and whose vomiting in their dormitory had motivated Beatty to abandon football for acting. Cvercko, then a center for the Dallas Cowboys, arranged to meet Beatty at an abandoned motel near Victory, Texas, where the cast was filming.

"As I walked up, they had security around the area, and I talked to one of the security people and wrote a note and said who I was, and all of a sudden, all the action stopped and lights switched on in our direction, and here came Warren with the whole entourage — Gene Hackman, Dub Taylor, Faye Dunaway, Michael J. Pollard — and I got to meet all those people." Cvercko found Beatty "pretty much" as he remembered him their freshman year in college. "He and I sort of flashed back, and went to his room. I was really surprised that he was very glad to see me, and I didn't expect to get that kind of attention . . . as a matter of fact, he had a little scrapbook of some of my press clippings. While we were talking, he said, 'Gee, you've become pretty well known,' and he told me about some articles he'd read."

Even actress Estelle Parsons, who had no expectations for *Bonnie and Clyde*, described that fall and winter in Texas as "a very exciting, creative atmosphere." The climactic scene, for the cast, was the "ballet of violence" conceived by Penn, in which the Barrow gang is ambushed in a slow motion storm of gunshots, a sequence inspired by Kurosawa's *Seven Samurai*.[237] According to editor Dede Allen, the scene was intended to evoke the Zapruder footage of President John F. Kennedy's murder in Dallas, Beatty's and Penn's social comment on the increasing violence of the sixties. "Arthur shot the ending like Kennedy's assassination."

Contrary to the later mythology that no one at Warner Brothers liked *Bonnie and Clyde*, its early champion there, Walter MacEwen, sent a letter to Beatty in November at the North Park Inn in Dallas, where the cast was staying, writing, "Bob Solo and I have been seeing every foot of the film shot to date. To say we are pleased with it is an understatement. Stay as sweet as you are, complete the goddamn show on schedule, and let's put it together as fast as we can . . ."[238]

"There was just something in the air while we were doing it," Michael J. Pollard would say later. "It was like electricity."

If, as Beatty later was to say, his personal life could be defined as "Before Annette [Bening]" and "With Annette [Bening]," his career would be considered pre–*Bonnie and Clyde* and post–*Bonnie and Clyde*, as the historic events of 1967 would demonstrate.[239]

38 *While he was still putting the finishing*
touches on *Bonnie and Clyde*, at the end of 1966, Beatty began to move toward his next grand obsession, *Reds*, a thirteen-year marathon that "[went]
through so many layers that by the time you're done, you almost forget why
you started it."[240]

His original fascination with Russia probably could be traced to Beatty's
romantic feelings about *Dr. Zhivago*, and its star, Julie Christie. It may also
have been kindled by Natalie Wood — Natasha, as her Russian-born parents
called her. After seeing *Zhivago*, Beatty felt a "kinship" with Russia, and Russians, that deepened when he began his love affair with Maya Plisetskaya.[241]
"We don't know enough about them," he said. "They don't know about us. I
think they will turn out to be the people we have most in common with."[242]

When Beatty returned from Texas in December, he started a script set in
Russia, which he hoped to film as a coproduction with the help of Russian
poet Yevgeny Yevtushenko, who had the popularity of a matinee idol in
Moscow. Yevtushenko was introduced to Beatty late in 1966, during a poetry
tour of the United States, and "loved Warren." He was dazzled by Beatty's
"incredible sparkling energy," which the actor demonstrated during their
first evening together, after showing Zhenia, the Russian pet name for
Yevgeny, a rough cut of *Bonnie and Clyde*. "Warren invited me to Hollywood bar," Yevtushenko regaled, in heavily accented English, "and that was
greatest show I've seen in my life."[243]

The charismatic Yevtushenko, who was known in Russia as a womanizer,
observed Beatty closely during their night's adventures, and later would compare his behavior to the character he played in *Shampoo*. "That was absolute
Warren." Beatty, the poet noticed, barely drank. "He was looking around the
bar for starlet girls like a hunter, and they looked to him, I could tell you, as
a rabbit to the python, absolutely, with trembling knees, and boobs . . . absolutely happy to be swallowed by him."

Beatty gave each woman his complete attention when he was with her,
asking questions about her background, observed Yevtushenko, "but he was
very quickly losing interest. He was not impolite, it was nothing insulting,
but he was going to other tables, inviting other girls, and I think probably in
couple of hours we shared about, probably, couple of dozen chicks. He
wanted more and more of them. He was insatiable . . . it was endless night.
We began to change bars, with other girls. Even I don't know myself, and

Warren probably could not explain himself, why he needed so many girls around him, because he couldn't deal with them properly."

Yevtushenko, who became a close friend, believed that "in a strange way, probably Warren was in love with each of them when he was connecting with them. He was like a child who is creating fairy tales from his life. His reputation of womanizer, it's just skirt-chaser — it was not like this. He was trying to make life more *romantical* than it was. But I think it was a kind of drug. Because a man with such a thirst for life, it's very difficult to find a response." In Yevtushenko's view, Beatty was using sex, or flirtatiousness, to blot out unhappiness, the same reason his father had turned to alcohol or his sister went on pilgrimages seeking inner peace. This recurring melancholia, which Kathlyn Beaty shared, may have had its origin, in part, in the family's Scots-Irish roots.

Like his father's drinking, Beatty's sexuality on occasion crossed a line, as it had in high school when he pretended to seduce his friends' mothers, or shortly after *Splendor*, when he dropped his trousers in front of Sue Umbs on a blind date. In the winter or early spring of 1967, when Beatty was in New York to help edit *Bonnie and Clyde*, Springer's associate Peter Levinson fixed him up with a fashion editor at *Mademoiselle* named Anita Alberts, who resembled Julie Christie. "She was very much of the sixties type, with the bangs and the long hair, and the ripped sweater." After the date, Alberts told Levinson that Beatty had been sexually aggressive. "She was kind of panicked, the way he was so sweet, and nice, and funny, and sexy, and then all of a sudden just grabbed her, and then didn't succeed, and then he left."

Unlike his earlier, similar experience with Umbs, Beatty was instantly contrite with Anita Alberts. "He called her either that night, or the next morning, and apologized profusely, and he wanted to be friends with her," said Levinson. Alberts, who became a publicist, married, and later died of cancer, talked about the disturbing Beatty incident with her husband, Wayne Cline, repeating what she had told Levinson. "And that's when she and Warren became friends," Cline affirmed, "and he treated her like a younger sister."[244]

Beatty seemed to be pulled in two different directions, as Kazan once described the character of Bud Stamper, his alter ego, the dutiful boy with "wildness, danger in him." Beatty the Hollywood star stalked starlets, while the "other Warren" telephoned Leslie Caron's children on Christmas Eve, after filming *Bonnie and Clyde*, making plans to see them in London on his way to Russia to visit Plisetskaya.[245] The good son celebrated that Christmas with his parents in Virginia, as he did most years, spending New Year's Eve of

1966 with his sister and his niece in Shirley's living room, "watching Guy Lombardo on TV," recalled MacLaine.[246]

Yevtushenko detected this internal conflict in Beatty when he studied him the first night they picked up women together. To the poetic Yevtushenko, Beatty, like him, was on a romantic's quest for his ideal woman. "It was like to taste fruit, or pick up many flowers, looking for another, which could be 'the one.' I remember that once I said to him, 'you remind me of my friend, a writer, who always was trying to find one woman with a virgin piece of snow between her legs. I understand you, because probably I'm also looking for same thing—because otherwise I'm crazy.' And I remember that Warren was laughing before, very happily, and he suddenly changed his face. He was thinking about it, and he very suddenly said, it was in absolutely different moment, he said, 'Probably.' And this was moment I remember."

Beatty revealed this longing for a soul mate, for a traditional marriage, a few months later in an interview, expressing concern about the changing sexual mores of the sixties. "My overall feeling," he said, "is that too little time is spent discovering the ability to get to know one person and to live with one person and the productivity that can come out of—the happiness that can come out of—simply living a life with someone else. There's a tremendous anti-romantic trend . . . it's very, very easy to avoid a relationship now. It's so easy to get a divorce. It's so easy not to get pregnant . . . it makes a promiscuous point of view easier."[247] For Beatty, who was living one lifestyle but whose mind-set was in another, this dichotomy created confusion, and uncertainty, about his identity.

Yevtushenko, who was in discussions with Beatty about their possible film collaboration in Russia, considered him "a rare person. He was one of the real men who deserved to be loved very deeply, because he had something very natural, poetical, inside him."

Dede Allen, who spent time with Beatty editing *Bonnie and Clyde* in Dallas and New York that winter/spring, was aware of his dream to make a movie in Russia, which she said he already had determined. "We were in, I think it was a Chinese restaurant, one day, and he said, 'Have you ever heard of John Reed? I'm going to do a film on him someday.' Warren had gone to the Soviet Union to see a ballerina, and he went to the place where this young American was buried, I guess just touring around, and he made up his mind he was going to do that. He's the kind of a person—when he gets an idea and it's a good one, he's a most incredibly tenacious man. Eventually he does it. Sometimes he has to *wait* to do it. He's remarkable that way."

Beatty's tenacity was centered on *Bonnie and Clyde* that spring, as it would remain throughout 1967. Dede Allen, whose quick-cut editing style would make her a legend among filmmakers, was to call Beatty "the best producer I ever had. On *Bonnie and Clyde*, it was down to the speed of the motor, and taking the old cars, making sure they would look like they'd go fast . . . all of his pictures have perfection written on them. Tremendous perfectionist." One of Beatty's important contributions to the film was to amplify the sound of the gunshots by putting a shotgun in a trash can for a heightened sound effect, a technique he learned from director George Stevens, who invented it for his classic Western, *Shane*.

On June 2, the Warners' sales force in New York saw an early cut of *Bonnie and Clyde*, "and all of us are impressed," Dick Lederer wrote in a memo, "especially with the exciting style."[248] The obstacle, in-house, was the old lion Jack Warner, who had sold the studio to 7 Arts and was preparing to relinquish his throne. "He was angry because he didn't want to make it in the first place," recalled colleague Robert Solo. "It was just another cheap gangster movie to him and Benny [Kalmenson]."

When Beatty and Penn brought the rough cut to Hollywood for a screening at Jack Warner's mansion, the mogul, known as "the Colonel," "hated the edit," according to Beatty. Warner, who judged the quality of a movie by how many times he "got up to pee," left the room to relieve himself countless times.[249] "After the lights came up," recalled Beatty, "Warner said, 'How long was that movie?' And someone said, 'It's two hours, fifteen minutes, Colonel.' And Warner said, 'Well, that's the longest fucking two hours and fifteen minutes I've ever spent.'"[250] Attempting to flatter him, Beatty told the Colonel that *Bonnie and Clyde* was an homage to the old Warner Brothers gangster movies, "and Jack Warner said, 'What the fuck is an homage?'" remembered Penn.[251]

Sensing that his "little cowboy movie" was about to get shot down by Jack Warner, Beatty came up with the bold bluff of offering to buy it back. Before acting on the idea, he sought counsel from producer Hal Wallis, the shrewd veteran who discovered his sister, Shirley, in *Pajama Game*. As Wallis's widow, actress Martha Hyer, was to recall, "I remember that meeting because it was late in Hal's life, and he wasn't doing so many pictures. Warren wanted Hal's advice on should he do it. And I think in the discussion my husband leaned against it. But Warren did the right thing."[252]

Beatty, who had shaped his career learning from the masters, this time followed his own instincts, asking Warner Brothers' chairman Ben Kalmenson if he could buy back *Bonnie and Clyde* for the studio's purchase price,

$1.8 million. It was a move that took "cojones," Harrison Starr would comment, since the actor did not have the money. "Well," recalled Beatty, "that really perked up [Jack] Warner's interest. He wouldn't sell it to me, but they got a little more interested in it."[253] Beatty reruited his longtime press agent John Springer, whose publicity campaign had made him a movie star, to help promote the picture, asking the screenwriters, Benton and Newman, to write the advertisements.

While Beatty was coordinating the marketing, film critic Judith Crist, his great fan and friend, became *Bonnie and Clyde*'s next female guardian angel. "Arthur and Warren showed me an early print, and I fell madly in love with it." Crist recommended the movie to Rock Demers, chairman of the Montreal Film Festival, who decided to open the festival on August 4 with *Bonnie and Clyde*. "I was absolutely astonished by the film," remembered Demers. "The studio thought it was a catastrophe." When Demers told a Warner Brothers executive he planned to "really create an event out of it by inviting Faye Dunaway, Warren Beatty, and Arthur Penn," the studio began to show more interest.[254]

Soon after, on June 21, Warners held a sneak preview at the Village Theatre in Westwood, the first public screening of *Bonnie and Clyde*. Robert Towne, who had predicted to a dubious Beatty and Penn that the film would gross $30 million, was at the sneak. "When Warren's name came on the screen as producer, there was audible tittering and laughter in the audience, and then, 'Yeah, right.' Not jeering, but a certain amount of incredulity at seeing his name as producer. There was no laughing at the end." As Michael J. Pollard recalled, "It got applause, and people *screaming!* I never heard of that in a movie! It was phenomenal from the beginning."

What caught Pollard's eye that night, as well as Towne's, was Beatty's date for the sneak preview. "Annie, my wife, leans over and said, 'Guess who's sitting next to Warren?' And I said, 'I don't know, who?' She said, 'Julie Christie.'"

The secretive Beatty had found an entrée to the English actress in May, when he noticed that Dean Tavoularis, the talented young production designer he had hired on *Bonnie and Clyde*, was in San Francisco as the art director on Christie's film *Petulia*. As Tavoularis recalled, "He said, 'Well, uh, you're working on this film. And Julie Christie is there?' I said, 'Yes, she's wonderful.' And he said, 'Do you think I could be introduced to her?' I said, 'Well, so what do you want me to do?' He said, 'Give her my name and phone number and see if she'll call me.'"[255]

Beatty later told Tavoularis what happened. "Warren said, 'Well you know, it all turned out so badly in the beginning. I talked to her two or three times on the phone and finally persuaded her to let me come up to see her, but she was not very friendly. And so I flew up to San Francisco, and there was some mix-up with the car rental.' So Warren rented a limousine and drove out to Sausalito, where Julie Christie was living in one of those little Sausalito cottages. So now there he is looking for this address, with the big, stretched-out white Cadillac limo barely making the little roads because the car was so big and the roads were so small. When he went in, she said, 'Oh, I saw this white limo going around and around a couple times.' And it certainly was not an impressive introduction from her point of view. So they went for a walk, and it went kind of sour. He said she was looking at him like some Hollywood hotshot—everything she didn't like. And he knew that. That's the reason he liked her, is that she was not impressed with Hollywood superstars. She was a very straight person. But they became a couple."

Robert Towne, who would consider Julie Christie and Beatty as family after they became involved, said of her, "Julie was not at all what anybody would have thought from seeing her on film; she was almost the opposite. Julie truly, more than any human being who's ever been a movie star, was the most indifferent. It was hilarious, and just wonderful. She thought *Dr. Zhivago* was big and splashy. Savaged the movie."

What Beatty and Julie Christie shared, in addition to a penetrating intelligence and a compulsion for privacy, was a high regard for the truth. As Towne affirmed, "Julie's honesty is matchless. I'm not saying she's always right, but, boy, is she always honest. She's like a touchstone."

Beatty seemed almost spellbound by what his poet friend Yevgeny Yevtushenko, another Christie admirer, described as her "immortal beauty." "I've never seen a face like that," Beatty said once.[256] The bonus, for Beatty, was her character. "The integrity in that face. That person. It's never faltered!" he would remark in his fifties.[257]

Beatty and Christie each would require several months to disengage themselves from other relationships. In Christie's case, it was her boyfriend of several years, English artist Don Bessant. For Beatty, the entanglements were dancers Maya Plisetskaya and Juliet Prowse, as well as Barbara Harris, the talented comedienne who won the Tony Award that spring for *The Apple Tree*, with Beatty as her date at the ceremony.

The spoiler in this otherwise golden year in Warren Beatty's life was a "nightmare" profile of him in the August issue of *Esquire* by Rex Reed, called "Will the Real Warren Beatty Please Shut Up." John Springer, who had persuaded Beatty to do the interview after Reed told the publicist he had seen *Mickey One* four times and was a fan, referred to the piece as an "attack," revealing later that lawyers found fourteen libelous statements "and I can't tell you how many more untruths."[258]

Beatty was stunned by the article, commenting that Reed "seemed dewy-eyed" during their interview, "[and] said he thought I was the best actor of my generation and that he'd seen these films of mine over and over again."[259] Beatty later told a college journalist, "I only spent an hour talking to him, certainly an hour of mistake. He made up the article largely out of things cut out of columns. He had me involved with women I'd never met and in all sorts of incidents that never took place. I would say the whole thing comes out of his homosexual anxiety . . . I think that the man is contemptible, dishonest, and a very hostile creature."[260]

The failurephobic Beatty, already press shy, found the piece a "very painful experience," according to Springer, who later made the comment that Rex Reed was "working out some of his own personal problems." Reed retaliated by saying he had no personal problems then, "I was just desperately trying to get something out of someone who wasn't willing to help."[261] Shirley MacLaine cackled at Reed's profile of her brother a few years later, telling the *Los Angeles Times*, "I'd like to do one on Rex — that's my idea of a good time."[262] The piece was a watershed experience for Beatty, who decided not to sue because it was "too costly."[263] The effects on his psyche would manifest themselves months later.

The day after Reed's article came out, a downcast Beatty attended an elite screening of *Bonnie and Clyde* at the Director's Guild, where the guests he invited included his former girlfriends Joan Collins and Natalie Wood, along with the directors, producers, and agents who had mentored him, a number of whom, like Renoir, Stevens, and Feldman, he not only loved but revered. When the end credits rolled, the audience, made up of other greats such as Billy Wilder, Frank Sinatra, and William Wyler, applauded for three solid minutes. Years later, Beatty would name this as his "best memory" of *Bonnie and Clyde*. "I had invited a lot of those people who were my betters when I started in the movies . . . it was like watching the basketball go through the net the first time."[264]

His next triumph was opening night at the Montreal Film Festival, the world premiere of *Bonnie and Clyde*. As promised, Rock Demers rented a fleet of cars from the 1930s in which Beatty, Dunaway, Penn, and Warner

Brothers executives could arrive in spectacular style. "And the reaction was absolutely overwhelming," remembered Demers. "It was a twenty-minute, standup ovation at the end of the film, and after that, the studio guys said, 'Well, maybe we didn't evaluate the film properly.' I remember shaking hands with a very happy Warren at the beginning, and a very, *very* happy Warren at the end. It was a never-ending ovation."

The fly in the ointment was Bosley Crowther, the *New York Times* film critic who had been Beatty's nemesis since *The Roman Spring of Mrs. Stone*. The aging Crowther was the only American print journalist at the festival, and his report from Montreal in the *New York Times* on August 7 dismissed *Bonnie and Clyde* as a "slap-happy color film charade," denouncing the crowd that cheered it as "delirious."[265] It was the opening shot in what would be a personal showdown between Beatty and Crowther, and, by extension, New Hollywood versus the Old Guard. On a larger scale, *Bonnie and Clyde* symbolized the rebellion of sixties youth disenchanted with the political establishment.

"It was very interesting," Estelle Parsons was to comment, "that it should become just the right film in the right time of the movement of our culture." Ironically, the opposing generals in this American civil war of culture, Warren Beatty and Bosley Crowther, were both from Virginia.

After Crowther's snipe, Beatty flew to New York to sneak into a press screening of *Bonnie and Clyde*. Joe Morgenstern, the thirtyish film critic for *Newsweek*, was startled to see the star of the movie he was reviewing sitting next to him in the back row. "I remember Warren trying to read my notes by the light of the projector," Morgenstern would recall, chuckling, conceding that Beatty's presence was intimidating. "In retrospect, I really respect him for [being there]. It bespeaks his gifts and determination as a producer."[266]

Bonnie and Clyde opened in two theaters in New York on Sunday, August 13, part of Warner Brothers' plan to introduce the film gradually to other cities, hoping public interest would increase due to positive word of mouth and good reviews. The day after it opened, the *New York Times* published a second full-length review by Crowther denouncing *Bonnie and Clyde* as a "cheap piece of bald-faced slapstick comedy that treats the hideous depredations of that sleazy, moronic pair as though they were as full of fun and frolic as the jazz-age cut-ups in *Thoroughly Modern Millie*."[267] It was the formal declaration of war between Old and New Hollywood.

Roger Ebert, the young critic for the *Chicago Sun-Times*, was in the vanguard of the antiestablishment view, proclaiming that Penn and Beatty "went into the desert and created a masterpiece."[268] Six other national critics, including Penelope Gilliatt of *The New Yorker* and the film's self-proclaimed "flaming advocate" Judith Crist, praised *Bonnie and Clyde* the week it was released, but "what really hurts," Beatty told Ebert at the time, "is that one lousy review in the *New York Times*. Bosley Crowther says your movie is a glorification of violence, a cheap display of sentimental claptrap and that's that. The *New York Times* has spoken, hallelujah."[269]

That Friday, Joe Morgenstern, who had written what he later called a "rather anal dismissive review" of *Bonnie and Clyde*, which would appear in *Newsweek* on Monday, decided to take his wife, actress Piper Laurie, to see the movie, thinking she might like the costumes and the music. "And the audience was going wild. The audience was just going berserk, and cheering, and yelling. And I felt the cold sweat on the back of my neck and realized I'd missed the boat. And I turned frantically to my wife and said, 'Do you have anything I can write with?' . . . and I started desperately scribbling notes."

On Monday, Morgenstern persuaded his "absolutely fearless" editor to let him write a second review of Beatty's film, which appeared in *Newsweek* on August 28. Morgenstern's new piece began, "Last week this magazine said that *Bonnie and Clyde* . . . turns into a 'squalid shoot-'em up for the moron trade' because it does not know what to make of its own violence. I am sorry to say I consider that review grossly unfair and regrettably inaccurate. I am sorrier to say I wrote it."[270]

Newsweek's "unprecedented about-face" in its review of *Bonnie and Clyde* made national headlines, giving the film a jolt of electricity as it was opening in Los Angeles, "and I think it emboldened Warner Brothers to put some more juice into that marketing campaign," observed Morgenstern. Benton defined Morgenstern's reversal, later, as a "turning point."

Years afterward, in the false mythology that would enshrine *Bonnie and Clyde*, it would be said that someone influenced Morgenstern to change his review—either his wife, Piper Laurie; Beatty; or critic Pauline Kael—but as he clarified, "my motive all along was just to dig myself out of a deep hole that I had gotten into. I had no idea that no mainstream critic had ever done this before."

Beatty not only was ecstatic, he was impressed. "Can you picture it?" he asked Ebert at the time. "The guy's honest enough to change his mind."[271] Morgenstern would recall, "I got a phone call from Warren—how could I make this up?—from poolside at the Beverly Wilshire . . . I was a very provincial New Yorker at that time, and getting a call from poolside, from

Warren Beatty, who said, 'That was really great, I appreciate that,' or words to that effect . . . I was pretty dazzled."

Bosley Crowther responded to the wave of enthusiasm sweeping *Bonnie and Clyde* to prominence by writing two more searing pieces in the *New York Times* lambasting the film's violence. His attack provoked an angry stream of letters to the *Times*, including one from movie critic Andrew Sarris, who claimed Crowther had "set back the American film industry by refusing to recognize a great film."[272] As Penn later noted slyly, "It was great publicity."[273]

When Beatty and Penn flew to London around September 10 for the film's United Kingdom release, they were shocked to see people on the streets dressed in clothes similar to Theadora Van Runkle's costumes for *Bonnie and Clyde*. "It went through the roof," as Beatty would exclaim, recalling eleven people who fainted during the first London screening.[274] The actor, who made a habit of personally checking the sound systems in theaters to make sure the gunshots would register as loud as in *Shane* to shock audiences, reacted with alarm at the London screening when the first shot fired by Clyde was barely a pop. "So I'm running up eight flights of steps to the projectionist," Beatty would recall, in a favorite story, "and I came into the booth, and of course the projectionist was not used to the star coming up there. And I said, 'Hello. Is something wrong with the sound?' and he said proudly, 'Oh no, no, I fixed it!' He said, 'I haven't had a picture this badly mixed since *Shane*.'"[275]

Beatty went directly from the London screening to catch a red-eye for the studio's red carpet premiere at the Campus Theater in Denton, Texas, on September 13. The event, which attracted thirteen hundred people, was preceded by a Texas-style barbecue, a parade, and a press conference at the Holiday Inn, with the stars of the movie answering questions from forty reporters bused in from around the country.[276] "It was so *big*," exclaimed a still-dazed Michael J. Pollard, thirty-six years later. "It was like the Beatles or something. It just built and built." The following day, when the movie opened at the Majestic in downtown Dallas, a euphoric Beatty, who owned 40 percent of the profits in the deal struck with Jack Warner, told a reporter that he expected *Bonnie and Clyde* to gross $25 million — $10 million short of the final figures, which were close to Robert Towne's original estimate.[277]

Bill Rives, a local columnist, observed the star before the movie premiere in a long conversation with a pretty Denton girl. "I asked the young lady later if Beatty had asked for her telephone number. 'Well, yes,' she said, 'but he didn't get it.' 'Oh,' I said, 'you wouldn't give it to him, eh?' 'No,' she said, rather wistfully. 'I don't have a telephone.'"[278] Robert Benton would recall a similarly amusing story about Beatty and fiftyish actress Loretta Young at the first screening in New York. "We all went out to dinner at a restaurant called La Fonda del Sol afterward," said Benton, "and Warren was doing his best to get Loretta Young into bed. She was really — at whatever age she was — an absolute knockout, and incredibly charming. And she brushed him aside, but he was so charmed, and so relentless with her. It was wonderful."

At the end of October, when *Bonnie and Clyde* ranked fourth in national box office receipts, *The New Yorker* published a seven thousand-word rhapsody on the film, and its stars, written by critic Pauline Kael, who would become the voice of the new generation of filmmakers and briefly a producing partner of Beatty's. The passionate tribute by Kael — another female to the rescue — along with the film's spectacular success in England, inspired editors at *Time* to assign a cover piece on *Bonnie and Clyde* for their December 7 issue, according to Stefan Kanfer, who wrote it.[279] For Beatty, the cover story in *Time* was sweet vindication, since the magazine's music critic, Alan Rich, had reviewed the film the previous August as tasteless "claptrap."*

Kanfer's lengthy piece in *Time*, which featured Warren Beatty and Faye Dunaway on the cover rendered by artist Robert Rauschenberg, compared *Bonnie and Clyde* to *Citizen Kane* and *The Birth of a Nation*, heralding Beatty's American New Wave film as a "watershed picture, the kind that signals a new style, a new trend."[280]

A few days before the *Time* cover appeared on newsstands, Bosley Crowther was removed from his position as film critic at the *New York Times* and given the title "critic emeritus." As his son recalled, "There were a group of people at the *Times* who were considerably younger than my father, and felt that Bos lost his touch with the young crowd. He was a very philosophical guy who said, 'Well, this is what happens in life. The young bucks, the young Turks start to take over.'" As Robert Towne described it, more bluntly, "Warren got Bosley Crowther fired." Years later, even Crowther would reevaluate Beatty's groundbreaking film, acknowledging that *Bonnie and Clyde* was "indeed a passover into a new style and thrust in social films."[281]

The end of January 1968, Faye Dunaway accompanied Beatty to Paris for the French premiere of *Bonnie and Clyde*. "That's when I knew something

---

*Rich quit his post at *Time* soon after to write exclusively about music. "If you talk to Warren Beatty," he would say in 2003, "will you please convey my apology?"

incredible was happening," remarked Dunaway. "I got out of the car into this sea of berets. It was stunning. I thought, 'Oh my God, everyone looks like me.'"[282] When Beatty returned to the United States after his triumph in France, he continued to badger Warner Brothers. "I pushed and shoved a hell of a lot to get the film re-released . . . and you know, with that time for gestation, we did five times as much business as we did in the first go-round."[283]

In April, a week after Beatty's thirtieth birthday, *Bonnie and Clyde*, his first film as a producer, won two Academy Awards, for Best Cinematography and Best Supporting Actress, given to Estelle Parsons. It was nominated for eight more Oscars, including Best Picture, Best Director, Best Screenplay, and Best Costume Design, along with acting nominations for Faye Dunaway, Michael J. Pollard, Gene Hackman, and Beatty, who had given his finest performance since *Splendor in the Grass*. "What was serendipitous for the movie," analyzed Towne, "is that in great and small ways, an unusual number of passionate, gifted people found their way in working on the same movie . . . and of course there's only one person you have to attribute that to, and that's the producer, Warren."

Shirley MacLaine said simply at the time, "My brother is a genius."[284] In her view, the violence in the movie expressed the rage her brother had suppressed in childhood as a silent observer of their father's alcoholic fury. "I know my brother, I know the fire under there. I know the turmoil and the hostility under there. That's what's so brilliant about *Bonnie and Clyde*. He turned his torture and his rebellion into a work of art."[285]

Bonnie and Clyde's original godmother, Elinor Jones, who, with her brother, had tried to realize Benton and Newman's *Jules and Jim*–inspired pipe dream for eighteen months before Beatty stormed Hollywood with it, said in retrospect, "The fact that we didn't make any money, it doesn't bother me, if you want to know frankly. I always felt very proud of *Bonnie and Clyde*, because we bet on the right horse."

For Warren Beatty, *Bonnie and Clyde* allowed him to achieve his definition of success: "when you don't know whether you're working or playing and you can do what you want to do and still get paid."[286] It was a philosophy inspired by the sacrifices of Tat and Ira Beaty—Tatira—who gave up their fantasies for a conventional life in Virginia as a real estate salesman and a housewife devoted to Shirley and Warren.

The Pro

"Oh, grow up.
You never stop moving. You never go anywhere.
Grow up! Grow up, grow up."

SHAMPOO
by Robert Towne and Warren Beatty, 1975

Warren Beatty at his home on Mulholland Drive, shortly after the release of
Shampoo in 1975, photographed by Harry Benson.

39 *After the extraordinary success of* *Bonnie and Clyde,* Warren Beatty's options seemed limitless. "Put it this way," he told a London reporter, revealing his characteristic dry wit, "right now if I went to somebody and said I wanted to make a musical of 'The Last Supper,' they'd probably say, 'Okay, let's talk about it.' But I don't think I'm any different than when I made *Splendor in the Grass* for Elia Kazan."[1]

Beatty's fidelity to the person he was before he became a movie star or a filmmaker would play a significant role in the choices he would make in the coming years. His freedom to pursue things he felt passionate about was made possible by the fact that *Bonnie and Clyde* made him "financially secure enough never to have to work again."[2]

Beatty used his freedom to become involved in politics, his fascination since childhood. His initiation was in March 1968, the month he turned thirty-one, when Robert Kennedy announced his candidacy for the presidency. Beatty, who had had an emotional connection to John F. Kennedy as a politician, and as a person, since he was Kennedy's choice for *PT 109*, campaigned with Robert Kennedy in Oregon, "activated" by his own opposition to the Vietnam War.[3] "Bobby was a greater influence on me than the President. I knew him better, and that's when I really began to be active in politics, is working with Bobby." Beatty described himself later as "an old-fashioned Kennedy liberal, a guy who had a romantic idea about what government could accomplish."[4]

By his admission, Beatty was "a little shy" initially, but as Ted Kennedy would recall, "Bobby especially appreciated his support — but what really impressed him was that Warren had studied and mastered the issues. When Warren became politically active it was in a genuine and serious way."[5] His movie star presence, however, created a stir. "Boy, all the little girls in the office went nuts," recalled Bill Rosendahl, a Kennedy campaign worker who first encountered Beatty in Oregon. "And so everybody went to meet Warren at some street corner where he was doing his politics for Bobby Kennedy. His whole purpose was to excite the canvassers who were doing the real grunt work, banging on the doors."[6]

Beatty's political involvement brought him back to his Virginia values, and to the political legacy in his family, helping him to purge a "certain amount of guilt" about the lifestyle he had adopted since becoming a movie star, a decision he still viewed with ambivalence. "I have led a very indulgent life," he told the *New York Post* in the seventies, "almost indescribably indulgent."[7]

Beatty said later he tried to keep his behavior "within reason," comparing himself to a "kid in a candy store."[8] His temptations increased with the sexual liberation of the sixties and seventies, and through the influence of friends such as Victor Lownes, the head of the London Playboy Club, and director Roman Polanski, who offered him the lead in *Rosemary's Baby*, which the high-minded Beatty turned down as "not important enough."[9] Their indulgences were sexual, not psychedelic, according to Lownes, who threw the stag party for Polanski in Europe before his wedding to Sharon Tate, attended by Beatty. "None of us were into drugs or anything. I mean there wasn't any point to it."

Beatty also spent time with Polanski in Los Angeles, where the Polish director rented a bungalow at the Chateau Marmont, the communal residence for a clique that included Dick Sylbert. "When I got to Hollywood in 1968, I became part of that group," recalled Sylbert's twin brother, Paul, also a production designer. "Polanski was having parties regularly on Friday night." Sandy Whitelaw, Beatty's English friend, would observe, "The thing that I find remarkable about Warren and about American males generally is that they seem to be so innocent in many ways, and at the same time they're actually much more experienced sexually than you think. I remember I had a video machine, and it was one of the first ones ever — Warren saw this thing and immediately imagined the possibilities."

Whitelaw, who went on the prowl with Beatty in Los Angeles, London, and Paris, said of him, "I think Warren was a much more *playfully* sexual human being than people think; that is, I think that his *method* of seducing had a lot more to do with sort of giggles, and actually really being kind of a lot of fun toward these girls . . . and he's not at all a boaster, and he will never say anything that would be harmful. I really do think that Warren is one of the nicest people that I met in Hollywood. I don't have very, very fond memories of my eleven years there, but certainly the time I spent with Warren was fun . . . what we mostly talked about was girls, women — who was available, who was good-looking, who we'd like to fuck, and who we didn't want to."

Cockney actress Judy Carne, the spunky redhead who became famous on *Laugh-In* in 1968, wrote about her affair with Beatty in this period, mentioning his interest in sexual "threesomes" — as would other women he dated briefly in the late sixties through the eighties, some of whom would describe them in tell-all books.[10] "I went through exactly the same sexual revolution as the country went through," Beatty said at sixty-two, describing those decades as his opportunity to "act out" in the way he should have during his "repressed Protestant" youth. "When the sixties came, it was different."[11]

At the same time, Beatty felt the need to atone, the vestiges of his Baptist upbringing and a source of recurring moral conflict. "I think my interest in politics has saved my . . . soul," he said later.[12] For Beatty, a confessed romantic, politics symbolized what John Reed represented to him, "that thing about people working together . . . it had to do with idealism, and not to turn one's back on idealism. Idealists move me. John Reed moves me."[13]

In 1967, Beatty went to Harvard to read a collection of the leftist journalist's poems and letters "and got lost in it," identifying with the handsome and sensitive Reed, whom Upton Sinclair once called the "Playboy of the Western Revolution."[14] Reed, a Harvard graduate whose eyewitness account of the 1917 Russian Revolution, *Ten Days That Shook the World*, became a classic, further stirred Beatty because of the striking parallels to Beatty's magnetic uncle Alex MacLeod, who had edited a left-wing journal, was the first witness to the intervention against Spain's fledgling democracy in 1936, and became the last Communist in the Canadian Parliament. Reed's love affair with writer-photographer Louise Bryant, who joined in his crusade for communism and workers' rights, evoked romantic childhood memories for Beatty of his actress aunt Ginny, who spoke on the radio in Canada to support MacLeod's human rights causes.

Beatty's reawakening to politics became more profound after Robert Kennedy's assassination, in June 1968, which Beatty described as a "horror" in a handwritten letter to Jean Howard, Charles Feldman's first wife, a week later. "I have never been so depressed," he wrote. "It was the worst thing that's ever happened in this country and the saddest. God, will it ever end. What that family has been through. I went to the funeral and on the train to the burial in Washington and I still can't believe it."[15]

Beatty responded by becoming chairman of the Artists' Emergency

Committee for Gun Control, giving speeches in which he drew a few boos, and once had a bottle thrown at him. "What I tried to do, really, since Bobby Kennedy is to live a political life as much as I wanted to. It's kept me alive to be politically active."[16] Ted Kennedy would describe Beatty as a "good and trusted friend" in the years after Robert Kennedy was shot.

Beatty suffered the loss of two other significant male figures in the same several-month period. One was his role model in the family his prominent uncle Mansell MacLean. The other was his Hollywood role model Charles Feldman, with whom he had reconciled the previous year, after Feldman was diagnosed with cancer. Beatty visited Feldman almost daily, "and sat beside his bed for days and nights of anguish," recalled Pierre Salinger's then wife.[17] If Feldman was asleep, Beatty left notes.[18]

"Warren is very good about dying," as Jane Fonda would observe. "Warren shows up when you're dying. He showed up for Charlie . . . he shows up when you're in trouble, too. It's interesting. He's a loyal friend." Grace Dobish, Feldman's longtime secretary, wrote to Feldman's first wife after his death, "Warren was a wonderful person throughout this sad affair."

On the night of the Oscars for *Bonnie and Clyde*, Feldman sent a wire to Beatty expressing how he felt, cabling, "DEAR WARREN: MY THOUGHTS ARE WITH YOU TONIGHT. YOU ARE GOING TO WIN EVERYTHING. YOU DESERVE IT. YOU ARE A WONDERFUL FRIEND AND I LOVE YOU. CHARLIE."[19]

Beatty was deeply affected by this trio of deaths in 1968, which reminded him of his mortality at the young age of thirty-one, and would inspire him, in the future, to make *Heaven Can Wait*, a film that offered the hope of life after death. "I learned that life is short," he said years later, "that movies are written on water, that the quality of your own life is the ultimate reality, that the important thing is to enjoy life rather than stack up wealth and fame."[20]

Beatty's yearning for a life beyond movies was reflected in statements he made in the late sixties, when he was in his thirties. "I don't have as many roots as I would like," he told a writer in New York. "In Hollywood, I even live on the roof of a hotel — and that's not right. I'm going to do something to change that."[21]

The fact that Beatty had fallen in love with the free-spirited Julie Christie in 1967 made this aspiration for a more traditional life, or a family, less likely. As costume designer Rita Riggs, who got to know Christie during *Petulia* when she began dating Beatty, would recall, "Julie used to sleep on the roof of Tony Walton's apartment in New York in a sleeping bag. She's a wonderful, offbeat character."[22] Christie was also a strong-minded feminist who believed in monogamy but saw "[no] reason for getting married unless you're religious, which I'm not."[23] She was also disinclined to have children. "I don't want to give away ten years of my life to a child," she said later, ". . . of course, I can imagine that once you've got a child, that's it. You're in love and it's marvelous."[24]

Ira and Kathlyn Beaty did not interfere in their son's personal life. As Beatty would comment after their deaths, "my parents never encouraged me to get married."[25] He almost certainly felt their hopes for him, however. Judy Evans Lang, one of Shirley MacLaine's close friends from high school, ran into Kathlyn Beaty in Arlington in the late sixties. "Mrs. Beaty and I ended up at the Grand Union one day," recalled Lang, "and she recognized me. I was married then and probably had my youngest with me, and I thought it was so funny because she was—typical mother, she was so worried that Warren would never get married. And I just thought that was so dear, that as a mother that was still her main concern. And of course, he was dating everybody and anybody. She said, 'I don't think Warren's ever going to get married.'"

Yet Beatty's next movie after the revolutionary *Bonnie and Clyde* was an old-fashioned throwback to Hollywood romances of the fifties, costarring Elizabeth Taylor. Set in Las Vegas, the movie follows two lead characters who, after many struggles, decide to get married, with the implicit message that marriage conquers all, a theme that would recur in Beatty's films. It was called *The Only Game in Town*.

Beatty turned down *Butch Cassidy and the Sundance Kid* to star in *The Only Game in Town* as a favor to aging director George Stevens, who called him at the Democratic Convention in Chicago in the summer of 1968 after Frank Sinatra, the original lead, dropped out. Though he correctly perceived the movie was a "9,000-ton soufflé" waiting to collapse, Beatty said yes immediately, sensing rightly that it would be the legendary director's last film.[26] When *Butch Cassidy* became a hit and *The Only Game in Town* quickly disappeared, dismissed by critics as "thin," the sentimental Beatty stood by his choice. "I always thought that it was probably one of the most sensible decisions I had made because I got the chance to work with George . . . ultimately it was more rewarding to me to have made a sort of an unsuccessful picture with him."[27]

Stevens impressed Beatty with his "unlimited patience" with Elizabeth Taylor, who had persuaded the studio to reconstruct Las Vegas in Paris in order to accommodate a "little tax matter" of hers, and who delayed production for months due to her recurring back pain.[28] Beatty later discussed with George Stevens, Jr., what he had learned from the director, whom he called the "Super Chief." "Warren did say to me that through all of this turmoil, trying to get this done in Paris, he said that he never heard my father raise his voice. He said that was one of the lessons he took away, and that when he made *Reds*, he made it a point never to shout."[29]

Elizabeth Taylor would compliment Beatty afterward to John Springer, their common press agent, telling Springer that Beatty was "more patient, thoughtful and considerate than any actor with whom she has worked."[30] Springer, whose friendship with the Kid dated back to Beatty's years as a cocktail pianist in New York, wrote to him after seeing *The Only Game in Town*, in which Beatty played a piano player in a Vegas lounge: "This character is more like you as I know you than any you have ever played. You are very funny, you are very touching at times, you could not be more attractive and it may be the 'nicest' character you have ever played. You are so likable in it."[31]

The movie plainly had a personal meaning for Beatty, beyond the opportunity to work with Stevens and Elizabeth Taylor. A year later, he disclosed that he would like to be married and have children, saying, "That movie, *The Only Game in Town*, didn't get the greatest reviews in the world, but it said something very important to me. A true thing. That while the institution of marriage seems to have fallen on bad times, it's still the only game in town. No matter how we try to push away from it, we're left with only one abiding thing, the family unit."[32]

During filming, Beatty paradoxically lived up to his Hollywood image as a playboy.[33] He occasionally commuted to Geneva, where Julie Christie was filming *In Search of Gregory*, and spent his nights in Paris with, among others, actress Brigitte Bardot, a stewardess for SAS, and Princess Elizabeth of Yugoslavia, whom he had met through Taylor and Richard Burton.[34] "It was one of the best times *I've* ever had on a movie, I can tell you," Beatty would admit mischievously in 2004, "and mostly it was after and before hours. We worked what they call 'French hours,' 12:00 to about 7:00. Usually we wouldn't get started till about 2:00, and so you can *imagine* what I was doing with the nights, in the '60s . . . it was an amazing time in Paris."[35]

The liberated Christie, who believed in being true to one person without getting married, was in a catch-22 with Beatty, who promised he would be faithful only if he took wedding vows. "I know when I was at Tony Walton's studio and she was up on the roof," recalled Rita Riggs, "she was confiding a little bit about rough times with Warren." Years later, Christie would reflect, "Even though it was sometimes painful, I learned a lot. Warren knows a lot of people involved in politics, and it was probably the first time I met people who were in positions of power, mainly American politicians."[36]

Beatty's interest in politics "crystallized" on November 2, 1968, the night Richard Nixon was elected president. "I had difficulty believing it," he said later.[37] What appalled Beatty was the hypocrisy of the Americans who had voted for Nixon. "We knew he was a crook, and we knew he would be surrounded by crooks, long before it was actually proved to us."[38] Beatty saw a parallel between what he considered the hypocrisy that led to Nixon's election, and the hypocrisy behind the sexual revolution. "Essentially, we've all been living lies," as he explained it. "Politically and sexually, marriage, 'til death do us part. The phrase 'sexual politics' puts it all together."[39]

When he returned to Los Angeles after finishing *The Only Game in Town*, Beatty suggested to Towne that they incorporate sexual politics into their comedy about the Don Juan hairdresser. He and Towne jettisoned their eunuch subplot and decided to make an "Our Town 1968," a satire about the sexual mores of Beverly Hills as seen through the perspective of an oversexed hairdresser on the eve of Nixon's election. They had lost their original title, *Hair*, to the Broadway musical that opened in April 1968, and temporarily used the title *Up and Down*, a sexual double entendre taken from the hairdresser's then standard query, "Do you want to wear your hair up or down?"

While Towne revised the script in 1969, Beatty and Julie Christie went to Moscow to retrace John Reed's steps. While they were there, Beatty was approached by representatives of Russian director Sergei Bondarchuk, who had seen him in *Bonnie and Clyde* and wanted Beatty to play Reed in a Russian film biography.

During the conversation, Beatty heard about an eighty-five-year-old former ballerina named Eleanora Drapkina, who lived outside Moscow and claimed to have had an affair with Reed, "so I wrangled my way out there with a KGB spy. I had just a minimal amount of Russian but I could speak to her. And I said, 'So you had a love affair with John Reed?' And she said, 'I fucked him.' And I of course fell in love with her."[40]

As Beatty recalled, "She had been a beautiful fifteen-, sixteen-year-old girl . . . I said, 'My God, how do you feel about Stalin?' She said, 'Only hate.' I said, 'Really.' She said, 'Yes. But of course the revolution is in its early stages.' It was at that moment I thought, I have to make a movie about that kind of passion. And I'm gonna make it without the Russians. And I'm gonna make it just the way I want to make it."[41]

Beatty's enchantment with the eighty-five-year-old Drapkina was similar to his childhood reaction to his grandmother MacLean, and the fact that he and John Reed both had had romantic involvements with Russian ballerinas increased his feeling of a "mystical connection" between him and Reed.

At the end of 1969, Beatty had another personal motivation to make the film when his uncle Alex MacLeod was hit by a car, and died several months later. The last lines of MacLeod's obituary underline his similarity to John Reed, and make it clear where Beatty derived his idealism: "Mr. MacLeod's persistence in counseling the [Human Rights] Commission to fight social injustice unflinchingly and with integrity, wherever it existed, was unparalleled. His memory and deeds will not be forgotten."[42]

When his uncle died, the loyal Beatty brought his younger cousin David Lehigh MacLeod, the only male in his generation on both sides of the family, to Los Angeles to be an assistant on the movie that would be Beatty's homage to Alex MacLeod as much as to John Reed. At the time, David MacLeod, who had the slender, refined look of the MacLeans, was an English teacher in Ontario, and wrote speeches for Pierre Trudeau. "MacLeod was like a brother to Beatty," noted screenwriter James Toback, who became close to both men. "I mean, MacLeod basically ran his life for twenty years. The only person who knew exactly what was going on with Beatty was MacLeod."[43] The reverse would prove not to be true.

Around the time Alex MacLeod died, Beatty wrote a treatment for the John Reed film, asking playwright Lillian Hellman to prepare a first draft script, according to Hellman's executor, novelist Peter Feibleman. "The Commie scare in the States was very high then," recalled Feibleman, a close friend of Beatty's as well as of Hellman's. "It wasn't that long since McCarthy, and the Red-baiting, and it was an extraordinary idea for somebody in Hollywood to have at the time for that reason. Hollywood was still under the shadow of Red-baiting, and Pinkos, and Commies—those words were still slung around. It was very courageous of Warren to do."[44]

It would be nine years before Beatty the perfectionist starting filming his movie about Reed. His procrastination, like his perfectionism, was his insulation against failure. He later would admit that he "waited too long" to make *Reds*, telling one of his co-writers he "should have made it in the late sixties or early seventies."[45] Beatty had high ambitions for his personal *Dr. Zhivago*. "Warren is looking for another masterpiece to top *Bonnie and*

As Bud Stamper in *Splendor in the Grass*, the character William Inge based on the young Beatty. With him is director of photography Boris Kaufman.
Photo by Sam Shaw; copyright Shaw Family Archives

On the set of *Splendor in the Grass* in 1960 with director Elia Kazan, whom Beatty revered.
Photo by Sam Shaw; copyright Shaw Family Archives

Wardrobe tests for *Splendor* from Kazan's private album show a playful Natalie Wood and a more pensive Beatty. *Wesleyan Cinema Archives*

According to Jane Fonda, Beatty patterned himself after suave agent/producer Charles Feldman, his Hollywood mentor and surrogate father. *Photo by Larry Shaw; copyright Shaw Family Archives*

For *The Roman Spring of Mrs. Stone*, director Jose Quintero rehearses Beatty on the proper way to kiss a lady's hand to play the gigolo Paolo, a character the once devout Baptist found loathsome. *Photo by Sam Shaw; copyright Shaw Family Archives*

On the London set of *The Roman Spring of Mrs. Stone*, March 1961, as costar Vivien Leigh and girlfriend Joan Collins vie for Beatty's attention. *Archive Photos France*

Beatty was falsely accused of breaking up Natalie Wood's marriage to Robert Wagner in 1961—as a couple, he and Wood were so famous, paparazzi slept in the halls outside their hotel rooms.

Actress/photographer Jean Howard took this photo at a Beverly Hills garden party hosted by agent Minna Wallis *(standing)*, one of Beatty's legion of older female champions. He and Natalie Wood are seated to Wallis's right.
American Heritage Center, University of Wyoming

The July 1961 table reading of *All Fall Down*, where Beatty made an unfortunate first impression. *From left:* Karl Malden, Angela Lansbury, Brandon de Wilde, William Inge, John Frankenheimer, Warren Beatty, Eva Marie Saint. *Copyright ZUMA Movie Stills Library, ZUMA Press*

The troubled *Lilith* production, the summer of 1963. *From left:* Peter Fonda, Jean Seberg, unidentified grip, Beatty. Robert Rossen is in a white cap and sunglasses (*background at center*). *Courtesy of Tibor Sands (pictured at far right)*

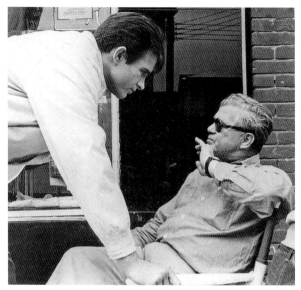

Beatty transferred painful, unresolved issues with his alcoholic father, Ira Beaty, onto director Robert Rossen *(right)* while they were making *Lilith*. *Courtesy of Carol Eve Rossen*

Beatty demonstrated his talent on the piano, his first love, in *Mickey One*, costarring Alexandra Stewart *(left)*. He portrayed a piano player again in *The Only Game in Town* and *Ishtar*; ironically, all three were commercial failures. *Courtesy of Alexandra Stewart*

The studio publicist reported that Beatty spent his free time with "six different young ladies" while filming *Kaleidoscope* in Monte Carlo, mid-February 1966. This photograph is from director Jack Smight's scrapbook, identified as "Star & twins!" *Courtesy of Jack Smight and Alec Smight*

Warren Beatty's first glimpse of girlfriend Julie Christie, captured in a photo. Christie *(at left)* shakes hands with Queen Elizabeth at the royal premiere of *Born Free* on March 14, 1966, as Leslie Caron *(next to Christie)* smiles at the queen while Beatty turns to look at Christie. Actresses Catherine Deneuve, Ursula Andress, and Raquel Welch can be seen on Beatty's left. *Photofest*

Beatty brought his then-love, Bolshoi prima ballerina Maya Plisetskaya *(at right)*, to the set of *Penelope* in June 1966 while trying to persuade ex-love Natalie Wood *(at left)* to costar in *Bonnie and Clyde*. *Courtesy of director Arthur Hiller (pictured between Wood and Plisetskaya)*

One of Curtis Hanson's stunning photos of Faye Dunaway that helped to persuade Beatty to cast her as Bonnie. *Photograph by Curtis Hanson*

Costume designer Theadora Van Runkle's original vision of Warren Beatty as Clyde Barrow, with his hair parted in the middle. Beatty rejected this period hairstyle, just as Faye Dunaway refused to wear 1930s marcel waves to play Bonnie. *Courtesy of Theadora Van Runkle*

Arthur Penn, Beatty, and Faye Dunaway bask in their twenty-minute standing ovation for *Bonnie and Clyde* on opening night at the Montreal Film Festival, August 4, 1967. *Courtesy of Rock Demers*

Beatty turned down *Butch Cassidy and the Sundance Kid* in 1968 for the chance to work with veteran director George Stevens on *The Only Game in Town*.
Courtesy of the Academy of Motion Picture Arts and Sciences by permission of George Stevens Jr.

Bearded to resemble his Virginia paternal ancestors for *McCabe & Mrs. Miller*, Beatty and Shirley MacLaine attend a Vietnam Moratorium party in Washington in May 1970. Their liberal leanings derived from their mother's family. *Copyright* Washington Post, *reprinted by permission of the D.C. Public Library*

Beatty rejected *The Godfather*, *The Sting*, and *The Way We Were* to work for Senator George McGovern's presidential campaign, when he invented the fund-raising concert. *Springer/Photofest*

Beatty and his longtime love, British actress Julie Christie, with publicist-mentor John Springer in the early 1970s. He told Springer that Christie turned down his marriage proposal.
Courtesy of Gary Springer

Legendary architectural photographer Julius Shulman photographed 13671 Mulholland Drive, the Bauhaus fortress Warren Beatty purchased in 1974 from the estate of Danish opera star Lauritz Melchior, who named it the Viking. The master bedroom features wraparound windows, where the Lion of the Loin—writer Carole Eastman's nickname for Beatty—could view the kingdom of Hollywood, but no one could see him.
Courtesy of Julius Shulman

For his role in *The Fortune* the fall of 1974, Beatty (with girlfriend Michelle Phillips) emulated Howard Hughes, who fascinated him. *Photofest*

Beatty's favorite moment associated with *Reds* was when he screened the picture privately for Diane Keaton, who inspired him to get it made more than a decade after he first conceived it.
Photo by PARAMOUNT PICTURES/ZUMA Press; copyright © 1981 by PARAMOUNT PICTURES

Beatty's glamorously leftist Canadian aunt and uncle, actress Virginia MacLeod and M. P. Alex MacLeod, the private inspiration behind *Reds*.
Archives Publiques De L'Ontario

Beatty holds his "Best Director" Oscar for *Reds* in 1982, congratulated by Loretta Young, the Golden Age actress he tried to woo fifteen years earlier after a screening of *Bonnie and Clyde*. *Photofest*

Dustin Hoffman and Beatty's lounge act in *Ishtar*, costarring French actress Isabelle Adjani *(center)*, Beatty's lover of several years, was based on his early struggles as a cocktail pianist in New York. The failure of the film in 1987 coincided with the most difficult period in Beatty's life. *Photofest*

Clyde," his sister told *Look* at the time, "and that's the impossible trap. The thing that cripples us from expressing ourselves in a growing way is the fear we won't make it better than we did before."[46]

If Beatty had made *Reds* sooner, Julie Christie likely would have played Louise Bryant. Her presence in *Zhivago* had helped to arouse Beatty's passion for Russia, and they were "desperately looking for a project to do together" in 1969, according to producer David Foster, who offered them the unconventional Western *McCabe & Mrs. Miller* in January 1970, while they were in London.[47] Originally called *The Presbyterian Church Wager*, the story was about an eccentric drifter named John McCabe who meanders into a frontier town on horseback with lofty dreams, falls in frustrated love with the local madam, and dies in a snowdrift during a fierce blizzard.

Foster, a first-time producer, had been a successful publicist, "and two things crossed my mind. Warren Beatty was a great actor, and Julie Christie was a great actress, and they had never worked together. And I said, wouldn't this be a coup publicity-wise?"[48] Foster's choice to direct was Robert Altman, "and the truth is, at that point no one really knew, except ten people, who Bob Altman was." Foster had seen an early print of *M*A*S*H*, Altman's irreverent comedy about war, "and I said 'Whoa, this is fantastic,' and by the end of the movie I made a shake-hands deal."

Beatty, who heard about *McCabe* originally through director Roman Polanski, was drawn to the story because it reminded him of tales he had heard as a child from Maggie and Bertie Beaty, his great-aunts in Front Royal, about Beatys such as their circuit-riding ancestor, John, settling in Virginia's Shenandoah Valley.

"I think," he said later, "that there were a lot of things about the character of McCabe that I imagined to be a part of things I've been told about my family's past, or about people they've known."[49] For the strong traditionalist in Beatty, the film held great appeal. "Then, I heard that Altman had made *M*A*S*H*, and when I stopped off in New York, I went to see it. There was a line two blocks long where the film was playing, and I said to myself, now wait a minute. Next day I saw a matinee, liked it, and called up Altman to say I'd like to do his film. The whole movie just, well, happened."[50]

Beatty grew a Robert E. Lee beard, wore his hair shaggy, and donned a derby hat to play McCabe, concealments that foreshadowed an increasingly shrouded private life, which he was taking steps to protect as a Virginian would. He already had stopped giving interviews except to promote a film, partially as a result of Rex Reed's toxic 1967 profile, a policy that made his longtime publicist and early mentor, John Springer, obsolete. As Springer wrote to an editor that year:

> The very fact that I have been involved with Warren so long illustrates one of his virtues which is quite extraordinary for his particular world — his loyalty. I did a good job for him when he was starting and again at "Bonnie and Clyde" time but much of the time there is so little I can do for him — not because there isn't a demand but because he himself will do almost nothing in the way of publicity. Yet he keeps me on — completely out of loyalty. Once, in a fit of despondency over collecting a regular retainer for doing so little, I tried to resign but he refused to accept the resignation.[51]

During the filming of *McCabe & Mrs. Miller,* in Vancouver in the fall and winter of 1970, Beatty and the equally reclusive Julie Christie, who described herself as an introvert, rented a house on Horseshoe Bay. Their personality differences became apparent in the way each responded to being directed by Altman, who considered the script "just a schedule" and encouraged actors to improvise.[52] Christie thrived, later naming *McCabe* as one of her favorite movies. Beatty, groomed by the meticulously organized Kazan, spent his nights feverishly writing his lines for the next day, shaping John McCabe in the model of his Beaty forebears, using dialogue lifted from "things I have heard in southern Virginia."[53]

"They're very different," Altman's then assistant, Anne Sidaris, observed of the director and Beatty. "Altman's a master manipulator, and he uses that very effectively with his actors. And before you know it, you're frothing-at-the-mouth angry, because he'll be very personal, if that's what it takes to get you to be what he wants you to be. And then he'll let you go, and it's your own anger that's coming through, or your own laughter — and I think he had trouble manipulating Warren, because Warren's pretty strong-minded. Warren knew who he was, and that made him a different challenge."[54]

Altman rolled his eyes at Beatty's fastidious technique, a clash of styles that led to a signature Beatty climax when the director was shooting an eight-minute John McCabe soliloquy on a cold Vancouver night. "We did it about forty times," related cinematographer Vilmos Zsigmond, ". . . when Robert said, 'Warren, you know, it's not getting better. I told you that take eight was perfect for me, and you kept going. I'm happy with take eight.' And Warren says, 'I want to do one more.' And then Robert said, 'Okay, Warren, I tell you what. I'm tired. I'm going to go home. You do as many takes as you want to. These boys are going to take it for you. Just finish it when you want.' And then he went home."[55]

"Bob was pissed," confirmed Altman's assistant. "I probably gave him some brandy or some scotch or something." Sidaris respected Beatty for his efforts. "We shot and shot and shot. We were there way into the night, and the snow was coming through the rafters and we were freezing to death. I might have been grousing about being up so late, but in the long run, we were all going for the same thing, a good project. And I think that reinforces my feelings about Warren being such a perfectionist . . . and how he's doing what he believes is true."

In many respects, *McCabe* was reminiscent of *Mickey One* for Beatty, who felt trapped in another obscure art film that was exquisitely pho-tographed, with hip music, by a director who, in his view, was experiment-ing. "I think," mused producer David Foster, who was in Vancouver throughout filming, "in general, Warren was thrown by Bob's style in every which way. He just does things the way he does them, and either you go with it or you don't. And I would imagine it would have unnerved Warren."

Beatty would create one of his more soulful and endearing characters in the drifter McCabe, whose signature line, "I got poetry in me," was Yev-tushenko's description of *Beatty*. His performance was a mirror of the confu-sion he was feeling about his life, expressing what critic Roger Ebert would call "a yearning for love and home that will not ever come."[56]

While he was in Vancouver, Beatty became friends with actor Jack Nicholson, who was there filming *Carnal Knowledge* for director Mike Nichols. The two film companies intermingled at a "pre-start" party given by Foster and his wife that everyone in town seemed to crash, according to Fos-ter. "It was this wild party, I want to tell you. And it got to be scary. Everyone was stoned out of their minds. It was insane."

Beatty, influenced by the example of his father, was the exception. He made his views about drugs known earlier that year, when he said, "This is one of the most serious problems we're facing today. We'd better do some-thing about it, and do it fast. Even those who say they 'only smoke pot' have no concept of what it's really all about. I think liquor and pot are equally dan-gerous, and it hasn't been proven to me yet that marijuana does *not* cause chromosomal or brain damage."[57]

Their mutual pal Paul Sylbert described Beatty and Jack Nicholson's friendship as "a Mutt and Jeff thing" with respect to drugs and alcohol, "a kind of unity of opposites." What bonded them in 1970, in Sylbert's view, was their "similar view of life, that it's there to be appreciated. I don't think they're hedonists. Warren doesn't sit around with gourmet dinners. Jack lives very simply. It's just . . . getting the things they *like* out of life, whether it's a basketball game, or a girl, or whatever the hell it is. I can't put it on a profound level. It's just two guys who discovered that they had similar orientations. With Jack, it's you only live once, and he knows what it's like to be on the down side."

When Beatty and Julie Christie returned to Los Angeles, they posed for a portrait for *Look* magazine to promote *McCabe & Mrs. Miller,* showing a bearded Beatty with Christie in her character's unruly turn-of-the-century corkscrew curls. The *Look* photographs of the ultraprivate couple, published in an issue with a cover story on the reclusive Howard Hughes, fixed Warren Beatty and Julie Christie as the archetypal New Hollywood couple of the 1970s, just as Beatty and Natalie Wood had personified old-fashioned Hollywood glamour in the early 1960s.

As Foster recalled, "Every magazine, every newspaper, every wire, *everybody* wanted to come and cover the 'lovers at work.' Warren and Julie wouldn't do any of it. They agreed to do one thing, and that was *Look* magazine."

Behind the classic photographs, Beatty and Julie Christie were already showing signs of strain. They lived apart during patches of *McCabe,* as Altman's assistant would recall. "I didn't see a lot of exhibition of affection . . . I was under the impression that their relationship was not what it had been, and let's face it, in those days Warren was not a very faithful guy. But he would be loyal and protective of anybody he cared about, whether the relationship was still in full force or not. Warren's a very loyal person."

40 *Beatty went directly from "McCabe"* into a forgettable heist film called $,* which he shot in Germany and Norway the first four months of 1971. He was impressed with the director, the experienced Richard Brooks, whom he quizzed about camera angles and complimented as "well-prepared," a relief after his frustrations with the unstructured Altman.[58] According to the on-set photographer, the crusty Brooks had a habit of grumbling and of calling everyone "Bullshit Charlie."

*Sometimes referred to as *Dollars.*

"He'd talk to Beatty, suggesting something about a scene, and then as he walked away, he'd mutter under his breath, 'Nobody listens, nobody cares, nobody listens, nobody cares.' It's probably true."[59]

Beatty's costar was the ebullient Goldie Hawn, who had just won an Oscar as Best Supporting Actress for her third film, *Cactus Flower*, but was better known from the television series *Laugh-In*. The two met for the first time in Los Angeles at a restaurant in one of the canyons with Julie Christie, who would become a close friend of Hawn's through the seventies.

"Warren was always such a romantic figure," Hawn recalled of that first lunch. "But I found his sense of humor just really funny. He disarms you with his charm . . . and Julie, too — oh my God! — 'cause I was also falling in love with Julie. She had on these overalls, and little T-shirt underneath. She's so full of style, and wonderful detail, and they were just great together . . . the difference, the space between them, is what made them so compelling. She was not a woman of Hollywood, didn't really want to be in Hollywood. She was a girl who liked to milk cows, or be on the farm . . . very, very earthy girl. And of course Warren was sort of the man-about-town, and all the girls falling over him, and Mr. Hollywood, who knew everybody there was to know."[60]

Once they got to Germany, Beatty made a pass at Goldie Hawn, which she would analyze, after years of observing him, in much the same way as his poet friend Yevtushenko, who felt that flirting was like a drug for Beatty. Hawn compared it to an electrical charge. "I mean he seduces children, men, women . . . he's a man who enjoys the moment, that moment of connection where there could be a potential spark. I watched him with boyfriends of mine, just wow them, and it's part of his nature, there's no question. He is charged by the person, therefore they become charged by him." Beatty's Arlington pal Tom Calhoun witnessed it in high school as the power to mesmerize. "Over the years, I've seen this happen," concurred Hawn, "because men are terribly threatened by Warren until they meet him. And then they fall in love."

Hawn rejected Beatty's sexual advance because she was married and he was involved with Julie Christie. "That's not to say that there wasn't any modicum of attraction there. I'd be insane to say that there wasn't. Come on! He was beautiful, artistic, smart, analytical, talented, a musician — all of it, all the great stuff. So as fate would have it, I didn't become one of Warren's 'girls,' and I'm very happy about that, because I had the joy of becoming a family member."

While they were in Europe filming $, Goldie Hawn got to know the "real" Warren. Like Beatty, Hawn grew up around Washington, D.C., with a father who played the violin. "I always think that anybody whose father plays the violin has been given something that they're not even aware of, like my dad. There's a spirit that goes along with a man that learned that incredibly high vibrational instrument. And we talked about our dads, and we related a lot to our histories together as two people who came from the same part of the world, who had very similar kinds of conservative upbringings. Not conservative in political ways, but conservative in family values, and what it is that we believed would make a successful life. Warren has an extremely strong work ethic, and my work ethic is very, very similar. I recognize it. And because I've had the pleasure of meeting his mom and dad, knowing his sister, knowing the family—I speak from a very deep level, and not necessarily the level of people that may have come into contact with Warren over the years. He's a very deep person . . . if I had a brother in this world—and I did have a brother, he was born before I was, but he died about four weeks after he was born, so I never had a brother—Warren is my brother. He has become the brother that I never had, and will always be till the day I die."

Not only was Goldie Hawn a touchstone to Beatty's Virginia values, her exuberant personality was the perfect counterpoint to his occasional moodiness, the Scots-Irish temperament he and Shirley MacLaine had both inherited. While MacLaine could be antic, Beatty offset his serious nature with wry, often self-deprecating humor. "If you're going to hang out with Warren, you have to have wit," observed his friend Marshall Bell. "Everybody he has in his life is funny . . . what people miss is how funny *he* is. It's a kind of interior humor that's spontaneous and situational."[61]

As actors, Hawn and Beatty had radically different styles, something Hawn, accustomed to the fast pace on *Laugh-In*, discovered while making $ the winter of 1971. "Warren is notorious for long takes, and doing lots and lots of takes, and I wasn't used to that, coming out of television. Three takes, and I'm done. I always thought that Warren's early takes were sometimes his best takes, but you can't tell anybody that. It's just a function of his wish for perfection. And this is not a perfect art, and these mistakes are just as important as our plans. But he just had trouble letting go of the take, and so he would do it until he felt he got it."

While Beatty was in Germany, Robert Towne sent him the rewrite of their hairdresser satire after months of writer's block. "And I actually thought he would like it," said Towne, "and I didn't hear from him for months. And then, when we finally did speak, he just said he didn't think it was particularly funny."

After completing $ in April, Beatty devoted the rest of 1971 and all of 1972 to Senator George McGovern's campaign for the presidency, turning down *The Sting* (which he considered "boring"), *The Way We Were* ("I said, 'Come on Barbra, you're kidding. Why don't I play the girl and you play the guy?'"), *The Great Gatsby* ("I didn't like the deal they offered me"), *The Godfather* ("the idea didn't motivate me that much"), and *Last Tango in Paris*.[62] "I had spent so much time involved in the pursuit of my own affairs — business and, uh, so forth — that it seemed very much in order for me to do something less selfish," he said later.[63] As a critic of Nixon, Beatty also felt an obligation "to be a participant in the great changes that need to take place."[64]

Beatty had discovered a truth about himself during the Kennedy campaign. "I can't mix making movies and working in politics," he observed, "because I can't dabble in either one of them."[65] Beatty could only make "total commitments," whether it was to people, or to projects, another reason he took his time making decisions.

Beatty gave his time and energy to George McGovern because he considered the senator from South Dakota "terribly honest, terribly forthright. When I checked his record as Senator I found his stand on all the issues was impressive."[66] Or as the actor told a group of students on the campaign trail, "I've never caught him in a lie and that's why I'd take the time to go out and support him."[67]

McGovern later would add, "Warren couldn't stand Nixon. And he was very impressed with my positions on the issues that he cared about — the war in Vietnam, economic and social justice here at home, and the call for the United States to live by its highest principles and ideals rather than engage in power politics, and corrupt politics, and all the rest — so I think he saw an opportunity to influence the direction of the country in a more hopeful and constructive way, and I think that's what drove him."[68]

As McGovern remembered it, Shirley MacLaine, who had been active politically for several years, hosted a fund-raiser for him prior to her brother's participation, although Beatty would insist, "I was involved in the McGovern campaign before she was," suggesting there was residual sibling rivalry from their childhood games of King of the Mountain, and that he was still sensitive at being perceived as copying his sister.[69]

Both Beatty's and MacLaine's strong support for the Democratic Party, and for social causes, had its roots in their mother's extremely liberal family tree, as well as from their great-uncle Ira Partlow, whose visits to the house in Arlington while he was attorney general of West Virginia in the late forties — talking politics, mentioning his friend Truman — helped to form their political consciousness.

Ira Beaty remained resolutely Republican. When journalist Barbara Howar was hosting a political talk show in Washington in 1970, "every afternoon when I came off the set there would be a phone call from an elderly male viewer in the Virginia suburbs, who politely took me to tedious task for my liberal views. His identity remained a mystery until one hot and humid day in a mammoth antique mall, where he introduced himself and insisted I meet his son . . . I edged away, only to glance over and see Warren."[70]

During the seventies the outspoken MacLaine made barbed jokes about Ira Beaty's politics, telling the *New York Post* their father thought Agnew should be president, and other comments that made her brother wince.[71] Beatty took a higher road. As Barbara Howar would recall her encounter with father and son at the mall in 1970:

> We stood there in the sweltering heat, listening to the senior Mr. Beaty spout Republican rhetoric, doing it so articulately I wondered . . . where his other child, Shirley MacLaine, had gleaned her Democratic dictums . . . Beatty, though totally respectful of his dad's diatribe, only shifted patiently from one foot to the other, his thoughts inscrutable; and then, suddenly, he unhooded his eyes to merrily signal that he in no way shared his father's sentiments.

Howar began to discuss politics "in sundry phone conversations" with Beatty afterward, discovering the actor "was better informed than I was as a journalist."

McGovern would observe the same thing during his campaign for the presidency. "Warren couldn't stand the war in Vietnam. And he had read a lot about it. He used to live in those days in the penthouse of the Beverly Wilshire Hotel, and when you walked into that apartment it was in total disorder. He had stacks of magazines around the floor, against the wall, just stacked — *The Nation, Harper's, The Atlantic Monthly, The Progressive,* and various other publications that he had just accumulated, things he'd read. He'd just throw the magazines over there. But I had the strong feeling, as I got to know Warren, that he read the *New York Times, Los Angeles Times,* liberal magazines, and anything else he could get his hands on, many books.

He must be a rapid reader. He told me recently that he just finished reading four books on the Bush administration, and you know, a lot of people talk about having read everything, but he actually does."

Before Beatty started *McCabe*, he and Julie Christie met McGovern's campaign manager, Gary Hart, a handsome, rather shy young lawyer from Denver, at a dinner party at George Stevens, Jr.'s, house in Beverly Hills. "We didn't really get to know each other then," recalled Hart. "I'm not even sure he knew who I was, nor would he or should he have known, and I wasn't seeking out movie stars."[72]

The two nonetheless made a connection, sparked when Hart mentioned that he had been a student activist for John F. Kennedy and a volunteer in Robert Kennedy's campaign. Beatty, sensing a kindred spirit, gave Gary Hart his telephone number "and said to call him sometime to go out to dinner or something."

The friendship would not begin to blossom until September 1971, when Beatty flew to Milwaukee for a series of McGovern rallies in the Midwest. While he was introducing McGovern at the University of Wisconsin, Beatty had an unnerving experience that would alter his political activism and ulti- mately inspire him to come up with a revolutionary idea for campaign fund- raising. As McGovern recalled:

> I was sitting on the stage behind him, and there were youngsters down in the front who I think were pretty well doped up, maybe nothing but marijuana, certainly at least that, and they started to heckle him. And he had just flown in from London, and prior to the trip he had to have a tooth pulled. So he had an aching tooth, and his jaw was swelled on one side, and he had flown all night to get there, and they started heck- ling him. Well, he couldn't believe it. He's used to cheers, and Acad- emy Awards, not used to a bunch of college kids heckling him, but they did.
>
> And so at one point I just stepped up to the mike, because he was kind of flustered, didn't quite know what to do — we're supposed to be having a love-in here, how come you people are trying to give me a bad time? So I just stepped up to the mike and I said, "Listen, Warren Beatty flew all night to get here to talk to you people, now shut up and listen to what he has to say. I don't want another word out of anybody here. I want you to sit there and listen to a thoughtful and talented man, and this is the end of this heckling. If you want to heckle, get the

hell out of here, because the rest of the people here are serious about this campaign, and serious about the issues we're talking about, and it's a rare opportunity for you to hear one of the most talented men in this country get up and explain his views on why he's in this campaign." Well, for some reason or another they quieted down, that was about it, and he got along fine after that.

The incident "embarrassed" him, Beatty said later, something he could not tolerate, a legacy from his father.[73] (That same year, MacLaine similarly admitted that she had a "terror of being laughed at."[74]) Beatty was also concerned that people might perceive him as a political dilettante, a "self-forwarding, publicity-seeking, capricious artist who would like to attach some mood of seriousness to his persona by participating in public affairs."[75] He stopped introducing McGovern, as Gary Hart would recall, "wanting to know what he could do to help that would be a more pragmatic involvement." According to Hart, Beatty made effective suggestions concerning the media, "how to make things dramatic, and most politicians don't know how to do that or wouldn't think of that."

As they continued on the campaign trail, Hart and Beatty became close friends, struck by the number of things they had in common in addition to their Kennedy idealism. "I came from Kansas," as Hart would recount, "from a reasonably strict religious environment. And his was not all that different. Warren didn't come from as small a town as I did, but Arlington — though it's near a large town — isn't. His mother was a more dramatic figure than mine, probably, but it was a similar background. And I also had an older sister who was flamboyant . . . so there are a lot of parallels."

What surprised Hart, a soft-spoken intellectual who was brought up in the austere Church of the Nazarene, was Warren Beatty's devout Baptist background. Gary Hart was one of the few people Beatty trusted enough to reveal his religious past. He told Hart how meaningful his baptism was to him, that he had taught Sunday school, that his mentor was a Baptist youth minister, "and I never would have expected that of him."

As the campaign progressed, noticed McGovern, "I had the impression that Warren and Gary were made for each other." Hart would concur, adding, "and we're so close in age. There's only six months between us." As a further symbol of a friendship that seemed almost mystic, Hart's middle name, he would note, is Warren. To Beatty, Gary Hart — the good son who finished college, married his childhood sweetheart, went to law school, and got into politics — represented the road not taken. Hart, who loved movies and had what Beatty called an artist's soul, took vicarious pleasure in his movie star friend. "In terms of lifestyles and everything," as McGovern would note, "Warren was in a pattern that Gary found intriguing, and romantic, and so on."

Once they became friends, "Warren would make these phone calls around two or three in the morning," recalled Hart. "It would go like this. I get a call at two A.M. 'Um. I'm a hairdresser. My clients are all having affairs and they're lying about it. Oh — and it's about Nixon's election.' And he wouldn't identify himself. It took me awhile to get into the pattern. And then he'd say, 'What do you think?' I didn't know what to say. So I'd always say, 'Sounds good, Warren. Do it.'"

Beatty continued his love affair with Julie Christie throughout the years of the McGovern campaign, while trying to conceal his brief romances with an array of women, including the English model and actress Twiggy, writer Kathleen Tynan, models Carole Mallory and Jennifer Lee, Swedish actress Britt Ekland (who praised him in her memoir as "a fabulous lover . . . kind and generous"),[76] and singer Carly Simon, whose famous 1973 song "You're So Vain" Beatty acknowledged in 1999 was written about him, saying, "Oh, let's be honest. That song *is* about me. It's not about Mick Jagger. It's about me."[77] Newsman Sander Vanocur, a close friend of Shirley MacLaine's in the seventies, dubbed Beatty "the Phantom of the Beverly Wilshire," recalled Gary Hart. "Because you never saw him. He had a private entrance and a private elevator and he slipped in and out."

Henry Kimelman, McGovern's finance manager, referred to Beatty with affection as the "playboy of the Western world." Kimelman's favorite Beatty story took place in Washington, D.C., during McGovern's frantic quest to replace Thomas Eagleton as his running mate. Beatty, who had offered to approach Senator Walter Mondale, phoned the senator to ask if they could change the location of their meeting from Mondale's house to Beatty's hotel. "Warren says, 'Frankly, Senator, can I speak to you man-to-man?'" Kimelman would recall. "And Mondale says, 'Certainly, Mr. Beatty.' Warren says, 'Well, I haven't had any action, Senator, since I've been here, and I got a gal coming down from New York to be with me. Would you mind coming to the hotel?' And Mondale says yes. That sums up Warren Beatty . . . Warren is, to me, a great American citizen. He cares about his country. He wants to be involved in the best way that he can, while being the big movie sex symbol."[78]

Abe Lastfogel, the high-powered agent who represented him on *Bonnie and Clyde*, detected that Beatty was unfulfilled by his lifestyle, saying in the early seventies, "Warren is a simple, very sweet, lonely young man. Often he just drops in for dinner, eats a lot of radishes, and scares me with his business acumen."[79] Beatty's friend Paul Sylbert compared the actor's penthouse lifestyle at the Beverly Wilshire to a sophomore dorm, the same concern Beatty expressed five years earlier when he said he wanted to put down roots. The closest he came to achieving this after falling in love with Julie Christie was to rent a beach house with her in Malibu. Christie, whose idea of happiness was to stroll the English moors, described herself later as someone who "was always just passing through in Hollywood. I stayed for one year after another but I always felt that I didn't really live there."[80]

Beatty's strong feelings about family life were well known to Ira and Kathlyn Beaty's friends and neighbors in Virginia, who would see him on his frequent visits back home, and were aware that he and MacLaine bought their parents a new house in 1972, when the Beatys were nearly seventy. "I can tell you this," said Mason Green, Jr., Ira Beaty's real estate colleague until he retired, "in the latter years, Shirley and Warren were very kind to their parents. And they were all very close. Of course Ira was proud of them, but he very rarely would talk about them unless you asked, and didn't talk in any way that would have been disloyal to his children. It didn't go to his head, let's put it that way. He was the same old Ira Beaty that everybody ever knew, in spite of their success."

Like the home where Warren and Shirley grew up, the one-story white brick traditional they purchased for their parents in 1972 was unpretentious, in a cozy Arlington neighborhood. Charles Holmes, the son of Kathlyn Beaty's cousin Jean, who still lived on Cape Breton Island, stayed with Tat and Ira on occasion. As he recalled:

Ira took us and drove us all around Washington, D.C., in this car, a convertible — some kind of Ford Galaxy that Warren had bought him as a gift. Tat loved poetry, as I remember her. As an adult, she enjoyed reading, and in their home in Arlington, there was a room, and she referred to it as the "birdhouse," because it was all glass all the way around, and she could see the birds in the trees. That's where we used to have morning coffee and things like that. She always read the newspaper, had to be up-to-date on everything that was going on. The room would be just festooned with newspapers and things like that. They were quite articulate people, and they spoke at great length about different world issues that they were concerned about.

It was nothing for Shirley to pop into the house and she'd say, "Mom, I've brought somebody . . . I'm just in Washington for a few hours and I wanted to come in and visit." "Well, isn't that lovely, Shirley, we weren't expecting you." And Shirley said, "Now I just want you to play it cool, but I've taken a friend along." "Really, who's your friend?" "Well, I think you might have heard of him." And in would come Henry Kissinger.

In their later years, when I stayed with Tat and Ira in Virginia, Warren and Shirley had made arrangements for two people to come to live with them and look after them . . . and when we sat down, even the three of us, Tat always rang the dinner bell. And Nester came in with the cloth over his arm.

Beatty's struggle to reconcile the values he was taught in Virginia with his lifestyle as the Phantom of the Beverly Wilshire compelled him to write his own draft of the satire about a promiscuous hairdresser that he and Towne still called *Up and Down*. "If I didn't have straight-laced beginnings myself, I wouldn't have had to make *Shampoo*," Beatty said later.[81] To him, the film was an expression of what he considered his own hypocrisy. "I think part of it comes out of the fact that we were all kind of set up and programmed to live a certain kind of a life, and I think that sexually, that's a part of it. We're all taught one way, and we wound up living another way, I guess. Feeling bad and guilty, and lying about it. I think we're now in the process of changing the rules maybe, or something."[82]

His attention was diverted from the hairdresser script during most of 1972, while Beatty devoted himself to McGovern's efforts to defeat Nixon in the November presidential election. When the campaign almost ran out of money in the spring, Beatty, who had been looking for a practical contribution of his time, came up with the idea for a series of concerts to raise money for the campaign, something that had never been done before. Gary Hart, the campaign manager, first heard of Beatty's brainstorm in a two A.M. phone call, with the actor whispering, "*Concerts. Concerts. Concerts.*"

Beatty volunteered to produce the events, "even though neither one of us knew anything about concerts or concert booking," conceded Hart. The star used his powers of persuasion to coax singer Andy Williams, composer Henry Mancini, and the phenomenally popular but stage-shy Barbra

Streisand, whom he had met back in 1957 when she was a babysitter in Clinton, to perform at benefit concerts in Nebraska, San Francisco, Cleveland, and Los Angeles. It was Beatty's inspired touch to use "celebrity ushers" to seat ticket holders.

"He was crucial," revealed McGovern, "because that was a lean operation that we were running. I didn't have the big money crowd behind me. But Warren produced huge batches of cash in crucial times. He produced three hundred thousand dollars at the Forum. That's a lot of money to get during the California primary, which was crucial to me winning the nomination. If we had lost California, we probably wouldn't have won the nomination."

The climax, on June 14, was another Beatty masterstroke, a "reunion concert" called "Together for McGovern." Held at Madison Square Garden, the concert reunited performers who had broken up, such as Simon and Garfunkel, Mike Nichols and Elaine May, and Peter, Paul and Mary, and featured thirty celebrity ushers, including Beatty's sister, Goldie Hawn, and Jack Nicholson.

The concerts produced by Beatty raised a million dollars for McGovern's presidential bid and set two important precedents for future political campaigns. "Warren invented the political concert," Hart would state succinctly.

Beatty's other contribution was even more historic. In McGovern's view, Warren Beatty transformed the relationship between Hollywood and politics. "That campaign generated far more Hollywood participation than any previous campaign. We had the bulk of the major figures in Hollywood. We'd never seen anything like that before. As a smalltown South Dakota guy who had admired these people for years, I never expected to have them out there cheering me on and participating in fund-raisers all over the country. Warren was the key factor . . . for the first time, somebody was telling celebrities what they could do to change America, and he was very convincing."

As John Springer, Beatty's publicist and one of his surrogate fathers, wrote to him that spring, "Dear Kid — 'Kid' doesn't sound quite right for one of our more formidable political 'behind-the-scenes' characters . . ."[83]

The experience crystallized what Beatty would continue to consider the most important political concern of modern times: campaign finance reform. "Until that issue is solved," he once told the *New York Times*, "the right people can't be elected."[84]

Nixon's victory over McGovern in November 1972 cemented Beatty's conviction to produce his satire about sexual and political hypocrisy, though

he had made a previous commitment to star in *The Parallax View* for director Alan Pakula. "I wanted to come in and work as an *actor* with a director I
liked," as he explained his choice.[85]

Beatty was also in what was euphemistically described as a "career
slump," caused by his two-year hiatus to campaign for McGovern, and the
dismal reaction to the three films he had starred in since *Bonnie and Clyde*,
beginning with *The Only Game in Town*. At the end of 1971, the *Washington
Post* predicted that $ "may end Goldie Hawn's career," and Beatty, according
to director Robert Altman, was so furious with the nearly inaudible soundtrack of *McCabe & Mrs. Miller* when it was released in the summer of 1971,
"he accused me of ruining his career . . . he went back in to Warner Brothers
and insisted that he loop or rerecord most of his stuff."[86]

McCabe continued on its parallel path to *Mickey One*, receiving initial reviews so bad that critics "drew blood," in the description of the *Hollywood Reporter*.[87] The notable exception was Pauline Kael, who considered *McCabe* a
masterpiece, just as Judith Crist had worshipped at the altar of *Mickey One*.
McCabe & Mrs. Miller would acquire a cult following, but as its producer
David Foster noted dryly, "you can't go to the bank with a cult film."

In *The Parallax View*, shot in the spring–summer of 1973, Beatty played
a reporter investigating a conspiracy behind the assassination of a political
figure, an "important subject and a film I respect," he said later.[88] The topics
it addressed, paranoia and assassinations, were often on Beatty's mind-be-
cause of his personal associations with both John F. Kennedy and Robert F.
Kennedy.

He was also eager to work with cinematographer Gordon Willis, whose
photography on *The Godfather* had brought him deserved acclaim. Willis
found Beatty to be "a charming guy" while he was shooting *The Parallax
View*. "Open and friendly . . . always concerned." The cinematographer also
observed Beatty's weaknesses as an actor — "not enough craft" — and his tendency to be inhibited. In Willis's view, Beatty spent "too much time working
his way around things he felt uncomfortable with. [He had] a great concern
about how he looked, or might be perceived."[89]

Beatty later conceded he had a difficult time going back to films after his
two years campaigning for McGovern, and at thirty-six, he was showing concern about the signs of aging on-screen, which he had been taking precau-
tions to delay, or ideally eliminate, since he was twenty-three. Craig Baxley,
his stuntman on *The Parallax View*, said, "I remember we were down at the

sports arena, and I walked by one day, and Warren had the little silver tanning thing, to tan his face, and he had cucumbers on his eyes. He was always — he was a young man then, he didn't need to be doing any of that stuff . . . he was always thinking about his mortality. That's Warren."[90]

Beatty's strengths, as ever, were as a filmmaker, even though he was not producing *The Parallax View*. Gordon Willis would remember him in a perpetual huddle with director Alan Pakula, engaged in "in-depth discussions about everything." Baxley, who would work with Beatty on several films and became an admirer, commented, "I'd be very surprised if any director that worked with Warren on a film wouldn't say that Warren was as responsible for that film as that director was. Warren was a true collaborator and he did it in such a way that it was such a positive experience."

In the fall of 1973, after he finished *The Parallax View*, Beatty contemplated running for governor of California. He was encouraged by a private poll that October naming him as the favorite in a survey of possible successors to former actor Ronald Reagan, whose election to office in 1966 had "astonished" Beatty.[91] "I think that got to him a little," admitted Hart. "He thought, 'I'm just as bright as he is. I'm just as qualified.'" Although he downplayed his interest in later years, saying he "thought about it for twelve seconds," Beatty was seriously considering the governorship, according to Craig Baxley, who was around him frequently then.

As further proof of how intent he was to present himself as a viable candidate, the actor sent his private secretary, Helen Feibelmann, on a concentrated search for a house, with instructions to find one "up high, with privacy and the other things I wanted."[92]

Beatty's personal incentive for house-hunting that fall may have been an attempt to salvage his relationship with Julie Christie, which had become severely strained. As in all of his previous romances, Beatty's infidelity was the leading cause, although with Christie, there were fundamental incompatibilities. "They were always arguing," observed Michael J. Pollard, who nevertheless considered Christie his old friend's greatest love, with Joan Collins a close second. "He *really* liked Julie."

Beatty had fallen in love with an *ideal*, with the face of Lara in *Dr. Zhivago*, an image of beauty and strength of character — before he even met Julie Christie. In their real lives, as their mutual close friend Goldie Hawn would observe, "when you say opposites attract — opposites attract, they don't always stay together." Beatty told John Springer that he proposed to Christie, who turned him down.[93] When she was forty-seven, Christie would say her decision not to marry or have children "is certainly not a regret. It's all been a choice I've made for myself." She described herself as "not a follower of the system and not a do-as-you're-told woman."[94]

An additional source of tension arose between Julie Christie and Beatty that fall over an extremely explicit love scene she did with Donald Sutherland the previous March in Venice, for the supernatural thriller *Don't Look Now*. After seeing the film, Beatty confronted the director, Nicholas Roeg. "I was at a party in Hollywood," recalled Sandy Whitelaw, "and Warren was there, and Nick Roeg, the director. Warren was furious. And he went outside with Nick Roeg, and he wanted to talk. He said, 'You promised that you would not make Julie do dirty sex stuff in your movie.' I had, of course, found that film incredibly tame, a perfectly ludicrous sex scene. But this upset Warren a lot, which means that he is fairly sensitive about all that stuff."

Weary of Beatty's philandering, most recently with actress Liv Ullman, Christie ended their romance around this time. According to Beatty, she phoned him at the Beverly Wilshire to tell him it was over. He could sense, he said later, that Christie was with somebody else.[95] "I think I was always rejected at the end of relationships," Beatty reflected when he was sixty-two. "I don't think I was a particularly easy person to be involved with, but I am pretty close friends with the people I have been involved with."[96]

Baxley, who observed Beatty with Christie when she visited the set of *The Parallax View* in the summer, witnessed the actor's broken heart later that year. "She was probably the best thing that ever happened to Warren, and he probably wouldn't want me to say this, but I also thought Julie Christie was something that got away that shouldn't have. She was just the most gracious person. They were amazing. I can tell you that he was very much in love with her, and she in love with him."

After eight years of fits and starts, Beatty raced to make his Don Juan film that December, a movie he conceived, in part, as a starring vehicle for himself and Julie Christie. Robert Towne, who had given up hope that the film would ever get made, came up with a title to replace *Up and Down*. "It was that time when Paul Newman was doing all these one-word titles, like *Hud*. Tough-guy movies. And then I thought, 'Warren Beatty in *Shampoo*.' *Shampoo*? I thought, 'You know, that's a great fucking word. It's like a John Hall movie with Maria Montez.' And so I tried it out on Warren and he said, 'Yeah, yeah, I think that'll work.' And so it became *Shampoo*."

Beatty produced *Shampoo* with the same conviction and derring-do as he had *Bonnie and Clyde,* putting up a million dollars of his own money before Columbia agreed to finance the film, a gamble that was considered risky. Once he finally made a decision, as Towne would observe, Beatty was "hysterically committed." He assembled a crew with his characteristic eye for talent, bringing in three key team players of Kazan's whom he'd met and admired on *Splendor in the Grass:* Dick Sylbert, Charles Maguire, and Bob Jiras.

At the last minute, Beatty decided he still was not ready to direct, the same concern he had expressed on *Bonnie and Clyde.* He shrewdly chose Hal Ashby, "someone who thought along similar lines" and would be willing to "collaborate," Beatty's euphemism for ceding control to Beatty.[97] In a burst of "adrenaline and rage," Beatty and Towne, who went in and out of agitation with each other over the various drafts written through the years, locked themselves in the Beverly Wilshire with Ashby and secretary Helen Feibelmann and emerged six days later with the script that became *Shampoo.*

"We had a very volatile time, I remember," said Towne, "and Hal was in the middle, and thank God he was. We'd talk about it, and then I'd go into the next room and write ferociously and come out. We were all a little thrown by the surprising quality of the work, and the speed . . . it just really came out well, and I don't know how or why to this day. Suddenly, after all the years of beating the shit out of each other and everything, that didn't exactly stop, but it stopped long enough for us to bang, bang, bang, bang, bang — just bang, it happened, and there the script was, and then after that I suddenly realized, Jesus Christ, we may actually make *Shampoo.*"

Beatty's key contribution was to set the sexual satire on the eve of Nixon's election in 1968, with party scenes inspired by Renoir's *Rules of the Game.* He was also responsible for a pivotal moment at the end. In the scene, his character, George Roundy, a charming but promiscuous hairdresser, tries to win back his ex-girlfriend, played by Julie Christie, by asking her to marry him. Beatty's suggestion for George, whom he described as "a little" of himself, was very telling.[98] "I think he's a person who believes that he can triumph," analyzed Beatty, "and who hopes to live happily in this era of new permissiveness or sexual revolution, and in his moment of desperation after the traumatic failures, he reaches into his past and says, 'Maybe the answer is what I was taught when I was a child — let's get married.' If the girl had said 'Yes,' I think he would say, 'Well — could I think it over?'"[99]

In most other respects, the character of George was based on the lusty Gene Shacove, the ex-husband of Towne's ex-girlfriend Barrie Chase, with elements of Shacove's "hairdressers to the stars" partners at the Razor's Edge salon: Jay Sebring, Richard Alcala, and Dusty Fleming.[100] "Autobiographical of me?" Beatty later would exclaim. "Oh, God, no! . . . if you look at that poor guy who couldn't get the money to open up a hairdressing shop, he's a man who's just out of gas — a guy who had no political sophistication whatsoever and had no overall ambitions . . ."[101] In fact, Beatty said, then and later, he identified more with the wealthy older businessman played by Jack Warden than he did with George the hairdresser.[102]

The week before he started to film *Shampoo*, in early March 1974, Beatty found his dream house. It was hidden behind a gate and situated like a castle on the highest point of Mulholland Drive, the winding canyon road separating Los Angeles from the San Fernando Valley, known, appropriately, as a lovers' lane because of its stunning views. The property was called "the Viking," named by its second owner, Lauritz Melchior, a Wagnerian tenor from Denmark, who purchased the five-acre property in 1941 from its original owner, Jascha Veissi, once the principal violist for the San Francisco Symphony. Beatty — who associated the violin with his father's lofty dreams, revered artists of stature, and had a nostalgic feeling about opera singers because of his grandmother MacLean — instantly romanticized the Viking.

The house, built in his favorite era, the thirties, was designed by architect Frederick Monhoff in an Art Moderne style, and featured an oval swimming pool, a trophy room with busts of animals shot by Melchior, a Norse "club" room, and a master bedroom with a mirrored wall and wraparound windows looking out over the kingdom of Hollywood. When Beatty arrived, a portrait of the recently deceased opera star, resplendent in black tie and tails, hung in the foyer. Melchior's married granddaughter Helle Wengrow, who was living on the property, gave the star a tour. "The real estate person introduced us very quickly, and I really didn't catch the name or pay any attention. So I actually didn't have any idea who I was talking to. I spent an hour with him, and every so often he'd kind of look at me. He had a lot of questions about my grandfather, and about the house."[103]

What caught Beatty's fancy, noticed Wengrow, was a story she told "about the fact that Clark Gable had always wanted to buy the house from my grandfather. But my grandfather had always refused him, had always said no way would he ever sell, but Clark Gable would always make these grand offers for the house. And when [Beatty] was leaving, he walked halfway down the stairs, and he turned around and looked at me. I still thought it was sort of strange, but nothing else. And my girlfriend, who was there visiting, as soon as I closed the door, said, 'Oh God, I can't wait to tell my husband I met Warren Beatty.' And I said, 'Where did you meet him?' I just had no idea."

Beatty returned for a second tour of the Viking, bringing Julie Christie. "She came across to me as being very shy," said Wengrow, who had tea with them. "And I was struck by the fact that she was wearing something that I would think someone would wear to clean house in, and [she had] a scarf around her head, and she sort of looked like, in those days, a cleaning woman." Wengrow's impression was that Beatty was buying the house for him and Christie to live in together. "It was clear they were a couple."

If so, it was not to be. Goldie Hawn, who played Beatty's girlfriend in *Shampoo*, would recall of the shoot, "Things were not great between him and Julie, which doesn't make for smooth sailing. I guess you could say it was like bottled-up emotion. And Julie was like a little flower. She was like a forget-me-not, like a little wildflower, and she needed water. As tough as she was, because she was tough, she was definitely set on the various things that she believed in, but at the time, she seemed very fragile. And a lot of it was because she had her own very strong beliefs about right and wrong, and what we should and shouldn't do, which also made wonderful sparks between her and Warren. And I know that Warren was very careful about how he approached Julie about many of those things . . . I was the one there that he didn't have to handle, is what you could say. It was hard to make the movie, because it was very close to everybody's chest, it was very personal. It might have been more personal for Warren, a message he wanted to get out, a part of his story that he wanted to talk about."

Beatty's similarity to the Don Juan hairdresser quickly became apparent to actress-writer Carrie Fisher, who would make her film debut in *Shampoo*, playing a teenager who boldly propositions George with the provocative line, "Do you want to fuck?" The scene was even more shocking because Fisher's mother was actress Debbie Reynolds, who was considered America's sweetheart from the innocent *Tammy* movies of the fifties.

When Carrie Fisher met Beatty to be considered for the part, he talked to her instead of asking her to read from the script. "The 'I am nothing like my mother' type of thing might have come up," described Fisher. "And I was doing everything in the world to indicate that by my dress and my attitude, and I'm certain that my language indicated that. However, though I may have used a four-letter word, I in no way was suggestive in my manner. I was a virgin. And I believe I may have mentioned that. I liked being the foulest-mouthed virgin anyone ever met. And Warren liked that, and offered to alleviate the incredible burden of my virginity. And I probably should have done it, because it was so sort of random.

"But I wanted to make an impression on Warren . . . because I knew that everybody wanted him, and he slept with a lot of people, and that was his thing. And I was going to be this person that Warren could not charm. I remember saying to him, something like, 'What makes you think that I would want to be someone that, just like all the others, make the difference?' Because I — at seventeen, I knew that each of them wanted to be the one that would reform him . . . and I wanted him to know that I had that kind of knowledge."[104]

Before casting Fisher, Beatty sought the blessing of Debbie Reynolds. "He came over and played the piano for my mother. It was very sweet . . . and my mother wanted to change the 'fuck' word to 'screw.'" Carrie Fisher's girlish impression of Beatty, throughout the filming of *Shampoo*, was as "a seducer. But not just that. That was one of the things that he was. He's an immensely talented person. So that is something that he does — like a collector. He wants to see his impact on people. I wanted to reduce him to just being this Lothario or something, but he is not that."

Just as his filmmaker mentor, Kazan, gave the script of *Splendor in the Grass* to a psychoanalyst, Beatty asked his psychiatrist, Dr. Grotjahn, to evaluate *Shampoo*. The therapist later offered his analysis of Beatty. "Warren is different from other actors I have seen," Grotjahn said in 1989. "He can do almost anything very, very well. But that is a superhuman temptation and can lead to great trouble. He does not know, is he an actor, a lover, a producer, a director?"[105]

Many of Beatty's talents were in evidence in *Shampoo*, which he co-wrote, produced, starred in, and, according to Towne, Hawn, and Fisher, effectively co-directed with Hal Ashby. "Warren and Bob wrote it," remarked Hawn, "so the two of them were holding their babies around, and we'd get three different directions — one from the director, one from Bob, and one from Warren. There were times when we'd say, 'Guys, get together, can one person give me a note?' So it became difficult."

Towne, who, as a close friend, was aware of Beatty's ambivalence about acting, was an asset to his performance in *Shampoo*, helping him to shake off his inhibitions. "I definitely take him into account when I am writing scenes for him, because I feel that I know what he does well. I feel that Warren always has to be tougher than he thinks. He presents a peculiar problem as an actor because he is a man who is deeply embarrassed by acting . . . you have to constantly force him, one way or another to use himself . . . Warren has the instincts of a character actor. He'd rather hobble around on one foot in *Bonnie and Clyde,* or wear a gold tooth in *McCabe & Mrs. Miller.*"[106]

By the end of filming, in June 1974, Beatty felt pride in accomplishing what he had set out to accomplish in *Shampoo,* his search for meaning in the lifestyles of the rich and famous in Beverly Hills during the sexual revolution. "It's not a frivolous movie," he would say several months later. "It's a movie about frivolous people, and not only exists as a comedy of manners, but there's also a rather sad undercurrent."[107]

He was experiencing that undercurrent in his own life. As Beatty confessed at the time, "I *need* to be with someone I know well, who knows me well. It is very lonely for me to live without a woman, without relating life with and to another person."[108]

That summer, he turned his attention to the Viking, which he had purchased at the bargain price of $167,000, well below its value, which would increase tenfold within a few years. The lissome blonde who moved into the Art Moderne house on Mulholland where Beatty would live for the next two decades was not Julie Christie, as he had fantasized, but occasional actress Michelle Phillips, the flaxen-haired flower child who sang with the Mamas and the Papas, and was the ex-girlfriend of Jack Nicholson, Beatty's new neighbor.

It was the beginning of another era for Warren Beatty, one in which he would depart from his hotel lifestyle of eighteen years, begun at the Blackstone in 1957, for an opera singer's secluded Bauhaus fortress at the top of a mountain, behind locked gates.

41 *Beatty would devote the mid-1970s to* the massive renovation of his mansion on Mulholland, a process that began when actress Candice Bergen, who was auditing classes at UCLA, recommended to him Tim Vreeland, the head of the architecture department. Vreeland was acquainted with Beatty through his mother, Diana Vreeland, the aristocratic former editor of *Vogue* and another of Beatty's close women friends over age seventy. "Warren used to drive down and pick her up in the evening and take her up to some house on Mulholland — maybe it was Jack Nicholson's — and we would hear wild stories the next morning at breakfast where my mother described what went on at these parties."[109]

After Beatty hired Tim Vreeland, they would meet on the roof of the Beverly Wilshire to go over drawings for the house. "Warren has, as I've discovered, a lot of difficulty making up his mind, and in fact he admitted that. I remember at one point he said, 'Tim, I can't even figure out what I'm going to wear when I get up in the morning.' And the funny thing was, that most of the time that I was working with him, he was wearing the clothes from *Shampoo* . . . his girlfriend at the time, Michelle Phillips, often made the decision, because she was someone who made quick decisions, so Warren would just defer to her."

Although Beatty was "elusive" with Gary Hart about whether he wanted to run for governor of California, his political ambitions were made clear to his architect after Vreeland completed the glass-enclosed porch next to the pool. "I also designed for that room," Vreeland revealed, "a very elaborate Art Deco black-and-white marble floor. The marble was all cut in Italy, and it was almost like a jigsaw to put all these pieces of black-and-white marble together, because no two were the same. And Warren went out to see it. And he was spending a great deal of time with [political consultant] Pat Caddell. Warren was seriously thinking of entering the political fray, and Pat Caddell was often up there advising him. And Warren came back and he said, 'No, this floor is impossible. It will not fit my Democratic image.' So I said, 'You don't *have* a Democratic image, you're a movie star' . . . and the whole floor was scrapped . . . all he did was salvage some of the pieces of white marble, which then were recut and used on the bathroom floor."

As his psychiatrist analyzed, Beatty was unable to make up his mind as to who "Warren Beatty" was. After ripping out the marble floor because it was too "Hollywood" for a Democratic gubernatorial candidate, Beatty sent Vreeland to movie producer Robert Evans's mansion to copy Evans's opulent private screening room. "So I went over there," recalled Vreeland, "and Robert Evans met me in a terry cloth robe, and took me into the screening room. I thought later about the white terry cloth robe, because my brother had always told me that he admired Hugh Hefner because he always had his business meetings in silk pajamas — it was sort of a power thing. Well, in my meetings with Warren on the roof of the Beverly Wilshire, he often simply had a white towel wrapped around his waist, and I thought, well that's sort of the ultimate."

Beatty also sought design advice from actor Jack Nicholson, who lived nearby on Mulholland, next door to Marlon Brando, and was at a career pinnacle after *Chinatown*. "Nicholson was constantly advising Warren, I know," said Vreeland. "Often Warren would come to me — I remember he wanted to put a sauna in his house, and so I designed a sauna as part of the house, and then later he said, 'Look, I've just talked with Jack, and Jack said that's impossible. If you have the sauna in the house, everyone will be visiting you, and sitting around the sauna, you'll never get rid of them,' and so we designed a separate sauna house." According to Gary Hart, Nicholson named Beatty's mansion the "Hospital Ship," "because it was big and white."

Warren Beatty and Jack Nicholson's "unique friendship" was the partial inspiration for *The Fortune*, a screwball comedy in which they agreed to star in the fall of 1974. It was written by Nicholson's close friend from Jeff Corey's acting class, Carole Eastman, the younger sister of Nicholson's friend Charles Eastman, who wrote *Honeybear, I Think I Love You*, the Truffaut-inspired comedy Beatty had been trying to buy for thirteen years.

A former model with the intellect and high standards of her brother, Carole Eastman based *The Fortune* on a true story she had read in a thirties newspaper.[110] She turned the piece into a dark comedy about two fumbling friends in a ménage à trois with an heiress to a sanitary napkin fortune they ineptly scheme to drown so they can collect her inheritance.* Once Eastman knew that Beatty and Nicholson would be the stars, "the triangle aspect was probably influenced by Warren and Jack sharing gals," she observed.

The whip-smart Eastman, who had known Jack Nicholson since the late fifties and had written *Five Easy Pieces*, his classic 1970 film, called him "the Bull of Mulholland," and dubbed Beatty "the Lion of the Loin," nicknames inspired by a trait of Nicholson's. "Jack, more than anyone I know, is given to renaming people. Once he does, he owns you; you're now what he's named you to be." Eastman became "Speed," short for "faster than the speed of light," and Peter Fonda was "the Patrician." "Jack named himself the Weaver," revealed Eastman, "which I took to mean that he's the one who

---

*Carole Eastman's original title was *The Mousebed Fortune*, inspired by her brother Charles's childhood name for sanitary napkins: "mouse beds."

weaves the spell." Nicholson's name for Warren Beatty, replacing the Kid, was "the Pro."

Michelle Phillips was the girlfriend Beatty and Nicholson had in common in 1974, though unlike the scenario in *The Fortune*, it was not at the same time. Phillips and Nicholson had ended their romance by that summer, when she and Beatty began "camping" in the master bedroom of the Viking part-time during the renovation. There they'd mix up "health milkshakes" made with chopped liver and crushed vitamins, the protein shakes Beatty's character would drink in *Heaven Can Wait*.[111]

Phillips described her romance with Beatty as "exciting at first," but she was anxious to make a name for herself after being "in the shadows" of Nicholson and, before that, musician John Phillips.[112] Beatty's phobia about privacy frustrated those goals. "Warren has kept me locked away," she told a reporter in London the next year. "He doesn't want anyone to know I'm here. He is so anxious to protect his private life that sometimes I say to him, 'Can we go out tonight, please?' We stay at home a lot because he is so recognizable. I cook for him. I'm the best cook in Hollywood."[113]

Another strike against the relationship was Beatty's disenchantment with marriage at the time he met Phillips, the cumulative effect of his sexually permissive movie star lifestyle, mingled, perhaps, with his disappointment over losing Julie Christie. Jennifer Lee, an aspiring actress who dated Beatty on and off in the seventies and later married Richard Pryor, would recall being invited to join him and Michelle Phillips in ménages à trois.[114]

Beatty's public statements in this period reflected his disillusionment. He told journalists in 1974 and 1975 that he had "no intention of getting married," that marriage for life was a "collapsed reality," a "contract with loopholes," and pondering, "it could be that short relationships where you can tell the truth are better than longer ones where the truth becomes more painful."[115] His true concern was revealed in an interview he gave in London, when he said, "I think that divorce would be very painful for me. It would mean failure."[116]

Despite these public denials, Beatty yearned for a family, embarrassed that it would seem "corny." "When I designed [my] house," he confessed in 1991, "I put a little room right off the master bedroom. That was designed for a baby."[117] His other designated space was for his grand piano, which Beatty now could play in immaculate privacy, looking out at Hollywood through floor-to-ceiling windows where no one could look back.

Carole Eastman, who was writing *The Fortune* for him and Jack Nicholson, would recall an unsettling, but revealing, experience with Beatty after he bought the house on Mulholland. An opinionated redhead like Shirley MacLaine, Eastman often discussed with Beatty their similar backgrounds. Each had an older sibling in the same profession, their mothers were from Cape Breton, and there was alcoholism in each of their families — parallels that made them "close in some kind of weird way that is almost inexplicable," as Eastman put it. "In a way I am Shirley to him, and in a way he is my brother to me, and there is a different complexity to that." Beatty confided to Carole Eastman that he was "hesitant to have a family life, because he came from a background of drinking. It may be a terrible cliché, but there it is; there's a formation there that's so inveterate. The whole existentialist 'do I want to get involved?'"

One night, as they were leaving a restaurant, Beatty blocked Eastman from getting into her car, saying, "I want to take you someplace." When she resisted, Beatty held her arm so tightly he left bruises. "He said, 'I want to take you up to show you this property up on Mulholland. Because you're going to live there.' And I said, 'Oh, no. Why am I going to live there?' And he said, 'Because I'm going to marry you.' And it's becoming more and more absurd, and more and more difficult to talk to him, and he's kind of smiling, and I can't take any of this seriously until it turns out that one of the things he says is that 'this is a gonadal matter,' and that he wants smart children."

Beatty bullied Eastman into his car, and when she resisted, "that's as far as it got for reasons which are not quite clear. Now that was a weird episode. Certain men do think that way, that they want smart children, and they are thinking genetically of how to breed up, as they say in the animal world. I think that his sister is intelligent, that he is, and that Warren would not have married someone who was not. I didn't take it serious at the time, but at the same time it was difficult. It was very odd when he started to physicalize it. Warren is very desirable, and also horrible, but that's the strange duality."

Carole Eastman's perception was that Beatty's odd marriage proposal sprang from his insecurity about making the adjustment "from living like this strange bachelor in this penthouse [to] . . . do I want to live in this house by myself? He was dealing with a big transition in his life, and it would make it easier for him, and less threatening, this big step — but it was all mixed in with this Don Juan compulsive-seductive behavior."

Beatty's affection for children was proven again by his close relationship with Michelle Phillips's young daughter Chynna. Chynna Phillips, like

Leslie Caron's daughter Jenny Hall, would have "fond memories" of Beatty, who had a sunken trampoline built in the backyard of his hilltop house to surprise her. Poignantly, Chynna, at seven, had a more realistic sense of her mother's romance with Beatty than Michelle Phillips had at the time. "I knew in my heart that Warren wasn't right for my mom," she would say. "I don't think he's really one for commitment."[118]

That August, Beatty and Jack Nicholson started *The Fortune*, directed by their friend Mike Nichols, the wildly witty former comedy partner of Elaine May, whom both had gotten to know in Vancouver during the simultaneous filming of *Carnal Knowledge* and *McCabe & Mrs. Miller*. Nichols was given the *Fortune* script by Nicholson before a flight to Poland to purchase Arabian horses, "and he said he was sitting on his suitcases in Warsaw laughing," recalled Eastman.

Mike Nichols anticipated that directing the movie would be a great time with "the boys," Jack and Warren. Nichols also expected they all would *make* a fortune from *The Fortune*, "which of course God always punishes you for immediately. I mean we were all too young to know that. That's the kiss of death. Even for a moment if you think something so stupid, it's over, it will cost you a lot of money . . . be careful."[119]

Eastman had similarly high hopes when she met Mike Nichols, believing he was the "dream director" for the comedy she envisioned as a sophisticated variant of Preston Sturgis's *Faithfully Yours*. "Mike is a delight. He is funny as hell. He makes you laugh. Maybe it wouldn't make other people laugh, but one day, in an office, someone came in with some bump in the road, and he said, 'Well, have *our* Jews talk to *their* Jews.' And I laughed and laughed. He's Jewish, so he gets away with it."

By the start of filming, Eastman and Nichols were barely speaking.

In Eastman's view, she had written a "chaotic unfinished first draft" of *The Fortune* and asked Nichols not to proceed until it was polished, "and he decided to do this movie even in its rocky first stages." Nichols's position was, "I couldn't get an ending from Carole at all. The script was hours long, but it had no ending. And that's where I began to discover there were going to be difficulties between her and me . . . and that's sort of where it started, and where it remained, and how it ended."

The pickles in the middle were Beatty, Nicholson, and actress Stockard Channing, who was making her film debut as the heiress the Beatty and Nicholson characters were clumsily plotting to kill. Beatty, who signed to do the picture as "just a fun, silly story about two ne'er-do-well idiots," found himself part of a magazine piece in the offing by Frank Rich, who was on the set, to be called "Notes on the Making of a Bad Film."[120] Nichols later described the feeling he had while directing *The Fortune* as "a little tickle in the back of your mind that something isn't quite right." Eastman, who intended the script as a satire, not as slapstick, was upset from the first day, "when Jack goes sky-high, to the broadest kind of comedy, and the crew laughs and Mike falls out of his chair. I remember Warren and I looked at one another . . . so Warren's situation was, 'Well, I thought we were going to do something else,' and he did his best. He's not a farcical actor, and I think he did very goddamn well in terms of that. It wasn't what he was prepared to do."

Known as an actor's director, Nichols carefully observed his two legendary costars. "I think that people's processes are so mysterious, and the better they are, the most mysterious their processes are . . . you can do anything with Jack, and he'll go along and he'll be your partner. With Warren, it tends to be quite numerous takes until he gets going, as it were. And what that is, it's something that he knows about and he trusts. It can panic people, because you wonder, how many takes are there going to be? But he knows what he's doing and why. And then when it begins to heat up, he's very much there. It's just that his inner mechanism, whatever it is, starts later than that of some others." Nichols likened Beatty to director William Wyler, "who was famous for doing many, many, many, many takes — sixty-four and more." In his opinion, both Wyler and Beatty were trying to get to a point where it no longer seemed like an actor performing, but "something happening before your eyes."

Unlike others, Mike Nichols did not consider Beatty and Nicholson opposites in terms of their personalities. "I find them to be far more similar, and true friends, and share many characteristics, and help each other in a thousand ways." One of the characteristics they shared was "horniness," the director observed. "We sat around and talked about girls. And they ask nothing, and want nothing, in the behavior of their friends. Everyone is free to be however they are."

As movie stars, Nichols felt that Beatty and Nicholson shared "a sense of being experienced at controlling their situation, and the business, without visible technique or method, but always being in control. Not being, as so many actors find themselves, a pretty thing to be moved around by others, but being the intelligence at the heart of whatever they're doing. I think that unites them, and to whatever degree, it makes them unusual."

Eastman, their other close friend on the film, had a more female viewpoint. "Warren and Jack were like two puppies in the litter box. Not that they were sloppy like puppies, but they just get along in this kind of gruffy, male manner that's more verbal, because both of them have verbal skills, and they seem to be very comfortable. The competition between them is very . . . on the sidelines. Not that it's not there at all, because it's sort of in the genes, but not brought into play, and not used too roughly. And this is something nice — Warren has never, to my knowledge, said an ill word about anyone that he was in love with. I have never heard him say, 'Oh, Julie this,' or 'Leslie Caron that,' or 'Natalie Wood this' — never. He's been like the most perfect kind of gentleman. Neither does Jack."

Character actress Florence Stanley, who replaced Nicholson's then girlfriend Helena Kallianiotes as the landlady in *The Fortune*, felt Beatty's performance was undervalued. "I thought he was wonderful in the movie. It's funny because everybody said, 'Oh, Jack was so cute and fun in the movie,' and he was, but when they say that, they don't also say how wonderful Warren was, and Warren was quite wonderful in a very difficult part. He was a very serious, sort of self-important con man who was also a bumbler. Jack Nicholson was a bumbler to the nth degree, but Warren was a bumbler in this movie also, but very serious, determined, taking himself very seriously — the character was. It was not easy. And I was very, very impressed with that performance, which was not an easy one to do."

Patterning himself after Howard Hughes, Beatty grew a moustache and combed his hair back slickly for *The Fortune*, which was set in the thirties, the style of his house on Mulholland. His fascination with Hughes was as strong as in the early stages of his romance with Leslie Caron, when they spied on the millionaire at the Beverly Hills Hotel. Beatty had even taken on some of Hughes's paranoia, asking Tim Vreeland to design a "safe room" in his house. "I'd never heard of this before," said the architect. "I didn't realize that such a thing existed, and Warren explained to me that someone in his position really might need this in case someone would try to kidnap him." Beatty, with Hughesian secrecy, had done extensive research on the millionaire and was developing a film about him, which he was calling the Phantom Project.[121]

After finishing *The Fortune*, Beatty shaved off his Hughes moustache and attended the Democratic miniconvention in Kansas City in December 1974 as a delegate-at-large from California. He would be less involved in Jimmy

Carter's presidential campaign over the next two years than he had been during his "total commitment" to the Democrats' campaign to oust Nixon during the early seventies, admitting he was "still smarting" over McGovern's loss.[122]

Beatty was also riding an enormous wave of critical and commercial success after the release of *Shampoo* in the spring of 1975, which resurrected his struggle to choose between theater and politics—one that began when he was a child in Richmond, torn between his interest in his mother's drama productions and his father's scholarly bent for history and the law. He told a writer that year, "I have a reasonable sophistication about politics . . . I don't know if I have the generosity of spirit to give up the ego-gratifying and increasingly satisfying artistic power I have for a life of grueling compromise."[123]

Beatty's guilt about placing politics second to movies spurred his compulsion to make a picture honoring John Reed, the "poet-journalist" who represented his idealistic side and whose selflessness he admired. As he told a film writer, "Reed tended to abdicate his personal and artistic life for the political experience that he passionately believed would be dominating the twentieth century."[124] Beatty had already begun to seek out people still alive who knew John Reed or Louise Bryant, and was filming the conversations on 16 mm, research that would lead to his unique idea to weave pieces of the interviews throughout the movie *Reds*.

"I met all these old people of that whole period of the development of the American Left," recalled Beatty, "and I fell in love with this thing about the fact that you get such contradicting interpretations of everything that happened. And I thought, 'I've got to get that on film somehow, and I want them to contradict one another, as they do,' so I had this sort of in my head."[125] The project was ideally suited to Beatty, who had revered his elders from the time he was a small child, dressing up for his grandmother at three, or sitting raptly at his great-aunts' feet while they spun stories about the Civil War.

The specter of his childhood values greeted Beatty when he promoted *Shampoo* in Virginia, where he wore glasses and a tweed suit to an interview for a Richmond newspaper, similar to the way his father was dressed in his official portrait as principal of Westhampton School in the 1940s. Beatty impressed the reporter, who was worried that Virginians might find *Shampoo* "decadently immoral." After interviewing him, the Richmond reporter wrote, "Warren Beatty doesn't seem much like a Movie Star. More like a thinker than an actor."[126]

When *Shampoo* came out in Arlington, Realtor Mason Green, Jr., would recall, "Ira came in the office and my mother said, 'Well, how are the children doing, Ira?' and he said, 'Oh, they're doing wonderfully.' And my mother said, 'Well, I want to see Warren's latest movie.' And Ira turned around, he came back, and said to my mother, who was about sixty-five then, 'I don't think you'd like that one.' She was Southern Baptist, and she grew up as a teetotaler."

In truth, there were very few sex scenes in *Shampoo* and no nudity, another reflection of Beatty's conservative Virginia upbringing, and a characteristic of the movies he produced. Most would feature love scenes that were highly romanticized, Beatty's preference, as William Inge had observed after *Splendor*. "Sex scenes bore me," Beatty confessed in 1994. "[I]f you look back at *Shampoo* now, it's hilarious. I don't know how to do those scenes except to make jokes about them."[127]

Critic Pauline Kael compared Beatty's second film as a producer to Ingmar Bergman's *Smiles of a Summer Night*, or to the films of Renoir, the model Beatty and Towne aspired to emulate with *Shampoo*. Beatty and Towne were nominated for an Oscar for their screenplay, which won awards from the Writers Guild and from the National Society of Film Critics.

In his personal life, Beatty was becoming increasingly isolated. He lived on the top of a mountain; his father figure in Hollywood, Charles Feldman, had been dead for several years; and in the mid-1970s he became estranged from two of his closest male friends. Mitch May stopped speaking to Beatty when the actor declined to intervene in a delicate family matter. As May's widow Gita Hall recalled, "It's just something that Mitch wanted Warren to do for him, and he didn't do it. And I didn't feel that Mitch should have asked him to do it anyway, so I have only pleasant feelings about Warren, but he and Mitch were no longer friends."

Beatty also had a falling-out for several years with Robert Towne, due to a conflict over the profits on *Shampoo*. As Towne would describe their period of estrangement, "I've said harsh things about Warren, Warren's said harsh things about me, but we love each other, and we respect each other. And above all, both of us have to accept the fact that close friends say things about you that you'd rather not have been said. As a close friend, that's part of what you have to do. But we've been friends, and we've *earned* the right to be indiscreet with one another, to say these things."

Screenwriter Jeremy Pikser, a friend of both, observed, "I'm sure that in the middle of one of those vendettas, if Towne needed help and would actually ask, or even if he wouldn't ask for it, Warren would be there, and part of that is unquestionably that he's a very, very loyal friend, and another part of that is he's a megalomaniac, and he likes to be the powerful one that rides to the rescue that everybody depends on."

In an interview during this period, Beatty admitted he was occasionally lonely, saying, "Being alone is fine, but to be lonely implies some kind of unhappiness. I think spending a certain amount of time alone is important to clarify your thinking."[128]

His attitude toward marriage began to soften, and rumors circulated in the summer of 1975 that Beatty planned to marry Michelle Phillips during a holiday they took to Bali, rumors with some foundation in fact. As architect Tim Vreeland, who discussed the design of the nursery with Beatty, recalled, "Warren one night said to me that he really did want to marry Michelle and live like married folk. I remember being surprised when he said that. I thought, gosh, I'm really providing them with a home."

Unlike Julie Christie, Michelle Phillips was anxious to marry Beatty, admitting later, "For a very long time, I did desperately want it to work between us."[129] Beatty told Phillips he wanted to get married and have a baby, later attributing his hesitation to his Southern Baptist upbringing.[130] "I never looked at it as something you try and see how it works and get out of it if it doesn't work. Why do it unless you mean it?"[131]

Beatty was also still seeing Julie Christie occasionally. "It's very strange," Michelle Phillips remarked at the time, "because I don't think they even like each other any more."[132] Phillips expressed her increasing frustrations toward Beatty while they were in Australia promoting the foreign release of *Shampoo*. "She stood in his shadow," noticed a marketing executive who spent time with them, "and she later said, 'If you want a shallow relationship, I can recommend Warren Beatty.'"[133]

In the summer of 1976, Michelle Phillips ended her two-and-a-half-year relationship with Beatty, just as her predecessors had. The ambitious Phillips, who was cast in the film *Valentino* shortly before she moved out, had figured out Beatty's pattern, which had also held true with Joan Collins, Natalie Wood, Leslie Caron, and Julie Christie. "The closer he gets, the more afraid he gets. And so he goes off and has another meaningless affair . . . he doesn't want to take the responsibility of anything not working out. I realized it would always be a part of his personality to evade the issue, and I'd have to make the decision. I finally faced up to it and got out."[134] The underlying reason, which he confessed to Phillips, was Beatty's secret fear "that marriage isn't a happy, productive life."[135] That fear came from listening to his parents argue throughout his childhood, strife that sent Beatty to the sanctuary of the closet in his bedroom.

After Michelle Phillips left, Beatty attended the Democratic National Convention in New York, going from there to Mike Nichols's wedding in Connecticut. While he was at the reception, Beatty met Trevor Griffiths, a respected English playwright with Marxist principles. Eight months later, after phone calls and meetings with Beatty in New York and London, Griffiths would begin the official draft of *Comrades*, the first title of the script that would lead to *Reds*. "I was terrifically impressed by Warren," Griffiths would recall. "He was utterly different to the image that had been created around him. I think that he had begun to think that in some ways John Reed's life corresponded to his own."[136]

Beatty shrewdly decided to produce a more commercial film before trying to set up *Reds*, realizing it was going to be difficult to persuade a studio to finance what he described, tongue in cheek, as "a 3½-hour story about a Communist who dies at the end."[137] He was also aware that two years had passed since his "face was on the screen," and *The Fortune* had performed so poorly that he would tell critic Gene Shalit, "I don't even want to *remember* that picture!"[138] In future years, critics would acknowledge the film's sly humor, as well as the goofy charm of Beatty and Nicholson as a latter-day Laurel and Hardy. But as director Mike Nichols would observe, "There's no question that it was a failure. One of its distinctions, I think it's the only movie I've ever heard of that is not on VHS."

The idea Beatty had in mind for his next "comeback" was a remake of the 1941 film *Here Comes Mr. Jordan*, a fantasy about a boxer who dies prematurely because of a mix-up in heaven. His soul is placed into the body of a selfish millionaire, he falls in love with a principled woman, and has to convince her of his worthiness. The sentimental story appealed to Beatty the summer-fall of 1976 as a diversion from the "heavy" films he was developing on Reed and about the reclusive Howard Hughes, who had died the previous April, revealing sad truths about the last years of the former Hollywood producer and ladies' man.

Beatty, who had become an expert on Hughes—to the point of soliciting Dr. Grotjahn to psychoanalyze him—considered the obsessive-compulsive mogul as "the opposite of this social animal that was John Reed."[139] Reed and Howard Hughes, each of whom was an alter ego of Beatty's, represented the conflicting sides of his nature: John Reed the good son, and Howard Hughes, the enfant terrible. What Beatty found compelling about Hughes, he said later, was "what he did with his unlimited wealth, how it isolated him from other people, how he lost everything that was meaningful in life."[140]

The analogy to himself was not lost on Beatty, who admitted that he was "a little depressed" at the time. "I kept returning to the idea of [making] a romantic fantasy . . . something about the size of the theme didn't seem small. It was dealing with death and reincarnation. That made me want to see it particularly."[141]

Beatty and his sister were exploring the same theme at roughly the same time, although they would go about it in extremely different ways. A year before, Shirley MacLaine had written *You Can Get There from Here*, recounting her involvement in the international women's movement in China, feminist leanings that harkened to Blanche MacLean and the legacy of MacLean women at Acadia. While Beatty became a lay expert in medicine in the tradition of their maternal grandfather, MacLaine spent the seventies experimenting with psychic healing, leading to her conviction that she had experienced past lives, which she would write about in the eighties in a series of bestsellers.

Beatty's religious beliefs were more traditional than his sister's, as they had been in childhood. He publicly acknowledged that he believed in life after death, "and if you asked me do I believe in reincarnation, then that's a horse of another color . . . that's a long answer which I would elect not to be reductive about."[142]

Beatty found the concept of being reincarnated "hard for me to rationally and scientifically deal with," but at the same time, he considered it "maybe the most appealing thing in life."[143] His interest in a film on that topic coincided with turning forty, a milestone birthday. As writer Jeremy Pikser, who would work closely with Beatty on *Reds*, and later *Bulworth*, observed, "Warren really would like to live forever. He really doesn't want to get sick, he really doesn't want to die, he doesn't want to wear out, and that has made him obsessively interested in medicine . . . I think it comes from being a movie star from an early age. Everybody wants to live forever, but it's only when you achieve a superhuman status that you start to think, well maybe I can. I can buy everything else, why can't I buy that?"

Beatty became a de facto diagnostician, partly from treating his own fragile health, beginning with his hepatitis in the fifties, expertise he considered a skill inherited from his grandfather.[144] Mike Nichols had a favorite story about Beatty, which took place at the Beverly Wilshire, when the actor picked up the phone and discovered there was a crossed line. "It was two women talking, perhaps two hookers, and because it was two women, Warren was entertained enough to continue to listen. Anyway, the girls were talking, and one said, 'I have to go into the hospital for surgery tomorrow.' And the other one said, 'Surgery!' And she said, 'They're going to remove my gallbladder.' As the woman was explaining it, Warren cut in and said, 'Excuse me, but you don't need surgery. What you have is hypoglycemia.' The girl thanked him, and I think maybe they exchanged numbers."

Beatty's random acts of kindness to friends, even strangers, with medical conditions would become well known in his circle. "It's what is so brilliant about him," said Nichols. "If you're worried, most people just stay there and keep worrying. Warren does the work. There's no doctor who knows everything that Warren knows, so that he can make sure that he, and the people he cares about, are doing the wisest thing medically. He has become brilliant and quite far advanced at it. I had a friend who was about to go on dialysis, and was highly diabetic, and Warren sent him to a doctor who made a lot of arcane and unusual tests, and changed his medication, and changed this, and changed that, with the upshot that his diabetes is completely under control. So Warren's knowledge and generosity in these areas has made a big difference to a lot of people. He always has time if somebody has a problem, even people he doesn't know."

His writer friend Pikser saw "a proselytizing aspect" to Beatty's medical interventions, possibly the traces of his Baptist background. "If he knows you, if he likes you, he wants you to benefit from his great medical understanding and involvement."

This wish to transcend modern medicine, and the religiosity Beatty kept private, were part of what inspired him to make *Heaven Can Wait*, the title he gave to his remake of *Here Comes Mr. Jordan*. In many respects, the film was a reflection of the "real" Warren Beatty, the private man from Virginia only his family, and intimate friends, knew. "It was a movie that I wanted to see. I thought something that was clean and funny and romantic would be a good way to spend an hour and a half."[145]

Paul Sylbert, who would win an Academy Award for the production design, recalled that when he sent Beatty sketches depicting what heaven would look like, "he called me up and he said, 'You know, I cried when I saw them.' I think he's affected by lots of things and we don't realize it. Weeping over sketches is an indication."

Beatty's original instinct was to cast Muhammad Ali as the boxer in *Heaven Can Wait*, after meeting Ali on an airplane and becoming "infatuated" with him. "I thought what an interesting idea if we took Ali and we brought him back in the body of a white man. I thought it'd be very funny. Ali's funny. We talked about it, but Ali wouldn't stop fighting. So I said, I'm just gonna change it to a football player and play it myself."[146] Beatty made Joe Pendleton, his character, a quarterback for the Los Angeles Rams, the position he had wanted to play while at Washington-Lee. Like Beatty, Joe Pendleton drank protein shakes, played a musical instrument, and had a tender heart similar to that of Bud, the high school football player in *Splendor in the Grass*, whom Inge patterned after Beatty.

Beatty co-wrote the script with the droll Elaine May, whom he had approached years earlier to write *What's New, Pussycat*, and asked Mike Nichols, May's former stand-up partner, to direct. "I got turned down by ten or eleven people, and finally thought it's time to face facts and just direct it myself."[147] As it got closer to filming, Beatty decided to hire a "codirector" to share the burden so he could also produce the movie, co-write the script, and play the lead character, exercising almost total creative control over the film, the position he had been inching toward since he overpowered the director on *A Hatful of Rain* at the Clinton Playhouse in 1958.

Lindsley Parsons, Jr., the Paramount executive supervising *Heaven Can Wait* in the summer of 1977, recalled, "I caught Barry Diller, who was our chairman at the time, in the hall, and I said, 'Barry, you're gonna be in a hell of a lot of trouble. You've hired Warren Beatty as your writer, your producer, your director, and the star.' He said, 'So . . . ?' I said, 'Well when the picture gets in trouble, which one are you gonna fire?'"[148]

Beatty's choice for a codirector was the playfully acerbic Buck Henry, who had a small part in the movie and would contribute to the script. His reason for choosing Henry revealed the lingering influence of Tat and Ira Beaty. "I worry and get uptight," said Beatty. "Buck insists on having a good time. He won't not have a good time. I can get through Monday, Tuesday and Thursday, say, but on Wednesday I can be *way* down, and that's no good."[149]

To further reveal his identification with the character, Beatty would cast only Julie Christie as the crusading idealist whom Joe Pendleton loves at first sight. Christie resisted for both personal and professional reasons. "I think she was weary of working with Warren," commented Buck Henry, "and because her philosophy about films suggests that this would not be the kind of thing that she thinks a sensible grown-up woman should do. She hated what she called the 'dolly' style of her hair and her dresses, and she thought the enterprise was frivolous. Or at least that's her pose." Henry described Christie as "contemptuous" of Beatty then, "but in that way that, at its best, is like an old movie — old comedies about divorced couples who love each other. So he had to lean on her very hard to get her to do it."[150]

Years later, Beatty explained why he was so insistent. "I don't know that I could have functioned in that [movie] without Julie Christie. Julie has something in her being that made that romantic fantasy work for me. Now, this was long after my romance with Julie. But Julie was that ideal, and I said, 'That makes the plot work for me.'"[151]

Christie's feelings about costarring with her ex-lover are crystallized in an incident that occurred while they were shooting one of the most romantic scenes in the film, a long shot of the couple strolling intimately through a rose garden. "What's-his-name's gorgeous music is playing," recalled Buck Henry, "and they're walking and kind of toying with each other, and he's looking at her, and they're talking, but you can't hear it." Henry and the sound engineer, who had headsets on, could hear Christie's private conversation with Beatty while their characters were supposed to be falling in love. "Julie was basically saying, 'I can't believe you're still doing this piece of crap when there are people all over the world making films of value, that have real meaning, that have political structure.' And Warren's going, 'Huh? Yeah, yeah, you're right.' He's just going along with it. It was hilarious."

Beatty would refer to this later, obliquely, when he talked about *Heaven Can Wait*. "Julie's own preferences don't lean to the linear film, and she's decidedly not sentimental. She'll always tell you what she thinks, with clarity, and the directness of an arrow. The pain, too. But it's valuable. And whatever it is you sense about her is what holds the film together — that intensity you feel about her."[152]

The filming of *Heaven Can Wait*, much of which was shot on location at the Filoli estate near Palo Alto, California, went on for four and a half months. "I don't know quite how to describe it," said Buck Henry. "Ideally, Warren would never, ever, ever finish anything, 'cause there's always got to be a better way to do something — the shot, the edit, or the scene, or the line, something. And in some cases, he will rewrite something out of extinction,

have it rewritten until it no longer makes any sense, because he's so determined to make it better than it was. And he'll do the same thing with costumes, he'll do the same thing with . . . everything."

Over the summer, the Hollywood trades began to report problems on the
set. "The picture was in trouble," averred Lindsley Parsons, Jr., the executive
in charge. "And I went up there, and Warren was there with the cucumbers
under his eyes, to take the wrinkles out, to look younger. And we went out
under a huge oak tree, just the two of us, and Warren told me all the things
that he was going to do in the future to bring the thing back within the pa-
rameters we had discussed. He was running over schedule already, and over
budget. And when he got all done, he said, 'What do you think?' And I said,
'Warren, I think that everything you say you obviously believe, but I just
don't think it's going to happen.' He said, 'Well, tell that to Barry [Diller]
anyhow.' And that's the way the picture went from then on. It became Warren's picture. The studio was a captive audience . . . but the film looked
good, so we weren't really concerned there."

Heaven Can Wait would mark the last time Warren Beatty costarred with
Julie Christie, a screen pairing he had hoped would join the ranks of Tracy
and Hepburn, or Gable and Lombard, according to Paul Sylbert. It was also
the definitive ending to their on-off romance. Astrologer Robert Aiken, who
prepared a chart for Christie after filming was completed in October of
1977, would recall, "She was 'finished' with Warren and not impressed with
the picture. Her choices were to remain in Hollywood or return to her native
England. I suggested she leave. Quite happily, she did." Christie said later,
"At some point you either stop passing through, or you go home. So I
went."[153] She had great respect for Beatty, Aiken observed. "She spoke of
how much Warren had taught her about politics, money, power dynamics,
Hollywood, show business, the world."

This was a recurring theme among Beatty's ex-girlfriends, who, for the
most part, would remain friends with him. Natalie Wood invited him to her
second wedding. Leslie Caron, who arguably was the most wounded by her
involvement with Beatty, credited him for having encouraged her to take up
writing, which led to her second career, late in life, as an author. In her late
fifties, Michelle Phillips would describe her interlude with Beatty by commenting, "We had a unique relationship for three years, and I learned a lot.
It was an interesting and important time in my life." Phillips wanted to say
more, but felt constrained by Beatty, who preferred that she keep the details
private.[154] "Warren is a good and loyal friend," Julie Christie would say in

2003. The fiercely private Christie, like Beatty, had a policy never to discuss personal relationships publicly, "because of the way I feel about celebrity in general, and about being a celebrity."[155]

According to Craig Baxley, his friend and stuntman, Beatty "still had a thing" for Julie Christie during *Heaven Can Wait*. After it was filmed, Ira Beaty told an English reporter, "Julie used to visit us with Warren so many times. She's such a little lady . . . we really loved her, Mrs. Beaty and me, and it would suit us just fine if Warren married her . . . but sometimes I wonder if Warren will ever really settle down. He's a nomad, like Shirley."[156] When the Beatys attended the Washington, D.C., premiere of MacLaine's film *The Turning Point* that November, Kathlyn Beaty told the *Washington Post* she was still hoping that her son would provide her with a grandchild, saying, "Warren is just waiting for the right girl to come along."[157]

Several months later, *Heaven Can Wait* opened in Arlington after mostly rapturous reviews praising the movie's "wonderful innocence" and describing Beatty as "endearing" in his role as the earnest football player who communicates with angels and wants to be united with his true love.[158]

John Raymond, the Baptist youth minister in Arlington whom the young Warren Beaty emulated as a second father, took his wife, Mary, to see *Heaven Can Wait* in the summer of 1978. "I don't think there were very many films that Warren was in that my husband didn't go and see. We saw *Heaven Can Wait* a number of times. And my husband told me, 'That's the biography of Warren's life.'"

Beatty's two opposing seventies screen personas — George Roundy, the hypersexual hairdresser, and Joe Pendleton, the pure-of-heart football player — represented the star's moral conflict between his Hollywood lifestyle and his Virginia upbringing. What the two characters had in common was the hope that they could achieve happiness by marrying a soul mate, the theme of most of Beatty's movies and the leitmotiv of his life.

Heaven Can Wait would make eighty million dollars and would put Warren Beatty on the cover of *Time* magazine on July 3, 1978, with the headline, "Mr. Hollywood." The *Time* cover piece, Beatty's second, lauded his Midas touch as a producer, citing his perfect track record of three movies, all phenomenal successes: *Bonnie and Clyde, Shampoo,* and *Heaven Can Wait*.

Beatty would begin the 1980s with his most daring artistic triumph, *Reds*, followed by what would be the worst setback of his career since "The Curly-Headed Kid."

42 *"Heaven Can Wait" would be the golden* chariot Warren Beatty rode to bring to fruition his decade-long dream to make his personal *Dr. Zhivago*. The huge success of the movie restored Beatty to the position of power he had occupied after *Bonnie and Clyde*, when he joked that he could get funding to make a musical version of the Last Supper. Inveigling Hollywood studio executives to finance a costly picture about John Reed's reportage of the 1917 Russian Revolution fell into nearly the same category, a fact that would have deterred filmmakers less impassioned than Beatty, who wanted to create a masterpiece that would honor his uncle Alex MacLeod's humanitarian ideals, and express his politics through his art.

Another key element fell into place for Beatty in the spring of 1978, when he began a significant relationship with actress Diane Keaton, who would sustain him through the grueling three-year production, and also portray Louise Bryant, the role Julie Christie would have assumed if hers and Beatty's lives had taken different turns.

Beatty's attraction to Keaton, then thirty-two, followed the precedent of his earlier serious romances, in which he became infatuated with an actress after seeing her photograph (his experience with Joan Collins), or fell in love with an idealized image (as he had with Leslie Caron's resemblance to the young girl in his favorite Renoir painting and Julie Christie's soulful beauty as Lara in *Dr. Zhivago*). In Diane Keaton's case, it was her intense performance in *Looking for Mr. Goodbar* in 1977 that infatuated Beatty. According to director Richard Brooks, Beatty saw the movie and was "overwhelmed" by Keaton.[159]

In another of his classic patterns, he became involved with Keaton shortly after she won the Academy Award as Best Actress in April 1978 for *Annie Hall*, recognition that distinguished her as a serious thespian in the tradition of the actresses in Beatty's family. Moreover, like his sister, Shirley, Diane Keaton was an eccentric, with a distinct, at times unusual, personal style. Her previous boyfriend was the unglamorous Woody Allen.

The willowy, self-deprecating Keaton, who never thought she was "pretty enough," privately questioned why Beatty would be interested in her. "I wasn't the Warren Beatty type, but there I was. He was just so . . . overwhelming in every way. He was so beautiful, which was very alluring to me.

I remember looking at his face and just going, 'How am I here with this?' The brilliance and the talent, you get caught up in it."[160]

Diane Keaton had qualities that reminded Warren Beatty not just of his sister but also of himself. Two of the more important ones were her devotion to the truth, and her obsession with privacy. Soon after they met, Beatty stopped giving interviews altogether, a moratorium that would last for more than a decade.[161]

Although Keaton later would describe herself as "nervous and hesitant" in her personal relationships with men, she acknowledged that her "demands were a little excessive," another characteristic that was familiar to Beatty.[162] In later years, he would express a few of his thoughts on Diane Keaton, saying she was "never boring . . . she's highly strung, she's artistic and she has a strong moral core."[163]

Part of the attraction, as Keaton later would admit, was their mutual fame. "There was an element of the world of acting and make-believe and pretending . . . that was very exciting."[164] This fusion, or confusion, of their romance with their celebrity status, and also with the characters they played, occurred soon after they became involved, when Beatty intensified his efforts to set up *Reds* as a love story, casting himself in the role of John Reed, and Diane Keaton as Reed's lover, writer Louise Bryant.

"It sometimes seemed I had very little interest in making a movie until I was romantically motivated," he explained in 1991. "You need and want that in order to build, to produce, to direct, to schedule, to act in, to finance . . . if Diane Keaton had not made *Reds*, I don't know what I would have done. I was in love with her when I made that movie, and, more importantly, before I made that movie. In her, I saw myriads of possibilities . . . I love her work, and she makes me laugh, she makes me cry, and in that sense, the old thing, you know: character is plot. Diane is a plot."[165]

They spent their first summer together in meetings with Jeremy Pikser, a youthful John Reed scholar who was collaborating with Beatty and Trevor Griffiths on the script for *Reds*. "Warren was forty-one, so he was the age of a family man then," observed Pikser. "And his relationship with Diane, it was sort of like a middle-aged married couple in a lot of ways. You know, a lot of drama. His reaction to her demands and stuff would be, 'Oh, she's busting my balls again.' He may have been screwing around a lot, but he didn't have the behavior, form, style, tone of a twenty-five-year-old stud."

There were red flags, however. According to producer Robert Evans,

Beatty phoned him early in the Keaton romance for his blessing to pursue actress Ali MacGraw, Evans's ex-wife, within an hour after MacGraw ended her relationship with actor Steve McQueen. "No wonder he's called 'the pro' by his friends," Evans later wrote in a memoir. "Until his marriage, Warren stood alone as the single most competitive person I've ever known. His obsession in life was to be *first* — first with the new hot girl in town, preferably model or starlet, first to be shown the new hot screenplay . . ."[166]

This dichotomy in Beatty was manifest in the two semiautobiographical films he produced and co-wrote in the decade before *Reds*. *Shampoo* personified the promiscuous Hollywood "Pro" described by Evans and so named by Nicholson in the seventies; *Heaven Can Wait* represented the straitlaced "Kid" from Virginia, as Springer dubbed him in 1959, the Beatty whom Jeremy Pikser observed with Diane Keaton.

Keaton, who was insecure in the relationship for her own reasons, intuited that Beatty was not faithful, and became "a little guarded and wary."[167] As Paul Sylbert, who spent time with them, would comment, "Diane was very loopy, nice, but she's very straight. And I just don't think she could cope with any of that for very long. She's not a player, nothing like that at all in her past." Years later, Keaton would confess that her wariness kept her from falling in love with Beatty. "Not where I felt the moments were shared and we were going to have a future together, that romantic kind of complete feeling of being happy and hopeful."[168]

The actress, who was at the height of her fame from *Annie Hall*, fit the model of Beatty's other girlfriends, perhaps by his unconscious choice. "I know you're supposed to have children when you're younger," Keaton said in 2003, "but I don't think I could have. I was way too ambitious, too selfish."[169] One of the reasons for Beatty's mixed feelings about marriage was his lingering fear that his career would suffer, based on Tat and Ira Beaty's lament that they relinquished their artistic dreams when they got married.

Beatty's intense desire to make *Reds*, which he described as a "character study of a man trying to find out what he wants from life," was an exploration as much of his own confusion as of John Reed's.[170] Ira Beaty's longtime friend, Mason Green, Jr., recalled how Beatty "hid out" at his parents' home in Virginia to work on the script, and sought help from his father the academic. "I think both of his children, at least Warren, relied on him very much for advice. I can tell you that *Reds* was written in Arlington. That was one thing Ira did tell me, that Warren came and was writing that in seclusion."

According to Peter Feibleman, one of his *Reds* collaborators, Beatty had to rework Trevor Griffiths's script. "[Trevor] was Oxford English, and his idea of an American accent or way of speech was to put 'ma'am' after everything. And it was three times too long. But there was a structure in it that was salvageable." Beatty's rewrite provoked the playwright to quit after an attempt to write a second draft together in London.[171] "I won't say that was a happy experience," Griffiths admitted. "We parted with irreconcilable views about what should be done."[172]

Jeremy Pikser, who was in the hotel room as a consultant during their London script conferences, and later co-wrote *Bulworth* with Beatty, would recall the actor throwing things at Griffiths. According to Pikser, this was classic Warren Beatty behavior in a script meeting:

> Trevor could never work with Warren in that way . . . he considers himself a very important playwright, and some Hollywood star is not going to tell him he's a fuckin' asshole, and have him expect to stay in the room with him. Trevor Griffiths leaves the room when somebody throws things, and that's not because he's not passionate and doesn't like to yell, but he expects a certain amount of respect. Warren feels that for him to work with you is enough of an indication that he respects you and your work. And thereafter he doesn't have to say a nice thing about you or your work.
>
> Warren's a football player. He doesn't expect you to take it to heart. When a cornerback makes a particularly bruising tackle on a pass receiver, hoping he will drop the next pass in fear of being creamed, he wants you to take it seriously. He doesn't want you to take it *personally*, but he wants you to take it *seriously*. He wants to hurt you, because that will strengthen his position. And he sees it as a struggle: your ideas, his ideas. He wants his ideas to win, unless your ideas are strong enough to beat his ideas.

Despite their acrimonious parting, Griffiths would have undying respect for Beatty for coaxing a Hollywood studio into financing a major film about an obscure American Communist. "It is part of Warren's gift that he can achieve it, that he can pull something off in this area. It's very hard to see who else could have."[173]

Beatty timed his appeal to Paramount to buy *Reds* around February 1979, the month *Heaven Can Wait* was nominated for eight Academy Awards, including four personal nominations for him as Best Actor, Best Director, Best

Writer, and one for Best Picture. Then he used a wily Warren Beatty strategy on Charles Bluhdorn, the head of Gulf and Western, which owned Paramount. "The way you persuade people in the free market," he revealed, "is to tell them if you don't sell it to them, you'll sell it to someone else."[174]

After the deal was struck, as Beatty would tell the story, "Charlie Bluhdorn, God rest his soul, he said, 'Look. Do me a favor. Go to Mexico. Take twenty-five million dollars. Spend one million. Just don't make *this* picture . . .'"[175]

According to Pikser, Bluhdorn was unaware the subject of the movie he had just bought was a Communist. "I know that Warren wouldn't let Paramount see the script for a very long time, and that they in fact did not know what it was about. They just thought it was about a journalist."

Beatty spent the first part of 1979 revising Griffiths's script, collaborating with writers Peter Feibleman, Robert Towne, and Elaine May, and using Pikser as their historical advisor. "As a writer," Pikser observed, "Warren is a great synthesizer. Cobbling together different bits of things that other people have written into one thing. And that's also a form of writing. He's the one who's deciding what's in the script and what isn't, always . . . it's kind of a subtle thing to say who's written a scene. In terms of, if you counted the words in a page on *Reds*, more than anybody else it would be Elaine May."

Griffiths would complain that the new script created a "seventies feel" for Reed's relationship with Louise Bryant that made it seem more similar to Warren Beatty than John Reed.[176] Critics, in particular, would mock a sentimental scene in which Reed surprises Bryant with a puppy, an idea of Beatty's that duplicated a gift he once gave to Julie Christie. "Warren thought it was very important to balance all the radicalism with real cornball stuff," recalled Pikser. "He thought that's your ballast, that's what people can hang onto while they're getting this other very challenging stuff."

Beatty would say that his greatest talent as a filmmaker was to make a risky idea commercially viable. He explained this philosophy once to Charles Eastman, whose much-admired 1960 New Wave–style script, *Honeybear, I Think I Love You*, never got produced because Eastman refused to make "Hollywood" concessions. "I remember Warren telling me, 'I have no pity for you. The thing you never learned is Hollywood is the place to be *successful.*' He said, 'I don't mean this in any kind of demeaning way, but if you're going to be in that game, you must succeed at it.' That penetrated my armor. Warren is a smart man, and there was something very smart in that. I guess I should have said, 'Sure, here's *Honeybear*, let's do it with Sandra Dee.'"

Beatty's mix of politics with sentimentality in *Reds* reflected more than his commercial instincts. As two of his close friends from high school later would observe, "We thought it was so much like Warren that it just almost bothered us. We couldn't see the character in *Reds*, we're seeing Warren in person."[177]

The summer after he finished the script, Beatty crisscrossed the country with his gifted and elegant Italian cinematographer, Vittorio Storaro, filming thirty-six hours of interviews with the octogenarian "witnesses" to John Reed's life. Trevor Griffiths, his estranged screenwriter, later conceded that the witness interviews Beatty intercut with the story worked "brilliantly . . . I must admit that some of them brought me to the edge of tears. . . . Warren always had that idea in mind, and he used it against the advice of a lot of other people. I think he deserves a lot of credit for it."[178]

Diane Keaton directed a few of the interviews, and accompanied Beatty to New York to help charm Polish writer Jerzy Kosinski, then relatively unknown in the United States, into playing a part in *Reds*.[179] "Warren loved Jerzy's imagination," recalled Kosinski's widow, Kiki. "They enjoyed each other's thinking processes, sense of humor, and intelligence. And they enjoyed discussing politics, life, and the world in general."[180]

Beatty, who had a gift for imaginative casting, tried to persuade movie mogul Sam Spiegel to take a cameo role, and telephoned Yevgeny Yevtushenko from England to ask the poet to play Trotsky. "I said, 'Warren, are you crazy? Have you seen photograph of Trotsky?' And he said, 'We've got makeup people. Come over. I'll pay you good money. We'll have a wonderful time.'" Yevtushenko declined. "My political situation was a little too shaky." As a favor to Beatty, Gene Hackman, now an Oscar winner in demand at every studio, took a small part, refusing to accept a salary. "I don't know who I play," he said before filming began, "because I never read the script . . . I owe Warren a lot of my career for *Bonnie and Clyde*."[181]

For the crucial role of playwright Eugene O'Neill, who had a brief, sad affair with Louise Bryant, Beatty thought of playwright Sam Shepard, who had just given a memorable performance in *Days of Heaven*. When Shepard turned him down, Beatty turned to his friend Jack Nicholson, who would consider O'Neill closer to himself than any character he had played. "I'm not saying I'm as dark as he was . . . but I am a writer, I am Irish, I have had problems with my family."[182] Beatty later revealed how he manipulated Nicholson into taking the part. "One day, I asked Jack who he could see for the role of Eugene O'Neill. And I explained to him that I needed to find an actor the public believed was capable of taking Diane Keaton away from me. And Jack said, 'There's only one person: me.'"[183]

Beatty's thirteen-year fantasy to film a movie on location in Russia suddenly evaporated that spring when he refused to star in director Sergei Bondarchuk's Russian version of John Reed's life, forcing Beatty to substitute locations in England, Finland, and Spain. As he and Diane Keaton left for Europe to play Reed and Louise Bryant at the end of the summer in 1979, they stopped to see Beatty's parents in Virginia. Ira Beaty would mention their visit that September in a letter to his former students at Westhampton School:

> . . . Warren brought Diane down to Richmond a couple of months ago
> and showed her around Westhampton where we lived and saw the old
> familiar places. He is a very sentimental fellow and has tremendous
> feeling and regard for the people and places he loves. He says this John
> Reed picture is by the far the biggest thing he has undertaken. It scares
> me when I think of all it entails. I understand the Russians are now try-
> ing to out-do him in the story, but he has the head start on them and he
> has more "know-how" in the business . . . Fondly, I.O.B.[184]

Beatty's relationship with Keaton would not be able to survive the punishing fifteen months of location shooting in Europe that was to follow, which he later described as "mayhem." As the director, writer, producer, and star, Beatty compared his plan for the filming of *Reds* to "that thing that Napoleon was reputed to have said when they asked him how he formulated a strategy for battle. He said, 'Well, here's the strategy. First we go there and then we see what happens.'"[185]

Keaton later described the experience as "tumultuous," saying, "I had to pick up and go to England, and I was basically by myself, and the part I was playing was so — she was in such pain all the time."[186] Nicholson, who wrote poems for Keaton during filming, just as O'Neill had for Louise Bryant, was reputed to have fallen in love with Diane.[187] Years later, they both refuted the gossip.[188] "I think, in a certain sense," Keaton would reflect, "we had a polite distance."[189]

Keaton's strained relationship with Beatty was obvious to everyone. As Pikser, who had become a close friend of Keaton's and was on location as a consultant to Beatty, would observe, "Warren's relationships, before Annette

[Bening] anyway, always tended to have stormy aspects to them. And Diane's relationships, just based on how she is, also have a stormy quality. And they had some battles during that period, and I don't think it disappeared when they walked on the set."

Beatty alluded to the difficulties, saying, "The plain fact of the matter is, that if you have an off-screen relationship with someone that you are working on-screen with, it can go either way. It can set up all kinds of inhibitions and embarrassments and worries that you wouldn't ordinarily have . . . so you're playing with fire when you do that. It's a little like running down a street holding a plate of consommé and trying not to spill any."[190] As Nicholson would remark, "Just look at how many movies the Pro's made with his girlfriends. Of course, there are classic pitfalls. Making a movie is psychologically brutal."[191] The situation on *Reds* was exacerbated further by Beatty's *directing* Keaton, who later would assert, "that performance was not my performance. It was Warren's performance, even though I was playing the part."[192]

As a director, Beatty shot multiple takes of every scene in his quest for perfection, just as he preferred to do when he was acting. Keaton said later she respected him for this, even though it was arduous. "What I admire most about Warren is his chutzpah, his literal insistence that, say, in *Reds* would take the form of eighty takes."[193]

Beatty's attention to detail dominated the complicated shoot over several continents. "He was absolutely besotted with it," observed Nigel Wooll, Beatty's production manager in England during the two and a half years of production. "I have never worked with any director like Warren. He is a real, real good guy, and the shooting went on forever. Each country we went to three times. There was nothing that he didn't know about. He was absolutely extraordinary to detail, and involvement with the film. Everybody wants to be involved with Warren, everybody, and he's really well liked over here, because he's a proper filmmaker. He's a proper person."[194]

The opposing point of view was that Beatty's method of filmmaking was self-indulgent. "Everything was incredibly slow," complained Pikser. "It was not a well-run set, from an efficiency point of view. There's a lot of waste and waiting."

Beatty's passion for *Reds* and his all-consuming involvement as star, director, producer, and co-writer, took its toll. Pikser, who was with him daily, would recall, "Warren said to me more than once, 'You and I are the only people in this entire fuckin' place who care about this story. Everybody else is just making a movie,' . . . and he feels very lonely in that regard. He knows that for almost everybody else there, it's just a job."

Barry "Baz" Richardson, an English hairdresser and close friend of Julie Christie's whom Beatty fondly called "The Comb," styled the actor's hair for *Reds*, their third film together. Richardson would remember Jack Nicholson offering his unconditional loyalty to Beatty, as the director, throughout the six weeks he was around to play Eugene O'Neill. "Warren would say, 'We're going to do this, we're going to do that,' and Nicholson will say, 'Okay Pro, anything you want.'"[195]

Beatty's other source of emotional support was his cousin and associate producer, David MacLeod, whose father, Alex, was the unspoken inspiration behind *Reds*. As Pikser recalled, "Warren would tell me about his uncle who was a Communist. I felt he was sort of trying to impress me with the fact that he had great affection for a family relative who was a Communist, and David MacLeod's dad." Jerzy Kosinski and his then girlfriend Kiki von Fraunhofer, later his wife, had met MacLeod in Los Angeles. "We continued to be quite close to David throughout filming," Kiki Kosinski said later. "He was a considerate, calm, and very pleasant man."

By the end of 1979, five months into filming, Paramount executives began to worry that *Reds* was headed toward financial disaster. The tide began to turn at Christmas, though, when the head of the studio, Barry Diller, who had stopped talking to Beatty, saw five hours of film and told him that he believed *Reds* held the promise of "real greatness."[196]

When the production moved to Spain in the spring of 1980, Beatty's romance with Diane Keaton started to unravel. "It was sort of over," she said later, "and what was I going to do? I had to keep living."[197] In her fifties, Keaton would comment, "To be with me was just too hard. I think Woody [Allen] said that being with me was like walking on eggshells."[198]

Beatty's former stunt coordinator Craig Baxley, the unit director in Spain, noticed that Keaton was struggling. "I don't think she was lost, maybe unfocused. The personal relationship started to break up in Madrid. I was around when that was going on, and with any performer, if their focus isn't where it should be — and Warren never, never loses focus — Warren would be very up front about it. He would speak his mind." Jerzy Kosinski took photographs during filming, at times capturing both Beatty's and Keaton's agitation. "It was not easy directing Diane," Kosinski later told *Rolling Stone*.[199] Journalist George Plimpton, who had a small part in the film, empathized with

Keaton, whom he felt had been "broken" by Beatty's fastidious insistence on thirty or forty takes.[200]

Nigel Wooll, the production manager, saw an underlying tenderness. "Diane Keaton's a very, very good actress, but sometimes maybe she would miss the words. I don't know what it was with her, but Warren was very patient with her, and 'please do it again,' and you'd see with her when he got it right, he got it right. It was just a sort of special look, you know, a special reaction. But he took the trouble."

The breakup was also difficult for Beatty. Kiki Kosinski, who accompanied Jerzy Kosinski to Spain, recalled, "By the time we got there, Warren was quite lonely." When the company set up production near Granada, where filming went on for weeks, Beatty arranged to stay in the back of a tiny cottage Kosinski shared with Kiki, and would ask the couple to keep the door open to their room so he could hear their voices and not feel alone. The primitive conditions in the cottage mirrored John Reed's. "We'd return from a hot dusty day on the set in the desert to find no hot water," said Kiki, who made toast for the three of them each morning by balancing bread over a naked flame. "We had these little bare beds, and they would make up our beds every night — folding back our sheets, with a fly swatter placed on each bed." Beatty sought relief in Jerzy Kosinski's absurdist humor.

By then, observed the Polish writer and his fiancée, Beatty's identity had blurred with John Reed's.* "It was totally schizophrenic," commented Kiki Kosinski. ". . . Jerzy felt that Warren *became* John Reed. In the movie where Reed was sick, Warren actually became sick. He was sick and exhausted because the filming and preparations were so demanding and had gone on for so long. We'd get home, and Jerzy and I would collapse, but Warren would be on the phone with the studio for many hours late into the night because of the time difference, but still be up early to direct and act." While they were in Spain, Beatty told Kiki that he believed *Reds* would be "his most important work, and that perhaps it had a stronger pull on his heart than anything else."

The film's most moving scene, when Reed is reunited with Louise Bryant in a train station, was choreographed in Spain entirely by Beatty, according to Kiki Kosinski, down to the single tear falling from Diane Keaton's face. "It

---

*According to Kiki Kosinski, Jerzy Kosinski also felt that *he* was closer to John Reed, "intellectually and as a person," than to the character he played, Zinoviev, "the kind of bureaucrat he despised."

was very, very, very much Warren's direction. He didn't want an exaggerated, 'Oh my God, I've found you.' He just had Diane put her arms around him, and just one tear rolls down her cheek. He knew exactly what he wanted from that scene." The romantic embrace at the train station, which would become the poster for *Reds*, was, in reality, the final farewell for Warren Beatty and Diane Keaton, though they would drift in and out for a time, as Beatty had done with Julie Christie.

IN THE FALL OF 1980, Beatty shot exterior scenes for *Reds* in New York City and Washington, D.C. He would spend the next year in New York working with a team of editors, headed by Dede Allen, meticulously piecing together what had become miles of film footage. "It was a tangled kind of emotional experience when it stopped, because it had been so much a part of our lives," as Allen would reflect. "We were in a building where Studio 54 was in the basement, and Warren would walk over, and he always wore John Reed's clothes, those wonderful pants that are corduroy that are slightly wider. And to this day, when someone comes up to me [like that], I think it's Warren."

That November, when he began editing *Reds* in New York, Beatty initiated a romance with actress Mary Tyler Moore, then forty-three. Moore had just filed for a divorce from television executive Grant Tinker, and was considered a top contender for an Oscar nomination for her taut performance in *Ordinary People*, which she would receive in February. The relationship, which Dick Sylbert's wife, Sharmagne, who was around Beatty frequently then, observed as "pretty serious," would continue through the fall of 1981, although it was not exclusive.[201] Beatty was also seeing Charlene Gehm, a dancer with the Joffrey Ballet, and had casual affairs with models Bitten Knudsen and Janice Dickinson.

Dickinson would later write about an evening in Beatty's suite at the Carlyle, the elegant Manhattan hotel he began to frequent in the seventies — replacing Delmonico's, which he left after playwright Lillian Hellman chided him for staying in a "fleabag."[202] According to Dickinson, while she was waiting for him in the next room, Beatty juggled calls from two girlfriends. "He was talking to Diane Keaton, one of the women in his life, but I could tell he gave good phone . . . then the second line rang and he had to ask her to hold, and it was the other woman in his life, Mary Tyler Moore. He made her feel deeply loved, too . . . of course I did eventually sleep with him . . . he was great, if you must know."[203]

Diane Keaton, who was filming the wrenching family drama *Shoot the Moon* in San Francisco during the first few months of 1982, chose not to talk about the "Big W," as her director, Alan Parker, referred to Beatty. Dana Hill, a young actress who was playing her daughter, found Keaton, whose character was going through a painful divorce, crying in her trailer one day between scenes. "The movie reminded her that she doesn't have that much longer to have kids. It was just after she broke up with Warren Beatty and it was difficult for her."[204]

Political advisor Pat Caddell later boasted that he almost persuaded Beatty to marry Keaton, who would assert, at fifty-seven, that she had never received a marriage proposal from anyone.[205] When Beatty was anticipating his first child with actress Annette Bening in his fifties, he would concede that he possibly had been "overcautious" about becoming a father, making sure "that it was the right thing to do at the right time and in the right circumstances."[206] Actor Dustin Hoffman, who would become a good friend in 1985, was of the opinion, "Warren has an extraordinarily delayed reaction to life. He thinks, 'Well, maybe I should get married.' He poses the question and then he mulls it over — for decades! And by the time he makes up his mind the girl is gone."[207]

In the case of Diane Keaton, their timing was off, and as Keaton was to say, she was not the sort of woman "to throw herself at a man."[208] To the self-effacing Keaton, Warren Beatty remained a "dream-like character," slightly beyond her reach, though as she reflected at the time, "I think everybody longs for those things you can't really have completely, so what can you do?"[209] Like Julie Christie, the independent Keaton would remain unmarried by choice; unlike Christie, she would adopt the first of two children when she was forty-nine, prompted by the death of her father. "I can't imagine what it would have been like to stay with [Warren]," she reflected in 2003, "and I'm sure [he] feels the same way about me . . . it wouldn't have worked long-term with Woody or Warren."[210]

Beatty was still under siege from *Reds* when he and Keaton parted in 1981, mired in editing the film that had consumed the past three years of his life, as well as parts of the decade before that. He began to question what was missing in his life that August, after he hosted a party at a private club in Washington, D.C., to celebrate Ira and Kathlyn Beaty's fiftieth wedding anniversary.

His close friend Goldie Hawn observed his aging parents' effect on Beatty, observations that went to the very core of who he is:

What I got from [his parents] was that they had a very strong connection. They were in love. And I'm not saying that there weren't problems, [that] life didn't take its toll, or there weren't issues with them . . . but the one thing that I really got was they loved each other, and I remember I did speak about that to Warren. I told him that was what I thought.

I was so happy to see that they were so proud of him. To see the joy that they were taking when they were remembering him as a young boy—just who he was, sort of this great kid. He was a football player, you know. I could see their eyes just dancing.

It's kind of like I looked at my mom and dad, too. . . . there was so much energy between them, that you knew that they were meant to be together, and they'd always be together through eternity. . . . Warren was very moved. He was very moved. We were both very moved, because I was afraid I was never going to see his daddy again, his daddy was not well then.

There's a groundwork of a marriage or a union or a relationship of any kind . . . Warren has those things. He was never going to get married until he knew it was forever. He was never going to bring children into the world unless he could be the right father, a good father, the correct father, a loving father.

Beatty channeled all of his unfulfilled longing in his personal life into finishing *Reds*, the film he hoped would be his legacy, declaring, "I felt I had made it just the way I wanted to make it."[211] One of the first people he screened it for was Elia Kazan, the director father figure he had tried to emulate. But his most emotional memory of *Reds* "was when I showed it to Diane Keaton. There was no audience, it was just her. And there's some very fragile stuff early in the movie and I saw her response to it and I thought, 'Oh, okay, good' . . . she's just wonderful in that film."[212]

Like Kazan in the fifties, Beatty refused to do publicity for *Reds*, saying, "A movie should speak for itself. You don't describe a song before you sing it or tell about a painting before you show it. You don't reveal the recipe before you serve the dish. You taste it."[213]

On December 23, 1981, after *Reds* had been out a few weeks, the *New York Times* reported it was "increasingly likely" it would be a "box office failure," blaming Beatty's refusal to promote it, along with Paramount's decision not to open it as an "event" film.[214] Critically, Beatty's personal statement about one man's choice to sacrifice his personal life for a higher cause was embraced as one of the best films of the year. Reviewers praised its ambition, if not its romanticism, with several critics comparing it to *Dr. Zhivago*, Beatty's private standard. Trevor Griffiths would call *Reds* "imperfect though it may be . . . the most important film about politics ever to have come out of the Hollywood system."[215] The movie, which cost roughly thirty-six million dollars, "did make a little money," Beatty later would assert with pride.[216]

Early in December, Beatty attended a private screening of *Reds* at the White House for then president Ronald Reagan, an ironic admirer. "He was very impressed that I had done all those jobs on the movie and still acted in it," Beatty would recount. "He said he wished the movie had a happy ending . . . he was funny. Reagan was funny."[217]

Seeing a former actor in the Oval Office, a few months after celebrating his parents' golden wedding anniversary, was another bittersweet reminder for Beatty, that year, of roads not taken. "After *Reds*, I thought I was not going to make any more [movies]," he revealed years later.[218] "You've gotta have a life," was his rueful explanation.[219] Jeremy Pikser, who had been at Beatty's side for three years on *Reds*, noted, "There was a period between Diane and Annette where he really was struggling with wanting to be married, not wanting to be married, not knowing if it was the women who didn't want to marry him, or him who didn't want to marry the women."

The actor later would confess he had been ready to have a baby "for a long, long time, but you don't do it alone, particularly if you're a man."[220]

Beatty would achieve the highest accolade of his career at this low point in his personal life. In February 1982, *Reds* was nominated for twelve Oscars, including four for Beatty personally, the same distinction he had achieved with *Heaven Can Wait*. The recognition for *Reds* made Warren Beatty the only person to receive four Academy Award nominations for a single film in two different years,* an honor that Johnny Carson announced, as host, at the March 29 Oscar ceremony. When Beatty won the Oscar as Best Director for *Reds* that night, he thanked, among others, "Miss Keaton," who attended with him and Jack Nicholson, though they were no longer romantically involved. He ended his acceptance speech saying, "I know I do one thing well: I get good people."

Hollywood's "Renaissance Man," as the *New York Times* would label

---

*Orson Welles is the only other person to receive four personal Oscar nominations for a single film (*Citizen Kane*).

Beatty after the 1982 Oscars, devoted the greater part of the next two years to his friend Gary Hart's campaign for the presidency, an office Beatty admitted he had considered for himself.[221] For Beatty, politics had become not only his saving grace, but also a substitute for a more rewarding personal life. "You've gotta relate to people. Otherwise you'll make movies about movies and it just won't be very interesting . . . and my avenue into life, my way of getting to know people, has been political."[222]

While Beatty and Jack Nicholson were filming *The Fortune*, the two stars had flown to Colorado for a public appearance to raise money for Gary Hart's successful campaign for the Senate. Toward the end of 1983, when the Colorado senator announced his candidacy for the Democratic nomination in the forthcoming election against Reagan, his trusted confidant Beatty became what Hart called his "stage manager." In effect, Beatty would serve as Hart's media strategist and behind-the-scenes counsel in his race for the presidency. Beatty said simply, "I tried to be a good friend and I tried to help in any way that I could."[223]

Shortly before Gary Hart's surprise victory over Walter Mondale in the New Hampshire primary in February 1984, Beatty was introduced to the French-Algerian actress Isabelle Adjani during a trip to Paris. Adjani would become his first serious romantic involvement since the self-questioning interlude Jeremy Pikser had observed, a period that coincided with Beatty's detachment from *Reds* after thirteen years. As his editor, Dede Allen, explained, "when you're on a film for a long time, it's like a separate out-of-reality experience which ends suddenly, like a parting in a very specifically entangled kind of relationship with the characters. *I* went into a big depression."

Actress Britt Ekland, who fell in love with Beatty in the early seventies, saw him at a party in the eighties, and made the telling observation that "his college-boy looks were becoming slightly crumpled . . . much of the charm was still there, but the old magic was missing. It looked like Warren had made himself too available . . ."[224] Beatty still made his legendary midnight phone calls in the early eighties, whispering, "What's new, Pussycat?", but the actresses he called sensed, at times, that he was simply lonely.[225]

Beatty's moral schism was still in evidence when he met Adjani. While the Lion of the Loin invited up-and-coming actresses to his lair on Mulholland for "some penetration," the "other" Warren brightened Lillian Hellman's last days with the tenderness of a son, carrying the grande dame of letters, then in her seventies, into restaurants when she was no longer able to get around.[226] Peter Feibleman, their mutual close friend, recollected:

> Towards the end of her life, she was staying with me in L.A. and Warren took her out to dinner. And Lillian was legally blind, and almost half-paralyzed from stroke. They went to the restaurant, an old one. It was a rather elegant one, and Lillian at that point — just the idea of being taken out to dinner by a guy was wonderful. And Lillian said afterwards, "That's the only interesting actor I've ever known," which is pretty much my take on it. Lillian didn't really like theater people; she avoided them all her life. She had two friends in the theater. She had Mike Nichols and she had Maureen Stapleton. And she had Warren, and that was it.
>
> After that particular dinner, I remember Warren saying what a feminine woman that is, and how interesting, how fascinating she is. It took Warren to see it, because at that stage, Lillian was apt to leave her teeth in her overcoat pocket. It took somebody who was willing to put up with a certain amount of inconvenience in her walking, in her sitting in a restaurant, all of it, to get what was under it, and Warren has that ability, he just does.

The exquisite Isabelle Adjani, Beatty's new love in 1984, was a throwback to the exotic brunette beauty of Natalie Wood and Joan Collins, his sixties flames. Like Wood, Adjani had been an intuitive child actress who specialized in tragic roles that reflected an underlying sadness. Adjani acknowledged that her melancholia was a legacy of her "dark and depressive" father, a family dynamic she had in common with Beatty.[227] Like him, Adjani was in search of happiness, something she once discussed. "I believe that life has things to give you that you might not be able to see for awhile, because you have so much work to do to get out of this dark chamber which childhood might have put you in."[228]

More than his other lovers, Isabelle Adjani, the "Garbo of France," shared Beatty's intense need for privacy and secrecy, even refusing to identify the father of her young son. She was known to be shy and sensitive, like Beatty, with a similar desire for control and a driving ambition. In the tradition of the women Beatty loved, Adjani had been nominated for an Oscar at twenty, for *The Story of Adele H.*, and was on the cover of *Time* at twenty-two, close to the same age Shirley MacLaine was when she made the cover of *Time* in 1959.

Similar to that of Joan Collins, Leslie Caron, and Julie Christie, Isabelle Adjani's beauty represented an ideal that transfixed Beatty. During their relationship, he would frame covers of the ethereal Adjani from French magazines and display them throughout his house on Mulholland. According to Adjani, the man she loved in the mid-eighties was not the Lion of the Loin. "I wouldn't have dated *the* Warren Beatty—that's not the person I dated. I didn't date the ladies' man. I dated a man who wanted to be with a lady. Okay? When I knew Warren, he was considering getting married and having a family; otherwise I would have never dated him."[229]

As with all of Warren Beatty's previous relationships, there was an inherent obstacle to deter him from marrying Adjani, who was twenty-eight to his forty-six when they met. "I was not ready," Adjani later acknowledged. "This would have meant living in L.A. Having another totally different life. I had too many other things to work out. But I always knew this man—as a married man, and as a father—would be the greatest company. And the most stable person."[230]

When Beatty returned to Los Angeles from Paris the spring of 1984 with Isabelle Adjani, it was his sister's turn in the spotlight. The year before, MacLaine had finally divorced Steve Parker—twenty-nine years after her brother and her parents warned her not to marry the slick aspiring producer she had met as a naïve nineteen-year-old chorus girl in *Me and Juliet*. "It was time. That's all I want to say," the normally garrulous MacLaine told *Playboy* in 1984, conceding that the promise she made, until death do us part, "was a mistake."[231]

MacLaine's three-decade delay in divorcing the husband who effectively abandoned her a year after they eloped was partly to insulate her from an intimate relationship with anyone else, something she and her brother feared would result in the strife they had witnessed as children. "We were apart most of the time," admitted MacLaine. "Steve went to Japan in the second year. So my emotional security was a symbol, somehow."[232] The actress's stubborn refusal to get a divorce was also guided by the same Protestant beliefs that had formed Beatty's value system. "Divorce was considered very progressive in our family," Beatty said a few years earlier, "which is why my sister's relationship with her husband could still be termed one of friendly estrangement."[233]

Ten years after her 1983 divorce, MacLaine would reveal that she had ended the marriage because she discovered, after hiring a detective, that Steve Parker had "bilked" her of millions of dollars, transferring her money to his girlfriend's account in Tokyo. He had also deceived MacLaine, she learned, about nearly every aspect of his past. "Steve was one of my greatest teachers," was MacLaine's eventual spiritual reaction to Parker's fraud. "I learned that we're all responsible for what happens in our lives."[234]

Beatty, who at seventeen had tried to protect his older sister from the man he was convinced would not be good for her, expressed his deep love for MacLaine with a special gift in April of 1984 that made her cry. The occasion was her fiftieth birthday, the same month MacLaine won an Academy Award as Best Actress for her favorite role, as Aurora Greenway in *Terms of Endearment*, costarring Beatty's close friend Jack Nicholson. "It was the most caring present I have ever received," she said. "Very complicated, with many parts, five of which I have figured out the meaning of. It took him months of thought to put it together. I have asked Warren what the other parts mean, but he won't discuss anything personal!"[235]

Both Warren Beatty and Shirley MacLaine paid homage to Ira and Kathlyn Beaty that spring, after they had become the rare siblings to have each received an Academy Award, possibly the most successful brother and sister in Hollywood history. Beatty wanted to bring their Oscar statuettes "home" to Virginia to give to their parents.[236] MacLaine expressed her gratitude by inviting the Beatys to watch her stage show at the Gershwin Theater on Broadway, where she performed songs highlighting her thirty-year career. Near the end of the show, she stepped offstage into the third row to sing a song to her mother and father, choosing the sentimental "As Time Goes By." When she finished, MacLaine turned to the audience and said, with her voice breaking, "Anybody who can dream it can do it," a message with a powerful personal meaning to her, to Warren, and to their parents.[237] She would say later it was the best year of her life.

The next month, MacLaine, like Beatty, made the cover of *Time* for a second time. The cover story celebrated her Academy Award and the success of *Out on a Limb*, MacLaine's new book about spirituality and what she believed were her past lives, the second highest–selling hardcover in her publisher's history. Ira Beaty, who had aspired to be a philosopher and to earn his Ph.D., "being a teacher, was more impressed by my books than by anything else I had ever done," revealed MacLaine.[238]

Her brother's higher calling was to advance Gary Hart's campaign for the presidency that spring and summer. "I have always felt very strongly about justice and equality," said Beatty, "which in our so-called democratic society does not fully exist. I wanted to do my bit to change things. My political motives were entirely altruistic."[239] His house on Mulholland became the command post for Hart, who met with advisors there to rehearse for a televised presidential debate in June. When he was in Los Angeles, Hart stayed with Beatty, a choice considered politically risky because of the star's playboy image.

"In a way," explained Hart, "it's easier for the *president* to relax than when you're *running* for president. Because the president has the White House, and there's a gate, and he can retreat behind that. And you need a place to genuinely relax, and have someone to talk to that you can genuinely trust, and kick off your shoes at the end of the day and discuss things with. And Warren was that person. And he had a gate."

When Hart lost the bid to become the Democratic nominee to Walter Mondale in the summer of 1984, Beatty had second thoughts about his decision to quit the movie business. He had been circling several projects, including his long-planned biographical film on Howard Hughes, a possible remake of the 1939 film *Love Affair*, and a gangster picture about the life of Bugsy Siegel, who had intrigued him since he met Mickey Cohen in 1959. Beatty also had an interest in playing the comic-strip detective Dick Tracy in a movie, and had approached Martin Scorsese to direct it.

Terry Semel, then a production chief at Warner Brothers, had been trying to set up the Hughes film with Beatty for years. "Warren started scheduling meetings," Semel would recall. "And week after week after week, month after month after month, I'd be going up to his house and having these long, long *interesting* meetings . . . and he wouldn't show me any of the pages. He'd have these mystery meetings all the time." Semel's explanation was that Beatty "is very stubborn, he thinks about things a lot. And he's very bright, so he re-thinks and he re-thinks and he re-thinks."[240]

Beatty's close friend Robert Towne considered Beatty's thought process, perceived as procrastination, to be a virtue. "Warren is a guy who is quite capable of thinking two opposite things at the same time, and thinking they both may be true. Which is where his reputation for dithering comes from. It really isn't dithering; it's a guy who can make an excellent case out of either side. He knows what generals know. You can have a brilliant battle plan, and it may turn out to be the battle of Marengo, and an equally brilliant battle plan that'll turn out to be Waterloo. An excellent case can be made for both. So he's always been keenly aware of alternate possibilities." The negative side of Beatty's caution ultimately would prevail with respect to Howard Hughes, a man he was born to play, in a film he would grow too old to star in.

In the spring of 1985, Beatty surprised everyone, particularly Terry Semel, who was expecting to start the Hughes film with him, by announcing that he would appear in a comedy then called *Blind Camel*, directed by writer Elaine May.[241] The project evolved from a trip that Beatty, May, and Peter Feibleman had taken to Costa Rica a few years earlier, with a "vague idea for a political comedy" set in Central America.[242] When the political idea became "undoable," Beatty offered to produce any script May wanted to write and direct, an act of friendship that would lead to *Blind Camel*, renamed *Ishtar*.

May came up with the concept at a party earlier that year, when she and Beatty had a conversation about his struggling early years in New York as a cocktail-bar pianist. Her idea was to write a "what-if" comedy about a pair of passionate but untalented lounge singers who get mixed up in political intrigue when they are invited to perform their mediocre lounge act in a third world country. May suggested actor Dustin Hoffman, a trained pianist, to play Beatty's exuberant but musically challenged partner, envisioning *Ishtar* as a takeoff on the Bing Crosby–Bob Hope *Road* pictures that began in the forties. In May's screwball eighties version, Dustin Hoffman would play the Crosby role of the ladies' man, with Beatty as the Bob Hope lovable schmuck. Beatty's girlfriend, Isabelle Adjani, who hoped to become better known in the United States, took the part Dorothy Lamour would have played opposite Hope and Crosby, updated as a feminist.

"Elaine's original idea, I believe, was to do a road company picture, the old Bing Crosby–Bob Hope movies, with reverse casting," recalled Feibleman, who was with May when she thought of the title. "It was at a spa in Mexico, the name of which amused me, and Elaine and I went down there—I worked on a novel, and she worked on *Ishtar*, and early on she started calling it 'Ishtar,' I remember."

According to Paul Sylbert, who was hired to do the production design, "Warren asked me to do *Dick Tracy*. And this hung fire for a bit, like all his projects, and then he called me with the news that he was gonna do *Ishtar*. He couldn't get Scorsese to direct, and he didn't want all of the stress of directing and writing. Warren wanted to play with Dustin. And I got the script for *Ishtar*, and it was a very funny script by the way, much funnier than the movie—it was lost in the movie."

In July 1985, shortly before filming, the *Los Angeles Times* reported the film's budget at between $30 and $45 million, publicizing Beatty's and Hoffman's individual $5.5 million salaries, and predicting that the movie would have to make $100 million to break even. Beatty and Hoffman, who had offered to defer their salaries to keep costs down at Columbia, believed from the first that the press had a "contract out" to destroy *Ishtar*.[243] Beatty later would describe the film as "a really good comedy, a very eccentric movie . . . with the publicity that surrounded it, it did not have a chance in the world."[244]

The production, which dragged on from summer 1985 to spring 1986, was both charmed and cursed by Elaine May's eccentric talent. Composer Paul Williams, who wrote the intentionally bad songs for Beatty and Hoffman to sing in the movie, recalled, "I began meeting with Warren and Elaine at his place in L.A., and I couldn't get him to commit that I had the job . . . I think, ultimately, it was Warren honoring Elaine's creative freedom. For the longest time, he was trying to get Elaine to say what she wanted. I'd write songs, and she would kind of go, 'I don't know.'"

From Williams's perspective, the first half of the film, which was shot in New York, was hilarious. "The songwriting scenes in the opening of that picture are probably as authentic as anything that's ever been done. That's exactly what it's like, and Warren and Dustin pulled it off just brilliantly, I thought." Williams, who coached both stars for their musical scenes, advising them to sing like Perry Como, felt that Beatty could have made a living as a singer, his secret ambition since childhood. "Warren's got a good voice. Dustin was a challenge. I can see Warren — having a lot of really bad luck — winding up in a piano bar . . . 'Here's one for the little lady on the end,' you know?"

The downfall of *Ishtar* was May's decision to shoot the second half in Morocco instead of on the Columbia lot, a choice that proved financially disastrous. The tone was set when she sent the crew on a six-week search through "every camel lot in Morocco" for a blind camel, and then came back for the first camel they saw, which had been made into "camel hamburgers" by then.[245] The blind camel became a metaphor for the movie. Soon after, May fixated on finding sand dunes that would appear flat, instead of undulating, for the desert scenes.[246] "We went all over the world looking for dunes," remembered Sylbert, the production designer, "and when Elaine finally got to the dunes, she said, 'Dunes, what do you mean by dunes?' She wanted Brighton Beach. We raked out a mile and a half of dunes with bulldozers — she had no idea what to do with them . . . she just couldn't cope, and no one could help her."

Beatty, who respected Elaine May's genius and was grateful for her crucial writing on *Heaven Can Wait* and *Reds*, gallantly supported her. "It just amazed me, his patience for her," observed Paul Williams, who went to Morocco with the company. "Elaine's approach to directing is 'I'll know it when I see it.' There was one point where I actually picked up an imaginary Elaine and started choking her, and rolling around on the floor, because I couldn't get an answer from her about what she wanted. It was an odd, strange moment. I was pretty loaded at the time, but it was one of Warren's favorite moments, I think. It was frustrating for everybody to not have more direction."

Nigel Wooll, the production manager on both *Reds* and *Ishtar*, perhaps said it best: "There are so many stories about *Ishtar*. And every single one is true. I regard Elaine as an absolutely brilliant writer, sensational writer, I really do, but she shouldn't direct." In Sylbert's view, Beatty felt "sandbagged" on *Ishtar*, "and he was such a gentleman in the fundamental sense that he could not take the picture away from Elaine. He tried everything to help her." Paul Williams, who took to calling Beatty "uncle" because he was so nurturing, kept a picture in his mind from *Ishtar*: "Warren standing on the bow of the ship with his face into the wind — that's the image of that movie that is the strongest. Just his patience, and his creative integrity — to say, 'This is what I committed to with her, and we go forward, and she's brilliant, and it'll work.'"

When the company was back in New York in March of 1986, Beatty flew to Arlington to spend time with his father, who had been diagnosed with leukemia. Dustin Hoffman, who had brought his wife and children to Morocco and invited Beatty to their New York apartment occasionally for dinner, encouraged him to start a family. "He makes us sad, and we don't quite know why," Hoffman said at the time. "There's an essential loneliness in him . . . there's something about Warren that reminds me of Howard Hughes. I mean, I can see him dying alone, with nobody there to love him or hold his hand."[247]

Beatty's troubles continued that summer after *Ishtar* wrapped, during the filming of another movie he set up as a favor. The recipient of his generosity was his younger MacLean cousin David MacLeod, whom he gave the opportunity to produce a comedy starring Robert Downey, Jr., and Molly Ringwald, written by Beatty's friend James Toback. While the film was in production, MacLeod was arrested in Times Square for soliciting three runaway boys, his "dark, sad secret," as Jeremy Pikser, who befriended MacLeod during *Reds*, would call it.

MacLeod's "proclivity," in Toback's description, had been rumored on location toward the end of *Ishtar*.[248] According to Paul Sylbert, it was MacLeod who suggested that Elaine May shoot *Ishtar* in Morocco, "because of the boys there. Nobody knew it at the time." Nigel Wooll, who was on the production team in Morocco with David MacLeod, would reflect, "We had many, many evenings together. He was a very quiet, gentle man. I just felt he was very lonely . . . he certainly wasn't surrounded by boys. He had his dark glasses on, and was just by himself all the time."

Beatty, who revered his distinguished uncle Alex and aunt Ginny MacLeod, stood up for his only male cousin in 1986. "Even the cops were sympathetic at the time," said Paul Sylbert, who was the production designer on MacLeod's film. "Warren went right to bat for him . . . we were all fooled, Warren included." The name of the film MacLeod was producing when he was arrested for solicitation ironically, was *The Pick-up Artist*. It was based on a character not unlike Beatty as a young man in New York, a charmer who picked up girls he passed on the sidewalk.

The summer of Beatty's discontent ended with a stream of gossip in newspapers and the trades reporting that *Ishtar*, which had been delayed six months for further editing by Elaine May, was in trouble. "There was almost a sense of revenge to the articles," noted Paul Williams, who was recording the songs with Beatty and Hoffman then. "The picture was doomed." Beatty, who blamed the new head of Columbia, British producer David Puttnam, would complain, "The man who ran the studio wanted it to fail. He refused to see the movie, never called me or sent me a letter, attacked me in the press . . . and here was one of the most eccentric, witty, gifted women in the country. She should be supported."[249]

The year 1986 ended with Ira Beaty's last battle with leukemia, ushering in perhaps the most trying year of Warren Beatty's life. He flew to Virginia to be at his father's bedside, where the good son would remain until Ira Beaty's death on January 15, 1987, four days before his eighty-seventh birthday. "Warren was very loyal to his father," in the observation of Virginian Mason Green, Jr. "When his father was in his terrible illness, he came and he stayed for quite some time and really didn't leave his side. So I think there was a very close bond there between Warren and Ira."

Beatty, who had never connected emotionally with his alcoholic, de-feated father the way he would have wished, said later, "We had a chance to get closer before he died. He seemed pleased with what I'd accomplished in life."[250] Shirley MacLaine, who was in Arlington with her brother, would re-call, "Before my father died, I talked to him a lot about his own feelings of failure, and asked if he could accept that Warren's success and mine were also his. In the end, I think he did see things that way, that maybe he had come into the world to help us and not himself."[251]

Privately, Ira Beaty, the scion of five generations of Southern Baptists, expressed concern to his daughter about Warren's spirituality, and talked to his son about MacLaine's New Age beliefs. "I remember my father sitting on the side of the bed," said Beatty, "his feet were kind of dangling, and he said to me, 'Warren, what do you think about these ideas of Shirley's?' I said, 'I don't know what to think of them.' He said, 'I just don't think I want to do what I have to do to find out.'"[252]

By a turn of fate, the Monday of Ira Beaty's funeral in Arlington, January 19, 1987, was the same date as a tribute to director Elia Kazan in New York, which Beatty was scheduled to host. Beatty sent Dustin Hoffman to replace him at the dinner honoring Kazan, the director he described as "the head of a family of grateful actors," while he eulogized his father at a private service in Arlington.[253]

The obituary for Ira Beaty in the *Washington Post* would identify him as a Ph.D., referring to an honorary doctorate from Johns Hopkins University that Beatty and MacLaine had arranged for their father to receive in 1982, sixty years after the academic slight that had blunted his adult life, and compelled them to overachieve. "I can always count on thinking of my father at the same time each day," Beatty later would say with emotion. "When I shave. He recommended a new shaving cream to me before he died, and he turned out to be right."[254]

After Ira Beaty's death that winter, Kathlyn Beaty moved to Los Angeles to live by turns with her son and daughter, as Beatty threw himself into Gary Hart's second campaign for the Democratic nomination for the presidency, announced on April 13, 1987.

By May, Beatty was in the throes of double disasters, as *Ishtar* was released to "vicious" publicity and was named as one of the ten worst movies of the year. In the same two-week period, Gary Hart was photographed on a yacht with a blonde on his lap, a scandal that punctured Hart's political dreams, and to some extent, Warren Beatty's.

Beatty viewed Hart as a "sacrificial lamb" of America's puritan past. "I don't think there is anything to be admired in lying and cheating, or philandering," Beatty said later. "But there might be something to be admired in not burning people at the stake because they have these weaknesses."[255] Beatty counseled Hart to stay in the race despite the compromising photograph. "Gary Hart is a sensitive man with a high level of love and concern for his family," he said later. "He didn't want them to be subjected to any more of that kind of humiliation, and it was a tragic event for the country. It was not only a terrible thing to happen to him, but it deprived the country of its leading conceptualist presidential candidate at a time when that kind of detailed thinking was urgent."[256]

Twenty years after his chance to become president was destroyed by an indiscretion made public, Hart would reflect, "In 1987, the boundaries fell, and I was in the middle of the change. Warren was a real friend. He was there for me. He would listen, and offer advice. He wanted me to get back in there and talked about the bold stroke, but I said, 'Warren, I've got two hundred people camped around my house, looking in my windows, and there are helicopters here.'"

After his fall from grace, much would be made of Gary Hart's close connection to "Hollywood sex symbol" Warren Beatty, criticism that made Hart bristle. "The mythology about that came up after I had retired from politics," he said in 2003. "The fact is that I never attended a party at Warren's house. There were no orgies in a hot tub or around the pool. There were never groups of women at Warren's house. Jack might come over, or Goldie—or whoever Warren was involved with, the three of us might go to dinner together. That's it. I've never seen Warren use drugs in my life. I think he's scared of them, really. I've seen him have fewer than six drinks in the thirty years I've known him."

With the media emphasis at the time on the titillating theory that Gary Hart wanted to be Warren Beatty, the real, and more interesting, story was overlooked; that it was Beatty who envied Gary Hart. "I can tell you," Beatty reflected three years later, "there is a significant part of me that would like to have children like Gary Hart has . . . Gary Hart has been with the same woman for thirty-five years, and there is a part of me that envies that."[257]

For Beatty, who craved privacy and could not tolerate humiliation, the years 1985 to 1987 had been a nightmare, beginning and ending with *Ishtar*, then compounded by his cousin's arrest, the political defeat of his friend and alter ego, Gary Hart, and his increasing concern that he might never experience a fulfilling personal life. All of this was made more poignant by the death of his father, and the sobering reality that he had turned fifty.

Beatty would have an overwhelming desire to start a family when he filmed *Dick Tracy* in 1989, and he was fond of Charlie Korsmo, who played the Kid. He later sent Annette Bening to observe Korsmo's relationship with his mother after Bening became pregnant. *Courtesy of Deborah L. Ruf*

Tat and Ira Beaty attend the Washington, D.C., premiere of daughter Shirley MacLaine's musical *Can-Can* in 1960. Four years later, Warren would name his production company Tatira to honor them.
Copyright Washington Post, *reprinted by permission of the D.C. Public Library*

Redemption

"I think he may just be the ugly duckling that
doesn't know he's a swan and thinks
he's a duck and continues to behave like a duck
until he finds another swan.
Well, maybe he's found one."

LOVE AFFAIR
adapted by Robert Towne and Warren Beatty, 1994

Annette Bening and Warren Beatty in a scene from *Love Affair*, filmed in 1993.
ZUMA Press

43 *Warren Beatty's deeply held feelings*
for his late father, and for his early childhood in Richmond, were expressed
by his decision, at the end of 1987, to play Dick Tracy, the crime-fighting detective in the comic strip Ira Beaty used to read to him nightly when he was
four years old.

When his other choices for a director passed, Beatty reluctantly assumed
the demanding mantle of writer, director, producer, and star for a third time.
"Finally I just said, 'I've got to do this movie now, and the way to do it is to
just go ahead [and direct].'"[1] Part of his motivation was to purge the stigma
of *Ishtar*, which *BusinessWeek* reported had lost twenty-five million dollars
and the *Wall Street Journal* would identify, two years later, as "one of the
biggest flops of all time," but Beatty's true inspiration was highly personal.[2]
"The film he made could have been his own dissertation on his childhood,"
reflected Shirley MacLaine, "with his father as the leading character."[3]

Beatty associated his innocent years in Richmond — when Shirley was his
best pal and they hopped on the back of milk trucks or strutted in Charles
Boyer top hats, before their father's drinking created family strife — as the
happiest time of his life, a feeling that was symbolized for him by the simple
heroism of Dick Tracy. "It's a very personal trip back into my own childhood," Beatty said then. "*Dick Tracy* was the comic strip I learned to read by
and with. So the experience is indulgently personal for me . . . I think of
it . . . as a story involving the wish for family happiness."[4]

While he associated the comic strip with his father, it was Beatty who
identified with Dick Tracy, the straight-arrow crusader he believed "represents, I think, the puritan work ethic, fueled by sexual abstinence, that built
this country through the Industrial Revolution. Those are my roots, too. I'm
the product of Nova Scotia and Virginia Baptists."[5] Beatty came up with the
movie's storyline, which had his alter ego, Dick Tracy, struggling to resist the
advances of a glamorous chanteuse and remain virtuous to his girlfriend,
Tess Trueheart, a metaphor for the moral conflict Beatty was experiencing in
his own life between his Southern Baptist upbringing and his Hollywood

lifestyle. "I considered using the title, 'The Temptation of Dick Tracy,'" Beatty said revealingly. "This is not some cockamamie detective story . . . it's about the temptation of Dick Tracy's love life. My Dick Tracy is human. He's all goofed up by temptation."

In effect, Beatty was making *The Temptation of Warren Beatty*. As he later described it, *Dick Tracy* represented a battle between the superego and the id, "if you define the superego as the parent within us, who either approves or disapproves of our actions and says this is right, this is wrong."[6] Beatty's superego was the Good Son, Joe Pendleton in *Heaven Can Wait*, while his id was the Pro, the hairdresser in *Shampoo*.

Beatty further identified with the comic strip Dick Tracy as an "aging professional" who never married.[7] In the script Beatty revised with Bo Goldman in 1987, Tracy secretly longs to marry Tess Trueheart and adopt a cunning orphan called "the Kid," the nickname John Springer had given Beatty years before. "Dick Tracy desperately wanted a family," Beatty said later of his movie character. "He wanted to marry Tess Trueheart and adopt the Kid as his own. But everything about his job worked against having a family. That's what interested me. That's what I related to."[8] Years later, he would confess to journalist Charlie Rose, "Sometimes I think *Dick Tracy* is the most personal movie I made."[9]

Isabelle Adjani declined Beatty's request to play Tess Trueheart, a symbolic gesture that reflected the end of their three-year long-distance romance.[10] Adjani was consumed with her own passion project, a film about sculptress Camille Claudel. In the end, she and Warren Beatty perhaps were too much alike for their relationship to succeed, and Adjani was not prepared to abandon her career in France.

The parting, which a friend of Adjani's described as "by mutual understanding," left Beatty bereft.[11] "Warren is a very passionate man, always was," observed Peter Feibleman, an intimate of Beatty's who spent time with him and Adjani. "When Warren falls in love, it goes very deep. Not playboy style at all. He had that reputation, but I think it was mostly things like the *National Enquirer* that gave it to him. It wasn't like him. He doesn't take people lightly, men or women. And if it's a relationship with a woman, and he's in love, he's very vulnerable."

With Adjani out of the picture, Beatty began to consider actresses such as Kim Basinger and Michelle Pfeiffer for the flashier role of Breathless Mahoney, the sultry torch singer who tries to seduce Dick Tracy. When pop singer Madonna, who hoped to become a movie star, called him to say that she "really wanted" the part, "Warren liked the idea right away," said his then production assistant, Maggie Kusik.[12]

Beatty kept the ambitious Madonna at bay the first half of 1988 while he refined the script, assembled his support team from *Reds*, and switched studios to Disney after Fox backed out of its commitment to *Dick Tracy* that summer.[13] "I evolved a concept," Beatty recalled, "that it could recapture my point of view at the age of six or seven when I was really interested in the strip. Emotionally, I began to get interested in that childlike feeling about the thrill of bright, primary colors, the sight of the stars and the moon, and people with primary emotions. I could look at them the way I looked at them when I was a kid — a bad guy was bad, a good guy was good . . ."[14]

With the exception of Madonna, whom Beatty hoped would attract her cult of fans to the movie, he cast *Dick Tracy* sentimentally, giving parts to James Tolkan, an old friend from Stella Adler's class, as well as to Michael J. Pollard, Dustin Hoffman, and Estelle Parsons. Beatty's personal taste in music, and his fondness for the thirties, was in evidence in his choice of composers, Stephen Sondheim, whom Beatty asked to write "Cole Porterish 1930s nightclub-type songs" for Madonna.[15] He considered *Dick Tracy* a musical, and its visionary style, in some ways, was a forerunner to the revolutionary *Moulin Rouge* in 2001.[16]

As with *Reds*, Beatty gave a part of himself to *Dick Tracy*, a film equally personal for different reasons. "One of the things that is incredibly exciting and compelling about Warren as a filmmaker," said Jeffrey Katzenberg, who met with Beatty daily as head of the Disney Studios, "is when there is something that he is passionate about, he gives everything he has — his commitment is total. He really is unlike anybody else I've ever dealt with in the entertainment business. He works twenty-four hours a day, seven days a week. He lives it, sleeps it, breathes it, eats it, and dreams about it. There's no one who works harder in the pursuit of excellence than Warren. He is tough and demanding — but no more on others than he is on himself."

Before filming began in January of 1989, Beatty ended a seven-month romance with actress Joyce Hyser, a pretty brunette, and began a relationship with Madonna, then thirty, in which she admittedly was the aggressor. As she described getting the role, "I waited and waited for Warren to call me. He never did. Finally, I decided to be pushy and called him. It took a year to make up his mind."[17] According to actress-writer Carrie Fisher, who was preparing *Postcards from the Edge* for Shirley MacLaine, "The only thing I think Shirley didn't understand about Warren was Madonna."

Michael J. Pollard, who saw them "smooching away" during *Dick Tracy*, considered Madonna another in his old friend's succession of actresses at their peak. "Warren's always gotten girls that are at the top of their balloon, you know?" Like Joan Collins, Madonna represented the overtly sexual category of actress Beatty was introduced to at nine, when he developed a crush on his mother's glamorous leading lady, a different kind of thespian than his distinguished grandmother.

Madonna also possessed the quality that Beatty consciously sought in his male friendships to balance his introspective nature, and the negativism he feared he had inherited. "I'm drawn to her," he said at the time, "because she's fun to be around."[18] Madonna, who was known for her outrageous behavior and for breaking sexual taboos, was also a counterpoint to the puritan reserve Beatty could never fully shake. His screenwriter friend James Toback, another larger-than-life personality, would observe, "He's intrigued by people who have no inhibitions. I think one of his interests in Madonna was that she is really someone without even the vaguest of inhibitions about anything. But that doesn't mean that he could or would want to be that way himself."[19]

At fifty-one, with nearly a decade passed since *Reds*, his last success, Beatty also found it gratifying to his ego to date the most famous pop star in the world. "You won't believe this . . . ," he phoned one of his friends. "I'm sleeping with *Madonna!*"[20]

Deborah Korsmo Ruf, the mother of Charlie Korsmo, the precocious young Minneapolis actor who played the Kid, spent considerable time with Beatty, occasionally in Madonna's company. Ruf, an educational psychologist like Beatty's father had aspired to be, was able to observe the couple casually the first time they met, at Beatty's house on Mulholland. "It was an interesting day, too. We were sitting around the kitchen, and Warren invited Madonna over, and she made popcorn. Charlie and I were kind of looking at each other like, 'Well, this is bizarre.' It was clear that Warren had made it clear to Madonna that she shouldn't swear around Charlie. He was very interested in getting to know Charlie better, and what kind of kid he was, because he really enjoyed Charlie very much."

Away from the cameras, Ruf noticed, Madonna was down-to-earth. "I started to see the girl from Detroit, and so did Warren. She's smart, she's nice, she's warm, she's caring, and she's gone off on this tangent that is just too much." Marshall Bell, a good friend of Beatty's who was in *Dick Tracy*, and whose wife, Milena Canonero, designed the costumes, observed the same thing about his romance with Madonna. "I was around it, and it was normal. It was so like people dating. Period."

One of Ruf's other observations was that Beatty, whom Madonna affectionately, and revealingly, called Old Man, "really was having a hard time growing old gracefully, and there were a number of things that made that clear." One of them, according to Ruf, was to "soften" the lights during his scenes "so he wouldn't look wrinkled," a common practice among stars of a certain age. Beatty also elected not to wear the prosthetic beak nose and lantern jaw the makeup artists had created to resemble the cartoon Dick Tracy. With those on, "he looked like a Lebanese arms dealer," joked Dick Sylbert, Beatty's production designer and pal.[21]

Beatty's sensitivity about his age was at least a factor in his decision to fire twenty-nine-year-old actress Sean Young, who was playing Tess Trueheart, after a few days of filming.[22] Jeffrey Katzenberg, then the chairman of Disney, said, "It didn't work. Literally. Warren and the studio looked at some dailies and agreed that there was no spark between the characters. I don't think age was the primary factor. It may have been a secondary issue, but it was not what led us to the decision to recast the part."[23] Beatty issued a public statement afterward, asserting, "I made a mistake casting her in the part and I felt very badly about it."[24]

Sean Young, who had a reputation for provoking controversy, would publicly accuse Beatty of firing her because she "wouldn't sleep with him," a charge Katzenberg angrily refuted at the time.[25] "The rumor was that she got too demanding, and they just decided not to put up with it," said Ruf. "I can tell you one thing: Warren making advances toward her I'm sure would not be true. He really was a serial monogamist at this juncture. He was interested in Madonna, and he was respectful of that relationship. I'm a good-looking woman, and I was available, and I really have had to learn a lot of tricks over the years to keep men at bay, and Warren Beatty, for God sakes, he did nothing. And I saw him with other people, and he was not a flirtatious and inappropriate man."

Beatty, who was extremely fond of Charlie Korsmo, Ruf's ten-year-old son, had serious conversations with Ruf throughout the five-month shoot. "As we got to know him," she recalled, "he was very open. One of the things he really liked about me was that our relationship, Charlie's and mine, reminded him of his relationship with his mother. And he really valued that. He said that 'as a single man, the way I have been living is not wrong, and I always said to myself and others that if I were to marry, I would be totally committed to my marriage.' He made that very clear, and he looked very wistful as he was talking about this stuff. So he was really getting ready."

Ironically, Annette Bening, whom Beatty would marry three years later, was one of the actresses recommended to play Tess Trueheart, Dick Tracy's true love. Bening, who had been in only one film, a mediocre John Candy comedy called *The Great Outdoors*, had impressed casting directors with her performance on Broadway in *Coastal Disturbances* in 1986. According to Bening, she canceled an appointment with Beatty to discuss playing Tess, he canceled another, and they failed to meet for *Dick Tracy*.[26] The part of Tracy's sweetheart went to Glenne Headley, whose hair was dyed red for the role, like the women in Beatty's family.

Beatty's self-reflection during filming extended to Charlie Korsmo, "the Kid," in whom he plainly saw himself at ten. He advised Korsmo to go to college, saying he regretted dropping out of Northwestern. Beatty also shared with Korsmo his thoughts on being a celebrity. "He started talking about how he was famous so young," recalled Ruf, "and he said when you're famous really young you lose perspective."

The year 1989 ended on a tragic note for Beatty when his cousin David MacLeod was arrested for a second time, a few months after they had flown to Toronto together for Ginny MacLeod's funeral. The arrest took place following a three-month FBI investigation of MacLeod that led to multiple counts of criminal solicitation for luring young boys across state lines. On December 14, 1989, during a break at a hearing in the Bronx on his criminal case, David MacLeod left the courtroom to make a phone call and never returned. "Nobody knows where he is," his and Beatty's close friend James Toback said in 1991. "*That's* a character worthy of a fucking novel. He had been an English teacher . . . his father was the head of the Communist Party in Canada . . . what do you do when the only thing that excites you is something for which you can go to jail?"[27]

MacLeod's saga would end in heartbreak for Beatty in 1998, when the body of his only male cousin was found in Montreal near a freeway overpass, an apparent suicide. Beatty told the police he had not seen his fugitive cousin since 1989, mentioning how disturbed he was by the way David MacLeod had died. Beatty felt "a sense of tremendous frustration," according to Toback. "He does not like failure. Not that it's failure. It's just that the whole thing was a disaster. MacLeod was like a brother for him."[28]

For Beatty, to whom family was sacred, his cousin's second arrest at the end of 1989 was another devastating blow in a decade of emotional turbulence. His mother, Kathlyn, who was a frail eighty-six, moved in with him over Christmas, while he was editing *Dick Tracy*. Beatty pampered his mother in her old age as she had indulged him in his youth. He regularly drove Kathlyn Beaty to get facials at the Beverly Glen Centre, a tony hillside enclave of shops and restaurants off Mulholland, where Beatty rented office space and which he liked to call his personal Via Veneto. "He was like I wish any son would be," observed his production assistant, Maggie Kusik. "Just so loving, and very doting, and very worried about every little thing his mother ate . . ."

Shirley MacLaine said at the time, "She thinks the sun rises and sets on him . . . he flirts, tickles her nose. It's so cute. Puts his arm around her and bundles her up in some cuddly shawl and, oh, she just melts. It really is darling. They're very close. That's the key. I think he's always felt responsible for her. I don't know how that impacts on his personal decisions about women, but it's in there somewhere." Beatty's only niece, MacLaine's daughter, Sachi, observed then, "Warren and Grandma are very tied . . . when I look at them I see a little boy and a mother."[29]

Charles Eastman, the brother of Carole Eastman, the intellectual writer whom Beatty once wanted to have his child, recalled his thoughtfulness while Kathlyn Beaty was living with him. "Warren's mother Scotch and my mother were born at the same period of time, about ten miles from each other in Nova Scotia. They both married alcoholics, they both had two children in show business, they both had a brother who made it big in some kind of way, and Warren decided that they should become friends. He was always very charming to my mother, and invited us to dinner with him and his mother. He seemed trying to be a good son, at a time that might be difficult for her."

Beatty's relationship with Madonna, who was preparing her *Blind Ambition* tour, "was petering out" by then, according to Maggie Kusik. Sometime around Christmas, he tracked down Charlie Korsmo in Fargo, North Dakota, to ask the eleven-year-old Midwesterner to go to the Academy Awards with him in March, telling Korsmo's mother "he thought that would be a lot more political than trying to figure out which woman to take." When Korsmo declined, "Warren could not believe it. He said to Charlie, 'You're turning me down?' Charlie said, 'Well, you know, I don't have a tux.' *'I'll get you a tux.'* I mean he did everything he could to try and talk Charlie into coming out for that." Instead, Beatty went to the Oscars with Jack Nicholson.

Beatty's sister, who had become closer to Beatty since their mother moved to California, said later, half in jest, that his romance with Madonna caused a "family crisis" that spring. "You know Madonna — need any more be said? She was strange to have around, but none of us really took it that seriously."[30] Deborah Ruf, who was around the couple constantly during *Dick Tracy*, felt that Beatty had genuine feelings for Madonna. "He wanted her to be more refined, but it just wasn't working."

Their fundamental incompatibility was sharply drawn in a comment of Beatty's during the filming of a voyeuristic documentary about Madonna she commissioned that spring called *Truth or Dare*. When someone asked the singer if she wanted to make a comment off camera, the excruciatingly private Beatty, who could be seen in the background of her dressing room, wincing at being filmed, interjected, "She doesn't want to *live* off camera. Why would you say something if it's off camera? What point is there of existing?"

By the time *Dick Tracy* came out that summer, he and Madonna were no longer a romantic item. "I think it is fun to be a celebrity couple for a time," as Carrie Fisher observed of them, "and then reality sets in."

Beatty was forced into the camera's glare, and into the jaws of reporters, to promote *Dick Tracy*, a picture he was driven to see succeed after *Ishtar*, and that Disney publicized relentlessly, hoping for a summer blockbuster on the scale of *Batman* the year before. Beatty sat for his first major print interview in over a decade, for *Rolling Stone*, the night of his fifty-third birthday; placed his hands in wet cement for journalists at a *Dick Tracy* event at Disney World in June 1990; and appeared on a multitude of talk shows. He referred to himself sardonically as a "human publicity machine," and was overheard muttering that he had become "promiscuous with the press."[31]

Beatty even agreed to be interviewed by Barbara Walters for one of her ABC specials, their first encounter since his fiasco on the *Today* show to promote *Kaleidoscope* in 1966. He was upset afterward by the editing of Walters's 1990 special, which he thought deleted his serious comments and made him seem "mumbling and incoherent," a complaint about him by journalists that became so pervasive during the *Tracy* tour that it was dubbed "Beattybashing" by Peter Bart of *Variety*.[32] Bill Zehme, who was assigned the *Rolling Stone* piece, enumerated Beatty's pauses in the course of their interview, during which, he wrote wittily, "Broadway musicals could be mounted."[33]

Despite the complaints about Beatty's tentativeness during interviews, *Dick Tracy* became a modest hit, making $22.5 million in its opening weekend. A review in *Time* extolled its "wit and grace," calling it "great moviemaking."[34] For Beatty, the greater reward was a personal one. He took his mother, Tat, as his date to the Washington, D.C., premiere of the film he had made as a paean to his and his sister's childhoods, a benefit for the Johns Hopkins hematology research center, where his father Ira had received treatment at the end of his life. "Shirley understood where the roots of [*Dick Tracy*] were for me," Beatty said, "so she was moved by it in the same way I was."[35]

The Beatty bashing continued the rest of that summer, mostly over his eroding relationship with Madonna, which the *Washington Post* would describe rather cruelly as "a parody," characterizing Beatty as an "aging roué" who was "on the verge of becoming ridiculous."[36] Although Beatty, a man of great pride, took pains publicly to point out that he was alone, not lonely, he later would say, revealingly, "I stood a good chance of reaching the end of my days as a solitary, eccentric . . . fool."[37] That June, he revealed to Chicago film critic Gene Siskel that he would like to have a child.[38]

When Shirley MacLaine was interviewed for *Vanity Fair* late that same summer, she said poignantly that her brother claimed he was happy, "so who am I to say, 'You're wrong, because you look sad'?" The first thing that came to MacLaine's mind when she thought of Warren, she would tell Barbara Walters, was "unrequited love."[39]

Adding insult to injury, Jeffrey Katzenberg, the Disney executive who was Beatty's soul mate and self-described "biggest booster" on *Dick Tracy*, wrote a twenty-eight-page internal memo that was leaked to *Variety*. In it, Katzenberg criticized the time and money the studio spent on the film, blaming Warren Beatty for the excess. "This is why," Katzenberg wrote, "when Warren Beatty comes to us to pitch his next movie . . . we must hear what they have to say, allow ourselves to get very excited, then conclude that it's not a project we should choose to get involved in."[40] Beatty stopped speaking to Katzenberg after the slight. "It is fascinating," Beatty would comment, "that a man could have a picture that is as profitable as *Dick Tracy*, and try to put a negative spin on it because it didn't do as well as *Batman* . . . it was a completely pleasant experience for me making that picture over there. I really liked everyone tremendously . . . all of them."[41]

"Warren was furious at me," remembered Katzenberg. "And I think that behind his anger was an enormous amount of genuine hurt. We really had become partners and friends . . . Warren had been such a great collaborator, and to be publicly criticized and blindsided really was hurtful in a deeply personal way. We were friends . . . and he felt that I had violated his trust."

Katzenberg was embarrassed over his publicized memo. "I think the memo was a reflection of my frustration and my personal failing in the live-action movie business at the time. In trying to rationalize a bad streak, I was pointing fingers at other people when in fact I really should have been pointing at myself. We all had unreasonable hopes and expectations for *Dick Tracy* . . . we wanted to manufacture blockbuster status, but I cannot, either artistically or commercially, fault Warren. The quality of the product he delivered to us was exceptional."

The Disney chairman sent Beatty several peace offerings, including an olive tree and live white doves. "I tried many times to apologize to him, and he was always gracious, but the damage lasted a long time. It has taken many years for us to regain our friendship. . . . and to this day I regret having written what I did, because it was both unfair and untrue."

The movie that would redeem Beatty in his career, and in his life, as the nineties began was *Bugsy*, the gangster film he had in the back of his mind since *Dobie Gillis*, when Joan Collins took stripping lessons from Mickey Cohen's girlfriend. What intrigued Beatty about Bugsy Siegel, a handsome 1940s mobster whose grand obsession led him to build a casino in the desert town of Las Vegas, was Siegel's internal moral conflict, a trait Beatty possessed himself. "Certainly he knew he was a psychopathic killer," analyzed Beatty, "a man with a terrible dark side, but he was a real split personality because he had this wife and two daughters back East that he really wasn't honest with. He was strangely torn in so many areas."[42]

In the case of Bugsy Siegel, the glamour of Hollywood became a cloak for his criminal activity. "Bugsy himself is a terrific metaphor for Hollywood," Beatty asserted. "The man made himself over, got rid of his Brooklyn accent. He dressed well, he cavorted around with movie actresses . . . he developed a well-mannered, happy-go-lucky personality that concealed a real killer."[43]

Warren Beatty's duality was the reverse. His Hollywood sex symbol image concealed Protestant inhibitions, even though there was a part of him, as Kazan had psychoanalyzed, that was tempted by "wildness," like Bud, his dutiful alter ego in *Splendor in the Grass*. James Toback, who wrote the *Bugsy* script for Beatty, observed, "Warren combines an elegant and well-cultivated charm with a tensely impacted psychosis. The role gave him a historical person through whom he could express his wild extremes."[44] Toback, a Harvard graduate with a history of drug use, womanizing, and gambling, understood the concept of "wild extremes."

What made the movie work for Beatty was Bugsy Siegel's devotion to Virginia Hill, a feisty bit actress who stood toe to toe with him. "Romance runs through most of my movies," Beatty reflected at the time, "even going back to *Bonnie and Clyde* and *McCabe & Mrs. Miller*, which I sort of co-wrote, and *Heaven Can Wait* and *Reds*. Because I believe that love can conquer all."[45] The origin of this belief, Beatty once said, was his mother's unconditional love for him.

In the fall of 1990, Beatty, James Toback, and Barry Levinson, the director Beatty chose for *Bugsy*, compared notes on possible actresses to play the role of Siegel's spitfire mistress, with Michelle Pfeiffer the dominant early contender. Levinson was looking for "the right chemistry between the two leads. Virginia Hill had to be an equal of Bugsy Siegel. That's why he was so taken with her—because she challenged him all the time."[46] As Toback, who had written the screenplay, mused, "I imagined, what would this woman have sounded like to have hooked Bugsy? Because here's a guy who never really had been stopped in his tracks. This woman was attractive, but no knockout . . . obviously, she must have had a lot of other things that got to him."[47] The same would be said, in due time, about Annette Bening vis-à-vis Warren Beatty.

Bening's name emerged near the top of the list of candidates to play Virginia Hill that same autumn. Beatty reacted quite differently to Bening for *Bugsy* than he had two years earlier, when they failed to meet to discuss her as Tess Trueheart in *Dick Tracy*. In 1988, her only movie credit had been a small part in an unsuccessful John Candy comedy. In the interim, director Milos Forman had chosen Bening for the flashy role of the cunning Madame de Merteuil in *Valmont*, his lush and literate adaptation of *Les Liaisons Dangereuses*, after a reading Forman described as "just absolutely perfect, she was so true to the character."[48] Annette Bening's sly and confident performance as the marquise, which included a sensual bathtub scene featuring Bening in a clinging, diaphanous white dressing gown with nothing underneath, caught the eye of critics, and of Beatty, in November 1989, his first glimpse of Bening, then thirty-one. "I said, 'That is an amazing woman,'" he would recall.[49]

A serious stage actress trained in the classics at the American Conservatory Theater in San Francisco, Bening had faltered in an earlier effort to break into Hollywood. Her low point occurred when she was replaced after the pilot episode in a television series called *It Had to Be You*, starring Tim Matheson. When she returned to New York, director Mike Nichols noticed

Bening's theater work. She reminded him of the young Meryl Streep, an earlier Nichols discovery and Bening's favorite actress. In 1989, Nichols offered Bening a small but showy part in the comedy based on Carrie Fisher's semi-autobiographical novel *Postcards from the Edge,* starring Streep and Shirley MacLaine. The director then cast Bening as Harrison Ford's supportive wife in a drama Nichols began filming in the fall of 1990, while Beatty was looking for his Virginia Hill.

Like others in Hollywood that year, Beatty would remember Annette Bening from *Valmont* and notice her biting cameo when *Postcards from the Edge* came out in September, but what got his full attention was her career-making performance as Myra Langtry, the conniving sexual tease in *The Grifters.* Bening's comic but lethal portrayal of Myra, which had critics in ecstasy, featured a brief, full-frontal nude scene that inspired Pauline Kael to describe Bening in *The New Yorker* as "a sex fantasy come to luscious life" and a "stunning actress," the two qualities that attracted Beatty coexisting in the same woman.[50] By fortuitous timing, *The Grifters* previewed in Los Angeles in early December, just as Beatty was closing in on his choice for Virginia Hill in *Bugsy.* "I didn't meet with Michelle Pfeiffer or any of the others Warren and Barry met with," remembered Toback, "but Warren said all along: 'Annette Bening will be the one. I promise you.'"[51]

Beatty invited Bening to meet him for lunch at Santo Pietro, an upscale pizzeria in the Beverly Glen Centre, off Mulholland, where he had his production office and brought his mother for facials. Bening accepted warily, warned by her agent that Beatty was meeting "every actress in Hollywood," which implied that he had other motives.[52]

Warren Beatty later would say he knew within ten to thirty seconds after meeting Annette Bening at the pizzeria that "she would change my life."[53] In effect, he had fallen in love with Bening before she arrived, similar to the intense infatuations he had with actresses Joan Collins, Leslie Caron, Julie Christie, and Diane Keaton based solely upon seeing them on screen. Beatty, the son, grandson, nephew, and brother of actresses, confirmed a year later that it was Bening's acting that attracted him to her romantically. "I saw her in some movies, and I thought, 'Wow, that woman is the best young actress that I've seen around, and she's beautiful, and she's funny, and she's got all of this — she's got everything.' And that is what interested me in Annette Bening."[54]

To Beatty, Annette Bening represented the ideal woman: an actress who combined the rigorous stage training and talent of his mother, grandmother, and aunt, *and* the overt sexuality of the glamorous little-theater actress he proposed to at nine, revealed in Bening's erotic performance in *The Grifters*. In person, Bening's willowy frame, simple makeup, and minimalist style suggested Beatty's extremely proper Canadian mother and grandmother, who followed the etiquette of their schools for young ladies. Bening looked strikingly like Shirley MacLaine, especially when her hair was cut spikey short, and her animated style as a comedienne was similar to MacLaine's. She also possessed what, for Beatty, was the ultimate aphrodisiac: a trained voice that Bening could manipulate like the gears on a car, switching from low and throaty to a high-pitched girlish giggle in a blink, a skill that symbolized Beatty's elocutionist mother and grandmother and the feminine ideals he held dear. As he once said, "the voice means everything to me."

Carole Eastman, the screenwriter Beatty wanted to have his child in the seventies because of her similarities to Shirley, recalled him commenting once that Annette Bening reminded him of Eastman. "He made a remark about it, and I said okay. I just let it pass. The likeness is between Annette and *Shirley*. There's a physical resemblance . . . and Shirley is a very strong individual, I don't think you can screw around with her so much, and I think Annette is the same: that you have to shape up. Warren had to shape up. That's what *I* see. There is this central thing in his life, this central thing in mine that he's always acknowledged — it has to do with brother-sister."

Two of Bening's other traits Beatty would extol from their first encounter were her honesty and her intelligence. "It was very clear to me within about five minutes . . . the vision was very clear. It must have been similar to what a peasant in Eastern Europe felt in 1911 when he saw he had a chance to go to America. I thought, 'This person has everything I like.' It took me minutes, minutes."[55]

Beatty's checklist was with one purpose in mind. When he took Bening for a walk around the cul-de-sac after lunch, he steered the conversation toward her upbringing in Wichita and San Diego, which she described once as "definitely a Protestant-based, midwestern ethic of morality and sexuality," calling her parents "very conservative, Republican, churchgoing."[56] The post-lunch stroll sealed Beatty's intentions. "My surprise came when I first met Annette and I saw that she was a combination of this best of the young actresses, in my opinion, best-looking, for my taste — and at the same time, she seemed to come from a very well-balanced and happy mother and father, and had a sense of health about her whole family, and I was struck by that." It suggested, to Beatty, that Bening would "pay attention" to a baby.[57]

Annette Bening, who was unaware of Beatty's secret plan to make her the mother of his child, remembered the lunch solely in professional terms. "I was a little nervous at first meeting Warren Beatty," she admitted, until she noticed that "he seemed kind of nervous."[58] Bening, who was thirty-two, twenty-one years younger than Beatty, confessed later that she had never thought much about him. The first thing that struck her, she would say, was "how smart he is," followed by "his passion for his work, his judgment, his obstinacy, his tenacity, his vulnerability."[59] She would not recall Warren Beatty's incisive questions to her about her parents and her background, nor did she feel any special emotions that day. "I didn't have any sort of realization or anything. I was an actress going to an interview."[60]

Beatty, who had already planned their future together, was overcome after meeting Bening. "Driving down Benedict Canyon, I had to stop the car. What had happened to me was so fully engaging that I had to pull over. I sat there for about five minutes, and I thought it through. It was as if all the nines turned over and everything made sense. I thought I had had an unusual life; that I had been well rewarded in so many ways, but in other ways things had not come together as well. I was not shaking. It was not an emotional moment. Who knows what leads you to the moment where you are?"[61] He later conceded, "Sure, maybe it was due in part to timing. I was ready for this. But Annette is something special. I can't articulate why she makes me so happy, but she does. Annette is so unique. She just . . . is."[62]

What he felt when he met Annette Bening, Beatty said, was "relief." After three decades of intense love affairs with career-driven women from exotic backgrounds, punctuated by periods of loneliness, he had found a gifted and sensual actress with the same Protestant middle-class values he secretly embraced. Typical of Warren Beatty, he was also conflicted. "I was so elated to meet her, and yet at the same time, I began to mourn the passing of a way of life. I thought, Oh, everything's going to be different."[63]

Perhaps as a result, Beatty had a last fling as *Bugsy* went into production in January of 1991. His farewell to his bachelor years was with Stephanie Seymour, a twenty-two-year-old Victoria's Secret model disengaging from a relationship with rock star Axl Rose. Beatty treated his brief romance with Seymour as if it were an extended bachelor party before committing himself to Bening.

As his *Reds* consultant Jeremy Pikser recalled, "I went up to his house one time when he had Stephanie Seymour, and three other models, and a photographer there. And Warren drank a vodka and cranberry juice, which I've seen him do maybe three times in all the twenty years I've known him, and was necking with Stephanie Seymour in the living room, and he claimed to be — he said, 'I haven't had this good a time in ten years.' Now that was probably fun for an evening or two, or for a few months."

Three months before Annette Bening met Beatty, her estranged husband of several years, J. Steven White, a stage director and fight choreographer, filed for divorce. The two had met and courted at the San Francisco Repertory Company, after White directed Bening in a production of *Romeo and Juliet*, and they were married in May 1984. By the time Bening filmed *Valmont* in France in 1988, "the marriage was already rocky," according to director Milos Forman. When White became ill, Forman recalled, "Annette just invited him and brought him in and behaved absolutely admirably to him and was taking care of him beautifully. On a human side, she has my greatest admiration."

When she was cast as Virginia Hill in *Bugsy*, the end of 1990, Bening was living alone in a small house in the Hollywood hills and dating lanky blond character actor Ed Begley, Jr., a relationship that began during *Postcards from the Edge*, according to Carrie Fisher. At the time, Bening described her life as "very normal," saying that she spent her free time doing yoga, "and I like to go to the beach and walk. I like to ride a bike. Or be alone. Or write."[64] She also demonstrated the trait that defined nearly all of Warren Beatty's serious love interests, "fencing her way" through a *Rolling Stone* interview that winter to avoid revealing anything personal. "It's *my* life," she stressed to a frustrated reporter that January, "and I want to keep it private."[65]

On February 18, a few days before she started work on *Bugsy*, Annette Bening was nominated for an Academy Award for *The Grifters*, the icing on the cake for the talent-worshipping Beatty. Bening's first phone call, when she heard the news, was to her parents, an act that proved her to be a woman after Warren Beatty's heart. Shortly after Bening was nominated, on the day she and Beatty shot the scene in *Bugsy* where Virginia Hill coolly suggests that Siegel "run outside and jerk himself a soda," Warren Beatty declared himself to Annette Bening. "I told her, 'Don't worry about me. As much as I'd like to have some sort of relationship with you, I'm not going to bother you with that while we're making the movie . . .'"[66]

Having Bening as a costar seemed to draw out the reserved Beatty, playing the lovesick but psychopathic Bugsy Siegel, a volatile part his friend

Toback set up to "write him right out of the closet. I honestly believed until the last minute he wouldn't do the movie. The script is so far out, so excessive . . . he went all the way with it."[67] Joseph Cosko, Jr., the camera operator, noticed that Beatty "was just really involved with it. Who knows, maybe he related to Bugsy Siegel? He *was* the character."[68]

As he often did in the films he produced, Beatty inserted coded references in *Bugsy* from his own life, including having Siegel put cucumbers under his eyes to reduce wrinkles, as Beatty did, or using a tanning reflector. Another reference was hidden in a scene in which the gangster offers to buy opera singer Lawrence Tibbett's mansion in Beverly Hills, even though it is not for sale. This was a version of the story that opera star Lauritz Melchior's granddaughter had told Beatty about Clark Gable trying to buy the Viking, Melchior's house on Mulholland. The scene was fiction, Beatty's sly wink to Melchior, whose name was even mentioned in the dialogue.

Cosko, the camera operator on *Bugsy*, would recall the classic Beatty experience of eighty takes, which took place during a telephone scene. "We just basically canceled the rest of the day. Warren was the only one in the scene, and for whatever reason he just wanted to keep doing it over and over again. At one point, evidently he got a whiff of a groan-type attitude with the crew and he said, 'Listen guys, this isn't even close to a record. My record was such and such.'" Annette Bening, according to Cosko, impressed the crew of *Bugsy* as not only professional, but "a very open and happy person, and very polite and cordial — everything good you can say."

By the second month of filming, James Toback heard gossip linking Bening and his friend Beatty, which he disregarded until he saw them in a midnight conversation after a long day's shoot, and sensed the "vibes."[69] Bening, who attended the Oscar ceremony on March 25 with Ed Begley, Jr., as her date, bringing her parents, responded to Beatty's pursuit cautiously, cognizant of his reputation. "I didn't fall in love with him instantly," she said later. "I was wary."[70] That spring, the actress was offered the coveted role of Catwoman in the next *Batman* film, officially anointing Annette Bening as Hollywood's "it" girl of 1991, another woman Beatty pursued "at the top of her balloon."

Peter Feibleman, his close friend, noticed that Beatty "began to glow in a peculiar way" while he was filming *Bugsy*, a love-struck look that is visible throughout the movie, although Feibleman would not find out why until later. As Glenn Gordon Caron was to say after directing Beatty and Bening in *Love Affair* in 1994, "Warren told me the greatest thrill of his life was falling in love with Annette.[71] Consistent with Beatty's secretive nature, the director of *Bugsy*, Barry Levinson, had no idea that his costars were becoming involved. "Everybody thinks that's impossible, but it's true. And we were together all the time, the three of us, on the set. But they were never hanging around, kind of whispering in one another's ear, kissing in the corners and stuff, holding hands. They didn't do any of that stuff."[72]

The turning point occurred late in filming, when Bening's parents, Grant and Shirley, a San Diego insurance salesman and a paid soloist in the church choir, visited the set and had lunch with Beatty in his trailer. To Beatty, the Benings were a happily married version of his own parents, with an element of his aunt Ruth, the church pianist in Front Royal — reminders of a wholesome middle-class past that was familiar and dear to him. What Beatty found compelling was the Bening family philosophy, established by Annette's salesman father, who gave Dale Carnegie motivational seminars ("I still remember the five points of salesmanship," she said that year, "attention, interest, conviction, desire and close") and was a follower of Norman Vincent Peale's power of positive thinking. "You ask my dad how he is, and he says, 'good and getting better,'" Bening would say, laughing. "I was definitely raised in that positive atmosphere, and I very much use it as a discipline."[73]

To Warren Beatty, who had spent his life trying to step out of the shadow of his father's defeatism and inability to experience happiness, Annette Bening's Dale Carnegie optimism seemed like a life raft. "As [her parents] were leaving," Beatty would recall, "I took Annette aside and said, 'I want to tell you that I'm not making a pass at you, but if I were to be so lucky as to have that occurrence happen, that I want to assure you that I would try to make you pregnant immediately.'" Their first child was conceived that night.[74] As Beatty remembered, "I finally said, 'You know, we have one more scene to do in the movie before the picture's wrapped up, and maybe if we went to dinner it wouldn't be so much pressure on either of us,' and I asked Annette if she wanted to have a child. After a few minutes she said she did. And I said, 'Well, I would like to do that right away.' And we did . . . that's the truth. And that's a nice thing for our kids to know."[75]

Neither Beatty nor Bening would say, or seem to remember, whether he proposed to her before the conception.[76] What they agreed on, then and later, was that each of them had a strong desire for a child at that moment in time. "When I met Warren I was thirty-two and the biological clock was ticking," said Bening, ". . . if he hadn't wanted to have children, it wouldn't have worked."[77] By the night of their fateful dinner, Annette Bening had also become aware that she and Beatty had "very similar backgrounds, so there's a lot of basic things we share," and discovered that, as she expressed it, "Warren has a very strong and rooted morality."[78]

Shirley MacLaine observed eight years later, "Annette knew what a Southern conservative father he'd make. She knew what she wanted in life, and he was a means to that end."[79] Gary Hart, who would get to know her well, later analyzed, "Annette's smart in a personal relationship way. She has terribly good instincts about human nature; I guess that's why she's such a good actress. She's perceptive about Warren. She knew who he was, and what he was, before she married him. She's one in a million in terms of women who would be able to understand Warren, and be clever about it, and I don't mean that in a negative way."

The only person Beatty told immediately about Annette Bening's pregnancy that spring was his mother, Kathlyn. "She was really declining, in and out of *compos mentis*-dom, and I thought, even though we haven't told anyone else that we're going to have this baby, I want to tell my mother."[80] Before filming ended, he also sent Bening to the set of the film *Hook*, in production on the same lot, so she could observe Deborah Ruf with her son, Charlie Korsmo, the Kid in *Dick Tracy*, who had a part in the film. "Annette Bening ran up to me, fully dressed in her *Bugsy* clothes, and she said, 'Are you Debbie? Are you Charlie's mother?' And I said yes, and she told me who she was, and she said that Warren really valued my relationship with Charlie, and said some good things about what a good mother I am, and what a wonderful boy he is. I mean this meant a lot to her . . . I really got the impression Annette was a really good person. It was quite an age difference, but really, I thought it was a very good pairing."

By early summer, Beatty confided his secret to the people closest to him, which included his sister, and Gary Hart. "I was in London," remembered Hart, "and Warren called at four in the morning. And he said, 'Annette's pregnant,' so I knew who it was. He talked about whether he should get married or not. He told me earlier he wanted to be married and have kids. I think he felt, at a certain point, it had reached 'it's now or never.'"

On July 16, 1991, Beatty and Bening issued a joint statement to the press that they were expecting a child together, and that she was dropping out of her role as Catwoman, news that made instant headlines around the world. The *Washington Post*, Warren Beatty's hometown newspaper, announced his impending fatherhood at fifty-four, tongue-in-cheek, as "a watershed moment in the history of American civilization."[81] Columnist Ruthe Stein of the *San Francisco Chronicle* referred to Beatty as a social "archetype," the bachelor who would never settle down. "In his role as archetype, Beatty could have a major impact on single men and women," Stein speculated; ". . . it's nice to think that perhaps a lot of Warren Beatty types, inspired by their hero, will give in to it and soon be singing another tune. Do I hear a lullaby?"[82]

"I would be lying to you if I didn't confess I liked it," Beatty told columnist Maureen Dowd, referring to the headlines describing his fatherhood as the end of an era. "I also liked all the cartoons. One related it to the fall of Cuba. Nice to be noticed."[83] Annette Bening conceded, that December, she "rather liked" being known as the woman who had "tamed" Warren Beatty. "Warren has been famous for so long, and I guess he has represented . . . certain things in people's minds. So in a way, I suppose you could look at this as being the end of an era."[84]

Beatty's blessings continued when the reviews for *Bugsy* came out at the end of the year, with Janet Maslin of the *New York Times* praising his performance as "the role of his career," and Richard Schickel proclaiming in *Time* magazine "the picture belongs, in every sense of the word, to Beatty."

While Beatty was promoting *Bugsy* in December, a month before Annette Bening was due to give birth to their daughter, journalist Katie Couric, another upright Virginian from Arlington, teased him on *Today* that her extremely proper mother had asked her "why he doesn't marry that girl." Beatty told Couric, "You should ask your mother to call me . . . she's making the assumption that this is up to me, which is not necessarily a good assumption."[85] It was unlikely the decision *was* Beatty's, who once said, "If I were about to raise a family, I would have to get married. I would feel morally obligated to my children to do this . . . I and my sister Shirley come from a very conventional Richmond, Virginia family, and I'm afraid this kind of behavior might shock them."[86] All he and Bening would say about marriage was "we're in agreement on the subject."[87]

As an expectant father, Beatty experienced "the happiness I had as a small child," referring to the years in Richmond he viewed with such nostalgia.[88] He would name January 8, 1992, the date Annette Bening gave birth to their first child, as the happiest day of his life, and Bening would describe watching him give their daughter her first bath in the hospital the most romantic thing Warren Beatty had ever done.[89] "I kind of fell apart," Beatty admitted a few months later, "I was so moved by it . . . there's nothing quite like looking into the face of your child and seeing your father, who passed away a few years ago. That makes me feel better about everything, and it's a much deeper feeling than I ever had in relation to a film."[90] Beatty's first act as a father was to sing a Cole Porter song to his little girl.[91]

When he and Bening took their daughter home from the hospital, the nursery that Beatty had built eighteen years earlier was prepared for her arrival. "I'd begun to think it was impermissibly pathetic when people would say, 'What's the purpose of this little room here?' And I would go, 'Oh, that's just something I whipped up in the design of the house.' But when we got back and her room was all ready with a cradle, and I took her in there, well . . . that really was a very emotional moment for me."[92]

His mother "was in a state of ecstasy," recalled Beatty. A few months earlier, when he and Annette Bening found out they were having a girl, Beatty told his mother they planned to name her Kathlyn Bening Beatty. "My mother was enormously moved . . . I'll never forget the look in her eyes. She started to cry. Then she composed herself, tossed her head a little, and said, 'I just hope I live up to it. This means I'll have to act respectable, for her sake. I won't be able to run off with a younger man!' My mother always said things that made me laugh. Our bond was very strong."[93]

Becoming a father profoundly affected Beatty, in the opinions of his sister and his friends. Novelist Peter Feibleman, Kathlyn's godfather, noticed that he was much calmer, something Beatty observed himself, saying that his daughter had given him "license to relax, to be happy, to be more emotional."[94] Having a child also brought Beatty closer to his sister, who felt that the baby, and Bening, served as a bridge between her and Warren. "The child has really changed him," observed MacLaine. "He's a very responsible father. He really loves her. And I really like Annette, who's a fabulous mother."[95]

The lessons Warren Beatty said he wanted to teach his children were to be honest, the trait associated with generations of Beatys, and "that it's okay to be happy," the ingredient that was missing from his parents' recipe for life, and the quality in Annette Bening that drew him to her.[96] "She has the capacity to be happy, which is a great gift to me and an even greater gift to her children. That's the greatest gift you can give a child," Beatty commented later, admitting he had been only "reasonably happy" throughout his life. "I see it more as a responsibility now and less as an indulgence . . . and I think you can only be happy by dealing in the present or not dwelling on the past or worrying too much about the future. I mean all we have is now."[97]

When Yevgeny Yevtushenko passed through Los Angeles to receive a Freedom Award two months after Kathlyn was born, Beatty invited his old friend to stop by the house on Mulholland to meet her and Annette Bening. "I've seen him first time really happy," reflected the Russian poet. "Not like man on the drugs, but *really* happy when he showed me his first child, and I was sitting with him and Bening. Warren — he was like reborn, you know? He was so happy, so proud of Annette. She was realistic woman. She accepted him like he is, she understood him, and she loves him. She looked at Warren like a mother looking at her most beloved child. You couldn't deceive a poet."

When Yevtushenko asked Beatty to read the synopsis for a film Yevtushenko conceived about the diary of a womanizer, a part he thought Warren might like, Beatty declined. "It could be great film, but after he met Bening, he didn't want to *talk* even about this. He didn't want even to play *roles* of womanizer. And that I remember beautifully."

A day or so after Yevtushenko's visit, on March 12, 1992, Henry Warren Beatty married Annette Carol Bening in Los Angeles, appropriately using a confidential marriage license to keep it a secret from the press. Bening described the wedding as "perfect and very simple — I wore a dress I had in my closet. Our daughter was the only witness and she was the one who wore white."[98]

Soon after, Beatty told British journalist David Frost that his goal for the remainder of his life was to be a husband and a father, and to "know how to do that right."[99] As one of his political heroes, Senator George McGovern, who kept up his friendship with Beatty, was to observe, "I think, just like Warren wants to bring perfection to acting and writing and anything else he does, he wants to be a good father and a good husband. So I say, power to him. I think that's the biggest change in his life."

After he married Annette Bening, two weeks shy of his fifty-fifth birthday, Warren Beatty would question whether he was any different from his schoolteacher father Ira or his grandfather Welton Beaty, the Front Royal, Virginia, craftsman and laborer, who believed that having a wife and children was the most exciting thing in the world.[100]

In the end, many the same traits he once listed to describe his father could be said to be true of Warren Beatty: "He was a very reasonable man. Cerebral. Sentimental. Outwardly jovial . . . in a way that concealed a basic Baptist Puritanism. Let's just say that he wasn't overconfident. Or materialistic. He was married once."

44 *As soon as he became involved with* Annette Bening, Beatty dusted off his seven-year-old idea to remake *Love Affair*, the 1939 Charles Boyer–Irene Dunne tearjerker. In it, a suave older ladies' man finally finds true love and, through that, becomes a better man. Tragedy intervenes, leading to a poignant reunion in the last scene that confirms the power of love and the role of destiny in one's life.

Beatty, who had idolized and done impersonations of the debonair Boyer after watching him in Richmond matinees with Shirley, "loved the original, just always loved the yarn, it touched me from the start . . . there's something about the situation with these two worldly but unhappy people. They're kind of cynical about love when they meet . . . then they find redemption through love. You know?"[101]

The parallel to his own love affair with Annette Bening was at least a subliminal part of its appeal to Beatty. "Meeting Annette inspired me to get off my ass and work on the movie," he said. "She's inspiring to me."[102] Bening, who had never seen the Boyer film, watched it alone in the kitchen on Mulholland when Beatty suggested they star in a remake together. "I was a mess at the end of it," she would recall, saying it was typical of Warren to be attracted to such a sentimental story. "That's just the kind of man he is."[103]

The movie, like Beatty's new life as a family man with Annette Bening, was about redemption. "I never thought of casting anyone but myself in the part," Beatty told a reporter from Virginia; ". . . the movie is a male fantasy, I suppose, that we are all redeemable."[104] The line in the remake that would be associated with Warren Beatty when the film came out in 1994 was from the original *Love Affair* in 1939. "It's a great line. Charles Boyer said it twice," Beatty once remarked to a reporter, reenacting his childhood Boyer impersonation, using a French accent. "He said it this way, 'You know, Terry, I have never been faithful in my whole life.' Then he says it again, 'In my whole life, I have never been faithful.' Well you really can't make this movie if you're gonna be ashamed of making it."[105]

In January of 1993, seven months after their surprise wedding, Beatty and Bening announced plans to star in the *Love Affair* remake for Warner Brothers from a script by Robert Towne, a project that was steeped in sentiment. The original thirties film was not only close to Beatty's heart, but it was also personally meaningful to Steve Ross, the chairman of Warner Brothers, who died of cancer before filming began. It was also a favorite of the late Charles

Feldman, who not only resembled Charles Boyer but, like Warren Beatty at fifty-five, could relate to the sophisticated, aging Casanova.[106]

The movie acquired an emotional urgency for Beatty a month later, when his mother, Kathlyn, died suddenly from a bacterial infection at age eighty-nine, triggering what became an obsession of Beatty's to induce the ailing Katharine Hepburn to play his character's beloved aunt in a small but pivotal scene. Beatty's fixation to cast Hepburn in *Love Affair* clearly was in homage to his mother, Kathlyn, whom he had associated with Katharine Hepburn since boyhood because of the similarity in their names and back-grounds, as well as their "perpetual integrity." "I'd have done anything to get her to play that scene," Beatty said later.[107]

Beatty wooed the frail but feisty eighty-six-year-old Hepburn with teenage ardor — sending massive bouquets of wildflowers, Hepburn's favorite, to her apartment in New York and her home in Old Saybrook, Connecticut; flat-tering her over the telephone; flying east to charm her; slyly utilizing her namesake goddaughter, Kat Kramer (the daughter of director Stanley Kramer), as well as novelist Scott Berg, a late-in-life friend of the reluctant actress, as intermediaries to persuade her. "I don't think there was anything more important to him in that whole period in his life than getting Katharine Hepburn to be in that movie," observed Jeremy Pikser, who was meeting with Beatty regularly on a future project.

In another sentimental gesture, Beatty hired Marion Dougherty, the fa-bled casting director who had given him his break thirty-six years earlier in "The Curly Headed Kid," to cast *Love Affair*. Dougherty arranged backups in case Beatty could not coax Hepburn into playing his dowager aunt. "I have lists of every actress that ever was known in those days, and what their state of health was. Oh my God, he was determined to get Hepburn, and Hepburn said absolutely not. And we went through hell. We went through every single woman who had ever been a star. And finally, I guess Warren pursued. He could tell you that story, nobody else could. But I think he sent her flowers every single day, and called her, and he finally got her."

Bening and Beatty started filming the remake in August of 1993, two months after the release of the popular romantic comedy *Sleepless in Seattle*, which included recurring references to *An Affair to Remember*, a 1957 ver-sion of *Love Affair* that starred Cary Grant and Deborah Kerr. *Sleepless in Seattle* ended with its star-crossed couple, played by Tom Hanks and Meg Ryan, meeting for the first time on the observation deck of the Empire State Building, the location chosen by the lovers in both *An Affair to Remember* and *Love Affair* as the place they would reunite. In both versions of *Love Affair*, the couples are separated by an accident of fate until destiny reunites them in the emotional final scene. Annette Bening considered her two canceled meetings with Warren Beatty to discuss playing Tess Trueheart in *Dick Tracy* "our Empire State Building," a missed connection or twist of fate before destiny brought them together on *Bugsy*.[108]

Beatty, who always respected his elders, and the classics, chose to make *Love Affair* as an old-fashioned, faithful adaptation of the original 1939 film — which he equated with singing "Danny Boy" in the middle of a rap concert, a right he felt he had earned after the daring films he had made earlier in his career, such as *Bonnie and Clyde*. "If you like a movie enough to remake it," he explained, "you should respect it, and take as much as you can from the original."[109] He considered Nora Ephron's *Sleepless in Seattle*, which had made ninety million dollars, "a nice comedy that makes a joke about *Love Affair*," saying later, "I didn't want to make fun of it the way Nora did."[110]

Beatty's latest sentimental journey to the thirties was a rocky one creatively from the start. The trouble began when he and Robert Towne developed artistic differences over the script, causing a several-year rupture in their close friendship. "I opened it up with Warren as a former football player getting a prostate examination," explained Towne. "Then I put him on a fat farm. Warren didn't see it that way; he thought it was too funny and unglamorous."[111] Beatty, who possessed the propriety and bearing of his distinguished MacLean forebears, was not comfortable losing his dignity on-screen, the reason he turned down the role of Superman in the seventies after trying on a pair of long underwear, looking at himself in the mirror, and concluding "I just couldn't do it."[112]

Towne's suggestion that Beatty appear in the first scene of *Love Affair* in a proctologist's office, a visit Beatty barely tolerated in real life, was not a viable option. "I do not enjoy a prostate examination," he said once. "It's very, very . . . the whole idea of it offends me, and I always felt there was something unjust about it. One time my doctor said, 'Look, do you think *I* like it?'"[113] After three more drafts of the script, Towne quit the project, and Beatty enlisted a director to rewrite it with him.

His next creative struggle would be with the director he chose, Glenn Gordon Caron. Caron had impressed Beatty with *Clean and Sober*, his first feature film after directing the hit television series *Moonlighting*, starring the famously fractious Cybill Shepherd and Bruce Willis. "I think that's one of the reasons I was there, quite frankly," said Caron, "is he had the sense that I was of the moment, and would sort of bring that to the film."[114]

The young director, who was flattered to work with Warren Beatty and enamored of Annette Bening's talent, agreed to make *Love Affair*, even though it was not a movie he would have chosen. "Because it was Warren," Caron admitted, "it meant that you're going to be surrounded by top-flight people, and I thought why not . . . you have to be deaf not to understand that you're getting involved with someone who's complicated, and demanding in their own way, but I thought, oh I can handle this, I've been through *Moonlighting*."

Beatty took control of the film on the first day. "What makes it complicated," Caron analyzed after the fact, "is that Warren wears so many hats, and frankly most people are there not because I'm directing, but because he's starring . . . and additionally you've got Annette, who he's married to. It was a complicated thing."

The dynamic was established in the first scene Caron shot, one with Annette Bening that he printed after eight takes. "And Warren came over to me and he said, 'Would you mind if I talked to her?' And I thought wow, you're the star, you're the producer, you're her husband, and I said, 'No, go ahead.' He went over, and we did thirty, thirty-five more takes." The next day, after the director and Bening saw the dailies, "she turned to me," Caron recalled, "and she said, 'you were right . . . take eight.' And Warren came to me afterward and said, 'From now on, if you need to speak to Annette, why don't you speak with me and I'll speak with Annette.'"

In Caron's view, "Warren's attitude is, 'how can you be so damn sure? Why don't we do this scene every way possible, and then in the cool of the editing room decide what it's really supposed to be?' So he's very comfortable doing thirty, forty takes — laughing, crying, sad, happy — completely antithetical to my sort of process. So that was really for us, and I think if you look at his work with most directors where there's been any kind of conflict, that's really at the heart of it."

Actor Pierce Brosnan, who played Bening's jilted fiancé in *Love Affair*, considered Beatty's passion for the film "sweet but obsessed," expressing disbelief that Beatty requested twenty takes from all angles on a simple shot their first day.[115] As Beatty's wife, Annette Bening, who preferred fewer takes than her husband, bore the brunt of his perfectionism. She also found it difficult having their eighteen-month-old daughter on the set of her first film since becoming a mother. "Warren can always say, 'Please hold the baby,' but I can't do that as easily. I found it quite an adjustment in terms of concentration. I'd be preparing to do a big scene and found I couldn't have her around, because if I didn't come up with the right take, I'd be in trouble."[116]

Several years later, Beatty candidly acknowledged the tension his high standards created, saying, "Whoa," when asked if he would direct Bening in a movie. "There's nobody I'd rather direct, but I think there'd be a certain amount of agony involved . . . the better question would be asked to her, whether she would put up with it."[117]

Katharine Hepburn's intimidating presence toward the end of filming created another source of anxiety for Bening, who admitted she was "desperate to please her. She's great. And she's tough. No nonsense. She's not somebody who sits around and has a chat with you. I would love to have said, 'What was it like to have done this and that movie?' "[118]

According to playwright Philip Barry's daughter-in-law Patricia, Bening was interested in starring in a revival of *The Philadelphia Story*, the play written by Barry for Katharine Hepburn in the thirties and adapted into a Hepburn film in 1940. Warren Beatty's first lovestruck glimpse of Hepburn was in the movie version, in which she played the regal Tracy Lord opposite Cary Grant as her charming ex-husband Dexter Haven.

"We'd been having wonderful meetings with Annette," recalled Patricia Barry, "and she really wanted to do it, and we thought she'd be wonderful, and the idea was to get her pinned down, and then have Warren play Dexter. And it kind of fit in with their personal relationship as well. And so they were really excited about that, and Annette was too, and Annette is very bubbly. Of course it was a challenge, because Kate had originated the part, but Annette was really excited about it. And then one day Kate came in and turned to Annette in her cold, steely look and said, 'My dear, that has been done.' Well, Annette was so bruised by that that she just crept away from the project. She just wouldn't even consider doing it. Just popped her balloon."[119]

Beatty, unsurprisingly, found the grande dame Kate Hepburn captivating. His later recollection of the eighty-six-year-old actress on one of their last days of filming was reminiscent of his reaction to his grandmother MacLean when he was a boy of five. "She might've had some trouble moving around or remembering things, but she never seemed a day over 40 to me . . . or 20. Removing her makeup after her final day, she looked over and caught me sitting and staring at her, besotted."[120]

As Glenn Gordon Caron observed, "There was a certain kind of woman — Annette, Katharine Hepburn, his mother — those are the women that Warren most admires, wants to be near. And there is a certain similarity. He was completely enamored of Annette, and they were very much a married couple. They sort of know where the lines are, and what the limits are."

Beatty's professional concerns about aging, and how he would be lit for his scenes, caused the greatest conflicts on the set of *Love Affair*, according to the director. "He used to joke with me," recalled Caron. "He used to say, 'I'm a producer who has a leading man under contract.' Warren recognizes that that's part of his commodity, and he wants to protect that. At the same time, he wants to be genuine to the material."

A battle waged between Beatty and cinematographer Conrad Hall, with Caron struggling to support Hall's aesthetic. "I felt Warren was too concerned with how he looked," said the director. "Over time, we gradually worked out a lighting scheme that worked. Usually Connie was upset, and Warren was insistent, and I was the guy sort of carrying messages between the two of them."

Two days after Beatty and Bening finished *Love Affair*, on January 17, 1994, the Northridge earthquake blasted their house on Mulholland in the middle of the night "like a bomb," recalled Bening.[121] "We were traumatized. Kathlyn was only two. Her crib was moving — it was kind of bizarre she was not awake. There was a lot of glass. We went into the front yard and she said, 'Look at all the lights!' The city was dark and you could see the stars."[122]

With their house severely damaged, the Beattys moved into the Bel Air Hotel and then temporarily rented a place in Malibu. Beatty, who had purchased the Viking in 1973 with the idea that he, like Lauritz Melchior, would live the remainder of his days there, bought the Mediterranean mansion next door as his temporary headquarters and began to supervise the reconstruction of his first and only house into the perfect home, a project his friends joke may never be completed to his specifications. As Terry Semel would tease Beatty at a tribute in 2002: "I asked Annette tonight, how's the house coming? And Warren said, 'Well, we're working on plans.' And I said, same architect? 'No.' How many have you had? 'I've had so many that I'm the architect now.' So I have one word of advice to Annette: if you really want that new house, buy it!"[123]

The earthquake in January 1994 was the last major bump in the road for Annette Bening in her eighteen-month adjustment to becoming an instant celebrity, mother, and wife, scrutinized as the woman who had landed Warren Beatty. All this was capped by the, at times, trying experience of filming *Love Affair*. Ironically, the movie that created stress for Bening, "in Warren's mind was very much a Valentine to her," observed Glenn Gordon Caron. "It was very much him saying here's how much I care, here is the depth of my feeling."

Beatty constantly praised Bening, and married life, publicly. "For me," he told author Norman Mailer a few years into his marriage, "the highest level of sexual excitement is in a monogamous relationship," adding, "I would hate myself if I fail to live up to it."[124] On another occasion, Beatty said, "I simply like my life now so much better than that sort of adolescent life that preceded this."[125] Patricia Barry, who had known Beatty for years, and spent time with him during *Love Affair*, made the observation, "Warren's a totally different person since he's been with Annette. He's much more open. He was always kind of guarded before. But he's just so open, and loving, and fun now."

The internal conflict Warren Beatty felt about his Hollywood lifestyle versus his core Virginia values no longer tormented him. "It's funny," his sister told the *Los Angeles Times* in 1995, "Warren was always a conservative Eastern gentleman. That's where he was headed all along, and now he's there, now that he's found this wonderful wife. Those children mean everything to him. Whenever I get a chance I'm over there with them."[126] Christmas, the holiday that was Beatty's sentimental favorite since childhood, was celebrated at *his* house after his marrying Bening, according to MacLaine. "It has to be at their house. It was at my house for years before he had kids."[127]

Beatty and Annette Bening both wanted more children after Kathlyn, announcing soon after *Love Affair* wrapped that Bening was pregnant again. In a further illustration of Beatty's charmed second act in life, Bening gave birth to a boy on August 23, 1994, what would have been his mother Kathlyn's ninety-first birthday. The baby was called Benjamin MacLean Beatty, "Ben" for Bening's father, and MacLean to honor Beatty's mother, sister, grandmother, maternal aunts, uncle Mansell, and grandfather Murdo. "We're both just floored our second child is a boy," Bening said that fall. "Warren is seriously excited. We're in heaven."[128]

Kathlyn Beatty, who was then two and a half, inherited Warren's cherubic face in his toddler years, along with Shirley's curls at three, and the speech skills of both sides of her family. "Warren is completely enraptured," Bening observed then. "He's extremely respectful of her. She's a very verbal kid, and a lot of it is because he sits and talks with her. He's started taking her out to lunch with him near his office, just the two of them."[129]

Beatty, who was fifty-seven when his son was born, was even more acutely aware of his own mortality. One of the ways he demonstrated this was by leaving parties early. "Being a daddy has changed my perspective. You suddenly ask yourself, 'How much time do we have now?' Children are everything. They're the key to understanding what is important."*[130]

Professionally, Beatty suffered a setback when *Love Affair*, his personal statement about redemptive love, opened in theaters in the middle of October 1994 and was dismissed by critics as "schmaltzy." As a result, it barely played in theaters. Janet Maslin of the *New York Times*, who had praised *Bugsy*, disparaged the soft lighting Beatty had requested to blur his age, writing that "both stars are filmed in such a rosy, gauzy glow that a star actually seems to gleam off Mr. Beatty's teeth in one scene."[131] Annette Bening was chided by a different critic for "swanning" through the film like a "disembodied . . . diction-class graduate."[132]

Glenn Gordon Caron, who had been deprived of the final director's cut on *Love Affair*, which went to Beatty, found the experience "really frustrating and sort of heartbreaking . . . we had a very, very, very, very difficult experience. Having said that, I genuinely like Warren. He is relentlessly himself, and that's a rare thing, you know."

Beatty's triumph when *Love Affair* came out was uniquely personal. He and Bening flew to New York to do publicity, introducing a "new" Warren Beatty to the press, who found him open, relaxed, and conversational. As one reporter at the junket wrote, "Interviews with the voluble and charming Mr. Beatty ran long . . ."[133] Now that he had a wife and children to talk about, Beatty no longer felt torn about living a life that was at odds with his upbringing, which diminished the need to keep his private life a secret.

The guarded Beatty, ironically, was his wife. "The more reticent Miss Bening," observed a reporter at the *Love Affair* junket, "appeared to adhere fairly close to the program." Barbara Walters, who interviewed Bening for an ABC special the next year, noticed the same trait. "It was disappointingly bland," Walters admitted, "as Warren, I think, coached her to say as little as possible. She was adorable before and after the interview, relaxed and talkative, but not during the interview."[134]

According to Annette Bening, it was she who established her privacy zone, not her husband, and she was uncomfortable, at times, with Beatty's

*As a memorial to their childhood, and to their parents, Beatty and his sister still kept the house in Arlington where Tat and Ira Beatty lived.

proud peacock disclosures about their personal life. "I've always been a little more private. I don't go into all those details about my feelings. It's just something I like to keep to myself."[135]

As Jeremy Pikser, Beatty's occasional collaborator, would observe, confirming Bening's strong role in the relationship: "Warren's very devoted to Annette. I think he can be exasperating for anyone to live with, and I think she busts his chops, which is something he absolutely would need, and he gets that from her. She's very strong, and it really worked very well for him. I think she's very devoted to being his wife, I think she's willing to put up with a lot, but not quietly."

IN ROBERT TOWNE'S observation, Beatty was "upset" at the end of 1994 by the disappointing reaction to *Love Affair,* but his career concerns were not enough to pull him away from his new obsession, family life, or from his secondary passion, politics.[136] As he hinted then in *Vogue,* "I smell political work around the corner — but it's not running for office."[137]

Beatty involved himself in politics in the way he genuinely was most comfortable, and often the most effective, in the movie business: behind the scenes. During the nineties, he and Bening became fixtures at the Beverly Hills political salons hosted by Stanley K. Sheinbaum, an active fund-raiser for the Democratic Party, then in his seventies, dubbed "The Man Who Would Be Kingmaker" by the *Los Angeles Times.*[138] Sheinbaum, who was married to Jack Warner's niece, had met Beatty in the seventies through their mutual support of the ACLU, and served as a political mentor to him, just as Kazan, Feldman, and others had guided him through Hollywood. "I would spend many an evening with Warren," Sheinbaum recalled, "just having dinner or something."[139]

Another political crony of Beatty's was Bill Rosendahl, an amiable, well-informed Democratic activist with a long-running Los Angeles–based cable television show that addressed political issues. Beatty's acquaintance with Rosendahl dated back to Robert Kennedy's candidacy for president, and the two became close friends during the McGovern campaign. "What I liked so much about Warren and his sister was they weren't prima donnas," commented Rosendahl. "They rolled up their sleeves just like everybody else, and got engaged in the politics, got engaged in the fund-raising. They did whatever we asked them to do." By the time Beatty married Annette Bening,

Rosendahl was the person Beatty picked up the phone to call if he wanted to bat around the latest issues, or candidates.

In the midnineties, Beatty began to develop a political satire to express his cumulative trauma over the assassinations of John F. Kennedy, Robert Kennedy, and Martin Luther King, Jr., and Gary Hart's withdrawal from the presidential race in 1988 over the publication of a paparazzi photo. In Beatty's view, these were all assassinations, whether by a gun, a flashbulb, or gossip. "I have witnessed too many assassinations of people who were saying the right things," he lamented, "whether those assassinations were by bullet or tabloid scandal. Many people have been hurt by these assassinations. I have been hurt by them. I have strong feelings about them, and that is why I made this movie."[140]

Beatty's original intent was to make a quick comedy before the 1996 presidential election about a depressed politician who pays someone to assassinate him, and then changes his mind after falling in love, restoring his political faith. He started to write the screenplay, then called *Tribulations*, with James Toback, his *Bugsy* collaborator, then replaced Toback with Jeremy Pikser, his stalwart on *Reds*. Writer Aaron Sorkin, who was working on *The American President*, a romantic comedy costarring Annette Bening, contributed what he described as "a couple of wise-ass remarks" to the script over the course of a year.[141]

"Warren too frequently gets lumped into the stereotype of the Hollywood limousine liberal, and Warren simply isn't those things," observed Sorkin, who was creating the political drama *The West Wing* at the time. "He goes about working toward the political things that he believes in, in an extremely sophisticated, much quieter way . . . and my sense was that Warren was frustrated with the Democratic Party, a party for which he had worked most of his life, and very hard, and had a couple of things to say."

Beatty's disillusionment with the Democratic Party coincided with his friendship with Republican Senator John McCain, whom he met in 1980 through Gary Hart. Around 1996, "we started seeing each other and communicating quite frequently," McCain recalled.[142] The issue that brought McCain and Beatty together was campaign finance reform, Beatty's pet cause since the seventies. "We are far apart on some issues," observed McCain, "but we're in agreement as far as the need for reform. Reform is a theme that doesn't just have to do with campaign financing; it has to do with reform of the military, reform of the tax system, reform of the different bureaucracies in Washington.

So we have a commonality there. Now our solutions may not always be the same, but I think Warren is committed to reform, and I know he would hate to hear me say this, but so was Theodore Roosevelt, who was my hero."

Beatty and McCain, and their families, became close socially around 1997, when the senator invited the Beattys and their children to his Arizona retreat. "We have a lot of friends in over the Fourth of July to our place up near Sedona, and we'd been together socially a few times, and so Cindy and I invited him over for Fourth of July . . . and they've come over every Fourth of July, except the last couple of years, when Annette has been working. We have cookouts, and fireworks, and swimming in the creek, and it's just a general Fourth of July weekend, which is a lot of—very enjoyable."

As his friendship with McCain was deepening, Beatty's political diatribe, *Tribulations*, took on an added dimension. The trigger was Beatty's increasing disillusionment with President Bill Clinton, particularly during Clinton's campaign for reelection in 1996. Jeremy Pikser, who co-wrote the script with Beatty, observed, "I think Clinton represents to Warren the epitome of Democrats saying winning comes first, principles come second." Annette Bening, who grew up in a Republican family and evinced no visible interest in politics before marrying Beatty, strongly espoused her husband's views. A few years later, she would criticize Hillary Clinton in *Vanity Fair* for "doing what's politically expedient in the most transparent way . . . you feel like there's prevaricating, there's lying. You just don't trust them."[143]

Beatty decided to produce his biting political satire at Fox, where he could have total creative control, since the studio owed him money for canceling *Dick Tracy* in 1987.[144] Using this creative license, and electing to star, produce, co-write, and direct for the third time, he set out to make his bravest film since *Bonnie and Clyde*—one that dramatized his disappointment "in the way that liberalism has sold its soul," according to Pikser. "What that film is about for him is a Martin Luther King quote that unless you have something worth dying for, you don't have anything worth living for."

The lead character was a disenchanted Democratic senator named Jay Bulworth—a name Beatty derived from Teddy Roosevelt's Bull Moose Party—a thinly disguised alter ego of Warren Beatty, with a twist of Gary Hart. "I know what it feels like," said Beatty, "to be a suicidally depressed Democrat."[145] As the character of Jay Bulworth becomes more dejected in Beatty's dark political satire, he begins to spout rap lyrics during his political speeches, shocking audiences by telling them the truth instead of repeating the usual campaign platitudes.

The idea for Bulworth's musical mental illness came to Beatty from an incident in his childhood, as did most of his films. "In my great-aunt Bertie and great-aunt Maggie's family in Virginia, there was a lady who had a nervous breakdown. And when she had this breakdown, she could only speak with the words of Oscar Hammerstein, Dorothy Fields, Larry Hart, Cole Porter. So when you talk to her — and I was five years old — I would say, 'Mrs. Liebowitz, what do you think about such-and such?' And she would say to me, 'You are the promised kiss of springtime.'"[146].

Through the farcical rhyming of Jay Bulworth, Beatty was able to express his private frustrations about the flaws in the political system, including his and McCain's key issue, campaign finance reform, and his belief that the Democratic party had lost its "mission." Beatty made the film, retitled *Bulworth*, for his children, dedicating it to them in the credits. "I wanted to do something that would mean something to them in the future," he said afterward.[147] This goal became more poignant while Beatty was finishing the script in the spring of 1996, when Annette Bening discovered she was pregnant with their third child.

Jeremy Pikser, Beatty's co-writer, considered Jay Bulworth an incarnation of Joe Pendleton, the sweetly decent football player in *Heaven Can Wait*, who was an extension of Bud Stamper from *Splendor in the Grass*, William Inge's cinema alter ego of Warren Beaty, the good son. "*Bulworth* is *Heaven Can Wait* in a lot of ways," analyzed Pikser. "I think, in a way, I just 'get' what's funny about Warren. The humor in *Bulworth* is the same humor as *Heaven Can Wait* — the anomaly of someone of great power and position being completely unabashed, and innocent. It's the innocence that makes it so funny, because the character is in the body of someone who's completely not innocent." After the film was released, Beatty told the *Washington Post* that Jay Bulworth's true love, the beautiful black activist played by actress Halle Berry, was the same character he wrote for Julie Christie in *Heaven Can Wait*.[148]

Halle Berry, who "hounded" Beatty for weeks to cast her in *Bulworth*, and was embroiled in a difficult divorce during filming, would thank Warren Beatty three years later in her Oscar acceptance speech for *Monster's Ball*. According to Pikser, who lived in the Beattys' guesthouse throughout *Bulworth*, "Warren's been a very generous, and supportive, and loving person in Halle's life, from everything I've been able to see. He really cares about her, and he's been interested in her welfare. He was very upset about what she went through in her divorce. That was going on while we were shooting, and her husband really hurt her. I never got a moment's sense of any kind of impatience from Warren, or that this was an inconvenience that she was distracted." Berry later told *The Voice*, "My experience on the film was magnificent. I got to learn a lot because Warren wore all the hats. He let me in on all the different aspects of filmmaking."[149]

One of Beatty's hidden messages in *Bulworth*, like his wink to Lauritz Melchior in *Bugsy*, was a tribute to his mentor Charles Feldman's longtime secretary Grace Dobish, who had died the year before. He created a character named after Dobish, making her Bulworth's faithful secretary, and casting seventy-three-year-old character actress Florence Stanley, who played the landlady who spied on him and Jack Nicholson in *The Fortune*.

"Warren wanted me for this teensy-weensy part," recalled Stanley, who described being directed by Beatty as a joy. "When you talk to him, it's like he doesn't have anybody on his mind except you. There are certain people — and there are very few — that make the moment a moment. And when you're with Warren, and you're talking to him, that's all there is. The connection is the magnetism, and his interest in you is so complete. His focus is so intense, *intense*, and the intent is so strong . . . I liken it to my grandson, who is a year and a half, who when I walk in the door, he lights up like I'm the person that he has been waiting for all his life."

As an actor, Beatty let himself go emotionally as the truth-rapping senator in *Bulworth*, allowing himself to look ridiculous on-screen for the first time. He also shed his vanity. "I've done a lot of very stylized, carefully lit movies," he said candidly. "When I first talked to cinematographer Vittorio Storaro about *Bulworth*, I told him, 'This time I want to look ugly.' I knew he'd be very interested in that."[150]

Beatty later would confide to Pikser, his collaborator, that he considered *Bulworth* possibly his greatest role. "I think it's the best picture I've made because I didn't give a fuck how much money it would make," he told the *UCLA Daily Bruin* afterward. "Even when I made *Reds*, I still felt an obligation to have it do well. I made this movie way in advance and had complete artistic autonomy on it, and I had none of the marketing rights. I'm just lucky as hell to be able to do it."[151]

While Beatty was filming *Bulworth* in 1997, Annette Bening gave birth to their third child, this time on his *father's* birthday, January 18. In memory of Ira Beaty, Beatty and Bening named their second daughter Isabel Ira Ashley Beatty. As a baby gift, Shirley MacLaine sent her brother a framed copy of a letter Ira Beaty had written to Warren on his thirtieth birthday, March 30,

1967, at the peak of his success on *Bonnie and Clyde*. Beatty hung the framed letter in his bathroom, where he could see it every morning when he used the shaving cream his father recommended to him on his deathbed.

In May of 1998, Warren Beatty's daring experiment, *Bulworth*, was released to admiration from critics for its audacity, and described by Jonathan Alter in *Newsweek* as a "hilarious cry from a broken liberal heart." But the film's political subject matter and the studio's timing of its release, opposite the spring blockbuster *Godzilla*, gave it "no chance to build," as Beatty complained.[152] The star contented himself with an Oscar nomination for Best Screenplay, shared with Pikser, and a writing award from the Los Angeles Film Critics Association.

While Beatty was acutely disappointed, movies had ceased to be the most satisfying or important part of his life. They had been replaced by his children, who fascinated him. "One thing Warren talks about with me quite frequently is, why work?" mused Jeremy Pikser. "I think that's a pretty big issue at this point. Why should he keep working? He doesn't usually answer, he usually asks. And I always say if I had your money, I wouldn't work another day in my life. And he said, 'Well, what would you do all day?' and I said, 'Cook supper,' and he said, 'I've been thinking a lot about cooking,' which I *think* is a joke."

A few years later, Beatty would tell a reporter he was "getting more and more into" cooking. "Annette has no interest. But I cook for the kids. At their ages, it's hard to interest them in anything that isn't bland. But I have a particular way of making eggs with cheese and milk that, if eaten at the right time, is very fluffy and good."[153]

Both Beatty and Bening, to no one's surprise, protected their children's privacy, refusing requests to take their pictures, although they were happy to be photographed or to sign autographs themselves. "We don't know what it's like to be children of celebrities," observed Bening. "We were both living in middle-class homes in the suburbs when we were kids."[154] Beatty also took steps to prevent his children from being spoiled, hoping to recreate the Virginia childhood he recalled nostalgically. "We try to live like our own mothers and fathers lived, which was without nannies and household staffs and things. My mother and father were teachers and Annette's mother and father are not loaded. They live upper middle-class existences, so we try to do that."[155]

Beatty's friend Marshall Bell compared them to a fifties television family. "I don't want to call it *Ozzie and Harriet*, but it's kind of like that." As Jeremy

Pikser observed, "They don't strike me as being very unusual other than they're incredibly famous, and incredibly rich. I remember, actually, when Kathlyn was probably about four, and they put up some enormous wooden jungle gym on the side of the house, and Warren's saying to me, 'She's like some rich girl, isn't she?' And I said, 'Well, yeah. You can't avoid it. She is a rich girl, she will always be a rich girl, you can't pretend that she's not really.' He always says, 'How can you stay interested in movies when you've got this? It's so much more interesting.'"

Before he started *Bulworth*, Beatty had already committed himself to starring in a comedy of manners called *Town & Country*, a decision that would haunt him in the new millennium, when the film was released after years of Sturm und Drang to crushing reviews. On its face, the project seemed like a classic romantic farce. The producer was the talented veteran Fred Roos, who shared office space with Beatty along his Via Veneto on Beverly Glen, and the writer was Michael Laughlin, Leslie Caron's ex-husband, who knew Roos and Beatty as a producer in the sixties. As Roos recalled, "Michael suddenly came back into my life from Hawaii and said, 'I've written a script, here it is, *Town and Country*, you want to run with it?' I mean not those words, but . . . so I did. I liked it. Wasn't quite the script that we shot, but the basic concept was the same, and I thought it was very right for Warren, and got it to Warren."[156]

Laughlin and Beatty, who discussed the script as early as 1996, envisioned it as a "comedy about remarriage" inspired by the films of Jean Renoir, whom they both idolized and got to know through Leslie Caron. "I really was writing my version of *Rules of the Game*," said Laughlin. "The world that Warren and I come out of is very, very different than the world that exists in Hollywood now . . . he and I would talk on the phone, and he was a very sensitive, very thoughtful person. Not that there aren't other sides of Warren, there are, but there is this sort of core that's very sensitive."

While Beatty was filming *Bulworth* in 1997, Roos lined up a stellar cast for *Town & Country* that included Beatty's close friends Goldie Hawn and comedian Garry Shandling, playing a couple with marital problems; actresses Nastassja Kinski and Andie MacDowell as women who tempt the married architect portrayed by Beatty to stray; and Diane Keaton as the wife he loves, loses, and wants back. "It was a terrific cast," Beatty said later, "and it seemed like it would be a lot of fun."[157]

The outsider in the project was the director, Peter Chelsom, an Englishman best known for a charming art-house film he wrote and directed in 1991 called *Hear My Song*. As Michael Laughlin would remember, "I was in meetings with Goldie, myself, Warren, and Diane, and it all seemed . . . just what you'd think, funny, and fun, and not a great deal of attention being paid to the director."

Goldie Hawn later described her and Beatty's experience with Peter Chelsom, prior to filming, as "a nightmare for a lot of reasons." Their biggest concern was the script. "So I took my time, and Warren took his time, and he stayed over a couple of nights with the director to talk to him about it . . . this director, who was very nice—I don't want to say anything bad about him, but at the same time, it may have been over his head, he may have disliked Warren and me, I don't know. Whatever the reasons are, there was a sort of, I guess you call it passive-aggressive, where you think you're getting through and you're really not, and it was maddening. And the one thing, of course, that gets Warren angrier than anything, and more upset, is passive-aggressive behavior."

When Diane Keaton was hired to direct the film *Hanging Up* and needed to start *Town & Country* the summer of 1998, it was the prelude to a three-year disaster. "Warren and I tried to postpone the movie because the film wasn't ready," recalled Goldie Hawn. "So Warren lobbied, I lobbied . . . we don't want to look like jerks in the movie, like actors that went into a film that didn't have what you consider a real beginning, middle, and an end. We just wanted to try to make the movie better." Beatty later commented, "It's really very simple. The picture began shooting before the script was finished because Diane Keaton had a date when she had to go off and direct a movie. So the company took the gamble of beginning the movie before it had a finished script."[158]

After three months of filming and revised drafts from several screenwriters, Beatty or Roos made a frantic call to satirist Buck Henry to try to salvage the script. "I said no a number of times until they raised the price so high I couldn't," recalled Henry, who wrote "hundreds of pages, many of which weren't shot . . . it's a real amalgam."

By the middle of July 1998, the Hollywood trades were reporting "battles" on the set between Beatty and Peter Chelsom, the director.[159] "As the whole movie went," Hawn would remember, "there was rewriting, there was agreeing and disagreeing . . . it was terrible. And the movie went way over budget, and everybody seems to blame Warren. Well, guess what, he could be maddening in certain ways, 'cause Warren is the way he is, and he wants things to be right, and he can be his own stubborn self because things aren't going the right way, but he is not the one to blame for this, and I will stand up forever on that . . . I remember saying to the guy at New Line [studio], 'Who's in charge here? Warren's not producing this movie.'"

In producer Fred Roos's view, "There were just a lot of cooks there, and our director, he wasn't, what can I say, Mike Nichols, with that kind of reputation and power to sort it out, and be the total captain of the ship." Peter Chelsom, in one of his rare public statements about directing *Town & Country*, made the remark that "no one will ever know the truth" about the filming of the movie. "I have a journal. About three people have read it."[160]

Michael Laughlin, its original writer, would comment forthrightly, "*Town and Country* is just a Hollywood movie out of control, nothing more than that. It's not about Warren, and it's not about Peter Chelsom, either. It's not about me, really. It was just totally out of control." According to Laughlin, the movie went so far over budget, everyone connected "bought a house" with the money they were paid. "Absolutely everyone. Every secretary, everyone."

While Beatty was filming *Town & Country* in New York, he crossed paths with Tracy May, the daughter of Mitch May, his estranged best friend from the fifties, sixties, and seventies, and his benefactor during his early struggles in New York as an actor–cocktail pianist. "He got really teary-eyed, and he hugged me and he said, 'Oh my God, I don't believe it,' and he was very sweet. He said, 'How's your dad? I miss your dad so much. How is he doing?' He got really *ferklempt*, you know, seeing a bit of his life. I was probably thirty at the time, and I had never met him, and it had been so long since he had seen my father. He got really emotional about it, he really started to tear up."[161]

Soon after, when Tracy May phoned Beatty to say that her father had cancer, "I could feel that there was a little bit of fear in his voice. And then, honestly, when I called him to tell him that Dad had passed, I just left a message with his assistant, and he never called me back. So I kind of got the feeling that he has some kind of issue about death." Beatty would respond the same way in 2002 to the passing of John Springer, the publicist who was like a second father to him, and to the death that same year of his close friend Richard Sylbert.

According to Sylbert's brother, Paul, their deaths moved, and frightened, Beatty. After Dick Sylbert's funeral, Paul Sylbert spent two days at Beatty's house on Mulholland at his invitation to mourn Dick's passing. When Sylbert left, Beatty made him promise to get a body scan. "Warren hooked me up with his doctor and he had me do a complete body scan. There was nothing on it except a benign tumor, but he insisted I do it—I guess because Dick and I were twins."

Beatty, who was then in his sixties with three young children, took every precaution to prolong his life for their welfare, including taking a separate flight from Bening when they traveled together as a family so one parent would survive if the other plane crashed. His mortality became more of an issue in the summer of 1999, when Bening conceived their fourth and last child, the year Beatty turned sixty-three.

That same August, with a presidential election looming and Bill Clinton at the end of his second term, writer Arianna Huffington floated Warren Beatty's name in her column as a possible candidate for president in 2000, a test balloon she had discussed with him at a dinner party beforehand. Beatty and Bening frequently attended political gatherings at Huffington's estate, and the topic that August was the Democrats' need for an alternative to "centrists" Al Gore and Bill Bradley in 2000. Huffington called her piece "Put Bulworth in the White House."

When Huffington's column proposing Warren Beatty for president set off an avalanche of publicity, she contacted Bill Hillsman, a Minneapolis advertising expert who had masterminded wrestler Jesse Ventura's successful campaign for governor of Minnesota. Beatty was intrigued enough about entering the race for president to invite Hillsman to his house on Mulholland to discuss his prospects.

"Beatty said at the time that we had the meeting, that if there were a Paul Wellstone running in the Democratic primary, there would be no need for him to run," Hillsman recalled. "Some of the roles he plays in his movies are sort of these reluctant hero type things, and I think that's very much the way he looked at this. That it was a situation where if there was nobody else better than him—and he felt that there were plenty of people better than him to do this—but if nobody else was going to step up and to enter this race, then perhaps he had to."[162]

His concern, Beatty told Hillsman, was that Gore and Bradley were overlooking the social issues he considered important, such as universal health care, racism, and child poverty. "Annette Bening was there as well, and if anything, was more the aggressor on this . . . her position on this was if we have the opportunity to somehow make the world a better place for our children and other people's children to grow up in, then we need to do what we need to do . . . she was almost pushing it, and he was more reluctant to do it, which surprised me."

According to Hillsman, the conversation got serious enough for Beatty to discuss raising ten million dollars "to be effective in the primary," and to evaluate his viability as a candidate. "He's very careful and he's very calculated. As he told me, he's a control freak. He said when you get to that part of the discussion where you talk about potential skeletons in the closet, he said, 'I don't drink, I don't take drugs, I've never taken drugs; I'm too much of a control freak for that.' I thought that he was trying to calculate all these various angles and figure it out." Hillsman believed there were two kinds of candidates. "There's the candidates who are in there to win, first and foremost . . . and then there are candidates who run out of a sense of conviction." In his view, Warren Beatty was the second. "It was much more, 'Well, isn't it worth it if I can change the dialogue and inject these issues into what Democrats are talking about nationally?'"

After a well-received trial-run speech September 29, when he received the Eleanor Roosevelt Award from Americans for Democratic Action, Beatty dropped the idea of running for president. "I frankly never thought that Warren was gonna take that step," reflected Senator John McCain, who was Beatty's houseguest the weekend before Hillsman's strategy session, and was a presidential candidate himself that summer. "I just didn't think he was. I didn't discuss it with him; I just didn't think he was. He had four very young children, and a wife who's still very active in her profession. I thought that those factors would mitigate toward him not running for office."

Beatty, who could only commit himself with "total passion," committed himself to his wife and children with the fanatic attention he had given to *Reds, Shampoo,* and *Bonnie and Clyde.* "So many people pressured him to run," mused Peter Feibleman, Kathlyn Beatty's godfather. "He considered it seriously for a while, but Warren can't dabble. He does something or he doesn't do it. He's now raising a family. It would have been one or the other. He's an extraordinary father . . . he takes Ben out to the ballgame, he takes the kids to museums, he's a hands-on father. He's there. It touches me, particularly, because my own father never was. And to see a father as attentive and physically there, and loving, and understanding, and interested in the children is amazing to me. I've never seen it before."

Warren Beatty's fourth child, a girl, was born on April 8, 2000, a few days after the Oscar ceremony where Annette Bening was a Best Actress nominee for *American Beauty* and Beatty received the Irving Thalberg Award, the Academy's most prestigious accolade for a producer. For a third time, Beatty honored his mother in his child's name, calling his third daughter Ella Corinne, after Kathlyn Corinne.

Shirley MacLaine was a frequent visitor on Mulholland by then. "They are very different people," observed writer Jeremy Pikser, "but there's a warmth, and she's around a lot, especially now with the kids. I've run into her a number of times at the house. And when one has a birthday party, she's there. I remember at a Halloween party, she was there, wearing black stockings. She's at least seventy-two now, and her legs are still good."

Bill Rosendahl, Beatty's friend since the McGovern campaign, described family nights at the former bachelor's once-stark compound, behind the gates, as a scene Kathlyn Beaty would have relished. "The kids are just incredible. Three girls and a boy, and they—I mean you go to the house for dinner, and they'll sometimes play a role at the dinner. They'll perform, or they'll take your order from your menu. They're so cute! And Warren and Annette have people over for dinner—like a year ago they had George McGovern up, my old buddy, and we had this lovely dinner with the kids. Then there was another time, [historian] Doris Kearns was up there, and she and Ben, the boy, started to talk about presidents. He rattled every one of them off, every one of the presidents. And Doris said, 'Warren, this kid's incredible.'"

For Beatty, it was a déjà vu of his childhood, when his father, Ira, took him to baseball games "and Warren," as a friend remarked, "knew every single player on the 1949 Washington Senators."[163] Beatty enrolled Ben, a puckish replica of Bening, in Little League, and went to a Boy Scout camp with him in 2004. "Warren is very *involved*," observed Bening, who has described Beatty as "an incredibly thoughtful, sensitive parent. He's very good at discussing things and reasoning and going through things carefully."[164]

Bill Rosendahl thought of Beatty as a househusband, which Beatty seemed to embrace. As he described a typical day, "I'll spend a lot of time seeing what is said about public affairs. I watch C-SPAN . . . I spend it with my kids. I write. I've played the piano all my life."[165] Michael J. Pollard, his friend since *A Loss of Roses* in 1959, the year Hollywood discovered Beatty, said simply, "Warren's so *happy* now."

In 1999, during an interview with Howard Stern, Beatty publicly declared that he was faithful to his wife, the vow he pledged he would never make unless he could keep it. According to one friend, he still charmed every woman he encountered, "[but] now Warren shows pictures of his kids. So he still gets to flirt, which is probably most of the fun, to see if he *can*. The seduction is there, there's just not a sexual payoff."[166] The senior Beatty took a Virginian's view of the lifestyle he once lived as portrayed in *Shampoo*. "It was an amazing opportunity for a generation of people to see that this kind of freedom — or license, if you want a pejorative — is not the answer to happiness."[167]

In his sixty-seventh year, 2004, Warren Beatty received two of the highest honors given to someone in his profession, one in January and the other in December, bookends to his nearly fifty-year career. The first was the Milestone Award, chosen by the Producers Guild of America for historic contributions to the movie industry. It was presented to him by his closest friend, Robert Towne, of whom Beatty once said: "I've known writers like Tennessee Williams, Bill Inge, Paddy Chayefsky, Noel Coward, and if I had an opportunity to reincarnate any of them, I'd still take Bob Towne."[168] Towne had this, in part, to say about Warren Beatty:

> . . . Privacy and secrecy are protective impulses, and few men are as cognizant of their importance, as protective of himself, his friends and family, and not so incidentally of his movies, as Warren. His passion for privacy could once seem too discreetly genteel, or coyly narcissistic. But given today's world of invasive government, and indiscriminately nosy media, and intrusive information highways, it now seems uncommonly prescient, prudent, sensible, wise. My rakish friend has somehow morphed into Ben Franklin. His advice has become as legendary as those who seek it . . .

Beatty's second laurel, at the end of 2004, the Kennedy Center Honors, represented the ultimate accolade an artist could receive in America. Named after his political hero, John F. Kennedy, the statesman he was asked to portray, the ceremony took place in Washington, D.C., next to Warren Beatty's home town of Arlington, Virginia, presided over by the president of the United States, in a program produced by the namesake son of director George Stevens—a confluence with profound meaning for Beatty. Jack Nicholson, who gave the keynote speech honoring his friend and neighbor on Mulholland, would remark that night, "Sure goes by fast, doesn't it, Pro?" Beatty brought his wife and children — "the four little Bs," Nicholson called them — to witness his award from President George W. Bush.

"If you knew my mother and father," Shirley MacLaine would say that same year of her, and her brother's, accomplishments, "it's not amazing.

They were extremely talented, unrealized and partial geniuses, and I think both of us are fulfilling the dreams they didn't dream for themselves."[169] Beatty not only acknowledged his parents' influence by naming his first production company Tatira, but also by including their names in all four of his children's, his legacies to Tat and Ira Beaty.

A few summers before his Kennedy Center award, when his eldest daughter, Kathlyn — whom he proudly described as "off the charts" in intelligence — showed an interest in the Beaty and MacLean family trees, Beatty took her, his wife, Annette Bening, and their three younger children to Front Royal, Virginia. There he walked them through the house the first Henry Warren Beaty built around 1901, pointing out where he used to climb out the window and down a tree at night.[170]

"I grew up as a fairly puritanical, Protestant, football-playing boy in Virginia," Beatty once said, summing up his life. "I don't know that I've changed very much."[171]

On his way to receive the Kennedy Center Honors in December 2004, the only time Warren Beatty and Annette Bening have permitted a photograph of their children in public. All four are named after Ira Beaty and Kathlyn Corinne MacLean Beaty. *From left:* Isabel Ira Beatty (born on Ira Beaty's birthday), Annette Bening, Ella Corinne Beatty, Benjamin MacLean Beatty (born on Kathlyn Beaty's birthday), Kathlyn Bening Beatty, Beatty.

Photo © by Peter Heimsath/Photo Associates News Service

Baptist youth minister John Raymond, Warren Beatty's mentor in adolescence and the man he most admired. *Courtesy of Mary Raymond*

The house in Waverly, Virginia, where Shirley and Warren Beaty were conceived. *Photo by author*

Young Warren used to climb out the second-floor window and down the tree at night when he and Shirley visited their great-aunts Bertie and Maggie Beaty, and, later, their aunt Ruth Gasque. *Photo by Eleanor Chadwell*

Nine-Thirty North Liberty in Arlington, where Shirley and Warren spent the majority of their childhoods and where their parents would continue to reside for twenty-eight years. *Photo by author*

notes

PROLOGUE: ORIGINS OF FAME

1. Nancy Collins, "The Real MacLaine," *Vanity Fair*, March 1991.

2. Alan Ebert, "Warren Beatty," *Ladies' Home Journal*, April 1976.

3. Lyn Tornabene, "Who Can Resist Warren Beatty?" *Cosmopolitan*, January 1975.

4. Shirley MacLaine, *Don't Fall off the Mountain* (New York: W. W. Norton & Company, 1970); Shirley MacLaine, *Dancing in the Light* (New York: Bantam Books, 1985).

5. Shirley MacLaine, *Dance While You Can* (New York: Bantam Books, 1991).

6. David Wallace, "Gotta Dance," *Los Angeles Times*, 26 August 1990.

7. Andrew Beaty material from Warren County Heritage Society, Front Royal, Va. ("The Register Man's Column: William Welton Beaty," *Warren County Register*, 3/7/46; Oral history of Margaret Jane Beatty, AKA Mrs. John Lewin, *Warren Sentinel*, spring 1940, reprint, 7/23/70; Miscellaneous unsourced handwritten Beaty marriage records; Notes, oral history of Bertie Beaty-Ware, n.d., n.p.; Researcher's notes titled "Beaty," n.d., n.p.); Anna Rae White, interview with author, April 2004; Gregory Priebe, letter to author; Beatty Project 2000, Lineage 34, courtesy of Ray Beaty, Mike Allen, and Cynthia Beatty Johnstone.

8. Prieb.

9. Bertie Beaty-Ware.

10. Oral history of Margaret Beatty Lewin (granddaughter of Sarah Adams Beaty); Cindy Beatty Johnstone, letter to author, February 2004.

11. See note 7.

12. Beaty-Ware; Lewin; Beatty Project 2000.

13. Taken from United States census records: 69th District, Warren County, Va., 12 July 1850, Reel 113, Library of Virginia; Warren County, Va., 22 June 1860, Front Royal, Reel 146, Library of Virginia; Warren County, Va., 13 August 1870, Front Royal, Reel 169, Library of Virginia; Warren County, Va., 12 June 1880, Front Royal, Reel 220, Library of Virginia; Warren County, Va., 18 April 1910, Front Royal, Reel 341, Library of Virginia; Warren County, Va., 8 January 1920, Front Royal, Reel 382, Library of Virginia.

14. Suzanne Silek, interview with author, 26 August 2002.

15. Lewin.

16. Beaty-Ware.

17. Lewin.

18. Lavinia Owens Edmonds, see note 7; Beaty-Ware; Lewin; Beatty Project 2000.

19. Church records, Beatty Project 2000.

20. Anna Rae White interview; Maggie Sill, interview with author, 26 August 2002.

21. Michael Wilmington and Gerald Peary, "Warren Beatty," *Daily Cardinal*, 8 November 1971.

22. "The Register Man's Column."

23. Quincy Gasque Butler, interview with author, 1 February 2004.

24. Gary Younge, "Rebel with a Cause," *The Guardian*, 23 January 1999; Silek interview; Sill interview.

25. Laura Virginia Hale and Stanley S. Phillips, *History of the 49th Virginia Infantry C.S.A: Extra Billy Smith's Boys 1861–1865*, n.p., 1981; "The Register Man's Column"; Johnstone, Beatty Project 2000.

26. Hale and Phillips; "The Register Man's Column"; Beatty Project 2000.

27. Gary Hart, interview with author, 7 November 2003.

28. Annette Bening, U.S. State Department dinner, 4 December 2004; Younge, "Rebel with a Cause."

29. See notes 7 and 13; John Vogt and T. William Kethley, Jr., *Virginia Historic Marriage Register, Warren County Marriages, 1836–1850*, Athens, Ga., Iberian Press, 1983; *Warren County, Virginia Marriage Registry, 1854–1880*, Abstracted and Compiled by D. A. Buck, 1996, n.p.; Beatty Project 2000.

30. See notes 7, 13, and 29.

31. See note 13; Donna Dunn, "Together Again," *Northern Virginia Daily*, 3 April 1999; Interviews with Thomas Blumer, curator, Warren County Heritage Society, 2002–2004, Suzanne Silek, Anna Rae White, Maggie Sill, et al.

32. William Welton Beaty obituary.

33. Paul Sylbert, interview with author, 5 December 2003.

34. William Welton Beaty obituary.

35. Helen Dorsey, "Warren Beatty," *Family Weekly*, 6 April 1975.

36. Rowland Barber, "Hollywood's Most Unconventional Mother," *Redbook*, July 1961.

37. MacLaine, *Dance While You Can*.

38. Rappahannock County, Va., Register of Marriages, 1901, Virginia Bureau of Vital Statistics, Reel 42, Library of Virginia.

39. Bill Goldstein, "Write While You Can," *Publishers Weekly*, August 1991.

40. Burrell T. Partlow obituary, *Rappahannock News*, 2 June 1933; Rappahannock Historical Society archives, Little Washington, Va.; Ira Partlow entry, *West Virginia Blue Book 1949*, compiled and edited by J. Howard Myers, courtesy of West Virginia Division of Culture and History, Charleston, West Va.

41. *Northern Virginia Daily*, 3 April 1999.

42. MacLaine, *Dance While You Can*.

43. Ibid.

44. Jean Pomeroy, interview with author, 26 August 2002.

45. Ibid.

46. MacLaine, *Dance While You Can*.

47. George Mason Green, Jr., (hereafter Mason Green, Jr.) interview with author, 11 September 2002.

48. Suzanne Silek interview. William C. Trenary, interview with author, 26 August 2002; Anna Rae White interview.

49. Photo of Beaty: see MacLaine, *Dance While You Can*.

50. MacLaine, *Dance While You Can*.

51. Shirley MacLaine, *My Lucky Stars* (New York: Bantam Books, 1995).

52. Mason Green, Jr., interview.

53. Randolph-Macon Academy archives, Front Royal, Va.

54. Andrea Winchell (a granddaughter of Ira Partlow), interview with author, 5 January 2004. ("Anecdotally, I can tell you that there probably was a close connection between Ira Beaty and Ira Partlow," Winchell confirmed, "but I have no letters to substantiate this.")

55. MacLaine, *Dance While You Can*.

56. Ronald Southward, interview with author, 18 June 2002.

57. Ira Beaty transcripts, University of Richmond; Mary M. Maxwell, interview with author, June 2002; Registrars Office, Randolph-Macon College.

58. Mason Green, Jr., interview. (Warren Beatty told his publicist, John Springer, similar tales about Ira: Springer correspondence to *Show Business Illustrated*, 6 December 1961, from John Springer papers, courtesy of Gary Springer and June Springer [hereafter cited as Springer papers]).

59. From "Shirley MacLaine: Kicking Up Her Heels," Wombat Productions, PBS, 1996.

60. Shirley MacLaine, *You Can Get There from Here* (New York: W. W. Norton & Company, 1975).

61. MacLaine, *Dancing in the Light*; MacLaine, *Dance While You Can.*

62. MacLaine, *Dancing in the Light.*

63. Lillian Ross and Helen Ross, *The Player* (New York: Simon & Schuster, 1962).

64. MacLaine, *Dance While You Can.*

65. Ira Beaty's application for admission to the Faculty of Philosophy, 6/11/28, Special Collections and Archives, Johns Hopkins University (Beaty did not disclose what he taught, or at which schools, in Va. and West Va. 1926–28); Michael Shelden, "I Was Always an Oddball," *Daily Telegraph*, 18 February 2000.

66. James Stimpert, archivist, Ferdinand Hamburger Archives, Johns Hopkins University, interview with author, 3 April 2002.

67. Jane Moore Banks, interview with author, 19 February 2002; Mabelle Symington Moore, interview with author, 19 February 2002.

68. Historical Society of Baltimore County, Cookeysville, Md.

69. Ibid.; Jane Moore Banks interview; *Marylander* yearbooks, 1930 and 1931, Maryland College for Women, courtesy of Jane Banks.

70. Jane Moore Banks interview; Mabelle Symington Moore interview.

71. Jane Moore Banks interview.

72. *Marylander* yearbook 1930.

73. Winifred Wokal Morrison, interview with author, 28 February 2002.

74. Winifred Wokal Morrison interview.

75. MacLaine, *Dancing in the Light.*

76. Franklin Lehigh obituary, *Brockville Evening Recorder*, 29 February 1916.

77. Genealogical records of Lehigh descendants, courtesy of Dave MacKenzie and Lorna Johnston, letter to author, 28 February 2004.

78. 1851 census, Elizabethtown, Ontario, courtesy of Lorna Johnston; Franklin Lehigh obituary.

79. Blanche Henrietta Lehigh's name: Wall Street United Church records, Brockville, Ontario, courtesy of archivist Shirley Cowan; Kathlyn Beaty's Social Security application, Washington, D.C.

80. William Delorma Lehigh information from Lorna Johnston.

81. Wall Street United Church records.

82. Federal Census of 1881 (Ontario index, Archives Nationales du Canada, Wolford, Leeds and Grenville North, 1881, NA Film C-13231, p. 13).

83. Mary Lehigh obituary, *Brockville Recorder & Times*, 24 March 1925.

84. Mary Frances Richards: Death registration reel, 1925, Ontario; census records, see notes 82, 86, and 1901 census of Brockville, Ontario, courtesy of Lorna Johnston; Lorna Johnston and Dave MacKenzie.

85. Mary Lehigh and Franklin Lehigh obituaries.

86. Federal Census of 1871 (Ontario index, Archives Nationales du Canada, Leeds and Grenville North, Reel C-10,004); Katie Lehigh obituary, *Brockville Recorder & Times*, 9 December 1939.

87. D. S. Hoig, M.D., *Reminiscences and Recollections* (Oshawa, Canada: Mundy-Goodfellow Printing Co., 1933).

88. Leanne Fitzgerald, Historical Information Sheet, Demill Ladies College, 10 June 1997.

89. Katie Lehigh obituary.

90. "Commencement Exercises, Demill College, 1892," n.p., courtesy of Oshawa Public Library.

91. Fitzgerald, Historical Information Sheet.

92. Mary Lehigh obituary.

93. Elva E. Jackson, *Windows on the Past: N. Sydney* (Windsor, Nova Scotia: Lancelot Press, 1974).

94. Warren Beatty, "The First Ten Seconds — They Shape the Way Ahead," *Films and Filming* (April 1961).

95. Halifax Ladies College records, Public Archives of Nova Scotia; First Baptist Church records, Halifax, N.S.

96. Ibid.

97. Ibid.

98. Dilly MacFarlane, Dalhousie Alumni Director, interview with author, n.d.; M. T. MacLean class records, Dalhousie Medical Alumni Association, Halifax, N.S.

99. "Shirley MacLaine Brings Sparkle of Stardom," *Acadia University Alumni Bulletin* vol. 69, no. 3 (Summer 1985).

100. Al Kingsbury, "Moving Address Delivered by MacLaine," *The Acadian*, 7 May 1985.

101. Warren Beatty, "Katharine Hepburn," *Entertainment Weekly*, 6 January 2004.

102. Charles Holmes and Jean MacLean Holmes interview.

103. Kathlyn McLean poem, n.d., *Acadia Ladies Seminary Collection*, Esther Clark Wright Archives, Vaughan Memorial Library, Acadia University [hereafter cited as ALS].

104. Charles Holmes and Jean MacLean Holmes interview.

105. Charles Holmes interview.

106. Charles Holmes and Jean MacLean Holmes interview.

107. Charles Holmes interview.

108. Jackson, *Windows on the Past.*

109. Charles Holmes and Jean MacLean Holmes interview.

110. Louise Brownell interview.

111. Jean MacLean Holmes interview.

112. MacLaine, *Dancing in the Light.*

113. Charles Holmes and Jean MacLean Holmes interview.

114. Ibid.

115. Index of marriage license, Murdock T. McLean and Blanche Lehigh, 22 October 1902, Belleville, Ontario, courtesy of Karen McKay.

116. Linda Cann, interview with author, 12 May 2002.

117. *Acadia Athanaeum*, June 1924, n.p.

118. Charles Holmes interview.

119. Kathlyn McLean student reports, *ALS.*

120. Charles Holmes interview.

121. MacLaine, *Dancing in the Light.*

122. "Citizens of North Sydney Pay Last Tribute to Mayor MacLean," *Sydney Post-Record*, 3 July 1922.

123. Candace Boudreau, letter to author, 10 March 2002.

124. "Shirley MacLaine Brings Sparkle."

125. Charles Holmes interview.

126. *Acadia Athanaeum*, June 1924.

127. *Acadia Athanaeum*, 1923; Tom Prescott interview; Linda Cann interview; *Acadia Bulletin*, "Shirley MacLaine Brings Sparkle."

128. Charles Holmes interview; Mansell MacLean obituary, *New York Times*, 6 July 1968.

129. *Acadia Bulletin*, "Shirley MacLaine Brings Sparkle"; *Acadia Athanaeum*, June 1924.

130. Charles Holmes and Jean MacLean Holmes interview.

131. Heather Murray, *Working in English: History, Institution, Resources* (Toronto: University of Toronto Press, 1996).

132. MES catalogue, Public Archives of Nova Scotia.

133. Murray, *Working in English*; MES catalogue.

134. Mavor Moore, letter to author.

135. Murray, *Working in English*.

136. Ibid.

137. "Young Actresses Achieve Success," *Toronto Globe*, 11 June 1925.

138. "Diplomas Received by Girl Graduates," *Toronto Globe*, 12 June 1925.

139. Louise Brownell interview.

140. Senator Jennie Woodall Forehand, interview with author, 18 February 2002.

141. Watson Kirkconnell, *The Acadia Record 1838–1953*, Acadia University, 1953.

142. Catherine Dunphy, "Scarborough Air Helps Rebel Mellow," *Toronto Star*, 20 October 1991.

143. Estelle Woodall's diary, 1925–26, courtesy of Jennie Woodall Forehand.

144. Jay Carr, "With Two Movies and Two Babies," *Boston Globe*, 16 October 1994.

145. Louise Brownell interview.

146. MacLaine, *Dance While You Can.*

147. Louise Brownell interview.

148. Ibid.

149. Ibid.

150. Brownell interview.

151. *Acadia Athanaeum*, 1928; Mansell MacLean obituary.

152. Mabelle Symington Moore interview.

153. 1930 *Marylander*.

154. Winifred Wokal Morrison interview.

155. Kathlyn MacLean Beaty, letter to Acadia University for alumni profile, Esther Clark Wright Archives, Vaughan Memorial Library, Acadia University.

156. MacLaine, *Dance While You Can*.

157. Ira Beaty's graduate studies: Special Collections and Archives, Milton S. Eisenhower Library, Johns Hopkins University, Baltimore, Md.; Jack A. Taylor, *Arts Education Policy Review*, Helen Dwight Reid Educational Foundation, July 1993. (Author's note: Music psychology had just been introduced as a course of study ten years earlier, and it was encouraged as a dissertation topic in educational psychology at the time Beaty was in consideration.)

158. Johns Hopkins University archives.

159. Dale Keiger, "Piano Playing as Science," *Johns Hopkins Magazine*, April 2002; Taylor, *Arts Education Policy Review*.

160. Winifred Wokal Morrison interview; *Marylander* 1932.

161. Jane Moore Banks interview; Arthur and Carolyn Eberdt, interview with author, 30 December 2001.

162. Jane Moore Banks interview; Mabelle Symington Moore interview.

163. Johns Hopkins University archives.

164. Kirkconnell, *The Acadia Record*.

165. Jeremy Pikser, interview with author, 29 September 2003.

166. MacLaine, *Dancing in the Light*.

167. Senator Elmon T. Gray, interview with author, 25 January 2002.

168. "Beaty-MacLean."

169. MacLaine, *Dancing in the Light*.

170. Winifred Wokal Morrison interview.

171. Johns Hopkins University archives.

172. MacLaine, *Dancing in the Light*; Johns Hopkins University archives.

173. Mason Green, Jr. interview.

ACT ONE: THE GOOD SON

1. Kathlyn Beaty, letter to Acadia University, Esther Clark Wright Archives, Vaughan Memorial Library, Acadia University.

2. Mason Green, Jr., interview with author, 4 September 2002.

3. Nancy Collins, "The Real MacLaine," *Vanity Fair*, March 1991; Mal Vincent, "The Many Lives of Shirley MacLaine," *Virginian-Pilot*, 22 April 1996.

4. Elizabeth West Chamberlin, interview with author, 25 January 2002.

5. Pat Jones, interview with author, 29 December 2001.

6. "MacLaine Book," *New York Daily News*, 2 November 1991; Shirley MacLaine, *My Lucky Stars* (New York: Bantam Books, 1995).

7. Bart Mills, "Tunes of Endearment," *Los Angeles Times*, 19 November 1995.

8. Elizabeth West Chamberlin interview.

9. Mary Grammer Tyler, interview with author, 30 June 2002.

10. Billy Allen, interview with author, 27 January 2002.

11. Senator Elmon T. Gray, interview with author, 25 January 2002.

12. Laurie Latham, interview with author, 29 December 2002.

13. Elizabeth West Chamberlin interview.

14. Collins, "The Real MacLaine"; Stephanie Mansfield, "Beds," *Esquire*, May 1990.

15. Ira Beaty student file, Special Collections and Archives, Milton S. Eisenhower Library, Johns Hopkins University, Baltimore, Md.

16. Margaret Brittain Guerrina, interview with author, 30 January 2002.

17. Ronald Southward, interview with author, 18 June 2002; Bill Goldstein, "Write While You Can," *Publishers Weekly*, August 1991.

18. Senator Elmon Gray interview.

19. Jack Griffin, interview with author, February 2002.

20. Mary Grammer Tyler interview.

21. Jon Whitcomb, "The Healthy Ego of Warren Beatty," *Cosmopolitan*, February 1962.

22. Collins, "The Real MacLaine."

23. Thomas Thompson, "There's Something Awfully Peculiar About Warren Beatty These Days," *Los Angeles*, March 1975.

24. *Entertainment Tonight*, June 1990; Norman Mailer, "The Warren Report," *Vanity Fair*, November 1991.

25. Valerie Grove, "Still Kicking Over the Traces," *Life and Times*, 31 January 1992.

26. Warren Beatty, "Katharine Hepburn," *Entertainment Weekly*, 6 January 2004; Catherine Dunphy, "Scarborough Air Helps Rebel Mellow," Toronto Star, 20 October 1991.

27. MacLaine, *My Lucky Stars*.

28. Frank J. Sulloway, *Born to Rebel* (New York: Pantheon Books, 1996).

29. MacLaine, *My Lucky Stars*.

30. David Rensin, interview with Shirley MacLaine, *Playboy*, September 1984; Richard W.

Nason, "Offbeat Success Saga," *New York Times*, 24 May 1959; "The Ring-a-Ding Girl," *Time*, June 1959; Shirley MacLaine, "My Feud with Warren Beatty," *Photoplay*, August 1962; Vincent, "The Many Lives."

31. Parry Ann Marston, interview with author, 19 February 2002.

32. Eleanor Harris, "Free Spirit," *Look*, 15 September 1959.

33. Elizabeth Jackson, interview with author, n.d.

34. C. Robert Jennings, "Welcome Back Shirley!" *Los Angeles Times West*, 16 March 1969; Rex Reed, "Will the Real Warren Beatty Please Shut Up," *Esquire*, August 1967.

35. Anne George Singleton, interview with author, 10 February 2002.

36. Dr. Ben Wagener, interview with author, 18 February 2002.

37. "Shirley MacLaine's Ankle on Life," *Pix*, 6 May 1961.

38. Shirley MacLaine, *Dancing in the Light* (New York: Bantam Books, 1985).

39. Dorothy "Dottie" Rector Turmail, interview with author, 6 May 2002.

40. Collins, "The Real MacLaine."

41. Sue Reilly, "Shirley MacLaine Explains," *McCall's*, August 1976.

42. Warren Beatty, *Aspel & Company*, 21 March 1992, London Weekend Television, courtesy of British Film Institute, London.

43. Virginia Ingram Guest, interview with author, 2 September 2002.

44. Ronald Southward interview.

45. Joan Edwards, "Shirley, Remembering Richmond," *Richmond Surroundings*, December 1991.

46. Collins, "The Real MacLaine."

47. Gail Gilmore, "For Shirley MacLaine, Stage Fright Began," *Richmond News Leader*, 29 March 1984; Jean-Noel Bassior, "Shirley's Way," *Modern Maturity*, Jan./Feb. 2001.

48. Betty George Williams, interview with author, 21 February 2002.

49. *Pat Collins Show*, February 1975, courtesy of D. J. Ziegler; Bill Roeder, *Newsweek*, 24 February 1975.

50. Patrick Pacheco, "Love Connection," *Newsday*, 16 October 1994.

51. "Shirley MacLaine as Sweet Charity," *Look*, 9 July 1968.

52. Sulloway, *Born to Rebel*.

53. Shirley MacLaine, *Out on a Limb* (New York: Bantam Books, 1983).

54. "Shirley MacLaine as Sweet Charity."

55. Bill Zehme, "Being Warren Beatty," *Rolling Stone*, 30 May 1990.

56. Lillian Ross and Helen Ross, *The Player* (New York: Simon & Schuster, 1962).

57. Gary Younge, "Rebel with a Cause," *The Guardian*, 23 January 1999.

58. *Aspel & Company*.

59. MacLaine, *My Lucky Stars*.

60. Virginia Ingram Guest interview.

61. Ibid.

62. Collins, "The Real MacLaine."

63. Philip Wuntch, "Warren's Love Affair," *Dallas Morning News*, 16 October 1994.

64. Joan Dew, "Warren Beatty: More Than a Lover," *Redbook*, May 1974.

65. "Shirley MacLaine Brings Sparkle," *Acadia Bulletin*.

66. MacLaine, *My Lucky Stars*.

67. Dew, "Warren Beatty."

68. MacLaine, *Dancing in the Light*.

69. Peter Feibleman, interview with author, 20 November 2003.

70. A. A. MacLeod data: Lucille Giscome, "Man of the People: The Story of A. A.

MacLeod," Bellwoods Labor Election Committee (Toronto: Donetta Press, n.d.); "In Memoriam: Alexander A. MacLeod," *Human Relations* vol. 10, no. 18, Ontario Human Rights Commission, May 1970; Don O'Hearn, "The Y Man Swung Lustily Left," *Windsor Star*, 12 September 1968; Obituary, unsourced Toronto paper, n.d.

71. Jeremy Pikser, interview with author, 29 September 2002.

72. Warren Beatty, "The First Ten Seconds—They Shape the Way Ahead," *Films and Filming* (April 1961).

73. *Times Saturday Review*, 11 March 1990; *Observer Magazine*, 4 November 1990 [cited as both, otherwise unsourced, courtesy of British Film Institute, London].

74. MacLaine, *My Lucky Stars*.

75. Ruth Beaty Gasque obituary, *Washington Post*, 23 February 1997; Robert S. Craig, *The Virginia Updikes* (Parsons, W.Va.: McClain Printing Co., 1985); Quincy Gasque Butler, interview with author, 1 February 2004. Maggie Sill, interview with author, 26 August 2002; Kathryn Biggs, interview with author, 26 August 2002.

76. MacLaine, *Dancing in the Light*.

77. Shirley MacLaine, *Dance While You Can* (New York: Bantam Books, 1991).

78. Kathryn Biggs interview.

79. Maggie Sill interview.

80. Anna Rae White, interview with author, n.d.

81. Kathryn Biggs interview.

82. Jan Hodenfield, "Still Circling," *New York Post*, 15 February 1975.

83. Younge, "Rebel with a Cause."

84. MacLaine, *Dancing in the Light*.

85. Younge, "Rebel with a Cause."

86. Lorraine Butler, unsourced newspaper, June 1990, courtesy of British Film Institute, London.

87. *Aspel & Company*.

88. Younge, "Rebel with a Cause."

89. "Shirley MacLaine: Kicking Up Her Heels," Wombat Productions, PBS, 1996; MacLaine, *Dancing in the Light*.

90. *Vogue*, 1 January 1962; Joan Collins, *Past Imperfect* (London: Coronet Books, 1978).

91. Richard Lee, "The Kid from Arlington," *Washingtonian*, December 1981.

92. MacLaine, *My Lucky Stars*.

93. Anne George Singleton interview.

94. Edwards, "Shirley, Remembering Richmond"; Elizabeth West Chamberlin interview.

95. Anne George Singleton interview.

96. Clifford Terry, "Shirley MacLaine: Revved Up, Roarin', and Real," *Cosmopolitan*, August 1977.

97. Jane George Flowers, interview with author, 11 February 2002.

98. Anne George Singleton interview.

99. Shirley MacLaine, *Don't Fall off the Mountain* (New York: W. W. Norton & Company, 1970); MacLaine, *My Lucky Stars*.

100. MacLaine, *Don't Fall off the Mountain*.

101. Mailer, "The Warren Report."

102. Johns Hopkins University archive, Baltimore, Md.

103. Ibid.

104. Virginia Ingram Guest interview.

105. Mailer, "The Warren Report."

106. Goldstein, "Write While You Can."

107. Reilly, "Shirley MacLaine Explains."

108. MacLaine, *My Lucky Stars*.

109. MacLaine, *Dancing in the Light*.

110. Collins, "The Real MacLaine."

111. MacLaine, *Dance While You Can*.

112. Dew, "Warren Beatty."

113. *Forever Hollywood*, Esplanade Productions, The American Cinematheque, 1999; MacLaine, *Dance While You Can*.

114. MacLaine, *My Lucky Stars*.

115. Collins, "The Real MacLaine."

116. Carroll Johnston Hanson, interview with author, n.d.

117. Martha Blount, interview with author, 22 February 2002.

118. Mike Wilmington and Gerald Peary, interview with Warren Beatty, *The Velvet Light Trap* (Winter 1972).

119. Anne George Singleton interview.

120. Carroll Johnston Hanson interview.

121. Maggie Sill interview.

122. Lee, "The Kid from Arlington."

123. Reilly, "Shirley MacLaine Explains."

124. Grace Johnston, interview with author, 10 February 2002.

125. Ross and Ross, *The Player*.

126. MacLaine, *Dance While You Can*.

127. Jay Carr, "Dick Tracy Speaks," *Boston Globe*, 10 June 1990.

128. Wuntch, "Warren's Love Affair."

129. "Shirley MacLaine as Sweet Charity."

130. Carr, "With Two Movies."

131. MacLaine, *Dance While You Can*.

132. "Shirley MacLaine: Kicking Up Her Heels."

133. Reed, "Will the Real Warren Beatty."

134. *Forever Hollywood*.

135. Lyn Tornabene, "Who Can Resist Warren Beatty?" *Cosmopolitan*, January 1975.

136. Lee, "The Kid from Arlington."

137. Virginia Ingram Guest interview.

138. Ibid.

139. Carr, "Dick Tracy Speaks."

140. National Film Theatre, interview with Shirley MacLaine, 28 March 1971, British Film Institute, London.

141. Parry Harper Marston, interview with author, 18 February 2002.

142. Warren Beatty, *Oprah Winfrey Show*, Harpo Productions, 20 December 1991.

143. Patricia Stewart, interview with author, 4 April 2002.

144. Collins, "The Real MacLaine."

145. Robert Chalmers, "Earth to Shirley," *Independent on Sunday*, 20 April 2003.

146. Collins, "The Real MacLaine."

147. Ibid.

148. Mailer, "The Warren Report."

149. Patricia Stewart interview.

150. Judy Michaelson, "The New Stars," *New York Post*, 12 September 1963.

151. Julie Christie, filmed interview, San Francisco Film Festival, April 25, 2002.

152. Ross and Ross, *The Player*.

153. *Bergen Evening Record*, 3 April 1959; MacLaine, *Don't Fall off the Mountain*.

154. "The Other Star in the Family," *Time*, 14 May 1984.

155. Adam Edwards, "Shirley MacLaine: My Brother, Warren Beatty," *Sunday Woman*, 15 July 1979.

156. "The Other Star in the Family."

157. "Sizzling Session with Shirley," *Modern Screen*, September 1962.

158. Patricia Stewart interview.

159. Tornabene, "Who Can Resist . . . ?"

160. "Viva Interview: Warren Beatty," *Viva*, July 1975.

161. Ross and Ross, *The Player*.

162. Ibid.

163. Mailer, "The Warren Report."

164. Florabel Muir, "The New Great Lover," *New York Sunday News*, 15 October 1961.

165. Dew, "Warren Beatty."

166. Letter from Kathlyn Beaty to Ira Partlow, 10 November 1951, courtesy of Andrea Winchell.

167. MacLaine, *My Lucky Stars*.

168. Collins, "The Real MacLaine."

169. Carr, "Dick Tracy Speaks."

170. Joe Hyams, "No Thought for Tomorrowsville," *Show Business Illustrated*, March 1962.

171. Carr, "Dick Tracy Speaks."

172. *Aspel & Company*.

173. O'Hearn, "The Y Man."

174. MacLaine, *My Lucky Stars*.

175. "Star Warren Beatty Goes Back to Films," unsourced Richmond paper, 20 April 1975, Warren Beatty file, Richmond Public Library, Richmond, Va.; Jeremy Pikser interview.

176. MacLaine, *Dance While You Can*; MacLaine, *Out on a Limb*.

177. MacLaine, *Out on a Limb*.

178. MacLaine, *Don't Fall off the Mountain*.

179. MacLaine, *Dance While You Can*.

180. Ibid.

181. Ibid; Jean-Claude Loiseau, "Le Defi de Warren Beatty," *Premiere*, October 1990.

182. Charles Holmes, interview with author, 9 April 2002.

183. Stephen Hunter, "Beatty/Tracy," *St. Louis Post-Dispatch*, 15 June 1990.

184. Ross and Ross, *The Player*.

185. John Kenrick, *History of the Musical Stage*, n.p., copyright 1996 and 2003.

186. Richmond paper, unsourced, n.p., 14 February 1971, Richmond Public Library, Beatty file.

187. Ross and Ross, *The Player*.

188. Caroline J. Brown, *Early History of the Arlington County, Virginia Juvenile and Domestic Relations District Court*, March 1983, by permission of Patricia M. Romano, Arlington Court Services Unit.

189. Mason Green, Jr., interview.

190. Brown, *Early History of Arlington*.

191. Thomas Calhoun, interview with author, 12 January 2002, here and throughout.

192. Mike Durfee, interview with author, 8 September 2002, here and throughout.

193. Letter from Kathlyn Beaty to Ira Partlow, 10 November 1951, courtesy of Andrea Winchell.

194. Brown, *Early History of Arlington*.

195. Collins, "The Real MacLaine."

196. Tornabene, "Who Can Resist."

197. Deborah Korsmo Ruf, interview with author, 29 December 2003.

198. Collins, "The Real MacLaine."

199. Dew, "Warren Beatty."

200. Ibid.

201. Henry Gris, "Warren Beatty and Julie Christie," *Coronet*, October 1971.

202. Henry Gris, "What Are You, Warren Beatty?" *Photoplay*, October 1963.

203. Muir, "The New Great Lover."

204. Ibid.

205. MacLaine, *Out on a Limb.*

206. Judge Paul D. Brown, interview with author, 3 April 2002.

207. Jeremy Pikser interview.

208. Favius Friedman, "Is He the Sexiest Thing Around?" *Silver Screen*, October 1961.

209. Ross and Ross, *The Player.*

210. Brown, *Early History of Arlington County.*

211. *Arlington Sun*, 21 September 1946.

212. Shirley MacLaine, *You Can Get There from Here* (New York: W. W. Norton & Company, 1975).

213. Rensin, "Shirley MacLaine's Ankle."

214. MacLaine, *Dancing in the Light.*

215. Kathlyn Beaty letter to Acadia.

216. MacLaine, *My Lucky Stars.*

217. Evelyn Ross, interview with author, 4 April 2002.

218. Ibid.

219. Heather Harris, interview with author, 22 February 2002.

220. Annette Bening, U.S. State Department dinner, Washington, D.C., 4 December 2004.

221. "Mrs. M. T. MacLean Death Is Mourned," *Cape Breton Post*, n.d.

222. Mason Green, Jr., interview, here and throughout.

223. Shelden, "I Was Always an Oddball."

224. Kathlyn Beaty letter to Ira Partlow, 10 November 1951, courtesy of Andrea Winchell.

225. MacLaine, *My Lucky Stars.*

226. Goldstein, "Write While You Can."

227. "Shirley MacLaine's Ankle."

228. Rowland Barber, "Hollywood's Most Unconventional Mother," *Redbook*, July 1961.

229. Jennings, "Welcome Back, Shirley."

230. Goldstein, "Write While You Can."

231. MacLaine, *Dancing in the Light.*

232. Zehme, "Being Warren Beatty."

233. Pacheco, "Love Connection."

234. Collins, "The Real MacLaine."

235. *Ladies' Home Journal*, January 1997.

236. Ronald Rynning, "Another Affair to Remember," *Film Review*, October 1995.

237. MacLaine, *Don't Fall off the Mountain.*

238. David Lewin, *Daily Mail*, 26 March 1965.

239. Susan Morse Durfee, interview with author, 8 September 2002, here and throughout.

240. Mary Lou Munson Woodruff, interview with author, 6 May 2002.

241. Dr. Michael Durfee, interview with author, 8 September 2002, here and throughout.

242. Susan Morse Durfee interview.

243. Collins, "The Real MacLaine."

244. Henry Louis Gates, Jr., "The White Negro," *New Yorker*, 11 May 1998.

245. "Star Warren Beatty."

246. Younge, "Rebel with a Cause."

247. "The Other Star in the Family."

248. Beatty, "Katharine Hepburn."

249. Wuntch, "Warren's Love Affair."

250. Warren Beatty, *CBS This Morning*, 24 October 1994.

251. Michael Durfee interview; Dorothy "Dottie" Rector Turmail, interview with author, 6 May 2002.

252. Collins, "The Real MacLaine."

253. Ibid.

254. Ibid.

255. Ibid.

256. Zehme, "Being Warren Beatty."

257. Ed DeBlasio, "His Hometown Secrets," *Motion Picture*, May 1962.

258. Mary Lou Munson Woodruff interview, here and throughout.

259. Dorothy Rector Turmail interview, here and throughout.

260. MacLaine, *Dance While You Can*.

261. Phyllis Battelle, "International Shirley Writes Down Her Adventures," *New York World*, 6 May 1967.

262. William Mallon, interview with author, 2 May 2002, here and throughout.

263. Ibid.

264. Hodenfield, "Still Circling."

265. MacLaine, *Dancing in the Light*.

266. Martha Weinman Lear, "Shirley MacLaine," *Ladies' Home Journal*, March 1975.

267. Wuntch, "Warren's Love Affair."

268. Ibid.

269. Mary Lou Munson Woodruff interview.

270. Grace Munson Nichols, interview with author, May 2002.

271. Ross and Ross, *The Player*.

272. MacLaine, *Out on a Limb*.

273. Tornabene, "Who Can Resist."

274. Gavin Smith, "A Question of Control," *Film Comment*, Jan./Feb. 1992.

275. Warren Beatty, "The Books I Can't Ever Forget," *Seventeen*, April 1962 (here and throughout the page).

276. Ibid.

277. MacLaine, *Dancing in the Light*, *Dance While You Can*, and *Don't Fall off the Mountain*.

278. Carr, "Dick Tracy Speaks."

279. MacLaine, *Don't Fall off the Mountain*.

280. MacLaine, *Dancing in the Light*.

281. Mary Lou Munson Woodruff interview, here and throughout.

282. *New York Times*, 9 July 1951 (cast selected for Berlin Festival).

283. Kathlyn Beaty letter to Ira Partlow, 10 November 1951, courtesy of Andrea Winchell.

284. Bob Sandin, "Shirley Beaty Wins Spurs in 'The Trouble With Harry,'" *Washington Star*, n.d.

285. Kathlyn Beaty letter to Ira Partlow, 10 November 1951.

286. "The Ring-a-Ding Girl."

287. Kathlyn Beaty letter to Ira Partlow, 10 November 1951.

288. Mary Lou Munson Woodruff interview.

289. Susan Morse Durfee interview.

290. Mason Green, Jr., interview.

291. Judy Evans Lang, interview with author, 6 May 2002, here and throughout.

292. Ross and Ross, *The Player*.

293. Reilly, "Shirley MacLaine Explains."

294. Tornabene, "Who Can Resist . . . ?"

295. Ross and Ross, *The Player*.

296. Tornabene, "Who Can Resist . . . ?"

297. Dana Kennedy, "'Beethoven' Star Grodin on Himself," *Chicago Sun Times*, 14 April 1992.

298. Hyams, "No Thought for Tomorrowsville."

299. "The Rise of Geyger Krocp," *Time*, 1 September 1961.

300. Kathlyn Beaty letter to Ira Partlow, 10 November 1951.

301. Mary Lou Munson Woodruff interview.

302. DeBlasio, "His Hometown Secrets."

303. Judy Evans Lang interview, here and throughout.

304. Mary Raymond, interview with author, 10 May 2003, here and throughout.

305. DeBlasio, "His Hometown Secrets."

306. Mary Raymond interview.

307. DeBlasio, "His Hometown Secrets."

308. Betty Hawthorne interview.

309. Kathlyn Beaty letter to Ira Partlow, 10 November 1951.

310. Ira Partlow obituary, *Rappahannock News*, 19 June 1952, courtesy of Rappahannock Historical Society.

311. "In Memoriam: Alexander A. MacLeod."

312. Thomas Calhoun, interview with author, 12 January 2002.

313. Elissa Barnard, "MacLaine Comes Full Circle," *Wolfville Chronicle-Herald*, 7 May 1985.

314. Lloyd Shearer, "The Star Who Hates Hollywood," *Telegram Weekend Magazine*, 11 January 1964.

315. Mailer, "The Warren Report."

316. DeBlasio, "His Hometown Secrets."

317. Taped interview, Warren Beatty and Joe Laitin, 26 September 1961, courtesy of Peter Laitin [hereafter Laitin tape].

318. Lynn Hirschberg, "Warren Beatty Is Trying to Say Something," *New York Times*, May 10, 1998.

319. Thomas Calhoun interview, here and throughout.

320. Idell Simms Conaway, interview with author, 6 May 2002.

321. Tornabene, "Who Can Resist . . . ?"

322. Dr. Arthur Eberdt, interview with author, 30 December 2001, here and throughout.

323. Archer Winsten, "Rages and Outrages," *New York Post*, 15 August 1960.

324. Arthur Eberdt interview; Tom Calhoun interview.

325. Tom Calhoun interview.

326. Paul Sylbert interview.

327. *Bravo Profiles*, "Warren Beatty," 17 May 1998.

328. *Washington Post*, 18 March 1982.

329. Younge, "Rebel with a Cause."

330. Mailer, "The Warren Report."

331. Laitin tape.

332. Janet Smith Filia, interview with author, 3 February 2002, here and throughout.

333. Tom Calhoun interview.

334. Ed DeBlasio, "Spotlight on Warren Beatty's Hidden Past," *Motion Picture*, April 1962; Tom Calhoun interview.

335. Grace Munson Nichols interview.

336. Margaret Penman, "'I Love a Beautiful . . . Movie Actress,'" *Toronto Telegram*, 29 May 1965.

337. "The Ring-a-Ding Girl"; Joanne Stang, "The Shirley MacLaine You Never Knew," *Good Housekeeping*, September 1962; MacLaine, *Don't Fall off the Mountain*.

338. L.Q.C.L. McKittrick IV, "The Many Lives of Shirley MacLaine," *The Virginian*, Jan./Feb. 1988; Jeff Cronin, "Beatty and the Two Beauties," *Photoplay*, December 1961; Barber, "Hollywood's Most Unconventional Mother"; "Shirley MacLaine's Ankle."

339. Goldstein, "Write While You Can."

340. Dee Phillips, "When Shirley MacLaine Blows a Fuse," *Photoplay*, May 1956; MacLaine, *Don't Fall off the Mountain*.

341. MacLaine letter to Rector, 21 October 1951, courtesy of Dorothy Rector Turmail.

342. DeBlasio, "His Hometown Secrets."

343. Sidney Fields, "No More Insults," *New York Mirror*, 9 November 1961.

344. Hirschberg, "Warren Beatty Is Trying."

345. Charlotte Kehart Lang, interview with author, 24 June 2002, here and throughout.

346. Diary of Janet Smith, 13 December 1952, courtesy of Janet Smith Filia.

347. Janet Smith Filia letter to author, 15 February 2002.

348. Jeannette Smyth, "The 'Shampoo' Man and Warren Beatty," *Washington Post*, 13 March 1975.

349. Dew, "Warren Beatty."

350. Idell Simms Conaway, interview with author, 6 May 2002, here and throughout.

351. Mailer, "The Warren Report."

352. Paul Sylbert interview; Janice Dickinson, *No Lifeguard on Duty* (New York: Regan Books, 2002).

353. Bert Thurber, interview with author, 24 June 2003.

354. Dr. Ben Wagener interview.

355. Bert Thurber interview, here and throughout.

356. Mary Raymond interview; Bert Thurber interview.

357. Mary Raymond interview.

358. Program, Servel "Show of Stars," 1953.

359. Shirley MacLaine letter to Dottie Rector, 4 December 1952, courtesy of Dorothy Rector Turmail.

360. Penman, "I Love a Beautiful . . ."; Ross and Ross, *The Player*.

361. Mary Lou Munson Woodruff interview.

362. Head shot courtesy of Lorraine Havercroft.

363. *Dick Cavett Show*, 1 November 1972.

364. Barber, "Hollywood's Most Unconventional Mother."

365. Ibid; Pete Martin, "I Call on Shirley MacLaine," *Saturday Evening Post*, 22 April 1961.

366. "Kicking Up Her Heels"; John Mundy, "Sweet, Hot and Sassy," *Photoplay*, December 1955; Harris, "Free Spirit."

367. Lorraine Havercroft interview.

368. Arthur Eberdt interview.

369. Letter from Nancy Dussault to Grace Munson, 5 October 1953, courtesy of Grace Munson Nichols.

370. Mary Lou Munson Woodruff interview.

371. Grace Munson Nichols interview.

372. Judy Evans Lang interview.

373. Shannon Colgan Gabor, interview with author, 28 January 2002.

374. Younge, "Rebel with a Cause."

375. Ibid.

376. Lee, "The Kid from Arlington."

377. Edwin Miller, "New Kind of Hollywood Hero," *Seventeen*, May 1961.

378. Ross and Ross, *The Player*.

379. Carolyn Eberdt, interview with author, 30 December 2001, here and throughout.

380. Younge, "Rebel with a Cause."

381. 1953/54 Washington-Lee yearbook, courtesy of Dr. Arthur Eberdt.

382. Shirley MacLaine letter to Dottie Rector, 16 November 1953; Dorothy "Dottie" Rector Turmail interview.

383. Marble Collegiate Church records, New York, N.Y.

384. Lorraine Havercroft interview with author, 3 March 2002; Steve Parker, "My Life with Shirley," *Picturegoer*, 31 December 1955; MacLaine, *Don't Fall off the Mountain*; Harris "Free Spirit"; Peer J. Oppenheimer, "I Earn More Than My Husband," *Movie Mirror*, July 1956.

385. Lorraine Havercroft interview, here and throughout.

386. E.g., MacLaine, *My Lucky Stars*; "Kicking Up Her Heels"; Collins, "The Real MacLaine."

387. MacLaine letter to Dottie Rector, 10 December 1953.

388. Harris, "Free Spirit"; Barber, "Hollywood's Most Unconventional Mother"; F. Friedman, "The Only Thing . . .," *Motion Picture*, August 1960.

389. Barber, "Hollywood's Most Unconventional Mother"; *Don't Fall Off the Mountain*; Harris "Free Spirit."

390. Harris, "Free Spirit"; Lorraine Havercroft interview.

391. Parker, "My Life."

392. Havercroft interview; Parker, "My Life."

393. Mary Raymond interview.

394. Nancy Dussault letter to Grace Munson, 2 February 1954.

395. E.g. MacLaine, *Don't Fall off the Mountain*; Barber, "Hollywood's Most Unconventional Mother"; Sandin, "Shirley Beaty Wins Spurs"; "The Ring-a-Ding Girl."

396. Nason, "Offbeat Success Saga."

397. *Warren Sentinel*, May 1954; Unsourced Arlington paper, n.d., n.p.; Mike and Susan Durfee interview.

398. Mary Raymond interview; John Raymond, quoted in DeBlasio, "His Hometown Secrets."

399. Susan Durfee interview.

400. Tornabene, "Who Can Resist."

401. Martin, "I Call on Shirley"; MacLaine, *Don't Fall Off the Mountain*; Shearer, "The Star."

402. E.g. Sandin, "Shirley Beaty Wins Spurs."; Harris, "Free Spirit"; Stang, "The Shirley MacLaine You Never Knew."

403. Martin, "I Call on Shirley."

404. Parker, "My Life"; Harris, "Free Spirit."

405. "Kicking Up Her Heels."

406. Ibid.

407. Ibid.

408. MacLaine, *My Lucky Stars.*
409. *Washington Star,* 5 March 1955; Kirtley Baskette, "The Trouble With Shirley," *Modern Screen,* June 1956; "Shirley MacLaine: This Time Around," A&E *Biography,* 2000.
410. MacLaine, *Don't Fall off the Mountain;* Harris, "Free Spirit"; Jon Whitcomb, "Sassy and Off-Beat," *Cosmopolitan,* September 1959.
411. Parker, "My Life"; Harris, "Free Spirit"; Martin, "I Call on Shirley."
412. Lorraine Havercroft interview; Barber, "Hollywood's Most Unconventional Mother"; Harris, "Free Spirit."
413. "The Ring-a-Ding Girl"; Martin, "I Call on Shirley"; MacLaine, *Don't Fall Off the Mountain.*
414. Hal Wallis and Charles Higham, *Starmaker: The Autobiography of Hal Wallis* (New York: MacMillan, 1980).
415. Ibid.
416. Martin, "I Call on Shirley"; Shearer, "The Star."
417. Shearer, "The Star."
418. MacLaine, *Don't Fall Off the Mountain;* Martin, "I Call on Shirley."
419. "The Ring-a-Ding Girl."
420. Ibid.
421. Ibid.
422. Parker, "My Life."
423. MacLaine, "My Feud."
424. Ibid.
425. Shearer, "The Star."
426. Grace Munson Nichols interview.
427. Tornabene, "Who Can Resist."
428. Betty Hawthorne interview.
429. MacLaine, *My Lucky Stars;* "Kicking Up Her Heels."
430. "Kicking Up Her Heels."
431. Martin, "I Call on Shirley."
432. Whitcomb, "Sassy."
433. "The Ring-a-Ding Girl."
434. Whitcomb, "Sassy."
435. "The Ring-a-Ding Girl."
436. Whitcomb, "Sassy."
437. "The Ring-a-Ding Girl."
438. Letter from Grace Munson to Mary Lou Munson, October 1954, courtesy of Grace Munson Nichols.
439. *Photoplay* clipping, January 1968.
440. Melina Gerosa, "Shirley's Lucky Stars," *Ladies' Home Journal,* June 1995.
441. MacLaine, *My Lucky Stars.*
442. MacLaine, *Don't Fall Off the Mountain.*
443. Collins, "The Real MacLaine."
444. Grove, "Still Kicking."
445. Sandin, "Shirley Beaty Wins Spurs."
446. Arthur Eberdt interview.
447. Tom Calhoun interview; Arthur Eberdt interview.
448. DeBlasio, "His Hometown Secrets."
449. Mary D. Campbell, quoted in ibid.
450. Bert Thurber interview, here and throughout.

451. DeBlasio, "His Hometown Secrets."

452. Miller, "New Kind of Hollywood Hero."

453. Laitin tape.

454. *Bravo Profiles*.

455. Harris, "Free Spirit."

456. "Bright New Stars of 1955," *Look*, January 1955.

457. The Virginia Historical Society, Julia Mildred Harper Collection, Richmond, Va., MSS 1: M3598A325.

458. "Shirley on Way Up," *Life*, 14 March 1955.

459. MacLaine, *My Lucky Stars*.

460. Warren Beatty, *The Howard Stern Show*, 13 May 1998; Ross and Ross, *The Player*.

461. Susan Durfee Morse interview.

462. Lee, "The Kid from Arlington."

463. *National Enquirer*, 9 August 1977.

464. DeBlasio, "His Hometown Secrets."

465. Hedda Hopper transcript, Academy of Motion Picture Arts and Sciences, Margaret Herrick Library, Hedda Hopper Collection, 11 March 1962; Michaelson, "The New Stars."

466. Warren Beatty, Debate Club, Oxford University, 27 February 1992.

467. Arthur Eberdt interview.

468. *Cue*, 29 October 1977; Friedman, "Is He the Sexiest"; Reed, "Will the Real Warren Beatty."

469. Lewin, Warren County Heritage Society.

470. Hector Arce, "Couples," *Women's Wear Daily*, 15 December 1970.

471. Ibid.

472. Holdenfield, "Still Circling."

473. Andy Cvercko, interview with author, 27 August 2002, here and throughout.

474. Hirschberg, "Warren Beatty Is Trying."

475. Frank Rich, "Warren Beatty Strikes Again," *Time*, 3 July 1978; MacLaine, "My Feud"; Cronin, "Beatty and the Two"; Mailer, "The Warren Report."

476. Sargent Hoopes interview.

477. Mundy, "Sweet, Hot."

478. Eleanor Wood Walker, interview with author, 14 July 2002.

479. Cy Spurlino, interview with author, 25 August 2002.

480. Ibid.

481. Dennis Marlas, interview with author, 27 August 2002.

482. DeBlasio, "Spotlight."

483. Holdenfield, "Still Circling."

484. Charles Miron, "Some Apples Make the Best Pie," *Motion Picture*, September 1962.

485. MacLaine, *Don't Fall Off the Mountain*.

486. Rensin, "Shirley MacLaine's Ankle."

487. Clifford Terry, "Shirley MacLaine: Revved Up, Roarin', and Real," *Cosmopolitan*, August 1977.

488. Ross and Ross, *The Player*.

489. Ibid.; Mike Connolly, "Lies, Lies, All Lies," *Modern Screen*, December 1962.

490. Warren Beatty, *60 Minutes*, 10 March 1999; *Howard Stern*; Mailer, "The Warren Report."

491. Mailer, "The Warren Report."

492. Ibid.

493. Dennis Marlas interview.

494. Karen Skadberg, interview with author, 8 September 2002.

495. Dee Phillips, "Shirley's Wonderful 'Divorce,'" *TV and Movie Screen*, May 1959.

496. Dorothy Rector Turmail interview.

497. "Beatty Raps," *Eye*, March 1968; Tornabene, "Who Can Resist."

498. Hedda Hopper transcript.

499. Miller, "New Kind of Hollywood Hero."

500. "Beatty Raps."

501. Ibid.

502. Charles Mercer, "Arlington Lad Starring in TV Title Role Tonight," *Washington Star*, 26 June 1957.

503. Hedda Hopper transcript.

504. Ibid.

505. Andy Cvercko interview.

506. Friedman, "Is He the Sexiest."

507. Miller, "New Kind of Hollywood Hero."

508. Louella Parsons, "Screen's Newest Idol," *New York Journal American*, 19 November 1961.

509. Wilmington and Peary interview.

510. Gene Siskel, "Tootsie & Clyde Detour to Ishtar," *Los Angeles Life Weekend, Los Angeles Daily News*, 15 May 1987.

511. Michael Fessier, Jr., "An Intimate Chat with Shirley MacLaine," *Cosmopolitan*, June 1966.

512. Kirtley Baskette, "Warren Beatty: Heart Stealer," *Modern Screen*, January 1962.

513. Rich, "Warren Beatty Strikes."

514. Helen Dorsey, "Warren Beatty on Privacy, Marriage, Kids, Himself," *Family Weekly*, 6 April 1975.

515. Baskette, "Warren Beatty: Heart Stealer."

516. Ibid.

517. Gilbert Guez, "Warren Beatty, C'est l'Idole de Demain," *Cinemonde*, 28 November 1961; Cronin, "Beatty and the Two"; MacLaine, "My Feud."

518. Nikki Calisch, "Beatty in Shirley Booth Play," unsourced Richmond newspaper, 1 November 1959.

519. Hyams, "No Thought for Tomorrowsville."

520. Miller, "New Kind of Hollywood Hero."

521. "Beatty Raps."

522. Gris, "Warren Beatty."

523. John Weisman, "Success Has Mellowed Arrogant Mr. Beatty," *Detroit Free Press*, 25 July 1971.

524. Charles Carshon, interview with author, 9 June 2002.

525. Hirschberg, "Warren Beatty Is Trying."

526. Wilmington and Peary interview.

527. Gene Siskel, "Success Story That Goes On," *Valley News Sunday*, 17 September 1978.

528. Younge, "Rebel with a Cause."

529. Reed, "Will the Real Warren Beatty."

530. Letter from Lenn Harten to Mrs. Harten, July 1957, courtesy of Lenn Harten.

ACT TWO: ENFANT TERRIBLE

1. Warren Beatty, San Francisco Film Festival, 25 April 2002; Lillian Ross and Helen Ross, *The Player* (New York: Simon & Schuster, 1962); David O. Russell, "Diary," *Slate*, 25 June 1996.

2. San Francisco Film Festival.

3. Rowland Barber, "Hollywood's Most Unconventional Mother," *Redbook*, July 1961; Eleanor Harris, "Free Spirit," *Look*, 15 September 1959.

4. Harris, "Free Spirit"; Marble Collegiate Church records, New York, N.Y.

5. Harris, "Free Spirit."

6. Charles Champlin, "Beatty Sings a Song of 'Ishtar,'" *Los Angeles Times*, 26 April 1987.

7. Lenn Harten, interview with author, variously in 2002–2004.

8. Jon Whitcomb, "The Healthy Ego of Warren Beatty," *Cosmopolitan*, February 1962; Lenn Harten interview.

9. Lenn Harten interview.

10. Ibid.; *Modern Screen*, January 1962; Favius Friedman, "Wanted! Have You Seen This Man?" *Motion Picture*, December 1961.

11. Ross and Ross, *The Player*.

12. Thomas Thompson, "Under the Gaze of the Charmer," *Life*, 26 April 1968.

13. Biography prepared by Warren Beatty, December 1959, and Springer correspondence to *Sports Illustrated*, 6 December 1961, both from John Springer papers, courtesy of Gary Springer and June Springer [hereafter "Springer papers"]; Charles Mercer, "Arlington Lad Starring in TV Title Role Tonight," *Washington Star*, 26 June 1957.

14. Mercer, "Arlington Lad"; "The Rise of Geyger Krocp," *Time*, 1 September 1961.

15. Warren Beatty, *60 Minutes*, 10 March 1999; Warren Beatty, *The Howard Stern Show*, 13 May 1998.

16. Rex Reed, "Will the Real Warren Beatty Please Shut Up," *Esquire*, August 1967.

17. Eleanor Wood Walker, interview with author, 14 July 2002.

18. Gary Younge, "Rebel with a Cause," *Guardian*, 23 January 1999.

19. Louella Parsons, "Screen's Newest Idol," *New York Journal*, 19 November 1961.

20. Transcript, Dr. Margaret Brenman-Gibson interview with Warren Beatty, 21 June 1965; Dr. Margaret Brenman-Gibson, interview with author, 21 July 2003.

21. Tag Gallagher, "Warren Beatty: The Stud as Thoughtful Man," *The Village Voice*, February 1975.

22. *The Independent*, 3 August 1991.

23. Charles Holmes, interview with author, 9 April 2002.

24. "Beatty Raps," *Eye*, March 1968.

25. Howard Thompson, "Young Man Who Has It Made," *New York Times*, 10 January 1965.

26. "The Rise of Geyger Krocp"; Ed DeBlasio, "Spotlight on Warren Beatty's Hidden Past," *Motion Picture*, April 1962.

27. DeBlasio, "Spotlight."

28. Lenn Harten interview.

29. Michael Shelden, "I Was Always an Oddball," *Daily Telegraph*, 18 February 2000.

30. Rita Gam, interview with author, 17 June 2002, here and throughout.

31. Lenn Harten interview.

32. Charles Carshon, interview with author.

33. DeBlasio, "Spotlight."

34. Lenn Harten interview.

35. Debbie Sherwood, "Warren, I Knew You When," *Photoplay*, August 1962.

36. Ibid.

37. Verne O'Hara, interview with author, 21 May 2003, here and throughout.

38. Shirley MacLaine, *My Lucky Stars* (New York: Bantam Books, 1995); Shirley MacLaine, *Don't Fall off the Mountain* (New York: W. W. Norton and Company, 1970).

39. Ian Miles, "Marriage Was a Pain for MacLaine," *Sunday News of the World Magazine*, 4 November 1990.

40. Shirley MacLaine letter to Dorothy "Dottie" Rector, n.d., courtesy of Dorothy Rector Turmail.

41. *Great Character Actors*, n.p., n.d., p. 6.

42. Pamela Ilott, interview, with author, 9 July 2003, here and throughout.

43. Jan Hodenfield, "Still Circling," *New Post*, 15 February 1975; Warren Beatty, *Film Night*, 30 October 1975, courtesy of British Film Institute, London.

44. Lyn Tornabene, "Who Can Resist Warren Beatty?" *Cosmopolitan*, January 1975.

45. Gallagher, "Warren Beatty."

46. John Preston, "Warren's Peace," *Sunday Telegraph*, 1 March 1992.

47. Lenn Harten letter to Mrs. Harten, 2 April 1957.

48. Holdenfield, "Still Circling."

49. "Beatty Raps."

50. Helen Dorsey, "Warren Beatty," *Family Weekly*, 5 April 1975.

51. Gavin Smith, "A Question of Control," *Film Comment*, Jan./Feb. 1992.

52. "Beatty Raps."

53. Dorsey, "Warren Beatty."

54. Ross and Ross, *The Player*.

55. Charles Holmes and Jean MacLean Holmes, interview with author, 9 April 2002.

56. Susan Bluestein Davis, interview with author, 24 June 2001.

57. Mercer, "Arlington Lad."

58. Eleanor Kilgallen, interview with author, 11 June 2002, here and throughout.

59. Marion Dougherty, interview with author, June 2002.

60. Gilbert Guez, "Warren Beatty, C'est l'Idole de Demain," *Cinemonde*, 28 November 1961.

61. Smith, "A Question."

62. Eleanor Kilgallen interview; Eleanor Kilgallen letter to author, 27 June 2002.

63. Nancy Franklin, interview with author, 2 September 2002.

64. Paine Knickerbocker, "Kaleidoscope — A Romp," *San Francisco Chronicle*, 26 October 1966.

65. Richard Seff, interview with author, 25 June 2002.

66. Lenn Harten letter to Mrs. Harten, 12 April 1957.

67. Stella Adler, audiotape, courtesy of Lenn Harten.

68. Ross and Ross, *The Player*.

69. Bernie Harrison, "A Story to Curl Any Actor's Hair," *Washington Star*, 27 June 1957.

70. Marion Dougherty interview, here and throughout.

71. Mercer, "Arlington Lad."

72. Lenn Harten interview.

73. Marlon Brando, "I, Me, Brando," *Guardian*, 3 September 1994.

74. Nancy Malone, interview with author, 6 March 2002.

75. *Forever Hollywood*, Esplanade Productions, The American Cinematheque, 1999.

76. Bert Thurber, interview with author, 24 June 2003.

77. Favius Friedman, "Is He the Sexiest Thing Around?" *Silver Screen*, October 1961.

78. Eleanor Kilgallen interview.

79. Tornabene, "Who Can Resist . . . ?"

80. Smith, "A Question."

81. *Seventeen*, May 1961.

82. Mercer, "Arlington Lad"; *Screen Stories*, December 1960.

83. *Daily Variety*, 3 July 1957.

84. Tornabene, "Who Can Resist . . . ?"

85. Ibid.

86. Dorothy "Dottie" Rector Turmail letter to author, May 2002.

87. MacLaine letter to Dorothy "Dottie" Rector, 11 July 1957.

88. Lenn Harten letter to Mrs. Harten, 11 July 1957.

89. Lenn Harten interview; Lenn Harten letter to Mrs. Harten, 30 July 1957.

90. *New York Times*, 6 August 1957.

91. Tereska Levin, interview with author, 1 March 2002.

92. Ross and Ross, *The Player*.

93. *Daily Variety*, 13 November 1957.

94. Pat Hingle, interview with author, 7 September 1999.

95. Joseph Scully, interview with author, 18 June 2002.

96. *Daily Variety*, September 1957.

97. Ned Manderino, interview with author, 19 June 2002.

98. Lenn Harten letter to Mrs. Harten, 9 October 1957.

99. Michael Wilmington and Gerald Peary, "Warren Beatty," *The Daily Cardinal*, 8 November 1971.

100. Lenn Harten letter to Mrs. Harten, 15 October 1957.

101. *Modern Screen*, January 1962; *Photoplay*, December 1961.

102. *Modern Screen*, January 1962.

103. *Hollywood Citizen News*, 13 October 1967.

104. Warren Beatty, *The Oprah Winfrey Show*, Harpo Productions, 20 December 1991.

105. Lenn Harten interview.

106. Pamela Ilott interview; Lenn Harten interview.

107. Lenn Harten interview.

108. Julius (Jack) Kuney, interview with author, 18 April 2002.

109. Mrs. Harten letter to Lenn Harten, 5 November 1957.

110. Roger Englander, interview with author, 23 April 2002.

111. Bennye Gatteys Bail, interview with author, 24 April 2002.

112. Bennye Gatteys diary.

113. Kevin Thomas, "Diane Ladd Struggles for Stardom," *Los Angeles Times*, 3 February 1975; "A Gal in Orbit," *TV Radio-Mirror*, March 1959.

114. "He Can Still Leave 'Em Breathless," *People*, 2 July 1990.

115. Rona Barrett, *Miss Rona: An Autobiography* (Los Angeles: Nash, 1974).

116. Lenn Harten interview.

117. Clinton Archambaugh and Arch Whiting, interviews with author, 1 March 2003; *New York Herald Tribune*, 5 August 1957.

118. Ned Manderino interview.

119. Clinton Archambaugh interview.

120. Valerie Grove, "Still Kicking Over the Traces," *Life and Times*, 31 January 1992.

121. John Maynard, "Westward-ha!", *Photoplay*, July 1957.

122. MacLaine, *Don't Fall Off the Mountain*.

123. Ross and Ross, *The Player*.

124. Lenn Harten letter to Mrs. Harten, 17 March 1957.

125. Jon Whitcomb, "The Healthy Ego of Warren Beatty," *Cosmopolitan*, February 1962.

126. MCA accounting records, courtesy of Eleanor Kilgallen; Eleanor Kilgallen interview; *The Episode Guide*, The Classic TV Archive (website).

127. Eleanor Kilgallen interview; Ned Manderino interview.

128. Charlotte Harmon, interview with author, 26 March 2002, here and throughout.

129. Pamela Ilott interview; Lenn Harten interview; Eleanor Kilgallen interview.

130. Ross and Ross, *The Player*.

131. Ned Manderino interview, here and throughout.

132. Ned Manderino interview.

133. Sean Macaulay, "Stud Without a Money Shot," *New York Times*, 28 June 2001.

134. Elizabeth Hubbard, interview with author, 20 June 2002.

135. Reed, "Will the Real Warren Beatty . . . ?"

136. Ned Wertimer, interview with author, 13 June 2002, here and throughout.

137. Paul Tripp, interview with author, 10 April 2002.

138. Ned Wertimer interview.

139. Smith, "A Question."

140. A.W.T., "Powerful Play Presented at Clinton Playhouse," *Clinton Recorder*, 8 August 1958.

141. Tomas Milian, interview with author, 2 July and 6 July 2003, here and throughout.

142. Anna Maria Barraque Crossfield, interview with author, 19 May 2003, here and throughout.

143. Tomas Milian interview.

144. Harry Crossfield, interview with author, 13 May 2002.

145. John Connolly, interview with author, 3 March 2003; Whitcomb, "The Healthy Ego."

146. George Christian, "A Chat with Inge," *Houston Post*, 1 October 1961; Arthur F. McClure, *Memories of Splendor*, Kansas State Historical Society, 1989.

147. Elia Kazan, taped interview, 17 September 1981, William Inge Collection, Independence Community College [cited hereafter as Inge Collection]; Kazan letter to Inge, 7 June 1963, Elia Kazan Collection, Wesleyan Cinema Archives [cited hereafter as Kazan Collection]; "Tall Grass," *Newsweek*, 16 October 1961.

148. Kazan letter to Inge, 7 June 1963, Kazan Collection.

149. Kazan notebook, *Splendor*, 2 April 1957, Kazan Collection; Ross and Ross, *The Player*.

150. Ibid., April 1957.

151. Richard Sylbert, interview with author, 17 June 1999; handwritten notes, Inge script, Billy Rose Collection, Lincoln Center Library; Jon Land, "Happily Ever After," *Saturday Evening Post*, March 1979.

152. Bill Davidson, "Hollywood Throwback," *Saturday Evening Post*, 7 April 1962; Land, "Happily Ever After."

153. Letter to Kazan from Production Code, 15 September 1958, Margaret Herrick Library, Academy Collection Academy of Motion Picture Arts and Sciences, Beverly Hills; "Playwright Bill Inge and Producer Kazan Here for Short Visit," *Independence Reporter*, 8 October 1958.

154. Whitcomb, "The Healthy Ego"; William Inge letter to the editor, "The Sound and the Fury," *Esquire*, October 1967.

155. John Connolly interview, here and throughout, unless otherwise noted.

156. Whitcomb, "The Healthy Ego."

157. John Connolly interview; John Connolly taped interview, Inge Collection.

158. John Connolly interview, Inge Collection.

159. Ibid.

160. JoAnn Kirchmaier, interview with author, 7 March 2003.

161. John Connolly interview, Inge Collection.

162. Kazan interview, Inge Collection.

163. Warren Beatty, *The Dick Cavett Show*, November 1972, courtesy of D. J. Ziegler.

164. Joanne Stang, "The Shirley MacLaine You Never Knew," *Good Housekeeping*, September 1962.

165. Whitcomb, "The Healthy Ego."

166. Ibid.; *Hollywood Reporter*, 11 December 1958.

167. Bonnie Bartlett, interview with author, 10 April 2003, here and throughout.

168. Lucas Cooper, interview with author, 24 June 2003.

169. Jeanne Rejaunier, interview with author, 17 August 2003, here and throughout.

170. *Bergen Evening Record*, 6 December 1958.

171. Peter Biskind, "Chronicle of a Life Untold," *Premiere*, January 1992.

172. Wayne Tippet, interview with author, 1 March 2002.

173. *Bergen Evening Record*, 10 December 1958.

174. William Inge letter to the editor, "The Sound and the Fury," *Esquire*, October 1967.

175. Rodney Amateau, interview with author, 10 April 2003.

176. Josh Logan diary and news clippings, Joshua Logan Collection, Boxes 26, 38, 45, 87, 119, 147–48, Container 137, Library of Congress [cited hereafter as Logan Collection].

177. News clippings, Box 119, Logan Collection.

178. Joshua Logan, *Movie Stars, Real People, and Me* (New York: Delacorte Press, 1978).

179. Warren Berlinger, interview with author, 7 May 2002.

180. Sandra Church, interview with author, 18 June 2002.

181. Dorothy Rector Turmail interview.

182. Kirk Lang, interview with author, 6 May 2002.

183. Josh Logan diary, 30 January 1959, Logan Collection.

184. Jane Fonda, interview with author, 5 May 2003, here and throughout.

185. Letter to Josh Logan from Jane Fonda's agent, 15 January 1959, Logan Collection.

186. Logan, *Movie Stars*.

187. *Seventeen*, May 1961.

188. Tom Laughlin, interview with author, 11 May 2003, here and throughout.

189. Jane Fonda, interview with author, 5 May 2003; Michael Callan, interview with author, 13 May 2003.

190. Logan's diary, Logan collection.

191. Jane Fonda interview, here and throughout.

192. Biskind, "Chronicle."

193. *Seventeen*, May 1961.

194. Biskind, "Chronicle."

195. "The Rise of Geyger Krocp."

196. Daniel Petrie, interview with author, 4 June 2002.

197. *Hollywood Reporter*, 13 February 1959.

198. *Time*, May 1961.

199. Logan, *Movie Stars*; Logan Collection (Fonda contract and correspondence regarding Fonda and Beatty contracts).

200. Letter to Kazan from Steve Trilling, 4 February 1959, Trilling Collection, USC Cinema-Television Library, Los Angeles [hereafter Trilling Collection].

201. Kazan letter to Trilling 26 January 1959, Trilling Collection.

202. *Houston Post*, 1 October 1961.

203. Elizabeth Pope, "What Hollywood Does to Women," *Good Housekeeping*, June 1962; *Look*, 13 August 1962.

204. "Natalie Wood: Our Sexual Conscience on the Silver Screen?" *L'Officiel*, August 1980.

205. John Connolly interview.

206. Jane Fonda interview; Alexander (Sandy) Whitelaw, interview with author, 12 June 2002, here and throughout.

207. James Kaplan, "Warren's World," *Entertainment Weekly*, 20 December 1991.

208. Harry Crossfield interview, here and throughout.

209. Gita Hall May, interview with author, 30 April 2003.

210. Younge, "Rebel with a Cause."

211. *Seventeen*, May 1961.

212. Lenn Harten interview; Jeanne Rejaunier interview.

213. *Seventeen*, May 1961.

214. Ibid.

215. Maurice Zolotow, "Playwright on the Eve," *New York Times*, 22 November 1959.

216. Ibid.

217. Inge letter to Jerry Wald, July 1960, Jerry Wald Collection, "Celebration," Book 1, USC Cinema-Television Library, Los Angeles; Zolotow, "Playwright"; Gilbert Millstein, "Ten Playwrights Tell How It All Starts," *New York Times*, 6 December 1959.

218. Unsourced article, 26 February 1959, Billy Rose Theater Collection, *A Loss of Roses* folder.

219. Inge letter to Kazan, 11 March 1959, Kazan Collection.

220. Springer notes, December 1959, Springer papers.

221. Kazan letter to Inge, 24 March 1959, Kazan Collection.

222. Press release, 31 March 1959, n.p., Billy Rose Theater Collection, *A Loss of Roses* folder.

223. Peter S. Haigh, "Warren Beatty — The Unknown Star," *Film Review*, September 1961; Logan, *Movie Stars*.

224. Eleanor Kilgallen letter to author, 20 November 2002.

225. *Modern Screen*, January 1962.

226. Draft of Josh Logan letter to Jane Fonda, 3 July 1979, Logan Collection.

227. Biskind, "Chronicle."

228. *Daily Variety*, 1 May 1959.

229. Rodney Amateau interview; Herbert Bayard Swope, Jr., interview with author, 3 June 2003.

230. Rodney Amateau interview, here and throughout.

231. Barbara Baxley taped interview, Inge Collection; Inge telegram to Logan, 16 May 1959, Logan Collection; Inge letter to Logan, 1 June 1959, Logan Collection.

232. Lyn Hirschberg, "Warren Beatty Is Trying to Say Something," *New York Times*, 10 May 1998.

233. Kilgallen letter to author, 20 November 2002.

234. *Los Angeles Herald Examiner*, 10 May 1959.

235. Eleanor Kilgallen interview; Beatty letter to Eleanor Kilgallen, courtesy of Eleanor Kilgallen.

236. Joan Collins, interview with author; Joan Collins letter to author, n.d.; Erskine Johnson, "The Impetuous Miss Collins," *Los Angeles Mirror*, 24 February 1961.

237. Marvin Birdt, interview with author, 17 June 2002.

238. Judith Balaban Quine, *The Bridesmaids* (New York: Weidenfeld & Nicholson, 1989).

239. Harry Crossfield interview.

240. Richard W. Nason, "Offbeat Success Saga," *New York Times*, 24 May 1959.

241. Ibid.

242. Dorsey, "Warren Beatty."

243. Hirschberg, "Warren Beatty Is Trying."

244. Steve Trilling telegram to Inge, 10 June 1959, Trilling Collection.

245. *Book Review Digest 1958*, n.p.; *New York Journal-American*, 18 August 1958; *Hollywood Reporter*, 20 March 1959.

246. *Modern Screen*, January 1962.

247. Hirschberg, "Warren Beatty Is Trying."

248. Deborah Sherwood LaScala, interview with author, 26 July 2003, here and throughout; Debbie Sherwood, "Warren, I Knew You When."

249. Dwayne Hickman, interview with author, 23 April 2003, here and throughout.

250. Bob Denver, *Gilligan, Maynard & Me* (New York: Citadel Press, 1993).

251. Dede Allen, interview with author, 7 November 2003.

252. Hirschberg, "Warren Beatty Is Trying."

253. Whitcomb, "The Healthy Ego."

254. *Book Review Digest 1958*; Tornabene, "Who Can Resist . . . ?"

255. Nason, "Offbeat Success."

256. Ibid.

257. Philip Yordan, interview with author, 27 January 2003; *Seventeen*, May 1961.

258. Philip Yordan interview.

259. Gerald Medearis (aka Christopher Knight), interview with author, 12 February 2003.

260. "Author Objects to 'Studs' Pic," *Daily Variety*, 15 April 1960.

261. Tornabene, "Who Can Resist . . . ?"; Eleanor Kilgallen interview; Hirschberg, "Warren Beatty Is Trying"; Biskind, "Chronicle."

262. Virginia Campbell, "Hollywood's Secret Hideout," *Hollywood Life*, May/June 2003.

263. *Forever Hollywood*.

264. Michael J. Pollard, interview with author, 11 July 2003, here and throughout.

265. Margaret Penman, "'I Love a Beautiful . . . Movie Actress,'" *Toronto Telegram*, 29 May 1965.

266. *Modern Screen*, January 1962.

267. Ross and Ross, *The Player*; Reed, "Will the Real Warren Beatty . . ."; Warren Beatty, "The First Ten Seconds—They Shape the Way Ahead," *Films and Filming*, April 1961; "Warren Beatty in an interview with Gordon Gow," *Films and Filming*, August 1975; Jeff Young, *The Master Discusses His Films* (New York: Newmarket Press, 1999); Kazan interview, Inge Collection; Inge, "The Sound and the Fury," *Esquire*.

268. Kazan, quoted in "Penn. Ave. to Broadway," produced by Michael Wood, Inge Collection; Michael Wood, interview with author, n.d.

269. Smith, "A Question."

270. *Elia Kazan: An Outsider*, English Silk, 31 August 1985, British Film Institute, London.

271. Young, *The Master Discusses*.

272. "Penn. Ave. to Broadway."

273. Beatty, "The First Ten Seconds."

274. Jack L. Warner Collection, Box 28, USC Cinema-Television Library, Los Angeles.

275. *New York Post*, 16 June 1959; *Stage News*, 15 June 1959 and *New York Times*, 17 June 1959; Billy Rose Theater Collection, *A Loss of Roses* folder.

276. Arthur Penn, interview with author, 20 October 1999; John Connelly interview; Barbara Baxley interview, Inge Collection; Louis Criss, interview with author, 12 April 2002.

277. Ross and Ross, *The Player*.

278. "Never Say Never," *TV Guide*, 14 July 1990.

279. Deborah Sherwood LaScala interview, here and throughout.

280. Ibid.; Debbie Sherwood, "Why Warren Beatty Can't Resist . . ." *Modern Screen*, September 1964.

281. Verne O'Hara interview.

282. Anita Sands, interview with author, 11 April 2003, here and throughout.

283. Monique James memo to Maynard Morris and Audrey Wood, 21 July 1959, Daniel Mann Collection, *A Loss of Roses* file, Margaret Herrick Library, Academy of Motion Picture Arts and Sciences, Beverly Hills.

284. Louis Criss interview; Robert Vaughn, interview with author, fall 2003.

285. *Seventeen*, May 1961; *Motion Picture*, December 1961.

286. John Springer's notes from Beatty, December 1959, Springer papers.

287. *Hollywood Reporter*, 24 July 1959.

288. Sidney Skolsky column, *Los Angeles Herald*, 28 July 1959.

289. *Seventeen*, May 1961.

290. Hirschberg, "Warren Beatty Is Trying."

291. *Modern Screen*, January 1962.

292. Joan Collins interview, here and throughout; see also, e.g., Johnson, "The Impetuous"; *Los Angeles Sunday News*, 15 October 1961.

293. Friedman, "Is He the Sexiest."

294. Sandy Whitelaw interview, here and throughout.

295. Friedman, "Is He the Sexiest."

296. Press release, 5 August 1959, Billy Rose Collection, *A Loss of Roses* folder; Barbara Baxley interview, Inge Collection.

297. Burry Fredrik, interview with author, 11 April 2002; Louella Parsons column, 22 July 1959.

298. Beatty, "The First Ten Seconds."

299. Whitcomb, "The Healthy Ego."

300. Quine, *Bridesmaids*.

301. Friedman, "Is He the Sexiest."

302. *Seventeen*, May 1961.

303. Ibid.; Friedman, "Is He the Sexiest."

304. Smith, "A Question."

305. Warren Beatty, *Aspel & Company*, 21 March 1992, London Weekend Television, courtesy of British Film Institute.

306. Smith, "A Question."

307. MacLaine, *My Lucky Stars*; Whitcomb, "The Healthy Ego."

308. Michael Wood, "An Interview with Daniel Mann," *Kansas Quarterly* 18, no. 4 (1986).

309. *Theater World*, February 1960.

310. Hirschberg, "Warren Beatty Is Trying."

311. Audrey Wood with Max Wilk, *Represented by Audrey Wood* (New York: Doubleday & Co., 1981).

312. Burry Fredrik interview, here and throughout.

313. Oral history, Daniel Mann, Southern Methodist University, Special Collection, Academy of Motion Picture Arts & Sciences, Beverly Hills.

314. Mann, oral history.

315. Barbara Baxley interview, Inge Collection.

316. Press release, 3 November 1959; Shirley Booth letter to Philip Clarkson, 22 June 1962, Inge Collection.

317. Louella Parsons column, 5 October 1959, Margaret Herrick Library, Academy Collection, Beverly Hills.

318. Lenn Harten letter to Mrs. Harten, 2 October 1959.

319. Wood, *Represented by Audrey Wood*.

320. Mann, oral history.

321. Robert Webber, Ronald L. Davis Oral History Collection, 11 August 1988, Margaret Herrick Library, Beverly Hills.

322. Smith, "A Question."

323. Wood, *Represented by Audrey Wood*; Burry Fredrik interview.

324. Carol Taylor, interview with author, n.d.

325. Webber, Oral History Collection.

326. Mann, Oral history.

327. *New York Post*, 15 March 1969.

328. Wood, *Represented by Audrey Wood*.

329. Ibid.

330. Richard L. Coe, "Inge Play at National," *Washington Post*, 31 October 1959.

331. *Daily Variety*, 30 October 1959.

332. Jay Carmody, "National's New Play Frank and Fragile," *Washington Star*, 30 October 1959.

333. Ibid.

334. *Washington Post*, 3 November 1959; Burry Fredrik interview.

335. *Daily Variety*, 4 November 1959.

336. Burry Fredrik interview.

337. Reed, "Will the Real Warren Beatty . . ."; Jean and Maureen Coe, interview with author, 4 March 2002.

338. Jean and Maureen Coe interview.

339. Wood, "An Interview with Michael Mann."

340. Dennis Cooney, interview with author, 6 April 2002; Reed, "Will the Real Warren Beatty . . ."

341. Dennis Cooney interview.

342. Sheri Mann, interview with author, 19 March 2003.

343. Richard L. Coe, "Behind Each New Play Is 'The System,'" *Washington Post*, 8 November 1959.

344. *New Haven Register*, 17 November 1959.

345. Ross and Ross, *The Player*.

346. Zolotow, "Playwright."

347. Vernon Scott, "Broadway Flop Will Be Filmed," *New York World & Telegram*, 11 July 1962.

348. Burry Fredrik interview.

349. JoAnn Kirchmaier interview.

350. Scott, "Broadway Flop."

351. Reed, "Will the Real Warren Beatty . . ."

352. Author interviews with Carol Taylor (Haney's niece), 17 June 2002, Ellen Blyden (Haney's daughter), 17 June 2002, Michael J. Pollard, and Burry Fredrik.

353. Ross and Ross, *The Player*.

354. Lenn Harten interview.

355. *New York Herald Tribune*, 3 November 1959.

356. Judith Crist, interview with author, 11 October 2003.

357. *Theater World*, February 1960.

358. *New York Post*, 30 November 1959.

359. Dorothy Kilgallen, *New York Journal-American*, 30 November 1959.

360. Scott, "Broadway Flop."

361. Burry Fredrik interview.

362. "Director Sees Pollard as a Star," *New York Post*, 15 March 1969.

363. Scott, "Broadway Flop."

364. Guez, "Warren Beatty."

365. Dick Seff interview.

366. Tornabene, "Who Can Resist . . . ?"

367. John Springer letter to Warren Beatty, 27 July 1961, Springer papers.

368. John Springer, "Initial Notes on Beatty," 29 December 1959, courtesy of Arthur P. Jacobs Collection, Loyola Marymount, Los Angeles; Springer papers.

369. Springer letter to Warren Beatty, 27 July 1961, Springer papers; "Initial Notes on Beatty."

370. Springer, "Initial Notes on Beatty."

371. *Hollywood Reporter,* 10 September 1964.

372. Reed, "Will the Real Warren Beatty . . ."

373. Smith, "A Question."

374. Ibid.

375. Ibid.

376. Springer letter to Warren Beatty, 27 July 1961, Springer papers.

377. Springer letter to Warren Beatty, 23 September 1963, Springer papers.

378. Joe Hyams, "No Thought for Tomorrowsville," *Show Business Illustrated,* March 1962.

379. Peter Levinson, interview with author, 12 May 2002, here and throughout.

380. Springer, "Initial Notes on Beatty."

381. Ibid.

382. Burry Fredrik interview.

383. Springer, "Initial Notes on Beatty."

384. Dorothy Kilgallen, "Joan vs. Chris . . . Boom," *New York Journal-American,* 9 December 1959.

385. *Seventeen,* May 1961.

386. Ibid.

387. Joan Collins, *Larry King Live,* CNN, 11 November 2002.

388. Dorothy Kilgallen, *New York Journal-American,* 21 December 1959.

389. Dorothy Kilgallen, *New York Journal-American,* 10 December 1959.

390. Springer, "Initial Notes on Beatty."

391. Biskind, "Chronicle."

392. Sidney Skolsky, "Tintyped: Warren Beatty," *New York Post,* 12 November 1961.

393. Springer, "Initial Notes on Beatty."

394. Robert Wise notes, March 1960, unsourced.

395. Sidney Skolsky column, *Los Angeles Herald,* 25 January 1959.

396. *Theater World,* February 1960; Springer, "Initial Notes on Beatty."

397. Joan Fontaine letter to author, 31 March 2003.

398. Jane Ficker, interview with author, 26 March 2003.

399. Sidney Skolsky, "Tintyped: Robert Wagner," February 1959, Academy Collection Margaret Herrick Library, Beverly Hills.

400. Biskind, "Chronicle."

401. George Christy, "In Hollywood," *Interview,* December 1984.

402. Champlin, "Beatty Sings."

403. Gordon Gow, "Warren Beatty," *Films and Filming,* August 1975.

404. "Tall Grass."

405. Howard Thompson, "Inge's Kansas Through a Kazan Kaleidoscope," *New York Times,* 22 May 1960.

406. Kazan notebook, *Splendor in the Grass,* Kazan Collection.

407. Ibid.; Letter from psychiatrist, Kazan notebook, Kazan Collection.

408. Richard Lee, "The Kid from Arlington," *Washingtonian*, December 1981.

409. William Inge letter to Jerry Wald, July 1960, Jerry Wald Collection, USC Cinema-Television Library.

410. Warren Beatty, *Aspel & Company*.

411. Ronald Rynning, "Another Affair to Remember," *Film Review*, October 1995.

412. Quine, *Bridesmaids*, here and throughout.

413. John Springer memo, 6 April 1960, Springer papers.

414. Alan Nevins, interview with author, n.d.

415. *Aspel & Company*.

416. *New York Times*, 22 May 1959.

417. Donald Kranze, interview with author, 8 September 1999.

418. Kazan notebook, Kazan Collection; Murray Kempton, "Natalie Wood: Mother, Men and the Muse," *Show*, March 1962.

419. Transcript, Dr. Margaret Brenman-Gibson interview with Warren Beatty, 21 June 1965.

420. David Richards, "Elia Kazan: The Director and His Gifts," *Washington Post*, 4 December 1983.

421. Donald Kranze interview.

422. Richard L. Coe, "Conversation at the Shore," *Washington Post*, Spring 1962.

423. Smith, "A Question."

424. Pat Hingle interview.

425. *Seventeen*, May 1961.

426. Barbara Loden, quoted in Ed DeBlasio, "His Hometown Secrets," *Motion Picture*, May 1962, here and throughout.

427. *Seventeen*, May 1961.

428. Dorothy Kilgallen, *New York Journal-American*, 29 October 1958; David Wallace, "Heart to Heart with Liz & R.J.," *People*, 6 October 1986.

429. Bob Jiras, interview with author, 16 September 1999, here and throughout.

430. DeBlasio, "His Hometown Secrets."

431. Natalie Wood, "Life Story," handwritten/typed memoir, submitted to Peter Wyden, 1966 [cited hereafter as Wood memoir], courtesy of Lana Wood.

432. Guez, "Warren Beatty."

433. Richard Simmons, "Natalie Wood: Star into Actress," *Newsweek*, 26 February 1962; Stanley Gordon and Jack Hamilton, "Natalie Wood: Beauty and Violence," *Look*, 11 April 1961.

434. Earl Leaf, "Natalie Wood," *Teen*, December 1961.

435. Joan Dew, "Warren Beatty: More Than a Lover," *Redbook*, May 1974.

436. Kazan notebook, Kazan Collection.

437. Skolsky, "Tintyped: Robert Wagner."

438. Warren Beatty, "50 Stars Write Their Own Biographies," *Movie Stars*, September 1960.

439. Whitcomb, "The Healthy Ego."

440. John Connolly interview.

441. "Elia Kazan on 'The Young Agony,'" *Films and Filming*, March 1962.

442. Curtis Lee Hanson, "An Interview with Warren Beatty," *Cinema* 3, no. 5 (Summer 1967).

443. Inge letter to Kazan, 31 August 1961, Kazan Collection.

444. Preston, "Warren's Peace."

445. Robert Aiken, interview with author, 29 September 2003.

446. Whitcomb, "The Healthy Ego."

447. Larry Shaw, interview with author, 23 July 2003.
448. Mike Wilmington and Gerald Peary, interview with Warren Beatty, *The Velvet Light Trap* (Winter 1972).
449. John Hallowell, "I'm Going to Live My Life," *New York Times*, 9 March 1969; Natalie Wood, San Francisco Film Festival, 26 October 1976.
450. Natalie Wood and Elia Kazan, *The Merv Griffin Show*, May 1979; Joseph Lewis, "What Ever Happened to Baby Natalie?" *Cosmopolitan*, November 1968.
451. Dorothy Kilgallen, *New York Journal-American*, 10 June 1959.
452. "Sizzling Session with Shirley," *Modern Screen*, September 1962.
453. Reed, "Will the Real Warren Beatty . . . ?"
454. Michel Delahaye, "Elia Kazan: Interview," *Cahiers du Cinema*, March 1967.
455. Jessica Maguire, interview with author, 28 September 2003.
456. Larry Shaw interview, here and throughout.
457. *People*, 6 October 1986.
458. John Connolly interview, Inge Collection.
459. *Weekend*, n.p. 3–9 July 1968.
460. Robert Evans, *The Kid Stays in the Picture* (New York: Hyperion, 1994).
461. Kazan, quoted in "Penn. Ave. to Broadway," produced by Michael Wood, Inge Collection.
462. Kazan notebook, Kazan Collection.
463. Donald Kranze interview.
464. Elia Kazan, *Elia Kazan: A Life* (New York: Alfred A. Knopf, 1988).
465. "Warren Beatty: Bigtime Winner," *Glamour*, September 1964.
466. Bernard Weinraub, "Deliver the Goods," *New York Times*, 12 March 1999.
467. Warren Beatty, *The Dick Cavett Show*, November 1972.
468. Kazan, *Elia Kazan*.
469. Joan Collins interview.
470. Springer letter to Dorothy Kilgallen, 17 January 1960, Springer papers.
471. John Houseman, *Final Dress* (New York: Simon & Schuster, 1983); Dorothy Kilgallen, *New York Journal-American*, 9 September 1960.
472. JoAnn Kirchmaier interview.
473. *Seventeen*, May 1961.
474. Peter Biskind, "The Man Who Minted Style," *Vanity Fair*, April 2003.
475. Preston, "Warren's Peace"; Biskind, "The Man Who Minted Style."
476. Warren Beatty letter to Charles Feldman, 12 March 1961, Charles K. Feldman Collection, Louis B. Mayer Library, American Film Institute, Los Angeles [hereafter cited as Feldman Collection].
477. Beatty, "The First Ten Seconds."
478. *Los Angeles Times*, 25 December 1974.
479. Warren Beatty, *Film Night with Tony Bilbow*, 30 October 1975, BBC 2, British Film Institute, London.
480. Ross and Ross, *The Player*.
481. Hedda Hopper transcript, March 1962, Academy of Motion Picture Arts and Sciences, Margaret Herrick Library, Hedda Hopper Collection, Beverly Hills.
482. *Photoplay*, July 1968.
483. Hirschberg, "Warren Beatty Is Trying"; Biskind, "Chronicle."
484. Dr. Margaret Brenman-Gibson interview; Warren Beatty, interviewed by Christopher Cook for the British Film Institute, 6 July 1990, courtesy of British Film Institute [hereafter cited as WB interview, BFI].

485. Notes from interviews with Warren Beatty, courtesy of Dr. Margaret Brenman-Gibson.

486. WB interview, BFI.

487. Brenman-Gibson interview; Notes from interviews with Warren Beatty, William Gibson and Dr. Margaret Brenman-Gibson.

488. Brenman-Gibson interview.

489. Brenman-Gibson, notes from interview with Warren Beatty, 21 June 1965.

490. Clifford Odets journal, 8 October 1960; Virginia Rowe, interview with author, 8 November 2003.

491. Notes from Brenman-Gibson interview with Warren Beatty, 21 June 1965.

492. Robert Aiken interview; Robert Aiken, "Heaven Can Wait: Beatty for President?" *North Shore News*, 25 October 1999.

493. Notes from Brenman-Gibson interview with Warren Beatty, 21 June 1965.

494. Warren Beatty, San Francisco Film Festival, April 25, 2002; WB interview, BFI.

495. WB interview, BFI.

496. Michael Laughlin, interview with author, September 2003.

497. Brenman-Gibson interview.

498. WB interview, BFI.

499. *Modern Screen*, January 1962.

500. Gow, "Warren Beatty."

501. Warren Beatty letter to Eleanor Kilgallen, March 1961, courtesy of Kilgallen; Warren Beatty letter to Feldman, 12 March 1961, Feldman Collection; Dorothy Masters, "Warren Beatty Turns Tables on Reporter," *Sunday News*, 30 October 1960.

502. Bart Mills, "Yellow Streak of Heroism," *Guardian*, 2 July 1990.

503. Beatty, "The First Ten Seconds"; Haigh, "Warren Beatty."

504. Beatty, "The First Ten Seconds."

505. Kate Cameron, "Tennessee Williams' Story of an Aging Beauty and Gigolo," *Sunday News*, 17 December 1961.

506. Hedda Hopper profile of Jill St. John, 9 April 1961, Academy Collection, Margaret Herrick Library, Beverly Hills.

507. Cameron, "Tennessee Williams' Story."

508. John Connolly interview; Connolly interview, Inge Collection.

509. Verne O'Hara interview; Hyams, "No Thought."

510. Biskind, "Chronicle."

511. Ibid.

512. Gallagher, "Warren Beatty"; Biskind, "Chronicle."

513. Tennessee Williams and Marion Black Vaccaro expense vouchers submitted to Audrey Wood, 25–27 November 1961, Audrey Wood Collection, Harry Ransom Center, University of Texas, Austin, Tex.

514. *Los Angeles Sunday News*, 15 October 1961.

515. Dotson Rader, *Tennessee Williams Memoirs: Cry of the Heart* (New York: Anchor Press, 1983).

516. Tomas Milian interview.

517. Peter Yates, interview with author, 16 June 2003.

518. Springer letter to Warren Beatty, 27 July 1961, Springer papers.

519. Springer memo, 30 December 1960, Springer papers.

520. Dew, "Warren Beatty."

521. Ibid.

522. Wilmington and Peary, interview with Warren Beatty.

523. *New York Post*, 8 January 1962.

524. Wilmington and Peary, interview with Warren Beatty.

525. Gene D. Phillips, *The Films of Tennessee Williams* (London & Toronto: Philadelphia Art Alliance Press, 1980).

526. José Quintero, *If You Don't Dance They Beat You* (Boston: Little Brown & Co., 1974).

527. Taped interview, Warren Beatty and Joe Laitin, circa 26 September 1961, courtesy of Peter Laitin [hereafter Laitin tape].

528. Hugo Vickers, *Vivien Leigh: A Biography* (Boston: Little Brown & Co., 1992).

529. Jill St. John, Joe Laitin interview, 1962.

530. Laitin tape.

531. *Film Review*, September 1961.

532. Preston, "Warren's Peace"; Brad Darrach, "Dustin and Warren," *People*, 25 May 1987.

533. Alexander Walker, *Vivien: The Life of Vivien Leigh* (New York: Grove Press, 1987).

534. Howard Thompson, "Young Man Who Has It Made," *New York Times*, 10 January 1965.

535. Ross and Ross, *The Player*.

536. *TV Guide*, 23 October 1982, Billy Rose Theater Collection, Joan Collins folder, Lincoln Center, New York.

537. Warren Beatty, *The Howard Stern Show*.

538. Julie Newmar, *People*, 26 August 1991.

539. Susan Strasberg, *Bittersweet* (New York: G. P. Putnam's Sons, 1980).

540. Springer memo, 19 August 1963, Springer papers.

541. Logan letter to Kazan, 29 November 1960, Logan Collection.

542. Warren Beatty letter to Kilgallen, n.d., courtesy of Kilgallen; Josh Logan journal, Logan Collection.

543. Warren Beatty, San Francisco Film Festival, 25 April 2002; Hyams, "No Thought."

544. Houseman, *Final Dress*, here and throughout.

545. John Connolly interview.

546. Gow, "Warren Beatty."

547. *Show*, March 1962.

548. John Frankenheimer, taped lecture, Arthur Knight class at USC, 1961, courtesy of Ned Comstock.

549. Debbie Reynolds, interview with author, 21 December 1998; *Los Angeles Times*, 21 June 1961; *Los Angeles Mirror*, 22 June 1961.

550. Maryann Marinkovich Brooks, interview with author, 4 November 1999; Jeanne Hyatt, interview with author, March 2001; Robert Hyatt, interview with author, 10 May 1999; Lana Wood, interview with author, 19 August 1999; Roderick Mann, interview with author, 20 January 2000; *Los Angeles Herald-Examiner*, 26 June 1961 and 29 June 1961; *Hollywood Reporter*, 27 June 1961; *Daily Variety*, 30 June 1961.

551. Wood memoir.

552. Warner Brothers letter to Natalie Wood, 3 July 1961, Warner Brothers Collection, USC Cinema-Television Library, Los Angeles.

553. Springer memos, Springer papers.

554. Lyn Tornabene, interview with author, n.d.

555. Stephen Rebello, "The Dark Romance of James Toback," *Movieline*, October 1991.

556. Laitin tape.

557. Lyn Tornabene interview.

558. Warner Brothers press conference, taped by Joe Laitin, courtesy of Peter Laitin.

559. William Peper, "Mystery Surrounds Mr. Beatty," *New York World-Telegram and Sun*, 29 June 1961.

560. Springer memo, Springer papers; Hedda Hopper Collection, March 1962 transcript.

561. Dorothy Kilgallen, *New York Journal-American*, 29 June 1961.

562. Woodrow Irwin, interview with author, 24 May 1999; Dorothy Kilgallen, *New York Journal-American*, 12 September 1961.

563. Springer memo to Arthur Jacobs, 21 July 1961, and Springer letter to Mel Heimer, 24 July 1961, Springer papers.

564. Springer letter to Mel Heimer, 24 July 1961, Springer papers.

565. Ibid.

566. Josh Logan diary, 1 July 1961, Logan Collection.

567. Jane Fonda letter to Josh Logan, 3 July 1961, Logan Collection.

568. Richard Sylbert interview.

569. Norman Mailer, "The Warren Report," *Vanity Fair*, November 1991.

570. Delmer Daves letter to Guy Luongo, 12 July 1961, Box 60, Folder 35, Delmer Daves Collection, Stanford University, Palo Alto, Calif.

571. Thomas Thompson, "Natalie Wood: Hollywood's Number One Survivor," *Look*, April 1979; Maryann Marinkovich Brooks interview.

572. *Los Angeles Herald-Examiner*, 15 July 1961.

573. Wallace, "Heart to Heart."

574. *Los Angeles Mirror*, 18 July 1961; Springer letter to Heimer, 24 July 1961, Springer papers.

575. Springer letter to Heimer, 24 July 1961, Springer papers.

576. Houseman, *Final Dress*.

577. Brandon De Wilde, in Ross and Ross, *The Player*.

578. Karl Malden, interview with author, 29 July 1999.

579. "The Rise of Geyger Krocp"; Judy Michaelson, "The New Stars," *New York Post*, 12 September 1963.

580. Dorsey, "Warren Beatty."

581. Springer letter to Warren Beatty, 27 July 1961, Springer papers.

582. Whitcomb, "The Healthy Ego."

583. Lewis, "What Ever Happened."

584. Mailer, "The Warren Report."

585. Joseph Laitin, "Brash and Rumpled Star," *Saturday Evening Post*, July 1962.

586. Charles Champlin, *John Frankenheimer: A Conversation with Charles Champlin* (Burbank, Calif.: Riverwood Press, 1995).

587. Ross and Ross, *The Player*.

588. Martin Gottfried, *Balancing Act: The Authorized Biography of Angela Lansbury* (Boston: Little, Brown & Co., 1999) here and rest of paragraph.

589. Ibid.

590. Tornabene, "Who Can Resist . . . ?"

591. Wood memoir.

592. Ibid.; Lana Wood interview with author, February 2002; *After Dark*, October 1979; Dick Moore, *Twinkle Twinkle Little Star* (New York: Harper & Row, 1984); *Cosmopolitan*, August 1975.

593. Wood memoir.

594. Mailer, "The Warren Report."

595. Myth repeated in Warren G. Harris, *Natalie & RJ* (New York: Doubleday, 1988); David Thomson, *Warren Beatty and Desert Eyes* (New York: Doubleday, 1987); John Parker, *5 for Hollywood* (New York: Carol Publishing, 1991).

596. George Norbe, "Why Husbands Don't Like Warren Beatty," *Los Angeles Sunday News*, 19 July 1964.

597. Ibid.

598. *Los Angeles Sunday News*, 15 October 1961.

599. Peter S. Haigh, "Warren Beatty — The Unknown Star," *Film Review*, September 1961.

600. Adam Edwards, "Shirley MacLaine: My Brother, Warren Beatty," *Sunday Woman*, 15 July 1979.

601. "The Rise of Geyger Krocp."

602. MacLaine, *Don't Fall off the Mountain*.

603. Edwards, "Shirley MacLaine."

604. "The Rise of Geyger Krocp."

605. Hollis Alpert, "What Goes on Here," *Woman's Day*, 1961.

606. MacLaine, *Don't Fall off the Mountain*.

607. Sandy Whitelaw interview.

608. Warren Beatty, *The Oprah Winfrey Show*.

609. Springer interoffice memo, 25 September 1961, Springer papers.

610. Lee, "The Kid from Arlington."

611. Guez, "Warren Beatty."

612. Inge letter to Kazan, 31 August 1961, Kazan Collection [here and next several paragraphs].

613. Thompson, "Young Man."

614. *Seventeen*, May 1961.

615. Sidney Skolsky, 1961, Skolsky Collection, Margaret Herrick Library, Beverly Hills.

616. Wood memoir.

617. *Los Angeles Sunday News*, 15 October 1961.

618. Charles Champlin, *John Frankenheimer: Conversation with Charles Champlin*.

619. Laitin tape; Warren Beatty letter to Springer, 22 September 1961, Springer papers.

620. Laitin letter to Springer, 22 September 1961, Springer papers.

621. Peter Laitin, interview with author, 7 October 2003.

622. Warren Beatty comments to Laitin, Laitin tape, courtesy of Peter Laitin.

623. Springer letter to Warren Beatty, 8 December 1961, Springer papers.

624. Springer letter to Warren Beatty, 4 October 1961, Springer papers.

625. Jane Alderman, interview with author, 25 June 2002.

626. Todd Gold, "Warren Beatty," *Us*, 3 April 2000.

627. *Cue*, 14 October 1961.

628. *Films in Review*, November 1961.

629. Philip K. Scheuer, "Jazz Age Film Poignant Tale of Young Love," *Los Angeles Times*, 10 September 1961.

630. "It's Warren Beatty," *Life*, 3 November 1961.

631. Sidney Fields, "No More Insults," *New York Mirror*, 9 November 1961.

632. Guez, "Warren Beatty."

633. Sue Chambers, "Warren's Working Again," *Milwaukee Journal*, 5 May 1963.

634. *The New Yorker*, 13 January 1962.

635. *Cue*, 30 December 1961.

636. *Hollywood Citizen-News*, 30 December 1961; *Cue*, 30 December 1961.

637. *Films in Review*, January 1962.

638. *Daily Variety*, 30 November 1961.

639. *New York Times*, 24 December 1961.

640. "The Hollywood Scene," *Seventeen*, February 1964.

641. *Ladies' Home Companion*, May 1962.

642. Warren Beatty, *Bravo Profiles*, May 1998.

643. Senator Edward M. Kennedy, letter to author, 16 December 2003.

644. Muriel Davidson, "Warren Beatty: Public Image vs. Private Man," *Good Housekeep-*

ing, August 1970; Ronald Brownstein, *The Power and the Glitter* (New York: Random House, 1993); Jack L. Warner, *Jack of All Trades* (London: W.H. Allen, 1975).

645. Peter Biskind, "Warren and Me," *Premiere*, July 1990.

646. Helen Lawrenson, "Warren Beatty Has Been Wronged!" *Cosmopolitan*, February 1970.

647. Hyams, "No Thought."

648. Springer papers.

649. *Modern Screen*, December 1962.

650. Lawrenson, "Warren Beatty Has Been Wronged!"

651. Laitin tape.

652. Ibid.

653. "Tall Grass," *Newsweek*.

654. Hyams, "No Thought."

655. Chambers, "Warren's Working."

656. *Seventeen*, February 1964.

657. Hanson, "An Interview with Warren Beatty."

658. Morgan Brittany, interview with author, 19 August 1999.

659. Wood memoir.

660. Clifford Odets material herein from: Odets's journal; Warren Beatty conversations with Dr. Margaret Brenman-Gibson and/or William Gibson, per Brenman-Gibson's notes, courtesy of Virginia Rowe and Dr. Margaret Brenman-Gibson; Odets's notes for a play, courtesy of Virginia Rowe; author interviews with Odets's biographer and friend Dr. Margaret Brenman-Gibson and Odets's private secretary Virginia Rowe, 21 July 2003 and 8 November 2003.

661. Odets's journal, 13 March 1962.

662. Warren Beatty, San Francisco Film Festival, 25 April 2002.

663. Kempton, "Natalie Wood."

664. Inge letter, "The Sound and the Fury."

665. Skolsky, "Tintyped: Warren Beatty."

666. Sheilah Graham column, *Hollywood Citizen-News*, 22 March 1962.

667. Mark Whitman, "Warren Beatty Comeback?" *New York Times*, 6 September 1966.

668. Susan Umbs, interview with author, 13 May 2002; Jacqueline Eastes, interview with author, May 2002.

669. "The Hollywood Scene."

670. Mailer, "The Warren Report."

671. Cher, *Playboy* interview, December 1988.

672. Warren Beatty conversations with Dr. Margaret Brenman-Gibson and/or William Gibson, per Brenman-Gibson notes; Virginia Rowe interview.

673. *Motion Picture*, September 1961.

674. Chambers, "Warren's Working"; Charles Champlin, *John Frankenheimer, Conversation with Charles Champlin.*

675. *New York Times*, 12 April 1962.

676. "The Ring-a-Ding Girl," *Time*, 22 June 1959.

677. Wood memoir.

678. Bob Thomas, "Life Is Wonderful Says Warren Beatty," *Richmond Times-Dispatch*, 26 January 1967.

679. Springer memo, 2 June 1962, Springer papers.

680. Springer letter, 11 June 1962, Springer papers.

681. Thomas Thompson, "Natalie Wood and Bob Wagner Get It Together Again," *Cosmopolitan*, August 1975; Patricia Reynolds, "Natalie Wood's Own Story," *Pageant*, 19 July 1971.

682. Wood memoir.

683. Frank Rich, "Warren Beatty Strikes Again," *Time* 3 July 1978.

684. Wanda Hale, "Filmland's 'Homme Fatale,'" *Daily News*, 21 December 1964; *New York Times*, 4 July 1962.

685. *New York Times*, 4 July 1962; Harrison Starr, interview with author, August and September 2003.

686. Wood memoir.

687. Lana Wood interview, here and throughout.

688. News release for publication on 16 January and 22 January 1963, Springer papers.

689. Charles Eastman interview with author, 12 January 2004, here and throughout.

690. Preston, "Warren's Peace."

691. Springer memo, 8 January 1963, Springer papers.

692. Wilmington and Peary, "Warren Beatty."

693. Smith, "A Question."

694. Henry Gris, "What Are You, Warren Beatty?" October 1963.

695. Springer letter to Warren Beatty, 1 February 1963, Springer papers.

696. Thomas, "Life Is Wonderful."

697. Warren Beatty, San Francisco Film Festival, 25 April 2002.

698. Springer letter, 1 February 1963, Springer papers.

699. Phone logs and phone transcript, 27 February 1963, Delmer Daves Collection.

700. Ibid.

701. Feldman memo, 13 March 1963, Feldman Collection.

702. Robert Solo, interview with author, 18 August 2003.

703. *New York Times*, 10 January 1965.

704. Thomas, "Life Is Wonderful."

705. Gerrard Garrett, *Evening Standard*, 15 September 1967.

706. Thomas, "Life Is Wonderful."

707. Wood memoir.

708. Jean Seberg, "Lilith & I," *Cahiers du Cinema*, January 1967.

709. Feldman memo to Jack Gordean and Ira Steiner, 13 March 1963, Feldman Collection.

710. Telegrams from Warren Beatty to Feldman, Feldman Collection.

711. Sam Shaw letter to Feldman, 5 April 1963, Feldman Collection.

712. From Margaret Gardner letter to Springer, 26 March 1963, Springer papers.

713. Seberg, "Lilith & I."

714. Smith, "A Question."

715. Springer memo, 3 April 1963, Springer papers.

716. Ibid.

717. Carol Eve Rossen, interview with author, 14 June 2003.

718. Mailer, "The Warren Report."

719. Tom Bosley, interview with author, 4 August 1999.

720. Springer memo, 17 June 1963, Springer papers.

721. Wood memoir; Lana Wood interview; Henry Jaglom, interview with author, 23 June 1999.

722. J. R. Salamanca, interview with author, 13 May 2003, here and throughout.

723. *New York Times*, 16 June 1974, incomplete, Jean Seberg file, British Film Institute, London; Stanley Paley, "Interview With Jean Seberg," *Art Films International*, February 1964.

724. Donald W. LaBadie, "Everybody's Galatea," *Show*, August 1963.

725. Unsourced Sheilah Graham interview with Warren Beatty, n.p., 28 April 1963.

726. Peter Fonda, interview with author, 7 May 2003, here and throughout.

727. Carol Rossen interview, here and throughout.

728. Seberg, "Lilith & I."

729. Springer letter to Henry Ehrlich, 11 December 1970, Springer papers.

730. Afdera Fonda, *Never Before Noon* (London: Trafalgar Square, 1986).

731. Tibor Sands, interview with author, 11 November 2003.

732. Warren Rothenberger, interview with author, 18 July 2003, here and throughout.

733. Paley, "Interview with Jean Seberg."

734. Gow, "Warren Beatty."

735. Hale, "Filmland's 'Homme Fatale.'"

736. Hanson, "An Interview with Warren Beatty."

737. Wilmington and Peary, "Interview with Warren Beatty."

738. Judith Crist, interview with author, 11 October 2003.

739. Smith, "A Question."

740. Dorothy Tristan Avakian Hancock, interview with author, 23 July 2003.

741. Irving Buchman, interview with author, 10 June 2003.

742. Wilmington and Peary, "Interview with Warren Beatty."

743. Dorothy Kilgallen, *New York Journal-American*, 15 May 1963; Sheilah Graham, *Confessions of a Hollywood Columnist* (New York: William Morrow & Co., 1969).

744. Springer memo, 24 May 1963, Springer papers.

745. Springer memo, 28 May 1963, Springer papers.

746. Warren Beatty, *The Dick Cavett Show*, November 1972.

747. Seberg, "Lilith & I."

748. "Rambling Reporter," *Hollywood Reporter*, 5 February 1964.

749. Ron Base, "Star Status Still Surprises Gene Hackman," *Toronto Star*, 20 October 1985.

750. Jessica Walter, interview with author, 12 June 2003.

751. Paul Sylbert interview.

752. Springer memo, 8/5/63, Springer papers.

753. Hanson, "Interview with Warren Beatty."

754. Springer letter to Henry Ehrlich, 11 December 1970, Springer papers.

755. MacLaine, *Out on a Limb*.

756. Smith, "A Question."

757. Springer memo, 19 August 1963, Springer papers.

ACT THREE: A LEGEND IN THE MAKING

1. John Springer memo, 19 August 1963, part of John Springer papers, courtesy of Gary Springer and June Springer [hereafter cited as Springer papers].

2. Ibid.

3. Springer memo, 28 August 1963, Springer papers.

4. Gita Hall May, interview with author, 30 April 2003, here and throughout.

5. Joe Hyams, "No Thought for Tomorrowsville," *Show Business Illustrated*, March 1962.

6. Feldman letter, 2 April 1963, Charles K. Feldman Collection, Louis B. Mayer Library, American Film Institute [hereafter cited as Feldman Collection].

7. Peter Biskind, "Chronicle of a Life Untold," *Premiere*, January 1992.

8. David Blum, "The Road to Ishtar," *New York*, 6 March 1987.

9. Springer letter to Goddard Lieberson, 9 August 1963, Springer papers.

10. Gavin Smith, "A Question of Control," *Film Comment*, Jan./Feb. 1992; Production notes, *Mickey One*, Margaret Herrick Library, Beverly Hills, CA.

11. Helen Lawrenson, "Warren Beatty Has Been Wronged!" *Cosmopolitan*, February 1970.

12. Tony Crawley, "Arthur Penn on Personal Experiences," *The Movie Scene*, March 1985.

13. Harrison Starr, interviews with author, August-September 2003, here and throughout.

14. Todd Gold, "Warren Beatty," *Us*, 3 April 2000.

15. Dorothy Kilgallen, *New York Journal-American*, 19 November 1963 and 21 November 1963.

16. Bill Zehme, *Intimate Strangers* (New York: Dell, 2002); Anthony Summers, *Goddess* (New York: Scribner's, 1985).

17. *New York Sunday News*, n.d., n.p.

18. Richard Sylbert, interview with author, 17 June 1999.

19. *Movie Mirror*, November 1965.

20. Angela Levin, "Thank Heaven Gigi Still Can't Stop Herself," *Daily Mail*, 17 June 1995.

21. Freddie Fields, interview with author, 18 September 2003, here and throughout.

22. Leslie Caron, letter to author, 20 October 2003 (first meeting).

23. Suzie MacKenzie, "At Last Leslie Can Laugh at Life," *Evening Standard*, 4 October 1995.

24. Angela Lambert, "Passions of an Ingenue Who Never Grows Old," *Independent*, 26 January 1993.

25. Ibid.; Aaron Latham, "Warren Beatty, Seriously," *Rolling Stone*, 1 April 1982; Peter Hall and Shaun Usher, "Passion Plays," *Daily Mail*, 6 September 1993; Peter Hall, *Making an Exhibition of Myself* (London: Sinclair-Stevenson, 1993).

26. Roderick Mann, "Why Miss Caron Is So Different Now," *Sunday Express*, 9 June 1968.

27. Jenny Hall, "Why My Parents' Divorce Forever Haunts Me," *Daily Mail*, 22 October 1992.

28. Feldman letter to Warren Beatty, unsent, 16 April 1964, Feldman Collection.

29. Warren Beatty letter to Feldman, 1 March 1964, Feldman Collection.

30. Mike Wilmington and Gerald Peary, "Interview with Warren Beatty," *The Velvet Light Trap* (Winter 1972).

31. Ibid.

32. Andre S. Labarthe, *Cahiers du Cinema* 196 (December 1967).

33. Alexandra Stewart, interview with author, 26 May 2003, here and throughout.

34. Roberta Hodes, interview with author, 23 July 2003, here and throughout.

35. Curtis Lee Hanson, "An Interview with Warren Beatty," *Cinema* 3, no. 5 (Summer 1967).

36. Patrick Goldstein, "Blasts from the Past," *Los Angeles Times*, 24 August 1997; *Movie Scene*, March 1985.

37. *Forever Hollywood*, Esplanade Productions, The American Cinematheque, 1999.

38. Todd Gold, "Warren Beatty," *Us*, 3 April 2000.

39. Hedda Hopper column, *Chicago Tribune* syndicate, 12 April 1963.

40. United Press International, 6 April 1964.

41. Warren Beatty cable, Feldman Collection, here and throughout.

42. Louella Parsons column, *Modern Screen*, July 1964.

43. Leslie Caron letter to author.

44. Robert Benton, interview with author, 3 September and 24 September 2003, here and throughout.

45. Elinor Wright Jones, interview with author, 29 August 2003, here and throughout.

46. Antoine de Baecque and Serge Toubiana, *Truffaut* (New York: Alfred A. Knopf, 1999).

47. Norton Wright, interview with author, 29 August 2003, here and throughout.

48. Truffaut letter to Elinor Jones, 18 February 1964, courtesy of Elinor Jones and Bibliotheque du Film, Paris, France.

49. Robert Benton interview; Patrick Goldstein, *Los Angeles Times*, 24 August 1997.

50. Robert Benton interview.

51. Warren Beatty, San Francisco Film Festival, 25 April 2002.

52. Helen Lawrenson, "A Song of Love Is a Sad Song," *Cosmopolitan*, November 1964.

53. *Rolling Stone*, 1 April 1982.

54. Maureen Donaldson and William Royce, *An Affair to Remember* (New York: G. P. Putnam's Sons, 1989).

55. Roderick Mann, "I Want So Much Out of Life," *Sunday Express*, 14 June 1964.

56. "Leslie Caron, Beatty Misconduct Charged," *Los Angeles Herald-Examiner*, 17 June 1964.

57. "Leslie Caron Enjoined," *London Times*, 18 June 1964.

58. "Peter Hall Seeks Divorce from Miss Caron in London," United Press International, *New York Times*, 18 June 1964.

59. *Daily Mail*, 6 September 1993; Hall, *Making an Exhibition of Myself.*

60. Ibid.

61. Feldman letter, n.d. Feldman Collection.

62. Feldman Collection.

63. Richard Sylbert interview.

64. Biskind, "Chronicle."

65. Mark Whitman, "Warren Beatty Comeback?" *The Times* (London), 6 September 1966; Biskind, "Chronicle."

66. Chris Nashawaty, "The Warren Report," *Entertainment Weekly*, March 2000.

67. Aaron Latham, "Warren Beatty, Seriously," *Rolling Stone*, 1 April 1982.

68. Rex Reed, "Will the Real Warren Beatty Please Shut Up," *Esquire*, August 1967.

69. Jennifer Hall, interview with author, 2 November 2003, here and throughout.

70. Mann, "I Want So Much Out of Life"; Pauline Peters, "Gigi Grows Up," *Daily Mail*, 30 May 1998.

71. John Parker, *Warren Beatty: The Last Great Lover of Hollywood* (New York: Carroll & Graf, 1994).

72. Dr. Michael Grotjahn, interview with author, 22 August 2003.

73. *New York Times*, 21 September 1964.

74. Reed, "Will the Real Warren Beatty."

75. Truffaut letter to Helen Scott, 7 September 1964, Bibliotheque du Film, Paris, France; Truffaut letter to Elinor Jones, 7 September 1964, courtesy of Elinor Jones.

76. *Daily Variety*, 21 September 1964.

77. *Time*, 2 October 1964.

78. Gary Arnold, "So Much in Common," *Washington Times*, 23 October 1994.

79. Wanda Hale, "Filmland's 'Homme Fatale,'" *Daily News*, 21 December 1964; Gene Siskel, "Success Story That Goes On," *Valley News, Sunday*, 17 September 1978.

80. See *Hollywood Reporter*, 10 August 1964; *Daily Variety*, 12 August 1964 and 25 March 1965; Lawrenson, "A Song of Love."

81. Warren Beatty, *Aspel & Company*, London Weekend Television, 21 March 1992, courtesy of British Film Institute, London.

82. Gerrard Garrett, *Evening Standard*, 15 September 1967.

83. Emerson Beauchamp, *Washington Star*, 18 October 1964.

84. "Warren Beatty in an interview with Gordon Gow," *Films and Filming*, August 1975.

85. Stanley Rubin, interview with author, 27 July 2003, here and throughout.

86. Arthur Hiller, interview with author, 19 August 2003.

87. Parker, *Last Great Lover.*

88. Nikki Murfitt, "I Hated My Stepmothers for Taking Daddy Away," *Daily Mail*, 19 November 1995.

89. See *Hall v. Hall and Beatty*, High Court of Justice, United Kingdom; Hall, *Making an Exhibition of Myself; Daily News*, 6 February 1964; Dame Margaret Booth letter to author 22 August 2003; Hall and Usher, "Passion Plays."

90. Hall and Usher, "Passion Plays."

91. Hall, *Making an Exhibition of Myself;* Hall and Usher, "Passion Plays."

92. Hall, "Why My Parents' Divorce Forever Haunts Me."

93. Henry Gris, "Warren Beatty and Julie Christie," *Coronet*, October 1971.

94. *Daily Variety* and *Hollywood Reporter*, 1 July 1965.

95. Howard Thompson, "Young Man Who Has It Made," *New York Times*, 10 January 1965; Margaret Penman, "'I Love A Beautiful . . . Movie Actress,'" *Toronto Telegram*, 29 May 1965.

96. Penman, "I Love a Beautiful."

97. Lois Romano, "Caron's Country Fare," *Washington Post*, 20 August 1993.

98. Elinor Jones interview; Legal files, Robert Montgomery, New York, N.Y.

99. Truffaut letter to Elinor Jones, 2 July 1965, courtesy of Elinor Jones and Bibliotheque du Film, Paris, France.

100. Warren Beatty, interviewed by Christopher Cook for the British Film Institute, 6 July 1990, British Film Institute, London [hereafter "WB interview, BFI"]; Peter Biskind, *Easy Riders, Raging Bulls* (New York: Simon & Schuster, 1999).

101. Paula Parisi, "Alpha Beatty," *Hollywood Reporter*, 16 January 2004.

102. WB interview, BFI.

103. *Easy Riders, Raging Bulls* (documentary), produced by Fremantle Corp. and BBC, 2003.

104. Louis Menand, "Paris, Texas," *The New Yorker*, 17 and 24 February 2003.

105. Charles Thomas Samuels with Truffaut, "Encountering Directors," essay, September 1970.

106. Warren Beatty, San Francisco Film Festival, 25 April 2002.

107. Tom DeCola, "Words Take New Truth," *Denton Record-Chronicle*, 14 September 1967.

108. Warren Beatty, San Francisco Film Festival, 25 April 2002.

109. WB interview, BFI.

110. Warren Beatty, San Francisco Film Festival, 25 April 2002.

111. Robert Benton interview.

112. Elinor Jones interview; David Picker, interview with author, 10 September 2003, here and throughout.

113. Elinor Jones journal, 29 June 1965, courtesy of Jones.

114. Truffaut letter to Jones, 2 July 1965, courtesy of Jones and Bibliotheque du Film, Paris, France.

115. Ibid.

116. Truffaut letter to Jones, 25 August 1965, courtesy of Bibliotheque du Film, Paris, France; Elinor Jones interview.

117. Robert Montgomery letter to Leonard Davis, 27 September 1965; Elinor Jones interview.

118. Lou Ann Horstmann Persons, interview with author, 17 August 2003.

119. Bill Stamets, "Images Make 'Mickey' Memorable," *Chicago Sun-Times*, 27 December 1996.

120. Gordon Gow, "Metaphor," *Films and Filming,* July 1971.

121. Whitman, "Warren Beatty Comeback?"

122. *Daily Variety,* 21 September 1965.

123. Stanley Kauffman, *New Republic,* 9 October 1965.

124. "People Are Talking About . . . ," *Vogue,* 1 October 1967.

125. Feldman message for Warren Beatty, 25 June 1965, Feldman Collection.

126. Jean Renoir letter to Leslie Caron, 30 September 1965, Box 20, Folder 13, Jean Renoir Papers, UCLA Arts Library Special Collection, Los Angeles.

127. Warren Beatty transcript, 15 October 1990, Brunnetti Collection, Margaret Herrick Library, Academy of Motion Picture Arts and Sciences, Beverly Hills.

128. Jack Smight, interview with author, 24 August 2003, here and throughout; "Warren Beatty on Discretion, Valour, and Better Parts," *Films Illustrated,* May 1975.

129. Judy Klemesrud, "Warren Beatty — Back Where He Belongs?" *New York Times,* 13 March 1974.

130. Robert Towne, interview with author, 3 October 2003 and 18 March 2004, here and throughout.

131. Warren Beatty, *Film Night with Tony Bilbow,* BBC 2, October 1975, British Film Institute, London.

132. Garrett, *Evening Standard,* 15 September 1967.

133. Warren Beatty, San Francisco Film Festival, 25 April 2002.

134. *Films and Filming,* August 1975.

135. *Film Night.*

136. Jan Hodenfield, "Still Circling," *New York Post,* 15 February 1975.

137. Derek Malcolm, "Hair do," *Guardian,* 26 April 1975.

138. *New York Times,* 8 May 1966, no title, Beatty file, Academy Collection, Margaret Herrick Library, Beverly Hills.

139. *Hollywood Reporter,* 28 December 1965.

140. Jack Warner memo, 27 December 1965, Warner Brothers Collection, USC Cinema-Television Archives, Los Angeles [hereafter Warner Brothers Collection]; Jack Warner memo, 27 June 1966, Warner Brothers Collection.

141. Scrapbook of Jack Smight, courtesy of Alec Smight.

142. Dana Hodgson, interview with author, n.d.

143. Victor Lownes, interview with author, 27 October 2003.

144. Peter Evans, "Marriage to One Woman Takes Genius," *Daily Express,* 1 February 1966.

145. Clive Revill, interview with author, 7 August 2003.

146. Marion Rosenberg, interview with author, 21 September 2003.

147. Kevin Thomas, "Shirley's Quiet Role as an Activist," *Los Angeles Times,* 18 June 1968.

148. Clifford Terry, "Shirley MacLaine: Revved Up, Roarin', and Real," *Cosmopolitan,* August 1977.

149. Mal Vincent, "The Many Lives of Shirley MacLaine," *Virginian-Pilot,* 22 April 1996.

150. Bob Porter, "Bonnie and Clyde's Obscure Figures," *Dallas Times Herald,* 28 January 1968.

151. Stefan Kanfer, "Hollywood: The Shock of Freedom in Films," *Time,* 8 December 1967.

152. Maureen Dowd, "Bugsy in Love, On Stage and Off," *New York Times,* 8 December 1991.

153. Tom Carlile memo, 10 February 1965, *Kaleidoscope* file, Warner Brothers Collection.

154. Peter Evans, "Marriage to One Woman Takes Genius," *Daily Express,* 1 February 1966.

155. David Picker interview.

156. *Easy Riders* documentary.

157. Buck Henry, interview with author, 29 June 2003 and September 2004, here and throughout.

158. Warren Beatty letter to John Springer, 17 March 1966, Springer papers.

159. Michael Wilmington and Gerald Peary, "Warren Beatty," *Daily Cardinal*, 8 November 1971.

160. Brian Hutton, interview with author, 3 December 2003.

161. Roger Ebert, "Warren and Julie," *Chicago Sun*, 1 August 1971.

162. Warren Beatty, George Stevens tribute, Academy of Motion Picture Arts and Sciences, 2 October 2004; Outtakes, *George Stevens: A Filmmaker's Journey*, 28 October 1982, courtesy of George Stevens, Jr.

163. Madeleine Morgenstern, interview with author, 16 September 2003.

164. Ibid.

165. Peters, "Gigi Grows Up."

166. Levin, "Thank Heaven."

167. Robert Musel, "Warren Beatty Talks," *TV Guide*, 22 March 1969.

168. Reed, "Will the Real Warren Beatty . . ."

169. *Rolling Stone*, 1 April 1982; Parker, *Last Great Lover*.

170. Bob Jiras, interview with author, 16 September 1999.

171. Joseph Lewis, "What Ever Happened to Baby Natalie?" *Cosmopolitan*, November 1968.

172. Warren Beatty, San Francisco Film Festival, 25 April 2002.

173. Lester D. Friedman, ed., *Arthur Penn's Bonnie and Clyde* (Cambridge, UK: Cambridge University Press, 2000).

174. Ibid.

175. Labarthe, *Cahiers du Cinema* 196 (December 1967).

176. WB interview, BFI.

177. Will Hodgkinson, "Hard Time," *Guardian, The Guide*, 3–9 July 1999.

178. Goldstein, "Blasts from the Past"; *Films and Filming*, August 1975.

179. Goldstein, "Blasts from the Past."

180. Friedman, ed., *Arthur Penn's Bonnie and Clyde*.

181. *Daily Variety*, 21 June 1966; Tony Costello, interview with author, 27 April 1999.

182. D. Dedubovay, "A Couple of Flirts," *Courier-Mail*, 4 July 1987.

183. Henry Jaglom, interviews with author, June 1999, and Jaglom's journals, courtesy of Jaglom.

184. Theadora Van Runkle, interviews with author, 12 August 2003 and 1 September 2003, here and throughout.

185. Michel Thomas, interview with author, 13 June 2003.

186. George Christy, *Hollywood Reporter*, 19 September 1984; *Photoplay*, January 1972.

187. Goldstein, "Blasts from the Past."

188. Michael J. Pollard, interview with author, 11 July 2003.

189. Arthur Penn, interview with author, 20 October 1999; Goldstein, "Blasts from the Past."

190. Arthur Penn interview.

191. Tuesday Weld and Natasha Harz Anderson, interview with author, September 2003.

192. Florabel Muir, "Little Girl Grows Up," *Daily News*, 12 August 1966; Vernon Scott, "Whatever Happened to Anjanette Comer?" United Press International, 22 September 1981.

193. *Back Story: Bonnie and Clyde*, docuseries, American Movie Classics.

194. Catherine Getches, "The Original Pick-Up Artist," *Salon*, 3 July 2002.

195. Lewis, "What Ever Happened to Baby Natalie?"

196. John Hallowell, "I'm Going to Live My Life," *New York Times*, 9 March 1969; *Los Angeles Herald-Examiner*, 13 October 1974; Thomas Thompson, "Natalie Wood and Bob Wagner Get It Together Again," *Cosmopolitan*, August 1975; Lana Wood interview.

197. Tony Costello interview.

198. Robert Solo, interview with author, 18 August 2003.

199. Goldstein, "Blasts from the Past."

200. Stefan Kanfer, interview with author, 19 October 2003; Kanfer, "Hollywood, The Shock of Freedom."

201. Roger Ebert, "Warren and Julie," *Chicago Sun-Times*, 1 August 1971.

202. Goldstein, "Blasts from the Past."

203. Theadora Von Runkle interview, here and as follows.

204. Warner Brothers memo, 30 September 1966, Warner Brothers Collection.

205. Springer letter, 11 December 1970, Springer papers.

206. Philip Wuntch, "Gene Hackman Happy with His Career," *Chicago Tribune*, 14 November 1985.

207. Gene Hackman interview, *Photoplay*, July 1968.

208. Wuntch, "Gene Hackman Happy."

209. Goldstein, "Blasts from the Past."

210. Mike Selsman, interview with author, 16 September 1999.

211. Arthur Penn interview; Faye Dunaway, *Looking for Gatsby* (New York: Simon & Schuster, 1995).

212. *Back Story*.

213. Ty Burr, "The Long Road to '8 Mile,'" *Boston Globe*, 3 November 2002.

214. *Newsweek*, March 1968.

215. Estelle Parsons, interview with author, 27 October 2003, here and throughout.

216. Jack Warner Collection, USC.

217. Springer letter, 30 October 1972, Springer papers.

218. Barbara Walters, *How to Talk with Practically Anybody About Practically Anything* (New York: Doubleday, 1970).

219. Kathleen Carroll, "Beatty Ducks Answers but Quacks Questions," *New York Daily News*, 25 September 1966.

220. Goldstein, "Blasts from the Past."

221. Gene Hackman interview, *Photoplay*, July 1968.

222. Don Stokes, interview with author, 16 September 2003.

223. Ibid.

224. Hanson, "Interview with Warren Beatty."

225. Ibid.

226. Dean Tavoularis, interview with author, September 2003.

227. Goldstein, "Blasts from the Past."

228. Morgan Fairchild, interview with author, 10 September 2003, here and throughout.

229. *Back Story*; Dunaway, *Looking for Gatsby*.

230. Dunaway, *Looking for Gatsby*.

231. Ibid.

232. Robert Benton interview.

233. WB interview, BFI.

234. Sidney Skolsky, *Hollywood Citizen News*, 13 October 1967.

235. Don Safran, "Show Biz," *Dallas Morning News*, 7 December 1966.

236. Philip Wuntch, "Warren's Love Affair," *Dallas Morning News*, 16 October 1994.

237. *Movie Scene*, March 1985.

238. MacEwen letter to Warren Beatty, 2 November 1966, Warner Brothers Collection.

239. Peter Biskind, "She Stars, He Stars," *Vanity Fair*, February 2000.

240. Stephanie Zaharoudis and Lois Romanoost, "Personalities," *Washington Post*, 4 December 1981.

241. Todd Gold, "Warren Beatty," *Us*, 3 April 2000.

242. Earl Wilson, "Warren Beatty—Producer," *New York Post*, 10 August 1967.

243. Yevgeny Yevtushenko, interview with author, 2 December 2003, here and throughout.

244. Wayne Cline, interview with author, 23 April 2003.

245. *Dallas Morning News*, 29 December 1966.

246. Peer J. Oppenheimer, "Warren Beatty," *Family Weekly*, 24 March 1968.

247. "Beatty Raps," *Eye*, March 1968.

248. Warner Brothers Collection.

249. Friedman, ed., *Arthur Penn's Bonnie and Clyde*.

250. *Los Angeles Times*, 14 August 1997.

251. Friedman, ed., *Arthur Penn's Bonnie and Clyde*.

252. Martha Hyer Wallis, interview with author, 6 August 2003.

253. Goldstein, "Blasts from the Past."

254. Rock Demers, interview with author, 9 October 2003.

255. Dean Tavoularis interview.

256. Wilmington and Peary, "Warren Beatty."

257. Norman Mailer, "The Warren Report," *Vanity Fair*, November 1991.

258. Springer letter, 11 December 1970, Springer papers.

259. Wilmington and Peary, "Warren Beatty."

260. Ibid.; Wilmington and Peary, "Interview with Warren Beatty."

261. Jeffrey Wells, "10 Interviews That Shook Hollywood," *Movieline*, April 1992.

262. C. Robert Jennings, "Welcome Back Shirley!" *Los Angeles Times West*, 16 March 1969.

263. Warren Beatty, *The Dick Cavett Show*, November 1972.

264. Nashawaty, "The Warren Report."

265. Bosley Crowther, "Shoot-'em-up Film Opens World Fête," *New York Times*, 7 August 1967.

266. Joe Morgenstern, interview with author, 27 August 2003.

267. Bosley Crowther, "'Bonnie and Clyde' Arrives," *New York Times*, 14 August 1967.

268. Roger Ebert, "Interview, Warren Beatty," *Chicago Sun-Times*, 24 September 1967.

269. Ibid.

270. Joseph Morgenstern, "The Thin Red Line," *Newsweek*, 28 August 1968.

271. Ebert, "Interview, Warren Beatty."

272. Ibid.

273. Hodgkinson, "Hard Time."

274. Keith Shelton, "Capacity Crowd to see 'Bonnie and Clyde,'" *Denton Record-Chronicle*, 14 September 1967.

275. Warren Beatty, George Stevens tribute, 2 October 2004.

276. DeCola, "Words Take Truth."

277. Garrett, *Evening Standard*, 15 September 1967.

278. Bill Rives, "Views," *Denton Record-Chronicle*, 15 September 1967.

279. Stefan Kanfer interview.

280. Kanfer, "Hollywood, the Shock of Freedom."

281. Bosley Crowther, *Reruns: Fifty Memorable Films* (New York: G. P. Putnam's Sons, 1978).

282. Patrick Goldstein, *Los Angeles Times*, 25 August 1997.

283. John Weisman, "Success Has Mellowed Arrogant Mr. Beatty," *Detroit Free Press*, 25 July 1971.

284. Muriel Davidson, "Warren Beatty: Public Image vs. Private Man," *Good Housekeeping*, August 1970.

285. "Shirley MacLaine As Sweet Charity," *Look*, 9 July 1968.

286. Warren Beatty, *The Oprah Winfrey Show*, Harpo Productions, 20 December 1991.

ACT FOUR: THE PRO

1. Donald Zee, "Sailing on the Clyde," *Daily Mirror*, 18 March 1968.

2. John Weisman, "Success Has Mellowed Arrogant Mr. Beatty," *Detroit Free Press*, 25 July 1971.

3. Warren Beatty, *The Dick Cavett Show*, November 1972.

4. *Bravo Profiles*, "Warren Beatty," May 1998.

5. Senator Edward Kennedy, interview with author, 16 December 2003.

6. Bill Rosendahl, interview with author, 30 April 2003.

7. Jan Hodenfield, "Still Circling," *New York Post*, 15 February 1975.

8. Bill Zehme, "Being Warren Beatty," *Rolling Stone*, 31 May 1990.

9. Roman Polanski, *Roman* (New York: William Morrow & Co, 1984).

10. Carolyn See, "Two Women with Two (Sad) Stories," *Los Angeles Times*, 3 December 1985.

11. Gary Younge, "Rebel with a Cause," *The Guardian*, 23 January 1999.

12. Jay Carr, "Dick Tracy Speaks," *Boston Globe*, 10 June 1990.

13. Warren Beatty, interviewed by Christopher Cook for the British Film Institute, 6 July 1990, British Film Institute, London [hereafter cited as "WB interview, BFI"].

14. Charles Champlin, "Beatty and the Beast," *Los Angeles Times*, 30 January 1976.

15. Warren Beatty letter to Jean Howard, 14 June 1968, Jean Howard Collection, Box 3, Folder 4, University of Wyoming, Laramie, Wyo.

16. WB interview, BFI.

17. Muriel Davidson, "Warren Beatty: Public Image vs. Private Man," *Good Housekeeping*, August 1970.

18. Charles K. Feldman Collection, Louis B. Mayer Library, American Film Institute, Los Angeles [hereafter cited as "Feldman Collection"].

19. Ibid.

20. Peter Biskind, "The Man Who Minted Style," *Vanity Fair*, April 2003.

21. Cleveland Amory, "Warren Beatty," *This Week*, 12 November 1967.

22. Rita Riggs, interview with author, 3 September 2003.

23. "Haunting Icon of a Hollow Decade," *The Observer*, 16 July 1995.

24. Joan Goodman, "Julie Christie Strides On," *Cosmopolitan*, July 1982.

25. Younge, "Rebel with a Cause."

26. Warren Beatty outtakes, *George Stevens: A Filmmaker's Journey*, 28 October 1982, courtesy of George Stevens, Jr.

27. Ibid.

28. Warren Beatty, George Stevens tribute, Academy of Motion Picture Arts and Sciences, Beverly Hills, 2 October 2004.

29. George Stevens, Jr., interview with author, 3 September 2003.

30. Springer letter to Henry Ehrlich, 11 December 1970, John Springer papers, courtesy of Gary Springer and June Springer [hereafter cited as "Springer papers"].

31. Springer letter to Warren Beatty, 14 January 1970, Springer papers.

32. Davidson, "Warren Beatty."

33. Jessica Maguire, interview with author, 28 September 2003.

34. Sandy Whitelaw, interview with author, 9 May 2002; Thomas Thompson, "There's Something Awfully Peculiar About Warren Beatty These Days," *Los Angeles*, March 1975; Melvyn Bragg, *Richard Burton: A Life* (Boston: Little, Brown & Co., 1988).

35. Warren Beatty, George Stevens tribute.

36. Paul Mansfield, "Miss Julie," *Homes and Gardens*, September 1987.

37. Jeannette Smyth, "The 'Shampoo' Man and Warren Beatty," *Washington Post*, 13 March 1975.

38. Derek Malcolm, "Hair do," *Guardian*, 26 April 1975.

39. Smyth, "The 'Shampoo' Man."

40. Warren Beatty, San Francisco Film Festival, 25 April 2002.

41. Peter Biskind, "Chronicle of a Life Untold," *Premiere*, January 1992.

42. "In Memoriam: Alexander A. MacLeod," *Human Relations* 10, no. 18, Ontario Human Rights Commission, May 1970.

43. Brian D. Johnson, *Wild Nights: 25 Years of Festival Fever* (Random House Canada, 2000).

44. Peter Feibleman, interview with author, 20 November 2003.

45. Jeremy Pikser, interview with author, 29 September 2003.

46. "Shirley MacLaine as Sweet Charity," *Look*, 9 July 1968.

47. David Foster letter, 5 May 1969, *McCabe & Mrs. Miller* file, USC Cinema-TV, Los Angeles.

48. David Foster, interview with author, 3 September 2003, here and throughout.

49. Weisman, "Success Has Mellowed."

50. Ibid.

51. Springer letter to Henry Ehrlich, 11 December 1970, Springer papers.

52. Jacoba Atlas and Ann Guerin, "Robert Altman, Julie Christie and Warren Beatty Make the Western Real," *Show*, August 1972.

53. Michael Wilmington and Gerald Peary, "Warren Beatty," *Daily Cardinal*, 8 November 1971.

54. Anne Sidaris-Reeves, interview with author, fall 2004.

55. *Easy Riders, Raging Bulls*, produced by Fremantle Corp. and BBC, 2003.

56. Roger Ebert, "McCabe & Mrs. Miller," *Chicago Sun-Times*, 14 November 1999.

57. Davidson, "Warren Beatty."

58. Mike Wilmington and Gerald Peary, "Interview with Warren Beatty," *The Velvet Light Trap* (Winter 1972).

59. Phil Stern, interview with author, 9 September 2003.

60. Goldie Hawn, interview with author, 19 December 2003, here and throughout.

61. Marshall Bell, interview with author, fall 2004.

62. *New York Times*, 17 March 1974; Lyn Tornabene, "Who Can Resist Warren Beatty?" *Cosmopolitan*, January 1975; "Star Warren Beatty Goes Back to Films," unsourced Richmond newspaper, 20 April 1975, Richmond Public Library, Warren Beatty folder; "Warren Beatty on Discretion, Valour, and Better Parts," *Films Illustrated*, May 1975.

63. Thompson, "There's Something Awfully Peculiar."

64. *Evening Standard*, 18 April 1975.

65. Warren Beatty, *Tonight*, NBC, 20 March 1975.

66. Springer quote of Warren Beatty's statement, 26 June 1972, Springer papers.

67. Wilmington and Peary, "Warren Beatty."

68. Senator George McGovern, interview with author, 4 September 2003.

69. *New York Times*, 17 March 1974.

70. Barbara Howar, "Rebels with a Cause," *V-Life*, Oct./Nov. 2004.

71. *New York Post*, 28 November 1970.

72. Gary Hart, interview with author, 7 November 2003, here and throughout.

73. Ronald Brownstein, *The Power and the Glitter* (New York: Random House, 1993).

74. Shirley MacLaine, National Film Theater, taped interview, 28 March 1971, courtesy of British Film Institute, London.

75. Brownstein, *The Power and the Glitter*.

76. Britt Ekland, *True Britt* (New York: Simon & Schuster, 1984); Britt Ekland, "Britt and Beatty," *Us*, 5 January 1982.

77. Andrew Billen, "Warren Beatty: The Andrew Billen Interview," *Evening Standard*, 3 February 1999.

78. Henry Kimelman, interview with author, 16 May 2004.

79. Davidson, "Warren Beatty."

80. Mansfield, "Miss Julie."

81. *Daily Mail*, 18 April 1975.

82. Warren Beatty, *Tonight*, NBC, 20 March 1975.

83. Springer letter to Warren Beatty, 20 April 1972, Springer papers.

84. *New York Times*, 17 March 1974.

85. Ibid.

86. Robert J. Emery, *The Directors* (New York: Allworth Press, 2003).

87. *Hollywood Reporter*, 25 June 1972.

88. Warren Beatty, *Film Night with Tony Bilbow*, BBC 2, 30 October 1975, British Film Institute, London.

89. Gordon Willis, interview with author, n.d.

90. Craig Baxley, interview with author, 19 October 2003.

91. Warren Beatty, *Charlie Rose*, CNN, 8 May 1998.

92. Thompson, "There's Something Awfully Peculiar."

93. Verne O'Hara, interview with author, 21 May 2003.

94. United Press International, 29 October 1988.

95. *Easy Riders*.

96. Billen, "Warren Beatty."

97. Robert Towne, interviews with author, 3 October 2003 and 18 March 2004; "Warren Beatty on Discretion."

98. Warren Beatty, *Dinah!*, 27 June 1975.

99. Gordon Gow, "Warren Beatty," *Films and Filming*, August 1975.

100. "Behind the Scenes," *Movieline*, June 2002.

101. Chris Nashawaty, "The Warren Report," *Entertainment Weekly*, March 2000.

102. Warren Beatty, transcript, 24 February 1975, *Village Voice* interview, courtesy of British Film Institute, London; *Easy Riders* documentary.

103. Helle Melchior Wengrow, interview with author, 18 September 2003.

104. Carrie Fisher, interview with author, 1 December 2003.

105. Stephen Farber and Marc Green, *Hollywood on the Couch* (New York: William Morrow, 1993).

106. John Brady, *The Craft of the Screenwriter* (New York: Simon & Schuster, 1981).

107. Hodenfield, "Still Circling."

108. Alan Ebert, "Warren Beatty," *Ladies' Home Journal*, April 1976.

109. Tim Vreeland, interview with author, 8 October 2003, here and throughout.

110. Carole Eastman, interview with author, 5 January 2004, here and throughout.

111. Tim Vreeland interview.

112. Fiona Macdonald Hull, "Warren's Women," *News of the World*, 10 September 1978; *Sunday Mail*, 20 June 2004.

113. Roderick Gilchrist, "'Shampoo' Beatty," *Daily Mail*, 18 April 1975.

114. Jennifer Lee, *Tarnished Angel* (New York: HarperCollins, 1993).

115. Joan Dew, "Warren Beatty: More Than a Lover," *Redbook*, May 1974; Barbara Wilkins, "'Even the Promiscuous Feel Pain,'" *People*, 14 April 1975.

116. Gilchrist, "'Shampoo' Beatty."

117. Maureen Dowd, "Bugsy in Love, On Stage and Off," *New York Times*, 8 December 1991.

118. Jim Jerome, "Getting It All Together," *People*, 20 May 1991.

119. Mike Nichols, interview with author, 5 December 2003, here and throughout.

120. Warren Beatty, *Film Night*.

121. *New York Times*, 21 April 1976.

122. Malcolm, "Hair do."

123. Thompson, "There's Something Awfully Peculiar."

124. "Warren Beatty on Discretion."

125. Warren Beatty, San Francisco Film Festival, 25 April 2002.

126. "Star Warren Beatty Goes Back to Films."

127. Amy Longsdorf, "Love Affair Could be Bening-Beatty Story," *Morning Call*, 16 October 1994.

128. Helen Dorsey, "Warren Beatty," *Family Weekly*, 6 April 1975.

129. Fiona Macdonald Hull, "Warren's Women," *News of the World*, 10 September 1978.

130. *Los Angeles*, June 1990.

131. Tom Green, "Beatty on the Beat," *USA Today*, 12 June 1990.

132. Hull, "Warren's Women."

133. Paul Weston, "Queensland Film Buff," *Sunday Mail*, 20 June 2004.

134. Hull, "Warren's Women."

135. Ibid.

136. Adrian Hodges, "The Telephone Calls from Beatty That Changed Two Men's Careers," *Screen International*, 25 February 1982.

137. Warren Beatty, San Francisco Film Festival, 25 April 2002.

138. Charles Eastman interview; *Ladies' Home Journal*, October 1978.

139. Jeremy Pikser interview; WB interview, BFI.

140. WB interview, BFI.

141. Charles Champlin, "Warren Beatty: Two Sides to a Hollywood Story," *Los Angeles Times*, 28 January 1979.

142. Warren Beatty, *The Oprah Winfrey Show*, Harpo Productions, 20 December 1991.

143. *Rolling Stone*, May 1990.

144. Jeremy Pikser interview.

145. *Ladies' Home Journal*, October 1978.

146. Warren Beatty, *Aspel & Company*, 21 March 1992, London Weekend Television, courtesy of British Film Institute, London.

147. Ibid.

148. Lindsley Parsons, Jr., interview with author, 4 September 2003.

149. Champlin, "Warren Beatty."

150. Buck Henry, interview with author, 29 June and September 2003, here and throughout.

151. Norman Mailer, "The Warren Report," *Vanity Fair*, November 1991.

152. Champlin, "Warren Beatty."

153. Mansfield, "Miss Julie."

154. Michelle Phillips to author, 7 August 2003.

155. Julie Christie to author, December 2003.

156. Hull, "Warren's Women."

157. Donnie Radcliffe and Nancy Collins, "A Turning Point Weekend," *Washington Post*, 15 November 1977.

158. Bobby Shriver, "I'll Bet You Think This Story's About You," *Los Angeles Times*, 27 June 1978; *Newsweek*, 3 July 1978.

159. Jack Kroll, "Thoroughly Modern Diane," *Newsweek*, 15 February 1982.

160. Dana Kennedy, "Falling in Love? It's All Just an Act," *Los Angeles Times*, 14 December 2003.

161. Warren Beatty, *Aspel & Company*.

162. Kennedy, "Falling in Love?"; Diane Keaton, *Intimate Portrait*, Lifetime.

163. Kennedy, "Falling in Love?"

164. Ibid.

165. Mailer, "The Warren Report."

166. Robert Evans, *The Kid Stays in the Picture* (New York: Hyperion, 1994).

167. Kennedy, "Falling in Love?"

168. Ibid.

169. Ibid.

170. Clive Jacobs, "Secrets of Seduction," *Screen Stories*, December 1976.

171. Jeremy Pikser interview.

172. Hodges, "The Telephone Calls."

173. "Newsreel," *Newsweek*, December 1981.

174. WB interview, BFI.

175. Warren Beatty, San Francisco Film Festival, 25 April 2002.

176. Hodges, "The Telephone Calls."

177. Susan Morse Durfee and Mike Durfee, interview with author, 8 September 2002.

178. Hodges, "The Telephone Calls."

179. Yevgeny Yevtushenko, interview with author, 2 December 2003; Tibor Sands, interview with author, 11 May 2003.

180. Kiki Kosinski, interview with author, 4 November 2003.

181. "Hackman Knows His Limitations," *Los Angeles Herald-Examiner*, 29 March 1981.

182. Jack Nicholson interview, *Easy Jet InFlight*, 17 December 2003.

183. Jean-Claude Loiseau, "Le Defi de Warren Beatty," *Premiere*, October 1990.

184. Ira Beaty letter to Westhampton, 5 September 1979, courtesy of Betty S. Williams.

185. Warren Beatty, Hollywood Foreign Press Association, 15 October 1990, Brunnetti Collection, Margaret Herrick Library, Academy of Motion Picture Arts and Sciences, Beverly Hills.

186. Diane Keaton, *Intimate Portrait*.

187. Kroll, "Thoroughly Modern Diane."

188. Jennifer Frey, "A Star's Laugh Lines," *Washington Post*, 11 December 2003.

189. *Entertainment Weekly*, 14 November 2003.

190. Warren Beatty, *Today*, NBC, 20 December 1991.

191. Aaron Latham, "Warren Beatty, Seriously," *Rolling Stone*, 1 April 1982.

192. Nancy Mills, "I Am Woman," *New York Daily News*, 13 February 2000.

193. *TV Guide*, 26 May 2001.

194. Nigel Wooll, interview with author, 30 May 2003.

195. Barry "Baz" Richardson, interview with author, 15 December 2003.

196. *Rolling Stone*, 1 April 1982.

197. *TV Guide*, 26 May 2001.

198. Diane Keaton, *Intimate Portrait*.

199. Latham, "Warren Beatty."

200. Ibid.

201. Sharmagne Sylbert, interview with author, 26 August 2003.

202. *Guardian*, 12 May 1998.

203. Janice Dickinson, "Between the Sheets," *Toronto Sun*, 12 November 2002.

204. Kroll, "Thoroughly Modern Diane."

205. Brownstein, *The Power and the Glitter*.

206. Biskind, "Chronicle."

207. Brad Darrach, "Dustin and Warren," *People*, 25 May 1987.

208. Kennedy, "Falling in Love?"

209. Diane Keaton, *Intimate Portrait*; *You Magazine*, 23 August 1987.

210. Kennedy, "Falling in Love?"

211. Gavin Smith, "A Question of Control," *Film Comment*, Jan./Feb. 1992.

212. Michael J. Pollard, interview with author, 11 July 2003; Nashawaty, "The Warren Report."

213. *Rolling Stone*, May 1990.

214. Aljean Harmetz, *New York Times*, 28 December 1981.

215. Hodges, "The Telephone Calls."

216. WB interview, BFI.

217. Lyn Hirschberg, "Warren Beatty Is Trying to Say Something," *New York Times*, 10 May 1998.

218. Peter Goddard, *Toronto Star*, 10 June 1990.

219. Carr, "Dick Tracy Speaks."

220. Todd Gold, "Warren Beatty," *Us*, 3 April 2000.

221. Jacobs, "Secrets of Seduction."

222. Carr, "Dick Tracy Speaks."

223. Brownstein, *The Power and the Glitter*.

224. Ekland, "Britt and Beatty."

225. David Stenn, interview with author, n.d.

226. David Stenn, from Stenn's journal, 22 January 1985; *The Lives of Lillian Hellman*, produced by Julian Schlossberg, 1999, Thirteen/WNET and Castle Hills Productions.

227. David Applefield, *London Financial Times*, 1 September 2001.

228. Holly Millea, "Enduring Isabelle," *Premiere*, April 1996.

229. Ibid.

230. Ibid.

231. David Rensin, *Playboy* interview with Shirley MacLaine, September 1984.

232. Ibid.

233. Jacobs, "Secrets of Seduction."

234. Melina Gerosa, "Shirley's Lucky Stars," *Ladies' Home Journal*, June 1995.

235. "The Other Star in the Family," *Time*, 14 May 1984.

236. Shirley MacLaine, *Dancing in the Light* (New York: Bantam Books, 1985).

237. *Richmond Surroundings*, 1 July 1984.

238. Shirley MacLaine, *Dance While You Can* (New York: Bantam Books, 1991).

239. Jacobs, "Secrets of Seduction,"

240. Terry Semel, San Francisco Film Festival, 25 April 2002.

241. Patrick Goldstein, *Los Angeles Times*, 24 May 1987.

242. Charles Champlin, "Beatty Sings a Song of 'Ishtar,'" *Los Angeles Times*, 26 April 1987.

243. Dustin Hoffman, *Larry King Live*, CNN, 8 November 1997.

244. Gold, "Warren Beatty."

245. Nigel Wooll interview.

246. Ibid.

247. Darrach, "Dustin and Warren."

248. Paul Williams, interviews with author, 11 December and 15 December 2003.

249. Carr, "Dick Tracy Speaks."

250. Bill Zehme, "Being Warren Beatty."

251. Michael Shelden, "I Was Always an Oddball," *Daily Telegraph*, 18 February 2000.

252. Douglas Thompson, "Warren Beatty Has It All," *Mail on Sunday You Magazine*, 15 July 1990.

253. Jim Robbins, "Actors and Filmmakers Honor Elia Kazan at Museum Benefit," *Daily Variety*, 28 January 1987.

254. *Rolling Stone*, 31 May 1990.

255. Billen, "Warren Beatty."

256. *Rolling Stone*, 31 May 1990.

257. Brownstein, *The Power and the Glitter*.

ACT FIVE: REDEMPTION

1. Jack Mathews, "A Day and Night with Warren Beatty," *Los Angeles Times*, 10 June 1990.

2. *Wall Street Journal*, March 1989; *BusinessWeek*, 30 November 1987.

3. Shirley MacLaine, *Dance While You Can* (New York: Bantam Books, 1991).

4. Gavin Smith, "A Question of Control," *Film Comment*, Jan./Feb. 1992.

5. Gene Siskel, "Beatty's Dick Tracy," *Chicago Tribune*, 10 June 1990.

6. Peter Biskind, "The Magnificent Obsessions of Warren Beatty," *Premiere*, July 1990.

7. David Eimer, "Cover Story: Warren Beatty," *Sunday Times* (London), 24 January 1998.

8. Philip Wuntch, "Warren's Love Affair," *Dallas Morning News*, 16 October 1994.

9. Warren Beatty, *60 Minutes II*, CBS, 10 March 1999.

10. Georgina Howell, "Adjani Anew," *Vogue*, December 1989; Holly Millea, "Enduring Isabelle," *Premiere*, April 1996.

11. Siri Dharma Galliano, interview with author, 29 April 2003.

12. Maggie Kusik, interview with author, 3 January 2004; David Ansen with Pamela Abramson, "Tracymania," *Newsweek*, 25 June 1990.

13. Lyn Hirschberg, "Warren Beatty Is Trying to Say Something," *New York Times*, 10 May 1998.

14. Gregg Kilday, "Strip Show," *Entertainment Weekly*, 15 June 1990.

15. Mervyn Rothstein, "Stephen Sondheim Writes On," *New York Times*, 27 November 1989.

16. Smith, "A Question."

17. Biskind, "The Magnificent Obsessions."

18. Chris Nashawaty, "The Warren Report," *Entertainment Weekly*, March 2000.

19. Stephen Rebello, "The Dark Romance of James Toback," *Movieline*, October 1991.

20. Joan Cohen interview with author, n.d.

21. Ivor Davis, "Who Are Those Mask Men?" *Us*, 9 July 1990.

22. *Daily Mirror*, 10 June 1990. British Film Institute Collection, London.

23. Jeffrey Katzenberg, interview with author, fall 2003.

24. *Daily Mirror*, 10 June 1990.

25. Ibid.

26. Jay Carr, "With Two Movies and Two Babies," *Boston Globe*, 16 October 1994.

27. Rebello, "The Dark Romance."

28. Brian D. Johnson, *Brave Films Wild Nights* (Random House Canada, 2000).

29. Nancy Collins, "The Real MacLaine," *Vanity Fair,* March 1991.

30. Dean LaManna, "Shirley MacLaine Down to Earth," *Ladies Home Journal,* May 1994.

31. Warren Beatty, *Entertainment Tonight,* Paramount Television, June 1990; *USA Today,* 10 June 1990.

32. Mathews, "A Day and Night"; *Daily Variety,* 20 June 1990.

33. Bill Zehme, "Being Warren Beatty," *Rolling Stone,* 31 May 1990.

34. Richard Corliss, "Extra! Tracy Is Tops," *Time,* 18 June 1990.

35. Warren Beatty, *Aspel & Company,* 21 March 1992, London Weekend Television, British Film Institute, London.

36. Megan Rosenfeld, "Warren Beatty, Bringing Up 'Bugsy,'" *Washington Post,* 19 December 1991.

37. Peter Biskind, "She Stars, He Stars," *Vanity Fair,* February 2000.

38. Siskel, "Beatty's Dick Tracy."

39. Collins, "The Real MacLaine."

40. Jack Mathews, "Leaked Disney Memo," *Los Angeles Times,* 31 January 1991.

41. Peter Biskind, "Chronicle of a Life Untold," *Premiere,* January 1992.

42. Iain Blair, "Bugsy's Real Appeal," *Chicago Tribune,* 15 December 1991.

43. Jack Mathews, "Bugsy, C'est Moi," *Newsday,* 15 December 1991.

44. Richard Schickel, "A Killer Goes to Hollywood," *Time,* 9 December 1991.

45. Siskel, "Beatty's Dick Tracy."

46. Blair, "Bugsy's Real Appeal."

47. Bob Strauss, "Bugsy Is Beatty's '90s 'Bonnie and Clyde,'" *Chicago Tribune,* 27 December 1991.

48. Milos Forman, interview with author, 19 June 2003.

49. Warren Beatty, *CBS This Morning,* 25 December 1991.

50. *The New Yorker,* 19 November 1990.

51. Rebello, "The Dark Romance."

52. Biskind, "She Stars, He Stars."

53. Warren Beatty, *The Oprah Winfrey Show,* Harpo Productions, 20 December 1991; Ronald Rynning, "Another Affair to Remember," *Film Review,* October 1995; Mal Vincent, "Still Faithful After All Three Years," *Virginian-Pilot,* 22 October 1994.

54. Warren Beatty, *Today,* NBC, 20 December 1991.

55. Todd Gold, "Warren Beatty," *Us,* 3 April 2000.

56. Patrick Pacheco, "Love Connection," *Newsday,* 16 October 1994; *Daily Telegraph,* January 15, 2000.

57. Warren Beatty, *CBS News,* 24 October 1992.

58. *Showbiz Today,* CNN, 18 October 1994.

59. Pacheco, "Love Connection."

60. *Eye to Eye,* 6 October 1994.

61. Dominick Danne, "Love Story," *Vanity Fair,* September 1994.

62. Barry Koltnow, "Beatty at Peace in Domesticity," *Orange County Register,* 20 December 1991.

63. Biskind, "She Stars, He Stars."

64. Tom Green, "Annette Bening's Big Year," *USA Today,* 31 January 1991.

65. *Rolling Stone,* 16 May 1991.

66. Chris Nashawaty, "The Warren Report," *Entertainment Weekly,* March 2000.

67. Rebello, "The Dark Romance."

68. Joseph Cosko, Jr., interview with author, 31 December 2003.

69. Maureen Dowd, "Bugsy in Love, On Stage and Off," *New York Times*, 8 December 1991.

70. Vincent, "Still Faithful."

71. Wuntch, "Warren's Love Affair."

72. Laurence Chollet, "An Ace of a Director," *Bergen Record*, 17 December 1991.

73. Hilary De Vries, "Regarding Annette," *Los Angeles Times*, 7 July 1991; Pacheco, "Love Connection."

74. Biskind, "She Stars, He Stars."

75. Ibid.

76. Warren Beatty and Annette Bening, 20/20, ABC, 6 October 1994; *Eye*, December 1994.

77. Vincent, "Still Faithful."

78. Jeanne Wolf, "I'm a Mom First," *Ladies' Home Journal*, September 2003; Pacheco, "Love Connection."

79. Elaine Dutka, "The Aura of Annette," *Los Angeles Times*, 21 February 1999.

80. Biskind, "She Stars, He Stars."

81. Lloyd Grove, "Warren Beatty and the End of an Era," *Washington Post*, 17 July 1991.

82. Ruthe Stein, "Singles," *Orange County Register*, 4 August 1991.

83. Dowd, "Bugsy in Love."

84. William Arnold, "Beatty and Bening," *Seattle Post-Intelligencer*, 16 December 1991.

85. Katie Couric and Warren Beatty, *Today*, NBC, 20 December 1991.

86. Clive Jacobs, "Secrets of Seduction," *Screen Stories*, December 1976.

87. Koltnow, "Beatty at Peace."

88. Pacheco, "Love Connection."

89. Annette Bening and Warren Beatty, *The Oprah Winfrey Show*, Harpo Productions, 21 October 1994.

90. Warren Beatty, *Aspel & Company*.

91. Phyllis Posnick, "Father Figure," *Vogue*, June 1992.

92. John Preston, "Warren's Peace," *Sunday Telegraph* (London), 1 March 1992.

93. Wuntch, "Warren's Love Affair."

94. Ibid.

95. *Ladies' Home Journal*, May 1994.

96. Warren Beatty, *The Oprah Winfrey Show*, ABC, 30 December 1999.

97. *CBS News*, 24 October 1992; Dominic Dunne, "Love Story."

98. Jonathan Alter, "A Family Affair," *Sunday Express Magazine* (London), 6 November 1994.

99. Warren Beatty, *David Frost*, PBS, 28 February 1992.

100. Cindy Pearlman, "An Affair of the Heart," *Vancouver Sun*, 21 October 1994.

101. Gary Arnold, "So Much in Common," *Washington Times*, 23 October 1994.

102. Amy Longsdorf, "Love Affair Could be Bening-Beatty Story," *Morning Call*, 16 October 1994.

103. Pacheco, "Love Connection,"

104. Vincent, "Still Faithful."

105. Carr, "With Two Movies."

106. Dominic Dunne, "Love Story."

107. Rynning, "Another Affair"; Warren Beatty, "Katharine Hepburn," *Entertainment Weekly*, 6 January 2004.

108. Carr, "With Two Movies."

109. John Hartl, "Actor Warren Beatty Breathes New Life into an Old 'Love Affair,'" *Seattle Times*, 18 October 1994.

110. Arnold, "So Much in Common."
111. Michael Sragow, "Return of the Native," *New Times*, 3–9 September 1998.
112. Biskind, "The Magnificent Obsessions."
113. Ibid.
114. Glenn Gordon Caron, interview with author, 7 February 2004, here and throughout.
115. *Entertainment Weekly*, 17 December 1993.
116. Jennet Conant, "Bringing Up Beattys," *Redbook*, October 1994.
117. Warren Beatty, *Charlie Rose*, CNN, 8 May 1998.
118. Longsdorf, "Love Affair."
119. Patricia Barry, interview with author, 3 April 2002.
120. Beatty, "Katharine Hepburn."
121. Annette Bening, *The Oprah Winfrey Show*, Harpo Productions, 21 October 1994.
122. Alter, "A Family Affair."
123. Terry Semel, San Francisco Film Festival, 25 April 2002.
124. Norman Mailer, "The Warren Report," *Vanity Fair*, November 1991.
125. Gold, "Warren Beatty."
126. Bart Mills, "Tunes of Endearment," *Los Angeles Times*, 19 November 1995.
127. Donna Hanover, "Shirley MacLaine," *Good Housekeeping*, January 1997.
128. Conant, "Bringing Up Beattys."
129. Alter, "A Family Affair."
130. Vincent, "Still Faithful."
131. Janet Maslin, "A Romeo Plays a Romeo, Hmm," *New York Times*, 21 October 1994.
132. Lisa Schwarzbaum, "Love Affair," *Entertainment Weekly*, 7 April 1995.
133. Pacheco, "Love Connection."
134. Barbara Walters, e-mail to author.
135. Margot Dougherty, "The Lady Vanquishes," *Los Angeles Times*, 1 March 2000.
136. Corie Brown, "No Love Affair," *Premiere*, February 1995.
137. Posnick, "Father Figure."
138. Ronald Brownstein, "The Man Who Would Be Kingmaker," *Los Angeles Times*, 28 June 1987.
139. Stanley K. Sheinbaum, interview with author, fall 2003.
140. Barry Koltnow, "Marriage to a Notorious Playboy Makes a Sense of Humor Handy," *Orange County Register*, 18 May 1998.
141. Aaron Sorkin, interview with author, fall 2003.
142. Senator John McCain, interview with author, fall 2003.
143. Biskind, "She Stars, He Stars."
144. Jonathan Alter, "Beatty Goes Bonkers," *Newsweek*, 18 May 1998.
145. Ibid.
146. *Guardian*, 12 May 1998.
147. Jonathan Alter, "Beatty Goes Bonkers."
148. Donna Britt, "Try Again, Warren Beatty, You Missed," *Washington Post*, 22 May 1998.
149. Julia Toppin and Kathy Greene, "The Riper the Berry," *The Voice*, 25 January 1999.
150. Chollet, "An Ace of a Director."
151. Lonnie Harris, "Beatty Campaigns for 'Bulworth,'" *UCLA Daily Bruin*, 14 May 1998.
152. Warren Beatty, San Francisco Film Festival, 25 April 2002.
153. Gold, "Warren Beatty."
154. Wolf, "I'm a Mom First."
155. "Warren Takes the Rap for a Snipe at Politics," *Daily Telegraph*, 16 January 1999.
156. Fred Roos, interview with author, 4 September 2003.

157. Warren Beatty, San Francisco Film Festival, 25 April 2002.
158. Gold, "Warren Beatty."
159. *Hollywood Reporter*, 16 July 1998.
160. Fred Topel, Avanstar Communications, 23 September 2001.
161. Tracy May, interview with author, 14 May 2003.
162. Bill Hillsman, interview with author, fall 2003.
163. Marshall Bell, interview with author, fall 2003.
164. Wolf, "I'm a Mom First."
165. Gold, "Warren Beatty."
166. Jeremy Pikser interview.
167. Alter, "A Family Affair."
168. *Hollywood Reporter*, 19 September 1984.
169. Marc Malkin, "Q&A with Shirley MacLaine," *E Online*, E! 15 July 2004.
170. Warren Beatty, San Francisco Film Festival, 25 April 2002 ("off the charts"); Maggie Sill, interview with author, 26 August 2002 (Beatty climbed out window).
171. Pacheco, "Love Connection."

Prospect Hill Cemetery, Front Royal, Virginia. *Photo by Eleanor Chadwell*

Lakeside Cemetery, North Sydney, Cape Breton, Nova Scotia. *Photo by Gwen Rudderham*

television, stage, and film credits

TELEVISION

Lamp Unto My Feet, CBS, March 24, 1957 (as "Warren Beaty")

Kraft Television Theatre, "The Curly-Headed Kid," directed by Peter Turgeon, costarring Raymond Massey and Nancy Malone, NBC, June 26, 1957

Studio One, "The Night America Trembled," directed by Tom Donovan, narrated by Edward R. Murrow, starring Alexander Scourby, CBS, September 9, 1957

Look Up and Live, "The Family," directed by Roger Englander, costarring Edward Andrews, Louise Platt, and Bennye Gatteys, CBS, October–November 1957

Suspicion, "Heartbeat," directed by Robert Stevens, starring David Wayne, Pat Hingle, and Barbara Turner, NBC, November 11, 1957 (credited as "Henry Warren Beatty")

The Verdict Is Yours, starring Jim McKay, CBS, December 1957 (five episodes)

Hotel Cosmopolitan, directed by John Desmond, hosted by Donald Woods, starring Henderson Forsythe, CBS, February–March 1958 (seven episodes)

True Story, hosted by Kathi Norris, written by William Kendall Clarke, NBC, March 29, 1958

Lamp Unto My Feet, CBS, May 18, 1958

Love of Life, directed by Larry Auerbach, starring Bonnie Bartlett and Ron Tomme, CBS, December 1958

Look Up and Live, "The Square," directed by Tim Kiley, costarring Warren Berlinger and Sandra Church, CBS, January 25, 1959

The Brighter Day, directed by Erwin Nicholson, starring Hal Holbrook, CBS, January 26, 1959; February 11, 1959; February 17, 1959; March 3, 1959

Playhouse 90, "Dark December," directed by Franklin Schaffner, starring Barry Sullivan, James Whitmore, and Lili Darvas, CBS, April 30, 1959

The Many Loves of Dobie Gillis, "The Best-Dressed Man," "Sweet Singer of Central High," "Dobie Gillis: Boy Actor," "The Smoke-Filled Room," "The Fist Fighter," directed by Rodney Amateau, starring Dwayne Hickman and Tuesday Weld, CBS, October 6, 1959; November 10, 1959; December 1, 1959; January 12, 1960; January 19, 1960

Alcoa Presents One Step Beyond, "The Visitor," costarring Joan Fontaine, ABC, May 10, 1960

What's My Line, hosted by John Daly, CBS, September 11, 1966 (as "Mystery Guest")

The Larry Sanders Show, starring Garry Shandling, HBO, May 31, 1998

STAGE

Clinton Playhouse, Clinton, Connecticut: *The Happiest Millionaire*, directed by Ned Manderino, costarring Herbert Voland and Patricia Peardon, June 28–July 5, 1958; *The Boyfriend*, directed by Ned Manderino, costarring Paul Tripp, Ethel Colt, and Elizabeth Hubbard, July 14–July 26, 1958; *A Visit to a Small Planet*, directed by Ned Manderino, costarring Paul Tripp and Patricia Peardon, July 27–August 2, 1958; *A Hatful of Rain*, directed by Jerry Solars, costarring Allan Miller, Anita Cooper, and Ned Wertimer, August 4–August 9, 1958

North Jersey Playhouse, Fort Lee, New Jersey: *Compulsion*, directed by Brennan Moore, costarring David Rounds, Allen Joseph, Wayne Tippit, and Robert Ludlum, December 9–December 21, 1958

Eugene O'Neill Theatre, New York: *A Loss of Roses*, directed by Daniel Mann, costarring Betty Field, Carol Haney, and Michael J. Pollard, November 28–December 19, 1959

FILM (also designated as producer, director, and/or writer)

Splendor in the Grass, directed by Elia Kazan, costarring Natalie Wood, Pat Hingle, and Barbara Loden, 1961

The Roman Spring of Mrs. Stone, directed by José Quintero, costarring Vivien Leigh and Lotte Lenya, 1961

All Fall Down, directed by John Frankenheimer, costarring Angela Lansbury, Karl Malden, Brandon de Wilde, and Eva Marie Saint, 1962

Lilith, directed by Robert Rossen, costarring Jean Seberg and Peter Fonda, 1964

Mickey One, directed by Arthur Penn, costarring Alexandra Stewart, Hurd Hatfield, and Franchot Tone, 1965

Promise Her Anything, directed by Arthur Hiller, costarring Leslie Caron and Robert Cummings, 1966

Kaleidoscope, directed by Jack Smight, costarring Susannah York, Clive Revill, and Eric Porter, 1966

Bonnie and Clyde, directed by Arthur Penn, produced by Warren Beatty, costarring Faye Dunaway, Gene Hackman, Estelle Parsons, and Michael J. Pollard, 1967

The Only Game in Town, directed by George Stevens, costarring Elizabeth Taylor, 1970

McCabe & Mrs. Miller, directed by Robert Altman, costarring Julie Christie, 1971

$ *(Dollars)*, directed by Richard Brooks, costarring Goldie Hawn, 1971

The Parallax View, directed by Alan Pakula, costarring Hume Cronyn, William Daniels, and Paula Prentiss, 1974

Shampoo, directed by Hal Ashby, produced by Warren Beatty, written by Robert Towne and Warren Beatty, costarring Julie Christie, Goldie Hawn, and Jack Warden, 1975

The Fortune, directed by Mike Nichols, costarring Jack Nicholson and Stockard Channing, 1975

Heaven Can Wait, directed by Warren Beatty and Buck Henry, produced by Warren Beatty et al., written by Elaine May and Warren Beatty, costarring Julie Christie, Jack Warden, Charles Grodin, and Dyan Cannon, 1978

Reds, directed by Warren Beatty, produced by Warren Beatty et al., associate producer David L. MacLeod, written by Trevor Griffiths and Warren Beatty, costarring Diane Keaton, Jack Nicholson, Gene Hackman, and Edward Herrmann, 1981

Ishtar, directed by Elaine May, produced by Warren Beatty, David L. MacLeod, and Nigel Wooll, costarring Dustin Hoffman and Isabelle Adjani, 1987

The Pick-up Artist (producer only), 1987

Dick Tracy, directed by Warren Beatty, produced by Warren Beatty et al., costarring Madonna, Charlie Korsmo, and Al Pacino, 1990

Bugsy, directed by Barry Levinson, produced by Warren Beatty et al., costarring Annette Bening, Harvey Keitel, and Ben Kingsley, 1991

Love Affair, directed by Glenn Gordon Caron, produced by Warren Beatty et al., adapted by Robert Towne and Warren Beatty, costarring Annette Bening, Katharine Hepburn, and Garry Shandling, 1994

Bulworth, directed by Warren Beatty, produced by Warren Beatty et al., written by Warren Beatty and Jeremy Pikser, costarring Halle Berry, 1998

Town & Country, directed by Peter Chelsom, costarring Diane Keaton, Goldie Hawn, and Garry Shandling, 2001

acknowledgments

Documenting a life with the sweep of Warren Beatty's required assistance on many fronts. I am ever grateful to the hundreds of individuals who helped me construct this detailed portrait, contributing their time, and their reflections, as recorded in the end notes, in addition to letters, diaries, photographs, scrapbooks, journals, memos, and other memorabilia, and to Warren Beatty, for tolerating my intrusion into his private sanctums.

I am especially indebted to Robert and Luisa Towne, George Stevens, Jr., Robert Benton, Eleanor Kilgallen, Gary Springer, Lenn Harten, Elinor Jones, and Bill Rosendahl, for their thoughtfulness and generosity. Jane Fonda, Verne O'Hara, Joan Collins, Ned Manderino, Andrew Cvercko, Peter Levinson, Jeanne Rejaunier, and William Inge's niece, JoAnn Kirchmaier, deserve express acknowledgment for my depth of understanding about Beatty's early career years. Additional gratitude to Melissa Ruberson at the William Inge Collection in Kansas and to John Connolly; Caroline Sisneros at the American Film Institute, for her kind assistance with the Charles K. Feldman Papers; and to Leith Johnson, for early and privileged access to Elia Kazan's papers.

My abiding thanks to the late Dr. Margaret Brenman-Gibson and to Virginia Rowe, for their invaluable insight into Beatty's relationship with Clifford Odets. To Leslie Caron, Buck Henry, Goldie Hawn, Michael Laughlin, Peter Fonda, Madeleine Morgenstern, Carol Eve Rossen, Alexandra Stewart, Fred Roos, the late Jack Smight, Theodora Van Runkle, Norton Wright, Jeremy Pikser, Yevgeny Yevtushenko, and Senators Edward M. Kennedy, George McGovern, and Gary Hart, my sincere appreciation for your intimate contributions and your kindness.

My gratitude, as well, to Ned Comstock at the USC Cinema-Television Library; Barbara Hall at the Academy of Motion Picture Arts and Sciences; Marie-Christine de Jabrun of the Bibliotheque du Film in Paris; Allen Streicker at Northwestern University; Leslie Shores at the American Heritage Center; Polly Armstrong in the Department of Special Collections at Stanford; Ray Faiola at CBS; the staffs of the British Film Institute in London, the Harry Ransom Humanities Research Center in Austin, the Library of Congress, and

Martin Luther King Library in Washington, D.C., the Museum of TV and Radio in Beverly Hills, Loyola University, UCLA Special Collections, and the Billy Rose Theatre Collection at Lincoln Center. Particular thanks to Duncan Campbell, Alain Renoir, Peter Bart, Michael Ovitz, Joan Cohen, Michael Wood, Brent Wallis, Pat Broeske, Henriette Montgomery, Peter Felcher, Jill Warford, Bill Fagelson, Fran Gilman, Lynda Haubright, Betty Batausa, Arlene Hellerman, the always obliging Peter Gotlib, Amro Hamzawi, Stewart Brookman, Alan Nevins, Ron Mandelbaum, Larry McCallister at Paramount, and to the gallant Steve Weissman at Time-Warner.

Senator Elmon T. Gray, Dorothy Rector Turmail, Dr. Michael and Susan Durfee, Grace Munson Nichols, Thomas Calhoun, Janet Filia, Carolyn Eberdt, and the late Dr. Arthur Eberdt were exceptionally helpful during my exploration of Warren Beatty and Shirley MacLaine's childhood and high school years, as were Laurie Latham at the Waverly Library, and the librarians at the Virginia Historical Society, the Richmond Library, and the Virginia Room of the Arlington County Public Library.

Mason Green Jr., Jane Banks, Susan Mink, and Senator Jennie M. Forehand provided critical information or understanding concerning Beatty's parents and his Virginia background. Special thanks are due to the Warren Heritage Society (notably Dr. Tom Blumer and Chuck Pomeroy), genealogist Penelope Woodford, and Ray Beaty, Mike Allen, and Cynthia Beatty Johnstone of Beatty Project 2000, for confirmation in tracing the Beaty history. I am particularly grateful to Beaty family members Quincy Gasque Butler, Suzanne Silek, Jean Pomeroy, Jessie Deavers, and Andrea Winchell, as well as to the Rappahannock Historical Society, Maggie Sill, Eleanor Chadwell, Eunice Knight, the West Virginia Division of Culture and History, James Stimpert of Johns Hopkins University, and Mary Maxwell at the University of Richmond.

I am beholden to Charles Holmes and Jean MacLean Holmes for their first-person accounts of Beatty's mother's upbringing in Cape Breton, Nova Scotia, and to a scattering of gracious Canadians who assisted me with the MacLean background, including Tom Prescott, Linda Cann, Pat Townsend, Bill Parker, and Karen McKay in Wolfville; Lara Aase in Toronto; Gwen Rudderham, Tom Rose, and Candace Boudreau in Cape Breton; Lorna Johnstone and Dave MacKenzie in Ontario. My sincerest appreciation to Acadia University, especially Rhianna Edwards and Winnie Badden at the Esther Clark Wright Archives; to Anne Dondertman *et alia* at the Thomas Fisher Rare Book Library in Toronto; to Dilly MacFarlane at the Dalhousie Medical Alumni Association; and to the North Sydney Historical Museum.

In addition to rare photos from private albums, this book is enhanced by its fine art photographs, with warm thanks to Larry Shaw for his and Sam Shaw's early photographs of Beatty, as well as to Harry Benson, the estate of Jean Howard; Leith Johnson, for photos from Elia Kazan's *Splendor* notebook; the remarkable Julius Shulman; and to Rock Demers, for his never-seen photo from the Montreal premiere of *Bonnie and Clyde*. I am especially grateful to Curtis Hanson for permitting me to use his poetic portrait of Warren Beatty as the frontispiece and three other photographs from his private collection.

I could not have completed this Herculean task without the heroic Barry M. Grey, who assisted with interviews, and provided inspiration, as time was running out. My perpetual thanks to Amy Schireson, my aide-de-camp at the Academy, assisted at various stages by Scott Busby, Sheila Joan Harvey, Gloria Cahill, Natalie Finstad, Karl Ring, Mary Belton, and Adoley Odunton. My deepest gratitude to Molly Friedrich, and to Ellis Levine, for their guidance; and to my early readers, or others who offered counsel or support, including Harold and Elaine Finstad, Inga Danville, Bruce Finstad, D. J. Ziegler, Bill Judson, Sharon Lawrence, Wendei Spale, Barry Evans, Diana Rico, Lesley-Anna Mullen, Steven Stogel, Melinda Allen, Jeff Lee, and Bill Ogden.

And, of course, thanks to my enthusiastic editor, Shaye Areheart, who encouraged me to write a biography of Warren Beatty, an experience that enriched my life in unexpected ways, and to her diligent team, Julia Pastore and Julie Will, with my continuing appreciation to Jenny Frost, Philip Patrick, Linda Kaplan, Laura Quinn, Wendy Gardner, Bill Adams, Lauren Dong, Laura Duffy, Patty Bozza, Kira Stevens, and Tara Gilbride at Crown for their instrumental contributions.

To Judith Crist, a thousand thanks for your inimitable prose.

—SUZANNE FINSTAD
MAY 2005